BUILDINGS OF THE
DISTRICT OF COLUMBIA

SOCIETY OF ARCHITECTURAL HISTORIANS

BUILDINGS OF THE UNITED STATES

Buildings of the
DISTRICT OF
COLUMBIA

PAMELA SCOTT

ANTOINETTE J. LEE

New York   Oxford

OXFORD UNIVERSITY PRESS

1993

Buildings of the United States is a series of books on American
architecture complied and written on a state-by-state basis. The primary objective
of the series is to identify and celebrate the rich cultural, economic, and geographical diversity
of the United States as it is reflected in the architecture of each state. The series has been commissioned
by the Society of Architectural Historians, an organization devoted to the study, interpretation,
and preservation of the built environment throughout the world.

OXFORD UNIVERSITY PRESS

Oxford   New York
Athens   Auckland   Bangkok   Bombay
Calcutta   Cape Town   Dar es Salaam   Delhi
Florence   Hong Kong   Istanbul   Karachi
Kuala Lumpur   Madras   Madrid   Melbourne
Mexico City   Nairobi   Paris   Singapore
Taipei   Tokyo   Toronto
and associated companies in
Berlin   Ibadan

Copyright © 1993 by the Society of Architectural Historians
1232 Pine Street, Philadelphia, Pennsylvania 19107-5944

First published in 1993 by Oxford University Press, Inc.,
200 Madison Avenue, New York, New York 10016

First issued as an Oxford University Press paperback, 1994

Oxford is a registered trademark of Oxford University Press

Buildings of the District of Columbia has been supported, in part,
by grants from the National Endowment for the Humanities, an independent federal agency;
the Pew Charitable Trusts; the Graham Foundation for Advanced Studies in the Fine Arts;
and the Latrobe Chapter of the Society of Architectural Historians.

LIBRARY OF CONGRESS CATALOGING-IN-PUBLICATION DATA
Scott, Pamela.
Buildings of the District of Columbia / Pamela Scott and Antoinette J. Lee
p.   cm.—(Buildings of the United States)
At head of title: Society of Architectural Historians.
Includes bibliographical references and index.
ISBN 0-19-506146-2
ISBN 0-19-509389-5 (PBK.)
1. Architecture—Washington (D.C.) 2. Washington (D.C.)—Buildings,
structures, etc. I. Lee, Antoinette J. (Antoinette Josephine)
II. Society of Architectural Historical. III. Title. IV Series.
NA735.W3S36   1993
720'.9753—dc20   93-9187

10   9   8   7   6   5   4   3   2   1

Printed in the United States of America
on acid-free paper

Foreword

It is with pride and pleasure that the Society of Architectural Historians presents this volume to the public. It is among the first in the monumental series, Buildings of the United States, undertaken by the Society.

Buildings of the United States is a nationwide effort, indeed a national one. Heretofore, the United States was the only major country of the Western world that had not produced a publication project dealing with its architectural heritage on a national scale. In overall concept, Buildings of the United States is to a degree modeled on and inspired by The Buildings of England, the series of forty-six volumes conceived and carried out on a county-by-county basis by the eminent English architectural historian Nikolaus Pevsner, first published between 1951 and 1974. It was Pevsner himself who—years ago, but again and again—urged his American colleagues in the Society of Architectural Historians to do the same for this country. In method and approach, of course, that challenge was to be as different from Buildings of England as American architecture is different from English. Here we are dealing with a vast land of immense regional, geographic, climatic, ethnic, and cultural diversity, with an architectural history—wide-ranging, exciting, sometimes dramatic, as it is—essentially compressed into three hundred years; Pevsner, on the other hand, was confronted by a coherent culture on a relatively small island with an architectural history that spans over two thousand years. In contrast to the national integrity of English architecture, therefore, American architecture is marked by a dynamic heterogeneity, a heterogeneity woven of a thousand strands of originality, or, actually, a unity woven of a thousand strands of heterogeneity. It is this quality that Buildings of the United States will reflect and record.

Unity born of heterogeneity was a condition of American architecture from the beginning. Not only did the buildings of the Russian, English, Spanish, French, and Dutch colonies differ according to national origin, but in the transformation process they also assumed a special scale and character, qualities that were largely determined by the aspirations and traditions of a people struggling to fashion a new world in a demanding but abundant land. Diversity even marked the English colonies of the Eastern Seaboard, though they shared a common architectural heritage. The brick mutations of the English prototypes in the Virginia Colony were very different from the wooden architecture of the Massachusetts Bay Colony: they were different because Virginia was a plantation society dominated by the Anglican church, while Massachusetts was a communal society nurtured entirely by Puritanism. As the colonies became a nation and developed westward, similar radical contrasts became the way of America's growth. The infinite variety of physical environment, together with the complex origins and motivations of the settlers, made it inevitable that each new state would have a character uniquely its own.

This dynamic diversity is the foundation of Buildings of the United States. The primary objective of each volume will be to record, to analyze, and to evaluate the architecture of the state. The District of Columbia, as a distinct political entity as well as our nation's capital, takes its place with a separate volume along with those for each state. All of the authors are trained architectural historians who are thoroughly informed in the local aspects of their subjects. In developing the narrative, those special conditions that shaped the state, together with the building types necessary to meet those conditions, will be identified and discussed: barns, silos, mining buildings, factories, warehouses, bridges, and transportation buildings will take their place with the familiar building types conventional to the nation as a whole—churches, courthouses, city halls, and the infinite variety of domestic architecture. Although the great national and international masters of American architecture will receive proper attention, especially in a volume such as this, in which the architecture under consideration is so much the product of the preeminent architects of the nation, outstanding local architects, as well as the buildings of skilled but often anonymous carpenter-builders, will also be brought prominently into the picture. Each volume will thus be a detailed and precise portrait of the architecture of the state that it represents. At the same time, however, all of these local issues will be examined as they relate to the architectural developments in the country at large. When completed, therefore, the series will be a comprehensive history of the architecture of the United States.

The series was long in the planning. Indeed, the idea was conceived by Turpin Bannister, the first president of the Society of Architectural Historians (1940–1942). It was thirty years, however, before the society had grown sufficiently in strength to consider such a project. This happened when Alan Gowans, during his presidency (1972–1974), drew up a proposal and made the first of several unsuccessful attempts to raise the funds. The issue was raised again during the presidency of Marian C. Donnelly, when William H. Jordy and William H. Pierson, Jr., suggested to the board of directors that such a project should be the society's contribution to the nation's bicentennial celebration. It was not until 1986, however, after several failed attempts, that a substantial grant from the National Endowment for the Humanities, which was matched by grants from the Pew Charitable Trusts, the Graham Foundation, and the Latrobe Chapter of the Society of Architectural Historians, made the dream a reality. The activities that led to final success took place under the successive presidencies of Adolf K. Placzek (1978–1980), David Gebhard (1980–1982), Damie Stillman (1982–1984), and Carol H. Krinsky (1984–1986). Development and production of the first books has continued under those of Osmund Overby (1986–1988), Richard J. Betts (1988–1990), and Elisabeth Blair MacDougall (1990–1993). And all the while, there was David A. Bahlman, executive director of the SAH at the headquarters of the society in Philadelphia. In New York was Barbara Chernow of Chernow Editorial Services, Inc., who, with her husband, George Valassi, was a valuable resource during the initial stages of the project. A fine board of editors was established, with representatives from the American Institute of Architects, the Historic American Buildings Survey, and the Library of Congress. These first volumes have now been seen through production thanks to the very able work of the managing editor, Susan M. Denny, who joined the project in 1991. Buildings of the United States is now part of the official mission of the Society of Architectural Historians, incorporated into its bylaws.

In the development of this project, we have incurred a number of obligations. We are deeply indebted, both for financial support and for confidence in our efforts, to the National Endowment for the Humanities, the Pew Charitable Trusts, and the Graham Foundation for Advanced Studies in the Fine Arts. We also express our gratitude to a number of individuals. First among these is Dorothy Wartenberg, formerly of the Interpretive Research Program of the NEH, who was particularly helpful at the beginning, and our current program officer, David Wise. For the conceptual and practical development of the project, profound thanks go to the current members of the editorial board, listed earlier in this volume, and the following former members: the late Sally Kress Tompkins, the late Alex Cochran, Catherine W. Bishir, S. Allen Chambers, Jr., John Freeman, Alan Gowans, Robert Kapsch, and Tom Martinson. Next are our present and former project assistants—Preston Thayer, Marc Vincent, and Robert Wojtowicz. And there are the two previous executive directors of the Society, the late Rosann Berry and Paulette Olson Jorgensen. The Dean of the College of Arts and Science at the University of Missouri–Columbia supported the work of a graduate research assistant. The maps in this volume were prepared by the computer cartographers at the Geographic Resources Center in the Department of Geography at the University of Missouri–Columbia, thanks to the efforts and ability of Christopher Salter, director of GRC, Timothy Haithcoat, program director, and Karen Stange Westin and Robert Parsons III, project coordinators. Finally, thanks are due to our loyal colleagues in this enterprise at Oxford University Press in New York, especially Ed Barry, Claude Conyers, Marion Osmun, Stephen Chasteen, and Leslie Phillips.

The volumes, state by state, will continue to appear until every state in the Union has its own and the overview and inventory of American architecture is complete. The volumes will vary in length, and some states will require two volumes, but no state will be left out!

It must be said, regretfully, that not every building of merit can be included. Practical considerations have dictated some difficult choices in the buildings that are represented. There had to be some omissions from the abundance of structures built across the land, the thousands of modest but lovely edifices, often rising out of a sea of ugliness, or the vernacular attempts that merit a second look but which by their very multitude cannot be included in even the thickest volume. On the other hand, it must be emphasized that these volumes deal with more than the highlights and the high points. They deal with the very fabric of American architecture, with the context in time and in place of each specific building, with the entirety of urban and rural America, with the whole architectural patrimony. This fabric, of course, includes modern architecture, as, on the other end of the scale, it includes pre-Columbian and Native American remains.

As to architectural style, it was our most earnest intent to establish as much as possible a consistent terminology of architectural history: the name of J. A. Chewning, mastermind of our glossaries, must be gratefully mentioned here. The *Art and Architecture Thesaurus,* a comprehensive publication and database compiled by The Getty Art History Information Program and published by Oxford University Press, has also become an invaluable resource.

Finally, it must also be stated in the strongest possible terms that omission of a building from this or any volume of the series does not constitute an invitation to the bulldozers and the wrecking ball. In every community there will be structures not included in Buildings of the United States that are clearly deserving of being preserved. Indeed, it is hoped that the publication of this series will help to stop at least the worst destruction of architecture across the land by fostering a deeper appreciation of its beauty, richness, and historic and associative importance.

Antoinette Lee began this volume: she conceived the original organization, made the initial selection of buildings to be included, compiled many of the building research files, and drafted substantial portions of the text. When, because of an unexpected emergency, it appeared that she would be unable to complete the entire text within the deadlines, Pamela Scott was invited to complete the remaining chapters. Their contributions remain quite separate, as indicated in the table of contents, except for the chapter on the Capitol Hill neighborhood, to which each contributed. Both saw their portions of the manuscript to completion and were present at the end when the final details had to fall in place, for which the editors are deeply grateful.

The volumes of Buildings of the United States are intended as guidebooks as well as reference books and are designed to facilitate such use: they can and should be used on the spot, indeed should lead the user to the spot. But they are also meant to be tools of serious research in the study of American architecture. It is our earnest hope that they will not only be on the shelves of every major library under "U.S." but that they will also be in many a glove compartment and perhaps even in many a rucksack.

ADOLF K. PLACZEK
WILLIAM H. PIERSON, JR.
OSMUND OVERBY

Acknowledgments

The debts of gratitude incurred while researching and writing *Buildings of the District of Columbia* have ranged broadly and were often so extensive that mere acknowledgment of them here seems entirely inadequate. First thanks are due to the historians of American architecture whose vision formulated this series and thoughtfully guided this volume. Without the encouragement, advice, and, above all, patience of Osmund Overby, Adolf K. Placzek, William H. Pierson, Jr., and Damie Stillman, this book would not have been so valuable to so wide a range of readers. Each contributed far more than reading and commenting on the text. Carol H. Krinsky carefully reviewed the manuscript. David A. Bahlman and his assistants, Preston Thayer and Robert Wojtowicz, at the Society of Architectural Historians office made this job immeasurably easier. Susan M. Denny's and Carol Eron's editorial readings were sensitive and sensible. Research assistance by a large number of historians and preservationists contributed to the breadth and accuracy of the entries. Marilyn Harper and Joyce E. Nalewajk culled information from a large volume of published and manuscript sources. Elizabeth Nolin's cheerfulness and perseverance in expertly gathering and cogently arranging vast amounts of information merits particularly heartfelt thanks. Franz Jantzen's wonderful eye as an architectural photographer is matched by his exuberance as a colleague.

Washington's federal institutions employ many knowledgeable individuals whose helpfulness in preparing this book was extraordinary. Barbara Wolanin's staff in the curator's office of the Architect of the Capitol, Linnea Dix, Eric Paff, and Dana Strickland, answered innumerable inquiries on all the buildings under the architect's care. Particularly helpful was review of pertinent sections of the manuscript by William C. Allen and Pamela A. Violente, whose corrections were very welcome. Sue Kohler at the Commission of Fine Arts provided information, photographs, and advice that all improved the quality of this work. John A. Burns and Sarah Amy Leach of the Historic American Buildings Survey of the National Park Service facilitated use of the research files maintained by that office.

At the Library of Congress Ronald E. Grim and Richard Stephenson in the Geography and Map Division and Sam Daniels, Marilyn Ibach, Maja Keech, and C. Ford Peatross in the Prints and Photographs Division were especially cooperative. Brenda Corbin, librarian at the National Observatory, shared her knowledge and appreciation of the site's numerous structures. Gary Scott and Robert Sondeman at the National Capitol Region office of the National Park Service graciously allowed access to many unpublished research reports about Park Service properties. Kevin Kandt, Orden Lantz, and Diane Miller facilitated the copying of the files of the National Register of Historic Places. Sally Blackford at the Pennsylvania Avenue Development Corporation gathered together a packet of historical materials. Cynthia R. Field and her staff in the Office of Architectural History and Historic Preservation, Smithsonian Institution, Amy Ballard, Rafael A. Crespo, Heather Ewing, and Jennifer Frehling, aided in the research on the buildings under their purview. Priscilla Goodwin gave generously of her knowledge of the Supreme Court building.

Numerous architects, historians, librarians, and preservationists employed by the District of Columbia were equally helpful. David J. Maloney, Suzanne Ganschinietz, and Nancy Kassner at the Historic Preservation office facilitated the use of their important files and reports. Walter L. Hill II of the Department of Human Services provided historical information on St. Elizabeths Hospital. Roxanne Deane and her staff in the Washingtoniana Division of the Martin Luther King, Jr., Memorial Library—Rhoda Atkins, Matthew Gilmore, G. R. F. Key, Mary Pernes, and Katherine Ray—provided unfailingly gracious and incredibly competent on-site and telephone assistance seven days a week. John Fondersmith of the Office of Planning clarified many aspects of the city's recent planning history.

Martin Moeller and Betsy May at the Washington Chapter of the American Institute of Architects aided with identifying many examples of Washington's most recent fine architecture. Stephen Callcott of the D.C. Preservation League provided much information from its files. The staff of Special Collections at Gelman Library, George Washington University, David Anderson, Eva Kaminski, Christine Kehrwald, William Keller, Andrea Mark, Teresa Rains, and Suellen Towers, jointly unearthed many rare items. The volunteers working under Margaret N. Burri at the Historical Society of Washington who were particularly helpful were Jack Brewer, Mona Dingle, Frances Flecknoe, and Ida Offutt. At the National Cathedral, Jennifer Faircloth, Jean Grigsby, Margaret Lewis, and Alison Parsons all helped me to understand that complex building.

The generosity of Emily Eig in giving free access to the research files of her historical research firm, Traceries, was exemplary. Those of her assistants who merit special thanks are Katherine Grandine, Kim Welsh, and Kendall Shugart. Special assistance in emergencies was provided by Steven Bedford, William Bushong, Don Hawkins, Alison K. Hoagland, Richard Longstreth, Kathleen Sinclair Wood, and Thomas Wright. The pastor of the Metropolitan Memorial United Methodist Church, Bruce Poynter, graciously shared his knowledge of his church with me. All of the above deserve more thanks than I can adequately convey. I sincerely regret any omissions and thank everyone who aided in the research, writing, and production of this book.

P.S.

No book on the architecture of Washington, D.C., can be considered entirely original. By necessity, much of it rests on the work of earlier historians, architecutural historians, writers, and others who undertook to write now-treasured guidebooks and monographs on the subject. Much appreciation also is due to those who document buildings and places for historic designation at the local level, for listing in the National Register of Historic Places, and as part of Historic American Buildings Survey projects. Without these comprehensive and individual efforts, this project would have been impossible. We hope to have made an important, although admittedly incremental, contribution to the study of the city's architecture.

Much of the initial material and inspiration for several of the chapters in this book was gained in the 1970s, when I worked for Frederick Gutheim on the preparation of the manuscripts that resulted in *Worthy of the Nation: The History of Planning for the National Capital* (Washington, D.C.: Smithsonian Institution Press, 1977) and the essay "Washington Panorama: A Brief View of the Planned Capital City," in *The Federal City: Plans & Realities* (Washington, D.C.: Smithsonian Institution Press, 1976). The chapter "Looking at Washington, D.C." and the chapters on the Southwest Quadrant and the Federal Triangle, in particular, owe some of their perspectives to these earlier publications.

My interest in federal government architecture was enhanced considerably by my own work on a history of the Office of the Supervising Architect of the U.S. Treasury Department, a study sponsored by the Historical Society of Washington, D.C., funded in large part by the National Endowment for the Humanities and, to date, still in manuscript form. The late Karel Yasko of the General Services Administration encouraged my interest in federal government buildings, particularly the current GSA building (formerly the Department of the Interior Building) in the Foggy Bottom neighborhood, and generously shared his files with me.

As reflected in several entries in this book, public school buildings constitute another aspect of my interest in government architecture. My work on this building type was sponsored by the District of Columbia Public Schools and funded, in part, by Historic Preservation Fund grants administered by the District of Columbia Historic Preservation Office. I am grateful to Richard L. Hurlbut, director of the Sumner School Museum and Archives, for enthusiastically sponsoring my survey of older school buildings and for his sustained encouragement of my interest in this subject.

Other individuals and institutions were essential to this book. They include Tony P. Wrenn, archivist of the American Institute of Architects, who makes the archival records of the AIA available and coherent to numerous historians and researchers. Robert Lyle of the Peabody Collection at the Georgetown Branch of the District of Columbia Public Library and staff members of the Prints and Photographs Division of the Library of Congress, which holds the Historic American Buildings Survey collections, including those on the District of Columbia, were helpful and encouraging. Several architectural firms offered ready access to their files or took time to confirm facts about particular buildings.

They include the firms of Arthur Cotton Moore, Hartman-Cox, and Vlastimil Koubek.

I also thank Kathleen Sinclair Wood and Marilyn Harper for their invaluable research assistance. They pored over the major architectural journals—*Architectural Record, Progressive Architecture, American Architect and Buildings News,* and *Pencil Points,* among others—for articles on Washington, D.C., buildings. This search unearthed many heretofore unappreciated buildings in the District of Columbia, and their research materials formed the initial files for many of the building entries included in this book.

To all of the above and to the many others who, over the years, offered their insights into the many facets of the city's built form, I offer my heartfelt thanks.

A.J.L.

Contents

List of Maps, xv

Guide for Users of This Volume, xvi

Looking at Washington, D.C., *Antoinette J. Lee,* 3
  The Sum of Its Various Parts, 5; A City of Neighborhoods, 9;
  Components of Washington's Architecture, 11; The Model
  and Experimental City, 12

Two Centuries of Architectural Practice
  in Washington, *Pamela Scott,* 14

The Mall (ML), *Pamela Scott,* 62

Monumental Capitol Hill (CH), *Pamela Scott,* 113

White House and Lafayette Square (WH), *Pamela Scott,* 149
  White House and Grounds, 149; Lafayette Square, 158

Federal Triangle (FT), *Antoinette J. Lee,* 166

Downtown East (DE), *Antoinette J. Lee,* 178

Foggy Bottom (FB), *Antoinette J. Lee,* 204

Downtown West (DW), *Antoinette J. Lee,* 219

Southwest Quadrant (SW), *Antoinette J. Lee,* 231

Capitol Hill Neighborhood (CN), *Antoinette J. Lee and Pamela Scott,* 246

Southeast of the Anacostia River (SE), *Pamela Scott,* 271

North and Northeast (NE), *Pamela Scott,* 280

16th Street and Meridian Hill (MH), *Pamela Scott,* 297

Dupont Circle (DU), *Pamela Scott,* 317
  Connecticut Avenue, 319; Massachusetts Avenue, 325;
  New Hampshire Avenue, 332

Sheridan Circle and Kalorama (SK), *Pamela Scott,* 336

Rock Creek Park and Northwest Washington (NW), *Pamela Scott,* 361
    Rock Creek and Connecticut Avenue, 361; Cleveland Park, 366

Georgetown (GT), *Antoinette J. Lee,* 398

Notes, 417

Suggested Readings, 419

Glossary, 421

Photography Credits, 446

Index, 449

List of Maps

Washington, D.C., 4

The Mall, 63

Monumental Capitol Hill, 114

White House and Lafayette Square, 150

Federal Triangle, 167

Downtown East (DE01–DE11), 180

Downtown East (DE12–DE39), 188

Foggy Bottom, 205

Downtown West, 220

Southwest Quadrant, 233

Capitol Hill Neighborhood
(CN1–CN47), 249

Capitol Hill Neighborhood
(CN48–CN53), 267

Southeast of the Anacostia River
(SE1–SE6), 272

Southeast of the Anacostia River
(SE7–SE10), 277

Southeast of the Anacostia River
(SE11–SE12), 278

North and Northeast (NE01–NE04), 282

North and Northeast (NE05–NE08), 286

North and Northeast (NE09–NE11), 289

North and Northeast (NE12–NE18), 291

16th Street and Meridian Hill, 301

Dupont Circle, 318

Sheridan Circle and Kalorama
(SK01, SK04–SK28), 337

Sheridan Circle and Kalorama
(SK02–SK03, SL29–SK50), 341

Sheridan Circle and Kalorama
(SK51–SK75), 355

Rock Creek Park and Northwest
Washington (NW01–NW32), 363

Rock Creek Park and Northwest
Washington (NW33–NW41), 377

Rock Creek Park and Northwest
Washington (NW42–NW54), 387

Rock Creek Park and Northwest
Washington (NW55–NW60), 395

Georgetown, 399

Guide for Users of This Volume

This guide to the architecture of Washington, D.C., is arranged by neighborhoods and districts. Its starts, as do most visitors, with the Mall and the major public buildings. It moves on to the adjacent districts that are primarily commerical and then to the residential neighborhoods.

Each entry begins with an identifying code, a two-letter abbreviation of the district or neighborhood and the number of the property. The name of the property, and alternate names, if appropriate, follow the code. On the next line appear the date or dates of construction, the name of the original architect (if known), and the dates of major additions or alterations to the property (if applicable). Finally, there is a narrative description of each property.

Detailed maps of each neighborhood or district are provided that should prove adequate to guide visitors to the buildings covered in the book. Structures are identified on maps by entry number, without the alphabetic code. The detailed *Washington, D.C., Transportation Map,* prepared by the District of Columbia Department of Public Works and available from that office, may be consulted as a helpful supplement.

All of the properties described in this book are visible from public streets. Buildings that are open to the public are so noted at the end of the appropriate entries. Of course, we know that the readers of this book will always respect the property rights and privacy of others as they view the buildings.

BUILDINGS OF THE
DISTRICT OF COLUMBIA

Looking at Washington, D.C.

Antoinette J. Lee

FROM ANY VANTAGE POINT, WASHINGTON, D.C., IS A CITY DE-fined by the geometry of its street plan and by the interrelationships between major public buildings and urban nodes. Within the original L'Enfant City, the street system of radial avenues and grid streets spreads out toward the horizon, punctuated by towers, domes, and obelisks. Only when L'Enfant City merges into the rest of the District of Columbia and then over to the Virginia shore and along the Maryland rim do the forces of geometry lessen, and the built-up city reaches skyward.

The wide radial avenues and major grid thoroughfares knit together the open spaces of the Mall, Rock Creek Park, and the many smaller neighborhood parks scattered throughout the city. From the flatlands of L'Enfant City, the ground rises up through terraces and hills. The open texture of the city and the various vantage points located throughout allow for the viewing of the entirety of buildings and for the full appreciation of their architectural qualities.

In no other city is the architectural experience more dramatic. Most residents and visitors remember the first time they beheld the United States Capitol building and comprehended in actual terms the mythical scale of the structure as portrayed in picture books. Located at the western end of the Mall, the marble Lincoln Memorial reflects the changing colors of the day and of the season. From heights, such as the first ridge north of Florida Avenue, the city's wholeness is revealed as more than the interconnections of its major public buildings. Here, the viewer can see the monuments as well as the binding elements of row house residences, churches, schools, playgrounds, firehouses, and recreation centers. Some buildings, such as Founders Library at Howard University, define the ridge. The sum of the city is more than the combination of

3

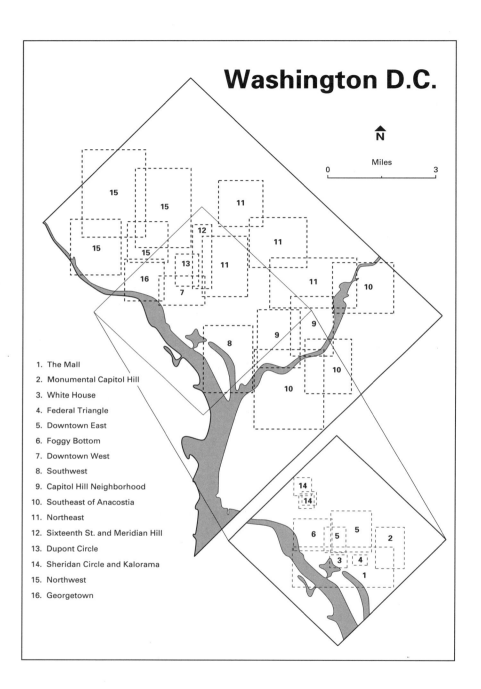

Washington D.C.

N

Miles
0 ——— 3

15
15
15
15
11
12
11
13
11
16
11
7
11
10
9
9
8
10
10
10

14
14
6 5 5 2
3 4
1

1. The Mall
2. Monumental Capitol Hill
3. White House
4. Federal Triangle
5. Downtown East
6. Foggy Bottom
7. Downtown West
8. Southwest
9. Capitol Hill Neighborhood
10. Southeast of Anacostia
11. Northeast
12. Sixteenth St. and Meridian Hill
13. Dupont Circle
14. Sheridan Circle and Kalorama
15. Northwest
16. Georgetown

major architectural features; it is the complete meshing of the official and residential uses with the topography of the site.

The architecture of Washington, D.C., is known throughout the world. Its Capitol, White House, and major monuments and memorials can be identified by many who have never seen the structures in person. However, the city is a conservative one by any architectural standard. The popular national styles hung on much longer than in other urban areas in the nation, many of which were pioneering new trends. This "burden of history" lingers over much of Washington's architecture, particularly in the twentieth century, when classicism gripped public building design well into the late 1950s.

The rarity of iconoclastic or eccentric buildings in the city can be ascribed to the desire of nationally influential architects to fit their buildings into the context of the city rather than to dominate it or defy convention. The works of trend-setting architects such as Frank Lloyd Wright, Louis Kahn, Helmut Jahn, and Frank Gehry would be out of place, except perhaps in isolated suburban spaces. Imaginative but often conservative architects, such as Paul Philippe Cret and I. M. Pei, have found a ready home for their works.

The creation of architecture in the city is heavily influenced by the statutory bodies that oversee projects. The deliberations of these bodies contribute to the conservative character of the city. The regulatory officialdom includes the federal agencies, such as the Commission of Fine Arts and the National Capital Planning Commission, as well as the municipal planning and development agencies. Myriad citizens' organizations also interact with the governmental agencies, including those with a citywide purview and those interested in a specific building, style, or historical period. The Committee of 100 for the Federal City represents citizens' concerns about how projects will affect the metropolitan area. The Art Deco Society of Washington, Save the Tivoli, the D.C. Preservation League, and the Washington Metropolitan Area chapter of the Victorian Society in America join with neighborhood-oriented citizens' organizations to influence the course of projects through review and public participation. As a result of public and private oversight, the architecture of Washington can be said to represent a consensus of a whole rather than purely an expression of an individual designer's creativity.

The Sum of Its Various Parts

"Washington, D.C.," is a catch-all label given to the Washington metropolitan area. The District of Columbia, originally 10 miles square, was designated by the Congress as the new national capital in 1790. The square was set at the head of navigation on the Potomac River and turned so that its corners pointed directly north, east, south, and west. Within its boundary were the thriving tobacco port cities of Georgetown on the Maryland side of the Potomac and

The City of Washington, engraving by George Cooke, 1834.

Alexandria on the Virginia side. "L'Enfant City," also referred to as Washington City, includes that portion of the original District of Columbia south of Florida Avenue (formerly Boundary Street) and east of Georgetown that Pierre Charles L'Enfant planned in 1791. Florida Avenue represents the northernmost boundary of the flat, basin lands before the first major steep rise to higher ground. Outside of Georgetown and Washington City spread the largely rural landscape of Washington County.

The 10-mile-square city was shorn of its Virginia portion in 1849, when it was ceded back to the Commonwealth of Virginia in anticipation that the Virginia lands would not be needed by the federal government. The lack of foresight in this decision became evident when, during the Civil War, a circle of forts located on high ground was constructed to provide protection for the federal city and included major vantage points in Virginia. The District of Columbia remains today a jurisdiction with perfectly straight edges except for the western corner and southwestern boundary, which follow the ragged edges of the Potomac River.

For many years separate governments administered Georgetown, Washington City, and Washington County. In 1871, these governments were replaced with a territorial form of government led by a lower house, elected by citizens, and a governor and upper house, appointed by the president of the United

States. The apparent excesses of expenditures on a massive public works program under Alexander "Boss" Shepherd caused Congress to abolish the territorial government in 1874 and to institute a governing system of three appointed District commissioners, one of whom was a member of the United States Army Corps of Engineers (the engineer commissioner). It was not until a century later, in 1974, that the District would elect its government again.

For much of the late nineteenth and early twentieth centuries, Washington was synonymous with the District of Columbia. Development continued along the major thoroughfares and filled the spaces in between, made accessible by electric streetcar and railroad lines. During the first three decades after the Civil War, many of the subdivisions in the District of Columbia were laid out according to their own street systems because the District government had not provided for a comprehensive street system beyond L'Enfant City. As development pressed farther into the formerly rural lands of the District, the lack of interconnected streets forced the issue. The Highways Acts of 1893 and 1898 finally extended the L'Enfant streets beyond Florida Avenue and grandfathered in the subdivisions that had been built prior to 1893. While some attempt was made to repeat the radial and grid patterns of L'Enfant City, the street plan of the turn of the century was primarily gridlike.

Handy Map of Washington, J. C. Entwistle, 1876.

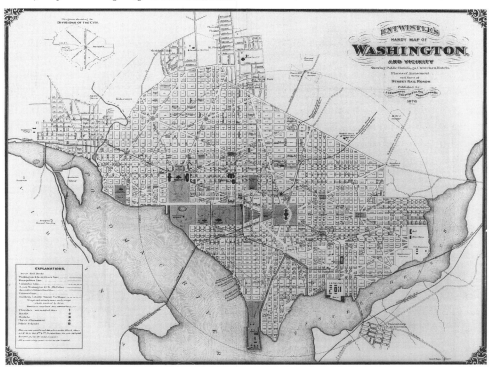

The McMillan Commission Plan of 1901–1902 is most often associated with the revival of classicism and the plan for the Mall, but using the model of the Boston Metropolitan Park System, it also devised a far-ranging plan for park development throughout the District of Columbia and the metropolitan area. The plan was intended not only to provide for parks and recreation as development moved outward from the central city but also to enhance the character of this later development. The plan was implemented during the following decades by the National Capital Park and Planning Commission (later the National Capital Planning Commission) and the Maryland-National Capital Park and Planning Commission as those agencies acquired parkland.

Today, Washington, D.C., envelops a virtual regional city, extending as far north as Baltimore, Maryland, and south toward Fredericksburg, Virginia. It also extends east to Annapolis, Maryland, and west to Leesburg, Virginia. Its center remains the monumental core of the national capital city defined by the Capitol, the White House, and the many buildings that make up the Executive Branch. However, federal government agencies have become more mobile and today need not be proximate to one another. Federal agencies are located along the long prongs of the Metro system in northern Virginia and Montgomery and Prince Georges counties in Maryland. Because of the wonders of computer technology, federal workers also are located in the farther reaches of exurbia, including West Virginia and the more peripheral counties of Maryland.

As the world of the federal government and government-related businesses becomes more diffusely spread over the regional landscape, new "edge cities" have developed. These quasi-independent urban centers, such as Tysons Corner in Fairfax County, Virginia, and Rockville in Montgomery County, Maryland, offer their own balance of employment, housing, commercial centers, and cultural facilities that rival those of the center of the District of Columbia. They are connected by beltways and interstate highways, rather than by the traditional radials and grids of the District of Columbia. These urban centers lack the character of true cities. However, they offer convenience, comfort, and relative safety from the hazards of the inner city.

The effect of these regional forces on the District of Columbia has been twofold. Many of the congestion and development pressures that might have befallen the District have been transferred to the less restrictive adjoining jurisdictions; thus, the District retains much of its unique historic and architectural character for residents and visitors to enjoy. On the other hand, the District's economic base is becoming diluted and worrisome. Its ability to retain skilled jobs for its residents is very much in question. The influential middle classes of all races have left the city for the surrounding jurisdictions and have relegated the District of Columbia to both the very rich and the very poor, who live in entirely separate spheres.

A City of Neighborhoods

Much of the L'Enfant Plan was centered on the location of public buildings to accommodate the needs of the federal government. Less well known was the system of urbanization that L'Enfant envisioned to provide the residential fabric of the nation's capital. The major public buildings themselves were intended to serve as centers of emerging residential development: the President's House was intended to be surrounded by an attractive and desirable residential enclave. The Capitol was also to serve as a magnet for the development of its surrounding neighborhood. But beyond these obvious centers, the major intersections of radial avenues and major grid thoroughfares were also to serve as centers for developing residential areas, reinforced by markets and parklands.

Much of what L'Enfant projected for the residential city came to fruition. Lafayette Square across from the White House served as an elite residential setting for much of the nineteenth century and well into the twentieth before commercial development transformed the area into a prime location for commercial office space, association buildings, and clubs. The activity around the Capitol generated the Capitol Hill residential neighborhood that spread eastward to the banks of the Anacostia River and connected with residential areas centered on the Navy Yard to the south. The major squares and circles in L'Enfant City also fulfilled their destiny: Mount Vernon Square, Dupont Circle, and Logan Circle became important late nineteenth-century neighborhoods of substantial red brick row houses.

The expansion of the electric streetcar and railroad lines allowed for residential development to occur well outside L'Enfant City. Neighborhoods such as Mount Pleasant, Columbia Heights, Le Droit Park, Brookland, Silver Spring, Takoma Park, Cleveland Park, and Chevy Chase offered residential living on higher ground, where the air was cooler. Mount Pleasant and Columbia Heights offered large row houses with ample backyards, while other streetcar suburbs provided detached houses and a more rural environment. As the city spread well beyond Florida Avenue, the spaces between these formerly sylvan settlements became filled in. For much of the Northwest Quadrant east of Rock Creek Park, the infill was of row houses, seemingly for blocks on end. The town house and row house clusters of Foxhall Village, Woodley Park, and Burleith were located in the Northwest Quadrant west of Rock Creek Park. The Northeast and Southeast quadrants retained their less dense character because they were less accessible.

With the coming of the automobile, the range of residential subdivision planning expanded. Neighborhoods such as Wesley Heights and Spring Valley surrounding American University in the Northwest Quadrant were designed beginning in the 1920s as comprehensive communities, complete with large single-family residences designed in popular historical revival styles, large pri-

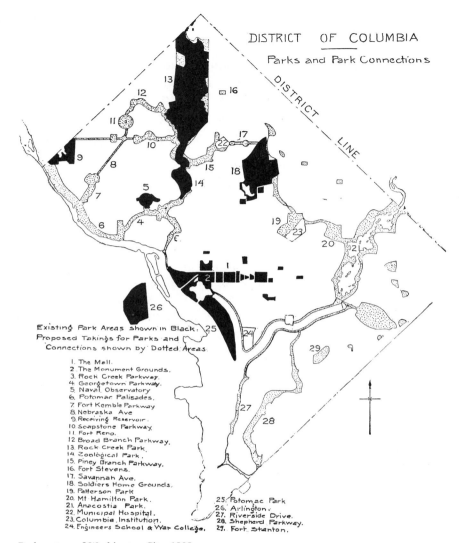

DISTRICT OF COLUMBIA

Parks and Park Connections

Existing Park Areas shown in Black,
Proposed Takings for Parks and
Connections shown by Dotted Areas.

1. The Mall.
2. The Monument Grounds.
3. Rock Creek Parkway.
4. Georgetown Parkway.
5. Naval Observatory.
6. Potomac Palisades.
7. Fort Kemble Parkway.
8. Nebraska Ave.
9. Receiving Reservoir.
10. Soapstone Parkway.
11. Fort Reno.
12. Broad Branch Parkway.
13. Rock Creek Park.
14. Zoological Park.
15. Piney Branch Parkway.
16. Fort Stevens.
17. Savannah Ave.
18. Soldiers Home Grounds.
19. Patterson Park.
20. Mt. Hamilton Park.
21. Anacostia Park.
22. Municipal Hospital.
23. Columbia Institution.
24. Engineers School & War College.

25. Potomac Park.
26. Arlington.
27. Riverside Drive.
28. Shepherd Parkway.
29. Fort Stanton.

Park system of Washington City, 1902.

vate lawns, and much of the natural land forms retained. Constructed by the W. C. and A. N. Miller Company after the model of J. C. Nichols's Country Club District in Kansas City, Missouri, Wesley Heights and Spring Valley included appropriately designed shopping facilities, recreational facilities, and protected parklands. These neighborhoods attracted those families formerly residing in the more congested neighborhoods closer to the center of the city or in gracious but limited apartment houses along Connecticut Avenue.

The Second World War had an impact on the city as well as on surrounding jurisdictions, as provisions were made to house the large number of war workers who had jammed themselves into existing housing. In 1941–1942, the Defense Homes Corporation developed the garden apartment communities of Naylor Gardens in the Southeast Quadrant and McLean Gardens in the Northwest Quadrant to the west of Wisconsin Avenue. During this period, defense housing also was built in Arlington County. With the scarcity of gasoline, however, development had to remain within reach of the public transportation system.

After World War II, the population of Washington, D.C., again became mobile and expansive. Suburban development spread into the remaining corners of the District of Columbia, Northern Virginia, and the adjoining Maryland suburbs in the form of detached low-slung ranch and split-level houses and upright Colonial Revival boxes. Accompanying this suburban boom were expanded shopping facilities, apartment houses along major thoroughfares, and sleek new schools. This form of postwar suburbia can be found in all quadrants of the city except for the Southwest Quadrant.

The Southwest Quadrant found its own special destiny in the urban renewal forces that swept the nation. As an alternative to the suburbanizing edges of the city, the Southwest Quadrant offered a rebuilt inner-city neighborhood with many of the amenities of suburbia, such as new housing, shopping centers, and schools. The project also offered a new beginning in race relations because it created a new neighborhood, free of traditional racially based residential patterns. Another urban renewal project, the new town of Fort Lincoln in Northeast Washington, also served as a viable and inclusive alternative to both central city living and suburban escape.

Components of Washington's Architecture

In order to appreciate Washington's architecture, one must look at its individual components. In a city so rich with buildings, landmarks, and districts, it is often difficult to distinguish the forest from the trees. The most common division of building types is the separation of the federal city from the local, residential city. Within each of these two major subdivisions are major building types. The federal city consists of the buildings of the executive, legislative, and judicial branches, all intended to house official functions. The federal establishment extends to the city's memorials and parks. The residential city includes the buildings in the downtown commercial core, neighborhoods, and industrial zones. Municipal buildings, recreation areas, schools, libraries, firehouses, churches, and commercial centers are essential to the functions of these areas as residential neighborhoods.

The residential city also identifies itself closely with important institutions outside of the monumental core, such as the several universities and colleges that defined the character of communities. Howard University has served as a magnet for the educated, affluent African-American population in the District. Catholic University is part of a larger grouping of Catholic institutions and schools. American University and Mount Vernon College were seen as decided assets in the development of the Wesley Heights and Spring Valley communities. The United States Soldiers' and Airmen's Home and Walter Reed Hospital serve as anchors of stability in their respective neighborhoods.

The nature of the city's business produced buildings unique to it, such as foreign embassies and association buildings. Many embassies occupy turn-of-the-century mansions. Others have commissioned their buildings as expressions of their own culture. Association buildings filled with lobbyists range from recycled older residences to association-commissioned buildings, many of which in some way convey their purpose.

Other than building types, the city is carved into distinct economic enclaves that affect the location and character of buildings. The city of affluence is populated by stately mansions, wealthy enclaves, and exclusive homes. The city's vast middle class of civil servants and their families is housed in communities of row houses, duplexes, and detached houses. Apartment houses serve the needs of singles, couples, and small families. The city of poverty is reflected in neglected areas and in public and subsidized housing. The demarcations between economic groups are not static; the lines shift over time as areas fall in and out of favor.

As the city straddles the Northern and Southern states, Washington has its own history of racial divisions. For much of its history, the city was influenced by the separation of the black and white races that was legalized in covenants and molded in everyday practice. Racial segregation resulted in separate housing, schools, and churches, the histories of which served to instruct as well as to inspire. While the binding of segregation has been removed from the law books, its influence can still be seen in the allocation of public services. Today, the city's absorption of new cultural groups has produced adjustments to the city's form. Recently arrived Hispanics and Asians have made their own imprint upon the city.

The Model and Experimental City

Washington also can be examined in the context of the contrast between the ideal and the real city. The city's special role in the nation gives rise to the notion that it is ruled by urban idealism and aspirations toward greatness. The L'Enfant Plan and its successor plans serve as national and international models for inspection and study. The interest of particular presidents in the planning and architecture of Washington inspired new designs for Pennsylvania Avenue, the Mall, and the White House environs, all of which were regarded by the nation's constituents as possible models for other cities.

The location of the federal government on the banks of the Potomac River has provided the city with not only unprecedented economic stability as compared with other cities throughout the nation but also with a ready laboratory of urban experiments. From the late eighteenth century, Washington has been a model in the evolution of national capital cities. Its extensive collection of public buildings and parks has spoken to other nations in succeeding centuries as new capital cities were planned. The city's affluent citizenry served as ready customers for the early neighborhood shopping centers designed for automobile commuters. Washington also became the location of the first and most fully developed urban renewal plan of the post–World War II era.

Even if the city were not a pioneer but a follower of national trends, it is unique. Its comprehensive metropolitan-wide system of parks developed after the inspiration of large park systems elsewhere in the nation. But where else could a park system find such a ready topography or linkages with such nationally significant locations? Likewise the subdivision plans of the early twentieth century that followed neighborhood development models elsewhere in the nation were shaped into the image of eighteenth-century graciousness.

More than any other city in the nation, Washington is both a unique city and a common, familiar city. Its uniqueness lies in its special functions and the monumental buildings that house them. Its commonness and familiarity are based in the building types that can be found in all other American cities. For this reason, the architecture of Washington, D.C., holds a special place in the affection of residents and visitors alike. It calls upon us to respect the symbols of the national government, and it reassures us that the seat of national government is part of the mainstream of American urban life.

Two Centuries of Architectural Practice in Washington

Pamela Scott

MEANINGFUL CULTURAL IDEAS AND WORTHY SOCIAL IDE-
als do not make good architecture; they merely explain why architectural forms, spaces, and details differ from one time and place
to another. Good architects make good architecture. Literature communicates
ideas and emotions through a written language, architecture via a visual one.
Instead of words, architects manipulate palpable form and abstract space and
light to create buildings that convey some meaning, whether intellectual, sen-
sory, or affective. As in literature, quality in architecture is dependent on the
talent and training of the practitioner, not on outside stimuli. Maya Lin did
not have to experience or understand war to design the Vietnam Veterans
Memorial; she had to understand architecture.

Architects practicing in Washington historically have been forced to respond
to a particularly difficult mixture of physical, social, and political circumstances.
Many were attracted to the city by the possibility of being involved in important
and highly visible structures, as public architecture has traditionally been viewed
as the highest calling. However, actually achieving beautifully designed public
buildings under highly politicized conditions where unqualified people, including presidents and members of Congress, have often had the decisive voice
required architects with strong personalities or great persuasive abilities. A
number of unusual factors have contributed to architects' practice of their peculiar fusion of art and profession in Washington: a largely transient population for nearly a century, the dichotomy between the public and the private
city, evolving bureaucratic structures established by the government to meet its
building needs, and, in the twentieth century, the presence of numerous planning agencies with overlapping areas of jurisdiction.

The entire range of Washington's architectural development, both public and

14

private, has been profoundly affected by the city's position as the national capital. This two-century history can be roughly divided into four fifty-year phases. During the first half century, few professional architects practiced in Washington, but they were among the most important in the country; their individual achievements, whether in the public or private realm, have had national significance. During the second half of the nineteenth century, two large and influential federal architectural offices employed numerous architects, engineers, and draftsmen, including many well-trained Europeans. With the extensions to the Capitol beginning in 1851, the Office of Architect of the Capitol burgeoned in relation to the magnitude of the work. In 1852 the Supervising Architect of the Treasury was formally established as a central office for design and construction management to meet the government's national architectural needs. In both instances architects working in these offices designed and built private and a few public structures during the era when residential neighborhoods were extending rapidly beyond the city's central core.

Many of Washington's resident architects during the early twentieth century were primarily involved in its private development, while its public buildings were designed either by federal architectural offices or commissioned from architects of national stature. In the late twentieth century, as elsewhere in the country, international movements and architects were competing with national and local ones as greater Washington grew far beyond the city's actual boundaries. As the national capital, Washington served as a laboratory for many government-sponsored mass and public housing projects beginning in the 1950s, as it had for large-scale urban and regional planning schemes since its founding. The historic preservation movement, in conjunction with planning agencies that were founded to regulate not just the growth but the ambiance of the city, has limited new construction. Much of the city's contemporary architecture is contained within older shells and hence is invisible to the general public.

Throughout its history, the consciousness of Washington's national (and more recently its international) importance has guided the layout and design of its public areas. The city's diverse population stimulated housing types and styles from elegant Beaux-Arts mansions to floating cabanas permanently docked along the southwest waterfront. The largest land area is covered by single-family homes; secure government employment produced a substantial middle class. Row houses dominate many nineteenth-century neighborhoods while major thoroughfares connecting downtown with suburban areas are lined with apartment buildings erected during the early twentieth century.

Washington contains remnants of each part of its diverse history, including habitation by native Americans. The Potomac as a major thoroughfare of the greater Chesapeake region was first explored and mapped by John Smith in 1608. He described the villages of Algonquin and Piscataway tribes as sometimes palisaded enclosures but more frequently as open with groupings of up to one hundred houses. The first European settlement in the area seems to have been about 1703, when Col. Ninian Beall, commander of the Provincial Forces of Maryland, patented 795 acres. While some original structures have survived in Georgetown, none on the actual site of the original federal city has survived, but they were noted on maps made during the 1790s. Some sites have been located in Rock Creek Park, but they are not identified in order to preserve the remains.

The national capital was located on the Potomac River as a result of a political compromise forged in Congress. From 1783 until 1790 more than fifty cities and towns were proposed, but the central location of the Potomac, its accessible but defensible position, the closeness of its headwaters to the Ohio River (and thus a vast area of inland country), and George Washington's sponsorship of the site led to the Residence Act of 1790. In 1785 Washington had been instrumental in organizing the Potomack Navigation Company to build a canal around Great Falls and Little Falls, the only obstructions in the river between Georgetown and Fort Cumberland.

In 1790, when Congress selected the Potomac River for the 10-mile-square federal district, two extant towns were to be incorporated into its boundaries, Alexandria, Virginia, and Georgetown, Maryland. Alexandria had been laid out in 1739 on a grid and was a sizeable and lively port town, the commercial center for a large number of Virginia plantations, including Mount Vernon. Georgetown, established as a tobacco warehouse depot in 1749, was still a modest commercial port when it became part of the federal district. However, its location just below the fall line of the Potomac River made it the logical place from which to ship goods—principally tobacco and wheat—brought down the river and its tributaries. Two towns in Maryland, Carrollsburg and Hamburg, were surveyed but not settled and fell within the boundaries of the federal city, a separate entity within the federal district.

The Residence Act of 1790 stipulated that Congress would move to the new seat of government in 1800. It gave President George Washington the authority to oversee erection of the public buildings therein, which was to be directed by three commissioners. The city was named in his honor on 9 September 1791. Washington devoted an enormous amount of his time during the last decade of his life to the federal city, becoming embroiled against his will in many personality clashes and minute details, in addition to choosing designs and architects. His secretary of state, Thomas Jefferson, was his closest adviser in all of these matters. Washington selected as commissioners Daniel Carroll and Thomas Johnson of Maryland and David Stuart from Virginia, a merchant, a landowner, and a physician, respectively, one of whom had had prior experience in architectural matters. Congress and the president were following the English precedent of selecting impartial men of good reputation who could be depended on to carry on the business aspects of architecture with honesty.

When Pierre Charles L'Enfant was appointed by Washington to design the federal city early in 1791, he supposed he was working directly for the president. In 1788 he had been selected as the architect of Federal Hall in New York, and his appointment as the designer of the new capital three years later was not the result of a competitive process. Rather it reflected Washington's belief that L'Enfant was the only person in the country capable of planning the new city and all of its public buildings. L'Enfant would have been familiar with this kind of deliberate choice, as public architects in France were appointed and held positions equivalent to other high executive officers. Washington's failure to make clear at the outset the lines of command between the commissioners and L'Enfant, as well as his own and Jefferson's level of participation, combined with the inexperience of the commissioners to make an explosive situation. In addition, there were opponents to the new federal capital who were located primarily in Philadelphia, and they were working behind the scenes to undermine the project throughout the 1790s. The entire process was tumultuous, and L'Enfant was fired within a year, a fate that was to befall numerous talented architects during the first decade of the city's existence. A long series of architects became victims of this process in the design and construction of the Capitol. Including L'Enfant, who submitted the initial design in 1791, seven architects were employed in designing and constructing the original Capitol before it was completed in 1829. Throughout its long and checkered history the Capitol was subject to the often uninformed opinions of numerous members of Congress, on whom funding depended.

The scale on which L'Enfant conceived the federal city was immense—6,100 acres—because he saw it as the symbolic representation of the entire country, which he referred to as "this vast Empire." Having traveled extensively in America both during and after the Revolution, he understood that the original states only began to represent the extent of the continent. In addition to expressing the country's size in his city plan, L'Enfant also incorporated in it the geographical relationship among the states. Streets named for the New England states were clustered in the northern part of the city, the central states in the middle, and the southern states on Capitol Hill. Moreover, the state avenues seem to have been associated with certain buildings in order to recall historical events associated with the establishment of the federal government. The most probable reason that New York Avenue abuts the White House grounds is that Washington was inaugurated the country's first president at Federal Hall in New York in 1789. Pennsylvania Avenue, in addition to being located in the center of the city (as Pennsylvania was in the country), joined both the grounds of the Capitol and of the President's House because of the significance and intensity of Revolutionary-era activity that took place there. Civic events included the signing of the Declaration of Independence and the constitutional conventions; military ones, the encampment of the Continental Army at Valley Forge during the winter of 1777–1778.

L'Enfant's response to the picturesque beauty of the local landscape was a

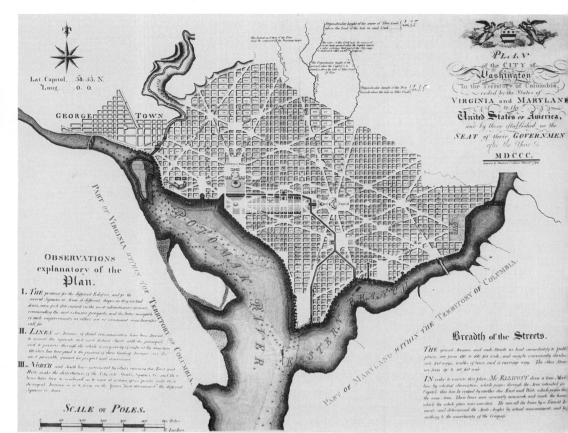

Map of Washington, D.C., by Thackara and Vallence, printed August 1792.

key factor in his design. His "Observations explanatory of the plan," written directly on the manuscript map and published in many newspapers beginning in December 1791, outlined the basic process by which he arrived at the city's major design elements. Prominent landscape features were to determine the sites of public squares; wide diagonal avenues would connect them for ease of communication and for "reciprocity of sight"; and, finally, an irregular grid of north-south, east-west streets would provide the underlying urban infrastructure. This matrix diffused the government's public and ceremonial functions throughout a city of numerous neighborhoods contained within the gridded sections. L'Enfant's intention was to address simultaneously practical, aesthetic, and symbolic issues. He was fired in March 1792 because he was unwilling to submit to the authority of the commissioners, whom he (and others) considered incompetent. His ideal of an entirely new "American" city began to be changed, an organic process that has continued to the present day.

Washington also chose the federal district's first surveyor, Andrew Ellicott, who in turn hired several assistants, including black mathematician Benjamin Banneker, to lay out the boundaries of the 10-mile-square district. Ellicott was later engaged in surveying and laying out the city's streets. In November 1791 Jefferson hired Ellicott to oversee the production of an engraved plan of the city, after L'Enfant's efforts at that task had failed. The first printed map was published in the March 1792 issue of the Philadelphia magazine the *Universal Asylum and Columbian Magazine*. L'Enfant's name appeared neither in the descriptive text nor on the map itself. The impression given was that Ellicott was the city's designer: "in order to execute this plan, Mr. Ellicott drew a true meridian line by celestial observation, which passes through the area intended for the Capitol." Washington and Jefferson promoted the engraved plans (there were four versions) as the official maps of the city, and distinguished between them and L'Enfant's manuscripts, which they viewed as preliminary essays.

Advertisements for designs for a capitol and president's house, drafted by Jefferson, were inserted in newspapers in March 1792 with entries due by July 15. A few professionally trained architects responded, but most were builder-architects with little or no formal academic training as designers. The eighteenth-century American traditions of the builder-architect, who executed his own designs, and the educated gentleman architect, whose designs for churches or public buildings were recognized by honorary rather than monetary recompense, slowly gave way to professional architects in the nineteenth century. The idea of architecture as a mental activity that required a specialized visual and technical education coincided with the need for large, three-dimensionally complex buildings such as the United States Capitol. During the next century, many of America's most talented architects vied to design buildings for Washington. Often they were plagued by inadequate public funding and a lack of professional standing.

During the twentieth century, architecture in general became a big business that required wide-ranging technical, aesthetic, and economic skills. The government's phenomenal size and complexity mandated that buildings be multifunctional, primarily to serve as offices, and that they also express national character. The preponderance of domestic architecture built in Washington generally shifted from row houses to single-family units, most often built in groups by developers rather than designed for private clients. Personal wealth in America traditionally had been expressed in private houses; its dispersal among a wider population and its concentration in urban areas beginning in the late nineteenth century had particular import for Washington, where population shifts are cyclical and family or business dynasties are rare.

Because of the limited financial resources of the federal government, construction of the early public buildings was protracted. The White House, Capitol, and executive department office buildings were begun in the 1790s, but none was complete by 1800, when the city was officially opened. The new Treasury Building, Patent Office, and General Post Office, begun in the 1830s, were all built in stages, with the north wing of the Treasury not completed until 1869. The Smithsonian Institution and Washington Monument date from the 1840s; the monument's capstone was set in 1884. A similar halting growth pattern of widely scattered domestic neighborhoods is reflected in the sarcastic, but only slightly exaggerated, description by the then architect of the Capitol, Latrobe, that Washington was "the waste *the law* calls the American metropolis."[1] As late as 1842, Charles Dickens's more famous quip—"a city of magnificent intentions"—reflected how slowly the few developed parts of the 6,100-acre city were being connected to one another.[2]

Although it was incomplete, Congress and the Supreme Court moved into the north wing of the Capitol in 1800, and President John Adams took up residence in the President's House. Sporadic private development was concentrated along Pennsylvania Avenue between Georgetown and the President's House, on Capitol Hill, and along the southwest waterfront. By November 1801 there were 621 houses in the city, double the number that had existed eighteen months earlier. Although the building regulations published in 1792 stipulated that all houses were to be built of brick, only 207 were, while the remaining 414 were wood.

A few Georgetown businessmen and original proprietors of land within the city built some speculative housing, but most was undertaken by the wealthy developers Robert Morris, John Nicholson, Thomas Law, and James Greenleaf, who had invested heavily in Washington real estate during the mid-1790s. They hired excellent architects, such as the French-trained Stephen Sulpice Hallet, fired after three years as the superintending architect of the Capitol, and Joseph Clark, architect of the Maryland State House since 1785, who had submitted an unsuccessful federal city plan to President Washington early in 1791. The developers also employed a number of architect-builders, such as William Lovering, who were responsible for the largest number of dwellings erected throughout the city in the 1790s. Little of their work survives (see SW16, p. 242), but it provided the basic housing and services for working-class families, government employees, the diplomatic community, and the transient congressmen who only spent a few months in the city while Congress was in session during the winter months.

An overview of the background, education, and involvement in the city's social, intellectual, and political life of Washington's most significant architects provides a cumulative picture of the changing nature of architectural practice in America; discussion of individual buildings helps to explicate Washington's unique character. Only a few of the architects who had the greatest impact on the city's development have been native Washingtonians. Many in the twentieth century were not even resident in Washington for significant periods of time but viewed the city as an abstract design problem on which an ideal of urban beauty could be imposed.

Pierre Charles L'Enfant (1754–1825) arrived in this country in 1777 to participate in the American Revolution. He was a young engineer who also served as a courier for General Washington and illustrated Gen. Wilhelm von Steuben's manual on military training for the Continental Army. L'Enfant had received his artistic education in Paris from his father, a painter of military subjects; his formal training in architecture and engineering is unknown. In three American architectural projects he undertook in the 1780s—a garden structure in Philadelphia to celebrate the birth of the French dauphin, a pavilion to seat 6,000 participants in New York's parade commemorating the ratification of the Constitution, and Federal Hall in New York to house the First Federal Congress—one of his principal concerns had been to invent or employ a symbolic visual language appropriately expressive of the American experience. He repeatedly used accepted American symbols, such as the eagle from the Great Seal of the United States and the stars from the American flag, in an architectural context. His incorporation of the number thirteen in his designs to signify the importance of the union of the states under the federal government culminated in his plan for Washington.

L'Enfant was in Georgetown for only about eight months in 1791, but he made good friends among the original proprietors of Washington land who urged the president to retain his services again after he had been fired in February 1792. L'Enfant's subsequent career in America was negligible. He returned to Washington in the early 1800s and lived in the city or nearby in Maryland for the remainder of his life, petitioning Congress to be paid for his design and to have his reputation as the city's designer restored to him. In 1806, Architect of the Capitol Benjamin Henry Latrobe noted in his journal:

> Daily thro' the city stalks the picture of famine L'enfant and his dog. The plan of the city is probably his, though others claim it. It is not worth disputing about. This singular Man, of whom it is not known whether he was ever educated to the profession, and who indubitably has neither good taste nor the slightest practical knowledge, had the courage to undertake any public work whatever that was offered to him. He has not succeeded in any, but was always honest, and is now miserably poor. He is too proud to receive any assistance, and it is very doubtful in what manner he subsists.[3]

When Irish-born and -trained architect James Hoban (c. 1762–1831) won the competition for the President's House in 1792, he relocated from Charleston, South Carolina, where he had been practicing architecture for the previous five years. Hoban had studied architecture with Thomas Ivory in Dublin, winning a medal in 1780 from the Dublin Society for some architectural drawings. Although he had been in America from about 1785, little of Hoban's work prior to his Washington career can be documented; his papers and drawings were destroyed by fire in the 1880s. During his early years in Washington, Hoban and his builder-partner erected numerous row houses and at least one hotel as speculative ventures. Other than the White House, Hoban's best-known

Blodgett's Hotel (in the foreground) was designed by James Hoban and built 1793–1800. It housed the post office and the United States Patent Office until it burned in 1836.

architectural design was for Blodgett's Hotel (1793–1800), intended as a prize in a lottery to promote the city but ultimately serving as a government office building containing the post office and patent office until it burned in 1836. Hoban was intermittently in charge of the Capitol's construction during periods when there was no superintending architect in residence.

Hoban was active in numerous civic affairs, founding the first lodge of Freemasons in the city and serving on the city council, as a member of the Columbian Institute, and on numerous building committees for churches and public works, probably acting as their architect. With builders Colin Williamson and Elisha O. Williams, Hoban took the city's first census, dated 12 August 1793, noting that a great proportion of the city's 820 residents consisted of "artists in the different branches of building, and from the different parts of America & Europe."[4] Throughout his years in Washington, Hoban invested in real estate and was a major property owner when he died.

Under Hoban's superintendence, building the White House presented no great difficulties, as his design was for a type of structure familiar to architects and artisans alike, a mansion with no extraordinary structural features. The Capitol, however, presented numerous difficulties from the outset, as it called for a new type of building to express the uniqueness of the modern republican form of government. No design was chosen from among those submitted to the March 1792 competition. Rather, the French-born and -trained architect Stephen Sulpice Hallet (1755–1825) was employed to make further designs based on his submission to the competition, a peripteral classical temple, and on a design he had shown to Jefferson in Philadelphia before the competition, some time in 1791, perhaps while he was employed as L'Enfant's draftsman.

Between July 1792 and March 1793 Hallet submitted a total of five Capitol designs, four in response to suggestions made by the commissioners, Washington, and Jefferson. All were of exceptional architectural quality but costly to build. In January 1793 his fourth submission was judged against a Capitol design submitted by physician and amateur architect William Thornton. Thornton's plan was favored, but Hallet was allowed to present a fifth design, which he said reflected for the first time his own ideas of what form the Capitol should take. The outcome of a conference attended by the architects, Washington, and Jefferson was a composite design that incorporated elements from both Thornton's and Hallet's plans. The judges considered that Thornton had contributed most to the composite plan, but Hallet believed the opposite. Hallet was given the second prize and, as a professional architect, hired to build Thornton's submission. The cornerstone of the Capitol was laid on 18 September 1793; Hallet was soon fired for deviating from the adopted plan by substituting major features of his own, finally leaving the federal employ in 1795. Hallet's subsequent architectural career in America was negligible, the waste of his considerable design talents a sad loss.

William Thornton (1759–1828) was born in the West Indies but educated in England and Scotland, receiving a medical degree from Aberdeen University in 1784. He resided in Paris and then returned to Tortola for a short time before he emigrated to the United States. He became a citizen in 1788 and the following year won the competition for the Library Company in Philadelphia (demolished in 1884, but its facade reconstructed in 1954). Thornton's interests were broad, ranging from steamboat design to a language for the deaf to abolitionism. Upon acceptance of his Capitol design, Thornton moved to Washington, where he played a leading role in its civic, social, and official life for the next thirty-five years.

Washington appointed Thornton one of the three Commissioners for the District of Columbia in 1795, a position he held until May 1802, when the board was abolished. In this official capacity Thornton was able to monitor closely the work of the trained architects who were charged with carrying out his Capitol design. He quarreled with each of them successively, but most bitterly with Benjamin Henry Latrobe, who, under Jefferson's aegis, implemented extensive changes to Thornton's original design. In 1802 Thornton was appointed superintendent of patents, a job he held until his death; he saved the Patent Office from being burned by British troops in August 1814, the only public building to escape immolation.

Thornton's two most significant private commissions have survived in excellent condition, Tudor Place (see GT22, p. 411), designed for Thomas Peter, and the Octagon (see FB21, p. 216), John Tayloe's city house. In 1817 Thornton advised Jefferson on his plan for the University of Virginia and contributed drawings from which Pavilion VII was built. Thornton authored several treatises and was voted a member of the American Philosophical Society in Philadelphia in 1803 as a result of one of them. He continued his many intellectual pursuits in Washington, writing, promoting a national university, and helping to found the Columbian Institute in 1816.

In 1795 George Hadfield arrived in Washington to superintend Thornton's Capitol design, but he was fired within three years. One of the most talented architects to emigrate to America during this period, Hadfield had been born in Italy and trained at the Royal Academy in London, winning its gold medal in 1784. In 1798 his designs for the executive department office buildings flanking the White House were approved; his dismay at not being allowed to superintend their erection contributed to his dismissal from public service. Hadfield went on to have an important private practice in the city, designing the city's first theater, Carusi's assembly rooms (rooms for private assemblies, parties, and other gatherings), at least two important rows of houses, and the Branch Bank of the United States in 1824. All but the last were lost before the advent of photography.

In 1802 Hadfield became the first foreign-born Washington resident to apply for American citizenship. He lived in the city until his death in 1826; his fortunes varied. In 1804 he was elected to the Washington city council but later had to hock his gold medal (retrieved for him by fellow architect Benjamin Henry Latrobe) and was reduced to working as a draftsman at the Capitol under Latrobe. In 1800 Hadfield patented a brick-making machine and started a business making terracotta roof tiles some time during the next decade. In 1822 Jefferson wrote Hadfield's sister, Maria Cosway, that since Latrobe's death (in 1820) her brother was "our first Architect," doing well, but might do better "would he push himself."[5]

Little of Hadfield's exceptional quality architecture has survived to attest to his finely honed sense of proportional relationships and command of Neoclassical architectural principles. Two of his major public buildings, the Commandant's House at the Marine Barracks (see CN44, p. 264) and the Old City Hall (see DE06, p. 183), have been rebuilt and altered by additions. Only two private structures are intact, the Van Ness Mausoleum and Arlington House in Virginia, with its overscaled giant Doric portico designed as a stage set, intended to be visible from central Washington.

In 1801, two years after being fired as the architect of the Capitol, Hadfield advertised his intention to open an architectural academy in Washington, the first such venture in the city. William P. Elliot, son of his friend and city surveyor William Elliot, was Hadfield's only known student. Elliot claimed to have studied with Hadfield for five years before spending three years in London and Paris to finish his architectural education. He entered many architectural competitions, winning for his design of the Patent Office in 1836 and placing among five winners for the Senate Committee on Public Buildings plan for the Capitol extension in 1850. However, Elliot earned his living primarily as a patent agent. He designed and paid for Hadfield's tombstone at Congressional Cemetery upon the elder architect's death and seems to have inherited his col-

George Hadfield's Branch Bank of the United States, built in 1824.

lection of architectural drawings (now lost), as in 1836 he entered a design for the Washington Monument in Hadfield's name.

The giant among Washington's early architects was Benjamin Henry Latrobe (1764–1820). He emigrated to the United States in 1795 from England, where he had received an excellent training in architecture and engineering. In 1803 President Thomas Jefferson chose him to superintend the partially completed Capitol. With only a two-year hiatus during the War of 1812, Latrobe expended much of his professional time and energy on the building until he resigned his position in 1818. During these years he maintained an active architectural practice in both Philadelphia and Washington, undertaking additional engineering and architectural work for the government as well as private commissions to supplement his inadequate salary as Architect of Public Buildings. Saint John's Church (see WH10, p. 162) and Decatur House (see WH08, p. 160) remain as the sole exemplars of his buildings for private clients in the city. He had designed a house for John Tayloe, but Thornton received the commission; his H-shaped house for John Van Ness, located on the square that is now the site of the Organization of American States (see FB06, p. 209) at 17th Street and Constitution Avenue, was described in 1830 as "unexcelled by any private building in this country."[6]

In 1804 Latrobe was hired privately to design the canal that connected the

This H-shaped house for John Van Ness was designed by Benjamin Henry Latrobe. It was built 1816–1817 and was located on the present site of the Organization of American States.

Potomac to the Anacostia River. It represented one of his many engineering projects to improve inland transportation in the country, a heritage he passed on to his two most successful students, Robert Mills and William Strickland. One of Latrobe's most significant and lasting contributions to American architecture was to establish standards of professional practice in his own work and to impress their importance upon his students and clients. In 1806 Latrobe wrote Mills outlining the responsibilities and rights of the architect: in providing architectural designs that are comely, functional, and buildable, calculating their cost, and overseeing all of the artisans involved in their execution, the architect sells his education, talent, and time. In return he should be allowed to superintend his own design, be paid a set percentage of the total cost of a building (5 percent being common in Europe), and have a decisive professional voice in differences of opinion about design with his client.

Like Thornton before him, Latrobe was very much a part of Washington's elite social and professional circles and participated in its intellectual life to its fullest during his periods of residence. As a founding member of the Columbian Institute, Latrobe carried on his tradition, initiated while he resided in Philadelphia, of participating in scholarly societies. Jefferson accepted Latrobe as his equal and the two worked closely together on many projects to provide urbane, modern, and suitable architectural models for America. Latrobe left Washington in 1818 because he found the constant battle with Congress over funding the Capitol and continued interference with his professional judgment to be too debilitating.

Professional associations among builders, developers, builder-architects, architects, and engineers began to be organized in the early 1800s. The first were essentially labor unions comprising stonemasons, bricklayers, and carpenters who were hired on a daily basis to erect public buildings. Because congressional appropriations were erratic and inadequate, all available monies were often expended by the middle of the building season. Throughout the first half of the nineteenth century the workmen organized themselves in an attempt to regulate their terms of employment, wages, and medical and disability benefits. Their success in securing benefits from their employer, the government, seems to have been limited. Therefore they functioned as benevolent societies, taking care of their own unemployed or injured members. While some were general mechanics' unions, most were organized according to individual trades.

Numerous citizens' groups petitioned Congress for incorporation as developers. In 1804 many of Washington's leading citizens, including publisher Samuel H. Smith and mayors John P. Van Ness and Daniel C. Brent, formed the Washington Building Company to promote the erection of buildings and to provide fire insurance for them. Organized as a tontine, the impact of the Washington Building Company has never been determined. More than thirty years elapsed before another such organization is known to have been formed. In 1838 the Washington Building and Improvement Company sought incorporation to remedy the 25 percent rise in rents due to "want of sufficient buildings" in Washington and to counteract the migration of mechanics, noting, "The number of brick houses annually built has fallen in the last few years from 86 to 16."[7] The company consisted of the builders George Sweeny, John C. Harkness, and Samuel Burch. They were joined by attorney David A. Hall, Charles Bulfinch's son-in-law.

In 1818, when Bulfinch (1763–1844) was invited to take over the Capitol's superintendence from Latrobe, he was one of America's most prominent architects. A mature man of fifty-five, he had been responsible for much of Boston's architectural beauty, including the Massachusetts State House, completed in 1797. During the eleven years Bulfinch was in Washington as the architect of the Capitol, he undertook a few additional commissions, all unfortunately demolished. The first was to design the church of which he was a member, erected in 1821 at 6th and D streets NW. Stuccoed brick, the 50-foot-by-72-foot Unitarian church was entered through an enclosed porch set within a tetrastyle Doric portico, the porch also providing partial support for a cupolaed bell tower. This interpenetration of masses was more reminiscent of Baroque architecture than of the austere Neoclassicism for which Bulfinch was famous, but its walls retained a planar quality, with arched doors and windows cut directly into them. After serving as the police court, the structure was demolished in 1900.

Bulfinch's Federal Penitentiary (1827–1828), located on the site of Fort McNair, was razed in two stages, all traces disappearing by 1903. The central rectangular block consisted of an outer, two-to-three-story brick shell that housed a

Charles Bulfinch's design for the Unitarian church, which was erected in 1821 at 6th and D streets, NW.

self-contained, four-story structure of cells arranged along both sides of a central spine, a system that had been developed at the Auburn, New York, Penitentiary early in the century. Bulfinch's writings on prison design while he was in Washington were considered so significant that they were published in the *National Intelligencer,* as a government report, and in pamphlet form. Additional Bulfinch commissions while in Washington were the Alexandria, Virginia, Jail, the Washington City Orphan Asylum, and renovations and additions to Hoban's Blodgett's Hotel, which served as the Patent Office and Post Office until it was destroyed by fire in 1836. His tenure as the public architect had been so untroubled in comparison to his predecessors that Congress even paid his return fare to Boston in 1829.

Robert Mills (1781–1855) spent his formative professional years and the last quarter century of his life in Washington, where he built some of his best-known structures, the Patent Office Building (see DE15.2, p. 189), General Post Office (see DE15.3, p. 191), the Treasury Building (see WH04, p. 154), and the Washington Monument (see ML09, p. 100), all fireproof masonry structures employing solid and permanent vaulting systems. As a young man Mills had come to Washington to apprentice with James Hoban, then went on to spend nearly a decade as Latrobe's apprentice and eventually assistant, working part of this time on the Capitol. His peripatetic career in the 1810s and 1820s took him from Philadelphia and Baltimore to Richmond and South Carolina. Mills's move to Washington in 1829 was in response to Bulfinch's departure, as he rightly supposed that there would be future opportunities there for his knowledge and talents. Unable initially to find full-time architectural work, Mills accepted an appointment as a Patent Office clerk but was soon employed as the engineer in charge of widening the Washington City Canal in the early 1830s.

Mills's surviving correspondence and journals record many other public projects, large and small, few of which were ever realized. He did undertake some minor renovations at the White House, won second place in the Smithsonian Institution competition and was named its superintending architect, and for twenty years was the caretaker architect of the Capitol. Mills must have done some important private buildings in Washington but no record of them has survived. Toward the end of his life Mills had to go outside the city to find work, traveling to Charlottesville, where he designed an addition to Jefferson's University of Virginia Rotunda, and to Richmond, where for a time he was in charge of erecting Thomas Crawford's Washington Monument, having himself placed second in the competition for its design.

In 1831 Mills advertised the opening of a school of architecture in the *Washington Intelligencer*; his only known student was Francis Benne, who in 1841 sought Mills's aid in his own efforts to open in Washington an Architectural Drawing School. Benne went on to practice architecture in New Haven, Connecticut. In contrast to all of his predecessors in Washington, Mills never experienced European architecture, his strong sense of the palpable force of stone buildings having been learned from Latrobe, a few other works in America, and secondhand from illustrated books of architectural designs. Mills was himself the author of several books, including three guidebooks to Washington that described the major public buildings, their locations, and the function of the federal offices. His descriptions of the Capitol and its artworks are particularly valuable.

James Renwick, Jr.'s (1818–1895), experience of the Washington architectural scene differed considerably from that of many earlier architects who had sought employment here. His youth, education, intermittent involvement in Washington architecture carried on from his New York office, and the nature of the project that brought him to Washington heralded definite changes in the architectural profession. Renwick was twenty-eight years old when he won the competition for the Smithsonian Institution. He was the son of an eminent scientist and professor at Columbia College in New York, where the young architect had received a broad and excellent education in the classics and sciences, graduating with an M.A. degree in 1839. He spent four years as an apprentice engineer (both of his brothers were engineers) before launching his architectural career by winning the competition for Grace Church in New York, the most sophisticated interpretation of Gothic architecture yet built in America.

Each of Renwick's Washington buildings introduced a new architectural style to the city and set standards of academic correctness in their design, an achievement that was uncommon among American-born and -trained architects of the period. The Smithsonian Institution's (see ML05, p. 94) hauntingly beautiful skyline frightened Neoclassical sculptor Horatio Greenough, who rightly perceived that it was a harbinger of a new age in architectural aesthetics. Renwick was the first to introduce principles and details of French Baroque architecture to Washington in his 1859 design for the Corcoran Gallery (see WH15, p. 164). Banker William W. Corcoran was Renwick's patron for numerous other Washington buildings, now demolished, including two groups of fashionable row houses, an office building, and Corcoran's own residence located at 1611 H Street NW, within steps of Lafayette Square.

Renwick's renovation of an existing three-and-a-half-story house for Corcoran began in 1849 with additions of east and west wings. When his work was completed in 1854, the form of Corcoran's house, its landscaping (by Andrew

Banker William W. Corcoran was James Renwick, Jr.'s patron for numerous Washington buildings, including his own residence at 1611 H Street.

James Renwick, Jr. designed Trinity Episcopal Church in the Gothic Revival style. It was built in 1849 on 3rd and C streets and razed in 1936.

Jackson Downing), and its exterior detailing were unlike any other Washington residence in their sophistication and elaborateness. With the Corcoran house, Renwick added a third stylistic exemplar to his Washington repertoire, a building derived from the Italian Renaissance. His fourth was accomplished in his 1849 Gothic Revival design for Trinity Episcopal Church, located on the northeast corner of 3rd and C streets NW (razed in 1936). For the church, Renwick recycled the twin-towered frontispiece of his rejected Gothic design for the Smithsonian Institution. All of Renwick's buildings were successful experiments in recasting historical forms and details in an American mold, indicative of the young architect's range of knowledge as well as his questing and eclectic outlook. The age of architectural purism had passed, and all of the world's architecture was available to provide inspiration for a new country that was perceived as being free of the national and cultural fetters existing in Europe.

American sculptor Horatio Greenough referred to his *Aesthetics at Washington,* printed in Washington in 1851, as a "paper on Structure and Ornament." In it Greenough criticized most of Washington's public buildings with the exception of the White House, which he did not mention. He found them all wanting aesthetically with the exception of Thomas U. Walter's Capitol extensions, which he knew only from a model because Walter's design was not selected until 1851. As a result of his overview of the country's largest assemblage of public buildings, Greenough concluded that America needed both a national school of design and a better method of monitoring the design and construction of federal buildings than by congressional committees. A Neoclassical purist, Greenough was profoundly uncomfortable with any variations on accepted classical forms and suspicious of the multitude of historical styles in architecture that began appearing widely during the 1840s. He misunderstood Mills's Washington buildings but rightly recognized that the choice of a medieval style as the model for Smithsonian Institution building meant that the prevailing eclecticism in domestic architecture and some public architecture was destined to be applied to all classes and types of buildings.

By the middle of the century the American states extended to the Pacific Ocean. Washington necessarily grew apace, as the country's enormous growth was reflected in the complexity and expansion of the government. Beginning in 1851, massive and elaborate extensions nearly tripled the size of the Capitol, and in 1852 the Office of the Supervising Architect was established under the Treasury Department. Both offices attracted large numbers of architects and designers to the city. Many were Americans who had learned their profession principally through apprenticeships, but a large number of European architects, many German born and trained, came to Washington to work in these large architectural offices. Some went on to be involved in the city's private architectural development, designing houses and churches while employed by the government, or later establishing their own private practices.

Thomas Ustick Walter's (1804–1887) fourteen-year career in Washington, from 1851 until 1865, coincided with the building of his Capitol Extension design (see CHO1, p. 125). During the 1840s Robert Mills had presented two schemes to enlarge the Capitol, one with longitudinal wings added to the existing building and another with a single wing projecting to the east from the center of the building. The latter would have created a Greek-cross-shaped building that left the original Capitol visually intact when seen from the Mall. In 1851 Walter submitted a longitudinal plan similar to Mills's, which won President Millard Fillmore's approval. Part of Walter's success was due to his extraordinary drafting ability. His voluminous and beautiful watercolor renderings, whether perspective views or full-scale details, depicted buildings in all their corporeality, convincingly showing in two dimensions how they would appear in reality.

During Walter's years at the Capitol, his plans for additions to Mills's three major office buildings—the Treasury, the Patent Office, and the Post Office—were accepted and carried out in conjunction with engineer Montgomery Meigs and with Walter's assistant architect and successor, Edward Clark. Mills's obituary in March 1855 noted that the seventy-four-year-old architect never recovered from the seizure he suffered upon learning that Walter's and Meigs's designs to extend the General Post Office had been chosen over his own.

Born in Philadelphia into a family of builders, Walter apprenticed between 1819 and 1824 as a stonemason and bricklayer with his father, who was in charge of building William Strickland's Second Bank of the United States, the seminal building for American Greek Revival architecture. Walter's own spectacularly successful career—more than 400 commissions in fifty-seven years— began as Philadelphia's leading Greek Revival architect, launched by winning the Girard College competition in 1833. Although his formal education in architecture was sporadic, it was as complete as it was possible to obtain in America during the 1820s. As a youth Walter attended a small private school, where he was taught Euclidian geometry by a retired sea captain. During a long apprenticeship with Strickland, Walter learned the rudiments of architectural drawing as well the general principles of architectural design and practice. In 1824 he began attending the School of Mechanic Arts in Philadelphia, where he took classes in architecture from John Haviland (who was born and trained in England) and in landscape painting from William Mason. By 1841 Walter was named professor of architecture at the Franklin Institute; in 1860 Walter taught architecture at Columbian College, the forerunner of George Washington University, where the first formal school of architecture in the city was founded.

Although Walter is best known for his monumental Greek Revival structures, his competence in a wide range of historical styles dates from the beginning of his independent career as an architect. His work in Washington, both public and private, was dominated by the Italian Renaissance tradition, attested to primarily by his Capitol Extensions, but also evident in his Italianate villa Ingleside (see NW07, p. 364), renovations of Saint John's Church Parish House (see WH11, p. 163), and the Third Baptist Church, now lost, for which Walter provided a new facade design in 1860. Walter was an ardent Baptist; this church was his own congregation and the center of his private life in Washington. The 160-foot steeple he designed for it blew down in a storm in 1862. Located on the south side of E Street NW, between 6th and 7th, the church's two massive, quoined corner towers and five tall, arched windows exhibited the same sense of strong composition, substantial structural presence, and bold detailing as his earlier Greek Revival buildings had. Walter's experience of architecture was that of a highly educated builder who knew and loved every step in the process of architectural creation. George Hadfield represented the exact opposite sensibility, where materials and construction were visually subjugated to an academic ideal of form and proportional beauty. Yet each is responsible for great works of architecture.

In 1853 superintendence of the Capitol passed from Walter's complete control to shared responsibility with army engineer Montgomery Meigs. In 1865 Walter was dismissed altogether, and his legal efforts to collect payments for his designs of additional government buildings (which he had done outside of regular office hours), located both in Washington and elsewhere, were never successful. Walter had been named vice president of the newly founded Amer-

This 1860 facade of the Third Baptist Church was designed by Thomas U. Walter, who was a member of its congregation.

ican Institute of Architects in 1857 and became its president in 1876. The AIA was founded to gain for architects the same status as other professions where mental labor was a large component of the work. Even by midcentury ambivalent attitudes toward distinguishing between architect and builder still existed. The competing interests of engineers who sought recognition as designers as well as builders was an additional factor that architects had to reckon with for the next century.

In 1852 the Metropolitan Mechanics' Institute was founded with Smithsonian Secretary Joseph Henry as president. The thirty-three officers and directors were drawn from the city's leading citizens and builder-architects. On 24 February 1853, they held their first exhibition at the Patent Office. Four years later the Washington Mutual Building Association, led by David A. Hall, sought incorporation "to act as a body both in the Manufacture, Purchase, Sale, and delivery of Materials necessary for Building purposes."[8] Little is known of these organizations, as no corpus of papers exists to study their operations or effectiveness.

The Office of the Supervising Architect was established under the Treasury Department in 1852 because it was the executive office whose agencies required federal buildings at locations around the country. These were principally federal customhouses, marine hospitals, and assay offices, although designs for federal courthouses and post offices were also produced by the office. New England architect Ammi B. Young (1800–1874) was the first incumbent, a position he held from 1852 to 1862. Young worked under army engineer Alexander H. Bowman, chief of the Bureau of Construction from 1853 to 1860, on a series of prototypical models for these public building types, devising cast-iron construction and decorative techniques intended to ensure that each structure would be solid, permanent, and handsome. His imposing and severe granite customhouse and post office for Georgetown (see GT07, p. 403) is typical of those designed for forty-one towns and cities from Waldoboro, Maine, to Galveston, Texas.

Young's successor was also born and trained in New England. Isaiah Rogers (1800–1869) held the position for just over two years, from 1862 to 1865. Both men made the transition from talented builders to creative architects with little formal training, their outstanding talents leading them to the most significant position in American architecture during their lifetimes. In spite of their enormous impact on national architecture, their influence on Washington architecture, outside of their respective wings for the Treasury Building and Young's Georgetown Custom House and Post Office, is apparently negligible, as no private works in the city are known to have been designed by either.

The third Supervising Architect, Alfred B. Mullett (1834–1890), resided in Washington from 1861 until his death. He trained two of his sons as architects, and they joined their father in private practice. In addition Mullett apprenticed many other young men, both in his official and private architectural offices, who went on to practice architecture in Washington. Mullett came to Washington as a clerk in the office of the secretary of the treasury. Although Mullett was born in England, his family emigrated when he was nine years old. In 1860 Mullett visited Europe for three months, traveling from England through the Low Countries as far east as Munich, then spending three weeks in France, visiting Versailles, the Louvre, and numerous churches and cathedrals in and around Paris.

Mullett came to architectural maturity while serving as the Supervising Architect; his massive French-inspired, multifunctional buildings were erected to serve as combination post offices, courthouses, and sometimes customhouses in every major American city, forceful embodiments of the federal government's presence. Between his appointment in June 1866 and his resignation on Christmas Eve 1874, Mullett designed thirty-six government buildings. In Washington, his State, War, and Navy Building was the most prominent, but he also designed the District of Columbia Jail, a Greek-cross-shaped building with heavily rusticated walls coupled with a simple but strong fenestration pattern of tall, narrow, arched windows with circular windows above them. Among his private commissions done in conjunction with his sons is the Apex Building (see DE12, p. 187), a twin-towered, heavily rusticated building that also had a strong French flavor.

Mullett's successor, William Appleton Potter (1842–1909), was on the cutting edge of American architectural design when he was appointed in 1875. With his half brother, Edward Tuckerman Potter, Potter was a leading proponent of the English-inspired High Victorian Gothic style of architecture, totally different in inspiration and details from Mullett's work. None of Potter's government buildings were located in Washington, but just before resigning in 1876 he did a design for the Library of Congress, a domed Neo-Byzantine structure with minaret towers at its four corners. No private buildings in the city by him are known.

James G. Hill (1841–1913) had served a three-year apprenticeship with Boston architects Gridley J. F. Bryant and Arthur Gilman before entering the Supervising Architect's office in 1862. Fourteen years later Hill was appointed Supervising Architect but resigned in 1883 to establish a prolific and respected private practice in Washington. Twenty-three of Hill's buildings were published in the *American Architect and Building News,* America's first and most influential architectural periodical. During the 1880s and 1890s Hill designed sixteen stores, banks, and office buildings in Washington's commercial core, concentrated along F Street between the Treasury Building and the Patent Office. Those that remain, including the Riggs National Bank (see DE35.2,

Alfred B. Mullett's District of Columbia Jail.

p. 202) at 9th and F streets NW, and especially the National Bank of Washington (see DE13, p. 187) at 7th Street and Indiana Avenue NW, illustrate Hill's personal and sometimes very beautiful interpretation of the Richardsonian Romanesque idiom. Adoption of this distinct treatment of rusticated stone walls punctured by low, arched openings that were decorated with foliate ornament contributed to a conscious nationwide movement to promote it as an American architectural style that had developed on this continent with no immediate nineteenth-century European forebears.

Hill's innovative design to provide health and social services for the small army of government workers employed at the Government Printing Office brought him back into government architectural circles as a private architect. He had worked vigorously with many other American architects to pass the Tarnsey Act in 1893, which opened design of government buildings to architects in private practice. Architects generally believed that the staff of the Supervising Architect's office had become too entrenched and bureaucratic to respond adequately to rapidly changing trends in American design. Hill's contributions to the profession were recognized by the American Institute of Architects in 1888, when he was named a fellow. A decade later he served as the vice president and then the president of the newly established Washington chapter of the AIA. Although best known for his commercial work, Hill designed thirty-eight known residences in Washington and made additions or alterations to forty additional structures.

No subsequent supervising architect had the national reputation of the first five, although output continued to be considerable. The office was incorporated into the General Services Administration when it was established in 1949. The title of superivising architect continued until 1956, when it was changed to assistant commissioner for design and construction within the General Services Administration. By the mid-1950s, the Public Buildings Service had evolved into an essentially administrative organization.

The presence in Washington of the headquarters of the Army Corps of Engineers played an important role in Washington's building history, one that was often in competition with that of local professional architects. It was Thomas Jefferson who had recognized the role a well-educated national corps of engineers might play in developing as well as defending the country. When he founded the United States Military Academy at West Point in 1802, he included in the curriculum courses in architecture as well as in civil and military engineering. The Army Corps of Engineers under the War Department not only designed, built, and maintained the military installations in and around Washington but also exercised considerable control over many aspects of the city's civilian government architecture. Washington's bridges and canals were often designed by architects but frequently built by army engineers. As the Potomac's width was considerable and it often froze during the winter, early bridges with wood piling had to be replaced several times. The most unusual early bridge was the Aqueduct Bridge at Georgetown, designed by topographical engineer William Turnbull and constructed between 1831 and 1835 to carry the Chesapeake and Ohio Canal from Maryland to Virginia.

The technical expertise and organizational abilities of the engineers often led to their supplanting architects during the construction phase of public buildings. Thomas Lincoln Casey was appointed to complete the Washington Monument, the State, War, and Navy Building, and the Library of Congress, in the latter two instances against the wishes of the still-living architects. Smithmeyer and Pelz, designers of the Library of Congress, sued the government for the loss of their professional fees; they eventually won the case but were never appropriated the money.

Although the engineers and architects were often at odds about their respective roles, some engineers contributed significantly to Washington's architectural beauty. The most important was Montgomery Meigs (1816–1892), a graduate of West Point in 1836, who spent most of his career working in Washington; his lovely watercolor and pencil sketches recorded the city's bucolic urbanism before its great expansion and redevelopment. He designed the Washington Aqueduct in 1852, devising not only the system of aqueduct bridges and conduits to bring water from the upper Potomac into the city but also small Neoclassical structures for buildings to house the machinery. Meigs's Cabin John Bridge, erected as part of this system, was the longest masonry arch in the world until the twentieth century. As superintendent of construction for the Capitol extensions, Meigs suggested and directed some alterations to Walter's building, including placing the legislative chambers in the center of each wing and introducing pediments on their east-facing facades. Meigs's role in devising the constructional system of the Capitol's cast-iron dome was crucial to its form and erection. To recover from the strain of having served as quartermaster general during the Civil War, Meigs spent several months in 1867 touring Europe, where he became particularly interested in Italian Renaissance architecture. Two years later he designed his own house, a small rendition of a monumental Italian palace with its entire ground story rusticated; it stood at the corner of Vermont Avenue and N Street until 1962. Meigs returned to Europe in 1876 to study exhibition architecture for the government, later advising on the design of the National Museum. His most lasting contribution to Washington's architecture is the Pension Building (see DE07, p. 183). Its massive form dominates its local skyline, and its vast interior space has been used for numerous inaugural balls.

Washington during the Civil War was an armed camp located on the edge of enemy territory, protected by a series of sixty-eight forts and batteries around its outskirts, some of which remain intact today. Fort Reno with its grounds is now a park located between Wisconsin and Connecticut avenues; Fort De Russey, located just above Military Road in Rock Creek Park, is a picturesque ruin. Because of this surveillance the city did not suffer the ravages associated with

After touring Europe and becoming interested in Italian Renaissance architecture, in 1869 Montgomery Meigs designed his own house, a small rendition of an Italian palace.

war, as did many southern cities. Its public buildings were used for hospitals but were not damaged; bread for troops was baked in the basement of the Capitol, but the building was never attacked; a herd of cattle to feed the army was grazed on the Washington Monument grounds, but the monument itself was not defaced. The war left its impact on the city's streets, deeply rutted from the movement of cannon and other military armaments through them, and on its public squares, left in shambles.

The 1,100-acre estate in Arlington, Virginia, originally owned by Washington's adopted grandson, George Washington Parke Custis, was designated Arlington National Cemetery in 1864. In 1849 the area of the District of Columbia located south of the Potomac had been retroceded to the state of Virginia. In 1871 the remaining area encompassed by the original 10-mile square of the federal district—Georgetown, Washington City, and Washington County—was united under a single territorial government by congressional act. The effect was to mitigate the strong control the federal government had always had over local civic affairs. This factor contributed to Washington's post–Civil War architectural boom, dominated by massive city-sponsored civil works projects that provided the city with many modern urban amenities and by large-scale privately sponsored residential developments.

The Board of Public Works, established in 1871 under the direction of speculator and developer Alexander R. Shepherd (who later became mayor), expended upward of $30 million to level, pave, and extend streets beyond L'Enfant's boundaries and to install under them sewer lines and water mains. In 1883, Joseph West Moore wrote in *Picturesque Washington*:

> In ten years from the time the Board of Public Works began its improvements, the city was transformed. The streets were covered with an almost noiseless, smooth pavement. Fifty thousand shade-trees had been planted; the old rows of wooden, barrack-like houses had given place to dwellings of graceful, ornate architecture; blocks of fine business buildings lined Pennsylvania Avenue and the other prominent thoroughfares; blossoming gardens and luxuriant parks were to be seen on all sides; the squares and circles were adorned with the statues of heroes, and bordered with costly and palatial mansions; splendid school-houses, churches, market buildings, newspaper offices had been erected. The water-works and sewer system were unequalled in the country. Washington had risen fresh and beautiful, like the Uranian Venus, from stagnation and decay.

The city benefited enormously, but so did Shepherd, whose extensive real estate holdings increased greatly in value. In 1888 his building operations were said to have exceeded those of any other person in the United States and were valued at $10 million. Historians have noted that Washington's economic expansion during the last quarter of the nineteenth century was based on real estate investment. Shepherd was the leader, the first developer in Washington to build entire city blocks of row houses that followed coherent, architecturally integrated designs. Frequently Shepherd's architect was Adolph Cluss (1825–1905), among the two or three most important German-trained architects to have settled in Washington in the mid-nineteenth century. Cluss designed Shepherd's Row, built in 1872 on the northeast corner of Connecticut Avenue and K Street NW; the developer resided in the turreted corner house and Cluss was his next-door neighbor. These substantial, well-designed stone houses were typical of many of the upper-middle-class residences that Shepherd built in the city's fashionable and rapidly expanding northwest neighborhoods.

Cluss had been educated as an architect and civil engineer in Württemberg, Germany, the son and grandson of architects, graduating in 1846 and emigrating to the United States two years later. He held government surveying and drafting positions before joining the Supervising Architect's office in 1855, where he was in charge of one of the drafting rooms for four years before transferring to the Navy Yard's ordnance office. In 1862 Cluss won, with Joseph von Kammerhueber (a fellow German-born architect who worked under Walter at the Capitol), the competition for the Wallach School. Upon completion in 1864, the building committee noted, "Comeliness and beauty in a building are more dependent upon the taste and skill of the architect than upon the amount of money expended." In 1865 Cluss's Franklin School (see DE19, p. 195) was begun; an articulated model costing $1,000 was exhibited at the

Shepherd's Row was designed by Adolf Cluss and built in 1872. The developer resided in the turreted corner house, and the architect lived next door to him.

World's Exposition held in Vienna in 1873, where it excited the interest of educators and architects alike and won a Medal for Progress in education and school architecture.

Cluss's designs of numerous city schools and markets, including Eastern Market (see CN33, p. 195), Sumner School for black students (DW04, p. 222), and numerous churches and residences, placed him at the forefront of his profession in Washington during the third quarter of the century. His national stature was assured by his four highly visible buildings on the Mall, of which the Arts and Industries Building, erected as the National Museum (see ML04, p. 92), is the sole survivor. Cluss's work with the American Institute of Architects gave him considerable status within the profession. He was elected a fellow in 1867 and read several papers at its annual conventions, including one in 1876 entitled "Architecture and Architects at the Capital of the United States from its Foundations until 1875." Cluss often worked in partnership with other German-born and -trained architects, principally Kammerhueber and Paul Schulze. Cluss with Schulze and Paul Schoen placed third in the Library of Congress competition in 1871; they were awarded $500 for their design.

Thomas Franklin Schneider (1859–1938), a native Washingtonian and the son of German immigrants, entered Cluss's office in 1875 for an eight-year apprenticeship. During his first three years in private practice, Schneider designed about seventy-five detached and row houses for private clients. However, in 1886 he took the step that determined his career, becoming a developer as well as architect by undertaking to finance as well as design a group of fifteen row houses. The following year Schneider began development of the 1700 block of Q Street, by which time his philosophy toward architectural design was firmly established. Within a common framework of Richardsonian Romanesque forms and decorative language, details were varied to make each house unique. This turning away from the more "tasteful" uniformity of Cluss's rows toward a lively mixture of architectural elements in order to express individuality did not result in better architecture but did express an ethos that was more typically American.

Although John Granville Meyers (1834–1902) was born in Pennsylvania, his family's background was German (he changed his name from Johannes), and his father, a mason, and brother, a brick maker, were involved in the building trades. Meyers himself was listed in the Washington city directories as a carpenter or builder from 1865 until 1875, when he appeared as an architect. Although best known for his house for Washington's German brewer Christian Heurich (see DU36, p. 332), Meyer designed 115 documented buildings in Washington, principally residences commissioned by individual clients. His most active period was the decade of the 1880s, when three-quarters of his known buildings were erected. During the same years Meyers was granted five patents relating to improved building technology, particularly fireproofing methods. Although Meyers thought of and advertised himself as an architect, justifiably so as he designed the buildings he erected, he moved in a different level of society than his professionally trained colleagues. He never joined the American Institute of Architects but rather was a member of the Masonic order and the Odd Fellows.

John L. Smithmeyer (1832–1908), born in Vienna, Austria, and Paul J. Pelz (1841–1918), born in Silesia, Germany, both came to America as youths and learned their profession as apprentices in architectural offices, Smithmeyer in Chicago and Pelz in New York. Both came to Washington shortly after the Civil War to work in government architecture offices, Smithmeyer spending five years in the Supervising Architect's office, and Pelz working for the United States Lighthouse Board. In 1872 they formed a partnership, pooling their experience and talents specifically to enter the competition for the Library of Congress (see CH12, p. 142). In 1873 they won the first prize of $1,500, and for the next fifteen years their careers were dominated by the library commission, which went through several design stages and culminated in Smithmeyer's dismissal in 1888 and Pelz's four years later. Pelz was replaced by Edward Pearce Casey, the twenty-eight-year-old son of Gen. Thomas Lincoln Casey of the Army Corps of Engineers, who had been in charge of constructing the library since

1888 and was the cause of Smithmeyer's earlier departure. Although they had a successful private practice designing many buildings in and outside of Washington, Smithmeyer's failure to receive the fees he lost on the Library of Congress commission, which he had been awarded by a court, led to a suicide attempt in 1899. He died destitute in Washington in 1908.

The nature of clients, major commissions, and the education of architects changed considerably toward the end of the nineteenth century. Members of Congress began to maintain residences in Washington as the legislative terms lengthened due to the growth and complexity of the nation and its government. Many wealthy self-made men wintered in Washington if they were not socially acceptable in Boston, New York, or Philadelphia society. Both groups either bought or commissioned substantial homes and many invested in Washington real estate schemes. Sen. Francis Newlands of Nevada backed the Chevy Chase Land Company. Although this tract was outside the district's northwestern boundary, its development required the introduction of amenities that benefited city residents, including apartment houses lining Connecticut Avenue above Rock Creek and a trolley line that served Northwest residents as well as those in Chevy Chase.

Opportunities for those Americans who wished to receive an academic education in architecture were severely limited until the last quarter of the nineteenth century. Richard Morris Hunt had traveled to Europe to attend the Parisian Ecole des Beaux-Arts in 1845. He returned to America a decade later, spending a few months working at the Capitol under Walter before establishing himself in New York. Although the first architecture school in the country was founded in 1865 (at the Massachusetts Institute of Technology), many young students, whether or not they had attended or completed a course in architecture in America, chose to experience and study the sources of the Western architectural tradition firsthand. As the Ecole not only offered a highly evolved system of instruction but also had a tradition of welcoming students from many parts of Europe, it became a mecca for young American architects. The classical French approach to architectural design emphasized highly organized spatial progressions and universal principles of design applicable alike to city plans, public buildings, and private houses. Abstract ideals of beauty and harmony, it was believed, could be taught systematically and applied in any cultural context. In addition, the actual experience of architecture—walking around and through buildings—cannot be satisfactorily replaced by theoretical knowledge or two-dimensional information gleaned from engravings or photographs.

Washington offered some unique advantages for architects trained at the Ecole. The monumental core of L'Enfant's plan included public spaces that are similar to those of Paris. The 1902 Senate Park Commission Plan that transformed the city's central area from a fragmented group of buildings nestled amidst a densely planted picturesque garden into a coherent, orderly, and architecturally unified ensemble set in an open park was primarily inspired by

French academic ideals and carried out by American architects, some of whom had been students at the Ecole. Washington's residential neighborhoods, as delineated on L'Enfant's plan, contained numerous irregular lot shapes that are comparable to those in Paris, but they were also similar to those that students at the Ecole had been typically assigned as projects. Washington's rich complement of mansions from the Gilded Age in the Dupont and Sheridan circle areas and on Meridian Hill reflect historical architectural styles from the Renaissance to the mid-nineteenth century, primarily those found in France.

The greatest American architect to be trained at the Ecole was Henry Hobson Richardson, who spent the Civil War years in Paris. Many other American (and French) students viewed the Ecole's teachings, based upon the modern classical historical styles, as a method of rearranging the stockpile of classical elements into an infinite number of combinations and permutations to create new compositions. Richardson, however, imbibed the fundamental principles taught at the Ecole and applied them to a visually and physically powerful medieval architectural tradition, the French Romanesque, which he imported directly to America, it having no contemporaneous revival in France. Richardson was a hero to all American architects and the buildings he designed between 1866 and his early death in 1886 are scattered, but those by architects he influenced are found throughout America. He designed five major houses in Washington, only one of which survives (see MH22, p. 311); his entry in the

H. H. Richardson designed this double house for two of his Harvard College classmates, John Hay and Henry Adams. It was built 1884–1886 and demolished in 1927 for the Hay-Adams Hotel.

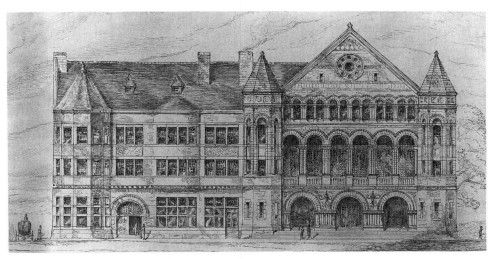

H. H. Richardson's unsuccessful entry in the competition conducted by the Washington Casino Association in 1883.

Library of Congress competition regrettably has been lost. Richardson's most significant Washington work, a double house facing Lafayette Square and 16th Street NW, was commissioned by two of his Harvard College classmates, John Hay and Henry Adams. It was demolished in 1927 for the Hay-Adams Hotel. Richardson conceived of the double house as forming an integrated visual unit with common materials, horizontal regulating lines, and his own invented language of architecture, the Richardsonian Romanesque. In his buildings Richardson repeatedly fused picturesque compositions with rational planning and intricate foliate decoration with massive stone walls, seemingly impossible combinations of incongruous opposites that he resolved and balanced to create great buildings of solid strength yet delicate beauty.

In 1883 several prominent Washingtonians, including two of Richardson's clients, formed the Washington Casino Association with the intention of building a cultural center. The facade of Richardson's entry in the competition shows a brownstone-trimmed brick building with the building's two main functions, casino and opera house, set side by side. Richardson's characteristic building up of arched openings from wide on the ground story to narrow on the top defines the opera house, while adjacent grouped rectilinear windows express the variety of public and private dining rooms, club rooms, and a ballroom. Richardson's design lost the competition; the project itself failed in 1874.

Joseph C. Hornblower (1848–1908) and J. Rush Marshall (1851–1927) formed an architectural firm in 1883 that was not dissolved until 1923. Their varied architectural educations, a mixture of American and European experiences, seem to have given them the design freedom to create an identifiable architectural image akin to Richardson's. They applied French academic planning and organizational principles to a mixture of "American" styles current at the turn of the century—Richardsonian Romanesque, Arts and Crafts, and Colonial Revival—to invent their own eclectic substyle. Both architects were active in Washington's intellectual and social clubs of the period: Hornblower was a member of six clubs in Washington and New York, including the Cosmos Club, to which he was elected in 1883. Marshall was also a member; they were jointly responsible for remodeling the club's headquarters at 1520 H Street NW. Both were also members of the AIA and active in its Washington chapter. In the early years of their partnership they employed many young architects who went on to establish their own firms, notably William J. Marsh and Walter G. Peter.

After graduating from Yale in 1869 with a degree in philosophy, Hornblower worked in Washington as an architectural draftsman in the Supervising Architect's office until his departure for Paris in 1874. He studied in the atelier, or studio, of Jean-Louis Pascal in 1875 and 1876, a common preparation for admittance to the Ecole. However, Hornblower returned to Washington in 1877 and began to practice architecture with the education he had obtained as an apprentice. Between 1895 and 1900 Hornblower was the head of the architecture department at Columbian College and continued to teach architectural history there until 1906. Hornblower made two additional trips to Europe, in 1902 and 1908, to study museum design in conjunction with the firm's commission for the Natural History Museum (see ML15, p. 108); he died at The Hague while on the second trip.

Marshall, whose father had been a professor at Dickinson College and later United States Consul in England, spent three years studying architecture at Rutgers College Scientific School beginning in 1868. After traveling in Europe with his father, Marshall entered the Supervising Architect's office in 1871, where he worked for the next twelve years before becoming Hornblower's partner. Marshall seems to have been the interior design specialist in the firm; his tasteful decoration of the great hall of the Pension Building for President William McKinley's inaugural ball in 1901 was widely praised. The firm's creative phase ended with Hornblower's death, as the office had no further major commissions.

Most Ecole-trained architects who practiced in Washington from the 1880s until the 1930s adhered to the formal, academic European styles taught in Paris. Jules Henri de Sibour (1872–1938) was born in France; his father was Vicomte Gabriel de Sibour and his mother an American. He was educated at Saint Paul's School in New Hampshire, graduated from Yale University in 1898, and spent the following year at the Ecole in Paris. His first professional experience was with Bruce Price's New York firm in 1902, where he stayed until 1908. Beginning in 1908 Sibour maintained offices in both New York and Washington, finally settling in Washington in 1911, where for thirty years he was one of the city's most prominent architects, designing a number of elegant mansions in academically correct American versions of French seventeenth- and eighteenth-century styles, including houses for Clarence Moore and Thomas

T. Gaff (see DU24 and DU29, pp. 325, 327). In 1924 Sibour's important works were published privately in *Selections from the Work of J. H. de Sibour, Architect, Washington, D.C.*

Nathan C. Wyeth (1870–1963) retired in 1946, after a distinguished career in both the public and private sectors of Washington architecture. He had graduated from the art school at New York's Metropolitan Museum of Art in 1889 and then spent ten years in Paris studying architecture at the Ecole. In 1899 he joined the Washington office of Carrère and Hastings and subsequently was employed both by the Supervising Architect's office and the Architect of the Capitol. Between 1905 and 1919 Wyeth designed a number of private mansions located principally in the Sheridan Circle and Meridian Hill areas, including residences for Gibson Fahnestock and Franklin MacVeagh (see SK20 and MH27, pp. 347, 314). His skills and practice, however, were not limited to such elite commissions, but ranged broadly to include bridges, hospitals, and the Battleship Maine Monument in Arlington Cemetery. During the First World War, Wyeth designed hospitals for the Office of the Surgeon General and spent the last dozen years of his career as the Municipal Architect of the District of Columbia.

The most popular society architect during Washington's Gilded Age was George Oakley Totten, Jr. (1866–1939), who almost single handedly created Meridian Hill's cosmopolitan ambiance in addition to designing several key structures on or near Sheridan Circle. Totten received his initial architectural education at Columbia University in New York, graduating with an M.A. in 1892. The following year he was awarded the McKim Travelling Fellowship, which allowed him to spend two years of advanced study at the Ecole in Paris. He immediately settled in Washington upon his return to America in 1895, where for three years he was chief designer in the Supervising Architect's office. He practiced in partnership with his college roommate, Laussat R. Rogers, until 1907, and thereafter independently. Totten's output was almost exclusively lavish residences or embassies, including one in Istanbul in 1908 for the Turkish Prime Minister. The overthrow of Sultan Abdul Hamid in 1909 curtailed Totten's appointment as "private architect to the Sultan of Turkey."

Totten's involvement with professional organizations was local, national, and international. He served as a delegate to eight International Congresses of Architects from 1897 until 1932, traveling to Brussels, Paris, Madrid, London, Vienna, Rome, and Budapest to represent American architects. He was president of the Washington Architectural Club in 1896–1897 and the Washington Chapter of the American Institute of Architects in 1932. In 1926 Totten published *Maya Architecture,* an illustrated scholarly study of native South American architecture that included color plates. Totten's especial interest in architectural decoration may have been a factor in his stylistic eclecticism, as he experimented continuously with a wide variety of western European historical styles, in many cases designing unique exemplars of them for Washington.

Other architects to practice in Washington who had the advantage of Parisian education included William Penn Cresson, who attended the University of Pennsylvania for two years before enrolling at the Ecole des Beaux-Arts and then the Ecole des Sciences Politiques. Cresson came to Washington in 1905, practiced architecture for just two years before becoming a Nevada cattle rancher, and eventually a diplomat with postings in England, Ecuador, Panama, Russia, and Portugal. Wyeth ended his somewhat unusual career as the Fletcher Professor of International Law at Tufts College in Massachusetts.

Waddy B. Wood (1869–1944) had a long and extremely prolific Washington career, active in federal, city, and private architectural circles, designing everything from bridges to apartment houses to the Interior Department Building (see FB20, p. 216). While working as a draftsman in several firms during the 1890s, Wood was granted permission to study all the architecture books in the Library of Congress in the evenings, a considerable undertaking. In 1903 he went into partnership with Edward W. Donn, Jr., who had been educated as an architect at the Massachusetts Institute of Technology and Cornell University, and with William L. Deming, an engineer educated at Columbian College in Washington. After 1914, Wood practiced on his own until his retirement in the late 1930s.

Perhaps the greatest legacy of the Wood, Donn and Deming firm was the large group of pleasant Colonial Revival, Spanish Colonial, and Arts and Crafts houses and row houses that provided quiet but lively streetscapes in the neighborhoods surrounding Dupont, Sheridan, and Kalorama circles. In 1906 a writer for the *Architectural Record* noted:

> They have developed the pictorial, they have demonstrated the value of color and texture, they have put some old materials to some good new uses, and have met, in measure at least the needs and requirements of a peculiar place and time. Their buildings are not all faultless, but are simple, dignified, and of fair proportion. They stand for integrity and character.[9]

While the majority of Washington's private buildings in the early twentieth century were designed by architects in practice in the city, the major government commissions went to architects with national reputations. Daniel Burnham (1846–1912) of Chicago, Charles Follen McKim (1847–1909) of New York, and Frederick Law Olmsted, Jr. (1870–1948), from Boston were responsible for redesigning central Washington under the auspices of the Senate Park Commission in 1901–1902. Burnham's career began in Chicago, where he was an apprentice in architectural and engineering firms in the mid-1860s. In partnership with John Wellborn Root from 1873 until Root's premature death in 1891, Burnham was a leader of the Chicago school during the years when the American skyscraper was formulated.

Burnham's talent for orchestrating large and complex architectural and planning projects, demonstrated in the Senate Park Commission Plan for Washington, had been tested in 1893 at the World's Columbian Exposition held in Chicago. It marked a distinctive shift in Burnham's architectural thinking away from the progressive and innovative ideals of the Chicago school to conservative and academic ones espoused by the American architects who trained in Paris at the Ecole des Beaux-Arts. In the decade following the fair Burnham's office designed large civic centers for a number of cities including Cleveland, Detroit, and San Francisco. Of all his urban plans his proposal for redoing central Washington was the most successful because the landscape matrix was already in place and because the precedent of L'Enfant's grand vision could be and was invoked to ensure its success.

Louis Sullivan, the major practitioner of the Chicago style, condemned the return to European precedents as "snobbish and alien to the land,"[10] and predicted that the pernicious influence of the Columbian Exposition would last for half a century, a prophesy that came to pass, as the Jefferson Memorial, completed in 1943, was the last major Beaux-Arts-inspired building erected in America. Burnham's success in overseeing the design and implementation of the Senate Park Commission Plan, including gaining the support of public and private groups and promoting it among congressmen and the general public, led to his commission as architect of Union Station (see CH10, p. 140), a key component of the plan.

A host of federal agencies, District of Columbia offices, and citizen's advisory groups have regulated the public and private development of Washington throughout the twentieth century. The earliest was the Commission of Fine Arts, established by Congress on 17 May 1910, "to advise upon the location, [models, and selection of artists] of statues, fountains, and monuments in the public squares, streets, and parks in the District of Columbia."[11] The Capitol and Library of Congress were excluded. Subsequent executive orders soon clarified the role the commission was to play. On 25 October 1910, William Howard Taft signed the order stipulating that all plans for public buildings erected by the government in Washington be submitted to the commission for approval. Three years later Woodrow Wilson extended the commission's purview to any new structures in the District erected under the direction of the federal government "which affect in any important way the appearance of the City."

Establishment of the Commission of Fine Arts replaced ad hoc committees, frequently composed of laymen appointed for the duration of each project, with a group of design professionals. The first chairman was architect Daniel Burnham, who served two years until his death in 1912; his successor was sculptor Daniel Chester French, who served for only three years. However, succeeding chairmen have been professional administrators in the fields of art, architecture, or planning who have served long tenures, committed to the orderly and harmonious development of Washington's public spaces. As the custodian of the Senate Park Commission Plan, the commission has reviewed tens of thousands of proposals to add to or alter buildings in Washington's monumental

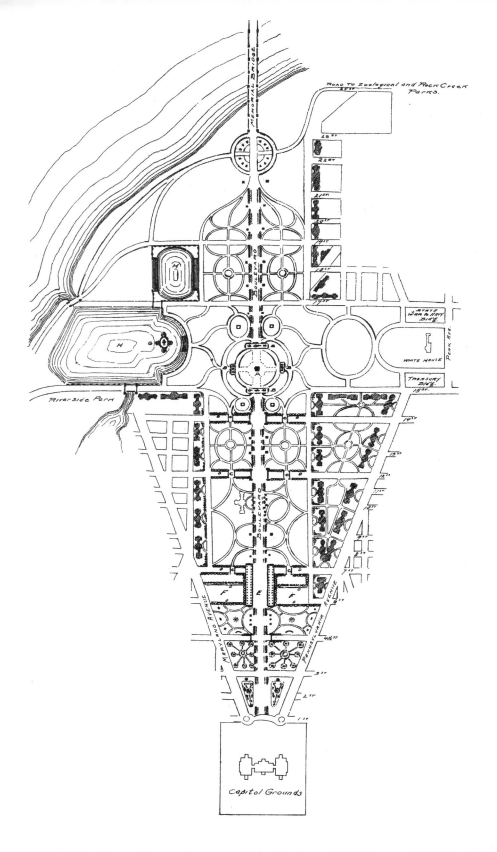

Capitol Grounds

core, defined at the present time to include all structures on public grounds (except the Capitol complex), the "private or semipublic buildings adjacent to public buildings and grounds of major importance," and all of Georgetown. The commission's design review process includes consideration of the overall impact of buildings on the city, including "height and appearance, color, and texture of the materials of exterior construction." Public hearings are an important part of the commission's process, and their decisions are legally binding. The commission's first major project was to review designs for the Lincoln Memorial; the most recent for the Holocaust museum. The commission's consistently conservative viewpoint has preserved central Washington's open, horizontal, and essentially classical ambiance into the modern era of vertical urban architecture.

Although there had been resident architects of the Capitol since 1793 and a formalized office structure had been in continuous operation since the early 1850s, the incumbents after Thomas U. Walter's departure in 1865 were caretaker architects without national reputations for their design abilities. Recognition of the importance of outstanding designs for the new Senate and House office buildings (see CH02 and CH03, p. 135) that obliquely faced the Capitol led to the selection of John M. Carrère (1858–1911) and Thomas Hastings (1860–1929) as their architects in 1905. Founders of a prestigious New York firm, both had been educated in Paris and had secured the commission for the New York Public Library in 1902, immediately recognized for its superior architectural quality. They were selected in 1906 to design the Carnegie Institution headquarters (see MH05, p. 302) because their work (specifically the library) was known and admired by members of the institution's board of directors. Their earlier renovation in 1901 of a Victorian house into one of Washington's most beautiful turn-of-the-century mansions for Richard and Mary Scott Townsend (see DU35, p. 331) had introduced their talents to Washington. More modest Washington residential commissions did not follow until 1929, neighboring brick houses at 2200 and 2222 S Street NW (see SK61 and SK62, p. 357) designed by the surviving partner Hastings during the last year of his life.

In 1900 the American Institute of Architects held its annual meeting in Washington. Glenn Brown (1854–1932) of Washington, secretary of the American Institute of Architects from 1898 to 1913, lobbied attendees to give lectures at the meeting (members of Congress were invited to attend) and prepare plans for modernizing central Washington so that American architects would play a key role in the inevitable development of the Mall and its surrounding areas, including its new extension to the west. Future public buildings, monu-

---

(Opposite) In 1900, the American Institute of Architects held its meeting in Washington and encouraged attending architects to prepare plans for modernizing central Washington. This plan was prepared by Glenn Brown, secretary of the AIA at that time.

ments, and sculpture were to be incorporated into a coherently designed landscape. Many architects participated; Brown's own scheme was published in the August 1900 issue of the *Architectural Review*. Cass Gilbert (1858–1934) presented a plan and outlined its principles. Brown included Gilbert's design and text in a group of essays entitled *Papers Relating to the Improvement of the City of Washington, District of Columbia* placed before Congress and published by the Government Printing Office in 1901. Brown's foresight led directly to implementation of the 1901–1902 Senate Park Commission Plan, which transformed monumental Washington into its current form.

Brown built a dual career in Washington as a prolific architectural writer and as a practicing architect, opening his office in 1879 after studying architecture at George Washington University and the Massachusetts Institute of Architects. His monumental two-volume *History of the United States Capitol*, published in 1900 and 1903, remains the seminal study. In an article, "Domestic Architec-

Cass Gilbert's plan for the modernization of central Washington, presented at the 1900 meeting of the AIA in Washington. Glenn Brown included this plan in a group of essays and plans published in 1901 and presented to Congress.

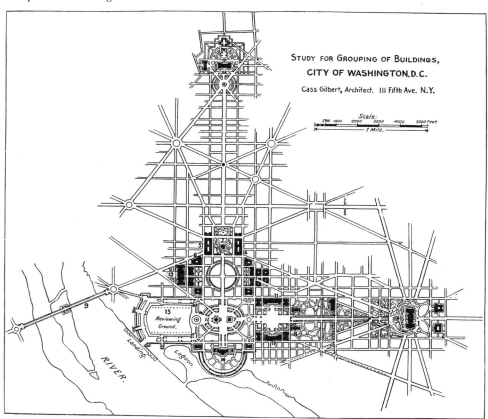

Cass Gilbert's 1900 plan for the modernization of Lafayette Square.

ture in Washington City," published in the *Engineering Magazine* in 1896 Brown analyzed numerous irregular house plans (including his own designs) occasioned by Washington's street patterns but focused on praising Richardson's great Washington houses, which he illustrated with photographs and plans. Brown himself designed more than a hundred Washington houses ranging in style from Queen Anne to Beaux-Arts; his greatest was for Joseph Beale (see SK18, p. 345).

Although best known for his skyscraper, the Woolworth Building (1913) in New York, Gilbert's reputation was established with complex Beaux-Arts public buildings, including the impressive Beaux-Arts Minnesota State Capitol, begun in 1895, and the New York Custom House, constructed between 1901 and 1907. Gilbert's involvement in Washington's early twentieth century development was extensive. He served as a member of the Commission of Fine Arts from 1910 to 1916; his two buildings facing Lafayette Square, the Treasury Annex (see WH13, p. 164) and Chamber of Commerce Building (see WH09, p. 161), were part of a larger scheme that would have implemented one element of the Senate Park Commission Plan, enclosing the square with monumental public buildings. Gilbert's greatest contribution to Washington architecture, the Supreme Court (see CH08, p. 138), came at the end of his career and during the last decade when monumental Beaux-Arts public buildings were deemed appropriate.

John Russell Pope's (1874–1937) influence on Washington's twentieth-century architectural development was profound. His highly visible public buildings include the National Archives (see FT08, p. 175), National Gallery of Art (ML16, p. 108), Jefferson Memorial (ML10, p. 102), Scottish Rite Masonic Temple (MH12, p. 305), American Pharmaceutical Association Building (FB10, p. 211), and Daughters of the American Revolution Constitution Memorial Hall (FB05, p. 208). The response of many in the architectural profession to Pope's work can be judged by critic Aymar Embury's 1921 statement, "Roman architects of two thousand years ago would prefer the Temple of the Scottish Rite to any of their own work."[12] The rightness of classicism as an appropriate American style of architecture, espoused by Thomas Jefferson more than a century earlier on political grounds, was reaffirmed in the early twentieth century on aesthetic ones. The interiors of two of Pope's elegant Washington residences are open to the public, those for Henry White and Irwin B. Laughlin (see MH17 and MH18, pp. 308, 309), neighbors on Meridian Hill, now owned by Meridian House International. This prodigious output of such high-quality buildings would be remarkable for an architect whose practice was located in Washington. Pope, however, designed major buildings for many parts of the country from his New York office, which he opened in 1903.

Pope's American and European education had been the finest obtainable. After earning a degree in architecture from Columbia University's School of Mines in New York, he won fellowships that paid for two years of study, in 1895–1896, in Rome at the American Academy. During these years Pope traveled extensively in Italy and Greece, concentrating on the study of ancient and Renaissance monuments. He then spent another two years in Paris at the Ecole des Beaux-Arts. By 1929, when Royal Cortissoz's three-volume work, *The Architecture of John Russell Pope,* was published, Pope had received many honors, including appointment by President Woodrow Wilson to the Commission of Fine Arts in 1917, yet the major Washington buildings for which he is best remembered were not designed until the final decade of his life. One of Pope's first acts during his five-year tenure on the Commission of Fine Arts was to propose covering Alfred B. Mullett's exuberant State, War, and Navy Building with a sedate Neoclassical exterior to nearly replicate that of the Treasury Building, thus attempting to impose the harmonious and symmetrical principles of classicism on existing and much-despised Victorian buildings.

In addition to his seventeen Washington buildings, Pope had been a major contender for the design of the Lincoln Memorial in 1916 and in 1925 was the successful competitor for the Theodore Roosevelt Memorial, planned to terminate the south axis of the White House where the Jefferson Memorial was ultimately located in 1939. With the Roosevelt Memorial's two massive Doric peristyles and four grandiloquent sculptural groups rising out of a long rectangular pool that traversed the Mall, Pope planned to frame the White House's

John Russell Pope's plan for the Theodore Roosevelt Memorial.

southern vista, rather than terminate it, as had been done at the Lincoln Memorial.

Paul Philippe Cret's (1876–1945) architectural background and career were substantially different from other architects whose impact on Washington has been as substantial. He was born and educated in France and came to the United States in 1903 after six years of study in Paris at the Ecole des Beaux-Arts to be the resident critic at the University of Pennsylvania's School of Architecture. Throughout his long and productive career Cret was involved in educating American architects; Louis I. Kahn was his most famous pupil. Three great Washington buildings and his five-year tenure on the Commission of Fine Arts (1940–1945) spanned most of Cret's architectural practice, beginning with his winning design for the Pan American Union (see FB06, p. 209) competition of 1907, continuing with the Folger Shakespeare Library (see CH15, p. 146), erected between 1928 and 1932, and culminating with the Federal Reserve Board Building (see FB08, p. 210), completed in 1937. The first is a canonically Beaux-Arts building while the last two, leading examples of Cret's modernized classicism (a fusion of ancient with modern architectural traditions), demonstrate the breadth of his creative ability as he led the way out of the conundrum of traditionalism versus modernism.

Washington's outstanding African-American architect, Hilyard R. Robinson (1899–1986), was a native Washingtonian. After study at Philadelphia's School of Industrial Design and service in France during World War I, Robinson traveled extensively in France before entering the University of Pennsylvania School of Architecture; he earned his B.A. in architecture at Columbia University in 1924 and eventually his M.A. there while teaching in Washington at Howard University's School of Architecture, where he joined the faculty in 1924. While still in college Robinson worked during summer vacations for Vertner W. Tandy, a talented black architect with a practice in New York.

Robinson's house for fellow Howard University faculty member Ralph Bunche (see NE05, p. 285) is one of his few single-family homes. His major interest was designing public housing following the social and aesthetic principles of modernism. During three European trips in 1925, 1931, and 1932, Robinson visited significant European housing developments in Holland, Austria, and Germany, and met and discussed their principles with Walter Gropius, Marcel Breuer, and Mies van der Rohe. Robinson's unrealized housing plan for "Howard City" on 12 acres adjacent to the university eventually led to his design for Langston Terrace (see NE02, p. 281) under the auspices of the Public Works Administration. Robinson designed seven additional government-sponsored housing projects in Washington, Baltimore, and Ypsilanti, Michigan. His other major works were educational buildings, including several at Howard University (see NE12, p. 292), and at Hampton Institute in Virginia and Jarvis College in Texas. Robinson's civic involvement was international as well as local; he was Technical Director for the Centennial Victory Exposition of the Republic of Liberia in 1947–1948 and a member of Washington's National Capitol Planning Commission from 1950 to 1955.

Hugh Newell Jacobsen (1929–), who located his architectural office in Washington in 1958, has had numerous national and international commissions. After graduating from Yale University's School of Architecture in 1955 he worked in the New York office of Philip Johnson for three years. Jacobsen's practice has been largely single-family houses (see NW30 and NW60, pp. 395, 397),

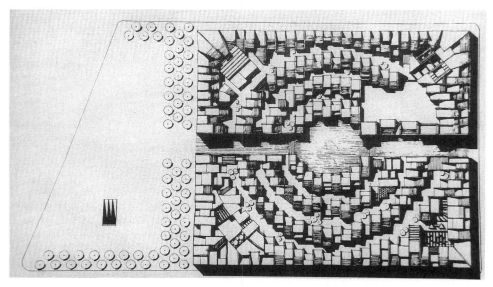

Hugh Newell Jacobsen's 1976 design for a block of houses for the Pennsylvania Avenue Development Corporation. It was planned for the site where Market Square was later built.

with many of his larger projects also residential in nature, such as the Half Moon Bay Hotel (1973) in Antigua and his dormitory for Georgetown University (see GT12.8, p. 407). In 1984 he renovated both the American Embassy in Paris, the eighteenth-century Hotel Talleyrand, and the American Embassy in Moscow, the Spaso House. His interest in preservation of historic buildings dates from two Washington projects, the Smithsonian's Arts and Industries Building and the Renwick Gallery. In 1976 Jacobsen designed for the Pennsylvania Avenue Development Corporation an entire block of houses to have been located where Market Square (see DE14, p. 188) was later built. It called for hotels and offices around the perimeter with staggered row houses set above them and in three concentric terraced rings organized around two half circles in the block's interior. Jacobsen's buildings have been widely published and repeatedly have won design awards from the American Institute of Architects as well as prestigious professional journals.

George Hartman (1936–) and Warren Cox (1935–) founded their architectural partnership in 1965 and have contributed a wide range of consistently excellent buildings to Washington and its suburban areas. Their numerous innovative office and mixed-use buildings have broken stereotyped molds while respecting and enhancing the historical context of their neighborhoods and of the city as a whole. Among the most notable are the Euram Building (see DU03, p. 320), the National Permanent Building (see DW17, p. 227), Sumner School, Van Ness Station (see NW29, p. 375), and Market Square. In addition to winning more than eighty local and national design awards, both architects have been involved in local and national architectural, intellectual, educational, and civic organizations. Hartman, who earned a Masters of Fine Arts at Princeton University in 1960, was a fellow at the American Academy in Rome in 1977–1978, president of the Washington Chapter of the AIA in 1975, president of the Cosmos Club in 1985, and named to the Commission of Fine Arts in 1989. Cox was educated at Yale University (M. Arch, 1961), where he edited *Perspecta, the Yale Architectural Journal.* His interest in the history of architecture is reflected in numerous lectures, films, and exhibits that have focused on contextualism in contemporary architecture. In 1981 Cox served on the board of directors of the Center for Palladian Studies in America and in 1986 was the director of the District of Columbia Preservation League. Both architects are fellows of the American Institute of Architects.

In 1924 the National Capital Park Commission was established by congressional act, to "provide for the comprehensive, systematic, and continuous development of park, parkway, and playground systems of the National Capital." It was composed of the chief engineer as well as the engineer in charge of public buildings and grounds from the Army Corps of Engineers, the engineer commissioner of the District of Columbia, the head of the National Park Service, and the chairpersons of the Senate and House committees on the District of Columbia. In 1926 the body was renamed the National Capital Park and Planning Commission, with its responsibilities extended to "preparing, developing and maintaining a comprehensive, consistent and coordinated plan for the National Capital and its environs." The federal agency functioned as a city planning office similar to those established in other major American cities around the beginning of the century; it was to oversee transportation, subdivisions, public building sites, sewerage, zoning, commerce, and industry.

In 1952 congressional legislation separated park management from city planning functions with the establishment of the National Capital Planning Commission (NCPC), whose purview was to ensure the "appropriate and orderly development and redevelopment of the National Capital and the conservation of the important natural and historical features thereof." Preparation of a comprehensive regional plan was a priority, with development agencies in Prince Georges and Montgomery counties in Maryland, and Arlington, Fairfax, Loudoun, and Prince William counties in Virginia consulting the comprehensive plan before implementing any local planning initiatives. In addition, NCPC has been involved in individual project planning as it coordinates the planning needs of federal agencies. Early commission members were professional planners and landscape architects who were related to pioneers in these fields. Frederick Law Olmsted, Jr., the son of the designer of the Capitol grounds in 1876, and Charles Eliot, whose uncle of the same name had designed the Boston Metropolitan Park System in 1893, contributed to implementing NCPC's goals. Commission members Frederic A. Delano, uncle of Franklin Delano

Roosevelt, and Ulysses S. Grant III had wide influence that extended to the White House to promote and implement planning issues dealing with the city's parklands, transportation system, and land-use concerns.

The National Park Service, a federal agency under the Department of the Interior, has jurisdiction over the care and interpretation of numerous historic sites, as well as national parks, throughout the country. In Washington, the Mall grounds, Washington Monument, Lincoln, Jefferson, and Vietnam Veterans memorials, East and West Potomac Park, Rock Creek Park, and most of the city's public squares are the responsibility of the Park Service. Designs for all proposed buildings or statuary to be located on these public grounds must be approved by the Park Service in addition to the Commission of Fine Arts and the National Capital Planning Commission.

Passage of the Home Rule Act of 1973 gave Washington's residents more autonomy over local municipal affairs. One provision of the act stipulated that the elected mayor share "procedures for appropriate meaningful planning process for the National Capital" with the National Capital Planning Commission. The present District of Columbia Office of Planning prepares and sends to the mayor and city council long-range comprehensive plans, ward plans, and small area plans. Their most important activity is land-use planning; under the 1984–1985 comprehensive plan the Office of Planning identified where development should occur and which neighborhoods should be protected from development. It also attempted to correct unbalanced growth in the city. The revitalization of the old downtown area during the 1980s resulted from recommendations made by the Office of Planning to other city agencies charged with housing and community development and historic preservation issues.

Since 1986 site and design approval of all commemorative works of art and architecture proposed for federal sites has been shared by the Commission of Fine Arts, National Capital Planning Commission, secretary of the interior, and administrator of General Services (successor to the Supervising Architect and since 1945 in charge of the construction and maintenance of government buildings).

Washington's architects have always played key roles in its intellectual societies. The Columbian Institute, founded in 1816 and disbanded in 1838, had eleven members who were directly involved in Washington's physical development, including Hoban, Thornton, Hadfield, Latrobe, Bulfinch, and Mills. In addition to holding monthly meetings at which lectures were often delivered, the Columbian Institute sponsored and developed the Botanic Garden at the foot of Capitol Hill and undertook the general beautification of the Mall, both of which were private initiatives to care for the city's most important public space.

The National Institute (later Institution) was founded in 1840 as a combination museum and scientific organization in order to be available to accept the bequest of English scientist James Smithson to found in Washington a society

Frank Lloyd Wright's 1939–1940 rendering of the Crystal Heights Hotel, a pioneering mixed-use project that was never realized.

for the promotion and diffusion of knowledge. Its membership, which included architect Robert Mills, was instrumental in formulating the program that eventually led to the Medieval Revival design for the Smithsonian Institution building. The National Institution's collections, which included artifacts of architectural interest, were displayed in their museum at the Patent Office before being transferred to the Smithsonian Institution. Throughout the 1840s lectures were given and papers read at meetings of the National Institution on historical and technical aspects of architecture. For example, Henry Wheaton sent drawings and lengthy descriptions of modern architecture in Germany, where he served as the American minister. The Smithsonian Institution continued this tradition, publishing in its annual reports studies on numerous aspects of building technology, including David Reid's "Ventilation in American Dwellings" in 1856, which later went through two editions in book form.

The Cosmos Club was begun in 1878 at the home of Maj. John Wesley Powell, second director of the United States Geological Survey, with many of its founding members leaders in Washington's scientific community. Its intention was intellectual and social fellowship rather than lectures or sponsored research and publication. The criterion for membership has always been high achievement; the Cosmos Club claims numerous holders of Nobel and Pulitzer prizes as members. During its first century there were 224 members whose professions were architecture or city planning, 2.5 percent of its total membership. Seven architects served as president of the club; those whose architectural work merited inclusion in this book include the partners J. Rush Marshall, president in 1895, and Joseph C. Hornblower, who served in 1903, and George Hartman, president in 1985.

In Washington more than in any other major American city, the urban character that its originators planned has been realized. For two centuries architects and planners have recognized and respected L'Enfant's vision of an American city, where a strong sense of place would be tied to a unique interweaving of landscape and architecture, public and private spaces. Nearly every American architect of significance has contributed something to Washington, albeit sometimes unrealized dreams and occasionally disdainful comment. In 1939–1940 in Crystal Heights, a pioneering mixed-use project planned for Washington, Frank Lloyd Wright foresaw that limited urban land and rising populations would make working and living in or near cities ever more unpalatable. He proposed a triangular 10-acre site on the northeast corner of Connecticut and Florida avenues NW, a vast complex in which 2,362 apartment units and about 140 hotel rooms (each with its own fireplace and balcony) would be contained in a cluster of faceted skyscrapers (the tallest 135 feet) along the site's northern perimeter overlooking a garden and plaza-parking lot. A total of twenty-one separate functions were to be accommodated in Crystal Heights, including theaters, a ballroom to accommodate 2,000 people, and a shopping center. The projected cost was $15 million. Wright commented about his prophetic design: "As the land rises and falls, so will the 21 parts vary in height," an affirmation of L'Enfant's original basic commitment to realizing the genius of the place.[13] Washington remains a green city where the natural and the man-made are in balance.

The Mall (ML)

Pamela Scott

T HE HISTORY AND SIGNIFICANCE OF THE WASHINGTON MALL
are embodied equally in its planning and institutions, which together
have produced a remarkable urban space, continuously green and constantly evolving. Pierre Charles L'Enfant regarded the Mall as the most important element in his design for the city, one that would attract many cultural
and economic enhancements. According to official boundaries established on 2
March 1797, the Mall was to enclose 227 acres and terminate at the confluence
of the Potomac River and Tiber Creek. Now considerably larger, the Mall extends 2.25 miles from the foot of Capitol Hill to the entrance to Memorial
Bridge. Its present irregular cross form and vast extent are not comprehensible
from any single point within its boundaries. Its twenty-one architectural works
span nearly two centuries, and plans call for a museum of the American Indian, a Franklin Roosevelt Memorial, and a Korean War monument.

Thomas Jefferson probably should be credited with the idea of linking the
capital's two major public buildings by an extensive garden, which he identified
as "public walks" on his February 1791 plan for the city. L'Enfant's Mall, a
more complex spatial and architectural treatment of the city's central core, consisted of a sunken, tree-lined promenade 400 feet wide, flanked on each side
by buildings raised on higher ground. In his description of the city written to
George Washington on 22 June 1791, L'Enfant characterized the Mall as a
"place of general resort" lined by theaters, assembly halls, academies, and "all
such sort of places as may be attractive to the learned and afford diversion to
the idle."[14] Prospects of the Potomac from all buildings in this central core
would be to the western, open end, and would, L'Enfant said, "acquire new
Swetness being had over the green of a field well level and made briliant by
Shade of few tree Artfully planted."[15] It was here, at the junction of the two

The Mall

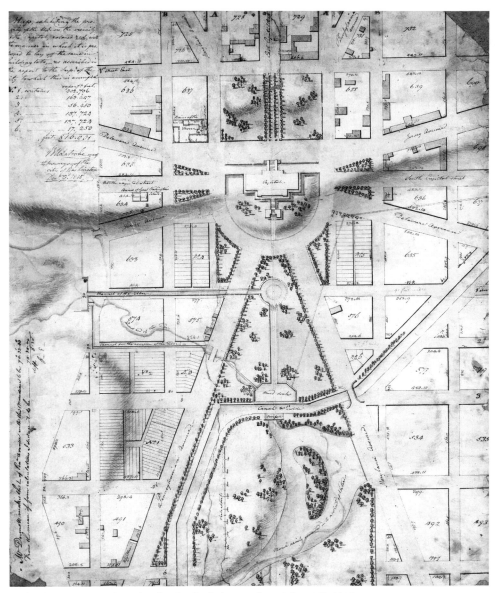

Benjamin Henry Latrobe's plan for the Capitol grounds and the Mall, 1815.

axes established by the Capitol and White House, that L'Enfant situated a bronze equestrian statue of George Washington authorized by Congress in 1783 to be located in the future national capital. At its eastern end, the Mall merged with the Capitol grounds, and L'Enfant placed there at the foot of the hill a sculpture group entitled *Liberty Hailing Nature out of Its Slumber,* his fundamental statement about the genesis and meaning of the city.

The major source for L'Enfant's arrangement of the Mall probably was the Parisian complex pivoting on the Place Louis XV (renamed the Place de la Concorde in 1795). The L-shaped relationship between the Madeleine church, Place Louis XV, Tuileries Gardens, and the Louvre was replicated in L'Enfant's plan of Washington by the President's House, a monument to Washington, the Mall, and the Capitol in a similar configuration and on a similar scale. L'Enfant was designing a city, not "a mere contemptible hamlet" (his words),[16] and Paris must have seemed an appropriate prototype for the national capital because of France's participation in the American Revolution.

Benjamin Henry Latrobe became the first architect to build on the Mall, beginning the canal depicted on L'Enfant's map. It began at the mouth of Tiber Creek, usurping land along the Mall's northern boundary, crossed the Mall at the foot of Capitol Hill, and drained into the Anacostia River. L'Enfant had planned the Washington City canal to supply markets in the interior of the city; it was not formally opened until 21 November 1815. Located under present-day Constitution Avenue, the canal continued in operation until after the Civil War and was slowly filled in during the 1870s. As an architect, Latrobe's main concerns were the appearance of the Mall and its possibilities as a physical and social environment. In 1815 he proposed landscaping in the English picturesque manner of Capability Brown, with an irregularly shaped lake and groupings of trees, leaving expansive meadows for public use in an enhanced natural setting. L'Enfant's "few tree Artfully planted" at the western end suggest that he, too, would have planted part of the Mall in this naturalistic manner. In 1822 Charles Bulfinch planned for a row of regularly spaced trees to be planted around the perimeter of both the Mall and Capitol grounds. Only those at the Capitol were planted.

In 1816 Latrobe designed for a committee of the House of Representatives a national university located on 34 acres between 13th and 15th streets. His U-shaped complex of buildings was influenced by, and in turn influenced, Jefferson's contemporaneous plan for the University of Virginia. A porticoed temple serving as an entrance and observatory was to be placed on the main axis of the Mall, at 15th Street, as was a freestanding domed church at 13th Street. Professors' houses, lecture rooms, and a medical hall connected with student lodgings, in the manner of English university colleges, were planned by Latrobe to be built incrementally between 1818 and 1830. No action was ever taken on this grand scheme.

In 1820, Congress granted a triangular site of 5 acres at the east end of the Mall to the Columbian Institute, Washington's first intellectual society, for a botanical garden. Within three years the grounds were fenced, pathways and flower beds laid out, and two ponds dug. The first greenhouse was erected there in 1850, to house exotic plants collected by the South Seas Exploring Expedition. Two larger glasshouses followed, including an octagonal Gothic Revival design of 1859 attributed to Thomas U. Walter. In 1856 it officially

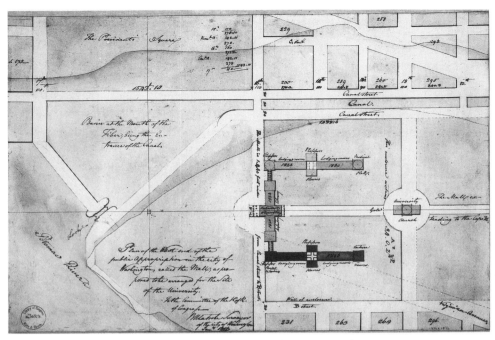

Plan for a national university on the Mall, 1816, by Benjamin Henry Latrobe.

became the United States Botanic Garden (see ML01); its greenhouses were rebuilt and enlarged in the 1870s. The Grant Memorial (Henry M. Shrady, sculptor) at the foot of Capitol Hill was mandated by the Grant Memorial Commission, which was founded in 1901. In 1909 the marble substructure designed by Edward P. Casey was erected at the expense of venerable trees and plants of the Botanic Garden. When the memorial was completed in 1922, an additional two hundred trees were destroyed and the greenhouses removed. The grounds and buildings of the Botanic Garden were then shifted to the south. The present conservatory, designed by Bennett, Parsons and Frost of Chicago, opened in 1933. Frederic A. Bartholdi's 34-foot fountain, originally made for the 1876 Philadelphia Centennial Exposition, stood in the Botanic Garden on axis with the Capitol until it was disassembled in 1927 and re-erected five years later on its present site at Independence Avenue and 2nd Street SW.

In 1841 Robert Mills was commissioned by the newly founded National Institution for the Promotion of Science to prepare designs for a rejuvenated botanical garden to be located on the Mall between 7th and 12th streets, the focus of which was to be a building for either the National Institution or the Smithsonian Institution, whichever Congress sanctioned first. The National Institution provided the basic direction. It was founded in 1840 with a dual purpose of public education through monthly lectures on a variety of topics and of the collection of objects of historical, anthropological, and scientific interest.

Its goals were reinforced by Congressman Robert Dale Owen of Indiana, head of the congressional committee charged with bringing the Smithsonian into being. His concerns were education for the masses and the development of an economical prototype for a style to serve all public architecture in America.

Mills's plan was remarkable in the range of architectural issues that it addressed as well as in the daring of its conception. This was the second of two plans that Mills prepared for the Mall. The first, in 1831, was made in conjunction with his scheme to widen the canal from 80 feet to 150 feet. The lockkeeper's house at the corner of Constitution Avenue and 17th Street NW was erected the following year by the engineer and stonemason Robert Leckie. The existence of the canal in L'Enfant's original plan created an imbalance in the width of the grounds along the Mall's central axis, resulting in the irregular placement of buildings within its boundaries. In both of his Mall plans, Mills maintained the cross axis established by the Capitol and the White House as the site for a monument to Washington. His 1831 plan for the Mall showed an equestrian statue, but by 1841 (five years after the competition for the Washington Monument) he had designed a rotunda wider than the 352-foot Capitol facade as a Washington monument. It was to sit in a fully developed pictur-

Robert Mills's plan of the Mall, 1841.

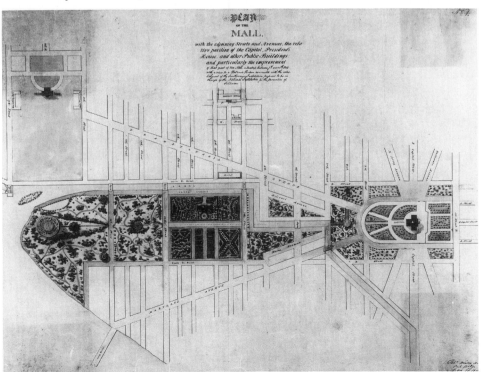

Robert Mills's design for the Smithsonian Institution, 1841.

esque garden amid winding pathways and clumps of trees. Mills had planned
this garden to complement his medieval revival building for the National Institution and to serve as agricultural experimentation fields. He favored a more
formal arrangement, reflecting the medieval medicinal garden, for the National Institution grounds, although he submitted an alternate plan making the
entire Mall picturesque.

Neither this proposal for the National Institution nor his design submitted
to the formal Smithsonian competition in 1846 was selected, but Mills was named
assistant architect to James Renwick, Jr., who was in charge of constructing the
Smithsonian Institution. The bequest of the English scientist James Smithson
to found at Washington an institution for the "increase and diffusion of knowledge among men" made a reality of L'Enfant's original vision of the Mall as a
place of learning and recreation.[17] As the criteria for the Smithsonian were so
liberal, the form it might take was interpreted by individuals in various ways.
A library, an astronomical observatory, and a scientific research center were
among possible functions vigorously promoted.

The search for an appropriate architectural image for this program, and for the best architect to realize it, was unprecedented in America. The Capitol and White House competitions of a half century earlier had simply invited participation through public notices in newspapers; by contrast, in the fall of 1846 Owen and the building committee of the Smithsonian actively sought out architects by traveling to Philadelphia, New York, Boston, and Cincinnati. Architects were asked to design an envelope around a functional plan carefully devised by the scientist David Dale Owen, brother of the congressman. This plan owed much to Robert Mills's 1841 design, as did the eventual choice of a *Rundbogenstil* style of architecture for the building. Although many talented and mature architects were practicing in America by the mid-nineteenth century, the Smithsonian competition attracted primarily a young (and unknown) generation of architects, perhaps because they were more comfortable with the medieval style mandated by the building committee. Twelve competitors submitted designs based on both Romanesque and Gothic styles of architecture.

The two entries submitted by James Renwick, Jr., of New York represented a manifestly more sophisticated handling of the medieval language than those of the other entrants. Partly to justify the decision of the building committee as being a knowledgeable one, rather than one based on rumored favoritism, and partly as a polemical tract to promote medieval architecture as a social and formal model for public architecture in America, Robert Dale Owen's *Hints on Public Architecture* was published in 1849. Like most of his contemporaries, Owen was an exponent of the enlightenment theory of associationism, believing that social, cultural, and political ideals of one time and culture could be nourished in another by replication of the historical artifacts of the earlier period. In promoting the medieval style as a model, not just for the Smithsonian building but also for future public buildings in America, Owen was selecting from history's storehouse an architectural system that he perceived had allowed for more variation and freedom of expression than was possible in the more rigidly hierarchical classical system. His ultimate goal was to participate in the creation of an American style of architecture: "to see spring up in our midst, a school of our own . . . to originate as well as to adopt."[18]

In 1833 the Washington National Monument Society had been founded by Washingtonians of local prominence, including several military officers and government officials. Their constitution, drafted by George Watterston, former librarian of Congress, mandated the largest monument in the world; the society saw size as a reflection of George Washington's greatness, just as L'Enfant had regarded the size of the city as a reflection of the vastness of the country. When in 1845 they selected Robert Mills's design for a 600-foot-tall obelisk on a circular base, they had to consider the reality of its scale, both in terms of its height and its 250-foot diameter. Its placement off the true east-west axis of the Mall seems to have been due to a combination of factors, although no explanation of its siting is found among the early records of the society. The

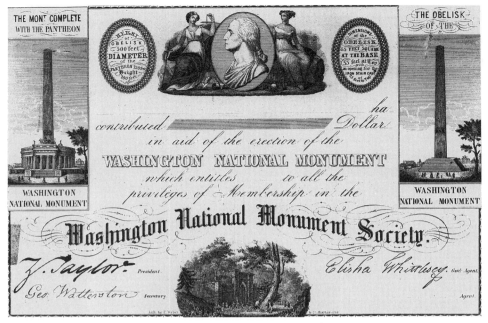

Membership certificate for the Washington National Monument Society.

actual crossing of the two important axes of the Mall was already occupied by the Meridian Stone, erected by President Jefferson in 1804 to be the point from which all future state lines were to be calculated. Its uppermost part has been excavated and may be seen at the crossing of these two axes.

Due to the 150-foot-wide expanse of the canal along its northern edge, the Mall was already inherently asymmetrical. The Smithsonian Institution (see ML05), begun in 1847, was placed 300 feet from the center line of the Mall (which was 1,440 feet wide), rather than along its southern perimeter. The site for the monument was chosen in January 1848. Its location south and east of two major axes would afford a view of both buildings from the Capitol (the principal viewing point of the city), and each would occupy its own distinct grounds in a panoramic view of Washington.

Throughout the 1840s, horticulturist and "rural architect" Andrew Jackson Downing had been promoting picturesque public parks for America to "soften and humanize the rude, educate and enlighten the ignorant, and give continual enjoyment to the educated."[19] The Washington National Monument Society and the Building Committee of the Smithsonian consulted him in 1848. His design to "ornament" the national capital, to influence the general taste of the country in the "natural style of landscape gardening," and to create an arboretum "to form a public museum of living trees and shrubs" was accepted by President Millard Fillmore in 1851.[20] The White House grounds would be the most formal, as they were to be the site of parades and military reviews. Appropriately, the Washington Monument grounds would be planted only with species of trees native to North America, and the grounds immediately adjacent were to be an evergreen maze, attractive especially in winter, for enjoyment by the increased population of the city during the months when Congress was in session. The Smithsonian grounds would be planted in a more natural style of open meadows, with tree species selected to echo either the pointed towers of the building or its round arches and, accordingly, carefully placed to achieve a reciprocal visual relationship with them. The natural style would be continued in the grounds of the Botanic Garden, where a small irregular lake would be introduced.

Although Downing died in 1852, before detailed planting plans were completed, and the program of specific garden types for each segment of the public grounds was never undertaken, his influence was considerable on the development of the Mall and the later planting of the Capitol grounds. For eighty years the Mall was a picturesque garden: trees from this period can still be seen in the vicinity of the Natural History Museum and the Department of Agriculture. In 1855–1856 the American Pomological Society erected a monument to Downing's memory, designed by his partner, Calvert Vaux, and sculpted by Robert E. Launitz. The 4-foot-tall, classically inspired urn rests on a rectilinear base that is inscribed with an affecting eulogy and quotations from Downing's writings. Once situated in Downing's picturesque landscape, it now is part of the Enid A. Haupt Garden (1987), a Postmodern version of a picturesque gar-

Andrew Jackson Downing's plan for the Mall, 1851.

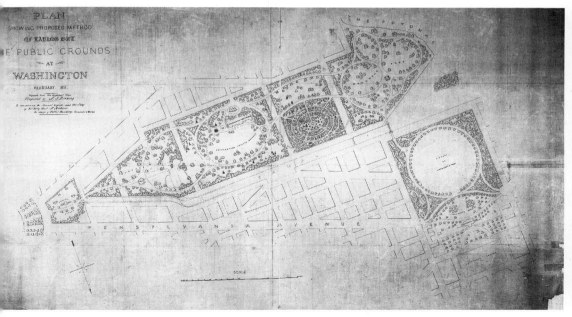

Plan of the Mall by Benjamin Franklin Smith, Jr., 1852.

den located just south of the Smithsonian Institution building, designed by Jean Paul Carlhian.

After Downing's death the public grounds were put under the supervision of the horticulturist Charles Breckinridge, and the Mall was densely planted without the varied spatial effects of open meadows contrasting with wooded groves planned by his predecessor. With no centralized control over its development, the Mall evolved in a laissez-faire manner during the second half of the nineteenth century. In 1855 the Washington Armory was erected on the northwest corner of Independence Avenue and 6th Street SW, where it served a variety of functions before being razed in 1964. Designed by Maj. William H. Bell of the United States Army Ordnance Department, it was constructed of brick in the Italianate style, with an internal structural system of cast- or rolled-iron columns, beams, and floors. Modest in scale, it was a rectangular block with hip roof, three-by-seven bays, a rusticated basement, and two-story, round-arch windows set within blind arches, an early Victorian transformation of a classical temple.

In 1856, the agricultural division of the Department of the Interior planted propagating gardens on the north side of the canal between what was then 4 1/2 and 6th streets NW (the site of the National Gallery). Greenhouses flanking a small circular Chinese pavilion were planned, though only the greenhouses were erected. When the Department of Agriculture was officially established in 1862, its dual purpose was to acquire and diffuse information on agriculture to the American people and to continue to "procure, propagate and distribute" seeds and plants to Americans. Both functions were carried out on the Mall. Adolph Cluss and Joseph W. von Kammerhueber designed the first Agriculture Department Building, constructed in 1867–1868 on a 35-acre site west of the Smithsonian and aligned with it in respect to the center line of the Mall. It was torn down in 1930. Constructed of pressed red brick with brownstone and terracotta trim, it was an eclectic Victorian design, German Renaissance Revival in style, but with a French mansard roof. Of modest size (170 feet by 61 feet) and I-shaped, it accommodated offices and laboratories. In the central section, however, two-story, round-arch, stained-glass windows lit a museum on the second floor. Decorative detailing related to the natural world; for instance, interior frescoes correlated the seasons of the year to the times of day and the ages of humankind.

A formal ornamental garden, in contrast to the naturalistic planting of the rest of the Mall, was laid out across the Mall by the Agriculture Department in 1868, following designs by the Scottish-trained landscape architect William Saunders. Beginning in 1871, this garden was terraced with two Second Empire style pavilions marking its entrance. Between 1868 and 1870 the propagating gardens, located since 1856 at the east end of the Mall, were moved to the north and west of the Agriculture Department building, and over the years two dozen structures, in addition to extensive greenhouses, were erected. The largest was the Entomological Building, in the same style as the Agriculture Department building. The most curious was a 50-foot-tall stump of a giant sequoia from General Grant National Park in California that functioned as a tree house from which to view the Mall. The buildings and formal garden were

Historical view, to the west, of the Department of Agriculture Grounds.

removed in 1931–1932, but many of the greenhouses remained until the outbreak of the Second World War.

The first substantial public building erected on the north side of the Mall was the Baltimore and Potomac Railroad Station, designed by architect Joseph M. Wilson of Philadelphia. Constructed between 1873 and 1878 on the southwest corner of Constitution Avenue and 6th Street NW, its major feature was a square tower marking the corner of an asymmetrical composition. Designed in the High Victorian Gothic style and built of brick with extravagant use of stone belt courses and trim, it was a veritable textbook of window and corbeled brick patterns. Its plethora of detail was finely proportioned to its relatively small scale. Although the double row of tracks serving it did not cross Pennsylvania Avenue, they crossed the corresponding avenue in the southwest sector, Maryland Avenue, and ran along 6th Street, then onto the Mall proper just before they entered the train sheds extending nearly the entire width of the Mall. With the station itself too modest to serve a growing tourist and official population, the tracks a serious safety hazard, and the sheds a substantial eyesore, the Baltimore and Potomac Station was destined for a short life. It was razed in 1907.

When the Philadelphia Centennial Exposition of 1876 closed, many of the exhibits were donated to the federal government for a national museum. The responsibility of housing and displaying this enormous collection of predominantly large objects fell to the Smithsonian Institution. In February 1877, the Smithsonian's Assistant Secretary, Spencer F. Baird, asked Congress to fund a building to be located on the grounds south of the Smithsonian building and attached to its south tower. Designs for an extension were prepared by both Montgomery Meigs of the Army Corps of Engineers, who in 1875 officially visited European museums and reported on their design to Baird and to Cluss, the architect who had been charged with rebuilding the Smithsonian after a fire in 1865. Two paramount concerns—fireproof construction and large, open, functional spaces that were inexpensive to build—led both architects to base their designs on recent exhibition architecture. Both proposed brick buildings 300 feet square; Meigs's had a central rotunda and dome, Cluss's a roofed square courtyard. Both proposals were pyramidal in composition, with each set of exterior aisles expressed by increasingly higher rings of shed roofs. Interiors were to be lit by clerestory windows.

Adolph Cluss in partnership with Paul Schulze was selected as the architect of the United States National Museum, now the Arts and Industries Building (see ML04). The architectural definition that Cluss gave to his functional shell was derived from his own German training and background and from the experience of the architecture of the 1873 exposition in Vienna, which in turn influenced the 1876 Philadelphia exposition. Colorful pressed and glazed bricks in conjunction with molded terracotta panels clad a building composed of round arches in what Cluss called "the modern Renaissance" style. The Arts and In-

Baltimore and Potomac Railroad Station, Joseph M. Wilson

dustries Building is the Mall's only surviving major building by Cluss, although his architecture dominated it for more than a quarter century.

The Army Medical Museum and Library, once located on the northwest corner of Independence Avenue and 7th Street SW, was also designed by Cluss and Paul Schulze. Begun in 1885 and completed two years later, the substantial U-shaped building housed 47-foot-tall exhibition galleries lit by monitor roofs in its east and west wings. Four stories tall and constructed of brick, it was the most restrained of the Victorian buildings on the Mall, with extensive, nearly unbroken runs of segmental and semicircular arched windows showing the influence of the rationalist aesthetic of contemporaneous Chicago school skyscrapers. Overlying this highly organized composition were elements associated with the *Rundbogenstil,* so much a part of Cluss's earlier work, including a corbeled cornice, polychrome lattice treatment of the spandrels of the main semicircular arches, inset brick panels, and molded brick belt courses. Robert Dale Owen's scheme to create with the Smithsonian a prototype for American public architecture based on the *Rundbogenstil* is often considered a failure, yet all the buildings erected on the south side of the Mall between 1855 and 1887 were predicated on such models. Adolph Cluss was the architect of three of these four buildings. Modern interpretative fusions of Romanesque and Renaissance traditions, they shared basic window shapes, sculptural forms, common materials and colors, and highly functional plans. All were inexpensive to build. The central preoccupation of nineteenth-century architects, the creation of an architecture expressive of their own time, had an added dimension in the United States, where architects from numerous cultural backgrounds came together to create not only a nineteenth-century style but also one that was American. Cluss may well have felt that his buildings, so prominently located close to the Smithsonian Institution, which its designer and its chief promoter proclaimed to be "American," were expanding the directions set by Renwick and Congressman Owen.

Between 1882 and 1900 the tidal flats west and south of the Washington Monument were reclaimed under the direction of the Army Corps of Engineers, nearly doubling the length of the Mall. In addition, the engineers created a tidal reservoir and a 2-mile-long spit of land facing the southwest waterfront. In 1900 the question of how to develop this area coincided with the centennial of the federal government's move to its national capital and with the maturation of Beaux-Arts ideas concerning the role of public buildings in parklike settings within an urban context. In 1900, James McMillan of Michigan, chairman of the Senate Committee on the District of Columbia, initiated the process leading to the Senate Park Commission Plan of 1901–1902, often called the McMillan Commission Plan. Two pragmatic concerns, larger offices and living quarters at the White House and the need for the Baltimore and Potomac Railroad to comply with recent public safety legislation, were major stimuli. McMillan suggested running a wide, oblique avenue through the Mall, called Centennial Avenue, to link the Capitol and White House to a new railroad station on the Mall and to a proposed Memorial Bridge crossing the Potomac at the Mall's western end. As McMillan sponsored recent legislation that had called for a much-expanded new station near the center of the Mall (necessitating at the same time elevated tracks above it), his promotion of a new plan for central Washington must be viewed as a political expedient rather than as an expression of advanced architectural or urban thinking. The architect Henry Ives Cobb of Chicago prepared the 1900 plan for McMillan.

Glenn Brown, secretary of the American Institute of Architects, played a key role by urging architects attending the institute's annual meeting, held in Washington in 1900, to present some general principles for developing the Mall. Many envisaged extending it to include the triangles formed by Pennsylvania Avenue on the north and Maryland Avenue on the south. Most retained some aspects of the extant Victorian gardens, interspersing serpentine pathways with a geometric overlay of long, broad boulevards. The landscape architect Frederick Law Olmsted, Jr., son of the designer of Central Park in New York and the Washington Capitol grounds, presented the most farsighted address, equating the city's greatness with L'Enfant's design and stressing that its formal qualities should be reinforced. Olmsted believed that the landscape in which public buildings are set must respond to their inherently stately aspects. Cass Gilbert, later architect of the Supreme Court, felt that the White House axis should be strengthened by terminating its southern end with a memorial building set in the tidal reservoir and its northern axis with a new presidential mansion on Meridian Hill. He proposed massing executive office buildings in a formal arrangement around the White House grounds, as well as a similar complex for the legislative branch.

With the advice of the American Institute of Architects, the Senate Park Commission was formed by Senator McMillan in February 1901. Architectural advisors were Daniel Burnham of Chicago and Charles F. McKim of New York, the design leaders of the World's Columbian Exposition held in Chicago in 1893. The landscape architect was Olmsted, whose father had worked with Burnham and McKim in 1893. Augustus Saint-Gaudens, the chief sculptor at the Chicago fair, was later added to the commission. The World's Columbian Exposition had been a full-scale model for exploration of the basic issues of formal and informal arrangements of buildings in relation to one another and to their appropriate landscapes. Its sources were avowedly grand-style European in origin, rather than an attempt to enlarge on the ideas and ideals of the contemporaneous native Chicago school of architecture. The lessons of the Chicago fair were seen by its designers and adherents as particularly applicable to the civic centers of American cities, a first step toward total urban revitalization. Public buildings, they believed, should be grouped in a landscape setting that included both water and formal plantings; they should be varied in form but derived from classical prototypes, be built of white or light-colored materials, have a common cornice line as well as other horizontal regulating lines, and harmoniously blend with one another.

By the spring of 1901, it had become evident that the commission would benefit from a study trip to major European cities. The opportunity to see anew familiar monuments and to discuss them on site with their colleagues would allow them to consider how the classic solutions to the numerous issues of urban design confronting them might be reinterpreted. Burnham, McKim, and Olmsted, accompanied by McMillan's secretary, Charles Moore, embarked on 13 June 1901. They returned seven weeks later, having visited Paris, Rome, Venice, Vienna, Budapest, and London. Olmsted recorded their journey with his camera; Moore later published some reminiscences from his diary. The architectural traditions of each country are discernible in the design they made during the fall and winter of that year. It was presented to President Theodore Roosevelt, Congress, and the public in January 1902.

The Senate Park Commission Plan embraced a huge, kite-shaped area of the city. It established a primary axis down the center of the Mall from the Capitol to a circle of radiating avenues on the Potomac 2.25 miles to the west, where a

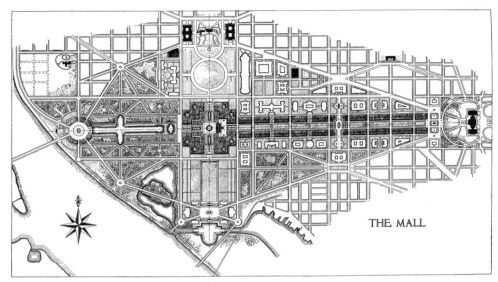

The Senate Park Commission Plan of 1901–1902.

great monument to Lincoln was proposed. The major cross axis ran from the White House through the Washington Monument grounds to a memorial complex, to be dedicated to the fathers of the Revolution. A minor cross axis at 8th Street responded to the imposing portico of the Patent Office and the open intersection that extended from Louisiana and Pennsylvania avenues as they met at 7th Street across to 9th Street. This great cross-axial arrangement of the landscape could now be likened justifiably to that of Versailles in its organization, extent, conjunction of buildings and landscape, and interpenetration of densely wooded, almost forested, areas with a few controlled and directed open areas. The entire Mall, with vast triangles attached to either side, would be more than quadrupled in size and was to be subjected to a rigid geometric discipline.

Four major groups of buildings were planned to accommodate present and future needs of both the federal government and the museum-going public. Executive department offices would replace all the homes facing Lafayette Square, as well as Saint John's Church. Fifteen buildings serving the legislative and judicial branches would join the Library of Congress in framing the Capitol. City government needs would be located in the triangle south of Pennsylvania Avenue between 6th and 15th streets. Everything that was not ordered, symmetrical, axial, white, or classical would be eradicated, including Downing's picturesque garden. All the Victorian buildings on the Mall would be replaced by classically inspired museums, organized in ranges along the Mall's perimeters. These future museums would face one another across a mile-long, 800-foot-wide lawn flanked by four rows of trees on either side, an arrangement that the commission members had seen at Hatfield House and Bushey Park in England.

The Washington Monument (see ML09) was allowed to remain, with its siting partially compensated for by realigning the east-west axis of the Mall, shifting it 25 feet to the south. The monument's location in respect to the north-south axis of the White House was too far out of alignment to permit modifications, so this fault would be turned to advantage by making it the focus of a terraced water garden on its west side. The plan included extensive parterres with formal garden elements synthesized from the Renaissance villa gardens the commission had visited in Italy and France. Charles McKim, who made preliminary drawings, envisaged the Lincoln Memorial as a standing figure facing the Capitol, silhouetted against a Doric colonnade that supported a quadriga. Lincoln would stand above an arcaded fountain wall in a manner reminiscent of a Hercules statue in the grounds of the French chateau at Vaux-le-Vicomte. Contained within a circle, the Lincoln Memorial would be separated from the Washington Monument by a reflecting pool shaped like a Latin cross, replicating on a smaller scale the cross-axial shape of the new plan.

South of the Washington Monument, a circular, porticoed temple based on the Roman Pantheon and enframed by smaller temples and a peristyle was planned as a memorial to the fathers of the Revolution. In all cases members of the commission determined that the models for buildings were to be Roman, because their sobriety was more acceptable than current flamboyant Parisian architecture. Rome's climate was similar to Washington's, and they found the image of lively fountains and still sheets of water a more appropriate adornment to the city than equestrian figures, a number of which had been erected after the Civil War. Although each major idea employed by the commission can be seen as consonant with European nineteenth-century urban planning principles, the result, an eclectic mixture, was typically American.

Under Daniel Burnham's direction the Senate Park Commission Plan far exceeded its mandate, and its budget. By dint of shrewd showmanship, spectacular presentation drawings and models, convincing the Pennsylvania Railroad to agree to an off-Mall site for their new station, and persuading Congress to pay for its tunnel, Burnham brought his vision to a wide and influential audience. The fundamental truth of Burnham's Mall is contained in the dictum often attributed to him (but which he did not originate): "Make no little plans, for they have not the power to stir men's minds. Make big plans."[21] Although violated over the years in numerous individual instances large and small, the Senate Park Commission's grand concept of the Mall gave Washington its identifiable image as a great city.

Implementation of the plan was an enormous struggle, leading to the establishment of the Commission of Fine Arts in 1910 to monitor the development of the monumental core of the city. The initial effort, begun in 1901, when the Agriculture Department needed a larger building, exemplifies the conflicting forces associated with the design and erection of public buildings in Washington. The winners of the 1901 invitational competition, Lord and Hewlett of New York, were replaced in 1903 by Rankin, Kellogg and Crane of Philadelphia, former associates of one of the judges, Charles McKim. As the latter firm had not been one of the ten original competitors and as Congress had slashed the original budget from $2.5 to $1.5 million, Austin W. Lord took his claim as far as the Supreme Court, losing in 1909. In addition, actual placement of the building within the Agriculture Department grounds was the subject of heated debate. Secretary of Agriculture James Wilson favored the site of the existing building, set back 300 feet from the center of the Mall, in line with the Smithsonian Institution building. Daniel Burnham and Charles McKim argued for its placement farther to the south, maintaining the 800-foot clearance established by the Senate Park Commission. Both parties enlisted the support of President Theodore Roosevelt, but it took the Mall Parkway hearings before the Senate in 1904 to decide the issue in favor of the architects, upholding the legal authority of the Senate Park Commission Plan.

Almost contemporaneously, the first building to be erected on the north side of the Mall as a result of the Senate Park Commission was begun. The United States National Museum, now the Natural History Museum (see ML15), was planned from the beginning to house the most extensive of the Smithsonian's collections, those relating to natural history and anthropology. As early as 1884, W. Bruce Gray proposed a design in brick and terracotta that would have nearly replicated the Arts and Industries Building on the corresponding site east of the Smithsonian building. Funds were not forthcoming. In 1901 Hornblower and Marshall (who were renovating the interior of the Smithsonian Institution building) were asked to prepare a design for the present location. A first design

Remnants of Andrew Jackson Downing's picturesque plan for the Mall.

of Italian Renaissance inspiration yielded to one made after the architects revisited Europe to study museums. The new building was based on Charles Girault's Petit Palais, erected in Paris for the 1900 World's Fair. The plans called for a monumental central arched and apsed entry, ribbed dome with oculi surmounted by a lantern in the shape of Bramante's tempietto, and a rich program of sculpture. This design proved to be too exuberant for the Smithsonian staff and Senate Park Commission members. The functionalist aesthetic in the tradition of economy and practicality associated with the history of the earlier Smithsonian buildings came into play. A spartan Roman model was called for, "substantial and dignified," with no "distracting architectural details."[22] The rationale was twofold: space for exhibitions and storage was of greater importance than architectural show, and no dome in the city should compete with that of the Capitol. As Hornblower and Marshall were unwilling to abandon their dome, Charles McKim, in his capacity as architectural adviser on the Senate Park Commission, produced the design for the Roman-inspired dome that was actually built.

The Natural History Museum was the first building to address consciously the problem of the natural slope of the Mall's terrain. As the Smithsonian Institution building stood about 50 feet higher than Pennsylvania Avenue, it was necessary to erect the Natural History building with north and south entrances on two different levels. It was also the first building on the Mall to conform to the siting criteria established by the Senate Park Commission, with its Corinthian portico centered on the porch of the Smithsonian 750 feet to the south and its main facade parallel to the newly established axis of the Mall and its east end canted 25 feet to the north.

Today there are six museums on the Mall (discounting James Smithson's original bequest), whose buildings and collections are gifts to the nation by individual Americans. The Detroit industrialist Charles L. Freer, a friend and business associate of Senator McMillan, was the first private donor. In 1906 he gave his pioneering collection of Chinese and Japanese art and American paintings of the Aesthetic period, along with the building and a million-dollar endowment, to the government to found the Freer Gallery (see ML07). Freer himself selected the architect, Charles Adams Platt, in 1913 and determined the spatial development of the building. His preference for a style based on sixteenth-century English manor houses was vetoed, however, in favor of a classical style in conformity with the Senate Park Commission guidelines. Although Platt was given the commission in 1913, the selection of site did not take place until two years later. Neither private initiatives nor further expansion by the Smithsonian resumed for another two decades until the second great private benefactor, Andrew W. Mellon, undertook to create the National Gallery of Art.

The Senate Park Commissioners, however, turned their attention to the Mall upon completion of Union Station in 1907; their first priority had been to

Lincoln Memorial and World War I temporary buildings on the Mall.

remove the Baltimore and Potomac train station and tracks from the Mall. The condition of the Mall west of the Washington Monument, an unkempt field of rubble, made it difficult for many people to envisage it as a grand urban space crowned by a great architectural monument. Opposition to memorializing Lincoln on this site delayed implementation of the entire Senate Park Commission Plan. In 1908–1909 Daniel Burnham prepared several circular designs for a Lincoln Memorial located between Union Station and the Capitol, but Congress reaffirmed the Mall site in 1909. A $2 million congressional appropriation establishing the Lincoln Memorial Commission in 1911 initiated an eleven-year process culminating in a masterwork of American architecture. Two architects, Henry Bacon and John Russell Pope, were asked by the commission (chaired by former President William Howard Taft) to prepare designs for the Mall and two other sites deemed physically and symbolically appropriate in relation to the major axes and monuments of the city. Meridian Hill, about a mile above the White House on 16th Street, and the Old Soldiers' Home, also on an eminence but north of the Capitol, were relatively undeveloped areas with commanding views to and from the city.

Of the various design solutions proposed by the two architects, three major ideas emerged, all incorporating a standing or seated figure of Lincoln. They all depended upon a columnar architectural framework that would be elevated above its surroundings. The largest and most impressive was a vast, circular double colonnade of Doric columns, which would be open to the sky and contain a seated figure of Lincoln. Pope proposed such a monument for the Old Soldiers' Home site, while Bacon planned a similar scheme for the Mall. A standing Lincoln before a Doric peristyle, rather than enclosed within an architectural space, was a second serious proposal. The third solution was a traditional classical temple with a cella to contain the statue; Pope suggested one for Meridian Hill based on the Athenian Parthenon. Henry Bacon's scheme for a variant on the enclosed temple for the Mall was selected by the Lincoln Memorial Commission on 3 July 1912. Bacon's design was closely allied to a design for a Lincoln Memorial proposed to the Senate Park Commission in 1901–1902 by Bacon's mentor, Charles Follen McKim. Each man designed a peripteral rectangle set perpendicular to the Mall's long axis.

With completion of the Lincoln Memorial in 1922 (see ML11), a major step had been taken toward the monumental development of central Washington. Gradually during the 1930s, buildings that had impeded development of the Mall were removed or relocated, principally the original Department of Agriculture building and the Botanic Garden. By 1937 four rows of trees on either side of the central parterres of the Mall had replaced most of the densely planted trees from Downing's original picturesque garden.

On 24 March 1937 President Franklin Roosevelt signed the congressional act that established the National Gallery of Art. Andrew W. Mellon had begun consciously collecting works of art to form the core of the National Gallery during his tenure as secretary of the treasury (1921–1932). His gift to the nation of this collection, as well as the building to house it, stimulated other major gifts, including those of Samuel Kress, Joseph E. Widener, Chester Dale, and Lessing J. Rosenwald. Suddenly the federal government became the guardian of an art collection of old masters that rivaled those of European museums.

Mellon selected John Russell Pope as his architect in 1936. Pope had previously designed major museum spaces in Europe as well as in America, including additions to the Tate Gallery and the British Museum in London, the Frick Museum in New York, and the Baltimore Museum of Art. His masterpiece was the National Gallery (see ML16), the plans for which were slightly altered during his lifetime (the gigantic doors on the east and west ends were substituted for porticoes) and further modified after his death in August 1937, two months after ground breaking. Pope's partners of fifteen years, Otto R. Eggers and Daniel Higgins, completed the building in 1941. Pope had sketched the plan and external massing of the museum, as it was eventually built, during a single meeting with Mellon in February 1936; it was a compendium of his earlier Classical Revival museums and the summing up of nearly a half century of American museum designs.

A year after the founding of the National Gallery, Congress established the Smithsonian Gallery of Art Commission in 1938. Its purpose was to erect on the Mall a museum of contemporary art dedicated to living artists; it would be located across the Mall from Pope's building. Joseph Hudnut, dean of the Harvard School of Architecture and an avowed modernist, was selected to oversee the competition. For the jury, he chose Frederic A. Delano, chairman of the National Capital Park and Planning Commission and Franklin Roosevelt's uncle; John A. Holabird of the long-established Chicago firm of Holabird and Root; Walter Gropius, former director of the Bauhaus in Germany and then professor of architecture at Harvard; the Philadelphia architect George Howe; and Henry R. Shepley of the Boston firm of Shepley, Bulfinch, Richardson, and Abbott. The ideological stance was balanced between modernists and traditionalists, with a slight edge given to the modernists.

The criteria outlined in the widely publicized competition program emphasized two aspects of the museum that predetermined a modern design. In direct reaction both to Mellon's National Gallery and to the recently established Museum of Modern Art in New York, it was to sponsor varied cultural activities rather than be a static repository for "great" works of art. This was translated into "maximum flexibility and freedom of extension," a major planning tenet of modern architecture. The preliminary open competition announced in January 1939 drew 408 designs. In May, ten of the competitors were invited to develop their ideas more fully. The best-known architects of this group were Paul Philippe Cret, Edward Durell Stone, Hugh Stubbins, and the father-and-son team of Eliel and Eero Saarinen. The unanimous decision of the jury was for the simple, elegant building, modern in its asymmetrical balancing of horizontal and vertical masses, designed by the Saarinens in conjunction with Robert F. Swanson. The architectural press hailed the selection as the first step in updating Washington architecture, which was viewed pejoratively as the stronghold of conservatism. Opposition to the Saarinen design was powerful, led by the Commission of Fine Arts, which found the modernist vocabulary alien to the site and destructive of the ideals of the Senate Park Commission Plan. Without an equally powerful supporter in Washington and a strong constituency fighting for its survival, the project never gained congressional funding.

Numerous attempts to erect a memorial to Thomas Jefferson in Washington also were unsuccessful until the Thomas Jefferson Memorial Commission was established in 1934. Sponsored by New York Congressman John Boylan, the commission initially wanted to place the memorial at the apex of the Federal Triangle, then nearing completion. The site—where Constitution and Pennsylvania avenues converge—was appropriate because Jefferson had helped to draft the Constitution and because his early involvement in the design of the city had included a landscape plan for Pennsylvania Avenue. When art historian and architect Fiske Kimball, the leading Jefferson scholar and restorer of Monticello, was named to the commission, he insisted that a monument to Jefferson ought to be of the magnitude and importance of the monuments to the two other presidents. He favored the site in the Tidal Basin on axis with the White House, planned by the Senate Park Commission as the location for a major monument complex, of which the central focus had been a rotunda. Jefferson's idea that the replication in America of Roman architectural forms and details would promote Roman civic ideals among his countrymen, as well as his use of the Roman Pantheon as a prototype for the rotunda at the University of Virginia, influenced Kimball to promote this structure as the model for Jefferson's monument.

No competition was held; John Russell Pope was considered the only living American architect capable of providing a classical design of significant dignity, grandeur, and correctness. In the spring of 1936, he submitted three designs for four sites: a domed pantheon for either the Tidal Basin site or the termination of East Capitol Street on the banks of the Anacostia River; an open colonnade on the Mall opposite the National Archives; and a Doric temple in the middle of Lincoln Square, twelve blocks east of the Capitol. The pantheon scheme located at the Tidal Basin was favored, and during the following winter Pope clarified his thinking, presenting two alternatives, both located in a newly designed, formal Tidal Basin. Dredging of the Potomac in the 1880s and 1890s had created the irregularly shaped, low spit of land enclosing the Tidal Basin, where the first cherry trees were planted, a gift of the city of Tokyo in 1912. Pope's redesign of the pond into a rectilinear reflecting pool would have eliminated the trees, already a venerable part of Washington life.

Both of Pope's treatments of the pantheon called for a building one and a half times the size of the Lincoln Memorial to be elevated on a high podium. He favored a colonnaded rotunda with its portico facing the White House; a second design had porticoes facing the four cardinal directions. In mid-February 1937, the commission met with President Franklin Roosevelt, who had been closely involved with the project from the beginning. The president favored the single portico design; the Commission of Fine Arts gave its official approval, but the National Capital Park and Planning Commissioners withheld theirs. Opposition to the design came from many quarters: from those who deplored destruction of the cherry trees, from modernist architects who found the design hopelessly old fashioned ("Pope's arrogant insult to the memory of Thomas Jefferson," according to Frank Lloyd Wright),[23] and even from conservative architects who viewed it as a hackneyed design, particularly as Pope had just designed the National Gallery of Art on the Mall with a similar dome and portico. Despite Pope's death the project went forward, as his partner Otto Eggers had been largely responsible for drawing Pope's numerous ideas. A compromise struck in March 1938 cut the size of the building in half and left the landscaping of the Tidal Basin essentially intact (see ML10).

During the two decades following completion of the Freer Gallery, the Smithsonian Institution had concentrated its energies on research and collection development. With the appointment in 1953 of Leonard Carmichael as the sixth secretary of the Smithsonian, a program of expansion (with seven new proposed buildings) and modernization of exhibits was undertaken. Carmichael's concern was to gain a wider audience and to display and explicate the institution's extraordinary range of objects more effectively. The National Museum of American History, founded as the National Museum of History and Technology in 1955, was established to correct an imbalance in display that had favored science over history, art, and technology. Its initial holdings were those collected by the National Institution for the Promotion of Science, which had been particularly interested in the fledgling industrial productions of the country. These were first displayed in the Patent Office because of its association with American inventiveness. The Cold War and the technology race of the 1950s provided the major impetus to display American superiority in matters of science and technology in a museum setting in Washington. Visiting consultants from the German Museum of Technology, however, advised against isolating industrial, technological, and scientific collections from those representative of wider concepts of cultural history.

The Smithsonian's establishment of the National Portrait Gallery and the National Collection of Fine Arts (now the National Museum of American Art) in the historic Patent Office building (see DE15.2, p. 189) at a location off the Mall in 1968 proved to be the most significant stimulus to research and collection of American art in the country. Acceptance by the Smithsonian in 1966 of Joseph H. Hirshhorn's gift of his six-thousand-item personal collection of late nineteenth- and twentieth-century art stipulated that the museum bear Hirshhorn's name and be located on the Mall. Because Hirshhorn's collection was particularly rich in sculpture, it necessitated both a building and a sculpture garden (see ML03). Initially the Hirshhorn Museum was to be located on the north side of the Mall along Constitution Avenue at 8th Street, against a high embankment on the Mall; it was also planned to keep the 8th Street axis open in conformity with the Senate Park Commission Plan. Hirshhorn objected; he agreed to the aboveground corresponding site along Independence Avenue. In conjunction with Secretary of the Smithsonian S. Dillon Ripley, Hirshhorn selected the architect Gordon Bunshaft. From the beginning, Bunshaft's response to the axis running south from the National Archives was to terminate it with a circular building. As modernist architectural theory and practice were unconcerned with maintaining contextual relationships with adjoining buildings, and as its nearest neighbor, the Arts and Industries Building, was itself such a strong architectural statement, Bunshaft's building deliberately turned inward.

The National Air and Space Museum (see ML02) had been visited by 100 million people within a decade of its opening on 1 July 1976. Its current exhibits are constantly updated, reflecting the most recent advances and adventures in a field where America has been a leader from the advent of modern air travel. A Smithsonian museum to celebrate this area of knowledge was particularly appropriate, as the institution's research arm has had direct involvement in American aeronautics since it began using balloons in 1857 to collect weather data. In 1946, Congress established the National Air Museum ("space" was added in 1966) as a bureau of the Smithsonian and authorized construction of a building to house it a dozen years later. However, $40 million in construction funds were not appropriated until 1972. During the six years between Gordon Bunshaft's design for the Hirshhorn Museum and Gyo Obata's for the Air and Space Museum, the antihistorical bias of modernist architecture began to break down. While Bunshaft designed his museum to be independent of the earlier classically derived museums on the Mall, Obata abstracted from them major principles that he applied to a thoroughly up-to-date structure.

When the National Gallery of Art began experiencing overcrowded conditions, particularly for its expanding scholarly programs and library and archival collections, its board planned a second building to the east of the existing museum. A large area was needed for offices, while the museum was to house expanding permanent collections and substantial temporary traveling exhibits, a particular phenomenon of modern museology. In 1953 the successor firm to John Russell Pope, Eggers and Higgins, had proposed a centralized building, a short rectangle with four shallow arms, placed at the west end of the trapezoidal site to avoid its narrow east end. In 1967 Pietro Belluschi was hired to advise on the best strategy for the future expansion. Two important requirements emerged: a tunnel connecting the buildings to maintain constant atmospheric conditions when moving works of art and a design that responded to the strong longitudinal axis of the Pope building. One possibility considered was to connect the two buildings by a skyway over 4th Street rather than by a tunnel. When I. M. Pei was commissioned in 1968 to design the East Building (see ML17), however, he felt strongly that the original building should remain untouched.

In the tradition of the Senate Park Commission's 1901 trip to Europe, the museum's director, J. Carter Brown, took Pei on a tour of his favorite American and European museums. Brown's preference was for domestically scaled rooms where works of art are seen in settings on a scale for which they were created. Pei was charged with creating a series of such spaces in the East Building, although it was recognized that the monumental scale of the Mall had to be maintained in his overall design. From the outset Pei conceived the office block as being housed not in leftover spaces of the museum but in a building of its own. His solution to the difficult geometry of the site was to place two triangles beside one another and connect them with a third triangle at roof level. Zoning laws require that buildings facing Pennsylvania Avenue and the Mall be set back within their blocks so that the sense of a continuous urban wall broken only by intersecting cross streets is maintained. Within these confines, Pei designed the East Building complex with four distinct facades responding to external prospects and internal functions. The Mall facade of his original design was criticized for not presenting a properly monumental appearance for such an important aspect. Pei then replaced offices on the Mall side with a library reading room, creating a glass facade that is ambiguous in its relationship to the Mall. Its location, shape, and materials seem to imply entry, a logical but mistaken assumption. The resulting facade is more in keeping with its location overlooking the Mall. The East Building opened in 1978 to worldwide acclaim, unprecedented for any Mall structure. Primarily a gift to the nation of Ailsa Mellon Bruce and Paul Mellon, children of Andrew Mellon, the gallery's founder, it remains the finest work of monumental modern architecture in Washington.

Constitution Gardens, located on the north side of the Mall parallel to the reflecting pool, was a bicentennial project sponsored by the National Park Service. The garden replaced temporary office buildings erected during the First World War that were finally removed in the 1960s. Designed by Skidmore, Owings and Merrill as a picturesque interlude with a duck pond surrounding an island, with gently rolling and winding pathways and with a variety of shaded bowers, these gardens were intended to provide an intimate natural setting in contrast to the open, formal nature of much of the Mall. Although pleasant, this landscape is so obviously contrived in comparison to the apparently inevitable and compelling experience of the nearby Vietnam Veterans Memorial that it suffers by its close proximity.

The genesis of the most recent museum on the Mall, the Arthur M. Sackler Gallery and the National Museum of African Art (see ML06), was S. Dillon Ripley's wish as secretary of the Smithsonian (1964–1984) to build a center to foster international relations on a cultural, rather than political, level. Because the Freer Gallery's collections had expanded by tenfold and the African Art Museum had developed rapidly after it was acquired by the Smithsonian in 1979, larger exhibition and storage space was needed. A complex of buildings to house several new or expanding functions of the Smithsonian was designed in 1978–1979 by the Japanese architect Junzo Yoshimura. He proposed two pavilions located in the south forecourt of the Smithsonian Institution building to serve as entrances to the underground museums and an international center. The pavilion adjacent to the Freer Gallery was modeled on a Japanese house, and a low, vaulted structure reminiscent of African adobe construction to its east was to stand next to the Arts and Industries Building. In 1979 the Smithsonian chose the Boston architects Shepley, Bulfinch, Richardson, and Abbott to carry out the project. The design underwent inevitable changes with a third element added, but the basic concept of underground museums with aboveground entrance pavilions set in a densely landscaped garden remained. When the complex opened to the public in 1987, it contributed an example of Postmodern architecture to the Mall, a style that consciously returns to pre-Modern historicism and often takes its design motifs from the immediate architectural context.

The announcement in 1980 of a competition for the Vietnam Veterans Memorial invited American artists to design a memorial that would be a "symbol for national unity and reconciliation after the controversy of the Vietnam War."

In the same year, Congress approved a 2-acre site on the north side of the Mall contiguous to the Lincoln Memorial. Conceived in 1979 by veteran Jan Scruggs after seeing the film *The Deer Hunter,* the memorial was sponsored by Vietnam veterans, who raised the money and administered the entire project. A jury composed of architects (Pietro Belluschi and Harry Weese), landscape architects (Grady Clay, Garrett Eckbo, and Hideo Sasaki), and sculptors (Richard H. Hunt, Constantino Nivola, and James Rosali) judged 1,421 designs, the largest competition in the history of American architecture. They awarded $20,000 to twenty-one-year-old Yale architecture student Maya Lin for her "simple and forthright" design, a V cut into the earth by two, 200-foot-long polished black granite walls set asymmetrically on the site, which pointed to the Washington Monument to the east and the Lincoln Memorial to the southwest (see ML13). The wall was to be inscribed with the names of the 57,692 men and women who died in the war, a prerequisite set by the competition program. Lin said of her design:

> The memorial is composed not as an unchanging monument, but as a moving composition to be understood as we move into and out of it; the passage itself is gradual, the descent to the origin slow, but it is at the origin that the *meaning* of this memorial is to be fully understood. . . . Walking into the grassy site contained by the walls of the memorial, we can barely make out the carved names upon the memorial walls. These names, seemingly infinite in number, convey the sense of overwhelming numbers, while unifying those individuals into a whole. For this memorial is meant not as a memorial to the individual, but rather to the men and women who died during the war, as a whole.[24]

Response to the design was immediate and divided: supporters were overwhelmed by its subtle beauty, while detractors, many of them veterans, found it impersonal and lacking an image with which they could identify. While private funding was being raised, inclusion of a sculpture group of three armed soldiers on patrol by Frederick E. Hart was considered. Placement of the sculpture, whether close to Lin's work or in a wooded area, was resolved in meetings of the veterans, the Commission of Fine Arts, the National Capital Planning Commission, and the National Park Service. Construction took place over a two-year period with Lin consulting with the Washington firm the Cooper-Lecky Partnership, the architects of record. Some alterations have been made: the walls had to be lengthened due to the incorrect official number of dead provided by the Pentagon; the approach and paved pathway were built to accommodate the large number of visitors (grass was intended to extend to the wall), and in-ground lights have been installed; all have marred the original design in small ways, but nothing has destroyed its essential quality. No one predicted the extraordinary response to the memorial. Its dedication on a cold, wet 11 November 1982 marked the beginning of pilgrimages by millions of

Americans, many of whom have left memorabilia of their dead (all of which have been catalogued and preserved). The Vietnam Veterans Memorial is now the most visited of our national monuments. A measure of its power is that both "hawks" and "doves" believe the memorial expresses their view of the American involvement in Vietnam. As its sponsors intended, the Vietnam Veterans Memorial truly has contributed to an American catharsis. The visceral reaction it prompts demonstrates how architecture of exceptional quality fundamentally affects the human psyche.

The Washington Mall is a paradigm of American architecture in its extent, eclecticism, and constant flux. The scale of L'Enfant's public grounds inhibited their early development, but once begun they became the locus of an extraordinary sweep of activities. The Mall grew as the city itself expanded, filled with museums and monuments, and has now nearly reached its capacity. The variety of its landscapes and buildings is a direct expression of the great historical and cultural change characteristic of the modern era. Buildings whose antecedents range over time and the globe are a peculiarly American phenomenon, reflecting the scope of the country's population, drawn from around the world. The individual nature of each building, designed to respond to specific programmatic and symbolic functions of its own time, exists within a framework at once ordered and slightly incoherent. The Mall's glory is its variability and freedom of access at any point, a triumph of disciplined energy. Given the pragmatic nature of American public architecture, it is amazing that L'Enfant's original intention of the Mall as a "place of general resort" has been respected. In totality the Mall represents mythmaking on a gigantic scale, always evolving and changing as we constantly redefine ourselves.

ML01 United States Botanic Garden

1931–1933, Bennett, Parsons and Frost. Southeast corner of the Mall between Independence and Maryland avenues SW

In this late example of Beaux-Arts design, the Chicago firm Bennett, Parsons and Frost combined a French-inspired orangery with a glass conservatory. Ultimately derived from the orangery at Versailles, the arcaded and balustraded 40-foot-tall building has the clarity and rhythmical grace of its seventeenth-century antecedent. The beautifully proportioned and detailed limestone orangery is essentially a 200-foot-long, 17-foot-wide entrance hall to the domed palm house (by Lord and Burnham), as well as fifteen climate-controlled rooms for the display of plant groups ranging from temperate to subtropic. The planar surface of the shallowly channeled rusticated walls is punctured by fifteen arched doorways whose sculpted keystone

ML01 United States Botanic Garden

mascarons show classical figures traditionally associated with nature. Here Pan, Pomona, Triton, and Flora represent different kinds of gardens: wild, agricultural, water, and flower.

ML02 National Air and Space Museum

1972–1976, Gyo Obata of Hellmuth, Obata and Kassabaum. South side of the Mall between 4th and 7th streets SW

Gyo Obata's solution to the anticipated huge crowds and the nature and scale of the objects to be displayed in the Air and Space Museum was to design a very elegant airplane hangar. He cites the influence of John Russell Pope's National Gallery of Art in the formal massing, plan, and materials of his design. Facing the Mall are four monolithic blocks that are clad in the same pink Tennessee marble as the National Gallery. They are connected by a bronze glass longitudinal spine that runs the entire 635-foot length of the building and rises through both floors of exhibition space. These alternating solids and voids were placed and proportioned to respond to the corresponding projections and recesses of the gallery that sits directly opposite on the Mall. Equivalent volumes face Independence Avenue, but the recessed, glass-enclosed bays of the Mall facade have been replaced by unbroken floating marble cubes cantilevered to be flush with the south facade to avoid excessive retention of heat. A similar inversion of negative and positive space exists on the two main facades of the Freer Gallery, a short distance to the west. The adjoining Hirshhorn Museum offered a detail that Obata adopted: the long slit of the balconies and deeply recessed windows cut into each block create dramatic black shadows, a kind of inverted cornice line. Again Obata used negative space as a positive element that is abstractly expressive of what would have been solid in an earlier architectural tradition.

The entire building is raised on a long, low, two-level terrace that provides a solid base for it in the classical manner. Other markedly classical aspects of the Air and Space Museum include its symmetrical composition, entries on the central axis marked by staircases, and its emphatic rectilinearity. The Air and Space Museum's open interiors are legible from the exterior. We know that the high-tech exposed tubular steel truss supports the gray glass walls and ceiling, yet they barely touch. The objects and museum experiences offered were to be very diverse and to encourage active participation by the public, and the spaces had to be designed to accommodate the variety of uses. One- and two-story open spaces, as well as enclosed galleries, theaters, and a planetarium, were mandated; they are served by continuous concourses on both exhibition levels. The direct manner in which Obata approached his architectural problems suggests simple solutions, but the design of the Air and Space Museum is more subtle than it initially appears. The marble slabs were laid with the grain running horizontally, which results in a basket-weave effect and a three-dimensional textured appearance on the planar cubes. The 2-by-5-foot panels are hung as a curtain wall on a steel lattice, rather than as a facing to a precast concrete core. Shadows in the interior are cast not just by the exposed structure but also by planes and rockets suspended from it. Response to changing exterior atmospheric conditions is immediate, as sunny or stormy skies quickly change interior lighting and atmosphere. This interface between inside and outside was intentional, for Obata wished to connect the museum's objects with the element they conquered.

Advances in heat-resistant glass technology allowed Obata to add in 1988 a glass pavilion at the east end for a 1,300-seat restaurant. Although he designed a more plastic form, Obata continued the high-tech interior structure and the same gray glass of the original building in the pavilion.

ML03 Hirshhorn Museum and Sculpture Garden

1966–1974, Gordon Bunshaft of Skidmore, Owings and Merrill. South side of Mall at 8th St. and Independence Ave. SW

ML03 Hirshhorn Museum and Sculpture Garden

The Hirshhorn Museum is aggressively modern in its architectural language, both in response to the avant-garde art it houses and in defiance of the preciousness of the Freer and the National Gallery, which create an almost sacred ambiance for the art they display. Gordon Bunshaft placed his cylindrical museum in a paved courtyard (300 by 400 feet) to control physical and visual access to it. The three-story hollow drum is raised on four curvilinear piers in conformity to a Corbusian-inspired belief that reinforced-concrete construction allowed for, even demanded, exploitation of its structural properties to achieve a dramatic and exciting spatial interrelationship between building and site. Bunshaft originally intended to encase the entire building in a veneer of pink travertine, which would have resulted in a building with light, elegant surfaces to counteract the solidity of the forms. Because of budget restraints and federal laws limiting importation of foreign materials for government buildings, exposed concrete was used instead. The aggregate he chose, a mixture of buff-colored sand and chips of pink granite, has been sandblasted to reinforce the clarity of a single volume. Recessed planes at the top and bottom of the drum and alternation of vertically placed concrete panels with narrow horizontal bands (indicating the building's division into three stories) were intended as subtle surface modulations in order to diminish its mass. In spite of these refinements, the drum (231 feet 7 inches in diameter) is stolid and ponderous. A view along its main axis presents most effectively the interaction between its massive curvilinear volume and strong horizontal planes. The emphatic lines of the 70-foot-wide balcony, the only opening on the exterior of the drum, are repeated by the courtyard and garden walls, but they do not give the much-needed scale.

The common approach beside high, battered walls limits one's response to the museum's sculptural qualities at the expense of some of its formal ones. In direct and conscious opposition to the National Gallery, whose monumental stair reaches out to draw one into its interior, entry into the Hirshhorn is through negative space. The glass enclosure containing the vertical circulation system is situated at the end of the main axis, requiring full penetration of the building's core when entered from the Mall. This was a conscious rebuttal of pre-Modernist planning principles so well represented by the National Gallery. At the Hirshhorn, entry is not a ceremonial experience but one intended to bring the visitor into direct contact with the art as quickly as possible. Entry and circulation are too controlled, with visitors forced to enter and exit through a single revolving door on Independence Avenue, as those facing the courtyard have been closed. Inside, vertical circulation is confined to a single bank of escalators.

Gallery spaces differ according to their use. A wider outer ring lit by artificial light is for the display of paintings from a period when canvases were often very large and limitless in their own internal boundaries, demanding plain, uninterrupted fields on which to be seen properly. No barriers, such as layering of the wall surfaces with architectural detail, interrupt the immediacy of interacting with the art; this is appropriate in a building sheltering art created for consumption by a wide public audience rather than for the pleasure of a select few. The more intimate interior ring for sculpture receives ample natural light from courtyard windows, but the view into the courtyard is dull. The architect created a sympathetic ambiance for the works of art, but it is one that lacks architectural excitement.

ML04 Arts and Industries Building

1881, Adolph Cluss and Paul Schulze. South side of Mall between 8th and 10th streets SW

Nineteenth-century exposition buildings, beginning with the 1851 Crystal Palace in Lon-

ML04 Arts and Industries Building

don's Hyde Park, were intended to be temporary occupants of great urban parks. Traditionally they were quickly erected of inexpensive materials and depended on iron and glass to achieve high, open, airy interiors. Within this context Cluss and Schulze designed the Arts and Industries Building to contain objects representative of American arts and manufactures created for the 1876 Centennial Exposition in Philadelphia. Specifically it was based on James Windrom's Government Building, which had been erected at the Philadelphia fair. Both were inspired by the architecture of the Vienna Exposition of 1873, where the central building was a vast multicolored brick, terracotta, and iron structure designed in what was termed at the time the Renaissance style. We now view this eclectic mixture of medieval and Renaissance principles and motifs as a Victorian style that was developed in Germany and exported to this country; it found wide acceptance because of its low cost, simple method of fireproof construction, and its versatility. It was termed *Rundbogenstil,* or Round Arch style, referring to the common use of round-headed windows set close together in imitation of Renaissance arcades and of corbel tables used extensively in Romanesque cornices. As the Mall was Washington's urban park, construction of a building to replicate the fairlike atmosphere of the original exposition building that had housed its exhibits was seen as perfectly appropriate.

Set slightly to the south of the Smithsonian Institution building so as not to obscure the view of it from the Capitol, the Arts and Industries Building continued the broken and varied skyline of the earlier building. In plan it is a Greek cross inscribed in a square. All four facades are the same: broad, double-towered entrances are connected to square corner pavilions by arcades whose windows are so large that they give the appearance of being open, as Renaissance arcades were. The mass of the structure rises in stepped tiers to a central octagonal rotunda; the interiors are lit by numerous multilevel round-arch windows. Above the Mall entrance Caspar Buberl's sculpture group, *Columbia Protecting Science and Industry* (1881), executed in plaster-coated zinc, was the only one of four planned sculptures to be installed.

The Arts and Industries Building is the best remaining example in Washington of brick polychromy, where red, black, blue, and tan bricks are used in striated and geometric patterns to enrich the surface of an inexpensive building. In conjunction with molded terracotta roundels, corbeled brick cornices, and banded voussoirs in the arches over the windows, the brick is a colorful skin encasing an iron skeletal structure, a modern rendition of traditional forms and compositions. Hard-burned bricks with their smooth surfaces were used, an innovation introduced at the Vienna exposition to counteract urban grime that had accumulated on earlier porous brick buildings. Their use in conjunction with the thin metal roof and voluminous windows enhances the sense that the exterior surfaces are just a shell or tentlike cover for a vast and complex interior space. The portals are finely carved white marble—a change in color, texture, and material typical of Victorian architecture.

The present interior differs considerably from the original expansive, two-story space divided by tall, arched brick walls. All four corners have been closed to create offices and a bookstore, with the museum confined to four arms radiating from the octagonal rotunda. Large and small segments of light, both colored and clear, stream into the four halls and rotunda through clerestory windows. The thin steel rods of the king post trusses, the insubstantial roof, and the faceted light contrast with the solidity and mass of the brick walls. The cast-iron balconies were added between 1894 and 1897 by Hornblower and Marshall.

The present decorations of painted stencils, etched glass, and encaustic tile floors were designed in 1976 by Hugh Newell Jacobsen using nineteenth-century prints and photographs to replicate the ambiance of the original, but they are not historically correct restorations.

ML05 Smithsonian Institution

1846–1851, James Renwick, Jr. South side of Mall on Jefferson Dr. between 9th and 12th streets SW

Renwick was twenty-nine years old when his design for the Smithsonian Institution was chosen in 1847. Trained at Columbia College as an engineer, he was self-taught as an architect, learning the principles and details of historical styles from the repository of architectural literature that had grown rapidly during the previous century. Renwick's prior experience as an architect had been as a designer of Gothic Revival churches in New York, principally Grace Church (1843–1846), which still stands. This dual background in which he brought up-to-date structural knowledge together with a learned interest in medieval architecture was excellent preparation for realizing a building that was planned to be, and is, the premier example of the picturesque movement in America. Growth in nationalism, scientific investigations that challenged previously held beliefs, recognition of the richness and diversity of world architecture, and awareness of nature as a vital force are some salient factors that contributed to this romantic attitude.

In architecture the picturesque represents not a style but a mind-set comparable but opposed to the classical mind-set, dealing with a whole series of principles about how buildings were to be composed, ornamented, and placed in harmony with nature. By the beginning of the nineteenth century, educated Europeans and Americans perceived that the broad range of historical styles offered the possibility of choice, and they linked the function of a given building with an architectural tradition with which that type was associated. Medieval revival styles of architecture were considered appropriate for educational institutions such as the Smithsonian because such great European universities as Oxford and Cambridge were founded during the Middle Ages. Combining elements from many examples within a common tradition (not necessarily limited to national boundaries) was an acceptable method among designers who believed that architecture would be invigorated by the interbreeding of national styles. The goal of architects was the creation of a modern style that assimilated Western architectural traditions with new building materials and methods, principally iron used as both a structural and decorative element. The Smithsonian Institution is an outstanding example of this creative process of eclecticism.

Renwick presented alternative designs for the building. One was English perpendicular Gothic in inspiration and the second, selected by the building committee, fused Romanesque and Renaissance traditions of arcuated compositions and structural methods to create the international *Rundbogenstil,* or Round

Arch style. The earliest examples in the United States, of which the Smithsonian is one, were much more deeply rooted in the medieval tradition, while later examples (such as the Arts and Industries Building) drew more inspiration from the Renaissance. Moreover, we know the specific books, principally German, that Renwick used in selecting forms and details for the Smithsonian. In particular he relied on compositional components and decorative elements from Georg Moller's *Denkmäler der deutschen Baukunst* (1815). We can speculate that in Renwick's search for a new idiom he was influenced by the wave of creative young German architects who immigrated to New York in the 1840s or by the preeminence of nineteenth-century German educational and scientific institutions. Initially Renwick planned to ornament the building exclusively with American flora, enlarging on Benjamin Henry Latrobe's use of American orders at the Capitol. However, as realized, these elements were stock repetitive geometric elements derived from English Romanesque or Norman architecture and simplified foliated capitals and pendants copied from Moller, seen most readily in the porte-cochère on the north front.

Renwick's first choice for building materials was a yellow sandstone, but the quarry could not produce a sufficient quantity. The red Seneca sandstone used, with its deep hue and artificially roughened surfaces, is the perfect complement to the dramatic masses and sculpted layering of wall surfaces. The main block with its major entry and double towers on the north, or Mall side, is balanced by a single tower on the south. Longitudinal wings are attached to the central building by lower, intermediate hyphens. This five-part arrangement met the needs of the Smithsonian because future additions were intended for the east and west through a series of hyphens and wings. In fact, a major reason for specifying a medieval revival design was its flexibility. Medieval structures were composed of clearly articulated masses expressive of their varying functions. Because of this breakdown of the building into several component parts, additional components would not mar the symmetry of a composition; in any case, asymmetrical balance of irregularly shaped forms was preferred.

The building committee selected an asymmetrical design for the north side's central towers. Six additional towers marked edges or entries. Each was of a different size, shape, and height, and each was detailed in a slightly different manner. These towers present a veritable encyclopedia of possible combinations of round-arch fenestration, methods of buttressing, and rooflines. This approach to design was particularly apt (and probably consciously done), because Congressman Robert Dale Owen, the Smithsonian Institution's principal supporter in Congress, saw the building as a model for future American public buildings. The full effect of the picturesque broken skyline created by these varied towers and masses is evident when the building is seen from an oblique angle. The most advantageous site from which to view the Smithsonian Castle in all of its architectural glory is still the Capitol terrace. The towers are still silhouetted against the sky so that the interrelationship of their balanced forms is as vivid an architectural experience today as it has been for nearly a century and a half.

The internal organization of the Smithsonian Institution building had been established through the collaborative efforts of the scientist David Dale Owen and the architect Robert Mills and is more symmetrical in plan than one initially supposes from viewing the exterior. All functions were assigned specific spaces tailored to their purpose, hence their differing scale, form, and orientation. The ground-floor central hall was divided into a library and principal lecture room; the equivalent area on the second floor was to serve as a museum, as were the two rooms on the west end of the building (the arcaded hyphen and what appears to be a chapel). All the rooms on the east end of the building were associated with the institution's scientific researches. Smaller tower rooms were used for meetings, offices, and display. When Joseph Henry was appointed the first secretary of the Smithsonian Institution in 1846, he saw the Smithsonian as primarily a research institution rather than as a museum and altered the internal disposition of space while it was still under construction. The large lecture hall was moved to the second floor and flanked by a picture gallery and apparatus room. The library was moved to the west wing. The central hall was fitted out with three levels of glass cases to display unusual natural history specimens oriented to the specialist rather than to the general public. Research facilities and offices accounted for the remainder of the rooms, with the exception of the east wing, which was Henry's residence. In its present incarnation the building contains a visitors' center in the principal ground-floor rooms, a restaurant in the art gallery–chapel, and offices in the remainder of the spaces, with the exception of the restored regents' room located on the second floor of the south tower.

ML06 Arthur M. Sackler Gallery, National Museum of African Art, S. Dillon Ripley Center, and Enid A. Haupt Garden, Smithsonian Institution

1983–1987, Jean Paul Carlhian of Shepley, Bulfinch, Richardson, and Abbott. Independence Ave. SW at 10th St.

The three above-ground buildings that serve as entrances to the Smithsonian's Quadrangle museum and office complex partially frame a garden containing several submerged structures and sculptural elements. Many serve to skylight underground passageways, but two brick and granite enclaves—one inspired by Arabian fountains and the other by oriental gardens—function as visual clues to identify the culture represented by each museum entered through its own rectangular pavilion. The geometries of these paved gardens are based on the circle and the octagon, forms associated with the major cosmological ideas and aesthetic traditions of the Far and Near Eastern worlds. The architect Jean Paul Carlhian intended this symbolic language of geometric forms to guide the visitor through his compact maze of garden and architecture and partially to link his museums to the eclectic group of extant buildings that defined the site. He selected the Freer Gallery and the Arts and Industries Building as the major form givers. The circular motif derived from the semicircular arches of the Freer Gallery was used on the National Museum of African Art, located adjacent to the Arts and Industries Building, while its angular roofs were the genesis for the irregular octagon that became the leitmotif of the Arthur Sackler Gallery, a collection of oriental art and thus logically located near (and connected underground to) the Freer Gallery. The geometries of the garden fountains are the reverse, as moon gates are associated with Chinese gardens and octagons with North African gardens.

Architectural links to the earlier buildings were also made through color and materials. The pink granite of the new museums harmonizes with the deep red sandstone of the Smithsonian Institution Building and the brick of the Arts and Industries Building, while the gray granite was intended to respond to the Freer Gallery. Carlhian accounted for the form of his third structure, a scalloped-roofed circular kiosk that serves as the entrance to the S. Dillon Ripley Center, on historical grounds unrelated to the immediate environment. He cited exotic circular pavilions as an integral part of English picturesque gardens (specifically a pavilion design by Humphrey Repton), the tradition from which some major aspects of the Enid A. Haupt Garden are drawn. He was unaware that a Chinese-inspired garden structure had been proposed for the Mall nearly a century and a half earlier.

The entire complex of old and new buildings (and gardens) is an intense visual and historical experience. The old and new buildings create a welcome sense of closure, an intimate interlude within the greater Mall area, but one where stylistic diversity verges on visual chaos. The confusion is partially intentional and partially a result of America's diverse and constantly changing built environment. The convergence on one small plot of American ground of six structures representing widely disparate historical, cultural, and artistic traditions is almost too fantastical. Carlhian intended to give them cohesion through geometry, but his own buildings are so strong that they add to the admixture rather than neutralize its riotous variety.

The interiors of Carlhian's two museum pavilions are organized spatially in a similar fashion, with their respective geometries dominating their formal vocabularies from

ML07 Freer Gallery of Art

window shapes to handrail designs. One enters into spacious halls vaulted by either six domes or six pyramids and circulates through a sales or reception area before descending to the main gallery levels by double circular or octagonal staircases. Unfortunately, rectangular Indiana limestone blocks that are the same gray color as concrete blocks (and set together with wide mortar joints in the same manner as concrete blocks) give a cold and cheap appearance to what are meticulously detailed (and expensive) surfaces. Galleries are clustered around three sides of the vertical circulation spaces. A series of interior perspectives creates spatial ambiguities where the visitor can see rooms that are in close proximity but can discern no clear pathway leading to them. This layering of space gives a three-dimensional element to rational and logical plans but confuses rather than simplifies the experience of visiting them.

The third major public space, the S. Dillon Ripley Center concourse, opens onto extensive, multilevel underground offices. Descent by a circular stair and then an escalator leads one to a colonnaded rotunda that shifts the axis to one parallel to the Smithsonian Institution Building's south facade. Interpenetration of vertical and horizontal space by skyways, glass walls, and layering of three levels of wall surfaces assure a comfortable and open space amply lit by natural and artificial light. The classic French device of reciprocal wall mirrors creates an illusionistic cross axis at the midway point of the promenade while its extent is lengthened illusionistically by Richard Haas's mural of a classical ruin that emerges from the site and opens a view of

the Arts and Industries Building, the structure actually located where the painted image places it.

ML07 Freer Gallery of Art

1913, originally planned; 1923–1928, constructed, Charles Adams Platt. 1989–1993, Cole and Denny. 12th St. and Jefferson Dr. SW

The serene and calm Freer Gallery, measuring 228 feet by 185 feet, is only one-third smaller than the Arts and Industries Building (which flanks the Smithsonian building on the east side), yet it seems diminutive in comparison. Self-contained and turning inward to its 65-foot-square open courtyard, the Freer Gallery was built at a time when technological advances allowed for interior climate and light control without needing to resort to huge interiors for air circulation. Constructed of gray Milford, Massachusetts, granite, the Freer's horizontal massing is organized as an Italian Renaissance palace, its height determined by the roofline of the Smithsonian's west wing as well as by guidelines established by the Senate Park Commission.

From the Porta Nuova in Verona (1533–1540), by the Italian Renaissance architect Michele Sanmicheli, Platt derived a single-story elevation with full facade rustication. The main front on the Mall is a five-part composition with a triple-arcaded entry in the center, reminiscent of Giulio Romano's Palazzo del Te (1524–1534) in Mantua. The refined use of Platt's Mannerist sources was perhaps intended to create a strong image to compete with the Freer's robust Victorian neighbors to the east and the French-inspired Agriculture Department to the west. This strategy was not altogether successful, as the main facade facing north is never directly, and rarely obliquely, lit by sun, contributing to its recessed and forbidding appearance.

The entire building is a study in contrasts, ranging from its overall form to its minute details. The dichotomy of closed exterior versus open interior is continued by the spatial inversion of its two main facades, where the projecting elements of the north side are recessed on the south and vice versa. The Mall entrance loggia is sleek, linear, and delicate in contrast to the heavily rusticated wall treatment, particularly the articulation of its two framing bays with their blind arches and empty niches forming the transition from the open entry to the blank end walls. The Doric entablature is surmounted by a parapet of equal height, balustraded, sculptural, and open where the wall is solid below, yet unbroken and planar where the wall gives way to the triple-arch entry. Other horizontal regulating lines—the frieze and belt course—are also manipulated in such a way that their traditional functions are called into question. While the entablature as a whole is continuous around the building, the Doric frieze of triglyphs and metopes is confined to the north and south entries, where the order is alternately expressed overtly (Doric pilasters on the north facade) and suppressed (flat Doric capitals alone on the south facade). The latter detail is probably derived from another Italian source, Giacomo Vignola's Palazzo Farnese at Caprarola (1559). The belt course composed of the running wave motif (the function of which is to mark divisions between stories) is broken by the corner quoins (which are barely discernible) but also by other modulations of the wall planes. These deviations from the strict rules of the classical language of architecture may have been intended to express consciously the difference between the appearance and the reality of the granite wall, apparently ponderous and thick but actually quite thin and dependent on steel frame construction. The issue of expressing the "truthfulness" of structure was an important concern in American architecture beginning in the mid-nineteenth century.

At the same time that Platt manipulated the Renaissance vocabulary on which he drew, he also enriched it. In the triple-arch loggia he reinterpreted a classic Renaissance theme, the integration of the trabeated system of construction, represented here by six Doric pilasters, with the arcade, tenuously supported by thin Tuscan pilasters set at right angles to and buttressing the taller Doric order. The composition of frame around frame around frame on this facade is a complex interweaving of lines and shallow planes, one so sophisticated that the Tuscan entablature of the arches slips in and out, emerging finally as the entablature of the blind niches in the framing bays. The metope sculpture at the main entrance—sheaves of wheat, amphorae, ships, and drinking horns—all classical symbols of fortune, probably were chosen to place the client of the building, industrialist and art collector Charles L. Freer, in the company of Renaissance merchant princes and art patrons whose residences bore these same sym-

bols. While Platt's treatment of the frieze was very academic and correct (including folding of the metope rosettes around corners, for example), it denied the basic rules of the Renaissance by an asymmetrical and disordered arrangement of the metope sculpture. Platt's design is not a pastiche of Renaissance elements but an integrated synthesis, one in which he has created a new sense of order for the Renaissance palazzo in the same spirit that the Renaissance architects whom he was emulating had renewed an earlier classical tradition.

Only one story, the single floor of exhibition rooms, is actually raised above a basement containing offices, storage areas, study rooms, and an auditorium. All are lit by windows at ground level, with heavy exterior grills that deny their intended light-transferring function. These basement rooms and a connecting tunnel to the Sackler Gallery were the major focus of a 1989–1993 renovation by Omaha architects Cole and Denny. Transition from the exterior to the interior is dramatic, through the groin-vaulted loggia into a cubical vestibule with a flat Renaissance coffered ceiling. A triple-arched screen separating the vestibule from the corridor is starkly silhouetted against a brilliantly lit courtyard. Platt's background in landscape architecture is evident in the courtyard, where once peacocks were kept. These arcaded facades are treated in a similar manner to the main entry facade but with the use of a fluted Doric order.

The Freer's plan is beautifully and economically organized. The axis established by the Mall entry is a visual one that passes through the entire building; it is more than a mere pathway. Two primary circulation corridors run counter to it and are connected by four north-south passageways, two of which are closed by glass doors and serve the courtyard. All of the exhibition rooms are rectangular, of differing sizes, and domestically scaled. Their arrangement within the block of the building varies, as does the manner of their interconnection. With two exceptions, all rooms open onto the corridors; most connect with just one neighbor. The only sequential treatment is in the Chinese galleries located in the northeast segment. Whereas the exterior is a masterful resolution of linear tensions, the interiors are wholly volumetric, beautifully proportioned spaces, with restrained use of classical details. Groin-vaulted

ML08 Agriculture Department Building

hallways are complemented by cove-ceilinged exhibition rooms with curved skylights barely breaking their lines. Artificial lighting has been concealed behind the white glass of the skylights for those occasions when natural light needs to be intensified, and movable canvas louvers can be used to control it.

The same quiet environment was created for all the art—Chinese, Japanese, and American. The intentional subtlety of the architectural experience was to mirror the refined nature of the collections for which the building was expressly designed. Freer's extensive collection of paintings and etchings of the American expatriate artist James A. M. Whistler culminated in his acquisition of the Peacock Room, originally the dining room in the Frederick R. Leyland House in London. The filigreed shelving and Renaissance-inspired pendant drop ceiling were designed in 1870 by Thomas Jeckyll to display Leyland's collection of blue and white Chinese porcelain. Its brown leather-covered walls were repainted by Whistler in gold and turquoise in 1877 to provide an appropriate setting for his painting *Rose and Silver: The Princess from the Land of Porcelain*, which was hung over the fireplace. Freer acquired the Peacock Room in 1904 for his Detroit residence because of the strong oriental feeling it evoked. He had it installed in the Freer Gallery in 1919.

The Freer Gallery is architects' architecture, a building most beautifully proportioned and planned, subtly and imaginatively detailed, and totally integrated with its purpose. Yet Charles Platt, trained as a painter, had no formal education after the age of seventeen and came to architecture by way of

landscape design. Frank Lloyd Wright, his contemporary, said he "was a very dangerous man; he did the wrong thing [academic architecture] so well."[25] The Freer Gallery, Platt's masterpiece, is one of the most satisfying architectural experiences on the Mall.

ML08 Agriculture Department Building

1903–1908, 1928–1930, Rankin, Kellogg and Crane. 14th St. and Jefferson Dr. SW

The Agriculture Department occupies the only building on the Mall that does not currently participate in the Mall's public life. Aggressive and imposing, it is the public facade for a massive and anonymous group of buildings containing 4,300 offices covering three blocks on the south side of Independence Avenue. The latter complex was designed by Supervising Architect Louis Simon and constructed between 1926 and 1936. But for budget cuts and bureaucratic interference, the main building by Rankin, Kellogg and Crane would have been a much better work of architecture than it is. The two L-shaped wings containing laboratories and offices were constructed between 1904 and 1908, but the boldly projecting central block was not finished until 1930. During both building campaigns, economy of construction, comprehensible interior planning, and advanced mechanical equipment were of greater importance than architectural merit. Each of the 256-foot-long wings, with pedimented Ionic porticoes enclosing thirteen unarticulated bays, is an adaptation of one of the most popular models for American office buildings in the early twentieth century, Jacques-Ange Gabriel's Gardes-Meubles (1755–1774) on the Place de la Concorde in Paris. The rusticated basement story provides continuity to the 750-foot expanse of the entire front, a continuity lacking in the materials—granite for the base, white Vermont marble for the superstructure of the wings, and a gray marble for the later central section. Moreover, an additional story inserted into the center disrupts the window rhythm. The change from a garlanded Ionic in the wing porticoes to Corinthian in the center also contributes to the disjunction of the various parts.

Botany is the theme of the meager sculptural program, with the pedimental sculpture of the four wing porticoes, executed by Adolph A. Weinman in 1908, representing fruit, flowers, cereals, and forestry. An invented American order in the lobby and the vestibule leading to the secretary of agriculture's office features cornstalks and gives some architectural interest to the interior, as does a two-story, interior, skylit courtyard replacing the dome originally intended.

ML09 **Washington National Monument**

1845–1854, Robert Mills. 1876–1884, completed by Thomas Lincoln Casey, U.S. Army Corps of Engineers. On the Mall between 15th and 17th streets NW

The tallest structure in the world when it was completed in 1884, the Washington Monument is the one work of architecture in the city that it is impossible to erase mentally, so inevitable does it seem, so deeply rooted, and so crucial symbolically, as the icons of American history and government revolve around it. Its greatness lies in the initial conception to make such a stupendous mark on the land and to achieve such purity of geometric form on such a scale. The Washington National Monument Society was founded on 26 September 1833 to erect a monument "whose dimensions and magnificence shall be commensurate with the greatness and gratitude of the nation which gave [George Washington] birth [and] whose splendor will be without parallel in the world."[26] The society envisaged that the projected million-dollar cost would easily be raised through public subscriptions of $1 per American, as they desired a "People's Monument." The members abandoned this idealistic goal after four years, when less than $25,000 had been collected, and agreed to accept any amount offered.

ML09 Washington National Monument

Public funds were not used to construct the monument until Congress undertook its completion between 1876 and 1884.

When the initial design competition was held in 1836, no site had been selected. Robert Mills's design, finally chosen on 18 November 1845, probably differed from the one he submitted to this competition, as the society felt none submitted had been "coextensive with the Nation." By 1845 various social, cultural, and political forces made a monument to the entire revolutionary era more acceptable than one to the president alone.

Hence Mills's design was composed of two parts: a 600-foot obelisk as the monument to Washington and a colonnaded base 250 feet in diameter and 100 feet high to serve as a pantheon honoring civic and military heroes of the Revolution. His prototypes were Egyptian obelisks and modern reconstructions of ancient tombs, particularly Hadrian's tomb and the Mausoleum of Halikarnassos. Sculpture played an important part in both segments: a single star at the summit of the obelisk would symbolize Washington's immortality with relief sculpture depicting four of his major victories to decorate each face of the obelisk where it met the roof of the pantheon. Further, Mills placed a chariot driven by Washington atop the projecting portico of the terrace. The pantheon was to be encircled by thirty Doric columns, 45 feet high and 12 feet in diameter, representing the number of states in 1845; bronze civic wreaths enclosing each of the state seals were placed above each column in the entablature; and statues of the signers of the Declaration of Independence were set in niches cut in the rotunda wall. Inside there were to be statues of the fathers of the Revolution and a cycle of history paintings. It was hoped that Washington would be reinterred in the monument, and catacombs in the basement were planned for tombs of other distinguished Americans.

The roof of the pantheon formed a balustraded terrace from which to view the city and the relief sculpture on the obelisk. Through four cupolas lighting the gallery below, one would see the sculpture and paintings. The pantheon also was to contain a museum and the society's archive, including a record of each American who had contributed to its erection.

In 1848 a committee of the Monument Society, in considering whether the height of the monument ought to be limited to 300 feet, asked Mills and James Renwick, Jr., to study the design for possible modifications. Their report suggested an intermediate solution until funds for the pantheon could be raised: the stepped pyramid base buttressing the obelisk could be treated as actual steps into which the names of statesmen and heroes could be cut, thus retaining some semblance of its original commemorative intention. Mills and Renwick also suggested changing the order of the future pantheon columns from Doric to "American" (presumably the corn capitals and shafts used in the Supreme Court vestibule at the Capitol) and using white marble for the exterior stone. They also suggested a pyramidal termination to the obelisk. Mills and Renwick saw the design as modular, capable of being built at any height between 300 and 500 feet. The society resolved that the obelisk's height should be 500 feet; their minutes do not record any discussion of the base.

Speaker of the House Robert Winthrop gave the oration at the laying of the cornerstone on 4 July 1848, before "masses such as never before were seen within the shadows of the Capitol," an estimated 15,000 to 20,000 people.[27] In October, Mills submitted the final drawings to the society. The base was 55 feet square with walls 15 feet thick. Two Egyptian Revival battered doorways with cavetto cornices decorated with winged orbs

were constructed on the north and south facades. It was planned that visitors would ascend to the terrace level by stairways, but to the summit of the obelisk "by an easy graded gallery, which may be traversed by a railway,"[28] possibly an elevator based on the principle of cog railroads. The materials employed were Symington's white crystal marble from quarries near Baltimore for the exterior and Potomac gneiss for the interior. Tests showed that the marble's compressive strength equaled that of granite.

To sustain public support of the monument, the society in 1849 solicited memorial stones from each state and from private organizations, 197 of which are in the interior stairwell. Other nations also donated stones. Construction of the monument was halted at about 170 feet, in 1855, following the theft of a stone donated by the Vatican and the consequent reorganization of the society. Work did not resume until January 1879.

By an act of 2 August 1876, Congress undertook to finish the monument, placing responsibility for construction under a joint commission consisting of the president, supervising architect, architect of the Capitol, chief engineer of the United States Army, and the Washington National Monument Society. As a result of vigorous lobbying for a new design by the *American Architect and Building News*, numerous sculptors and architects proposed in vain a variety of mid-Victorian solutions incorporating the 150-foot shaft and 20-foot stepped pyramidion base. The society, however, wished to see the obelisk completed.

When Lieutenant Colonel Casey was placed in charge in 1876, he found faulty the society's 1848 decision for a 500-foot obelisk. The American ambassador at Rome, George P. Marsh, determined that the correct proportional relationships of base to shaft in Egyptian obelisks there was a ratio of one to ten, so the height was set at 555 feet. Casey designed a 50-foot-tall pyramid for its top, an excellent decision, as one perceives the obelisk in its totality at any distance. Casey removed the original Egyptian Revival door frames from the exterior in order to obtain absolute geometric purity, but their interiors are still visible.

The 3,300-pound monolithic capstone of Maryland marble was set on 6 December 1884. Its tip was the largest piece of cast aluminum at the time, measuring 9 3/4 inches and weighing 100 ounces. It recalled the Egyptian practice of using a gold pyramidion to reflect the first rays of morning sun. Marbles from quarries ranging from Massachusetts to Virginia were used in the monument's completion. There are 897 steps, its actual height is 555 feet 5 1/8 inches, and it weighs 80,378 tons. The cost was about $1.5 million, and the monument remains the world's tallest masonry structure.

Five years after its completion, the monument was surpassed in height by the Eiffel Tower. As the great monument to modernity was rising in the old world, that to antiquity was completed in the new. Ironically, we now perceive the Washington Monument as modern and timeless because of its abstract form and the Eiffel Tower as expressive of nineteenth-century daring and ingenuity. Each serves as the symbol of its respective city.

ML10 Jefferson Memorial

1939–1943, John Russell Pope; Eggers and Higgins. Raoul Wallenberg Pl. (formerly 15th St. SW), across East Potomac Walkway, West Dr., in West Potomac Park

Ideally, one would view the Jefferson Memorial from the air. Only then can one fully appreciate its placement in the center of radiating concentric circles, like a stone dropped in a pond. The best approach is by paddleboat across the Tidal Basin, confronting the broad podium and Ionic portico along its main axis. The common approach is oblique for pedestrians coming either from the Mall or along the parking lot located to the south. This informal picturesque approach increases the sense of drama that the memorial's design and siting imply. Like Pope's contemporaneous domed central space for the National Gallery of Art (also partially inspired by the Roman Pantheon), the Jefferson Memorial rotunda is opened in the four cardinal directions by columnar screens. In direct contrast to the National Gallery, Pope placed his Ionic colonnade on the exterior of the rotunda rather than within it. The resulting relationship between the two buildings is a familial one, yet the dynamics of the two spaces are radically different. Although its sponsors specifically suggested the Roman Pantheon as an apt prototype for a memorial honoring Jefferson, Pope's transformation of that model also proved to be appropriate. The Pantheon is a closed space, lit only by the oculus of the

dome, while the Vermont marble exterior colonnade and open cella walls of the Jefferson Memorial suggest eighteenth-century classical pavilions erected in English picturesque gardens. The closest model is William Kent's Ionic Temple of Ancient Virtue (1734) at Stowe, a garden visited by Jefferson during his English garden tour in 1785 in the company of John Adams. Although larger in scale, the Jefferson Memorial functions as a garden pavilion within the greater landscape of the Mall. It was intended to collect and dispense vistas and to serve as a contemplative retreat. Unfortunately, the present view to the south is of a superhighway, but that to the White House on the north has been consciously kept open. Dense perimeter planting of many varieties of trees and shrubs has created a miniature picturesque garden atop the grassy 25-foot-high podium, thus limiting east and west vistas.

Rarely do visitors pass beyond the frontal plane of the standing figure of Jefferson to explore these gardens. Movement within the interior fostered by the four openings is countered by a stronger sense of stasis. No oculus breaks the thin, coffered ceiling of the dome; articulation of the wall planes is by shallowly incised pilasters and framing elements; the entablature barely projects from the wall surface; the Ionic columns are unfluted. This emphasis on smooth, linear surfaces of palpably solid elements focuses architectural energies inward. The sculptural force of the triple row of columns is not strong enough to draw one outside except on brilliantly sunny days when light is the primary mover. Unlike the Lincoln Memorial, where visitors linger, the Jefferson Memorial is an exquisite work of perfectly proportioned architectural sculpture with primary architectural impact from afar, best seen from across the Tidal Basin nestled in its miniaturized landscape as one traditionally experiences garden pavilions.

Pope intended the memorial to synthesize the major aspects of Jefferson's multiple public contributions as statesman, architect, president, drafter of the Declaration of Independence, adviser on the Constitution, and founder of the University of Virginia. It is a canonical example of Beaux-Arts design in its axial planning and transformation of meaningful historical prototypes for modern usage, lacking only painted images to explain its purpose. Architectural form (a pantheon),

ML10 Jefferson Memorial

ML11 Lincoln Memorial

sculpture (Jefferson's statue), and the written word (quotations from his writings) all explicate the building's function.

Shallow pedimental sculpture executed by Adolph A. Weinman depicts the members of Congress selected to write the Declaration of Independence. Benjamin Franklin and John Adams are on Jefferson's left and Roger Sherman and Robert R. Livingstone on his right. Unfortunately, Rudolph Evans's standing bronze figure of Jefferson (19 feet 6 inches) lacks the vitality of Daniel Chester French's Lincoln. Stolid and heavy, it combines Jefferson's seventy-eight-year-old body from Thomas Sully's 1821 portrait with Rembrandt Peale's portrait, painted when Jefferson was fifty-seven. Jefferson's own statement of his life's purpose is engraved in the frieze, "I have sworn on the altar of God eternal hostility against every form of tyranny over the mind of man." Inscriptions record his beliefs and excerpt his most significant writings. The exterior and dome are constructed of Vermont marble and the interior walls of

white Georgia marble, but the coffered ceiling is of limestone.

ML11 Lincoln Memorial

1912–1922, Henry Bacon. West end of the Mall at the foot of 23rd St. NW

The sense of quiet and repose essential to the experience of the Lincoln Memorial derives from its placement in the extended landscape created especially for it and from the perfectly balanced relationship between Daniel Chester French's great statue of Lincoln and the equally great architecture that Henry Bacon designed to shelter and display it. The ideal of monumental Beaux-Arts public architecture was the dynamic fusion of landscape, architecture, sculpture, painting, and the written word to draw the spectator toward, into, and through an architectural space that culminates in some transcendent meaning. Bacon saw the building as the logical conclusion to the historical development of the Mall, with the Capitol symbolic of American government, the Washington Monument dedicated to the founder of that government, and the Lincoln Memorial to its savior. Consecrated to Lincoln as the emancipator and preserver of the Union, the building's meaning was closely linked to McKim, Mead and White's Arlington Memorial Bridge, designed to connect it visually with Robert E. Lee's home located in Arlington Cemetery. This relationship was seen as a symbolic healing of wounds between the North and South.

The building itself is a paradigm for the union of the states. Thirty-six Doric columns (and double wreaths in the entablature above them) represent the states at the outbreak of the Civil War. The easily read names of each state with the date of admission into the Union were intended to make this relationship manifest. Forty-eight festoons in the recessed attic represent the states at the time of the memorial's erection. (A bronze plaque with information on Alaska and Hawaii was installed at the foot of the approach stairs in 1985.)

Bacon's spatial and organizational frame was designed not only to display this historically potent iconographic program but also to enhance its meaning by providing an appropriate setting and approach, as well as a subdued and supportive interior space. The monument's physical isolation and elevated position were intended to reflect the character of Lincoln, who was seen to be above petty politics. The progressive experience of first viewing the gleaming white temple at the end of the reflecting pool, then approaching it off axis, and finally arriving at the broad plaza was meant to make visitors feel that they were entering a sacred precinct. The intensity of the experience gradually increases as one mounts the staircase, first by gradual ascents and finally by a steep rise requiring a real effort. One's initial impression on arrival is of a single-volume, lofty interior, so powerful are the east-west directional forces. The sense of *gravitas* emanates from French's statue and from the high and uncluttered cella that Bacon provided for it. Subdued daylight seeps though the double roof (ridged on the exterior) that is glazed with thin translucent panels of marble set within a framework of bronze beams. Screens composed of four 60-foot-tall Ionic columns create two antechambers. On the south wall Jules Guerin's mural entitled *Emancipation* spans its upper portion, while Lincoln's "Gettysburg Address" in bronze letters is inscribed below. On the north wall

Guerin's *Reunion* is paired with Lincoln's "Second Inaugural Address."

Although the dimensions and proportional relationships (188 feet long by 118 feet wide by 74 feet high), cella sculpture, and details of the Doric columns all suggest the Athenian Parthenon as the major inspiration for the Lincoln Memorial, its orientation with the entry on the long side (rather than at the narrow end, as at the Parthenon) and its high attic rather than a sloping roof indicate that the memorial was not derived from any specific prototype. Classical precedents existed for roofless temples and those entered on the long axis, as we know from the Roman writer Vitruvius. Refinements to make the entire building appear perfectly rectilinear and symmetrical when viewed from afar include the entasis that modulates the 44-foot-tall Doric columns and the increased intercolumniation in the center of the east facade; this nearly square (45 feet by 44 feet) entrance creates a dark backdrop that needed to be lightened. The exterior is of white Colorado marble. Interior floors and wall bases are of pink Tennessee marble, with Indiana limestone on the upper walls. An underground catacomb of floating reinforced concrete arches spreads beneath the long staircase approach to the memorial and on the other three sides.

The reflecting pool was intended to mirror the Washington Monument from the top step of the Lincoln Memorial, but it had to be shortened to accommodate the foundations necessary to support the memorial, which was being constructed on what a quarter-century earlier had been tidal flats. Thus the obelisk is not reflected in its entirety.

ML12 Arlington Memorial Bridge

1926–1932, McKim, Mead and White. Potomac River at west end of the Mall

A bridge between Washington and Arlington, Virginia, was frequently proposed during the nineteenth century, but its site and orientation were not fixed until the Senate Park Commission included it as a formal and symbolic element in its 1901–1902 plan. Visually connecting the Lincoln Memorial to the Custis-Lee Mansion (Robert E. Lee's home) in Arlington National Cemetery, it is a metaphorical as well as an actual bridge. In 1922 the Arlington Memorial Bridge Commission began developing the bridge's dual role as a

ML12 Arlington Memorial Bridge

monumental approach to the city and to the cemetery. After determining its major elements, the architects McKim, Mead and White were chosen from a short list that included Charles Adams Platt and Paul Philippe Cret. The commission wanted the bridge complex to extend beyond the bounds of the river. It is organized around three traffic circles. The first redirects the Mall's axis (behind the Lincoln Memorial), the second acts as a traffic collector (on the Virginia banks of the Potomac), and the third is an entrance to the cemetery. Pylons surmounted by sculpture mark each transition, and an apsed wall terminates the vista at the cemetery end as seen from the Lincoln Memorial.

The reinforced concrete bridge (2,138 feet long; 90 feet wide) consists of nine low arches and an electrically operated draw. Its formal inspiration was Roman aqueducts. The arch voussoirs and rusticated spandrels are faced with dressed North Carolina granite. Six-foot-tall heads of bison in the keystones were sculpted by Alexander Proctor; eagles in relief roundels set between fasces on the piers are the work of C. Paul Jennewein as are the eagles atop the pylons at the Arlington end of the bridge. Two monumental groups of equestrian sculpture at the Lincoln Memorial circle were part of McKim, Mead and White's design. Leo Friedlander's *The Arts of War* flanks the entrance to the bridge, and James Earle Fraser's *The Arts of Peace* leads to Rock Creek Park. Commissioned in 1925, these gilded bronze statues were not cast and put in place until 1951. Both sets recall the European use

of similar equestrian sculptures in an urban context, particularly the four groups on the Place de la Concorde in Paris. This intense historicism in conjunction with thoroughly contemporary engineering, so typical of the period, resulted in a work that contributes considerably to Washington's monumental core.

ML13 Vietnam Veterans Memorial

1982, Maya Lin, Cooper-Lecky Partnership. North side of the Mall between 21st and 22nd streets NW

Although most American monuments commemorate collective actions, the naming of individuals dates at least from the Civil War, when monuments that recorded lost local heroes by name were erected in numerous towns and cities. On the national level, thousands

of names are inscribed on the First and Second Division Memorials (see WH01 and WH02, p. 152) erected after World War I. In all cases recognition of each person by name was subsidiary to the architectural forms, most often derived from columns, obelisks, or triumphal arches. The Vietnam Veterans Memorial differs in that the names are the primary content, but its form is as deeply embedded in ancient memorial architecture, recalling Roman tabularia and the Western ("Wailing") Wall in Jerusalem.

Its aesthetic and emotional impact derive from multiple interactions between architecture and spectator, written word and image. Although apparently open and set in a free-flowing landscape, the approach and circulation are tightly controlled. Visitors are subtly forced to enter at either end and remain on the narrow, paved path close to the wall. This confrontation personalizes everyone's visit, as names replace the anonymity of numbers, and as faces reflected in the highly polished black granite turn spectators into participants. The living meet the dead. It is a commonly accepted truism that buildings only come alive when their three-dimensional qualities are actually experienced by humans moving around and through them. At the Vietnam Veterans Memorial, visitors' shifting reflections animate the static stone, a brilliant interpretation of the fundamental interchange between architecture and user.

Open to the south, two 250-foot-long, wedge-shaped walls are set at a 125-degree angle so that they point toward the Washington Monument to the east and the Lincoln Memorial to the west, establishing a fundamental relationship with the two earlier American monuments associated with major wars. Connections established between the living and the dead through the names and reflections are continued by the monument's form, which cuts into the earth, literally bringing the visitor underground to the land occupied by the dead. Lin organized the names to establish continuity with the earth where the dead are symbolically buried. Each wall is composed of seventy-three black granite slabs, seventy of which are inscribed with the names of those dead or missing between 1959 and 1975 in the Vietnam War. The names start at the top of the east wall, continue chronologically to its apex, and then begin again as the west wall emerges from the ground, climaxing as the end meets the beginning where

the walls abut against one another. With great economy of formal and material means, the architecture forms a complete aesthetic episode at the same time that it symbolically closes an historical era. These two completed cycles foster the sense of wholeness and integrity we feel.

Because the names are listed chronologically, day by day, those who died together are remembered together. All names are equal; officers are not singled out and no individual hero is honored. The competition program specifically forbade entrants to comment about the validity of the controversial and divisive war. Lin's design demonstrates that it was not 58,000 American soldiers who were sacrificed but identifiable human beings, the real enormity of any war. Elemental things—names, faces, stone, earth, basic geometry—fuse the personal and the abstract. The memorial's aesthetic and popular success is due to the power generated by these physical and metaphorical forces acting so strongly on us that we know we have been struck. We recognize why, but we are not sure how. Truth is beauty; beauty, truth.

ML14 National Museum of American History (National Museum of History and Technology)

1955–1964, McKim, Mead and White; Steinman, Cain and White. North side of the Mall between 12th and 14th streets NW

Congressional approval in 1955 for the Museum of History and Technology and its site on the north side of the Mall next to the Natural History Museum was accompanied by a $36 million appropriation. Secretary of the Smithsonian Leonard Carmichael's attitude was at once conservative and innovative. He wished the new museum to fit into the "prevailing architecture" of Washington, yet he wanted the interior to function as a model of architectural futurism to match up-to-date exhibit methods and contents that demonstrated American superiority in science and technology. That is, the museum was to be built from the inside out, with the exterior form unrelated to its innovative interiors. The once-great firm of McKim, Mead and White, founded in 1879, was selected to design the building in 1956. Its architects had continued to design in a conservative tradition well into the modern era, attempting to fuse principles

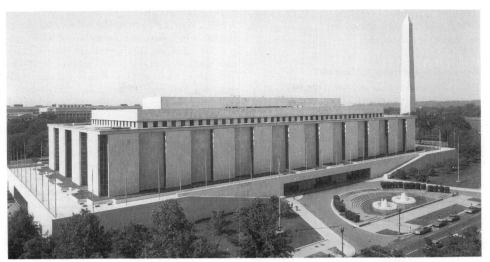

ML14 National Museum of American History (National Museum of History and Technology)

of two inherently antithetical traditions. Unfortunately, counterproposals from within the government's architectural community to select an architectural firm that would produce an inspired modern design (Saarinen and Saarinen were vigorously promoted) were unsuccessful.

James Kellum Smith was responsible for the initial design of the modernized Beaux-Arts shell of the museum. At his death he was replaced by Walker O. Cain of the successor firm of Steinman, Cain and White. The building's broad terrace seen from the Mall serves as the roof of a full-story level set against the embankment fronting on Constitution Avenue. Its compact rectangular mass culminates in a recessed attic story, a typical Beaux-Arts solution to diminish the height of large buildings. All four facades were composed in a uniform manner; in fact the museum was conceived as a modern rendition of a peripteral temple on the model of the Lincoln Memorial. Regularly spaced, rectangular slabs of wall set vertically that rise from the podium to the cornice line are treated as a modern equivalent of columns. They are held away from the inner wall by vertical windows of solar gray glass, creating the alternation of light and shade associated with columnar architecture. At the Mall entrance, these slabs provide a surface for inscriptions relating to American history and invention, another instance of Beaux-Arts influence.

Although the design itself is a bland at-tempt to modernize traditional architecture, many of the structural aspects were innovative at the time. The remarkably thin (16 3/8 inches) walls consist of a sandwich composed of structural precast concrete panels, rigid insulation, and a facing of pink Tennessee marble sandblasted to give a uniform surface. The structural joints used to hang these panels, so that they appear as freestanding units floating on the surface, were devised for this building. The interior plan was adapted from designs proposed in 1946 by Frank Taylor for a modern museum of science, engineering, and industry. In Taylor's plan a central rotunda flanked by two square storage rooms provided a core surrounded by a continuous unbroken gallery where exhibits might merge with one another in a continuum of history and technology or be subdivided by movable walls. This flexibility of space was allied to new concepts of museology by which visitors were encouraged to participate in the exhibits, even to handle objects. Although these planning and display concepts responded to the reality of huge numbers of visitors occupying the museum at the same time, the lack of clear architectural order and hierarchy have resulted in incoherent interiors, where visitors are disoriented and regularly have to be directed to exits, as the architecture does not provide the necessary clues. Signs are so numerous (and intrusive) as to become a meaningless jumble. Such an internalized experience, where natural light and a view to the outer world are excluded, requires a simple but sophisticated spatial structure to guide one through the maze.

ML15 Natural History Museum

1901–1911, Hornblower and Marshall. 1963, additions, Mills, Petticord and Mills. North side of the Mall between 9th and 12th streets NW

Although it contains some of the Smithsonian's most venerable objects, the Natural History Museum is one of the least architecturally exciting buildings on the Mall. This is due to functionalist attitudes and economizing measures on the part of the Smithsonian rather than to the quality of the local architectural firm of Hornblower and Marshall, for whom this was their major work of public architecture. With the defeat of their fine 1904 French-inspired design, the architects focused on the central octagon, an advanced system of fireproof construction, and spacious exhibition and storage areas. Although the white granite-clad exterior of the building is a stereotypical treatment of the four-story Beaux-Arts institutional envelope, its proportional treatment and sunken basement control the mass of a building covering 4 acres.

The adoption of Charles McKim's suggestion of a dome inspired by the Roman Pantheon predicated a Corinthian portico with elaborate capitals derived from the Temple of Jupiter Stator in Rome. The central dome is buttressed by four extended gables broken by thermal windows, a motif frequently used by McKim, Mead and White. An octagonal version of such a dome was simultaneously under construction at the Army War College (see SW14, p. 241). The dome covers the building's best architectural feature, a three-story irregular octagon with a Guastavino tile vault, modeled on that of McKim, Mead and White's Low Library at Columbia University (1898). The Natural History Museum's octagon has doors and loggias set within short pier walls that make the transition from the octagon to the circular dome. Longer walls that run between them contain triple-tiered balconies for ease of circulation on each level. Three levels of columns are not the usual Doric below Ionic below Corinthian, possibly because the bottom two stories (Ionic above Doric) are the same height, and the third story (Ionic) is shorter. Indiana limestone walls and variegated marble columns were a concession to architectural grandeur for the building's main space; the remaining interior walls are covered with glazed terracotta tiles.

Steel frame construction allowed for three 116-foot-wide skylit main halls with no permanent interior walls, thus maximizing flexibility of exhibition areas. The second-floor north hall on the main axis, the present Hall of Dinosaurs, is the only area today where this dramatic span is still visible. The diameter of the octagonal hall is 81 feet 6 inches along its main axis. The dome's diameter is 75 feet and its total height is 165 feet.

ML16 National Gallery of Art, West Building

1936–1941, John Russell Pope. North side of the Mall between 4th and 7th streets

John Russell Pope was an architect for whom refinement and reinterpretation of a few canonical archetypes held greater creative possibilities than invention of new forms. His transformation of the Roman Pantheon as the central motif at the West Building of the National Gallery of Art is only one instance of his reinterpretation of the famous pagan temple. Comparison of the West Building with Pope's Jefferson Memorial (see ML10), under construction simultaneously, demonstrates how an architect of his ability could modify the same prototype for use in buildings serving such disparate functions yet create distinctly different architectural experiences. Both were conceived as temples, one dedicated to a man of true republican principles and one a sanctuary to house refined and valuable artworks. One is open; the other closed. Both reveal Pope's architectural sensibility to have been subtle, refined, and precise within the context of monumentality. Although ancient buildings were his starting point, Pope was strongly influenced by sixteenth-century Roman architecture for his surface treatments and details. To overlay Renaissance details onto antique forms was well within the tenets and practice of the American Beaux-Arts tradition. As a significant proportion of the art in the National Gallery was Italian High Renaissance, Pope consciously designed a modernized Renaissance setting in which to display it.

The West Building sits in the center of a two-block-long site removed from its immediate surroundings by high, moatlike walls along its wings on both the Mall and Constitution Avenue sides. In exemplary Beaux-Arts fashion the relationship between plan and elevation is expressed clearly by the exterior volumes. The 782-foot longitudinal spine (31 feet longer than the Capitol) passes through the entire building, intersecting three great cross-axial masses before it emerges from both ends. Shorter parallel setback roofs contain the skylight system for the central sculpture galleries and garden courts. Six distinct rectilinear volumes, unbroken by windows, suggest spaces appropriate for the display of paintings. These volumes are articulated by the traditional horizontal and vertical regulating lines associated with the classical system of ordinance, a complex shallow layering of pilasters, moldings, architraves, and panels. The continuous, unbroken surface of the moat walls tends to concentrate the architectural forces on the porticoes and dome. The linear articulation of the unfenestrated wing walls contributes to this movement, which builds in intensity as the wall surfaces become more densely gridded toward the center of the building. This interplay between the linear and the volumetric, which at first one supposes reveals the influence of modernist geometries on Pope, was present in his earliest

work and derived from his interest in Italian High Renaissance architecture.

Andrew Mellon chose the pink Tennessee marble, seven shades of which are used on the exterior. The graduated hue from pink at the base to near-white at the cornice is a subtle factor in keeping the huge masses from being too ponderous. The marble is not a veneer but solid blocks of stone. The lightest color was reserved for the dome. An additional color refinement is that the outer columns of the porticoes are a darker hue while those at the center are lighter. From the Mall one ascends a tall, broad staircase to the main entrance portico. Twelve Ionic columns are distributed in two rows, with the inner ones framing three doors. The portico on the Constitution Avenue facade is similar but set high above the street with entries cut into its solid base. Both are simple without being severe, largely due to their attenuated proportions. With the exception of the Ionic order repeated in the rotunda, the more austere Doric is employed for pilasters throughout and for the freestanding columns of the garden courts, as simplification of volumes and surfaces was fundamental to Pope's aesthetic and contributes greatly to the calm ambiance of the museum.

The rotunda of the National Gallery is an interior space of great power. The primary circulation axis of the museum as well as its symbolic core, a double circle of columns, is overlain by a Greek cross with arms of unequal length. Sixteen monolithic 36-foot-tall green Italian marble columns circumscribe the inner circle and carry the limestone entablature and parapet. Double columns mark entry into each of the arms, while empty niches are carved out of the rotunda walls. By attempting to reconcile the dichotomy between circular and cross-axial movement, Pope created a space where access is tightly controlled but movement is constant. Diffused light filling the galleries and portico arms draws one from the rotunda to the circulation pathways, while the width of the Mercury fountain requires deviation from the main axis within the rotunda. The contrast of shiny, dark column shafts against grainy, light walls, dome, and column sculpture is an arresting moment of drama within the serene play of manners which characterizes the museum as a whole. This interplay of light and shadow and of dark and pale materials enhances the complex changing perspectives as one enters

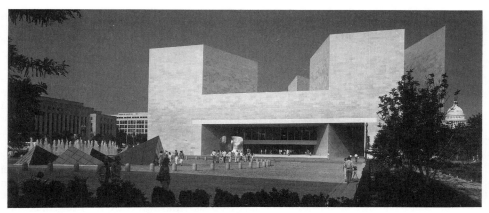

ML17 National Gallery of Art, East Building

and passes through the rotunda. Pope may have intended his rotunda to pay homage to two famous unexecuted plans for the Capitol. William Thornton's 1793 design called for a ring of columns set within his central rotunda, and both Benjamin Henry Latrobe's 1806 and 1817 schemes had large niches set diagonally.

The intensely cerebral nature of Pope's architecture continues in his treatment of materials and architectural details. Contradictions abound. Sleek, thin rusticated walls on the ground story give way to unpolished matte surfaces on the main floor. Architectural details—such as the guttae in the garden court frieze—just appear, apparently from nowhere, as they are not logically connected to the seemingly correct classical system. The marble seems alternately so hard that it can only be used in shallow rectilinear or curvilinear sheets, then so malleable that a thick spiral of it can be molded into a sinuous stair rail–baluster–newel post whose curve sweeps one upward. Interior walls display the same subtle surface modulations as the exterior, with layered shallow planes often merging with the ordinance system as walls become extended pilasters. Decoration is held to a minimum: elongated scroll brackets (reminiscent of those used by the Renaissance architect Antonio de San Gallo the Younger) provide three-dimensional structural ornamentation as architectonic as the rest of the building. The constant interplay of the linear and volumetric is as clear and structured as the plan, the whole a temple not just to display but to enhance the paintings and sculpture it contains.

Decorating each gallery to the historical period and place of the art it was to contain was not Pope's decision but rather that of the gallery's director, David E. Finley. Creation of such modern "period rooms" allied the gallery with American turn-of-the-century museums that collected actual historical rooms. The sensitive ground-story renovation creating a bookstore, café, and sculpture gallery is the work of Keyes Condon and Florance. Completed in 1983, it is thoroughly consonant with the elegance of the original building.

ML17 National Gallery of Art, East Building

1978, I. M. Pei and Partners. Pennsylvania Ave. and 4th St. NW

I. M. Pei's East Building addition to the National Gallery of Art is a complex interweaving of two- and three-dimensional geometries. The entire structure is a trapezoid, a form dictated by the 8.8-acre site just west of the apex of the triangle where Pennsylvania Avenue converges with the Mall. In plan the trapezoid is formed by an isosceles triangle—the museum—and a right triangle—the Center for Advanced Study in the Visual Arts. The separation of these two forms is evident at the southwest and northeast corners where a skylight spans an external corridor between them, creating a tenuous connection between the two geometries and functions. The triangle as a building module is a difficult one, and its application at the East Building is not entirely successful, as Pei relentlessly applied it to every space and detail. Twenty-five tetrahedral skylights cover the museum's open atrium. Three lozenge-shaped towers marking the apexes of the museum triangle are composed of two isosceles triangles set side by side, their inner points converging in the center of the skylight. Interior and exterior spatial forces are focused there just as the cross axes of the major spatial thrusts of the West Building are focused on its dome. Here we perceive that Pei's conscious connections between the two buildings go far beyond reopening a Tennessee quarry to obtain the same shade of pink marble as was used on the West Building. The East Building, the only museum on the Mall with no entry facing the Mall, addresses the West Building in an inversion of positive and negative space similar to the skylight-dome symbiosis that exists between the centers of the two museums. Although the two buildings are not strictly aligned with one another, Pei's two west towers correspond to the setbacks of Pope's east facade, not just duplicating their position but also approximating their volumes. Pei's wide, low entry is a horizontal response to Pope's vertical doorway and its surrounding frame.

The north and south facades, where one expects to enter the museum, are distinct compositions. In response to the importance of Pennsylvania Avenue, the north facade is similar to the west one in that it is shaped as an emphatic letter H, replicating the seemingly impossible cantilever of the entry. Where the receding aperture of the west entry draws the visitor into the building, a low garden wall (as at the West Building) shuts off physical and visual access from the north. These two similar facades define the museum. Skylights are not visible; one reads only the prismatic geometry of solid volumes silhouetted against the sky, and low, deep shadows. Unbroken surfaces monumentalize the building's symbolic role and internalize its functions, in the tradition of the West Building. In position, scale, form, and materials, the East Building proclaims its public nature yet there is an aura of mystery. The architecture is emphatically antibureaucratic, anti–mass production—a sacred enclave dedicated to the creative achievements of individuals rather than mass society.

Distant views of the south facade are cut off by the Mall's elms, and the grove of cherry trees in its immediate vicinity obscures what

might be read as entry—the diagonal glass wall that recedes into the study center's mass. The small triangular plaza formed by this wall (which lights the reading room of the library) and its adjacent solid marble wall are seemingly dead spaces resulting from too strict adherence to the triangular theme at the expense of the area's function. In reality, the heat and glare of the southern sun are mitigated by the relative positions of the two walls. The fine balance of vertical and horizontal masses on this facade is reinforced by the way the materials are used: horizontal marble panels measuring 4 feet by 8 feet are countered by vertical glass ones. The weakest facade is the uninspired glass curtain wall on the east that lights the offices of the study center. This is particularly unfortunate, as the point from which buildings on the Mall were meant to be seen to their best advantage was the terrace of the Capitol.

Contradictions between the exterior and interior begin with the dichotomy between the symbolic entry and actual access to the museum. The progression from street to plaza to covered porch gradually draws the visitor to a wide glass wall where one expects numerous choices, only to be funneled through two revolving doors. Immediately one is in a low, dark, and undefined space from which one is drawn forward by the intensity of light. The atrium is an explosion of light-filled multidimensional space in direct contradiction to the closed and formal exterior. Movement is the leitmotif: Alexander Calder's mobile slowly revolves; shadows cast by the skylight fade and intensify; people move along bridges, stairs, and escalators.

In late twentieth-century museums, cultural and historical artifacts are a form of consumerism for much larger and better-educated audiences than at any other period in American history. Pei's East Building responds to this phenomenon on many levels. The atrium serves as the traffic artery for large crowds moving among numerous exhibition spaces. At the same time, it serves as a public park with trees, benches, and sculpture. Most of all, it is a space of great architectural potency meant to excite, to give a sense of place. To misquote Gertrude Stein: there is there there. Within the atrium, no two circulation modes are the same, forcing visitors to be actively involved with the building as they move through it. In contrast, most of the galleries are subdued, perfect foils for the display of painting and sculpture. The result of this architectural self-consciousness is that the building vies with its contents for aesthetic supremacy.

To achieve his dramatic effects, Pei advanced architectural technology in many areas. The tetrahedral skylights are composed of brushed chrome tubes laminated between two layers of glass and set within a steel space frame. They introduce light and control the interior climate, reducing glare, melting snow, and admitting fresh air to the intake system. The high-quality craftsmanship of the build-ing is the result of careful planning of details and customized elements. The 3-inch-thick marble veneer panels (2 feet by 5 feet) were hung by steel plates on the cast concrete core. This allowed for custom cutting of corners, as in the acute angle of the study center on 4th Street. Neoprene gaskets instead of mortar joints between the marble panels allow for expansion and contraction and are maintenance free. Marble dust was mixed with the concrete aggregate to harmonize the two materials. God was in the details.

Monumental Capitol Hill (CH)

Pamela Scott

G EORGE WASHINGTON AND THOMAS JEFFERSON REGARDED the Capitol as the most important architectural component in the design of the federal city. In his first report to Washington, dated 26 March 1791, Pierre Charles L'Enfant wrote that the public buildings should be placed on eminences so that they held commanding views and "might be seen From Twenty mile off." In a letter to Washington on 28 June accompanying the first map he submitted to the president, he explained the basic principles that guided him in the general design of the city and in the selection of sites for public buildings. Reciprocal vistas linked to existing landscape conditions were a fundamental design consideration. He placed the Capitol (Congress House) on the west end of Jenkin's Hill, "which stand as a pedestal waiting for a monument." In 1813 L'Enfant recalled that he and an "eminent Italian sculptor" planned to place a sculpture group at the foot of Capitol Hill entitled *Liberty Hailing Nature out of its Slumbers.* This expressed L'Enfant's view of the meaning of the federal capital: liberty, in the form of the unique American system of government, was to create a major metropolis, the center of a "vast empire," out of a virtual wilderness. The building where the representatives of the people met embodied this concept of liberty.[29]

L'Enfant's Capitol, the plan of which has been obliterated from the only surviving manuscript map of the city attributed to L'Enfant, is depicted on later engravings. They show a disproportionately large building, probably a function of the small size of the original engraved plate, but its size may have been a bold refutation of skeptics in Philadelphia and New York who opposed the creation of the federal city. The most salient feature of L'Enfant's Capitol was a vast circular room projecting from the west front. This space was probably the "conference room," a space large enough to hold joint sessions of Congress,

Monumental Capitol Hill

an essential part of the building program as outlined in the competition guidelines drafted by Jefferson. The conference room, like the House of Representatives, was to accommodate 300 people, the Senate chamber to cover 1,200 square feet. All three of these rooms, with their lobbies and antechambers, were to be double-storied, while twelve 600-square-foot offices would be of one story. No provision was made for the Supreme Court, as the Capitol was not originally intended to house the judiciary. Jefferson expressed his preferences for the Capitol in a letter to L'Enfant of 10 April 1791. He hoped the building would be based on "some one of the models of antiquity which have the approbation of thousands of years."[30]

The complicated history of the competition and construction of the Capitol until 1800 can be given here only in outline. Competition designs were due on 15 July 1792. Having received a letter from the physician and amateur architect William Thornton announcing his intentions to submit a design, Washington and Jefferson did not award the commission at this time. Rather they retained the services of Stephen Sulpice Hallet, whose design was the most sophisticated and professional of the competition entries. His surviving plan shows that Hallet proposed a peripteral temple, on the model of Jefferson and Charles Clérisseau's 1784 design for the Virginia State Capitol, the first monumental building in the modern world to exploit an ancient temple as a prototype. During the next several months both Thornton and Hallet submitted designs for approval by Washington and Jefferson. Thornton's were refinements of his original submission, which had derived from eighteenth-century English Georgian mansions. Hallet's designs underwent a similar process, but he began with a seventeenth-century French chateau. Both arrived at a compact horizontal block with a large circular conference room projecting to the west, probably guided to this resolution by Washington and Jefferson. Thornton's plan was preferred, and on 5 April, he was awarded the $500 first prize and a gold medal. Hallet received the second prize of equal value, but as he was a professional architect, he was hired to build Thornton's design.

Thornton's lost original plan was unique and highly irregular in that it apparently called for two domed spaces on the same structure, both based on that of the Roman Pantheon. The one facing the Mall contained a conference room (as in L'Enfant's plan); by 1797 Thornton had designed a high colonnaded dome above it to serve as a monument to George Washington. Thornton's House of Representatives, located in the south wing, set an elliptical colonnade in a two-story rectangular room. His Senate chamber, in the north wing, was a semicircular room facing east. A disproportionate amount of floor space on both levels was given to corridors and grand staircases, particularly an oval staircase in the center of the north wing.

Hallet was dismissed in June 1794, when he was discovered to be laying the foundations for his own design for the central area rather than Thornton's. The English architect George Hadfield, winner of the Royal Academy gold

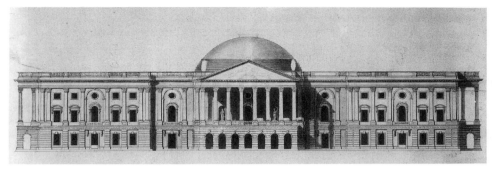

Plan for the east elevation of the Capitol, by William Thornton.

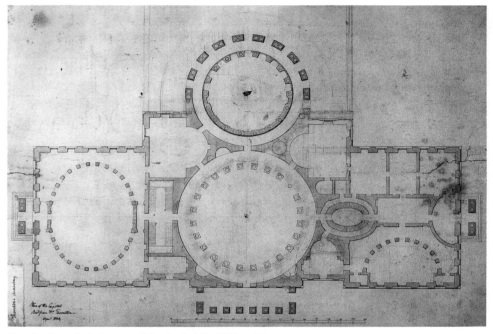

Plan for the principal story of the Capitol, by William Thornton.

medal in 1784, was placed in charge of the Capitol until 1798, when he also was discharged. He remained in Washington until his death in 1826, however, designing many beautiful buildings, most of which have been destroyed or thoroughly altered. The only part of the Capitol that unquestionably reflects his tenure is the exterior guilloche belt course. James Hoban, whose successful supervision of the White House was nearing completion, was put in charge of finishing the north, or Senate, wing of the Capitol in time for the reception of Congress in 1800.

Construction did not resume until 1803, when Jefferson, at that time president, hired Benjamin Henry Latrobe to carry the original Thornton design to completion. Latrobe was given a series of plans by various individuals (including Thornton), all purporting to be the original design of the Capitol, each of which differed in detail from the others. After a close study of the documents Latrobe concluded that both the original design and the existing fabric were faulty, necessitating rebuilding the interiors of the extant north wing and redesigning the south wing and central section of Thornton's design. His scheme for completing the building according to a more realizable scheme was to have a single, low, saucer dome covering a central rotunda. He redesigned the elliptical House of Representatives chamber to be two semicircles joined by a rectangle in order to be more easily constructed. Contrary to his own judgment, he accommodated Jefferson's wish for a room domed with long narrow skylights set between vertical wooden ribs. Jefferson had seen such a dome on the recently completed Halle au Blé in Paris while there as the American minister in the 1780s. On the exterior facade, Latrobe redesigned both the east and west porticoes in order to link the north and south wings visually and physically and thus to diminish the importance of Thornton's walls, which he disliked. On the east, Latrobe placed an octastyle portico before a wide screen of columns, the whole approached by a monumental staircase with a carriage drive passing beneath it. On the west an octastyle, unpedimented portico with columns set in antis spanned the entire central section of the building, as did that of the east portico.

Latrobe's Capitol was carried forward in two building campaigns, the first lasting until his tenure was interrupted by the War of 1812. During the first campaign he built the Supreme Court chamber, rebuilt the Senate chamber, and erected the House wing. The Capitol was partially burned by British troops in August 1814; the House chamber and Library of Congress were destroyed, the Senate severely damaged, but the Supreme Court survived almost intact. Between 1815 and 1817 Latrobe returned to rebuild the badly damaged building. He made two major changes to his 1806 scheme. The House was redesigned as a semicircular room on the model of Jacques Gondouin's surgery theater at the Medical School (1775) in Paris, the first modern adaptation of an ancient theater for an auditorium. The western wing was extended in order to increase office space and relocate the Library of Congress, which he placed across the width of a new projecting west wing that overlooked the Mall. Upon his departure in 1817, Latrobe left a set of drawings to complete the Capitol, but they were only partially followed.

Charles Bulfinch was hired in 1818 to finish the building. He carried out Latrobe's designs for most of the interiors of the north and south wings and the east portico but substituted his own scheme for the west portico, rotunda, and dome. His final work was to landscape the grounds and to erect gate houses, a fence, and a terrace continuing the ground level of the east plaza along the Capitol's north, west, and south sides. When the Capitol was completed in 1829,

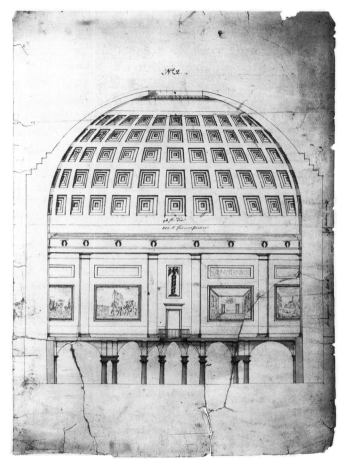

Section of the Capitol rotunda, by Charles Bulfinch, c. 1822.

office space and the size of the two legislative chambers were already inadequate. In 1845, Robert Mills and the Army Corps of Topographical Engineers both made plans for its extension. Their schemes included lateral wings attached directly to the old building, lateral wings with an intervening hyphen, and replication of the original building on the grounds to the east separated by a courtyard. In 1851, a year after a Senate-sponsored competition, President Millard Fillmore selected Thomas U. Walter's design that extended the Capitol with new lateral wings attached to the original building by hyphens.

The cornerstone was laid on 4 July 1851 for wings that located the legislative chambers at their western perimeters. After an 1852–1853 congressional investigation of Walter's superintendence of the project, control passed to Montgomery C. Meigs of the Army Corps of Engineers, although Walter retained his position as architect. Meigs moved the chambers into the center of each .

wing, placing them perpendicular to the long axis of the building, and added sculpture-filled pediments to the east porticoes. The House occupied its new chamber in 1857; the Senators theirs in 1859.

In 1855 Congress had voted to replace the original dome with one of cast iron designed by Walter. Although its construction was temporarily halted by the outbreak of the Civil War, it was advanced enough by 1863 to raise Thomas Crawford's statue of *Freedom* atop it. By 1865 the extensions and dome of the Capitol were finished except for some of its decoration. The Italian-born and trained Constantino Brumidi had begun to execute his great cycle of fresco paintings in 1855, but it remained unfinished at his death in 1880. The pedimental sculpture of the north, or Senate, wing entitled *The Progress of Civilization* was designed by Thomas Crawford in 1853, while he was resident in Rome; the figures were carved in marble at workshops on the Capitol grounds and put in place in 1863. Paul Wayland Bartlett's pedimental sculpture for the south wing, *Apotheosis of Democracy,* was unveiled in 1916.

Major renovations of the Capitol in the twentieth century include restoration of the original House and Senate chambers in 1901, redecoration of Walter's House and Senate chambers in 1949–1950 under Architect of the Capitol David Lynn, addition of a 32-foot-deep marble replica of Latrobe and Bulfinch's east facade between 1958 and 1962, and restoration of the original Senate and Supreme Court as museum rooms for the bicentennial in 1975–1976.

In 1874 Frederick Law Olmsted began redesigning the Capitol grounds, whose mature plantings were densely packed, obstructing views of the building. Olmsted's plan replaced the original central walkway on the west with a lawn and created two lateral approaches connected to Pennsylvania and Maryland avenues. On the north and south he opened oblique and side views across expansive lawns and created outdoor rooms walled with specimen trees in the grounds to the east. Curved roadways and walkways connected the grounds to the surrounding city following picturesque principles. In addition to these landscape elements, Olmsted planned new and elaborate stone terracing on the north, west, and south sides of the building, greatly extending Bulfinch's earlier terraces. Architectural features of the terrace, entrance gate posts, and retaining walls were designed by the English architect Thomas Wisedell under Olmsted's supervision and constructed between 1886 and 1892. The double monumental approaches flanking a great arcaded hemicycle mask two basement levels of the center section of the building and provide a broad, stable base to unify the 751-foot west front of the building. In the northwest quadrant of the grounds are Olmsted's rustic stone tower, actually a ventilation shaft (another is located in the southwest quadrant). There, too, is his grotto, planned as a cool retreat and public water fountain, where, in the tradition of grottoes, nature's architecture is shown in conjunction with man-made architecture.

The Library of Congress was located in the Capitol until a separate building was opened in 1897. It was to be an apsed rectangular room across the hall from the Senate chamber and was designed by Benjamin Henry Latrobe in the Egyptian Revival style, but plans for the facility were only partially implemented. Following the 1814 fire, the library was relocated in the western projecting wing and built following Charles Bulfinch's design. This was the room that housed Thomas Jefferson's private library, some 6,700 volumes purchased by the government for $23,950 after the original library was burned. Its double-story alcoves ranged along both sides of the long, narrow reading room, a common library arrangement. The library room was again a victim of fire in 1851; its successor was designed by Thomas U. Walter in 1853. Erected in cast iron to be fireproof, this, the third Library of Congress, was Renaissance Revival in style and followed the same general spatial organization as the two earlier libraries. In 1900–1901, after the Library of Congress building was completed, the library facility in the Capitol was dismantled and replaced by offices.

A separate library became necessary by 1870 with passage of the copyright law, which required that two copies of each work protected by the law be deposited there. Librarian of Congress Ainsworth Spofford established detailed criteria for the 1873 competition: a stone exterior measuring 340 by 270 feet to house at least 2 million volumes was to focus on a central circular reading room patterned on the British Museum library. Interiors entirely of iron would render the building fireproof. The height of its dome was limited to 70 feet so it would not compete with the Capitol dome. Although it was assumed that the new building would be contiguous to the Capitol, no site was selected prior to the competition.

On 22 December 1873, the newly founded firm of Smithmeyer and Pelz was awarded the $1,500 first prize from among twenty-six entries for its Renaissance Revival design (see CH12). Sen. Timothy O. Howe, a competition judge and chairman of the Joint Committee on the Library, led a congressional junket to numerous European national libraries in 1874. The congressmen later instructed the architects to prepare a larger building with more grandeur; many additional architects, including William Appleton Potter and H. H. Richardson, entered a second competition, held in 1874.

The site for the larger building became an issue. Judiciary Square, the Mall, and Capitol Hill were all suggested. A substantial addition on the west front of the recently completed Capitol was also considered. Between 1874 and 1886 Smithmeyer and Pelz prepared drawings specific to each location, with Italian and French Renaissance designs to the east of the Capitol, Italianate and Romanesque on the site of the present Botanical Garden on the Mall, and Gothic and German Renaissance for Judiciary Square (where the Pension Building was erected in the 1880s). In all cases their designs were predicated on the same plan, a rectangular building organized around a central reading room attached to the exterior envelope by arms containing book stacks. Although the clothing of the exteriors differed dramatically, all the designs maintained the same basic pattern of their 1873 winning design: an imposing central pavilion linked to corner pavilions by curtains that could vary in length depending upon the ultimate scale of the building.

Although professional librarians voiced the opinion that the new national library should be a model of functionalism, John L. Smithmeyer was an outspoken exponent of the library as "a museum of literature, science, and art . . . the mecca of the young giant Republic." He viewed the building not simply as the repository of the books containing all human knowledge but also as the visual exposition of "an insight into the colossal array of knowledge which the human mind has accumulated and still gathers together."[31] In 1882 Congress paid Smithmeyer's expenses for a European trip to study national libraries in London, Paris, Rome, Berlin, Munich, and Vienna (Smithmeyer's native city). This experience reinforced his attitude that the Library of Congress should have three separate systems, one for the storage of books, one for scholars, and one to display for the general public American achievements within the context of world knowledge.

In 1886 Congress approved an 1885 "version" of the winning design to be erected on Capitol Hill. Although Frederick Law Olmsted devised a plan in which the library would be situated on its present two-block site without obstructing the view of the Capitol along Pennsylvania Avenue from the southeast, Smithmeyer insisted on placing his building centrally on the land acquired for it, thus cutting off a major vista in the city. In 1888, Thomas L. Casey of the Army Corps of Engineers took charge of construction. He named as architect his twenty-three-year-old son, Edward P. Casey, who had just graduated from architecture school. Smithmeyer and Pelz sued the government for the fees they had lost, claiming they had devoted a major portion of their careers to providing designs for the library. They never received additional compensation, and Edward P. Casey's name was placed above theirs on the cornerstone as one of the architects.

No further significant development took place on Capitol Hill until the relevant parts of the great Senate Park Commission Plan of 1902 were carried out in the first decade of the twentieth century. This master plan envisaged circumscribing the Capitol grounds with a series of Beaux-Arts-inspired buildings to serve the needs of the legislative and judicial branches, the genesis for the present arrangement of the House and Senate office buildings and the Supreme Court. A crucial feature of the plan was the removal of the Baltimore and Potomac Railroad Station from the edge of the Mall at 6th Street and Constitution Avenue. Washington's new train station was named Union Station because it brought together under one roof all of the railroad companies operating lines to the national capital. Upon acquiring the Baltimore and Potomac Railroad, Alexander Cassatt, president of the Pennsylvania Railroad (and brother of the painter Mary Cassatt), was persuaded by Daniel Burnham (the chief architectural mind behind the Senate Park Commission Plan) to relinquish its prime location on the Mall and move to a site north of the Capitol where Massachusetts Avenue is intersected by Delaware Avenue, Louisiana Avenue, and 1st Street NE. In exchange Congress agreed to provide partial funding for construction of a tunnel necessary to serve all traffic to and from the south. Burnham was chosen as architect of Union Station in 1903; it opened to the public five years later (see CH10). Architects of contemporaneous railroad stations in other major American cities also saw these stations as significant modern building types, symbolic of progress and destined to participate in the transformation of American life. These stations were divided into two distinct parts, the functional train sheds—very wide to accommodate numerous tracks—and the passenger stations, which served simultaneously as symbol and container of the unpredictable movement patterns of the large numbers of people using them.

Burnham connected Union Station to the city through numerous traffic arteries converging on a great semicircular plaza. A rendering of his design, published in 1906, depicts trolley cars, horse-drawn carriages, two automobiles, and numerous pedestrians filling the plaza that Burnham visualized as the focus for a monumental ensemble of public buildings. In 1986 plans to use the corresponding site to the east of Union Station, then a parking lot, for a government office building resulted in Edward Larrabee Barnes's Federal Judiciary Building to house administrative offices of the United States courts (1989–1992). The competition for its design was unusual in that teams of developers and architects working together were asked to submit proposals. Burnham intended connecting Union Station to the Capitol by developing Delaware Avenue NE as a monumental architectural approach. In 1908, when erection of the Lincoln Memorial on the Mall was halted temporarily, Burnham suggested placing a seated figure of Lincoln within a huge open colonnade on the Union Station plaza. In 1912, in collaboration with the sculptor Lorado Taft, he designed the Columbus Fountain. During World War I, the adjoining blocks to the south were covered with temporary dormitories for women war workers; these same blocks were landscaped by the Office of the Architect of the Capitol between 1927 and 1932. In 1968 Congress passed legislation transforming Union Station into the National Visitors' Center in anticipation of the millions of tourists expected during the bicentennial year of 1976. The building continued to function as Washington's train station during its occupation by the National Visitors' Center (1976–1985). It continues to serve that function as well as an urban mall, which opened in 1988, designed by Benjamin Thompson Associates.

Two of the six Senate and House office buildings are of great architectural merit. The Russell Senate Office Building (see CH03) and the Cannon House Office Building (see CH02) were the initial steps in implementing the Senate Park Commission's suggestion to circumscribe the Capitol with a frame of classically inspired office buildings. In 1904 the New York firm of Carrère and Hastings agreed to the terms set by Architect of the Capitol, Elliott Woods: the architects would produce designs for the two buildings for a set fee, and Woods's office would produce the working drawings and oversee construction. Carrère and Hastings were the principal exponents of using French, particularly Parisian, prototypes (as opposed to classical Roman models associated with the firm of McKim, Mead and White); Woods selected the firm, even though he was wary of the "excesses" of modern French ornamentation. The problem was to provide buildings of appropriate richness and importance that would not compete visually with the Capitol. The sites of both buildings were identical, irregular rectangles bounded on one side by a diagonal boulevard. This site condition was a major factor in their design, as the architects chose to place the main entrances on the obtuse angles diagonally facing the Capitol, thus emphasizing their relationship to the central object they were to serve. The Cannon Building—whose space needs were greater—was designed around a central courtyard, enclosed on all four sides, while the Russell Building was initially U-shaped, with its fourth side not added until 1931–1933. Construction took place simultaneously on both buildings between 1905 and 1909. Upon completion they became instant classics, models copied elsewhere in the city and around the country.

Before occupying the room Benjamin Henry Latrobe designed for it in the Capitol, the Supreme Court was located in various temporary quarters in the building. The court did not sit in its own specially designed chamber until 1810, only to move four years later when the Capitol was burned by the British. In 1819 the court returned to its ground-floor location on the east front of the north wing where it remained until 1860. In that year the former Senate Chamber on the main floor of the Capitol was remodeled for its use until the present building was completed in 1935. The only external feature of the Capitol to attest to the court's residence therein is Thomas Crawford's sculpture entitled *Justice and History* (1863), located over the east door of the 1851–1859 Senate wing.

The 1901–1902 Senate Park Commission, in allocating plots on Capitol Hill for future government offices, placed the Supreme Court at the corner of East Capitol and 1st streets NE (see CH08). The building conforms to the trapezoidal site, with the narrow end facing the Capitol. On 25 May 1926, Congress passed the law authorizing acquisition of the site and in November the Public Buildings Commission began proceedings to purchase or condemn the land at an eventual cost of more than $1.75 million. Among those buildings destroyed was Latrobe's Old Brick Capitol, erected for the temporary accommodation of Congress in 1815.

In 1928 the United States Supreme Court Commission was formed, consisting of the chief justice (former President William Howard Taft, who had been its major promoter), an associate justice, congressmen, and the architect of the Capitol. Taft resigned in 1930 and was succeeded by Charles Evans Hughes, who saw the building completed. Taft suggested Cass Gilbert of New York as architect. Surviving sketches dating from as early as November 1927 indicate that Gilbert anticipated his appointment. From a first plan with the building in the center of East Capitol Street until his final design of 1932, Gilbert consistently conceived of the building as a dominant temple form intersecting a lower rectangular mass, thus visually and physically separating the court's main function and symbolic content from its day-to-day operations. Gilbert aligned his raised octastyle porch axially with Walter's east portico of the Capitol's north wing and expanded on Crawford's theme of the interrelationship between justice and history to develop an appropriate and extensive iconographical program.

Gilbert was uncompromisingly Beaux-Arts in his approach to what he may have considered to be the last of the really significant government buildings to be erected in Washington. The opulence of design and materials of the Supreme Court initially seems odd, considering that its building history coincided with the worst years of the Great Depression. It was, however, only one of hundreds of public buildings undertaken by the federal government during the 1930s to help stabilize the American economy. It was erected for nearly $100,000 less than the initial appropriation of $9.74 million.

In 1928 industrialist Henry Clay Folger selected Washington over Chicago, New York, and Stratford-upon-Avon to build a library to house his unparalleled collection of Shakespeareana. The Folger Shakespeare Library (see CH15), conceived as an important research institution, was located on East Capitol Street to be near the Library of Congress. Folger hired Alexander B. Trowbridge, former dean of Cornell University's College of Architecture, to advise him on selecting an architect and to act as his intermediary. Folger's initial preference for the stylistic clothing of his library was Elizabethan. Trowbridge convinced Folger that it was desirable to maintain uniformity of classical forms and principles in Washington's public architecture, particularly for a building close to the Capitol. Folger's desire for an Elizabethan interior, however, was honored.

Trowbridge recommended the French-born and -trained Paul Philippe Cret to Folger as an architect who would design a modern building in a classical spirit free from imitation of specific historical prototypes. Cret's earlier use of low-relief sculpture to convey the purpose of buildings influenced the choice, as Trowbridge had suggested to Folger that sculptural subjects drawn from Shakespeare's plays should ornament the library. Throughout the 1920s, Cret had experimented with ways to maintain the evocative qualities of historically derived architecture yet respond to the European modernist reactions against imitation and repetition. Cret's solution was to simplify his volumes by reducing their number and the complexity of interrelationships and by treating their surfaces in a more planar manner. He also rethought the role of architectural and sculptural decoration. This process of simplification resulted in two masterworks by Cret in Washington, the Folger Shakespeare Library and the Federal Reserve Board Building (see FB08, p. 210). Formal dedication took place on 23 April 1932, the 368th anniversary of Shakespeare's birth.

Tremendous growth in the holdings of the Library of Congress necessitated an annex building three decades after the original building was completed. The law funding the $8 million building was not passed until 1935, seven years after the land acquisition. Architect of the Capitol David Lynn was placed in charge of the project, and his office selected a Washington firm. When Pierson and Wilson, with Alexander B. Trowbridge as consulting architect, designed the annex to the Library of Congress they consciously responded to both the Library of Congress and the diminutive Folger Library that bordered its site. In composition, scale, and organization the annex was allied institutionally and iconographically to the main library building, but in horizontal massing, materials, fenestration patterns, and modernized classical detail the architects hoped to complement Paul Cret's masterpiece without overpowering it. Within these constraints, Pierson and Wilson successfully designed a modernized classical building with exceptional Art Deco details, particularly in the interiors.

CH01 United States Capitol

1793–1865, William Thornton, Benjamin Henry Latrobe, Charles Bulfinch, Thomas U. Walter, Montgomery C. Meigs. Capitol Hill

In its present state the United States Capitol exhibits four distinct architectural minds at work, those of its original designer, William Thornton; Benjamin Henry Latrobe, the architect responsible for erecting the major portion of the first building; Charles Bulfinch, responsible for redesigning and carrying out the central section including the rotunda; and Thomas U. Walter, the architect of the extensions and present dome. Montgomery Meigs of the Army Corps of Engineers worked closely with Walter on the structural aspects of the Capitol extensions and directed its elaborate decoration. As it would necessitate considerable backtracking to follow the Capitol's construction history, it is more practical to begin on the west terrace, comparing the exterior features of the original building with the later additions, before moving to the east, and then discussing the interiors.

The sole remaining exposed wall of the original Capitol consists of five bays to the north of the projecting west center wing completed by 1800 under George Hadfield (1795–1798) and James Hoban (1798–1800). The reciprocal bays on the south side were carried out by Latrobe between 1804 and 1807. These walls were built with brown Aquia, Virginia, sandstone, first painted white in 1818 and most recently restored in 1987 when eroded stones were replaced by Indiana limestone. The corresponding walls on the east front

have been covered by the 32-foot-deep addition completed in 1962, when the original sandstone walls were replicated in Georgia marble.

Office areas designed by Hugh Newell Jacobsen in 1991 fill the light courts between the original basement walls and the inside of the terraces. The basement walls are left exposed and are lit by skylights.

Thornton's design for the wall articulation was an elegant interpretation of a palace type, with a rusticated basement story, tall principal floor, and attic story. The compact original building has a balustrade masking the low roof, deep entablature, and guilloche frieze above the basement rustication. These horizontal lines are countered by the vertical organization of the windows into bays separated by two-story pilasters, producing a tightly woven abstract grid. In addition Thornton introduced numerous curvilinear elements into his composition, making the Capitol the first major building in the United States to be influenced by the eighteenth-century English Neoclassical style. Called the Federal style in America, it was characterized by horizontal massing, oval and circular rooms and wall elements, and delicate, attenuated proportions and details. In the center bay on each wing wall Thornton enclosed bull's-eye and arched windows within a shallow, semicircular arch to give a central focus to what was at the time in America a large expanse of wall. Segmental pediments over the principal floor windows continue the curved lines across the facade and were intended to be resolved visually in the center by two low saucer domes, one projecting to the west and the second

CH01 United States Capitol, exterior

contained within the main body of the building. The Corinthian order was employed because the Capitol was perceived as the most important building in the federal city and therefore merited the most lavish ornamentation.

Despite its long building history, the exterior of the Capitol as a whole is in harmony, but there are differences between Thornton's facade and those adjoining by Bulfinch and Walter that reflect their differing interpretations of the classical tradition. For the projecting west wing Bulfinch made both major and minor changes to the pattern established by the earlier building. As Thornton's north and south wings had segmental pediments over the piano nobile windows, Bulfinch continued their use on the north and south faces of the west wing. Thornton probably had intended that the Capitol sit on a level plateau, rather than project over the brow of the hill. To increase office space Bulfinch added a sub-basement story on his west wing, erecting a terrace in 1826–1827 to mask it. These walls were visible from the terrace until 1991, when the courtyard between the terrace and basement walls began to be filled with offices designed by Hugh Newell Jacobsen. All of the east front basement walls will be left exposed and visible from a hall in the new interiors. Rather than employ quoins on the edges of his building, Thornton had used the more elegant double pilasters to terminate his composition. Bulfinch, apparently to strengthen the corner where the west projection meets the original walls, placed double pilasters on the inside angle but neglected to put them on the outside western edge of the walls. He did, however, use double pilasters on both ends of the portico face of his wing, so the articulation is correct when viewed from the front.

Walter continued all of the horizontal regulating lines of the original building in his 1851–1865 marble extensions. He preferred triangular pediments for all his facades. Careful comparison of the relationship between the walls and windows indicates some fundamental differences in sensibility between the Neoclassicism of the original building and the subsequent Renaissance Revival (a Victorian interpretation of classicism of a half century later). The spacing between the pilaster edges and window frames of the first building campaigns produced an even, measured rhythm across the walls. Walter closed the gap, introduced more windows, and created a much more rapid, staccato movement. In the Thornton-Bulfinch facades, the wall is treated as a neutral plane onto which pediments, brackets, and window frames have been attached; Walter's facades are activated with the sculptural elements treated more three dimensionally. They not only are denser but also project more from the wall and contain more elaborate detail. The crispness and intricacy of Walter's walls can best be seen by viewing their profiles against the sky.

The central section of the Capitol has undergone many design changes. Thornton planned a projecting, circular west front and a pedimented octastyle portico raised on an arcaded basement on the east. On the west he planned blank lateral walls between the wings and the small, circular center temple; on the east, single recessed bays that repeated the arched windows of his main walls to intervene between the wings and the portico. When the conference room was deleted from the building's program and the double dome abandoned, Latrobe designed octastyle porticoes for both fronts. His east portico stood in front of a colonnade spanning the width of the center section. It was reached by a monumental stair above a carriageway. Because its shallow pediment did not rise above the top of the entablature, views of his saucer dome were unimpaired. Bulfinch built Latrobe's design for the east portico, making the pediment higher to accommodate sculpture for which Latrobe had not planned.

Latrobe's projecting west portico was unpedimented and set within a wide wall flanked by single window bays. Bulfinch redesigned the west portico to project in front of a wall with a series of arcaded windows. Two sets of double columns flank two single columns, an unusual arrangement he had used earlier on the Massachusetts State House (1795–1797), probably known from a portico on Sir William Chambers's Somerset House (1776–1801) in London.

Bulfinch's dome, constructed in 1822–1824, had an unusually high profile to accommodate the request of James Madison and John Quincy Adams. Set above an octagonal stone drum, the inner hemispherical dome was largely of brick and stone while the outer dome was constructed of wood. It was sheathed in copper but never gilded. In 1851–1859 Walter planned a new focal point for the Capitol. He chose a cast-iron dome because it would be fireproof, lighter, cheaper, and more quickly erected than one in traditional masonry construction. In 1860–1861 the foundry Janes, Fowler, Kirtland and Company of Brooklyn delivered to the site 1.3 million pounds of cast and painted iron parts to be bolted together for a double dome held together by an extraordinary system of thirty-six continuous trussed ribs, apparently devised by Walter's chief draftsman August G. Schoenborn. On 2 December 1863 the final piece of Thomas Crawford's cast bronze statue,

Freedom (19 feet 6 inches), cast in five parts by Clark Mills at his nearby foundry, was hoisted into position. Final weight of the ironwork was nearly 4,500 tons, the only dome of this size to be erected on an existing building.

Walter's design, with its four-part composition consisting of a thirty-six-column peristyle drum and intermediate attic, carrying the dome and tholos, traces its ancestry to Sir Christopher Wren's late seventeenth-century dome on Saint Paul's Cathedral in London. Auguste Ricard de Monferrand's cast-iron dome on Saint Isaac's Cathedral (1824–1858) in Saint Petersburg provided the most immediate model. The pyramidal composition of the Capitol dome—287 feet high, 135 feet in diameter at the base, and 88 feet at the cupola—resulted from structural necessity and aesthetic considerations. Even distribution of its weight on the rotunda and exterior foundation walls was of particular concern because of damage to the outside walls in the 1814 fire. A 14-foot iron ring was cantilevered out from Bulfinch's octagonal masonry drum and supported by seventy-two 15-foot brackets. Its iron skirt brought the base of the dome to the edge of the penultimate columns on the east front portico in an attempt to bring the new dome into visual harmony with both the original building and the new wings. Its size was calculated on the basis of the great length of the total building (751 feet) with its massiveness ameliorated by its openness. The skeletal cast-iron structure permitted vast expanses of glass on all four levels, flooding the interior with light, although only the drum windows are visible from the interior. Its sculptural three-dimensional quality in outline and in detail relates directly to the wings, drawing the whole into as much an integrated composition as possible given the disparate nature of the two architectural traditions represented.

Walter's wing extensions are attached to the main building by colonnaded hyphens, particularly successful in that they break the horizontal sweep of the Capitol into three manageable masses. Each rectangular wing was originally set perpendicular to and centered on the longitudinal axis of the main building, but the east front extension created an imbalance with the hyphen recess now deeper on the west than on the east. The honey-colored marble of the extensions came from Lee, Massachusetts. The infelicitous cold gray of the "white" Georgia marble used in the 1958–1962 east front extension is a poor match. Each one of Walter's three walls facing away from the original building has a portico spanning nearly its entire width. Raised on rusticated arcades, they are unpedimented decastyle on the west, north, and south. In deference to the central portico of the main building, the porticoes on the east front extensions are octastyle and pedimented, at Meigs's suggestion. Similar to Latrobe's much-admired design for the center, these porticoes stand in front of a colonnade that traverses the entire facade and are approached by imposing staircases above carriageways. The effect, whether seen obliquely or frontally, is of a richly columnar building, partly French-inspired, partly English. Walter's extended colonnades on all three facades function in apparently contradictory ways. While they impart a sense of grandeur to the building, they control the scale of the wings by breaking up their expansive wall surfaces and integrating them to the original Capitol without diminishing it. Walter used one hundred monolithic fluted Corinthian columns of Maryland marble for the extensions. The original east front Corinthian columns were designed by Latrobe and executed by Bulfinch with unfluted shafts, perhaps due to structural reasons or more probably for aesthetic ones associated with English Neoclassical tenets propounded by Sir John Soane (1753–1837).

Opinions as to which aspects of American history and ideology should be represented at the Capitol changed over time, as seen in the sculptural programs of the three east front pediments. President John Quincy Adams suggested the subject for the 81-foot 6-inch-wide central pediment, the *Genius of America*, the whole carved in sandstone by Italian-born sculptor Luigi Persico between 1825 and 1828. The originals were replaced by Georgia marble replicas when the east front was extended in 1958–1962. America, 9 feet tall, stands at the altar of liberty attended by Justice and Hope, classically garbed allegorical figures that harked back to the revolutionary era as its fiftieth anniversary was being celebrated.

A quarter century later the theme was manifest destiny, the belief that European-American dominance of the continent was preordained. Thomas Crawford's marble figures in the north wing pediment form a den-

ser and more sophisticated composition and iconographical program, entitled the *Progress of Civilization* (1863). The central figure of America is flanked on the north by Indians and frontiersmen representing the early history of America. On the south a soldier, merchant, two youths, a schoolmaster instructing a child, and a mechanic illustrate the country's development as numerous professions contributed to civilizing it.

Marble sculpture for the south, or House, wing was not completed until 1916 and reflects the aesthetic and symbolic concerns of a well-established culture. Paul Bartlett's complex three-dimensional arrangement of attenuated figures represents two major aspects of American life. Entitled the *Apotheosis of Democracy*, the central composition depicts Peace protecting Genius; the figures on the north relate to agriculture and those on the south to industry. Each wing pediment is 80 feet long and 12 feet high at its apex. The exterior sculpture continues iconographic themes present much earlier on the interior.

Latrobe's three chambers, originally occupied by the Senate, House of Representatives, and the Supreme Court, and their subsidiary spaces, are the architectural glory of the Capitol. Constructed during two building campaigns (1803–1812 and 1815–1819), they were the most architecturally sophisticated spaces in America, carried out despite labor difficulties, lack of continuous and adequate congressional funding, shortages of material, and opposition to Latrobe's proposed changes to Thornton's original plan. Latrobe's detailed reports and exquisite drawings have made accurate twentieth-century restorations possible.

Although the interiors of the north wing were completed and occupied by Congress when Latrobe began work in 1803, their construction was faulty. In his rebuilding, Latrobe changed many elements but left the outlines of many major interior walls, which contributed to the criticism of the hallways as ill-lit mazes. In his interiors, Latrobe above all was conscious of making a building that was small, compared with contemporaneous European public buildings, appear monumental. He achieved this by creating layers of space within each room or visually connected area. The Supreme Court vestibule, which is entered through the Law Library door to the north of the central stair, is an excellent example of this practice. The small apsidal rec-

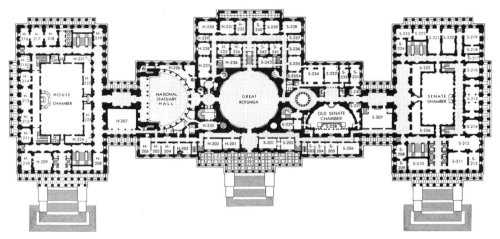

CH01 United States Capitol, plan for principal floor

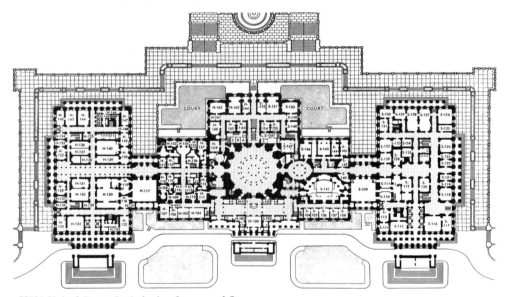

CH01 United States Capitol, plan for ground floor

tangular room is broken longitudinally by a series of spaces defined by half domes, domes, and barrel and groin vaults. These are carried on the six famous corncob and cornstalk columns that stand in front of unfluted pilasters and create the illusion that the walls are receding, not that the columns are intruding into the room. This illusion is reinforced by the final pair of columns (in front of the Supreme Court door) which support an arch that defines a shallow space apparently deeper than it actually is. This kind of spatial manip-

ulation was an important aspect of European Neoclassicism that Latrobe introduced to America. The opening opposite the main door was cut by Bulfinch; Latrobe planned the vestibule as primarily an entrance to the Supreme Court chamber with only one off-axis door to the main stairhall located behind the vestibule. Arched openings rather than doors and the multifaceted ceiling increase the sense of space in flux, pushing out rather than confining the visitor in a small space.

The corncob columns were the first of three

American orders Latrobe invented for the Capitol. Carved by Giuseppe Franzoni in 1809, they, and Latrobe's tobacco-leaf and magnolia orders, were well within the Western architectural tradition of inventing orders associated with appropriate symbols. These orders were Latrobe and Jefferson's attempts to begin an emblematic language for America based on native plants particularly associated with its agricultural richness and economy. Latrobe used Aquia sandstone, an unreliable material for exterior use, extensively and to great advantage on the interiors.

Rooms serving major functions were not normally found on the ground story of classically inspired buildings. The Supreme Court chamber was probably located here due to space constraints in the original building, and this placement was viewed as a temporary expedient. It was the first of Latrobe's rooms to be completed that followed the same spatial arrangement. In the Supreme Court, space is not confined within visible walls nor does the actual physical weight of the vaults oppress. Space appears to be expanding in all directions, resulting in the appearance and reality of monumentality. Semicircular with a screen of columns along its diameter and angled piers around its circumference, the arrangement was based on ancient theater forms and had been revived in European eighteenth-century auditoriums. Faced with the problem of creating a room that had to support a two-story space above it yet reflect architecturally its important function, Latrobe visually and physically diminished the mass of the individual supporting elements. For his six Doric columns Latrobe used as a model early Greek columns with the exaggerated echinus that expresses in its bulge the great weight each carries. However, Latrobe's columns and piers are remarkably slender, contributing considerably to the sense of openness in the room. Formerly, natural light entered through the three large east windows, but the 1962 east front addition necessitated static backlighting at these windows, destroying the important interplay between form and space that changes as natural light shifts throughout the day. The layer of space behind the columns and piers functioned as small meeting areas yet were visually open to the main body of the room. In addition, the half dome is not a continuous surface, broken only by shallow coffers, but rather a series of butterfly vaults set between substantial ribs

that spring from the polygonal piers. The language is classical but the principle of ribbed vaults is medieval. Latrobe's willingness to draw on numerous historical periods to solve structural and decorative problems at the Capitol resulted in unique spatial solutions. He achieved an eclectic mixture that was destined to become the hallmark of American architecture.

Adjacent to the Supreme Court is the two-story tobacco leaf rotunda set within oval walls that originally contained a major staircase of Thornton's design (destroyed by the fire of 1814). Latrobe's substitution of the rotunda with its own cupola brought light and air into the central circulation spine on both principal floors. The windows of the cupola have been closed and the rotunda is now lit by an inappropriate and vastly overscaled twentieth-century chandelier. The curved and arched piers on the ground floor obliterate the sense of being in an oval, a form that Latrobe disliked because of its geometric impurity and expensive construction. Yet Latrobe used the oval to create a subtle visual thread connecting the public circulation spaces on the ground floor. He cut the plan across its short axis and stood the resulting semicircle vertically within a semioval so that when one looks from the center of the tobacco-leaf rotunda through the crypt to the far hallway on the south, one sees a series of semicircular and semioval arches. Throughout the ground-floor halls, the walls are frequently articulated by open or blind semicircular openings set within half ovals.

The crypt was intended to function like ecclesiastical crypts, for it was hoped that Washington would be buried in a tomb below. The crisp profile of the entablatures and the general arrangement recall Sir Christopher Wren's crypt at Saint Paul's Cathedral. In addition, the center of the Capitol was the original prime meridian for the country (marked by the compass rose set in the floor). State lines were measured from this point, and the division of the city of Washington into its four quadrants was calculated from the center of the Capitol. In anticipation of large crowds visiting this space, Latrobe designed it (and Bulfinch executed it) to be as open and light-filled as possible. An outer double ring and inner single ring of slender, unfluted Doric columns carry elliptical vaults of an extraordinary lightness that are reminiscent of the vaults designed by Soane for

English Neoclassical buildings. The splayed echinus of the capitals lightly cushions the transition from the vaults to the columns, creating a sense of absolute balance between the vaults they support and the unfluted columns.

The present main staircase serving the south portion of the original building is an enlargement by Bulfinch of Latrobe's stair following the same constructional principles Latrobe had employed on the corresponding staircase on the north. Each marble tread is embedded in the wall and rests on the step below. Latrobe deviated from the standard practice of S-shaped steps, making his a quarter oval in profile, similar to stairs employed by the English Neoclassicist Robert Taylor. The scalloped outside edge of his steps particularly complements their curved form. The small octagon at the top of the stairs is Latrobe's oldest extant interior space in the House wing and the earliest surviving fragment of Greek Revival architecture in America; the Corinthian order is derived from the Tower of the Winds in Athens.

The present National Statuary Hall is the second chamber for the House of Representatives designed by Latrobe. The first, destroyed in 1814, was carried out between 1804 and 1807 in close collaboration with Thomas Jefferson as a double-apsed room, a compromise between the oval space of Thornton's plan, which Jefferson wished to build, and the semicircular room that Latrobe preferred. Latrobe's semicircular House chamber, built on the same semicircular plan as the earlier Supreme Court and Senate chambers, contained several inherent faults; these were due to the need to gain as much space as possible for an ever-expanding House membership by filling the rectangular envelope of the south wing. The acoustics were poor and it was difficult to heat. The curtains behind the columns replicate originals that only partially deadened echoes that plagued the room. Despite these problems, it is a beautiful room, but one marred by an inappropriate color scheme. To be historically correct and to harmonize better with the brown, gray, and white sandstone and marble structural elements, the turquoise should be light sky blue and the red a deeper burgundy; the curtains should also be darker.

The corner blocks contain staircases once open to the exterior and used by visitors to reach the second-story public gallery behind the columns. The gray shafts of the twenty Corinthian columns are Potomac Breccia marble; their elaborate capitals, based on those found on the Choragic Monument to Lysicrates in Athens, were carved in Italy of white Carrara marble at Jefferson's behest. The present cast-steel half-dome is decorated in clear, bold Greek Revival motifs in imitation of the original; it dates from 1901. Four white marble fireplaces are 1975 reproductions of the originals designed in 1812 by Giovanni Andrei and sculpted in Philadelphia by Adam Traquair. The originals had escaped destruction in the 1814 fire as they were in storage awaiting installation. In the center, putti, flanked by rings of thirteen stars, bind together the rods of the fasces. These symbols of authority and union are shown completed, carrying liberty caps, on the vertical supports of the mantles. Latrobe seems to have been the first to adopt these for an American symbol, although they had been common motifs during the French Revolution.

The north wing containing the old Senate chamber is the remaining part of the Capitol designed by Latrobe. He designed the tobacco leaf and flower order in 1816 for the sixteen columns of the rotunda outside the Senate chamber to replace a monumental double staircase damaged in 1814. The columns had to be more attenuated than Latrobe felt canons of classical taste allowed for in Ionic shafts, so he designed the tobacco leaf order to have "an intermediate effect approaching the character of the Corinthian order"[32] yet retaining a simplicity of outline agreeable to him. The capitals are now gilded and painted without any historical basis.

The inequality between the lengths of the east and west exterior walls of the north wing is resolved in the Senate vestibule, where the screen of Ionic columns masks the fact that the doors to the Senate to the east and offices to the west are not opposite one another. This vestibule, with its faceted corner piers and shallow dome carried on pendentives, is a little-remarked architectural gem of the building, a space where Latrobe proportioned and detailed each element with infinite care.

The Senate chamber as rebuilt after the 1814 fire retained its shape but was enlarged by about one quarter. The screen of gray Potomac Breccia columns with their Carrara marble Ionic capitals (modeled on those of the Erechtheum on the Athenian Acropolis) create, as in the House chamber, a semiprivate recess with a fireplace at each end. The corner blocks contained stairwells serving the original visitors' gallery above and behind the vice president's chair. In his initial plan for rebuilding the Senate chamber, Latrobe proposed two superimposed galleries, the upper to be supported by thirteen caryatid figures with the seals of the original states. Latrobe intended these figures to express emblematically the difference between the Senate ("the assembly of the states") and the House (representative of the majority of the people). Although models of the caryatids were made, they and the upper gallery where they stood were removed in 1828, when Bulfinch's cast-iron gallery around the room's semicircular perimeter was installed. The present cast-steel half-dome was installed in 1901. The room's excellent restoration was completed in 1976.

As in the Supreme Court chamber directly below, natural light from east-facing windows was cut off by the 1958–1962 addition, and artificial lights were installed. The Senate's most unusual feature is the skylight, now covered and backlit. Light to the chamber was filtered through a series of translucent circular windows set within the curvature of the half dome. In this way Latrobe devised a compromise between cupolas with vertical windows, which often admit inadequate, diffuse light, and skylights, where glare, condensation, and heat are disadvantageous. It was probably Jefferson's insistence on a skylit roof for the original House chamber that stimulated Latrobe to contrive this solution.

The rotunda is Charles Bulfinch's major remaining public room at the Capitol. His Library of Congress, decorated with the order based on the Tower of the Winds in Athens, traversed the west center front. It burned in 1851, and Bulfinch's stairhall leading to it from the rotunda was redone by Carrère and Hastings in 1901. Latrobe's plan for an astylar rotunda included four large niches between the doors to house statues and stairs leading to the crypt below. John Trumbull's cycle of eight history paintings, commissioned by Congress in 1817, was to be placed between the niches and doors. When Bulfinch assumed office as architect of the Capitol in January 1818, many areas were incomplete.

Under Bulfinch the iconographic program of the Capitol was expanded to honor pre-Revolutionary events and people. Four of the eight horizontal decorative panels contain portraits by Francisco Jardella of early explorers who came to North America: John Cabot, Christopher Columbus, René de La Salle, and Sir Walter Raleigh. Sculptural panels of Aquia sandstone in the rotunda and figures for the niches on the east front codified the belief that European dominance of the American continent was inevitable and just. The earliest event recorded occurred in 1607, the *Preservation of John Smith by Pocahontas,* carved by Antonio Capellano and placed above the west door in 1825. Enrico Causici's representation of the 1620 *Landing of the Pilgrims* (east door) was completed in the same year. Nicholas Gevelot's *William Penn's Treaty with the Indians* (1682), above the north door, was done in 1827. Causici's 1826–1827 panel above the south door depicts Daniel Boone fighting the Indians. The two standing figures of *War* and *Peace* on the east portico are 1958 replicas of Luigi Persico's 1834 marble figures carved in Italy. The present marble relief of *Fame and Peace Crowning George Washington* over the east door is a reproduction done in 1959–1960 of Antonio Capellano's 1827 original. None of the European-born and -trained sculptors remained in America, ending their careers in France or Italy.

The dome above Bulfinch's sandstone frieze with wreaths is of cast iron, glass, and painted plaster. The handsome grisaille frieze recounting major events in the formation of America from the landing of Columbus to the California gold rush is 300 feet in circumference and 58 feet above the floor. Designed by Constantino Brumidi in 1859 but not begun until 1877, the frieze was unfinished at his death in 1880 but completed over the next eight years by a fellow Roman-trained artist, Filippo Costaggini. Probably due to a miscalculation, a 31-foot segment was left blank; in 1953 Allyn Cox added depictions of the Civil War, Spanish-American War, and the Wright brothers at Kitty Hawk. The subject of the canopy painting executed by Brumidi is the *Apotheosis of George Washington.* It is suspended from the outer dome 180 feet above the rotunda floor and lit by windows not visible from below; until tours of the dome were limited, visitors could view the canopy painting from a balcony at its base, or from the gallery at the springing of the dome. Six groups of figures representing War, Science, Navigation, Commerce, Manufac-

CH01 United States Capitol, 1846, daguerreotype by John Plumbe, Jr.

tures, and Agriculture are located around the central composition of an enthroned Washington, attended by Liberty and Fame; he is facing east and wears a classical robe over his uniform. The thirteen figures completing this circle represent the original states. Brumidi's figures, executed in broad, sweeping brush strokes, have the three-dimensional quality necessary for them to be discernible from the floor. Moreover, they perfectly complement the sculptural qualities of the decorative cast iron of the inner dome that frames them. Because of the structural dictates of the iron— a giant Tinkertoy bolted together—the latticelike frame of the dome coffers is heavier and more elaborately decorated than the coffers themselves.

Although both Latrobe and Bulfinch worked within the Neoclassical tradition, their interpretations of the style differed considerably. Latrobe's penchant was for bold statements, and he freely mixed simple Greek orders, structurally articulated spaces derived from Roman architecture (perhaps directly or perhaps via English Neoclassical traditions), and medieval constructional principles to unify space and decoration. His creative spatial approach to architecture differed from Bulfinch's essentially decorative sensibility, which emphasized rich and elegant surface details. The decorative vocabulary Bulfinch employed was primarily Roman inspired. Areas of the building where he completed work begun by Latrobe suggest that he introduced decorative elements that were more delicate in scale and detail. In doing so, Bulfinch returned to the Federal style in which William Thornton had originally designed the Capitol.

The Capitol extensions contain some of the finest extant mid-Victorian interiors in America. Designed by Walter, Montgomery Meigs, and the Italian fresco painter hired by Meigs, Constantino Brumidi, they are characterized primarily by an exuberant explosion of color and pattern, making a more decisive break with the original building than do the extension's exteriors. The decorative vocabulary does not represent a unified vision but rather an eclectic mixture of Victorian versions of the Italian Renaissance style. Each wing is treated as a distinct composition, with the principal floor the most lavishly ornamented, following standard practice with Renaissance-derived buildings. Unfortunately, the present decoration of the current House and Senate chambers (done in 1949–1950 by Architect of the Capitol David Lynn) destroyed the two most important rooms, which combined brilliantly painted and gilded cast-iron decoration and an iron ceiling with inset glass panels evenly lighting the rectangular rooms. Numerous offices and committee rooms contain equally lavish interiors, albeit on a smaller scale, but there are few spaces open to the public where one can appreciate the true quality and extent of the architectural decoration of the Capitol extensions.

The walls and vaulted ceilings of the Senate (north) wing ground-floor corridors are covered uniformly with fresco and oil paintings on plaster carried out by Brumidi and his assistants. The most interesting are the northern east-west and western north-south corridors where the decorative framework is composed of native American plants and animals mixed together with the traditional spiraling mixed together with the traditional spiraling acanthus leaves of Roman-derived decoration. The acid reds, greens, browns, and ochers used by Brumidi were substantially correct copies of ancient tones. Paintings of historic American events, symbols, and inventions as well as portraits of important figures are set within an ornate system of Roman-inspired frames, with some empty fields reserved to record future deeds. The barrel and groin vaults enhance the effect of an extensive and complex building enriched throughout in imitation of Roman and Renaissance architecture. The floors on all three levels in the Senate wing are covered with profusely patterned encaustic tiles in colors that harmonize with the walls. The commission to provide these tile floors for the Capitol was so large that the English manufacturer, the Minton Tile Company, later advertised that they were "tile makers to the US Capitol."

Included in the spectacular architectural features of the extensions are the two marble imperial stairs for public use, adjacent to the east elevator vestibules in each wing. Lit by iron ceilings with glass etched and painted by the J. & G. H. Gibson Company of Philadelphia, these staircases are constructed of a richly veined, brown Tennessee marble. Unfluted columns on the second and third stories have black Corinthian capitals of cast bronze manufactured by Cornelius and Baker of Philadelphia. The coffered ceilings are of white Italian marble. The east front vestibules and their related staircases are among the few areas in the Capitol extensions where the color and opulence of the materials achieve a splendid effect without additional painting or gilding. The white marble of the vestibules is from Lee, Massachusetts, and the columns are one of Walter's two variants on the American order, where acanthus and tobacco leaves coexist harmoniously.

Both chambers are circumscribed by hallways open except for their entry vestibules

and two members' staircases located at their outer corners. Designed by Brumidi in 1857, the newel posts and rails for the dogleg stairs were modeled by Edmond Baudin and cast in bronze by Archer, Warner, Minsky and Company of Philadelphia between 1857 and 1859. Stars, eagles, deer, and squirrels are incorporated into a three-dimensional design of children intertwined with a continuous acanthus arabesque, again combining Renaissance and American motifs in an exuberant and unified design.

The Senate Reception Room (S–213) is the only major remaining space on the principal floor where visitors can see the richest of the Victorian interpretations of Italian Renaissance interiors. Based upon Raphael's frescoed rooms at the Vatican (1508–1517), the walls and shallow domes are overlaid with modeled and gilded plaster. Frames for paintings and deeply undercut rosettes of an astonishing variety display the technical virtuosity of master plasterer Ernest Thomas. The extravagant use of uncommonly deep yellow gold from California in this room (and many others) celebrated America's resources, as did the numerous varieties of marbles and scagliola used throughout. The gold also reflects the meager natural light, as heavy curtains traditionally protected elaborately painted rooms to prevent fading. When the gas chandeliers were in use, their flickering light also reflected off the intricately carved gilded surfaces, enhancing the preciousness of the interiors. This luminosity, the shallow arches and domes, and the overall pattern of somber and rich colors create rooms of great intimacy.

The Hall of Columns on the first floor of the House wing is the most spectacular of the architectural features open to the public in the south extension. Twenty-eight stopped-fluted Corinthian-cum-American columns form a monumental entrance to the Capitol that extends from the south door through the entire 142-foot width of the wing. The white columns of Massachusetts marble have capitals designed by Walter as one of his American orders in which a single row of acanthus leaves is superimposed on one of tobacco leaves and thistles. The floors, originally laid in a colorful variety of encaustic tile designs, were replaced by the simple black and white marble pattern in 1924. The trabeated construction was made possible by cast-iron beams, and the combination of structural systems results in a stately and dignified ceremonial route drawing one to the center of the building. Allyn Cox's 1974 and 1982 mural cycles, *Hall of Capitols* and *Great Experiment Hall,* are located on the main east-west cross corridor.

There are four cast-bronze historiated doors at the Capitol, all modeled generically after Lorenzo Ghiberti's famous *Gates of Paradise* for the Baptistery in Florence. The most magnificent are the Columbus doors, since 1871 at the prominent east central door opening into the rotunda. Designed and modeled by Randolph Rogers in Rome in 1858, they were cast in Munich in 1861 and installed between the original hall of the House and the new south wing in 1863. Thomas Crawford designed doors for the main entrances to both extensions between 1855 and 1857. The Senate doors were cast in America and put in place in 1868, but those for the House were not cast until 1903 and installed two years later. Their rectangular and circular panels depict allegorical scenes and actual events of the Revolution. The doors designed by Louis Amateis in 1910 for the west center door were installed only in the east House stairwell south of the crypt. Their iconography is allegorical, with the apotheosis of America in the transom. Panels containing portraits of Americans represent various trades and professions.

Throughout the Capitol extensions one senses that the opulence of materials and Renaissance Revival designs were meant to express that the torch had passed from the Old World to the New, from the age considered the epitome of European civilization to the maturation of American ideals as its east and west coasts were united.

CH02 Cannon House Office Building

1905–1908, Carrère and Hastings. Southeast corner of Independence and New Jersey avenues NE

CH03 Russell Senate Office Building

1905–1908, Carrère and Hastings. Northeast corner of Delaware and Constitution avenues NE

The original Senate and House office buildings exemplify the Beaux-Arts design tenet that facades should suggest the main elements of interior space. Here long repetitive ranges of arcades, colonnades on the main

CH02 Cannon House Office Building

facades on Constitution and Independence avenues, and pilastrades on secondary facades on New Jersey and Delaware avenues imply the existence of the offices behind them, as the central pavilioned block suggested some important room or nexus, not just entry into the building. Two-story circular entry vestibules act as collectors of circulation as well as suitably impressive introductions to important buildings. These rotundas, comprising a pier arcade below and Corinthian order above, were based on Jules Hardouin-Mansart's Chapel at Versailles (1688–1710) in their arrangement as well as their richness of ornamentation. Thomas Hastings (the designer in the firm) may also have intended to refer to Benjamin Henry Latrobe's two-story domed rotunda in the north wing of the Capitol.

In each building a double-flight grand staircase leads to a major room on the principal floor, the Senate Caucus Room in the Russell Building and the House Caucus Room in the Cannon House Office Building. Initially planned as semicircular rooms based on Statuary Hall, they were later made rectilinear and projected into the courtyard. Black-veined New Jersey marble Corinthian columns and pilasters define the rectangle measuring 54 feet by 74 feet, which is robustly decorated in the Louis XVI style. A flat, deeply coffered ceiling rising 35 feet alternates plain panels with ones of gilt rosettes and others of acanthus arabesques. The rooms are set at right angles to the axes established by the entrances. This axial conflict is not resolved, resulting in an impression of an interrupted, incomplete, or truncated space. The arrangement of the room is odd, as two paired sets of columns and a single set at each end frame three large arched openings along the long walls, while six pilasters (in the same arrangement as the columns) articulate the short end walls.

In the tradition of academic eclecticism in America, the exterior elevations were drawn from more than one easily identified prototype. Carrère and Hastings's preference for Parisian models led them to choose two functionally appropriate sources for these office buildings, Jacques-Ange Gabriel's Gardes-Meubles (1755–1774) and Claude Perrault's east front of the Louvre (begun 1667), in which regular cell-like rooms were contained behind their giant colonnades. Hastings saw that the scale relationship between the House and Senate office buildings and the Capitol was the major issue in relating the three buildings. Columns encompassing two or more stories set upon a full-story arcade, in conjunction with a flat cornice line, diminished vertical height; doubling columns on a long colonnade visually contracted horizontal extent. Hastings carefully calculated the proportional relationship of the parts of the entablature to his columns, comparing them not only with his French prototypes but also with the wings of the Capitol.

French ornamentation was kept to a minimum: slender fluted Doric columns decorated with a simple necking band established the mood of restraint characteristic of the buildings as a whole. Sculptural exuberance extended to garlanded brackets marking the entries, window brackets, and empty helmets in the attic of the pavilions. The white Vermont marble used on the exteriors and the public spaces inside retains its innumerable sharp edges, important in that the linear character of these buildings' exterior surfaces contributes to diminishing their mass. The Russell and Cannon buildings teach us that background buildings can achieve the same standard of excellence as the important buildings they support.

CH04 Longworth House Office Building

topped by tall entablatures (all marble), and a recessed attic story not readily visible from the street. The pedimented Ionic portico of the main facade is reminiscent of the early nineteenth-century architectural work of Robert Mills, whose position as one of the first of the government's architects was rediscovered during this period. The change in architectural character from sumptuousness in the Cannon Building to austerity in the Longworth Building was not just a shift from Neoclassical French to classical Roman prototypes but reflected a new sense during the 1920s, as the modern language of architecture began to be used for monumental buildings, of designing classically inspired buildings with thinner, more planar walls and sparser ornamentation. The Allied Architects, whose principals were Frank Upman, Gilbert LaCoste Rodier, Nathan C. Wyeth, and Louis Justement, prepared two designs during 1925 and were retained as consultants to the architect of the Capitol when one was selected in 1929 for the Longworth Building.

CH05 Rayburn House Office Building

1962–1965, Harbeson, Hough, Livingston, and Larson. Independence Ave. between South Capitol St. and First St. SW

Perhaps Washington's most maligned public building, the Rayburn Building covers eight former Capitol Hill residential blocks with four massive rectangular office wings separated by courtyards that open to the east, south, and west. The difficulties of designing in a historical style whose time has past by those untrained or ill-trained in its basic principles is manifested most obviously in the

CH04 Longworth House Office Building

1929–1933, Allied Architects of Washington. Independence Ave. between New Jersey Ave. and South Capitol St. SE

The narrow, steeply sloping, and irregular site of the Longworth Building was easily accommodated by the standard Beaux-Arts office building formula of rusticated basement (two to three stories in granite here), main stories spanned by giant columns and

Rayburn Building by the lack of a comprehensible human scale, the most fundamental legacy of the classical system of architecture. Although one can identify specific models employed by the architects—Piranesian cyclopean basement walls, sunken, vertically connected windows to re-create columnar rhythms in bays, a motif copied from its masterful use by Paul Philippe Cret at the Federal Reserve Board Building (see FB08, p. 210), massing of each block into three horizontal layers like those of the typical Beaux-Arts office building (see CH04)—the architects lacked the talent to make from them a new synthesis or a distinguished whole. The end result is a bombastic architectural expression of raw, arrogant, and uncontrolled power that dominates through sheer size rather than coexisting amicably with its neighbors or enhancing the art of architecture by contributing a viable new interpretation of its building type or architectural style.

CH06 Dirksen Senate Office Building

1947–1958, Eggers and Higgins. Northeast corner of Constitution Ave. and First St. NE

The most unsettling aspect of the Dirksen Building's exterior is the presence of a giant projecting and pedimented portico on its side facade on First Street NE with no doors in it. This portico is not even a symbolic entry; it merely functions as a visually symmetrical counterpoint to the portico on the facing wall of the Russell Building across the street. The actual entries into the Dirksen Building are on the main Constitution Avenue facade through doors in the center of three-bay wall projections at each end. These projections were intended as modern astylar, unpedimented expressions of porticoes, but they are

so integrated into the overall wall patterns that they do not immediately signify entry. Thus architectural legibility that is so much a part of the classical system has been subverted, with the front reading as the side and the side containing the only monumental exterior feature of the building.

The fenestration pattern of vertically linked windows recessed behind the wall plane and set within continuous metal frames is the dominant feature of the Dirksen Building. The motif was probably suggested by its use on Beaux-Arts buildings of the 1920s and 1930s, including the National Academy of Sciences (see FB09, p. 210) and the nearby Folger Library (see CH15). Alternation of windows with wall sections of equal width set up an even rhythm across the facades in imitation of the alternation of solids and voids found on classical buildings surrounded by columns or articulated with pilasters. This window motif in conjunction with appropriately proportioned basement and attic windows controls the large rectilinear mass of the Dirksen Building. Although the building is not particularly distinguished in its reconciliation of modern with Beaux-Arts architecture, it does attempt to continue the human scale of the Capitol Hill monumental buildings that preceded it.

CH07 Hart Senate Office Building

1973–1982, John Carl Warnecke and Associates. Second and C streets NE

The cost of the Hart Building ($137.7 million), which provides offices for fifty senators, was more than that of the East Building of the National Gallery, yet the architectural benefits to Washington are not comparable. The Hart Building is the first of Capitol Hill's legislative office buildings to be designed in the modern language of architecture without any historicizing detail, yet the architect did not create from that idiom a memorable building that befits the importance of its function or location.

Fortunately, it is not apparent from the Hart Building's main facade on Constitution Avenue that it encompasses more than one million square feet of interior space; only fifteen bays (273 feet) of the massive building front on the street. A major concern for energy-efficient design is reflected on all of the similar nine-story facades. Each facade is articulated by separate, three-dimensional gridded frames of Vermont marble that project from and frame each of the tall, rectangular windows. The frames function as brises-soleil, partially shading the windows of dark-tinted solar glass. Proportions of the windows and their regular alternating rhythm with the gridded frames link the Hart Building to the neighboring Dirksen Building behind which its vast bulk extends.

Below-grade entry into the Hart Building is unmarked by any special architectural features, less impressive than many commercial office buildings. Senators' offices, however, retain the 16-foot heights of the earlier legislative office buildings, but double-stacked staff offices in adjoining suites have 8-foot ceilings. To increase energy efficiency, the focus of the offices and circulation spaces is inward onto the central skylit atrium dominated by Alexander Calder's somewhat ponderous *Mountain and Clouds,* installed in 1986.

CH08 Supreme Court

CH08 **Supreme Court**

1929–1935, Cass Gilbert. Northeast corner of 1st St. and East Capitol St. NE

The relationship between the architecture of the Supreme Court and its landscaping is one of the most successful in Washington. The architect, Cass Gilbert, effectively disguised the irregular trapezoidal plot on which the building sits while totally controlling the approach, entrance, and passage through the building. The building is composed of three parts, a dominant temple of Roman derivation flanked by two wide horizontal wings. The temple, literally conceived of as the temple of justice, contains the most important functions, culminating in the Supreme Court chamber which terminates its 385-foot-long axis. The physical and symbolic pathway to this chamber begins on the plaza. A few steps above the sidewalk, a 100-foot-wide terrace— a square expanded by great apsidal ends— runs counter to the main east-west axis. The terrace is enclosed by the same low wall that surrounds the entire building and is paved in the gray and white marble pattern of alternating circles and squares seen at the Roman Pantheon. Immediately upon entering the terrace one encounters marble candelabra where low-relief panels depict Justice holding her sword and scales and the Three Fates weaving the thread of life. The bronze bases

of the flagpoles there, designed by Gilbert and modeled by John Donnelly, Jr., are decorated with numerous symbols of justice (scales and swords, books, masks and torches, pens and maces) as well as the four elements (earth, air, fire, and water). At the closure of the terrace a full-story staircase draws one upward onto the dipteral octastyle portico. Throughout this entire processional route, one is surrounded by white Vermont marble with an unusually high mica content. Reflections are so brilliant on sunny days that they almost blind the viewer. White glazed-tile roofs contribute to the luminous quality of the building. The opulence of these materials is complemented by the richness of the architectural and sculptural decoration and the intricacy of its allegorical theme.

Atop the long cheek blocks of the staircase James Earle Fraser's stern seated figures, the *Authority of Law* (on the south) and the *Contemplation of Justice* (on the north), guard the temple entrance. Sixteen columns (and eight pilasters) are Gilbert's American variant of the Corinthian order where heraldic eagles are set between splayed volutes. The frieze of braziers hung with garlands (symbolic of the plenty existing in an ordered society) is particularly lavish. In the pediment, Robert Aitken's central sculptural figures represent *Liberty Enthroned Guarded by Order and Authority.* They are attended by six allegorical figures symbolic of Counsel and Research who were modeled after Americans responsible for bringing the Supreme Court and its quarters into being, although they are all shown in Roman garb. The muscular reclining figures at the edges of the composition are Chief Justice William Howard Taft on the north and Chief Justice John Marshall on the south, both shown as young men. Next to Taft, the architect Gilbert converses with Secretary of State Elihu Root while the sculptor Aitken attends to Chief Justice Charles Evans Hughes. The inscription in the frieze, "Equal Justice Under Law," helps to explain how portraits of the architect and sculptor appear with those of eminent jurists: the sculpture proclaims equality in American society while it reflects the artists' optimistic attitude concerning the emerging role of the fine arts in America.

The rarely noticed pediment on the east front depicts a related theme, *Justice the Guardian of Liberty*. Hermon A. MacNeil's central figures are representations of great law givers, *Moses, Confucius,* and *Solon*. Their supporting figures are symbolic of the functions of the Supreme Court: *Means of Enforcing the Law, Tempering Justice with Mercy, Settlement of Disputes between the States*. In a secondary group is *Protection of Maritime Rights, Pondering of Judgment, Tribute to this Court,* and the *Fable of the Tortoise and the Hare*. This in-antis Corinthian portico, while less fully developed than the entrance, is symbolically important, as the chief justice's suite of rooms, directly behind it.

The bronze entrance doors and the frieze of the Supreme Court chamber are the two major remaining foci of Gilbert's iconographical program, and they both depict the historical development of law throughout the world. John Donnelly, Jr., modeled the thirteen-ton bronze doors, each with eight panels. On the left the scenes are derived from classical historical and literary sources, the Shield of Achilles (Greek law), Praetor's Edict (Roman law), and the Justinian Code (religious law). The panels on the right illustrate events in Anglo-American legal history: *Magna Charta, Westminster Statute, Coke, James I,* and *Story, Marshall*. On both doors, the most remote events are at the bottom, and they move chronologically to the top as they move from laws themselves to their application or enforcement. Hence, like its neighbor the Library of Congress, the Supreme Court places American achievements within the broad continuum of human history.

In canonical Beaux-Arts fashion, the extended experience of approaching and entering the Supreme Court continues inside the building as one moves along the central axis toward the court chamber. Gilbert employed two common Beaux-Arts methods of spatial division along his processional route: changes in level (both modest and dramatic) and screens of columns. The visitor passes through six distinct spaces before arriving at the courtroom. The colonnaded main hall has double rows of columns at each end and an additional screen masking its apsidal termination. The lateral columns standing close to the niched and pilastered side walls create a measured and stately approach to the courtroom. All are Roman Doric in white Georgia marble and carry an entablature whose frieze is composed of classical heads in profile on the model of classical coins, as well as numerous abstract symbols associated with the law. Busts of justices alternate with the columns and are set within the niches. The space is emphatically trabeated with the flat, coffered ceiling of painted plaster (red, white, and blue) made possible by the use of a steel frame.

The courtroom cannot be experienced as Gilbert intended, for he planned it to be brightly lit from side windows that are now covered with heavy curtains. The light was to be filtered through two sets of double Ionic columns, one set within the courtroom and the second across intervening halls that separate it from courtyards on either side. Gilbert may have had in mind Leon Battista Alberti's dictum from his *De re aedificatoria* (c. 1450) that the place where justice is dispensed should be flooded with light, a metaphorical statement. The Supreme Court chamber is a near cube with the top third composed of an attic story with four marble friezes in low relief sculpted by Adolph A. Weinman after pencil sketches by Gilbert. Above the justices' bench is the *Majesty of Law* and opposite it the *Power of Government*. On the west wall is *Justice and Divine Inspiration*. On both sides are portraits of the world's law givers, including Confucius, Augustus, and Napoleon. John Marshall is the only American represented. Costly and sumptuous materials were used throughout, including colored marble from Africa and Europe. Bronze screens with repetitive small-scale Roman ornaments are set between the side columns and cast intricate shadows on the interior surfaces when the curtains are drawn.

The office wings are raised on a walled podium. E-shaped, they are attached to the sides of the temple, creating four internal courtyards. These are highly developed architectural spaces with Corinthian columns or pilasters on all four facades as they are viewed from important rooms and were intended to be used as rooms themselves. The plasticity of the temple with its strongly three-dimensional architectural and sculptural elements contrasts markedly with the compact and restrained wings. Thin, unfluted Ionic pilasters barely break the wall surface; unframed vertical windows puncture it in a correspondingly shallow depth. Panels of low-relief garlands above the windows, the plain and planar entablature, and blind end bays all contribute to the shallow wall treatment and further emphasize the dominance of the temple over the wings.

CH09 **United States Post Office**

1915, Graham, Burnham and Company. 2 Massachusetts Ave. NE

When Daniel Burnham designed Union Station (CH10), he did not envisage it as an isolated object in the landscape but rather as the central piece of a three-part composition where flanking subsidiary buildings would provide a properly monumental, yet subdued, frame for his greater building. Burnham's successor firm completed the post office just three years after his death, using what was to become a common facade treatment for monumental Beaux-Arts public buildings that primarily contained offices. The post office's giant Ionic colonnade imbedded in the wall effectively masks several office floors, as does the attic story set above and slightly back from the main entablature. The architects used a number of techniques to link the two structures: continuation of Union

Station's material (white Bethel, Vermont, granite), uniformity of its height at the entablature line, inscriptions above the end pavilion entries, and classical vocabulary that established axial relationships with architectural features between the two buildings.

CH10 **Union Station**

1903–1908, Daniel Burnham. Columbus Circle at Massachusetts Ave. and 1st St. NE

Railroad stations had no analogous building type in ancient architecture, so Daniel Burnham combined the triumphal arch and the public bath typologies to obtain a classical and meaningful image and to solve crucial interior circulation problems for Union Station. Triumphal arches were the gateways of Rome and bath complexes accommodated huge crowds constantly on the move. Burnham reordered the Arch of Constantine in his triple-arched entry, concentrating his iconographical program for the building here, which he entitled *The Progress of Railroading*. The entablature above six Ionic columns breaks forward to provide bases for 18-foot-tall allegorical figures by Louis Saint-Gaudens that represent Fire, Electricity, Freedom, Imagination, Agriculture, and Mechanics. Inscriptions in three central panels composed by Harvard president Charles Eliot reinforce the meaning of the sculpture, which elevates railroads to a status comparable to major cultural and historical institutions. Union Station was intended to represent the culmination of the emblematic program introduced at the Capitol in the 1820s when the push westward was seen as America's destiny. Railroads con-

CH09 United States Post Office

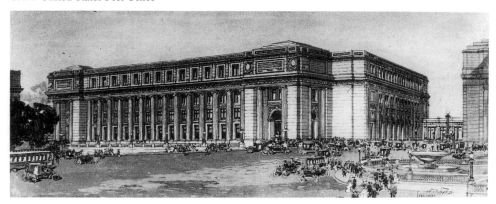

CH10 Union Station

quered the continent and recognition of this role, as well as their contributions to the country's great prosperity at the turn of the century, accounts for the architectural importance accorded Union Station. Although not erected until 1912, Burnham and Lorado Taft's *Columbus Fountain,* located on the plaza on the central axis, participates in this grandiloquent scheme. Columbus stands at the prow of his ship flanked by crouching figures representing the Old and New worlds. A globe supported by American eagles sits atop the entire composition. The fountain—the first element we encounter—symbolizes the link between the two continents while the station itself represents mastery of the North American continent.

This succinct and meaningful display of two fundamental facts of American history contributes to Union Station's greatness, but it might have existed on a building of lesser architectural merit. In its five-part organization Burnham established a hierarchy with the central portals dominant and the side arcades and end pavilions subordinate in scale, sculptural plasticity, and decorative (and thus emblematic) elaboration. This ordering gives clear spatial organization and a sense of compactness to a very large structure. The 626-foot extent of the facade's continuous vaulted loggia funnels people into either central or end doors. These arcades of Renaissance inspiration have two stories knit together by giant Ionic pilasters. Burnham maintained a kind of integrity in his eclecticism in that all the architectural detailing of the Renaissance-derived portion of the building is in Renaissance style and in the Roman-derived portion, Roman. The balustrades, for example, a Renaissance invention, mask the recessed

attic on the wings alone. Throughout the building, the arcuated and trabeated systems of construction interweave, a central theme of Roman architecture that was passed on to the Renaissance. Articulation of each of the minor components of the facade relates to their individual functions. The width of the west pavilion arch is determined by its original function as a carriage entry; the corresponding east pavilion served as the state entrance to the presidential reception room.

The clarity of the facade's organization is carried over into the interiors. The barrel-vaulted roof, clearly visible from all approaches to the building, offers a preview of the location, shape, and size of the major interior spaces. Above the central portico, the attic provides the backdrop for the inscriptions and buttresses the reinforced concrete barrel vault of the central waiting room. Above the arcades, the attic stories mask low barrel vaults with skylights that originally lit the ticket lobby, on the west, and offices and the dining room, on the east. These roofs reinforce the major longitudinal axis implicit in the wide facade. Burnham's placement of solid geometric forms above a facade that is repeatedly penetrated by deep recesses reveals his highly developed feeling for the architectural effects of light and shade. These roof volumes seem to be covered by a tightly stretched thin membrane (actually reinforced concrete tiles), in contrast to the thickness of the layered walls below. White Vermont granite of a quality and appearance similar to marble, a veneer applied over a steel frame and brick core, perfectly complements the building's forms and surfaces.

As one passes from the loggia into the waiting room, the logical route to the trains along the north-south central axis is evident, but it runs perpendicular to the central space, which contained all of the functions preparatory to boarding the trains. Here the three arches of the exterior are increased to five short barrel vaults with column screens below and thermal windows above. This arrangement is replicated opposite on the north wall, which opens onto the train concourse. Each barrel vault is set perpendicular to, and buttresses, the high, coffered elliptical vault (which is now gilded but was not when it was originally built) that runs along the dominant east-west axis. The intersecting spatial organization, scale (120 feet by 219 feet; 96 feet tall at the center), and articulation of the coffered vaults are patterned after the Baths of Diocletian in Rome. Column screens divided the waiting room from the ticket lobby and dining room. This open, light-filled interior has been maintained despite its present renovation into a shopping mall by the architects Benjamin Thompson Associates of Boston. The grand concourse (760 feet by 130 feet) was originally a skylit platform affording access to thirty-four trains whose individual platforms were attached to the back of the building. Unfortunately, this area has been poorly subdivided, with a sunken food hall and movie theaters below grade and a freestanding platform lifted above the concourse level (which still provides access to the trains). Comparison of this space-destroying arrangement (and its mundane detailing) with the greatness of Gae Aulenti's spatially exciting contemporaneous renovation of the Parisian train station, the Gare d'Orsay, into the Musée d'Orsay is a commentary on a culture dedicated to consumerism vis-à-vis one that extols—and consumes—its own cultural history. Large amounts of money were expended on gold leaf, rather than on architectural design that would enhance rather than diminish a great building, in order to convince the consumer that tenants of Union Station mall were specialty shops.

CH11 Federal Judiciary Building

1989–1992, Edward Larrabee Barnes Associates. Columbus Circle and Massachusetts Ave. NE

With the Judiciary Building the architect of the Capitol's office leaped into the mainstream of late twentieth-century architecture by selecting a Postmodern design that was neither the most conservative nor the most innovative among the five finalists, all major corporate firms with excellent design reputations. Unlike the other competitors, New York architect Edward Larrabee Barnes chose to have a solar glass entry wall (a remnant of modernism), literally wedging it between two historicizing wings whose wall articulations fuse elements from both Union Station and the post office. From the station came thermal windows, which Barnes balanced atop rectangular ones to replicate the rhythms of Daniel Burnham's arcades. The layering of the Judiciary Building's walls with vertical pilasters and pronounced lintels below the cornice line, and square attic windows above it, reinterprets elements from the post office's main facade. Corner pavilions from both earlier buildings reappear in the Judiciary Building as the ends of its two main blocks and become part of its faceted main facade as they frame the glass entrance. Their uneven widths and offset relationship to one another is in direct contradiction to the strict rules of symmetry and axiality adhered to by Burnham and his contemporaries. Obvious contextual references where elements of nearby historical architecture are consciously reused are at the heart of Postmodernism. Often, as here, they are reused in ways that are slightly jarring and require both a second look and rethinking.

The office of the architect of the Capitol has never considered the matching of shades of stones used on the twentieth-century buildings and additions as a priority. The cold gray of the "white" Chelmsford, Massachusetts, granite on the Judiciary Building is infelicitous seen in such close conjunction with the gleaming white Bethel, Vermont, granite used for the other two buildings on Columbus Circle.

CH12 Library of Congress, Thomas Jefferson Building

1871–1897, John L. Smithmeyer and Paul Pelz. Northeast corner of Independence Ave. and 1st St. SE

The Library of Congress was the first building in Washington to express fully the tenets of the Beaux-Arts system of architecture. Situated centrally on its own landscaped block and having a complex entry sequence integral to its design, the library exemplifies the nineteenth-century French planning thesis that

CH12 Library of Congress, Thomas Jefferson Building

the experience of approaching and entering a public building should prepare the user for its purpose and should indicate how to proceed through it to utilize its major and minor areas. In the library's Jefferson Building, the most fundamental of functions—the storage and easy retrieval of the library's diverse holdings—is rationally located and provided for, but it is hidden from view as the stacks are not open to the public. The library's mandate to serve researchers is expressed by the central reading room, but its position is subsidiary to the library's most public feature, its entrance pavilion, manifestly more important for the majority of the library's anticipated visitors. Here, and in the great hall that it contains, the unifying theme expressive of the library's symbolic purpose is presented in microcosm: integration of American contributions into the entire panoply of world knowledge and culture. This iconographical scheme provided visitors to the city, who comprised the growing tourist population at the time, a new locale in which to celebrate those American achievements that were not glorified at the Capitol.

The probable source of inspiration for Smithmeyer and Pelz was Charles Garnier's Paris Opera House (1861–1875). The major features of its main facade were slightly altered by the library's architects for their central pavilion. Many features were derived from the famous Parisian model—an arcaded entry enriched by allegorical figures, double giant columns that integrate single-bay flanking pavilions to the rest of the facade, bull's-eye windows that frame busts of great men, an attic story with segmental pediments containing emblematic sculpture. In addition, interior separation of the building's symbolic purpose (represented by the sculpture, mosaics, and frescoes of the grand staircases and promenade) from its actual functions (focused on the reading room) is similar to the division of the actual theater at the Paris Opera from its public promenades. The Library of Congress glorifies American contributions to world knowledge in the same hierarchical manner as the Paris Opera glorifies France's contributions to the performing arts.

Secondary attention was given to the corner pavilions on the exterior, which originally contained separate reading rooms for special collections, such as rare books, maps, prints, and manuscripts. Thirty-three keystones representing the races of humankind are located in arches above the entrance-story windows on all four sides of the building. Modeled by William Boyd and Henry Jackson Ellicott from evidence compiled by Otis T. Mason of the Smithsonian's department of ethnology, the heads are grouped according to their racial affinities. The biased presentation shows the European (located to the left of the main entrance) as a portrait of Beethoven, while many of the nonwhite races are depicted as savages. Although it was common on Victorian buildings to trace the development of plant and animal species, the Library of Congress may be the first attempt on a monumental public building to embody humankind's variety through racial models.

As the library's major architectural forms prepare the visitor for the location and size of important internal rooms, and its multi-level entrance staircase suggests the spatial progression to be encountered within, its program of exterior sculpture establishes the purpose of the building. Underlying the major theme of human knowledge is a parallel motif, the conceit of how it is acquired. The physical and allegorical pathway to knowledge begins at the bottom of the central axis on the sidewalk with Roland Hinton Perry's *Neptune Fountain.* Mythology, the lowest form of knowledge, starts a progression through five physical and intellectual levels culminating in Elihu Vedder's mosaic, *Wisdom,* which terminates the central axis at the top level of the great hall. This axis is a visual one, not a straight path: the road to wisdom is not direct but demands exploration of many branches of knowledge.

The sculptural program of the main entrance establishes the specificity within universality that characterizes the iconographical program of the entire library. The six spandrel figures above the triple doors were carved in granite by Bella Lyon Pratt and represent literature at the north door, science in the center, and the arts on the south. The reliefs on the bronze doors set within arched recesses allegorize the development of human communication from the storyteller to the printed page. *Oral Tradition* is linked with figures modeled by Olin Warner representing *Imagination* and *Memory* on the north doors. Frederick MacMonnies's *Art of Printing,* illustrated by *Humanities* and *Intellect* on the center doors, is associated with the development of science. Warner and Herbert Adams's *Art of Writing* is allied with *Research* and *Truth* on the south doors. Two stories above, nine busts placed in front of bull's-eye windows portray Benjamin Franklin, who is given pride of place, flanked by Europeans, the writer Johann Wolfgang von Goethe and the historian Thomas Macaulay. Americans Nathaniel Hawthorne and Washington Irving occupy the next positions; Ralph Waldo Emerson and Sir Walter Scott are in the pavilions. The busts on the sides of the pavilions, Dante on the south and Demosthenes on the north, represent the traditions from which modern literature evolved.

Beyond the entrance is a lavishly decorated and intricately developed series of spaces that spreads vertically as well as horizontally. The vestibule is presided over by *Minervas of War and Peace* who raise torches of learning. Passing into the main hall one encounters the dramatic richness of the multilayered and multileveled stairhall flooded with light from windows on three stories and a flat stained-glass ceiling. Signs of the zodiac revolving

around the sun are inlaid in bronze on the marble floor, the whole symbolic of the universe. Children above the fountains on the sides personify the four continents, a traditional method of succinctly representing the human portion of the universe. These figures were sculpted by Philip Martiny as were the children intertwined with garlands that line the staircases; they symbolize various intellectual and manual occupations. Bronze female torchbearers (electric lighting fixtures) preside over the hall. Names of famous writers are inscribed in gold in the ceiling vaults.

Throughout both levels of the main hall, painted lunettes and mosaics symbolically depict numerous branches of knowledge. Names of their renowned practitioners, ancient and modern, European and American, are linked to these images. Pertinent quotations (supplied by Harvard president Charles Eliot) are included on the mezzanine as the system intensifies. Those disciplines dependent on creative thinking are located just beneath Vedder's mosaic. *Wisdom* apparently is the culmination of the entire process, but closer inspection reveals two staircases that lead to a public balcony overlooking the main reading room. The octagonal reading room was specified by Librarian of Congress Ainsworth Spofford to accommodate a new system of organizing books (and hence knowledge) under eight hierarchical headings. Stacks on each wall of the reading room were to contain the reference books for each branch of learning identified by the allegorical figures atop each of the clusters of Corinthian columns marking the divisions. Appropriate quotations in cartouches above the statues continue the Beaux-Arts system of linking the visual arts with the written word to explicate the meaning of a building. Two statues of great men representative of each discipline stand on the upper balcony flanking the allegorical figures. *Religion* (Theodore Baur, sculptor) is represented by Moses and Saint Paul; *Commerce* (John Flanagan, sculptor) by Columbus and Robert Fulton; *History* (Daniel Chester French, sculptor) by Herodotus and Edward Gibbon; *Art* (François M. L. Tonetti-Dozzi after sketches by Augustus Saint-Gaudens) by Michelangelo and Beethoven; *Philosophy* (Bella Lyon Pratt, sculptor) by Plato and Sir Francis Bacon; *Poetry* (John Quincy Adams Ward, sculptor) by Homer and Shakespeare; *Law* (Paul Wayland Bartlett, sculptor) by Solon and James Kent; and *Science* (John Donoghue, sculptor) by Isaac Newton and Joseph Henry. Of the sixteen luminaries, Kent, Fulton, and Henry are Americans. The portrait statues of the individual practitioners were done by thirteen sculptors; the most significant are Bartlett's Columbus and Michelangelo, French's Herodotus, and Louis (brother of Augustus) Saint-Gaudens's Homer.

Encircling the oculus of the dome are allegorical paintings by Edwin Blashfield that depict historical contributions to civilization. In chronological order: Egypt gave written records; Judea, religion; Greece, philosophy; Rome, administration; Islam, physics; the Middle Ages, modern languages; Italy, the fine arts; Germany, printing; Spain, discovery; England, literature; France, emancipation; and America, science.

Creating a systematic order out of the multiplicity of world knowledge is a fundamental function of libraries, but also it was a preoccupation of the nineteenth century. The craze for classification demonstrated here continues the eighteenth-century Linnaean practice of identifying plants and animals according to a binomial system. In no other Washington building is the visible expression of iconography so intricately and inextricably connected with its architectural organization. The Library of Congress is a literal demonstration of the Neoplatonic belief that knowledge may be embodied in structure. The building is not a passive container of learning but an active participant in it.

Such profuse and colorful decoration, however, tends to distract one from some architectural dissonances. For instance, the double Corinthian columns forming the upper court of the stairhall do not turn the corners but are layered in the direction of the main axis. As a result the arcades and lunettes are of different widths. There is a conflict between the mosaic lunette on the west window wall in the poets' corridor (located in the south hall, entrance level) and the surrounding entablature, as the interior does not match the exterior fenestration. Although the Library of Congress has neither the control nor integration of the architecturally greater Boston and New York public libraries, there is a vigor in its overblown character. The iconography is so relentless that it transcends minor architectural infelicities, but it so overwhelms visitors that they need a guide to unravel it as well as a map to identify and locate specific rooms.

CH13 Library of Congress, John Adams Building (formerly Thomas Jefferson Annex)

1935–1939, Pierson and Wilson; Alexander B. Trowbridge. Corner of 3rd St. and Independence Ave. SE

A major concern of the architects of the Library of Congress annex was the proper contextual relationship among the three library buildings occupying the two adjacent blocks bounded by East Capitol Street on the north and Independence and Pennsylvania avenues on the south. Institutionally, Pierson and Wilson's building is allied to Smithmeyer and Pelz's 1897 Library of Congress, but spiritually, it responds to Paul Philippe Cret's Folger Library, completed in 1932. The challenge was to mediate between two such disparate interpretations of the classical tradition yet create a building with its own architectural character. In their design the architects successfully fused elements from both buildings and added a modernized decorative vocabulary, largely the work of sculptor Lee Lawrie.

The volumetric organization of the John Adams Building is similar to that of the Thomas Jefferson Building (see CH12): a rectangle with corner and central pavilions linked by wide, fenestrated curtains terminated by a high recessed attic story. Like the Folger, it has both ceremonial and functional facades. The Independence Avenue entrance is treated in a traditional Beaux-Arts manner with controlled progression up and into the building and with important interior spaces (fifth-floor reading rooms) strung along the main axis. However, these basic organizational elements are overlaid by features derived from modernist and Art Deco vocabularies. These include planar wall surfaces, sunken window frames, and stylized decoration, mainly variants on the honeysuckle flower ornament popular in American architecture since the early nineteenth century. Vertically linked window bays alternate with narrow strips of marble-clad walls, a modern expression of the basic rhythm of peripteral temples that Cret had exploited as a salient design feature at the Folger. Pierson and Wilson also adopted Cret's use of an anthemion frieze set well below the cornice line in place of a traditional entablature.

Materials—whether stone, metal, or plastic—are used in particularly elegant ways. The matte finish of the white Georgia marble and North Carolina pink granite on the exterior gives way to colorful and highly polished marble interiors from quarries throughout the country. Chased bronze surfaces on the seven pairs of exterior doors are complemented by shiny bronze and anodized aluminum interior panels and doors. Low-relief figures on the exterior doors represent individuals credited with giving the art of writing to their cultures. Modeled by Lee Lawrie, they were made by the Flour City Ornamental Iron Company in Minneapolis, as was the extensive interior metal decoration. Art Deco zigzags and streamlining were applied to the anthemion, producing designs of great vitality. The architects won an award in the National Plastics Competition for the use of formica, a new material used with aluminum for the catalogue cases in the catalogue room separating the two reading rooms on the fifth floor. The reading room table tops are also of formica. In addition to being a rigid material with a "satin-smooth" surface, formica was advertised as a good interior building material because it was cigarette, cocktail, and stain proof, and when imitating wood surfaces, such as the table tops, achieved "imperishable beauty."

The major spaces are all on the top floor; the monumental entry to them from the south is currently closed. The reading rooms are rectilinear with square columns creating recesses along the side walls. In addition to Art Deco detailing, these spaces are decorated with murals painted by Ezra Winter, showing friezes of Chaucer's Canterbury Pilgrims in the north reading room and scenes inspired by Thomas Jefferson's writings in the south reading room.

CH14 **Library of Congress, James Madison Building**

1966–1980, DeWitt, Poor and Shelton. Independence Avenue between 1st and 2nd streets SE

Nationwide concern among architects about the mundane quality of the Madison Building led to a federally mandated AIA committee review of its design in 1967. However, no perceptible changes were made to the monolithic, marble-clad rectangle, measuring 500 feet by 400 feet, that rises 70 feet to the first setback, 80 feet to the second, and 100 feet to the top of the penthouse mechanical floor. Each facade is essentially the same, with long ranges of spindly pillars spanning six aboveground stories held between massive unar-

ticulated walls. On one level these walls were intended to be modernized interpretations of classical facades in deference to its neighbors, and on another, mammoth (and ludicrous) visual metaphors of books on shelves contained by bookends. The sculpted screen of bronze books above the entrance was designed by Frank Eliscu and installed in 1983. Each of the four quadrants is color coded so one can determine his or her location within the architecturally undifferentiated interiors.

CH15 **Folger Shakespeare Library**

1928–1932, Paul Cret. 1985, Hartman-Cox. 301 East Capitol St.

In its style, scale, and materials, the Folger Shakespeare Library mediates between the monumental Capitol complex and the domestic neighborhood of Capitol Hill. Cret's design was for a low horizontal building to contain the library, an exhibition gallery, and a theater for the presentation of Shakespeare's plays in their original staging, and for lectures or concerts. He placed the library in the center of a U-shaped arrangement behind the gallery that runs nearly the width of the East Capitol Street facade. The east wing contains the theater and the west wing administrative offices and access to the library. Entries at both ends of the main facade serve the respective wings and allow access to the gallery. The east facade is a blank wall broken only by masks of comedy and tragedy. The west facade facing the Capitol is treated more prominently, as the main approach to the building is from the west, and both this and the East Capitol Street facade are often seen together.

A broad attic story broken only by inscriptions, a slight recession at the top, and an entablature of shallowly incised abstract classical ornament at the bottom emphatically cap the building. To achieve a harmonious balance between solid and void, Cret grouped nine window bays on the north facade and five on the west in the center of horizontal fields. In his fusion of historicist vocabulary with modernist forms, Cret emphasized the trabeated system of classical architecture by repeating pilasters with all intermediate openings emphatically rectilinear. Only suggestions of traditional architectural decoration have survived: fluting, friezes, and moldings associated with capitals and entablatures are stylized versions of the original forms. Cret transferred most of the decorative ornament from the walls to window and door screens, thus reinterpreting the traditional interplay of light and shadow across wall surfaces. Aluminum screens of Art Deco design cast ever-changing linear geometric patterns on interior surfaces equally geometric but Elizabethan in origin. The idealized naturalism of John Gregory's eight high-relief panels (1932) illustrating scenes from Shakespeare's most celebrated plays offers an interesting contrast to the stylized rectilinearity of the screens set against the windows just above them. On a classical building one expects sculptural panels to be associated with the entablature, but Cret brought them to ground level where they can be easily seen and interpreted. In conjunction with the quotations from Shakespeare in the attic and Brenda Putnam's *Puck Fountain* (1932) on the west front, these narrative panels announce the building's purpose, a remnant of the Beaux-Arts tradition in which Cret was trained.

The contrast between exterior and interior is one of historical style rather than architectural quality. The clarity of composition, consistency of scale of decorative elements, and craftsmanlike manner in which the materials are put together—whether the large marble panels on the exterior or the Elizabethan strapwork plaster ceiling of the gallery—attest to an architectural mind able to grapple with apparent inconsistencies of the three Western languages of architecture employed here and reconcile them into a unified whole. Cret offered a method by which contemporary architectural concerns could be integrated into historical architectural environments as diverse as those he found on Capitol Hill. The beautiful and sensitive 1985 addition to the library visible on the south facade is the work of the Washington firm Hartman-Cox.

CH16 Lutheran Church of the Reformation

1946, Porter and Lockie. 222 East Capitol St. NE

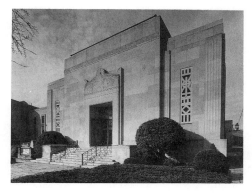

This church, classical in its massing and modern in its details, contrasts with the more typical nineteenth-century churches on Capitol Hill. It derives some of its presence from its location directly across East Capitol Street from Paul Philippe Cret's Folger Shakespeare Library. The Lutheran church's monolithic buff limestone exterior is composed of a sparsely articulated central cube projecting from and rising above a lower rectangle, the intersections marked by modern fluted pilaster strips and the corners by full-width pilasters. Single vertical windows, with limestone screens composed of Latin and Celtic crosses superimposed over Xs (the initial letter in the Greek spelling of Christ), admit light into the narthex. Additional classicizing details are the acroteria at the corners of the massive door frame and a frieze that marks the cornice line of the main block; its relief decoration shows symbols of the twelve apostles and grapes, symbolic of communion. The sculptor of the pedimental relief of the enthroned Christ is unknown.

While the exterior fuses classical and modern, the simple interiors with their subdued, well-crafted furnishings are primarily late Arts and Crafts in style. In the narthex the upper walls of rough plaster are divided from the simple oak paneling by a stenciled dado of abstract crosses. Eighteen historical variants on the form of the cross are used as symbolic decoration throughout the church, uniting the exterior and interiors. Eight pairs of stenciled beams joined by king posts support a wood ceiling, which covers the single volume interior in the tradition of north German and Scandinavian hall churches, the traditions from which this Lutheran church draws its inspiration. Ten predominantly blue and pebble glass windows made by Oliver Smith of Bryn Athyn, Pennsylvania, relate the life and teachings of Christ. The simplicity of the architectural space is complemented by subdued, rectilinear oak furniture and chancel furnishings, as well as faceted, hanging copper light fixtures, all finely handcrafted.

CH17 **Saint Peter's Church**

1889, James L. O'Connor. 313 2nd St. SE

Saint Peter's was the second Catholic parish established in the city. James Hoban was a member of the building committee (and probably the architect) of the first Saint Peter's church erected on the same site in 1820. The second church, a simple brick hall church with a central tower, reputedly designed by Mr. Lowe, was built in 1867. The cornerstone for the present Romanesque Revival structure was laid in October 1889, with the church dedicated in November of the following year. Owen Donnelly was the builder. The adjoining rectory in the same style was built in 1902. The massive church walls and tower are rockfaced Baltimore County marble throughout, with small rectangular blocks of many sizes laid in irregular courses giving its surfaces a faceted and fortified appearance. The asymmetrical facade composition masks a regular basilica form, the interiors of which were re-

CH17 Saint Peter's Church

built in 1940–1941 after being completely gutted by fire. Richardsonian ornament around the three doors, the wheel window in the center, and the top of the lofty tower lack the vigor of most Washington structures in the same style. Pedimental sculptures at the entrances depict Saint Peter meeting Christ above the south portal, Christ establishing the church with Saint Peter as the first pope in the center, and Saint Peter preaching on the north.

White House
and Lafayette Square (WH)

Pamela Scott

White House and Grounds

ON 30 MARCH 1791, PIERRE CHARLES L'ENFANT AND GEORGE Washington walked over the area designated for the federal capital and decided on the general locale for the President's House and executive department offices. In a letter to Washington that June, L'Enfant discussed in detail the site and his design for the "President's Palace." Located on a high ridge extending east-west, L'Enfant's final site selection was predicated on an advantageous southern vista down the Potomac and on proximity to the Capitol and legislative offices. L'Enfant described the President's House as a combination of the "sumptuousness of a palace" with the "convenience of a house and the agreableness of a country seat."[33] Although its plan has been partially obliterated on the only surviving manuscript map attributed to L'Enfant, the engraved plans (the first of which appeared in March 1792) show a complex, U-shaped arrangement of garden mound, forecourt, and flanking buildings leading to an elongated central block with a curved portico traversing the entire north facade. The two flanking buildings (shown with incomprehensible floor plans on engraved maps) were probably intended to house the executive department offices, then four in number.

In an April 1791 letter to L'Enfant, Thomas Jefferson noted his own preference for a President's House based on Parisian "modern" architecture, citing seventeenth- and eighteenth-century examples. There is no known response by L'Enfant. The competition for a design was announced in March 1792, just after L'Enfant was fired. Recognizing the limited resources of the government, Jefferson suggested that the competitors be told that the central section of the

149

The White House

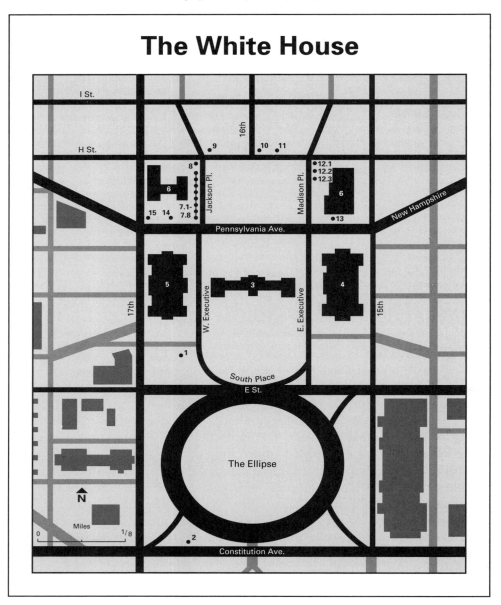

building might be constructed first ("with the appearance of a complete whole"), while the detached wing buildings could be erected later. Designs by six competitors survive, although nine entrants are known. Several sketches by Jefferson exist, but many probably date from his presidency between 1803 and 1811.

Between 1798 and 1800 two executive department office buildings, the Treasury Department and the War Office, were erected contiguous to the White

House. Designed by George Hadfield, they were large, rectangular buildings set at right angles to and aligned with the White House on the east and west. Like the President's House, which they were meant to complement, they were derived from Anglo-Georgian prototypes of a half century earlier, with raised basements and water tables, central projecting Ionic porticoes, belt courses dividing two equal stories, and high, dormered roofs. Burned by the British in 1814, they were rebuilt by James Hoban, who erected two additional buildings, one for the State Department and another for the Navy Department. They nearly replicated Hadfield's two earlier buildings and were located to the south of the extant buildings on 15th and 17th streets, thus framing the executive mansion with the State and Treasury buildings on the east and the War and Navy department buildings on the west. The Treasury Building, occupying the southeast position in the group, was a victim of arson in 1833. Robert Mills's new Treasury Building was begun in 1836; the State Department Building to its north was not demolished until 1867, during the last phase of the Treasury Building's four-part construction, which took place over more than three decades. Both William Strickland and Mills provided designs to enlarge the buildings for the War and Navy departments in the 1840s, as did Thomas U. Walter in the 1850s. The present Old Executive Office Building was built as the State, War, and Navy Building between 1871 and 1888, following a design by Alfred B. Mullett. The Treasury Department continues to occupy a building in the presidential park, but the other departments are dispersed throughout the region.

Major architects worked on memorial sculpture and miscellaneous buildings designed for, or now located within, the White House grounds. Two gate houses (c. 1828), miniature cubes that were originally the west entrance to the Capitol grounds, were moved to the southern corners of the Ellipse in 1874. Charles Bulfinch copied their articulation of channeled rustication and guilloche frieze directly from William Thornton's design for the basement story of the Capitol. Simple Roman Doric porticoes are surmounted with a rectangular panel of sculpted ornament identical to decorative panels Bulfinch had used in the Capitol rotunda. The McMillan Plan had designated an area south of the State, War, and Navy Building as the location for a monument. Cass Gilbert's First Division Memorial (WH01), an 80-foot, monolithic Doric column in pink Milford, Massachusetts, granite, was erected there in 1924. A private tribute by members of the First Division of the American Expeditionary Forces to commemorate their comrades lost in battle in France between 1917 and 1919, the slender column with its gilded, bronze-winged *Victory* by Daniel Chester French is based on Joseph-Louis Duc's *July Column* in Paris (1840). In choosing the delicate Parisian column (rather than the traditional Roman model with a helical sculptural frieze), Gilbert was doubtless considering its proximity to Mullett's French-inspired building, as well as responding to the taste of his own time. The names of all the dead from the 1830 Revolution in Paris had been inscribed on Duc's column, but Gilbert placed the 5,599 names of the First Division dead on bronze tablets set on the sloping surface of the main plinth, where they can be easily read. Two walls, to the east and west, which create an enclosure for the column, were designed by Gilbert's son in 1957; the west wall bears the names of the First Division dead in the Second World War, the east wall those who died in Vietnam (added in 1977).

The Second Division Memorial (WH02) (1936), located near Constitution Avenue just off the north-south axis of the White House, is John Russell Pope's modern rendition of a triumphal gateway. A single portal, framing James Earle Fraser's 18-foot gilded bronze sword, was cut from pink and gray Connecticut granites. The inside edges of the square-arched opening are curved, giving relief to its relentlessly rectilinear form. Two L-shaped arms were added in 1962 to memorialize the Second Division's losses in the Second World War and Korea.

WH03 White House

1792, James Hoban. 1600 Pennsylvania Ave. NW

With the exception of the winning design by the Irish-born and -trained architect James Hoban, entries in the 1792 competition for the President's House were by builder-architects rather than the few academically trained architects then practicing in this country. Hoban was awarded the $500 premium on 17 July 1792; the cornerstone was laid on 12 October for a building one-fifth larger, at President Washington's suggestion. During construction, the basement story was essentially eliminated, reducing the three-story residence to two stories raised slightly above-ground in the contemporaneous French manner. Hoban's design was a simplified co-lonial version of a mid-eighteenth-century Anglo-Palladian palazzo, a horizontally ori-ented rectangle with a tetrastyle Ionic portico attached to the north facade and a colon-naded porch spanning the entire width of the south facade. The plan called for a large square entry hall on the north on axis with an oval room, resulting in a central semicir-cular bow on the south. A large banquet room traversed the entire east side while three more intimate public rooms were distributed along the west facade. Private family quarters were on the second floor. At present there are 130 rooms in a much-enlarged complex of build-ings, the result of almost continuous renova-tions, additions, and redecorations.

Built of light brown Aquia, Virginia, sand-stone, the building was first whitewashed in 1797. Generally referred to as the White House

WH03 White House (north portico)

by Jefferson's day, it was not officially so designated until 1902. Hoban's source for the White House was Leinster House (1745–1751, Richard Castle, architect), originally the Dub-lin residence of the Duke of Leinster and today the Irish parliament house. Hoban may have used Robert Pool and John Cash's *Views of the Most Remarkable Public Buildings, Monu-ments, and Other Edifices, in the City of Dublin* (1780); he followed the fenestration pattern of Leinster House illustrated there (alternat-ing segmental and triangular pediments on the main story) rather than the continuous segmental pediments found on the actual building.

By 1800 the White House was occupied, but it was not completed until 1803. In 1807 Benjamin Henry Latrobe redesigned the north and south fronts, adding monumental porti-coes that were carried out in slightly altered form by Hoban in 1824 (south) and 1829

WH03 White House (south portico)

(north). Latrobe also redecorated the interiors, landscaped the grounds in a picturesque manner with terraces, and added low, single-story wings to provide for storage and other household necessities (as at Monticello) on the east and west. Hoban was again in charge of construction between 1815 and 1818, rebuilding after the August 1814 burning by British troops. The interiors were gutted, but the earlier walls remained sound.

As early as 1867, crowded conditions in both the living quarters and White House offices led Brig. Gen. Nathaniel Michler of the Army Corps of Engineers to suggest that a new presidential residence be built on one of eleven sites he had chosen and that the original building be retained as the official presidential office. Instead, public opinion and concern about the effective operation of the executive branch led the government to consider additions to the original building. In 1890, architect Frederick D. Owen, in collaboration with Mrs. Benjamin Harrison, proposed major additions to the White House. Two replicas of the original structure were to be attached to it at right angles via circular colonnaded pavilions, resulting in a U-shaped complex open to the south. A decade later Theodore A. Bingham of the Army Corps of Engineers, working with Owen, proposed that only the two-story circular pavilions be added to create much-needed office space. When Theodore Roosevelt became president in 1901, he selected McKim, Mead and White to design separate buildings for offices and to renovate the third-story attic into habitable rooms, thus separating the day-to-day work of the president from his ceremonial and family life. These wings were attached to the main block by new, extended colonnades. The west wing terminated in a "temporary" office building modeled on French eighteenth-century pavilions—geometric, sparsely decorated, and low to the ground. In 1909, Washington architect Nathan C. Wyeth extended this wing, creating the oval office to reflect the central oval room in Hoban's building. The setback raised roof of the west wing was designed by Eric Gugler during Franklin Roosevelt's administration; he also moved the oval office from the center of the building to its southeast corner. In 1942 architect Lorenzo S. Winslow reconstructed McKim, Mead and White's east wing, adding a Tuscan colonnade for the visitor's entrance. The balcony on the second-story level of the south front was added in 1948, when the interiors underwent extensive renovations. The present Tuscan porte-cochère and circular drive were added in the 1970s.

During Harry S. Truman's administration (1948–1952), the White House was gutted to create more space and to provide structural stability to the original walls. It was "reconstructed"; none of the original mantels and little of the original woodwork survive. During the early 1960s Jacqueline Kennedy redecorated the ceremonial first-floor rooms in the Federal style, recalling the period when the White House was first occupied; private

WH04 Treasury Building

areas have since been redecorated to reflect the tastes of subsequent presidents and first ladies.

Although pleasing in its proportions and details, Hoban's design for the White House was not an inspired, creative work of architecture. Rather, its origin in a suitable European prototype, expressing dignity but not opulence, was acceptable to most Americans. Throughout the last two centuries, considerable effort has been expended to maintain at least the symbol of republican simplicity originally desired. The White House was designed as a simple residence without any iconographic program expressive of power or dynasty such as was then common with the official residences of European heads of state. Yet the south portico, because it is so often filmed and illustrated, has become a worldwide symbol of the American presidency and, by extension, of the country's power and prestige.

WH04 Treasury Building

1836–1871, Robert Mills, Thomas U. Walter, Ammi B. Young, Isaiah Rogers, Alfred B. Mullett. Southwest corner of 15th St. and Pennsylvania Ave. NW

The Treasury Building was constructed wing by wing over a thirty-five-year period beginning in 1836. On 4 July 1836, President Andrew Jackson selected Mills's design over that of his only known competitor, William P. Elliot, Jr. This design called for an E-shaped building with the spine along 15th Street and three porticoed wings facing the White House. Under Mills's superintendence, the spine and central wing were constructed between 1836 and 1842; it was one of three impressive

office buildings he designed for Washington using fireproof brick-vaulted construction throughout. The major architectural feature remaining in Mills's section of the Treasury Building is the 466-foot unpedimented Ionic colonnade along 15th Street. The Ionic order he selected, with an anthemion necking band below the volutes, derived from the Erechtheum on the Acropolis. It was the most widely copied of the Greek Ionic orders in America. The present facade differs in two respects from Mills's original plan. The only pedimented pavilions in Mills's initial scheme were in the centers of the north and south wings; today there are pedimented pavilions at both ends of Mills's colonnade, a result of Thomas U. Walter's 1855 design for completing the building. Mills also constructed a double-ramped staircase on the sidewalk in the center of the facade that led to the main entrance behind the colonnade. It was removed during renovation in 1908. Mills's colonnade, originally constructed of brown Aquia sandstone, was replaced by granite in 1908, but behind the colonnade, the original coffered ceiling of sandstone survives. Four of the original Aquia columns were saved and form a picturesque ruin in Pioneer Park in Lincoln, Nebraska.

Mills's sources for this monumental colonnade drew upon antique and modern examples, such as the Temple of Diana at Ephesus, which inspired its size and staircase arrangement, and Alexandre Brongniart's instant classic, the Paris Bourse (1808). Two factors have altered Mills's facade: substitution of the bold and crudely carved sandstone columns by more refined granite ones in 1908 has robbed it of its elemental power. Raising the original basement was due to repeated street grading. It was refaced and Mills's staircase was removed, creating a high monolithic base.

The interiors of Mills's wings in the Treasury Building are the least spatially satisfying of any of his three Washington office buildings. The corridors are narrow and dark, the result of severe budget constraints and the need to create the maximum amount of usable office space. Unusual at the time was the regular spatial arrangement of groin-vaulted office cubes on both sides of the central barrel-vaulted corridors, the first large modular office building in the United States. At the Treasury Building (and the Patent Office Building [see DE15.2, p. 189] being constructed simultaneously), Mills capitalized on this system of fireproof vaulting in larger buildings than those where he had previously used it in South Carolina and New England. The most beautiful feature of his interiors is his fireproof double flying staircase carried through four stories, constructed by cantilevering each tread from the wall and corbeling the treads against one another. The complementary curves of the scalloped treads and converging semicircles of each set of stairs, combined with the airy lightness Mills achieved with the solid marble treads, make this staircase in company with his others at the Patent Office (DE15.2, p. 189) and General Post Office (DE15.3, p. 191) the most magnificent monumental stone staircases in America surviving from this period. A few of the original fireplace mantels remain; they are unique designs by Mills and the German-born and -trained sculptor Ferdinand Pettrich. Cast in a composition material and called "Etruscan," they are small in scale and crudely classical in their ornamentation.

In 1855, Thomas U. Walter proposed a design to complete the Treasury Building in the form of the figure eight. It called for imposing porticoes projecting in the centers of the south, west, and north facades and pedimented porticoes at each end of the east and west facades. The central portico facing the White House was the most fully developed, with its octastyle porch projecting in front of a colonnade in the same manner as Latrobe's much-admired east facade of the Capitol. The octastyle north and south porticoes masked deep colonnaded entries in a manner similar to the entrance to the Athenian Acropolis. This envelope was the basis for completing the exterior of the building,

but the interiors followed designs of the individual architects in charge of construction between 1855 and 1869. Recognition of the need for permanent materials in public buildings resulted in the use of Dix Island, Maine, granite on all three extensions. While Mills's interiors were barrel or groin vaulted in brick, in the extensions there are cast-iron columns and beams in conjunction with minor brick vaults, so interior spatial effects there are entirely different. With the exception of columns at the main staircase (derived from the Temple of Apollo at Delos), Mills's interior walls are unarticulated plaster; those in the extensions are punctuated by cast-iron Corinthian pilasters carrying an ornate cast-iron frieze.

Ammi B. Young was named Supervising Architect of the Treasury Department in 1852 and in 1855 was put in charge of constructing the south and west wings of the Treasury Building, although Isaiah Rogers took over the west facade in 1862, when Young retired. Young's plans followed Walter's three-story scheme but introduced the high staircase projecting from the south wing, due to the declivity of the land. Young spread his stairs below and in front of both cheek blocks, as on the east front of the Capitol.

Young introduced a pronounced grid effect by interposing horizontal bands between the second and third stories. These were not mere belt courses but plain bands that stepped forward and then back in triple tiers, introducing an additional three-dimensional element onto an already sculpted wall surface. The sharply defined edges of each unit in Young's facade were imposed by the hardness of the granite. He exploited the nature of the granite to achieve a contrast between the broad and relatively slick surfaces of the stone and the layered effect of the facade composition. One striking example is his window framing (especially notable in the lintels), where both the plain architrave and cyma reversa moldings of the jamb are cut from single blocks of granite. These refinements, probably an outgrowth of an austere style of granite building initiated by architects in Boston during the 1830s, were continued by the architects who followed Young on the east and north facades.

On the interiors of his south wing, Young replaced the acanthus leaves of the Corinthian order with eagles beneath the volutes and introduced keys grasped by a fist, the symbol of the Treasury Department. Some interior features of Young's south wing have been lost, principally bronze gaslighting fixtures designed by J. Goldsborough Bruff that incorporated cougars, rattlesnakes, and Indians hunting buffalo or seated before campfires (the gas jets) as well as the revived American corn order. Bruff's bronze balusters in the form of fasces connected by oak branches survive in the eastern stairhall of the south wing, as do carved marble fireplace mantels employing eagles and insignia of the trades and branches of commerce served by the Treasury Department.

Monolithic granite columns on the west wing exterior (1855–1864) were cut from the quarry on the diagonal, a remnant of Young's and Isaiah Rogers's New England training in the Boston granite style of construction. Between 1861 and 1863, Rogers was the engineer in charge of the Bureau of Construction of the Treasury Department and then served two years as the supervising architect. On the exterior, Rogers replaced the stone balustrade of the east and south facades with giant cast-iron anthemions, removed when the north wing was begun. The most interesting interior features of the south wing were the decorative cast-iron walls for four burglar-proof vaults designed and patented by Rogers in 1864 and constructed in the Treasury Building by George R. Jackson of Burnet and Company of New York. One example survives in the northwest corner on the main story. Two layers of cast-iron balls sandwiched between wrought-iron and steel plates rotate when struck by drills or other burglar's tools, preventing penetration of the wall. The outer layer of Rogers's vault is ornamented with gilded cast-iron heraldic eagles grasping the Treasury key and set within circular frames. They alternate with roundels containing the Treasury Department seal; both motifs are set off by large and richly decorated cast-iron anthemions.

Construction of the north wing was begun after the Civil War. Its forecourt had to be sunk to accommodate the full height of the building against the incline of the hill. This siting, in conjunction with its unlit facade, tends to diminish the impact of the north portico. To achieve a semblance of exterior symmetry, its architect, Alfred B. Mullett, had proposed narrowing 15th Street in order to build a monumental portico in the center of Mills's colonnade, but it was never carried

WH05 Old Executive Office Building (State, War, and Navy Building)

out. Although Mullett followed the exterior pattern established by his predecessors, he designed his interiors in the Renaissance Revival style while his predecessors carried over the Greek Revival of the exterior to their interiors. Mullett's most remarkable space was the Cash Room, a double-storied rectangular room (72 feet by 32 feet, and 27 1/2 feet tall) divided by a balcony with windows on the long south wall. It originally functioned as a bank for the government. With the exception of the iron-beamed flat ceiling, gilded plaster cornice, bronze balcony railing, and bronze doors (originally wood), seven varieties of variegated Italian and American marbles are used throughout. The subdued richness of these colorful materials is matched by well-proportioned architectural and emblematic decoration. Superimposed sets of double pilasters circumscribe the entire room, Corinthian below and composite above. The composite order carries a bracketed cornice composed of plaster shells. The bronze balcony railing by J. Goldsborough Bruff contains symbols of the supervisory responsibilities of various Treasury Department bureaus. Grapes, corn, and cotton relate to the agricultural basis of the American economy and shells and starfish to the commercial products; the caduceus refers to the Marine Hospital Service administered by the department. Three original bronze gas chandeliers were removed from the Cash Room in 1890; electrified replicas were installed in 1987. The Treasury Building contains some of the finest and least-known early and mid-Victorian interiors in America.

The landscape plan of the Treasury Building grounds by Arthur Cotton Moore in 1986 replaced East Executive Avenue with a pedestrian promenade.

WH05 Old Executive Office Building
(State, War, and Navy Building)

1871–1888, Alfred B. Mullett, Thomas Lincoln Casey, Richard von Ezdorf. Southeast corner of 17th St. and Pennsylvania Ave. NW

The Old Executive Office Building is one of only a handful of major government buildings designed by Mullett in the Second Empire style in the 1860s and 1870s that still exists intact. This flamboyant French-inspired style was introduced during Mullett's tenure as Supervising Architect of the Treasury between 1865 and 1874 as the number and size of federal buildings increased throughout the country. Most were structures that combined more than one function, including assay offices, courthouses, customhouses, subtreasuries, and post offices. The Old Executive Office Building, which brought the State, War, and Navy departments under a single roof, provided the architectural model for such complex administrative and bureaucratic interrelations. Mullett had altered several buildings under construction in the late 1860s to give them mansard roofs (the chief feature that distinguished them as French inspired) and began designing in a full-blown Second Empire style in 1869 with the New York City Courthouse and Post Office, but his masterpiece was the Old Executive Office Building.

The ground plan—in the form of the figure eight—was identical to that of the Treasury Building, completed by Mullett in 1869. Although the size of the area covered by the State, War, and Navy Building is the same as the Treasury, it seems to displace a great deal more space due to its extra story, faceted roofline, bold plasticity of forms, and four monumental central porticoes that project forward in giant steps to provide separate entries for the three executive departments. Each facade is composed of five parts with end pavilions joined to the central pavilion by curtain walls, a common method of composing large buildings in France and England from the seventeenth century onward, and in America in the nineteenth century. Mullett's own interpretation was viewed by his contemporaries with great disfavor, both because of its exorbitant cost and what was considered

its bombastic air for something as mundane as a government office building.

As in most historically derived, nineteenth-century American architecture, the design of State, War, and Navy was a synthesis of several European prototypes in which novel combinations of major elements were overlaid by motifs invented by the American architect. None of the distinctive elements of Mullett's building correspond to the recent additions in the Tuileries courtyard of the Louvre, always cited as a prototype for American Second Empire architecture. Instead Mullett turned to seventeenth-century models, such as François Mansart's Château de Maisons-Laffitte of 1642 and Jules Hardouin-Mansart's Church of the Invalides (1675–1706), where sculpture was subservient to architectural ordinance. Mullett's main porticoes share with Hardouin Mansart's church open and deeply recessed two-story porticoes where pairs of columns flank the central opening and seem to push it forward. In Mullett's porticoes the columnar elements extend vertically through three, four, or five stories. This pyramidal arrangement is strengthened by equally bold horizontal extensions. On the north and south facades the central porticoes are buttressed by double sets of columns, while on the longer east and west sides square bays flank the central portico and are connected to it by short screens of columns. The porticoes also extend back into the building, seeming to penetrate into its fabric, which in fact they do in the colonnaded entry halls. The faces of the corner pavilions on the long facades are also entries and are treated in a similar fashion, while their adjacent faces on the shorter sides merely terminate the composition and have no projections on the lower stories.

Mullett's interpretation of the classical rules of superposition may have been a response to the building material, a hard Virginia granite. Simple Doric capitals with a fluted necking band and incised echinus are used on the first, second, and third stories, while an Ionic order (also with a fluted necking band) is used at the mansard roofline of the center pavilions (one story on the north and south but two stories on the east and west). The Doric columns span the same height in all stories, but the Ionic columns of the central pavilions are shorter, contrary to the canons of classical taste. Mullett exploited the architectonic possibilities of the wall surfaces in his central and corner pavilions by covering them with columns and substantial pilasters, creating intensely three-dimensional walls, with decorative and emblematic sculpture relegated to dormer windows and segmental pediments atop the mansard roofs crowning the pavilions.

Full entablatures, rather than simple belt courses, divide the building into stories and provide projecting horizontal lines sufficiently pronounced to counteract the vertical of the orders. Mullett's window enframements also deviate from standard practice in that he reversed the order of their elaboration, placing the segmental pediments over first-floor windows, triangular pediments over second-story windows, and flat lintels on the top story. Insignia on the shields above each window identify the departments originally housed in each wing: the Navy Department was on the south, State on the east, and War on the north and west. The hard-edged stone surfaces are particularly pronounced in these frames, where the brackets with their bosses and triglyphs not only look as if they were produced by a machine but also take on the appearance of gears and ball bearings. The dramatic contrast between the smooth wall surfaces where mortar joints are barely discernible and the bold clusters of freestanding columns, engaged columns, and thick pilasters creates a scenographic effect through repetitive use of relatively simple and unadorned forms. In raking light, the gray Virginia granite takes on a violet hue, which, combined with the violet-gray of the slate and the verdigris of the copper in the mansard roofs, contributes to the overall richness of effect achieved by relatively simple means.

The interiors, as well as the detailing of the exterior, were largely the work of the Venetian-born and Austrian-trained engineer and interior designer Richard von Ezdorf. Ezdorf was responsible for the structural engineering of the internal cast-iron trusses as well as the cast iron visible on the interiors. Three miles of hallways were articulated by cast-iron pilasters carrying beams across halls that support shallow brick arches along their lengths. Offices (whose brass hardware on the doors bear the insignia of the original departments occupying them) are decorated with mahogany doors and marble fireplaces.

The three major rooms in the building are libraries typical of the nineteenth century, with bookshelves set on balconies overlooking a central reading room.

Lafayette Square

In L'Enfant's original plan, the President's Palace projected into a large square open on three sides, a hub for seven major radiating streets. An irregular U-shape, this square was modeled on Roman and Parisian examples rather than on an enclosed park. As L'Enfant designed 16th Street to be the same breadth as the diagonal avenues, it was intended that great prominence be given to the President's House by creating reciprocal views to and from numerous vantage points. The shape of the park was not firmly established until 1824, when Pennsylvania Avenue separated the president's grounds from Lafayette Park, named in honor of the French hero's American tour of 1824–1825. In the early 1830s Robert Mills suggested enlarging the executive department offices by covering the entire park with a single, vast building. Although the design was praised by Thomas U. Walter, local residents opposed it. In 1851, as part of Andrew Jackson Downing's design for the public grounds, Lafayette Square was landscaped in a picturesque manner. Clark Mills's equestrian statue of Andrew Jackson was dedicated on 8 January 1853, a cast-iron fence (perhaps designed by Robert Mills) was erected, and gaslights were installed.

Four groups of statuary were erected in Lafayette Park between 1891 and

1910. Reflecting Beaux-Arts ideals of public sculpture linking America with its European origins, all were dedicated to foreign heroes who fought in the American Revolution. Paul Pujol was the architect of the base for J. N. J. Falguière and Antonin Mercié's *Lafayette* (1891) in the southeast corner. The architects are unknown for Antoni Popiel's *Kosciuszko* (1910) in the northeast corner and J. J. Fernand Hamer's *Rochambeau* (1902) in the southwest corner. Thomas J. Johnson, with Cass Gilbert consulting, was the architect for Albert Jaeger's *von Steuben* (1910) in the northwest corner. The present landscape plan dates from the 1930s.

Private development around Lafayette Square was slow but produced some significant architectural works from an early date, principally Benjamin Henry Latrobe's Stephen Decatur House (see WH08) and Saint John's Church (WH10). Although other early nineteenth-century private residences on the east and west sides of the square were inhabited by a succession of important public figures, none was of the architectural quality of Latrobe's work. All the buildings on the square were endangered when Daniel Burnham and Charles Follen McKim proposed in 1902 that they be replaced by monumental executive department office buildings. Some of the early residential architecture was destroyed when, in 1917–1918, Cass Gilbert partially succeeded in an effort to carry the 1902 proposal into effect and when later private initiatives were effected. Two of the most unfortunate losses to Washington's architecture were houses that once overlooked Lafayette Square. James Renwick, Jr.'s, elaborate Second Empire William W. Corcoran residence was at 1611 H Street (1854, demolished 1922), and H. H. Richardson's magnificent double corner house for friends and former Harvard classmates John Jay and Henry Adams (1884, demolished 1927) was at 1603 H Street and 800 16th Street. Additional prominent works of architecture in the neighborhood that have been destroyed include Richardson's Nicholas Anderson House (1882, demolished 1925) at 1530 K Street and John Russell Pope's John R. McLean House (1907, demolished 1939) at 1500 I Street. Jackson Place and Madison Place, the two north-south streets enclosing Lafayette Square, were extensively restored during the 1960s when John Carl Warnecke's New Executive Office Building and Court of Claims Building were erected.

WH06 New Executive Office Building and Court of Claims Building

1968–1969, John Carl Warnecke. 722 Jackson Pl. NW and 717 Madison Pl. NW

Warnecke's two government office buildings were consciously designed to respond to the materials, scale, and historical context of Lafayette Square. They represent a landmark attempt by the government's architectural establishment, which had been erecting both impossibly monumental and unbearably dull buildings in Washington during the 1950s and 1960s, to be conscious of the city's earlier built environment. Each rises out of the center of the block east and west of Lafayette Square, with primary ground-level access through courtyards connected to the square in addition to entries on 15th and 17th streets. Their ten-story heights were determined by the height of the Old Executive Office Building (see WH05).

Brick walls, domestically scaled windows organized into vertical bays, projecting bay windows on the upper floors, and even modernized versions of mansard roofs to mask the mechanical equipment were modern references to the forms, materials, and architectural languages found among the nineteenth-century buildings in the immediate area, while adjoining monumental and classical twentieth-century structures, such as the Treasury Annex and Chamber of Commerce, were ignored. These choices reflect the historical architecture admired at the time, but the contextual "background" buildings that were intended are in fact aggressive intruders, primarily due to the sheer bulk of their planar brick walls.

WH07 Jackson Place

1840s–1870s

Both interior and exterior renovations on all the buildings on Jackson and Madison places were carried out when the New Executive Office Building and the Court of Claims (see WH06) were built; the interiors of many of the buildings were opened and connected internally to create expansive new government office spaces.

With one exception, all of the buildings on Jackson Place are three-story brick buildings, although six have additional attic stories above the cornice line. The only architect known for these houses is the one for Decatur House (see WH08). The Italianate Dr. Peter Parker House (WH07.1) (1860–1861, number 700) has an entry and a cornice that are similar to those of its earlier, undated neighbor, the Edward D. Townsend House (WH07.2), indicating that the latter building was probably renovated at the same time. The William P. Trowbridge House (WH07.3) (number 708), built in 1859, retains much of its simple Italianate decoration. The Henry J. Rathbone House (WH7.4) (number 712) is undated but stylistically appears to be from the 1840s with its mansard roof added later. Number 716 (WH07.5) was erected in 1867–1868 by Mary Jesup Blair as an investment property; the bracketed cornice, mansard roof, and Italianate door and window details are still intact. The five infill buildings, by John Carl Warnecke, at 718–726 and 740–744, although undistinguished themselves, maintain the nineteenth-century scale and regulating lines established by the bay systems, floor levels, and cornice lines of their neighbors. Those

at 718–726 include an entry to an interior courtyard, an important innovation in Washington where much space on the interiors of blocks is wasted.

The Italianate brownstone at 730, the William J. Murtagh House (WH07.6), with its finely carved, boldly projecting window frames, bracketed cornice, and doorway, is so beautifully proportioned as to suggest a skilled, but as yet unknown, architect. The date of the Charles G. Glover House (WH07.7) (number 734) is unknown, but its tall, narrow proportions and incised Neo-Grec ornament, particularly the gearlike character of the door brackets, indicate that it probably dates from the 1880s. The sophisticated composition of the William L. Marcy House (WH07.8) (number 736), with its two double window bays introducing the only round-arch elements on the street, indicates that it was also designed by a trained, but unknown, architect. The gradation and character of the decorative detail, from the most elaborately sculpted on the first floor to triangular pediments on the second story and flat lintels on the third, suggest a date in the 1870s.

WH08 Decatur House, National Trust for Historic Preservation (Stephen Decatur House)

1817–1819, Benjamin Henry Latrobe. 748 Jackson Pl. NW

Only a few of the many residences erected in America from Latrobe's designs survive. All have undergone later nineteenth-century modernizations and twentieth-century restorations. In 1871 the house built by naval hero Commodore Stephen Decatur was purchased by Gen. Edward Fitzgerald Beale, who changed both its exterior and interior appearance. Boldly projecting sandstone lintels on the front door and first-floor windows Victorianized the exterior of the house; interior changes consisted primarily of decorative embellishments. In 1944 Thomas T. Waterman freely restored the house's facade to its "original" appearance but introduced changes, such as cutting 15 inches off the top of the ground-story windows. Waterman also partially restored the interior. In 1956 Decatur House became the property of the National Trust, which has maintained it as a house museum that reflects its diversified history.

Latrobe's design was for an imposing, restrained, and nearly cubic (51 feet wide by 45 feet deep) three-story, three-bay corner house with a hip roof, the first private residence erected facing the president's park. He treated its brick walls as a tautly stretched membrane punctured by windows. The simplicity and elegance of the main facade is due to the fine balance Latrobe achieved between these openings, which float on the broad expanse of flat wall, unbroken either by horizontal or by vertical projections such as belt courses, inset panels, or pilasters. The survival of Latrobe's detailed drawings made possible the restoration of the main door, where attenuated pilaster strips frame side lights and their entablature, composed of shallow, undecorated planes, supports a semicircular lunette. The door's sandstone arch (Waterman's replacement of Latrobe's original brick arch) rests on rectangular blocks supported by the brick wall with neither vertical pilasters nor half columns, following the rational Neoclassical tenet that structural reality should be obvious. The wall supports the arch and the window lintels, with sunken bull's-eye terminations (projecting beyond the opening), a hallmark of Latrobe that was quickly adopted by local builders.

The vestibule is an exquisitely proportioned and spatially sophisticated entrance on a deceptively small scale. It is divided into three sections—a rectangle, a square, and a semicircle—by a barrel vault, a shallow dome,

and a half dome in its vaulted ceiling. Latrobe planned this subtle spatial sequence to divide circulation between the public and private areas of the house. The main staircase, which rises directly to the primary living quarters on the second story, is on the main axis and contained in a separate hall behind the curved doors that terminate the vestibule. A south door in the vestibule, to which one is subtly directed by the dome, opens to a suite of rooms from which Decatur conducted business. Latrobe planned no corresponding door on the north, as the rooms facing H Street (the Decaturs' bedroom suite but planned by Latrobe to contain the kitchen) were to be accessible only from the back hall, but a door was added. To divide private spaces for family life from rooms where the public was invited, he created suites of rooms on the model of eighteenth-century French city mansions, a principle Thomas Jefferson had implemented at Monticello. The present arrangement of rooms on the second story, with the double parlor traversing the front of the house, dates from 1871, when the sliding doors between the two rooms were removed. The parquet floors in the main parlor date from this period. Although the second story is now decorated in the Victorian style, the sense of spatial flow is due to Latrobe's original planning. Sculptural ornament is very restrained; the house's quality is dependent on Latrobe's architectonic sense that the shape of space, rational and legible organization, and balanced proportional relationships define great architecture.

WH09 Chamber of Commerce Building

1929, Cass Gilbert. 1615 H St. NW

Begun a year after completion of the Treasury Annex (see WH13) in 1928, the Chamber of Commerce Building employs the same general arrangement as the earlier building. It also occupies a corner site (in this case an irregular one) and has two identical facades. Yet one building is mundane and the other admirable. The architectural success of the Chamber of Commerce is due to its more finely tuned proportions, more direct relationship to the ground, and more refined details. Engaged giant Corinthian columns provide the vertical frame for the three stories with a simple Greek key frieze and recessed panels dividing the stories horizontally. The low relief of the carving is echoed in the shallowly channeled rusticated basement.

WH10 Saint John's Church

1816, Benjamin Henry Latrobe. 1525 H St. NW

Saint John's stood in its original form as a Greek cross church for only four years before the west transept arm was lengthened in 1820, turning it into a Latin cross. Although plans for enlarging the church were solicited from Charles Bulfinch, then architect of the Capitol, it was George Bomford, chief of the Army Ordnance Department, who directed the alterations, allegedly following Latrobe's own plan for its extension by extending the west transept arm and fronting it with a Roman Doric portico. Contrary to Latrobe's plan, a 40-foot triple-tiered steeple by an unknown designer was erected above the west transept in 1822, creating the exterior form essentially as it exists today.

A substantial eight-windowed cupola atop a shallow dome was part of Latrobe's original design, as were a clerestory light and large semicircular lunettes on the then three unaltered facades. Latrobe's drawings show lunettes with such intricate iron tracery patterns that they might be interpreted as a classicized rendition of Gothic windows. Windows on two stories of the short walls of each arm provided additional light. Hence, the small church built originally with eighty-six pews (number 28, selected by President Madison, is still reserved for the chief executive) was flooded with clear light. Subsequent alterations changed the plan and spatial sense as well as this abundant lighting.

Originally there were two entrances, the liturgically mandated west door facing 16th Street and a secondary one facing Lafayette Square and the White House on the south (closed off in 1836). Latrobe's furnishings were organized in a complex series of interlocking circles. He circumscribed a circular aisle within the Greek cross. Box pews were to be located in the arms, within two semicircles in the circular central aisle, and on a gallery on the second level. The wine-glass pulpit sat on a iron rail (so that it could be moved) within a circle that projected into the circle of pews under the dome. The gallery was carried by twelve columns. In 1842 they were replaced by more slender ones when a wooden floor was built on top of the original bricks. At the same time the box pews were replaced by low-backed rows of pews. These alterations may have been undertaken by Latrobe's pupil, Robert Mills.

On Latrobe's original exterior, stuccoed brick walls were broken only by the recessed doors (or blind arches) with their lunettes and by plain window frames. Horizontal lines were established by a simple water table, belt course, and entablature. His interiors were equally free of extraneous ornamentation.

Suggestions for enlarging the church by rebuilding it in a Victorian style were made by Montgomery Meigs in 1867 and T. S. Cheville in 1874. James Renwick, Jr.'s, plan was actually carried out in 1883. The original east end wall was replaced by marble Ionic columns carrying a shallow arch, as this end was lengthened and a Palladian window over the altar was added. One- and two-story appendages on the north and south provided space for a robing room, study, furnace room, and other necessities. Larger windows were cut for the installation of stained glass portraying the life of Christ and images from the Apocalypse designed by N. H. Eggleston of New York and made by Veuve Lorin, curator of glass at Chartres Cathedral. The interior was painted with colorful stenciled designs, and exterior sculptural elements, such as the columns and new window frames, were painted a dark color in contrast to the lighter walls.

WH09 Chamber of Commerce Building

raising the roof and adding a cast-iron bracketed cornice; the present mansard roof was added in an 1877 renovation, as was the front door. The ground-floor windows (raised above high basement windows screened by cast-iron panels) are elaborately treated with substantial balustraded balconies carried on consoles. The balconies and consoles are of sandstone, but the balusters are of cast iron. The window frames with boldly projecting triangular pediments supported by brackets are similar in both proportions and details to Walter's window treatment on the principal story of the Capitol extension. Bracketed flat lintel surrounds are used on the second story while the third-story windows are simply framed. The entrance lamps date from Walter's time.

In 1919, the firm of McKim, Mead and White was engaged to renovate Saint John's. On the exterior the architects added four buttresses to the north and south topped with Renaissance-derived volutes, and they enclosed the 16th Street vestibule, which they paneled in a Colonial Revival style. On the interior, they replaced the plaster Ionic capitals of the chancel screen with marble and lined the chancel with gray Siena marble. The Victorian stenciling was covered with off-white paint. Today Latrobe's proportional refinements, purity of unbroken wall surfaces, and interplay of interior circles clearly lit by semicircles are marred but still discernible to the discriminating eye.

WH11 Saint John's Church Parish House

1836, unknown. 1854, Thomas U. Walter. 1525 H St. NW

The original house, of which the present structure is a rebuilding, was erected in 1836 by Matthew Saint Clair Clarke, former clerk of the House of Representatives. A five-bay, hip-roof cube, it was devoid of surface decoration other than two central tripartite windows and an elegantly simple marble Ionic porch, never installed, which is now on the Enoch Pratt House in Baltimore.

In 1854, Thomas U. Walter transformed the house into an Italianate palace for a new owner. The exterior was stuccoed and was scored to resemble ashlar, and the elaborate sandstone window and door frames were added. The proportions were also altered by

WH12 Madison Place

between H St. and Pennsylvania Ave. on the east side of Lafayette Square

Madison Place derives its name, designated in 1859, from the corner house at its northern end (WH12.1). Built in 1818 for Dolley Madison's brother-in-law, Richard Cutt, from whom the Madisons obtained it in 1828, the house today has little intrinsic architectural merit, having been remodeled numerous times, most recently in 1968 by John Carl Warnecke and Associates. Its three remaining neighbors have also been extensively renovated and serve as offices for Warnecke's Court of Claims complex (see WH06). The William Windom House (WH12.2), adjacent to the Madison House, was built in 1874 by Henry

WH11 Saint John's Church Parish House

Reed Rathbone; its neighbor, the Robert G. Ingersoll House (WH12.3), four years later. The imposing three-bay brick house erected by Benjamin Ogle Tayloe in 1828 was a free-standing house next to an alley. Its projecting portico and cast-iron balcony may be original. Unfortunately, no definitive histories exist for these buildings, and they have been altered so often that it is difficult to judge them individually. Their remaining architectural value is that they maintain the domestic scale and period detail that Lafayette Square was designed to accommodate.

WH13 Treasury Annex

1917–1918, Cass Gilbert. Corner of Madison Pl. and Pennsylvania Ave. NW

This building was originally planned to extend the entire length of Madison Place. Following the scheme suggested by the McMillan Commission and stimulated by Robert Mills's east facade of the Treasury Building, Gilbert planned to frame the entire square with an almost continuous colonnade. Built of Indiana limestone, the Treasury Annex's two identical facades consist of rusticated basements set behind retaining walls and a giant Ionic colonnade framing three stories lit by floor-to-ceiling windows. The deep entablature masks a skylit story, and a recessed attic is partially obscured by the balustrade. This arrangement was a typical Beaux-Arts solution for minor urban office buildings that were meant to provide a contextual visual support for their more important and monumental neighbors. Instead of copying the style of the Ionic of the Erechtheum as it was used in the Treasury Building, Gilbert chose that of the Temple on the Ilissus in Athens, thus maintaining simple Greek lines but varying the details.

WH14 Blair House

1824, unknown. 1651 Pennsylvania Ave. NW

Blair House's unusually wide Federal style facade serves as the ceremonial front and entrance to five houses that now comprise the official guest house of the president. Built in 1824 by Dr. Joseph Lovell, the house's most important early historical associations occurred during its occupancy by Montgomery Blair, Abraham Lincoln's postmaster general.

Both the facade and interiors have been repeatedly rebuilt or restored in the twentieth century. Many of its interiors were acquired from demolished or denuded Federal period houses from other parts of the country. Some rooms are composed of elements from many different buildings, only a few of which are known. In the 1920s Maj. Gist Blair had the carved wood trim from Alexander Parris's 1801 Joseph Holt Ingraham House in Portland, Maine, installed in the then dining room and the small room to the right of the front entry.

WH15 Renwick Gallery, Smithsonian Institution (Corcoran Gallery of Art)

1859–1861, James Renwick, Jr. 17th St. and Pennsylvania Ave. NW

The only building in the city to be named in honor of its architect is the Smithsonian's museum for the decorative arts, originally designed as the Corcoran Gallery of Art. Renwick and his patron, banker William W. Corcoran, traveled together to Paris in 1854 to study museums as well as contemporary French architecture and to visit the 1854 International Exposition. Visconti and Lefuel's additions to the Louvre courtyard (1852–1857) revived interest in the architecture of earlier sections of the same building. Renwick's composition was a simplified and composite adaptation of the entire Louvre complex, with a central pavilion capped with a mansard roof of curved profile and corner pavilions with straight-sided mansards, the whole gathered together under a secondary, sloping mansard roof. All of the second-story exhibition rooms were skylit. The elaborately designed and sculpted principal floor, with double columns and pilasters carrying a projecting entablature, steps forward to frame what were once niches set into the wall surface. These contained 8-foot-tall statues of great European artists and American sculptor Thomas Crawford (their names are carved in the belt course). Here, and in the choice of the sculptural decoration of swags, roundels, and rich floral motifs in segmental as well as triangular pediments, Renwick turned to Pierre Lescot's original facade of the Louvre (1546). Renwick's use of brick walls with Aquia sandstone trim derived from another Parisian model, the Place des Vosges (1605).

The resulting building exemplifies nine-

WH15 Renwick Gallery, Smithsonian Institution (Corcoran Gallery of Art)

teenth-century American eclecticism and was the first major French-inspired structure to be erected in this country. One specifically American feature is difficult to see from the ground; carved corncobs nestle in the acanthus leaves of the Corinthian capitals. After serving as government offices and even a warehouse, the building returned to its original function when it was renovated by Hugh Newell Jacobsen between 1967 and 1972. Only three interior spaces approximate their original state: the massive staircase at the entrance, the grand salon encompassing the entire width at the back of the building (furnished and hung with paintings as it originally was), and the octagonal room in the center front, which was designed to display Hiram Powers's *Greek Slave,* the most famous of American nineteenth-century sculptures.

Federal Triangle (FT)

Antoinette J. Lee

T HE FEDERAL TRIANGLE IS A COHERENT GROUPING OF PUB-
lic buildings that joins the Capitol grounds with those of the White House.
Composed of nine distinct monumental structures spread over a flat land
surface, the triangle area reverberates with the design lessons of Pierre Charles
L'Enfant and Daniel H. Burnham. Two of the structures were constructed during the period from 1890 to 1910 and the remainder between 1926 and 1938.
The two earlier buildings, the Old Post Office and the District Building, represent tentative attempts to establish a public building enclave in the area. The
seven later buildings, all housing major federal government agencies and bureaus, reflect the fulfillment of a long-anticipated grouping of public buildings.

The Federal Triangle is located on a slice of land formed in the shape of a
right triangle. It is bounded by Pennsylvania Avenue (the hypotenuse), Constitution Avenue (the long leg), and 15th Street (the short leg). While the Federal
Triangle project dates primarily from the twentieth century, the area's development has deep roots in the late eighteenth and nineteenth centuries. Located
near the turning basin of the Washington City Canal at 8th Street, the area was
home to the sprawling Center Market and light industry. Its proximity to the
center of the city as it developed between the Capitol and the White House
also made it a focus of commercial development. However, its tendency to flood
and its poor drainage relegated it to marginal commercial enterprises, while
department stores and affluent establishments were located on higher ground
along F and G streets.

The Corps of Engineers' reclamation of the Potomac Flats and the filling in
of the canal signaled a new era for the area. Although soil and drainage problems lingered well into the twentieth century, the federal government indicated
a willingness to invest in the area. The Romanesque Revival Post Office Build-

166

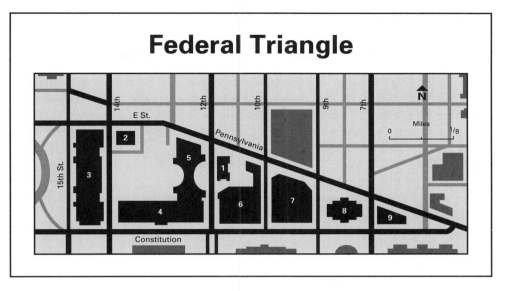

ing (see FT01) was constructed during the 1890s along Pennsylvania Avenue at 12th Street. While it did not usher in a grand scheme for the triangle area, the Post Office anticipated other federal government buildings in the future. The McMillan Commission Plan of 1901–1902 recommended the triangle area for a grouping of municipal buildings, the result of which would "assert the individuality of the District of Columbia." The plan presented a loose arrangement of low-rise monumental buildings as an illustration of what might develop. Later in that decade, the District Building (see FT02) was constructed at 14th Street facing Pennsylvania Avenue and housed the three federally appointed district commissioners and their staffs.

Ultimately the land within the triangle area proved too valuable for municipal functions, and the Municipal Center later developed around Old City Hall. In 1910, the Treasury Department sponsored a limited competition for the stretch of land bounded by Pennsylvania Avenue, 15th Street, Constitution Avenue, and 14th Street. The competition called for designs for three buildings, to house the departments of State, Justice, and Commerce and Labor. The winning designs were not implemented, but their Beaux-Arts and grouped character were harbingers of the Federal Triangle project.

The Public Buildings Act of 1926 set in motion plans for the Federal Triangle. Secretary of the Treasury Andrew W. Mellon hired Edward H. Bennett of the Chicago firm of Bennett, Parsons and Frost as his personal architectural advisor on the project. Bennett had been associated with Daniel H. Burnham on the City Beautiful plans for San Francisco in 1905 and for Chicago in 1908–1909. Bennett organized a board of architectural consultants, each member of which was assigned the design of one of the buildings. Louis Ayres of the New

York City firm of York and Sawyer designed the Department of Commerce Building (see FT03); Arthur Brown, Jr., of San Francisco the Department of Labor, the Interstate Commerce Commission, and the Departmental Auditorium (see FT04); William A. Delano of the New York City firm of Delano and Aldrich the new building for the post office (see FT05); Milton B. Medary of the Philadelphia firm of Zantzinger, Borie and Medary the Justice Department Building (see FT07); Louis A. Simon of the Treasury Department's Office of the Supervising Architect the Internal Revenue Service Building (see FT06); John Russell Pope of New York City the National Archives (see FT08); and Bennett the Federal Trade Commission Building (see FT09). The project, which flourished with the full support of the Executive Branch and Congress between 1926 and 1933, merely survived to near completion during the Roosevelt administration.

The effort Bennett oversaw was based on a comprehensive plan that addressed functional requirements of federal agencies and bureaus, city planning, architecture, landscape design, and decorative arts. It also spoke to the symbolic role of a harmonious ensemble of monumental buildings in inspiring the respect of the nation for federal government institutions.

At the time Congress approved plans for the Federal Triangle project, federal offices were spread throughout the central city in rented quarters. The simultaneous need of several federal government agencies and bureaus for new buildings set the stage for an entire group of public edifices. The grouping of functions promoted greater efficiency in communication among employees and between agencies and bureaus. Housing employees in government-owned buildings promised long-term savings in leasing costs. The grouping of buildings also provided an opportunity to create a monumental design effect unparalleled in the development of the capital city.

In the history of city planning in the United States, the Federal Triangle was one of the last City Beautiful plans in the nation. At the time it was initiated, the project found universal support among architects, planners, and politicians. By the time it was completed, the nation was in the throes of the Great Depression and attitudes toward planning and architecture had changed. By 1938, the Federal Triangle was viewed as passé and out of touch with the realities of the living city. Antipathy toward the Federal Triangle lingered well into the 1970s. During the past decade, a renewed interest in Beaux-Arts architecture and City Beautiful planning has reclaimed projects like the Federal Triangle from the heap of discarded planning ideas.

The design of the Federal Triangle bespeaks a range of design influences, from the treatment of large and monumental buildings such as the Louvre in Paris to the architecture of Rome and the grouping of governmental buildings at Whitehall in London. The Federal Triangle project also reflects the 1920s interpretation of the architectural and planning traditions of the city itself, particularly those of its first half century, from 1790 to 1840. Its plan placed a classical stamp on this section of the city and, while monumental in character, was subordinate to the Capitol and White House. As the project was implemented in the 1930s, Beaux-Arts Classicism gave way to an infusion of Art Deco and depression-era art.

An elaborate landscape plan tied together the buildings in the complex and organized the major structures around two great open spaces, the Grand Plaza and 12th Street. The plan also opened interiors with courtyards and gardens. As the project neared completion, however, the demands of the automobile compromised the landscape plan by transforming the Grand Plaza and some courtyards into parking lots and allocating other courtyards for entrances to underground parking.

The attention paid to decorative detail throughout the complex was an indication of the intended public uses of the buildings. The building exteriors were adorned with decorative sculpture and mottos. The building lobbies were lavish, intended to impress and instill awe in visitors. In the 1930s, art programs of the depression era left their mark on the buildings in murals and sculpture.

Through a comprehensive plan and consistency in building materials, design, and scale, the Federal Triangle buildings achieve a harmony of character unmatched by the Legislative Group around the Capitol or the Executive Group around the White House. The nearly full implementation of the Federal Triangle plan was a product of agreement among design professionals regarding the plan and unqualified political support during the project's early years. Unlike City Beautiful plans in other cities, which were only partially realized, the Federal Triangle is a mature exhibit of that movement's aspirations.

FT01 **Old Post Office**

1892–1899, Willoughby J. Edbrooke, Supervising Architect. 12th and Pennsylvania Ave. NW

The first public building in the triangle area, the Old Post Office has endured an uneasy relationship with its later neighbors. Built as the Post Office Building, it was renamed the Old Post Office when the new Post Office was constructed across 12th Street as part of the Federal Triangle scheme. It was the product of the Office of the Supervising Architect, a bureau within the Treasury Department, which assumed responsibility for federal government buildings throughout the nation. At the time the building was initiated, Willoughby J. Edbrooke of Chicago served as supervising architect. While he frequently is credited as the architect of the building, Edbrooke saw his position primarily as an administrator or an executive. By the 1890s, the office employed a large technical and clerical force, and Edbrooke's designers were responsible for taking charge of the entire design process associated with a public building. He served in the position for only two years, from 1891 to 1893, a brief tenure during which at least eighty-six federal government buildings were in the pipeline.

The completion of the Old Post Office in 1899 occurred at a time when the public taste, particularly in public buildings, had turned to classical forms. Numerous critics cited the large, somewhat ungainly Post Office Building as symptomatic of the inability of designers in the Supervising Architect's Office to produce public buildings commensurate with those designed by architects in private practice. The Supervising Architect's Office was taken aback by the criticism because, since the 1870s, the vast majority of the federal government buildings had been designed in the

FT01 Old Post Office

Romanesque Revival style. By the 1890s, these buildings were designed in a mature rendition of this familiar form. Neither this long tradition nor the fact that Romanesque Revival buildings were still being constructed elsewhere in the nation calmed the critics.

The Old Post Office was designed in a manner reminiscent of H. H. Richardson's Allegheny County Courthouse in Pittsburgh, with a large clock tower rising out of the massive granite structure. The building's exterior is articulated with a downsizing of the round-arch opening as the building ascends and with setbacks in the elevation above the front and side entrances. The treatment of the granite also separates horizontal sections of the building, from rusticated blocks at the base to smooth blocks above. Round towers capped with conical roofs accentuate the corners and ornamented dormer windows punctuate the roof.

The Old Post Office was at odds with the twentieth-century City Beautiful groupings of public buildings the nation's designers envisioned for the capital city. However, the McMillan Plan of 1901–1902 could hardly have recommended the building's removal so soon after its completion. But by 1926, the Federal Triangle plan was designed with another building in its place, one that would complete the Internal Revenue Service hemicycle. The economic crisis of the 1930s prevented the demolition of the incongruous but perfectly serviceable building. Efforts to upgrade Pennsylvania Avenue in the 1960s led to models showing the "completion" of the Federal Triangle, meaning the demolition of the Old Post Office, or the retention of only its tower, jutting out from a new building.

The preservation of the Old Post Office was the result of its survival to the 1970s, when historic preservation forces coalesced to bring about a revision in federal and District policies concerning older buildings in the capital city. The Old Post Office was transformed into a model of the federal government's efforts to create multi-use, publicly accessible federal government buildings. The firm of Arthur Cotton Moore/Associates designed the rehabilitation of the Old Post Office, reopening its covered center court, upgrading office space around the perimeter for federal government cultural and arts programs, and placing a two-level shopping arcade at the ground floor. While tourists and office workers alike benefit from the food services in the shopping arcade, this function also produces an odoriferous pall throughout the interior.

FT02 District Building

1904–1908, Cope and Stewardson. 1350 E St. NW

Located near the base of the hypotenuse of the Federal Triangle, the District Building resembles a marble outcropping in a limestone bedrock. It was located in the triangle area soon after the issuance of the McMillan Plan of 1901–1902, which suggested that the area be developed as a municipal enclave. The Philadelphia firm of Cope and Stewardson, well known for its collegiate buildings at Bryn Mawr College, Princeton University, the University of Pennsylvania, and Washington University in Saint Louis, won the competition for the building.

A stately symbol for the three District Commissioners and their staffs, the building serves a similar function today for the District of Columbia City Council. The District Building's design was in keeping with the classical theme of the Federal Triangle, but its compact and self-contained character, as well as its municipal functions, were out of sync with a plan that emphasized interrelatedness and federal government uses. The Federal Triangle models called for a monumental struc-

FT02 District Building

FT03 Commerce Department
Building

ture on the north side of the Grand Plaza,
including the District Building site, in order
to balance the Labor Department, Departmental Auditorium, and Interstate Commerce Commission complex on the south side.
Instead, the District Building stayed put but
became far removed from the Municipal
Center as it developed around the old City
Hall.

In an architectural setting dominated by
gray limestone, the District Building was constructed of white marble (now much yel-
lowed) over a gray granite base. The building
is divided into three horizontal planes: a rusticated base of one story and an exposed
basement, a three-story shaft or middle section, and an attic story. The horizontal lines
are accentuated with belt courses, heavy cornices, and balconies. An elaborate central
portal, projecting end pavilions, and monu-

mental Corinthian columns that rise from the
third through the fifth stories provide the
vertical forces. The three-story shaft is made
more complex with a different treatment of
window lintels at each story. At the attic level,
heroic sculpted male and female figures separate the windows and represent the arts,
commerce, science, and statesmanship. At the
entablature is a cartouche capped by an eagle
and flanked by reclining figures representing
justice and law. Although not set within a
supportive landscape, the District Building
symbolizes the important and dignified role
of municipal government in a city dominated
by federal government interests.

FT03 **Commerce Department Building**

1926–1932, Louis Ayres of York and Sawyer. 14th
and E streets NW

The Commerce Department Building forms the short leg of the Federal Triangle. It is located on the site that was the subject of the 1910 design competition for the departments of State, Justice, and Commerce and Labor. By the time the Federal Triangle plan was developed, the entire three-block site was dedicated solely to the Commerce Department, an agency that, through various bureaus and programs, promotes foreign and domestic commerce. When completed, the structure was the largest government building in the nation. Its dimensions staggered the imagination: its floor space covered 37 acres and was traversed by 8 miles of corridors.

The New York City firm of York and Sawyer had a special claim to the project because it had won the 1910 competition for the Commerce and Labor Building on a portion of the same site. Headed by former employees of McKim, Mead and White, York and Sawyer established a reputation for designing monumental Beaux Arts and Renaissance Revival buildings in New York City and elsewhere. Louis Ayres, the firm's partner and fellow disciple of McKim, Mead and White, represented the firm on the Board of Architectural Consultants for the Federal Triangle.

The building is arranged in a rectangular floor plan within which are six interior courts. Its steel frame is sheathed in gray Indiana limestone and crowned with an orange tile roof. The main elevation along 14th Street is divided into three sections such that, when viewed from either corner of the block, resembles a group of three buildings. The central section presents a grand colonnade of monumental Doric columns. The flanking end sections present a tripartite arrangement of a rusticated base, smooth shaft, and an attic story set behind a balustraded parapet. At each story, the window treatment varies from the story above and below with the size of the opening and the lintel design. On the 15th Street side, four projecting Doric colonnades support large triangular pediments, each cradling a heroic sculptural group. On both the 14th and 15th street elevations, triple-arched gateways lead to inner courts now relegated to parking spaces. Both the E Street and Constitution Avenue elevations are designed with a central colonnade. However, the E Street elevation opens into a large visitors' center through a series of arched openings.

The finished building served several urban design needs. It formed a monumental frame

along 15th Street, the east side of the Ellipse, and balanced the lineup of monumental buildings along the 17th Street side of the elliptical park. The 14th Street elevation provided an appropriately formal conclusion to the Grand Plaza, which stretched from 13th Street to 14th Street. The Commerce Department Building perfectly illustrates the advantages of City Beautiful groupings of monumental buildings. While each building in the group could stand on its own, the total effect is greater than the mere sum of its parts. Each building enhances its neighboring structures and contributes to reinforcing the relationship of the group to the larger urban fabric beyond.

FT04 United States Customs Service, Departmental Auditorium, and the Interstate Commerce Commission

1935, Arthur Brown, Jr. Constitution Ave. between 12th and 14th streets NW

Among the most challenging design assignments in the Federal Triangle group was the long building fronting on Constitution Avenue between 12th and 14th streets. It was intended to house the Labor Department (today that section houses the United States Customs Service), the Departmental Auditorium, and the Interstate Commerce Commission. The rear of the building framed the south side of the Grand Plaza and was to coordinate with the Post Office Building at the east end of that open landscape area. The long line of the building enhanced Constitution Avenue as it stretched westward toward the Lincoln Memorial and Arlington Bridge and eastward toward the Capitol.

The project was assigned to Arthur Brown, Jr., the well-known Beaux-Arts practitioner from San Francisco. His impressive list of accomplishments included the San Francisco City Hall and Opera House. His association with the development of the San Francisco Civic Center, another City Beautiful plan, no doubt drew him to the Federal Triangle project. His experience with both office structures and a performing arts center likely led him to this particular commission.

Brown designed the complex with the Departmental Auditorium as the centerpiece facing Constitution Avenue. Flanking the auditorium on the west was the Labor Department and on the east the Interstate Commerce Commission. The auditorium facade is designed as a projecting temple facade

FT04 United States Customs Service, Departmental Auditorium, and the Interstate Commerce Commission

FT05 Post Office Building

composed of a rusticated base supporting six monumental Doric columns. The columns support a large triangular pediment furnished with a heroic sculptural group. Open courts prefaced with freestanding Doric columns set off the flanking office blocks from the Departmental Auditorium and provide passageways from Constitution Avenue to the Grand Plaza. Each office structure is framed by a projecting Doric colonnade on both ends, each subordinate in scale but similar in design to the Doric temple facade of the Departmental Auditorium.

FT05 Post Office Building

1934, Delano and Aldrich. 12th St. and Pennsylvania Ave. NW

The Post Office Building is the vital center of the Federal Triangle group. Here the Grand Plaza, running east-west, is connected to the

major north-south thoroughfare of the group, 12th Street, through the 12th Street Circle. The Post Office hemicycle forms half of the circle, while the Internal Revenue Service hemicycle (never completed) was to form the other half. The Federal Triangle plan envisioned a special treatment for 12th Street, with the placement of pylons in the street, a traffic impediment that was never implemented. The pedestrian sidewalk passes under arched openings at the projecting ends of the half circles and continues around the circle through a sidewalk arcade. At the base of the circle, passageways lead to the Grand Plaza. On the other side of the passageway is the mirror image of the Post Office hemicycle, a suitable terminus for the partially enclosed Grand Plaza.

While the circulation pattern of the Post Office is one of its notable features, so is the architectural treatment. The 12th Street elevation is divided into three horizontal planes. The rusticated base is punctured by regularly spaced arched openings. The three-story middle section is separated vertically with a central projecting Ionic pavilion and two end pavilions of the same order. At the attic level, a slate mansard roof is embellished with windows trimmed with green copper. On the Grand Plaza side of the building, on the line of 13th Street, the roof returns to the orange tile material used throughout the Federal Triangle group. On the 13th Street side of the building, closest to Pennsylvania Avenue, the raw unfinished wall indicates the planned location of the northern enclosure of the Grand Plaza.

The New York City firm of Delano and Aldrich undertook this project. Made up of former employees of the firm of Carrère and Hastings, Delano and Aldrich established its reputation on private homes for America's wealthiest families. The firm also undertook the United States Government Chancellery at the Place de la Concorde in Paris and, several years after the Federal Triangle project, La Guardia Airport in New York City and the balcony of the White House south portico. No doubt, the firm's familiarity with Paris led it to employ the circular form in the Post Office building. Another source of inspiration could have been the much-published colonnaded crescent-shaped London County Hall on the city's embankment, completed in 1922 after designs of Ralph Knott.

FT06 Internal Revenue Service Building

1928–1935, Louis A. Simon, Supervising Architect. Constitution Ave. between 10th and 12th streets NW

The Office of the Supervising Architect commenced design work on the Internal Revenue Service Building before the Federal Triangle group had been planned. The reaction among private architects to the single building project accelerated the move toward a larger scheme. The resulting treatment of the Internal Revenue Service structure reflects a peculiar ordering of elements within the larger plan. Department headquarters were to be accorded monumental buildings "of the first class," while bureaus, of which the Internal Revenue Service was the only example in the Triangle, were to be housed in subordinate structures. As the Internal Revenue Service building became absorbed into the Federal

Triangle group plan, its design became dramatically scaled back and shorn of sculptural detail originally planned.

As completed, the Internal Revenue Service Building presents a simple Doric colonnaded elevation on the Constitution Avenue side. On the other sides, horizontal planes were divided between a two-story rusticated base, a middle section marked with long rows of fluted Doric pilasters rising from the third to the fifth floors, and an attic story set behind a balcony. Because the survival of the Old Post Office prevented the completion of the Internal Revenue Service Building, the latter exhibits raw edges of brick and limestone on the Pennsylvania Avenue and 12th Street elevations.

The history of the Internal Revenue Service Building illustrates the scant respect architects in private practice accorded Louis A. Simon and the Office of the Supervising Architect of the Treasury Department. An employee of the office from 1896, Simon served as its chief architect from 1915 to 1934 under James A. Wetmore, who held the position of acting supervising architect. After Wetmore's retirement in 1934, Simon was appointed Supervising Architect. Simon maintained a career-long cooperative attitude toward private practitioners, but in return, few regarded him as their creative equal.

The supporters of the Federal Triangle group no doubt included many who possessed a genuine desire to see a world-class architectural ensemble develop in such a key location. Other architects seized upon the project to further their contention that government architects were less able as designers than private practitioners. In arguing for a comprehensive Federal Triangle scheme, several private architects accused Simon's office of being capable only of "parking" the buildings on the triangle site, rather than grouping them. After the Internal Revenue Service was forced into a relatively spartan design in the overall group plan, private architects singled out the building as the least inspiring component in the complex.

FT07 Justice Department Building

1931–1934, Zantzinger, Borie and Medary. Pennsylvania Ave. between 9th and 10th streets NW

Of all the Federal Triangle buildings, the Justice Department is the one that best sym-

FT06 Internal Revenue Service Building

FT07 Justice Department Building

bolizes the transition from strictly classical forms to modernism. Laid out on a trapezoidal site, the building echoes the treatment of the Post Office and Internal Revenue Service buildings in the use of classical pavilions to emphasize corners. Their use on Constitution Avenue balances the classical pavilions on the United States Customs Service, Departmental Auditorium, and Interstate Commerce Commission blocks farther west. Long Ionic colonnades on the 9th Street and Pennsylvania Avenue elevations present a classical image to the viewer. On the other hand, spare blocklike fluted pilasters are employed along 10th Street and Constitution Avenue, except for the end pavilions, where Ionic columns appear. Art Deco and Greek decorative flourishes are evident throughout the exterior and interior.

The successful Philadelphia firm of Zantzinger, Borie and Medary undertook the design of the Justice Department. Charles C. Zantzinger and Charles L. Borie, Jr., collaborated with Horace Trumbauer on the Philadelphia Museum of Art, among the firm's most prominent commissions. The firm was experienced in designing large institutional and public buildings, which, while classical in proportion and massing, absorbed elements of modernism and individuality. In the Justice Department, the firm achieved a building that was in harmony with the Federal Triangle group but was also unique in the use of machine-age design influences.

New York City sculptor C. Paul Jennewein, who had collaborated with Zantzinger and Borie on the Philadelphia Museum, was commissioned to coordinate a comprehensive decorative arts plan for the building. He pro-

vided not only the sculptural forms but consulted with the firm on all architectural details. Exterior sculptural work and the abundant New Deal murals in the interior relate to the themes inherent in the role of law and justice in American society. Polychromatic tile embellished with gold-glazed snow cleats in the shape of anthemions cover the roof. Aluminum decoration was lavished on the building, in grilles, door leaves and surrounds, railings, window frames, and torchères. In the interior, aluminum was employed in stair railings, light fixtures, door trim, ceiling and wall panels, window frames, elevator doors, and selected sculptural work.

Elaborate mosaic work, executed by John Joseph Earley, adorns the entrance and lobby ceilings. The Justice Department's artistic program made it one of the most admired of the Federal Triangle buildings.

FT08 National Archives

1935, John Russell Pope. Pennsylvania Ave. between 7th and 9th streets NW

Located between two busy north-south thoroughfares, the National Archives occupies a strategic location in the city's plan. Its central portico looks north along 8th Street, a street that Pierre L'Enfant assigned for special treatment because it lay midway between the Capitol and the White House. Robert Mills's Patent Office building secured the importance of the thoroughfare between F and G streets.

In the early twentieth century, the Carnegie Library reinforced the street's importance to the north on K Street. The National Archives building at Pennsylvania Avenue provided an effective southern terminus to the 8th Street vista from the F Street entrance of the Patent Office. Thus, in a visual way, the Federal Triangle was tied to the larger urban scene to the north. The south elevation reinforced the monumental line of edifices that defined the grand thoroughfare of Constitution Avenue.

Few doubted that John Russell Pope was the most appropriate designer for this pivotal building. His designs for the DAR Constitution Hall and the National City Christian Church (see FB05 and NE17, pp. 208, 295) were welcome classical contributions to the city's central area. Pope had also designed the monumental Baltimore Museum of Art. His success with these commissions and the National Archives no doubt led to the Jefferson Memorial and the Mellon Gallery of Art, today the National Gallery of Art (see ML16, p. 108). The rapid succession of grand projects inspired fierce protestations from critics who were swept up in the oncoming wave of modernism.

The National Archives building serves two major functions. The first is expressed in the Constitution Avenue elevation, where a monumental staircase leads into a half-domed room in which documents sacred to the American republic are on exhibit. Stored in secure cases, these documents include the Declaration of Independence, the Constitution, and the Bill of Rights. The other function is indicated on the Pennsylvania Avenue elevation, the entrance to the reading rooms and archival vaults stored within a windowless stack.

As if to underscore the importance of 8th Street, the National Archives is taller than the other Federal Triangle structures. Its solid rectangular form is clad on all four sides with a Corinthian colonnade. On the Constitution Avenue elevation, the pedimented Corinthian portico extends out the center, meeting the staircase at its top. On the Pennsylvania Avenue side, the pedimented portico surmounts the base of the building, which contains a modest visitors' entrance. With the exception of the Constitution Avenue elevation, which is nearly windowless, the columns surrounding the structure partially mask vertical strips of windows. Heroic figures flank the north and south entrances and are set on pedestals incised with mottos relating to the study of history.

FT08 National Archives

FT09 **Federal Trade Commission Building**

1938, Bennett, Parsons and Frost. Pennsylvania Ave. between 6th and 7th streets NW

At the apex of the Federal Triangle is the Federal Trade Commission, an appropriate capstone for the ambitious building project and the most visible component of the complex from the east. The overall design coordinator for the Triangle project, Edward H. Bennett, was the designer. The apex building was the last major element to be undertaken and was almost dropped altogether because of the demands of the Great Depression. Its completion is testimony to Bennett's effective lobbying and willingness to strip the building of much of its classical detail in order to bring it into conformity with the spartan spirit of the times.

Like the other Federal Triangle buildings, the Federal Trade Commission Building is clad in limestone and rests on a granite base. The rounded corner facing the Capitol is accentuated with a monumental Ionic colonnade stretching from the third floor to the cornice line. The attic level is covered with the same orange tile found on other buildings in the complex. At the ground level, on each side of the curved corner, is a larger-than-life-size sculpture of a titanic workhorse being held in check by a muscular man. Winner of a nationwide competition for the work, sculptor Michael Lantz designed the figures to symbolize "Man Controlling Trade."

Other notable decorative features include the overdoor sculptural panels on the Pennsylvania Avenue and Constitution Avenue elevations. On the Pennsylvania Avenue side, industry and shipping are illustrated in panels executed by Chaim Gross and Robert Laurent. On the Constitution Avenue elevation, Concetta Scaravaglione and Carl Schmitz executed bas-reliefs depicting agriculture and trade. In embellishments of aluminum grilles, door reveal panels, and railings, the trade theme is further developed.

Downtown East (DE)

Antoinette J. Lee

A N EXPANSE OF LAND BETWEEN THE CAPITOL AND WHITE House, Downtown East is an underappreciated architectural enclave in central Washington. Incorporating the oldest commercial buildings in the city, the area exhibits a remarkably long architectural evolution of over a century and a half, including several cycles of redevelopment, with survivors from each.

Pennsylvania Avenue between the Capitol and the White House, location of some of the earliest residential and commercial settlement in the city, is the area's southern boundary. The commercial core extends north from it to Massachusetts Avenue, between 16th Street on the west and North Capitol Street on the east.

Distinctive areas in Downtown East are a result of special protective designations or treatment programs such as the Downtown Historic District, the 15th Street Financial Historic District, and the north side of Pennsylvania Avenue. Other enclaves developed around the parklike squares that Pierre Charles L'Enfant provided at the intersection of major thoroughfares, such as Franklin and McPherson squares, or from a clustering of similar uses, such as Judiciary Square, where municipal and federal courts are located. Still others, such as Chinatown, centered on H Street and the commercial thoroughfare along 7th Street, are a product of historical phenomena.

Topography and transportation routes helped define the geographical framework of Downtown East. From the flatlands of Pennsylvania Avenue, the land rises precipitously to F Street, an area secure from the flooding from the Tiber Creek and the Washington City Canal. Streetcar routes along 7th Street reinforced the development of that thoroughfare as the city's first major commercial street. Other rail lines along Pennsylvania Avenue and F Street completed the transportation network to the downtown core by the early twentieth century.

For much of the nineteenth and early twentieth centuries, aside from Pennsylvania Avenue and 7th Street, a good part of the area was residential. Shopkeepers frequently lived above their stores or close to their establishments, creating a kind of walking city before mass transportation enabled the population to separate living from working. By the 1920s, F Street, anchored by major department stores, reigned as the supreme commercial thoroughfare in the city. Commerce reached G Street, a secondary commercial artery, and then farther north as office buildings and shops opened on 14th and other north-south streets.

Downtown East served as the hub of immigrant groups. In the 1930s, when the Federal Triangle replaced the old Chinatown south of Pennsylvania Avenue, the Chinese community moved to H Street and adorned existing buildings with oriental motifs. As successive waves of ethnic groups occupied Downtown East, new churches were built and others were adapted. For example, synagogues were converted to Baptist churches that served predominantly black congregations.

Downtown East reached its peak as the city's commercial heart in the years between the world wars. By the late 1940s, in the face of suburbanization, the importance of the traditional downtown declined. Businesses and organizations sought offices in Downtown West, where new buildings were developed. After the riots that accompanied the assassination of Martin Luther King, Jr., in 1968, retail sales plummeted and Downtown East kept only a handful of department stores, marginal shops, and low-rent offices.

In order to reverse the downward trend, city officials attempted to revive the area through such devices as constructing a two-lane brick median strip in the middle of F Street between 13th and 14th streets to encourage pedestrian use of this block and of several others nearby. The Metro system opened several stations in Downtown East, and a gigantic convention center was viewed as a way to attract visitors, stimulate hotel construction, and generate additional tax revenues. At the southern end of the area, the Pennsylvania Avenue Development Corporation manages a separate development process that fosters innovative new construction and adaptive use of landmark buildings. Plans to reintroduce housing on the thoroughfare and elsewhere in Downtown East are also underway.

In the wake of these infrastructure projects and the filling out of Downtown West, real estate developers began to assemble sites and erect new buildings. By the late 1970s, as old buildings were being pulled down and new ones put up, the area's character changed dramatically.

City planners and developers hoped to avoid the mistakes of Downtown West. Moreover, by the 1970s, the city's consciousness of historic preservation had matured, and improved laws and regulations were in place protecting the

Downtown Historic District, the 15th Street Financial Historic District, and the Pennsylvania Avenue National Historic Site.

Most of the new office structures are designed in a Postmodern spirit, thus providing a different character to the new office blocks. Some retail shopping has survived in the area. Unlike Downtown West, Downtown East contains several important cultural and historical institutions, such as the Smithsonian Institution's National Museum of American History and National Portrait Gallery, the Martin Luther King, Jr., Memorial Public Library, the National Park Service's Ford's Theatre and the Petersen House (where Lincoln died), the National Building Museum, and the National Museum of Women in the Arts, all of which provide institutional and urban stability.

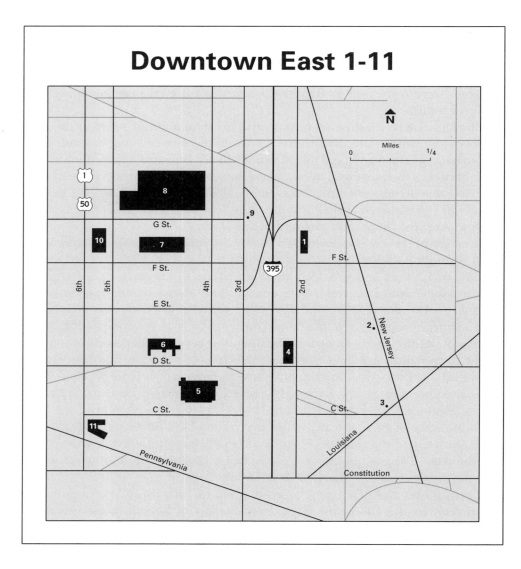

DE01 Georgetown University Law Center

DE03 Acacia Mutual Life Insurance Company

DE01 Georgetown University Law Center

1971, Edward Durell Stone. 600 New Jersey Ave. NW

At least 3 miles from the main campus in Georgetown, the Georgetown University Law Center is located near the eastern edge of the old downtown in order to provide its students with easy access to the District and federal courts at Judiciary Square and to the Supreme Court.

Edward Durell Stone designed the building in a large and dignified idiom expressive of the majesty and remoteness of the law. Like other of his buildings during that period, it is a rectangular box topped by an overhanging flat roof and flat attic floor above. Clustered pilasters separate vertical ribbons of windows and become narrower near the doorways. These pilasters provide a sense of depth and modulate the otherwise flat wall surface. At the rear of the block, the building is reached by a long staircase leading to a large terrace.

DE02 Hyatt Regency Hotel

1974–1976, Welton Becket Associates. 400 New Jersey Ave. NW

Located two blocks from the Capitol, the Hyatt Regency Hotel defied the tendency of hotels to locate in the far Northwest Quadrant or in the suburbs. The Hyatt Corporation saw in the empty lots and time-worn buildings an opportunity to provide services and hotel accommodations for lobbyists, industry representatives, and tourists who wished to be close to Capitol Hill. Within a decade and a half, the Hyatt was part of a larger area of rebuilding emanating from the massive Union Station project, a trend that saw the rehabilitation of older hotels nearby.

The major design difficulty was the reconciliation of the Hyatt trademark of a vast open lobby with Washington's height limitation and building codes. The architects therefore designed a sloping five-story lobby roof angled sharply downward, supported by a complex web of steel girders and trusses. The result was a compromise lightwell that is defined by the sides of the interior court and a 130-foot long bridge at the ninth and tenth floors. The exterior is clad with a tan brick punctuated by bronze-framed windows. A rooftop restaurant offers an oblique view of the Capitol.

DE03 Acacia Mutual Life Insurance Company

1936, Shreve, Lamb and Harmon. 52 Louisiana Ave. NW

The Acacia Mutual Life Insurance Company building is one of the few private buildings to face the Capitol grounds, only a block away. On the one hand, the design required a sense of civic responsibility to relate the building to the notable structures grouped about the Capitol. On the other, two practical considerations influenced its form: the need to provide a modern office structure with an adaptable plan and the equal need to deal with a site located over the Tiber Creek sewer.

The architects designed an irregularly shaped pentagonal building that could be constructed in phases around a central court. The absence of interior structural columns allowed a free arrangement of offices. The southeast facade facing the Capitol has a flat U-shaped plan, the bottom of the U being longer than the sides. The bay sides were placed at a slight angle to the long facade, which is articulated with fluted pilasters extending from the second floor to the fourth, separating vertical columns of windows. The facade is sharply demarcated into three zones—the rusticated granite base, the pilastered limestone shaft, and the fifth-floor "entablature" atop a projecting cornice. A balustraded terrace forms a high base for the building, thereby moving it back from the sewer close to Louisiana Avenue and allowing the elevator to serve the basement level. The design conformed to that of the buildings around the Capitol, although it is clearly subordinate to the Senate office buildings (see CH03 and CH06, pp. 135, 137).

DE04 United States Tax Court

1969–1976, Victor Lundy. 400 2nd St. NW

The Tax Court building is a dramatic arrangement of four office blocks set on a monumental pedestal. The architect claimed that the form of the building resulted from taking a monolithic block and breaking it apart, separating granite sections with sheets of bronze-tinted plate glass and crowning the whole with a clerestory that brings daylight into the recesses of the building. Each office block is structurally and mechanically an independent unit.

The most compelling facade is that facing the plaza on 2nd Street, where a 200-foot-long courtroom block is cantilevered 55 feet over the entry steps. This 4,000-ton block is supported by six columns at the rear and

DE04 United States Tax Court

more than a hundred post-tensioning cables secreted in the transverse walls and in the roof and third-floor slabs. The block holds three courtrooms and a series of judges' suites. The cantilevered section appears to be a floating concrete block to the pedestrian approaching the building from the entrance plaza, which itself is placed over a section of an expressway. The *Architectural Forum* pronounced the building "one of the most daring structures, in terms of engineering, ever proposed for the capital."[34]

The building houses nearly three dozen judges' suites and courtroom facilities, serenely expressed in granite and concrete and creating a dramatic contrast with the dynamic exterior.

DE05 Municipal Center

1934–1941, Nathan C. Wyeth. 4th to 6th streets, Indiana Ave. to C St. NW

The Municipal Center is a grouping of District of Columbia government buildings flanking John Marshall Place. The creation of a municipal center in the 1930s, far from the District Building at 1350 E Street NW, resulted from the dedication of the entire Federal Triangle project to federal government functions. Municipal Center's design retained a vista along John Marshall Place be-

DE06 Judiciary Square

tween Pennsylvania Avenue and Hadfield's City Hall, a configuration provided for in L'Enfant's Plan for the capital city. The central plaza broadened the vista and placed Municipal Center on a terraced court below Judiciary Square. The original scheme called for both municipal office buildings and a central public library.

The first two buildings to be constructed were the East and West buildings, both facing the Central Plaza. From a pink granite base, limestone walls rise six stories, with setbacks at the top three stories. The walls of the facade consist of recessed vertical strips of windows, separated at each floor with ornamental spandrels. Announcing the main entrance are three-story porticos supported by four square piers, each of which is incised to suggest column capitals.

DE06 **Judiciary Square**

1820–1881, George Hadfield. 1919, Elliott Woods. 1934–1939, Nathan C. Wyeth. Indiana Ave. and F St., 4th and 5th streets NW

The Old City Hall forms the centerpiece of a formal grouping of federal and District court buildings. It is located two blocks east of the location of the Patent Office Building (see DE15.2). Hadfield designed this building as well as other important commissions of this era such as the executive office buildings flanking the White House and the Van Ness Mausoleum.

The Old City Hall was constructed in several sections: the central section completed in 1820, the east and west wings in 1826 and 1849, respectively. The building served as the city hall until 1873, when the federal government took it over for use as courts. In 1881,

a north extension was added. Between 1910 and 1939, four compatibly designed public buildings were placed around Old City Hall. Capitol architect Elliott Woods supervised the design of the first, the 1910 Court of Appeals Building at 5th and E streets. Municipal architect Nathan C. Wyeth designed the remaining three buildings—the Juvenile Court Building at 4th and E streets, the Municipal Court Building on 4th Street, and the Police Court Building on 5th Street.

Old City Hall is one of the finest examples of Greek Revival architecture in Washington, aside from the Treasury Department and the Patent Office buildings, and it determined the design of the four succeeding buildings in Judiciary Square. A Greek Ionic portico set above a terraced stepped base defines the central section. Flanking the portico are hyphens with recessed round-headed windows at the first floor. At the ends of the building are wings with Ionic columns fronting an open recessed space with a round-headed opening at the rear. The Ionic order and the recessed round-headed windows were carried to the later limestone buildings of Judiciary Square.

DE07 **Pension Building**

1882–1887, Montgomery C. Meigs. F St. between 4th and 5th streets NW

Even by modern standards the size of the Pension Building, erected solely to serve the needs of Union veterans, is astounding, with its immense scale deeply imbedded in the history of its origins. During and immediately after the Civil War, Congress passed laws that greatly expanded the eligibility for pensions of the wounded, maimed, widows, and orphans of that particular war. Complying with the complex laws and adjudicating the increased number of claims produced by this legislation required a staff of 1,500 Pension Office clerks. Dispersed accommodations in four rented buildings proved inadequate and led to the erection of a single facility. By the time the majority of the monies had been dispersed in 1920, $500 million had been paid from the Pension Building to Union veterans during a time when the North became rich and industrialized and the South remained poor and agrarian.

The Pension Building was planned by army engineer and architect Montgomery Meigs to provide a naturally air-conditioned environ-

DE07 Pension Building

ment for its employees and a circulation system that was easily accessible to its users, who were often disabled. Designed in 1881, the massive structure was constructed between 1882 and 1887 of 15.5 million inexpensive bricks in response to the vastly expensive and ornate State, War, and Navy Building. Meigs based his design on an eclectic mixture of Renaissance palaces, fortified city houses into which families could retreat in time of war. His firsthand knowledge of such buildings dated from two extended sojourns in Italy, in 1867 and 1876. Like Italian Renaissance palaces, the Pension Building was designed with a single layer of rooms around the building's perimeter, each of which faced an interior courtyard; unlike its Italian models, the Pension Building's courtyard is covered by a roof.

Antonio da Sangallo's Palazzo Farnese (1515–1534) in Rome, the largest and most famous of all Renaissance palaces, provided the model for the exterior massing and articulation of the Pension Building. Meigs's initial design called for a building on the same scale as the Palazzo Farnese, but eventually he doubled its size to 400 feet east to west by 200 feet north to south. Other major changes were in the roofing of the courtyard and the introduction of a 1,200-foot frieze depicting the Union Army on the march. Similarities to the Italian model are the horizontal organization of the building into three nearly equal stories, duplication of the main-story fenestration pattern of alternating segmental and triangular pediments, development of a full third story rather than an attic, and imitation

of the details of its entablature. On the interior the brick staircases composed of deep treads and shallow risers, which are canted down, were derived from Palazzo Farnese staircases.

The elevation of the Pension Building's courtyard, two levels of arches outlined by simple, narrow moldings carried by slender columns, was based on Donato Bramante's Roman Palazzo della Cancelleria (1489–1511). Simultaneous with his careful adherence to its outward appearance, Meigs transformed his prototype in many ways. Four levels of open arches set back from the plane established by the two-story arcade (and the iron balcony suspended above it) were added to provide entry to the offices from the balconies. These office entrance arches were not aligned with the arcade openings (except in the center of each side), a violation of the Renaissance principle of axiality. As did other contemporaneous architects, Meigs used the image and meaning of historical architecture but manipulated many of its basic tenets and elements to meet his own pragmatic needs and different aesthetic outlook.

This Victorian attitude of combining partial quotations drawn from numerous historical precedents is further expressed by Meigs's odd placement of columns to span the top two stories on the four exterior corners. This Venetian architectural motif, the prominence of the main frieze above the ground story, and the sheer scale of the building all suggest that Meigs had carefully read John Ruskin's *Seven Lamps of Architecture* (1849), the most widely disseminated book on architecture in the nineteenth century. In his chapter entitled "The Lamp of Power," Ruskin considered the visual means by which a building generated a sense of power. His formula for achieving power included undivided geometric masses (consider the Pension Building's form), huge scale bounded by continuous lines "from top to bottom, and from end to end" (as exemplified by the projecting window frames, friezes, and entablature), and the "continuous series of any marked feature" (the relentless march of the Pension Building's windows and frieze elements around its 1,200-foot perimeter, for example). Ruskin noted the aesthetic importance of angle sculptures in modifying the three-dimensional bulk of the Doge's Palace in Venice. The corner columns on the Pension Building are too small in comparison to its immense scale to modify its magnitude, but apparently Meigs considered that they did, as they serve no structural purpose and are unrelated to its Roman antecedents. Meigs may have included these columns as a reference to the Venetian Renaissance tradition, viewing the building as a catalog of Italian palaces.

The Pension Building's decorative elements all mark it as a monument to glorify the victorious Union Army. Meigs named the four entrances gates, an additional allusion to fortifications. The north gate, the Gate of Invalids, is presided over by Justice; the south Gate of the Infantry, by Truth. Mars, the god of war, protects the east Naval Gate, and above the west Gate of the Quartermaster is Minerva, goddess of wisdom. Meigs reinforced the military character of the building with a belt course of crossed swords between the second and third stories and a frieze of exploding bombs and cannons just below the cornice. The sculptor was Bohemian-born Caspar Buberl (1834–1899).

Buberl was also responsible for the building's most meaningful and spectacular feature, the 1,200-foot frieze dividing the ground story from the main level. It was executed in 3-foot-tall bisque terracotta panels by the Boston Terra Cotta Company. Cavalry, artillery, infantry, navy, and quartermaster's corps are all shown in characteristic dress and pose. Twenty-eight individual panels of varying length (representing 69.5 feet of original design) are repeated, but their order is varied to disguise any impression of sameness. Although Buberl likened the frieze to the Panathenaic Procession on the Parthenon, its re-lationship to that Athenian monument is more generic than specific. Friezes depicting military exploits were, in fact, a venerable tradition, dating from pre-classical times. Meigs's formal sources for his frieze, as well as for the spandrel sculpture above the doors, were the frieze, decorative relief panels, and spandrel figures on Jean-François Chalgrin's Arc de Triomphe (1806–1836) in Paris. The sculptural program on the then largest triumphal arch in the world depicts Napoleon's campaigns, including his *Grande Armée* on the march. Meigs's and Buberl's association of the victorious Union Army with the most famous army in the modern world was a statement about the power of the military in American society (and in the federal government) at that time.

The regularity of the exterior composition, made up of so many distinct parts, implies numerous cubes of space, which in reality is the case. However, another interior dimension exists. Not even the building's huge external mass prepares the visitor for the experience of the Pension Building's courtyard. It was designed to serve as an immense chimney, dispersing the air that had been drawn into each office through vents (there are three bricks missing under every window), to circulate throughout the offices (originally there were no doors facing the courtyard) and then exit through large clerestory windows. The scale of the courtyard is emphasized by the presence of eight colossal Corinthian columns, which rise 75 feet to carry the superstructure that supports the roof. Constructed of 70,000 bricks with terracotta bases 8 feet in diameter and molded plaster capitals, each column was plastered and painted to imitate Siena marble, the latter embellishment not carried out until 1895. The abacus above each plaster capital (based on those in Michelangelo's Santa Maria degli Angeli in Rome) is cast iron, a material used throughout the structure of the building in conjunction with brick and terracotta for its fireproof properties.

Extensive renovations in 1984 included structural stabilization, exterior cleaning and interior decoration, including the present color scheme and marbleizing, reproduction of shallow urns for the edge of the upper arcade (planned by Meigs to contain plants), and commissioning of white plaster busts, related to the building trades, for the small niches of the central court to replace lost busts of soldiers. Like the Washington Monument, the Pension Building was built to be a sublime experience, and it succeeds. In 1882 Meigs wrote a friend that the building's effect could "hardly fail to be impressive," a judgment that posterity cannot dispute. (Pamela Scott)

DE08 General Accounting Office

1951, Gilbert Stanley Underwood. 441 G St. NW

Covering an entire city block and rising seven stories, the General Accounting Office is significant as the first block-shaped federal government office structure in the capital city. The block form was a direct result of the invention of fluorescent lamps in the 1930s, which allowed for glareless, uniform, and comfortable lighting for office workers without relying on natural light. Earlier government office buildings had to capture natural illumination through light courts or skylights. Air-conditioning throughout ventilated the interior spaces.

Gilbert Stanley Underwood, who served as Supervising Architect in the Federal Works Agency before the federal architectural functions were transferred to the General Services Administration, was responsible for the design. It recalls his pre–World War II work such as the State Department Building in Foggy Bottom. The long stone facades are articulated with a polished granite base and slightly projecting walls extending up to the fifth floor. A modest cornice frosts the projecting wall sections. Simple casement windows are placed at equal intervals throughout the elevation. On either side of the entrance are bas-reliefs by Joseph Kiselewski illustrating people performing various occupations. The building exemplifies the straightforward nature of the agency it houses.

DE09 Adas Israel Synagogue

1876, unknown. 3rd and G streets NW

Adas Israel Synagogue is a starkly simple religious structure, reminiscent more of an eighteenth-century Quaker meeting house than of many elaborate late nineteenth-century urban synagogues. The building features an elongated second story where the women's gallery was located. Wood sunburst designs and round brick lintels above the narrow windows and main entrance are the sole ornaments on the spartan red brick facade.

DE09 Adas Israel Synagogue

Originally constructed at 6th and G streets NW, the Adas Israel Synagogue was located in what was then the center of the Jewish settlement in the capital city. By 1907, however, the congregation moved to a more commodious building at 6th and I streets NW. The old building was turned over to a Greek Orthodox church, later to an evangelical congregation, and by the mid-1940s to a grocery. Plans for the transit system (Metro) headquarters structure on this block prompted citizens to have the city lease a new site at 3rd and G streets to which the synagogue was moved. Adas Israel, on a new foundation, was carefully restored and refurnished to house the Lillian and Albert Small Jewish Museum of Washington and the headquarters of the Jewish Historical Society of Greater Washington.

DE10 Metro Operations Control Center

1971, Keyes, Lethbridge & Condon. 600 5th St. NW

The Metro Operations Control Center exudes a purely modern and functional air, much like the underground Metro system it operates. The eight stories are divided by protruding concrete shelves, all punctured by concrete columns that rise through the building's full height. Bands of dark windows are recessed behind the columns. The upper floors house offices, while the basement levels contain computers, a parking garage, and a revenue collection area. The penthouse structure encloses the building's mechanical systems and refrigeration equipment for several nearby subway stations. The building occupies a whole city block and stands aloof from its historical surroundings.

DE11 Canadian Chancery

1982–1988, Arthur Erickson Associates. 5th St. and Pennsylvania Ave. NW

The Canadian Chancery demonstrates the tendency of foreign nations to choose their best architects for their Washington buildings. The only foreign mission to occupy a site along Pennsylvania Avenue, the building conforms to the area's height and cornice requirements. The U-shaped building opens to the avenue through a large rectangular entrance on the south side. The pedestrian encounters a cascade of steps and a corner rotunda ringed with twelve fluted metal columns, one for each of Canada's provinces and territories. The round form acts as a spool, pulling the horizontal glass and masonry bands around the corner. In the courtyard, a colonnade supports a barrel-vaulted skylight. The rotunda was derived from the curved corner of Edward H. Bennett's Federal Trade Commission Building (see FT09, p. 176), the apex of the Federal Triangle. The fluted columns echo those on John Russell Pope's National Gallery of Art (see ML16, p. 108) building across Pennsylvania Avenue. In this way the architect attempted to incorporate local forms into this modern design.

DE12 Apex Building

mid-1860s–1887, Alfred B. Mullett. 7th St. and Pennsylvania Ave. NW

The Apex Building is one of the most prominent structures along Pennsylvania Avenue. Its twin towers frame the left side of the view of the Capitol, looking east from the Treasury Department building. The building is a result of several accretions over a period of time. The original core was the Saint Marc

Hotel, framed in masonry and cast iron and dating from the mid-1860s and a characteristic example of earlier fireproof construction in the city. The rusticated stone facade is punctured at even intervals with round-arch windows, which are longest on the lower floors. In 1887, when the Central National Bank converted the hotel to office use, Alfred B. Mullett was hired to design the picturesque twin towers on the west elevation, each crowned with a conical roof and decorative finials.

As part of the rejuvenation of Pennsylvania Avenue, Sears World Headquarters expanded the building in the mid-1980s by adding a sixth floor to the original hotel structure. A new connection was constructed to the small Italianate commercial buildings to the east, one formerly housing Matthew B. Brady's studio and the other a drugstore. The connection is compatible with the original hotel building but differentiated from it with flat arch windows and a distinctive gable roof.

DE13 National Bank of Washington

1889, James G. Hill. 301 7th St. NW

The diminutive and picturesque National Bank of Washington, which now serves as the Washington branch of that bank, reflects the scale of the late nineteenth-century city. It is located on one of the triangular wedges of land at the juncture of diagonal avenues and grid streets, and it anchors the southern end of the nineteenth-century commercial strip that extends along 7th Street.

Constructed of pink granite ashlar, the

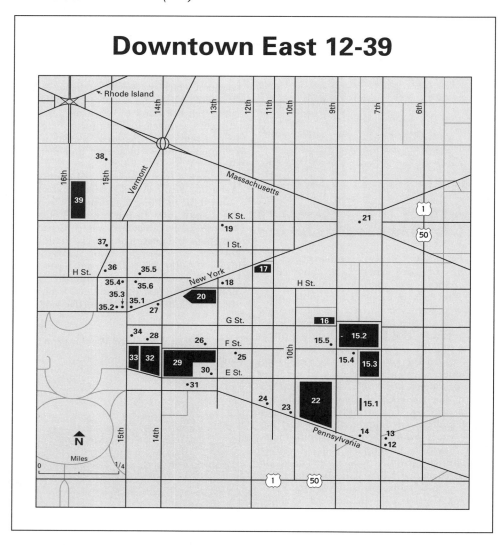

Downtown East 12-39

rough-hewn stone is crossed with bands of dressed stone at the window sills, window lintels, and water table. The round-arch entrance opens from a projecting entrance porch. Clusters of colonnettes mark its corners. A Byzantine capital and cornice band made up of scrolls and acanthus leaves crowns the porch. At the roofline are dormer windows ornamented with scrolled ornament. Double windows puncture the building walls. Wrought-iron grilles cover the transoms of the first-story windows. These delicate decorative elements offer grace notes to the otherwise weighty facades.

DE14 Market Square

1984–1990, Hartman-Cox and Morris Architects. 701 and 801 Pennsylvania Ave. NW

Market Square is the ultimate contextual building in Washington. It was designed to fit in with a complex set of design requirements at the important intersection of 8th Street and Pennsylvania Avenue, the mid-point between the Capitol and the White House. Winner of a competition sponsored by the Pennsylvania Avenue Development Corporation, Hartman-Cox designed Market Square to reinforce the significance of 8th

Street, from Carnegie Library at Mount Vernon Square to the north and then south to the Patent Office Building, the National Archives, and the Hirshhorn Museum on the Mall. It echoes the form and massing of the Federal Triangle across Pennsylvania Avenue and serves as a monumental element along Pennsylvania Avenue, a revitalized and rebuilt thoroughfare of new, rehabilitated, and restored buildings. Finally, the building provides a fitting backdrop to the new Navy Memorial, a circular space designed by Conklin Rossant of New York City and defined by a bronze map of the world and a solitary sailor sculpted by Stanley Bleifield. As *Architecture* noted, the building walks a "tightrope between foreground and background architecture."[35]

Market Square is made up of two buildings, each a mirror image of the other. The buildings part company at 8th Street and offer a clear vista north to the Patent Office Building. Each building forms a hemicycle that curves around the Navy Memorial before straightening out on Pennsylvania Avenue. The hemicycle is formed of a curved facade lined with a five-story Roman Doric colonnade and heavily rusticated base constructed of Indiana limestone that wraps around the corner on Pennsylvania Avenue with four columns. Its drama recalls the hemicycles of the Post Office Building in the Federal Triangle. The rest of the facade is constructed of buff-colored brick and resembles turn-of-the-century commercial facades common to the city's downtown. The tripartite arrangement of vertical sections between the base, shaft, and cornice also separates the buildings' functions. Retail uses occupy the base. Commercial office space is assigned to the shaft, while residential condominiums are located in the cornice.

Market Square is notable for its unabashed classicism. The architects looked for design inspiration from not only the Federal Triangle, but also the Treasury Building and the buildings of the 15th Street Financial District. While the building is neither a square nor a market, its name recalls the city market that once thrived on the location of the National Archives across Pennsylvania Avenue.

DE15 Downtown Historic District

An irregular T-shaped area centered on the Patent Office Building and extending along 7th St. to Pennsylvania Ave., north to I St., and west along F St. to 11th St.

DE15.1 Gallery Row

The Downtown Historic District incorporates many of the oldest commercial buildings in Downtown East, which clustered along 7th Street. Seventh Street emerged as a major commercial artery in the District of Columbia because it connected the Washington City Canal and the markets between 7th and 9th streets with the agricultural lands in the District beyond Boundary Street (Florida Avenue) and Maryland. F Street marked a plateau safe from the floods on the land rising to the north from Pennsylvania Avenue.

The Downtown Historic District includes major public and private buildings such as the Patent Office Building (see DE15.2), the United States General Post Office (see DE15.3), and the former Washington Loan and Trust Company (see DE15.5), but it is characterized more by anonymous low-rise commercial architecture of the mid-nineteenth to the early twentieth centuries, fragile survivors in an area undergoing redevelopment.

An example is the Germond Crandell Building (DE15.1) of 1877, designed by architect Germond Crandell and recycled as Gallery Row in the 1980s by Hartman-Cox.

DE15.2 Smithsonian Institution, National Museum of American Art, National Portrait Gallery (United States Patent Office, United States Civil Service Commission Building)

1836, Town and Elliot. 1836–1840, 1849–1952, Robert Mills. 1852–1857, Thomas U. Walter and Edward Clark. Block bounded by 7th, 9th, F, and G streets NW

The site chosen for the Patent Office in the 1830s had been allocated on L'Enfant's plan for a nondenominational church dedicated to American heroes. Public Reservation 8 sat on the same ridge of high ground that accommodated the White House. The Patent Office was seen as an appropriate substitute for such a national pantheon because ingenuity and inventiveness were perceived as the qualities most reflective of the American national character. As the repository of America's arts and sciences, it was not a shrine to military and civic heroes, as envisaged by L'Enfant, but honored the country's collective intellectual genius. In a broad sense, the current occupants of the building, two Smithsonian museums—the National Portrait Gallery and the National Museum of American Art—carry on L'Enfant's intention, as well as the original functions of the Patent Office, which contained a museum in addition to offices.

On 4 July 1836, Andrew Jackson selected a design proposed by Ithiel Town of New York and William P. Elliot, Jr., a young Washington architect who had been trained by George Hadfield. Town and Elliot's plan was for a rectangular building with a courtyard, which could be constructed wing by wing as needs dictated and resources allowed. On the same day Jackson placed Robert Mills in charge of construction. Mills immediately modified some details of the winning design, which in general form was similar to his own proposal, a temple of "massy" proportions (probably Greek Doric, as Town's and Elliot's design) that intersected a rectangular block. In 1851 Mills's and Elliot's dispute over authorship of the design was carried on in the pages of a new national magazine, the *Scientific American*.

Like the Treasury Building (see WH04, p. 154), the thirty-year period of construction of the Patent Office is reflected most noticeably on the interiors and barely discernable on each facade with the exception of the south wing, which was the first to be constructed. This portico and its flanking walls are the only substantial architectural fragment left in the city where the color and texture of Aquia, Virginia, sandstone, the material from which the early public buildings were mandated by law to be built, is still visible. When the marble wings were built in the 1850s the sandstone was painted white; earlier painting of external walls at the White House and Capitol had served as an effective vapor barrier.

The streets were lowered around the Patent Office during nineteenth-century public works projects, particularly those undertaken during the 1870s. As a result the building now sits several feet higher than the surrounding cityscape, little of which dates from such an early period. In addition, the present gray granite south entrance—caused by removal of a monumental staircase in 1936 when F Street was straightened—stands in sharp contrast to the color and texture of the brown sandstone portico and walls above and around it and the white marble wings. Once an integrated design that sat comfortably on its site, the building when now viewed along its principal axis seems an unhappy assemblage of barely related parts.

Each of the four facades is composed of similar giant Doric porticoes centered on walls articulated by wide Doric pilasters and terminated by pavilions. The north and south facades have octastyle porticoes; those on the east and west are hexastyle. Each is distinguished by a different entrance sequence: on the south, entry is through the base directly under the portico, on the east via a steep staircase that splays out in front of rusticated cheek blocks, on the north by a wide staircase contained between two low walls, and on the west by a shallow staircase divided into two parts by a short segment of rusticated wall. Thus they together represent a veritable catalog of possible monumental portico entrances.

In 1849 Mills was named architect of the Patent Office Extension, which commenced with the east wing. His design in marble for its 402-foot length created unpedimented square corner pavilions for the east and wings. In order to maximize interior space yet still retain a major staircase on the future north wing, Mills made adjustments to the fenestration pattern on the east wing, gradually increasing the space between the windows from south to north. In 1852, after Mills had carried the walls to the third floor, he was replaced by Thomas U. Walter, a result of the fourth and last of the politically motivated congressional investigations Mills had undergone since his arrival in Washington in 1830. It effectively brought his career as a public architect to a close. Walter was then placed in charge of constructing both the west and north wings; he introduced shallow pediments above the pavilions on the north and west wings. Walter's assistant, Edward Clark, was in charge of completing the west wing.

The interiors of each wing differ in their spatial configuration, structural principles, and architectural articulation. Mills's major change

DE15.2 Smithsonian Institution, National Museum of American Art, National Portrait Gallery

to the Town and Elliot design for the south wing was to introduce a double, semicircular, three-story flying staircase to project from the center of the north wall, which resulted in a broad three-story bay on the courtyard facade. This cantilevered and corbeled staircase is the most spectacular of Mills's stairs, graceful and elegant with the bottom curve of each tread responding to each floor's double semicircular rising curve.

Mills's south wing rooms consist of office cells on the east half and open, colonnaded halls on the west, originally storage on the ground level but a gallery to display patent models on the main story. The entire third floor of the south wing, designed by Mills as additional gallery space, was taller in proportion to the main-floor gallery but was organized in the same manner. Barrel-vaulted bays faced the windows with groin vaults down the center carried by columns that divided the rooms into thirds. The squat, massive Greek Doric columns that remain on the second story have fluted necking bands and bases, a detail Mills borrowed from those at the Temple of Apollo at Delos. The two lower floors of the east wing were designed for offices while the third floor, one vast room carried on tall square columns, was for additional gallery space.

Walter's north and west wing interiors continued the regularized office cells initiated by Mills, but they and the central halls were roofed following rectilinear trabeated principles rather than the curved arcuated ceilings of Mills's sections. Shallow brick arches run between cast-iron beams that span the hallways and each office to create a totally different spatial effect. Half of the north wing

entrance hall was designed by Walter as a double story vestibule, its rectilinearity emphasized by two levels of pilastered walls and its flat ceiling.

In 1877 iron roof girders in the west wing buckled when the top floor in that area caught fire. Although the damage did not extend to the top floor of the south wing, both large model rooms in the south and west were rebuilt in a Victorian style following designs by Adolf Cluss and Paul Schulze. The decorative appearance of the south wing's model hall, including stained-glass windows and paint and stencil scheme, date from a 1976 renovation, in which historical accuracy was not attempted. The Minton tile floor is original, as are the major architectural elements. Cluss and Schulze divided the wing into two doublestory side areas with a single-story domed central vestibule. Cast-iron round columns stand on top of square piers to support iron balconies in the side areas. The elaborate cast-iron capitals and the brackets above them reflect Cluss and Schulze's belief (derived from French Neo-Grec thinking) that when iron replaced the traditional building materials of wood and stone, its structural and decorative characteristics should not imitate earlier forms and principles. Instead iron, mass produced in parts and then bolted together, should have a hard-edged, mechanistic quality, evidenced by the stylized plant forms of the capitals. Iron's tensile strength should be exploited visually by showing its different structural properties, seen here in the brackets and beams they help support.

The relief panels and portraits in the model hall were designed by Czechoslovakian-born sculptor Caspar Buberl and cast in Keene's white cement. The four roundel portraits are of early American inventors: Benjamin Franklin, Thomas Jefferson, Robert Fulton, and Eli Whitney. The three panels on the north wall are allegorical depictions of Fire, Electricity and Magnetism, and Water; those on the south wall are Agriculture, Industry and Invention, and Mining. (Pamela Scott)

DE15.3 United States Tariff Commission Building (United States General Post Office)

Robert Mills, 1839–1842. 8th and F streets NW

Robert Mills's General Post Office is the least well known of his Washington buildings, yet he and his contemporaries considered it his masterwork. Louisa C. Tuthill in her *History of Architecture in the United States* (1848), the first critical history of American architecture published in this country, called it "one of the most splendid buildings in the United States." Although utilizing the same internal spatial organization and the same system of brick vaulted construction as his two better-known Washington works, the Treasury Building and the Patent Office, the General Post Office was designed on a much smaller scale. Originally organized as a U-shaped building facing E Street between 7th and 8th streets, a major addition by Thomas U. Walter in 1855 (following Mills's plan) transformed it into a rectangle with a central courtyard that filled the entire block up to F Street.

Mills's first proposal for the General Post Office was a three-story building with a hexastyle portico raised above an arcaded basement, which in turn was surmounted by a clock tower to be erected either in stone or iron. The actual building is entirely different, based on a traditional Renaissance palazzo, with a rusticated basement below and principal and attic stories knit together by giant Corinthian pilasters. This is the first use of the Italianate style for an important public building in America, although John Notman's Philadelphia Athenaeum (1847) is often accorded that honor.

The main, or south, front has a tetrastyle portico of engaged fluted Corinthian columns framed by single pilasters with narrow pilaster strips on their outside edge, thus making a subtle transition to the wall surface. The center is further emphasized by a tripartite window with a segmental pediment (in contrast to the triangular pediments elsewhere). Three tripartite windows are centered on the east and west facades of the original portion, with the central one framed by a portico of double engaged columns. This subtle layering of the wall surface in conjunction with a complex grid of vertical columns and pilasters, horizontals of basement, a belt course-cum-entablature supporting them, and a cornice and solid parapet at the roofline resulted in Mills's most sophisticated facade, one promoted as a model of additional government buildings planned in the 1840s. It is difficult to appreciate these qualities because the General Post Office has suffered considerably from repeated lowering of the streets. Excavation of its foundations and the subse-

DE15.3 United States Tariff Commission Building (United States General Post Office)

quent injection of a sub-basement, as well as the loss of an ornate cast-iron fence, have marred its original harmonious appearance.

In 1839 Mills was successful in demonstrating to Congress that repair costs to the Capitol and White House due to the erosion, spalling, and cracking of the Aquia sandstone had been considerable. For the new General Post Office, he was allowed to select a marble if he could find one at a cost comparable to granite, the preferred building material because of its durability. Marble buildings had been erected in Philadelphia and New York, yet none existed in Washington. To celebrate his victory, Mills changed the Corinthian capitals from some unspecified common variety to ones with intertwined volutes between the lateral volutes. The order Mills selected was identified by Palladio as that used on the Temple of Jupiter Stator, the first marble building erected in Rome. Unfortunately the inexpensive Westchester, New York, marble selected was of inferior quality, and both the decorative details and wall surfaces show severe cracking and weathering.

Although Mills employed the same regularized internal plan of a central barrel-vaulted corridor flanked by cubical groin-vaulted offices in his three major Washington office buildings, he created unique entries for each. At the General Post Office, two sets of niches, one outside behind the Doric in antis doorway and the second within the vestibule, create a simple but effective entry sequence of strongly architectonic elements. The vestibule is separated from the corridor by a screen of Tuscan columns, again set in antis. The ground-floor corridors are sparingly decorated with plaster ornamentation, but those of the second story carry a wide, richly sculpted anthemion frieze that projects boldly from the wall surface. Numerous bands and fillets of ornament outline the vaults, and large elegant rosettes mark the corner groins. These are Mills's most lavish interiors. Although his architecture was admired in the early twentieth century for its sparseness and geometric purity, Mills himself preferred ornamented architecture but could not find clients who would pay for it. None of the original marble mantles survives. The only major room is a rectangle on the top story traversing the center ten bays. Groin vaults carried by eight Doric columns derived from the Temple of Apollo at Delos divide the room into a central nave with side aisles. In the center is a small dome, the pendentives of which are decorated with the caduceus, Mercury's attribute as messenger of the gods and the symbol adopted by the Post Office.

With the completion of the General Post Office, Mills had provided for Washington three permanent exemplars of classically derived architecture, each with specific historical references of great importance. His Ionic Treasury was related to the stoa in form, his Doric Patent Office, a temple, and his Corinthian General Post Office was in the form of a palazzo. Their solidity of construction suggests that he was building for eternity; their scale and massiveness suggest an intention of monumentality. It is interesting to note that all three buildings have been in continuous use by the government since they were built and that the rigidity of the grid system of office spaces has not prevented them from being successfully adapted for modern office space.

Walter's addition tripled the length of the east and west facades, created a new northern facade, and introduced subtle changes to the exterior. Projections from his wall surfaces were slightly more three dimensional. The point of juncture can be discerned by his Corinthian capitals, which are more robustly sculptural. Unfortunately, the Maryland marble he employed was not conspicuously superior to the New York marble of the original building. In completing the rectangle, Walter provided an arched opening into the courtyard on the west for the cartage of mail; on the east he imitated Mills's south facade. The sculpture of the keystone and spandrels of

the arch was executed by Guido Butti in 1856. Fidelity is in the center, flanked by Electricity, who carries a lightning bolt, and Steam, who holds a steam engine. These allusions were apt. The first telegraphic message (sent over electric lines) was dispatched from this building in 1844 by Samuel F. B. Morse, and railroads, which were rapidly expanding during the 1840s and 1850s, provided for the swift movement of the mails.

Walter's north facade is a very different composition. Here he introduced a major recessed portico formed by four sets of double columns in antis above an arcade, a variation on the portico of the Capitol by Latrobe and Bulfinch. This change in facade treatment presaged a different spatial arrangement on the interior. The city post office was located on the ground floor. Above it was a large, two-story, skylit room with a cast-iron balcony around its perimeter that served as a sorting room for the dead letter office. As in all his additions to Mills's buildings, Walter used iron girders as roof supports, and iron beams to span the halls and offices, which resulted in rectilinear, trabeated spaces rather than vaulted ones. These subtle variations between Mills's and Walter's parts of the General Post Office herald the differences between Neoclassical and Victorian sensibilities in architecture. Availability of better materials and expertise in new building techniques played their part in promoting the change in taste. (Pamela Scott)

DE15.4 Le Droit Building

1875, James H. McGill. 800–812 F St. NW

Facing the south front of the Patent Office Building, the Le Droit Building is one of the most distinctive commercial structures along commercial F Street. The upper and lower parts are definitively distinguished by a projecting cornice, supported by simple Corinthian pilasters. The lower floors are devoted to shops, the upper to office spaces. Along the third and fourth stories are five rhythmic groups of triple windows, each group crowned with brick hood molds. A heavily bracketed cornice with one triangular and two segmental pediments crowns the building. The architect also designed the buildings for the development called Le Droit Park.

DE15.5 **Washington Loan and Trust Company**

James G. Hill, 1891. 9th and F streets NW

Now a branch of the Riggs National Bank, the Washington and Loan Trust Company is a commanding nine-story Romanesque Revival building located diagonally from the Patent Office Building (see DE15.2). The building's presence marks an abrupt transition on this thoroughfare between the classicism of the cluster of buildings defined by the Patent Office and the General Post Office and the surrounding buildings of Downtown East. The gray rock-faced granite ashlar gives a rich texture to the facade, over an internal frame of steel floor beams and cast-iron columns. Seen on the exterior, the lower two stories form the base of the design, the next four are treated as an elongated arcade, and the next two form a separate unit with flat-arch windows. At the top is a single story of small round-arch windows, the whole crowned by a modest cornice.

After leaving his position with the Supervising Architect's Office, Hill enjoyed a flourishing practice in Washington, designing buildings such as the massive Government Printing Office in the Romanesque Revival style and apartment houses and residences throughout the city.

DE16 **Martin Luther King, Jr., Memorial Library**

1969–1972, Ludwig Mies van der Rohe. 9th and G streets NW

Much of the downtown area of Washington is filled with modern buildings inspired by Mies van der Rohe's work, but the Martin Luther King, Jr., Memorial Library is the only structure in the city actually designed by Mies. The main part of the building is raised on stilts, creating a light and airy ground level enclosed by a cream-colored brick exterior wall; this is placed behind a row of the steel columns similar to those in much of his American work. The upper floors provide large reading and stack areas. The *AIA Journal* described the structure as "unadorned, its beauty being revealed in its quiet and harmonious proportions."[36] The life and career of King are celebrated in a mural that runs along the length of the interior of the main public room on the ground floor.

Like the early twentieth-century Beaux-Arts Carnegie Library it replaced, the King building perfectly expresses the city's desire for home rule and for separation from federal supervision in a civic structure. Its bold modern lines are at variance with many of the city's federal and municipal government buildings. Such buildings stand at the vanguard of the city's drive toward cultural autonomy.

DE17 Greyhound Terminal

1939, William S. Arrasmith. 1110 New York Ave. NW

The Greyhound Bus Terminal is one of the city's preeminent surviving Art Moderne buildings and one of the outstanding Greyhound bus stations in the nation. The architect designed dozens of other Greyhound terminals elsewhere in the country. In form, his buildings are symbols of the speed, efficiency, excitement, and modernity of passenger bus lines.

The building's curved surfaces can be appreciated in their entirety because the building was a freestanding "island unit." Constructed of reinforced concrete, it is faced with Indiana limestone and terracotta on the street frontage. Its tall entrance and clock tower in the center of the building bisect the curved walls of the building. A speeding greyhound dog originally capped the tower as well as the curved walls above the second story. A loading dock and concourse were located at the rear.

Ringing the circular waiting room were ticket offices, shops, and concession stands. In 1989, as part of an effort to preserve the building and construct a harmonious rear addition, sheet-metal cladding added in 1976 was removed, revealing the building's intact form and materials.

DE18 Masonic Temple

1908, Wood, Donn and Deming. 801 13th St. NW

The six-story Masonic Temple is located on a trapezoidal site formed by New York Avenue, H Street, and 13th Street where it is visible from several vantage points. The Masonic Temple provided facilities for large auditoriums, lodge rooms, a library, a banquet hall, and a mystic shrine. The steel-framed trapezoidal building is clad in Indiana limestone and a light gray brick. Large semicircular openings articulate its massive rusticated base. The superstructure is lined with a colonnade flanked with heavily rusticated piers. Above the attic, a balustrade gives scale to the whole.

After the Masonic Order abandoned the building and the Downtown East area became unfashionable, the building became a movie theater. As Downtown East once again became popular, the Temple's Beaux-Arts vocabulary inspired several new buildings nearby. Today, the building houses the National Museum of Women in the Arts.

DE19 Franklin School

1869, Adolph Cluss. 13th and K streets NW

The Franklin School, now an educational administrative center, was the finest of the half-dozen schools initiated in the 1860s by Mayor Richard Wallach, who intended to improve the quality of public education in the capital. The Franklin School reflected German-born Adolph Cluss's knowledge of school building architecture in Europe as well as in the United States. At its completion, the Franklin School was considered unsurpassed in its accommo-

DE18 Masonic Temple

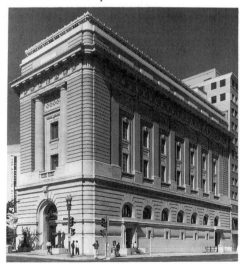

DE19 Franklin School

dation of educational functions and as a model of good taste.

In the Franklin School, Cluss combined elements of Second Empire style with the *Rundbogentsil*, or Round Arch style, which he learned in his native Germany and which he would also apply in his work on the Arts and Industries Building on the Mall (see ML04, p. 92). The school was constructed of red brick and trimmed in stone and cast iron. Octagonal towers flanking the central pavilion served as ventilating shafts. The vertical elements of towers, long windows, and pilaster strips are balanced by bold horizontal strips connecting windows on each floor, heavily articulated corbeled brick at the cornice line, and flat roofs over the end pavilions. A polychromatic slate-covered mansard roof over the broad center, which carries elaborate cast-iron cresting, crowns this rare Victorian survivor on Franklin Square.

DE20 Daon Building

1983, Skidmore, Owings and Merrill. 1300 New York Ave. NW

One of the largest nongovernmental buildings in the city, the Daon Building is one of its earliest Postmodern buildings. Its massive form bends around an awkward corner formed by New York Avenue and H Street. Its twelve stories are divided into a three-story limestone and granite base, a colonnaded midsection of buff precast concrete, and a robust cornice over an attic. Slim infill bands and intersecting "pilasters" of tan glazed brick set off buff concrete window surrounds. A monumental center arch opens to a lobby entrance and leads to an inner atrium faced in white and colored marble. The large inte-

rior court is lined with stepped balconies and a towering waterfall. Today, the building houses the Inter-American Development Bank.

DE21 Carnegie Library

1899–1902, Ackerman and Ross. Mount Vernon Square (intersection of Massachusetts and New York avenues between 7th and 9th streets NW)

Built as the Main Public Library of the District of Columbia, the Carnegie Library is serenely situated at the center of Mount Vernon Square amid winding walks. Like hundreds of other Carnegie libraries across the nation, it was a gift from Andrew Carnegie, who made a cash donation for the library with the stipulation that Congress provide a site. The building's design was obtained through competition, won by the New York firm of Ackerman and Ross, which subsequently designed other Carnegie libraries. Philip Martiny designed the sculptural elements.

The Carnegie Library was one of the earliest public buildings in the District to be designed under the influence of the Chicago World's Columbian Exposition of 1893. Constructed of white Vermont marble over a steel frame, the Carnegie Library was designed in the Beaux-Arts style. Its long, rectangular plan is articulated on the south side with a long, elaborate central section and two lower and plainer flanking wings. The central section contains the main entrance and is made up of an arcade formed of Ionic columns. Richly ornamented pedimented end pavilions are at the ends of the sections. A sculptured attic story contains three panels with inscriptions testifying to the Carnegie gift, the building's function, and the purpose of diffusing knowledge. The building's entrance is reinforced by a paved terrace with curved stone seats on either side. The rear of the building, the north side, reveals long, narrow window openings that indicate the location of the library book stacks. On the interior, a fine entrance hall greeted library patrons, while stairways on either side of the entrance led to the second floor and galleries. The wings were devoted to reading rooms.

The building served as the city's central library until 1972, when it was superseded by the Martin Luther King, Jr., Memorial Library on G Street. Today it is a facility of the

University of the District of Columbia. While its urban context has become dense and much commercialized, the Carnegie Library still serves as a reminder of the civic-mindedness of public architecture at the turn of the century.

DE22 **FBI Building**

1967–1972, C. F. Murphy. Pennsylvania Ave. between 9th and 10th streets NW

The FBI Building was one of the first major governmental buildings to rise along Pennsylvania Avenue as part of the revitalization of that thoroughfare. C. F. Murphy was the official designer, but the director of the agency, J. Edgar Hoover, influenced many of the building's particulars.

Organized around a courtyard that opens visually to Pennsylvania Avenue, the FBI Building rises eleven stories above grade and extends three below. The upper floors appear to be placed on stilts, which were intended to form an open arcade with shops and restaurants. Hoover vetoed the commercial facilities in the interest of security for the agency's employees, but the loss of the open arcade deadened the building and its surroundings. The 75-foot setback from the avenue allowed for rows of shade trees. The buff-colored precast window frames are set into cast-in-place corner piers that contain the building's services. The materials and window designs and the articulation of stories in groups recalls slightly earlier buildings such as Marcel Breuer's Department of Housing and Urban Development Building (see SW10, p. 239) in the Southwest Quadrant of the city and Boston's city hall, designed by Kallmann, McKinnell and Knowles.

As the FBI building neared completion, some critics viewed it as refreshingly modern when compared with the classically inspired Rayburn House Office Building and the Federal Triangle buildings. Others have justly criticized it as being out of step with its immediate environment.

DE23 **Office Building**

1980–1987, Hartman-Cox. 1001 Pennsylvania Ave. NW

This office building exhibits the best of new construction along the nation's ceremonial thoroughfare. The developers, Cadillac-Fairview, with the architects, Hartman-Cox, were challenged by the location to produce a new building that would be in keeping with the Federal Triangle across the avenue, the Evening Star Building (see DE24) to the west, and the FBI Building (see DE22) to the east, while at the same time retaining several small brick facades at the northwest corner of the building.

The building is sheathed in limestone and brick. The Pennsylvania Avenue facade features projecting one-bay pilasters punched with windows and deeply recessed sections four bays wide. Vertically, the building is divided into a base, shaft, and capital, echoing the typical American office building of the early twentieth century. The rear of the building, however, steps down in sections to meet the old brick facades. Although the retention of these facades can be criticized as mere tokens to preservation, as venerable fragments they lend variety to the design of the building. A distinctive interior feature is the seven-story octagonal atrium that connects with each of the entrances.

DE24 **Evening Star Building**

1908, Marsh and Peter. 11th St. and Pennsylvania Ave. NW

The Evening Star Building housed the offices of the former daily newspaper. Its convenient location between the White House and the Capitol placed it in the center of the news beat.

Ornamented with outbursts of decorative detail, it is one of the most exuberant buildings on Pennsylvania Avenue, thereby holding its own among more recent large office buildings. Newspaper buildings often used

DE24 Evening Star Building

M. Pei and Partners to design this large, rose and gray granite structure embellished with geometric motifs of a white square within a square below each window. Each of the entrances is indicated by a sharp vertical recess rising the full height of the facade. The whole is topped with an ornamental balustrade. An arcade at the ground floor level shelters pedestrians as well as the entrance to the retail shops. The huge atrium is created by a structural steel frame.

Columbia Square represents the minimalist modern forms closely identified with the Pei firm's work elsewhere, here in a building occupying an entire half block. With its size and repetitive design, the building is impressive rather than endearing.

attention-getting designs to attract free publicity. Its ornamentation is all the more pronounced given the tight constraints of its horizontal and vertical edges. The traditional demarcation between base, shaft, and capital is accentuated with round-arch windows, rustication, balcony treatments, heavy window frames, and prominent window pediments. A balustrade crowns the building. The heavy corner quoins appear to hold in the energetic elements.

DE25 Columbia Square

1985–1987, Henry N. Cobb of I. M. Pei and Partners. 555 13th St. NW

Columbia Square is a harbinger of things to come in Downtown East. It is a Texas-sized building, commissioned by Texan developer Gerald D. Hines. A self-styled "collector of buildings," Hines hired Henry N. Cobb of I.

DE26 Sun Building

1887, Alfred B. Mullett. 1317 F St. NW

Designed for the publisher of the *Baltimore Sun*, the nine-story Sun Building is one of the nation's oldest surviving skyscrapers, defined by its curtain walls, its internal metal structural frame, and the interior elevator. The soaring, three-bay exterior is divided into three major sections: a two-story triple-arch base, a five-story shaft of two tiers of projecting bay windows, and a crowning section marked by paired windows. The Sun Building also is of historic interest for its association with Alfred B. Mullett's postgovernment career, during which he contributed substantially to the early development of metal frame construction.

DE27 Bond Building

1901, George S. Cooper. 14th St. and New York Ave. NW

The seven-story Bond Building has been described as a "hectic wedding cake of classical revival motifs."[37] Its location at the prominent corner of 14th St. and New York Avenue is accented by its rounded corner, which is decorated with a range of rectangular and oval windows. From its heavily rusticated, two-story base, the three-story shaft is expressed with round-arch openings and occasional balconies. The two-story capital has one story with flat-arch windows and one with round arches. Recently, Shalom Baranes added four new upper stories of paired columns, ribbon windows, and a classical colonnade.

DE28 Garfinckel's Department Store

1929–1931, Starrett and Van Vleck. 14th and F streets NW

When the new Garfinckel's Department Store opened in the late 1920s at 14th and F streets, it had already garnered a reputation for quality and elegance at its earlier location, farther east on F Street. Its new store retained these qualities. As the foremost department store designer of the day, Starrett and Van Vleck of New York City based its design for Garfinckel's on its earlier successes such as Lord and Taylor, Abercrombie and Fitch, and Saks Fifth Avenue in the firm's home city. These buildings and the new Garfinckel's were constructed of smooth limestone and trimmed in classical detailing. The classical proportions and motifs were simplified and abstracted to bring them up to date.

Above the base with its large display windows, the third to the seventh floors were designed with a smooth stone surface and small windows, all crowned with an architrave. The eighth and ninth floors are set back from the front plane of the structure.

DE29 National Place

1978–1982, Frank Schlesinger. 14th St. and Pennsylvania Ave. NW

National Place is a large mixed-use complex that zigzags around the buildings of the National Press, the National Theater, and the National League of Cities. It connects 14th St. and Pennsylvania Avenue with 13th and F streets. Incorporating the Marriott Hotel and a shopping atrium, National Place is better appreciated from the interior, where a grand hotel lobby connects to ballroom levels and shopping arcades. Its bland brown brick exterior serves as a backdrop for the more exuberant Willard Hotel.

DE30 National League of Cities Building

1982, Frank Schlesinger. 1301 Pennsylvania Ave. NW

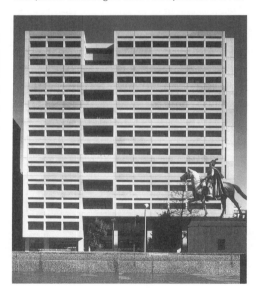

Named for its most prominent tenant, this twelve-story building was designed in concert with National Place. Its face of slightly tinted glass recedes behind precast concrete panels and sun screens. The south facade presents

a formal aspect to Pennsylvania Avenue, with a wide vertical niche admitting light to windows on the full height of the atrium adjacent to the elevator. On the more exuberant 13th Street facade, notches are carved out and setbacks create an interesting checkerboard effect. The modulation of the east side creates light wells for the offices and offers street views.

DE31 **Western Plaza**

1981, Venturi, Rauch and Scott Brown. Pennsylvania Ave. between 13th and 14th streets NW

The current appearance of Western Plaza is a much pared down version of the original concept. Its avant-garde architects conceived a flat concrete park bearing the outlines of the L'Enfant plan reproduced in marble and granite, with a grassy strip indicating the Mall. M. Paul Friedberg was named as an associate, as was sculptor Richard Serra, whose pair of 86-foot-high pylons and miniatures of the White House and the Capitol were to provide the third dimension to the composition. As it turned out, only the Venturi, Rauch and Scott Brown section survived. (Friedberg was commissioned to design the adjacent Pershing Park.) At one end of the park, planters surround a statue of Pulaski, while at the other end, a sheet of dark water in a reflecting pool pours over a granite curve. Quotations about the capital city dot the composition. Western Plaza remains a little bleak because of the partial realization of a more complex vision.

DE32 **Willard Hotel**

1900–1901, Henry Janeway Hardenbergh. 14th St. and Pennsylvania Ave. NW

The Willard Hotel is Washington's answer to New York City's Plaza Hotel and is referred to as the "Grande Dame of the Belle Epoque." Its recent restoration enabled it to regain its prominent position among Washington hostelries despite its abandonment for nearly sixteen years.

The Willard's steel frame is covered with a rusticated limestone base and a shaft of light-colored brick and terracotta, channeled to resemble stone masonry below. Its eleven stories, capped by a single story under a large convex mansard roof, are placed on a sloping site with ten stories exposed on F Street. The three-story Doric entrance portico is ornamented with balustrade and urn decoration. Pediments, iron balconies, large ornamental consoles, and ten large decorative dormers animate the exterior. The turret at the southeast corner provides a transition from 14th Street to Pennsylvania Avenue. The interior is notable for its lavish lobby, public rooms, promenade at the first-floor "Peacock Alley," and a ballroom at the twelfth floor.

Along with the recent restoration, Hardy Holzman Pfeiffer of New York City designed a new addition to the west. Rather than being a replication, it evokes the original, to which it defers by stepping its four pavilionlike sections around a courtyard, separated from the older building with a breathing space. Hardy

Holzman Pfeiffer left the project before its execution; Vlastimil Koubek executed their concept.

DE33 Hotel Washington

1917–1918, Carrère and Hastings. 15th St. and Pennsylvania Ave. NW

DE35.1 National Savings and Trust Company

The nine-story Hotel Washington, modified from an Italian Renaissance model, is one of a number of buildings by Carrère and Hastings in the capital city, including the Russell Senate Office Building and the Cannon House Office Building (see CH02, CH03, p. 135). The Hotel Washington acquires a certain dignity through such decorative elements as a smooth rusticated stone veneer that covers the steel frame below the third story. In the upper stories, Italian artists enlivened the dark brown brick with fine sgraffito decoration in the spandrels and around the windows. The rooftop garden overlooks the White House and the Executive Group.

DE34 Metropolitan Square

1986, Skidmore, Owings and Merrill. 15th and F streets NW

Metropolitan Square incorporates three landmarks and weaves the Garfinckel's Department Store building and several others into a complex covering an entire block. The project grew out of an eleventh-hour confrontation between the developer and the historic preservation community. The surviving buildings on the block, the Metropolitan Bank Building and the Keith-Albee Theater were preserved as facades in front of a new twelve-

story structure because review bodies preferred a continuous wall of Beaux-Arts facades along 15th Street. The third landmark, the interior of Old Ebbitt Grill, was located behind the Keith-Albee triple-arch entry arcade.

DE35 15th Street Historic District

1900–1930. 15th St. between Pennsylvania Ave. and I St. NW

The 15th Street Historic District is a three-block area based upon the Treasury Department building and inspired by the City Beautiful movement. By the early twentieth century, the former residential area had yielded to commercial buildings, especially the banks on 15th Street designed in the Beaux-Arts Classical style. Those on the north side of Pennsylvania Avenue facing the Treasury Building were especially important. As financial institutions clustered together and supporting office structures filled in the interstices, the area took on the character of a financial district.

Among the area's anchors are the large red brick National Savings and Trust Company (DE35.1), designed by James Windrim in 1888, located at the northeast corner of New York Avenue and 15th Street. Two classical-styled

DE35.3 American Security and Trust Company

DE35.5 Southern Building

bank buildings at the northwest corner of 15th Street and Pennsylvania Avenue, the Riggs National Bank (DE35.2) and the American Security and Trust Company (DE35.3), were designed by York and Sawyer. The Union Trust Building (DE35.4) with its Corinthian columns at 1500 H Street NW was a work of Wood, Donn and Deming. Daniel Burnham's firm designed the Southern Building (DE35.5) at 1425 H Street in 1910, a triumphant Beaux-Arts office building bearing some of the district's most elaborate terracotta detail. The Woodward Building (DE35.6) at 1426 H Street, designed by the Washington firm of Harding and Upman in 1911, is another example using terracotta on brick. In their common function, bulk, cornice line, and vintage,

these buildings represent the private sector's response to the extension of the McMillan Plan's Executive Group that surrounded the White House.

DE36 Lafayette Building

1941, A. R. Clas. 811 Vermont Ave. NW

The eleven-story Lafayette Building is one of the few privately developed office buildings constructed in the city during the Second World War. It was intended to house expanding government agencies bloated by the demands of wartime Washington. Clas designed the building in cooperation with Holabird and Root of Chicago. It was admired for its simplicity and direct, businesslike character. The building facade is divided into three major portions: a two-story base, a shaft rising from the third story to the tenth, and a setback eleventh story serving as the capital. The walls are of brick clad in limestone. At the base of the building, the narrow windows that are two stories tall suggest a colonnade. The nearly decoration-free structure was enlivened with a few limestone window frames.

DE37 University Club

1911, George Oakley Totten, Jr. 900 15th St. NW

The University Club occupied this diminutive five-story Renaissance Revival building. Its small classic form contrasts with the modern commercial behemoths that today ring Mc-

Pherson Square. Totten, a graduate of the Ecole des Beaux-Arts, used a pronounced cornice and a slight change in color to demarcate sharply the first two stories from the top three. At the second floor, large round-arch windows indicate the principal public and entertainment floors. When the University Club moved to the more commodious Racquet Club building on 16th Street, the interior was used as office space. Today, it houses the United Mine Workers Union.

DE38 Washington Post Building

1951, Albert Kahn, Associated Architects and Engineers, Inc. 1150 15th St. NW

Although designed and executed by the firm nearly a decade after Kahn's death, the Washington Post Building bears the unmistakable stamp of his classic industrial designs for the automobile industry in Detroit. Its facade is composed of ribbons of windows and limestone, with a decorative aluminum canopy and sign at the entrance. The building was designed to house the newspaper plant and offices in a single structure shoehorned into a tight downtown site. The huge presses occupied the two-story main floor, while on the second story were offices and a visitor's balcony. The third floor provided space for the mail room, the fourth story for composing and engraving departments, and the three top stories for offices. At its completion, the building attracted national attention in architectural journals because its facilities were stacked rather than "strung out in assembly-line fashion," continuing an innovation in publishing seen earlier in Raymond Hood's Daily News and McGraw-Hill buildings in New York.

DE39 Capital Hilton Hotel

1943, Holabird and Root; A. R. Clas. 16th and K streets NW

Constructed as the Hotel Statler in 1943, the Capital Hilton Hotel was rushed to completion in order to provide temporary housing for businessmen who had difficulty finding accommodations during the Second World War. Even with the critical shortage of building materials, the hotel project received permission to proceed.

The nine-story hotel occupies a half block facing 16th Street between K and L streets. The plan, a triple H, has three light courts that admit natural light to the hotel rooms. The light courts provided a strong rhythm of solids and voids in the 16th Street facade. The hotel's innovations included the partly covered motor drive from K to L streets to shelter arriving guests as they alight and guest rooms designed to be living rooms during the day and bedrooms by night. Architect John Root brought this multipurpose idea from observations of similar hotel rooms in Europe. At the time of its completion, it was the largest air-conditioned hotel in the world. Its massive banquet facilities were precursors of such facilities in postwar hotels.

Foggy Bottom (FB)

Antoinette J. Lee

FOGGY BOTTOM'S ORIGINS CAN BE TRACED TO 1765, WHEN Jacob Funk, a German immigrant, purchased a 130-acre tract in the area and laid out the town of Hamburgh. Also known as Funkstown, it was one of several ports located along the Potomac River, of which Georgetown and Alexandria were the most successful. Little came of the Hamburgh settlement; however, its distinctive German flavor lingered into the early twentieth century in churches, housing, and industry.

During the nineteenth century, topography influenced Foggy Bottom's urban form considerably: 23rd Street separated the high ground of an affluent, residential area inhabited by the military, diplomatic, and scientific elite from low ground and the modest dwellings of workers who labored in nearby glassworks, breweries, gasworks, and a cement company. Here, the entrance to the polluted and ill-constructed City Canal and the marshy lands along the Potomac River gave rise to the name "Foggy Bottom," where it was said that the incessant, nightly croaking of frogs furnished material for ghost stories.

After the reclamation of the Potomac flats and the filling of the canal during the 1870s, large federal, semipublic, institutional, and association buildings were built in Foggy Bottom. The convenient location, south of Pennsylvania Avenue between the White House and Georgetown, made Foggy Bottom an appropriate site for such buildings. The march of monumental buildings can be followed starting at 17th Street and New York Avenue, continuing south along 17th Street, then west along Constitution Avenue, and along the riverfront ending at Rock Creek Park. Federal government buildings, located in an area referred to as the Northwest Rectangle in order to balance the Federal Triangle on the other side of the Ellipse, were sited on the eastern end of Foggy Bottom. The complexes for the Interior and State departments are the largest of these structures.

204

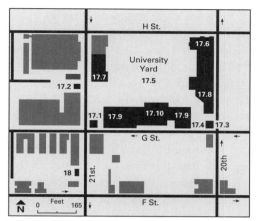

George Washington University

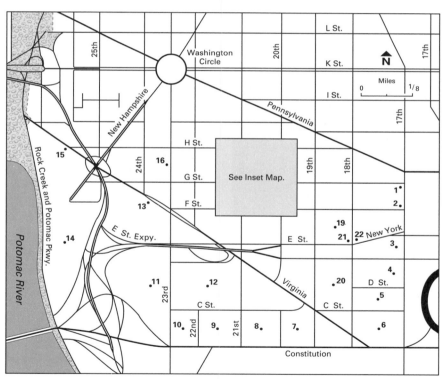

Foggy Bottom

Another trailblazer was George Washington University, which occupied buildings at 20th and G streets NW in 1912 and later acquired major landholdings in the vicinity. After World War II, the World Bank and the International Monetary Fund built large structures here for their expanding staffs.

Despite the influx of such organizational buildings in the 1940s and 1950s, many planners perceived decay and designated the area for a vast urban renewal effort. By the time the renewal plan was implemented in the form of Columbia Plaza in the 1960s, the character of the area had changed: Foggy Bottom had become fashionable. The construction of the luxurious Watergate complex of apartments, offices, hotel, and shopping center epitomized the new affluence.

Remnants of the nineteenth century survive in a few churches and blocks of modest town houses in the small Foggy Bottom Historic District and in the old Naval Observatory. Some of the city's best-known buildings can also be found here, among them the Kennedy Center, the Corcoran Gallery of Art, and the building that houses the Organization of American States.

FB01 **Federal Home Loan Bank Board**

1977, Max O. Urbahn Associates. 17th and G streets NW

In the mid-1970's, the National Endowment for the Arts called for the creation of lively federal government buildings; this mix of office, commercial, and recreational use, a small-scale version of New York City's Rockefeller Center, was the response. The L-shaped building of offices for the FHLBB over shops encircles a reflecting pool/skating rink. The mid-nineteenth-century Winder Building forms the south side of the complex. Between them, an open courtyard, designed by Sasaki Associates, leads to Liberty Plaza and the pool and makes possible a dialogue between the two buildings. The curved corner of the new building at the first floor invites the pedestrian, and covered arcades around the pool are appropriate for serving refreshments

during warm weather. The gray, reinforced concrete structure was skillfully designed to offer windows of varying widths, patterns of solids and voids, and a gradual stepping up of the building as it extends away from 17th Street. In building elements and color, it echoes the Second Empire Old Executive Office Building across the street. Some of the building's charm lies in the fact that it is lower than many surrounding office structures, a clear acknowledgment of its relationship to the Winder Building. The walkways are carefully placed to encourage pedestrian traffic through the complex.

The success of the project nearly permits one to forgive the General Services Administration for the destruction of a lovely early twentieth-century Riggs Bank on the site. The only remnants of that building are its gargoyles, now fixed in place in the waterfall at the lower level of the complex.

FB02 **Winder Building**

1848, unknown. 17th and G streets NW

A five-story brick structure coated with smooth plaster, the floors of the Winder Building were constructed of cast-iron beams with segmental brick vaults struck between them. This fireproof technique was introduced to Washington by James Renwick in part of the Smithsonian Building. Although privately financed as a speculative venture of William H. Winder and a modest building by com-

FB02 Winder Building

parison, the Winder Building is nevertheless of great historical importance because it was the first structure in the city to employ this new method throughout. The federal government purchased it for the War Department four years after its completion.

The just-restored look dates from the completion of the Federal Home Loan Bank Board building to the north and includes a modern brick retaining wall matching the brick of Liberty Plaza, which ties the Winder Building to the larger complex.

FB03 Corcoran Gallery of Art

1897, Ernest Flagg. 1915, Waddy B. Wood. 1928, west wing, Charles Adams Platt. 17th St. and New York Ave. NW

When the Corcoran Gallery of Art outgrew its Second Empire structure at the northeast corner of 17th Street and Pennsylvania Ave-

FB03 Corcoran Gallery of Art

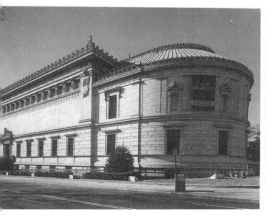

nue, the museum elected to move to a larger site, leaving behind the handsome building designed by James Renwick and erected in 1859–1861 (see WH15, p. 000). The new building, however, proved its equal aesthetically. Located three blocks south of Renwick's building, it foreshadowed the development of that area as the western boundary of the monumental frame for the Ellipse.

To entice visitors, the structure relies on proximity to the sidewalk and an elaborate Greek-inspired doorway flanked by reclining lions. The severity of the facade bespeaks the serious study of art. Three horizontal bands—a pink granite foundation, a smooth marble wall punctuated by fortified windows, and an elaborate Greek detailed entablature—insulate the interior. Square openings in the frieze, allowing for air circulation across the galleries in warm weather, provide a connection between street bustle and the sequestered interior. The copper roof contributes a sense of lightness to the heavy building.

As the visitor enters and climbs the lobby steps, the closed and protected structure opens into a large, airy enclosed court, originally Statuary Hall, supported by limestone Doric columns. Ahead is the main stairway, 16 feet wide, with pedestals on either side for sculpture. The stairway invites the visitor to the second floor, where picture galleries open from the atrium's encircling balconies.

The Corcoran building program also called for accommodations for the Corcoran School of Art, so a separate entrance staircase leads to the dramatic Hemicycle, which connects the gallery and the school and houses an auditorium and exhibition space. Designed by Flagg as a double-height room, the Hemicycle's interior was redesigned by Washington architect Waddy B. Wood as a two-story space in 1915. The addition of the Clark Collection to the Corcoran's holdings in 1928 necessitated an addition, the west wing designed by Charles Platt.

FB04 American Red Cross National Headquarters

1915–1917, Trowbridge and Livingston. 17th and D streets NW

A memorial to Civil War service primarily, the Red Cross Headquarters is unique in its attempt at symbolic reconciliation by recognizing the sacrifices of both the North and the South. In 1912, the State of New York

FB04 American Red Cross
National Headquarters

FB05 Daughters of the American
Revolution Continental Memorial
Hall

took up the idea of a monument in Washington to honor the women who tended the sick and wounded during the war. Officials persuaded Congress to appropriate funds and provide the site with the understanding that substantial private funds would also be raised. Trowbridge and Livingston of New York were selected as architects.

The white marble Classical Revival building gains appeal from its siting well away from the street, its gentle terraces, and long circular drive. A central projecting portico of four Corinthian columns rises two stories and supports a triangular pediment. Four identical engaged columns are placed on each side of the building. The building's third story is located discreetly behind a balustrade that encircles it.

Within the building, which evokes a solemn, respectful mood, the story of the memorial is developed. A marble tablet above the main stairway cites the contributions of women on each side of the conflict. Hiram

Powers designed busts of Faith, Hope, and Charity that are located on the stair landing. On the second floor in the Neoclassical/Federal Revival assembly room, a door contains three glass panels designed by Louis C. Tiffany showing the themes of wounded warriors; patron saint of the sick, Saint Filomena; and Truth with red roses.

In 1930 and 1932, two additions were built. The north addition lined with Ionic columns was conceived as a memorial to the women of World War I. The west addition is an office annex. The buildings frame a rectangular park, a welcome green space amid the area's monumental buildings.

FB05 Daughters of the American Revolution Continental Memorial Hall

1910, Edward Pearce Casey. 1923, Marsh and Peter. 1929, John Russell Pope. 1776 D St. NW

Designed in what the Daughters of the American Revolution termed the colonial style "modified only so far as will be necessary to apply modern improvements with classical lines,"[38] the white marble building was conceived as a monument to the founders of the republic, as an inspiration for patriotic sentiment, and as a headquarters for the organization. Designs were solicited twice for the building, but no single design was accepted. Rather, Edward Pearce Casey of New York presented an amalgamated plan calling for a 2,000-seat auditorium, a library, and a memorial room, which together provided a reception hall for 5,000 people. Thirty-three modestly sized period rooms, each sponsored by a state chapter of the organization, form the building's perimeter. The second floor contains offices, and the third floor, just visible behind the roof balustrade, houses a great dining hall. The auditorium, which serves as a genealogy and local history library, still exhibits its original grand scale and detailing.

The exterior of the hall presents three distinct facades. In the east, a great Ionic portico with tripled columns at the corners leads to a triple colonial doorway adorned with fanlights and swags. To the south, a semicircular portico projects 30 feet. Thirteen memorial columns and pilasters symbolizing the original states form a semicircle beneath a massive roof. From this portico, steps lead in to the memorial room or out to a grassy terrace. To the north, a long portico 10 feet deep is created by a row of seven Ionic columns.

When membership outgrew the building after two decades, the local firm of Marsh and Peter designed the administration building facing D Street, completed in 1923. In 1929, John Russell Pope contributed the adjoining classical style Constitution Hall, constructed of Alabama limestone; its auditorium seats 4,000. Notable are the Ionic portico and the pediment punctuated by a sculpted American eagle above the entrance.

FB06 Organization of American States Building (Pan American Union, International Union of the American Republics)

1908–1910, Albert Kelsey and Paul Philippe Cret. 1948, Harbeson, Hough, Livingston, and Larson. 17th St. and Constitution Ave. NW

The most exotic of all the monumental buildings in Washington's central core is Albert Kelsey and Paul Philippe Cret's Organization of American States Building. The architects drew from traditions of both North and South America in providing a headquarters for the organization, which promotes cooperation among Central and South American countries and the United States.

The triple-arched entrance of the principal facade on 17th Street forms an arcade flanked by huge pylons and two-story pavilions. One of two sculptural groups, each before a pylon, illustrates North America with a female figure and child. It was executed by Gutzon Borglum. On the south, a similar group, by Isidor Konti, symbolizes South America. Above each statue, bas-relief panels illustrate, respectively, George Washington, Simón Bolí-

FB06 Organization of American States Building

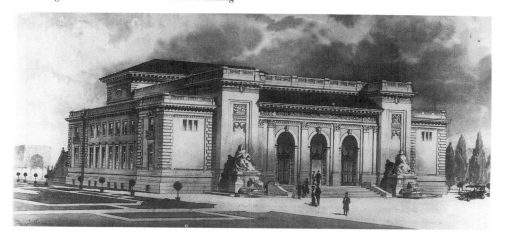

var, and José de San Martín. At the cornice lines of the pylons are an eagle, symbol of America, and a condor, associated with the Andes. Mayan motifs line the base of the pilasters and the top of the parapet and adorn two copper lamps at the entrance. A red tile roof and a classical balustrade crown the building.

The interior similarly incorporates cultural details drawn from Aztec, Incan, Mayan, and European art, all set in the context of spacious halls, patios, exhibition rooms, and the Hall of the Americas. The luxuriousness of the decorative details increases on approaching the interior tropical courtyard.

The more distinctively South American Annex, also designed by Kelsey and Cret, resembles a Spanish villa. Decorative elements drawn directly from Mexican models are seen in the tilework of the pool that is in the garden connecting the main building and the annex. Terracotta is also seen in large urns, the walls of the loggia, and in the building's polychromatic cornice and shield. The marble-clad administration building, located between 18th and 19th streets, was the last structure completed in this group. Constructed in 1948 after designs by Harbeson, Hough, Livingston, and Larson, it has a slightly bowed wall to emphasize the entrance and represents the firm's long association with classicism.

FB07 Interior South

1933, Jules Henri de Sibour. Constitution Ave. between 19th and 20th streets NW

This simple, four-story, white marble building is set in a terraced lawn thickly planted with trees and surrounded at the base by a balustrade. Aluminum window spandrels, each separated by fluted pilasters, and the gray tile roof provide a cool, restrained effect to the composition. The building originally housed Public Health Service offices and library.

FB08 Federal Reserve Board Building

1937, Paul Philippe Cret. Constitution Ave. between 20th and 21st streets NW

The last building to be constructed along Constitution Avenue west of 17th Street, the Federal Reserve Board is not traditionally classical because nearly all classical ornament

has been omitted from the exterior; yet, its symmetrical arrangement, white marble facade, scale, and placement on a large block are in keeping with its surroundings.

The form of the Federal Reserve Board Building was dictated in part by the building's supervisors. A Reserve Board representative, Adolph C. Miller, and Fine Arts Commission Chairman Charles Moore agreed that the building should rely on "conception, proportion, scale and purity of line" rather than "purely decorative or monumental features." The external appearance was so progressive that the *AIA Journal* reported, "This would appear to indicate that the reign of the column and pediment is nearing its close, even in Washington."[39]

After soliciting designs from ten nationally recognized architects, a jury unanimously selected Paul Philippe Cret of Philadelphia, a leading classicist. Cret's design demonstrates a clear development from his Beaux-Arts Organization of American States Building of 1908 to one in harmony with modernism. The dominating central portico is defined by four square pilasters supporting a flat cornice. An eagle of white marble sculpted by Sidney Waugh holds a central position on the cornice. The stark white marble sheathing of the H-shaped building contrasts with the bronze windows and polished granite spandrels with mounted bronze plaques. The approach features a series of terraces and star-studded steps flanked by formal gardens. The courts located on the east and west sides of the building are also landscaped according to Cret's designs.

A commanding central stairhall with wrought-iron railings executed by Samuel Yellin unites the four arms of the buildings. The rooms' spare Greek motifs on smooth walls echo the exterior and its chaste detailing.

FB09 National Academy of Sciences

1924, Bertram Grosvenor Goodhue. 1962–1970, Wallace K. Harrison. 21st St. and Constitution Ave. NW

An anticlassicist by inclination, Bertram Goodhue had hoped the building site for the Academy of Sciences would be located farther from the monumental core and so permit a freer design style. When it was not, he even suggested that another architect be hired. He

FB09 National Academy of Sciences

nonetheless produced a building of classical massing, but without columns or pediments, a fitting "frame" for the Lincoln Memorial 1,000 feet to the south.

The facade's warm-toned, white, New York Dover marble was cut in many different sizes and laid in recessed courses to form a battered wall. It has now mellowed to pale gold. Bronze, used in the window grilles and doors, and the copper of the roof and cresting provide the other dominant colors. A frequent collaborator with Goodhue, Lee Lawrie executed the bronze sliding doors with eight panels in low relief illustrating major figures in science. The window panels, also by Lawrie, represent scientific progress from the Greeks to the twentieth century.

The pale gold and green color scheme of the exterior continues into the foyer and beamed ceiling of the lobby. In the Great Hall a vaulted and domed roof is lined with profusely colored tiles depicting emblematic figures and bearing inscriptions related to science, the work of Hildreth Meière. The Great Hall represents Goodhue's aspirations for the building as a "temple of science."

Goodhue died soon after the dedication of the southern portion facing Constitution Avenue. From 1962 to 1970, the west and east wings and a new auditorium were added. Designed by Wallace K. Harrison, once a draftsman in Goodhue's office, the compatible wings are of the same marble with bronze window trim as the original block. The modern auditorium, also by Harrison, is in the form of a shell with long, narrow, diamond-shaped projections arranged in cycloid curves,

providing maximum sound distribution and an appearance that the general public sees as futuristic. The red, white, and gray color scheme was also considered unusual and up-to-date.

FB10 American Pharmaceutical Association Building

1933, John Russell Pope. Constitution Ave. between 22nd and 23rd streets NW

The American Pharmaceutical Association Building perches at the summit of a long sloping lawn, a position meant to foster public admiration of the achievements of this profession. Architect John Russell Pope's white Vermont marble building has a plain, windowless central projecting pavilion with four pilasters at the center. This entrance is embellished with allegorical bas-reliefs executed by Ulysses Ricci to portray the progress of pharmacy, as well as Light and Hope. The bronze entrance door is topped by a circular grilled transom and is flanked by bronze lamps.

An attic parapet heightens the effect of the building. On either side are two recessed bays. A balustraded terrace surrounds the entire composition.

While the project was a relatively modest one for Pope, who was also hired to design the National Archives, DAR Continental Memorial Hall, the Mellon Gallery of Art, and the Jefferson Memorial, it attracted favorable response even from modernists, largely for its compatibility with the Lincoln Memorial.

FB11 Old Naval Observatory

1843–1930s, several architects. 23rd and C streets NW

A steep rock formation at the conjunction of Tiber Creek and the Potomac River, the former site of Marine Corps headquarters, became the site of the Naval Observatory in 1843. As the city developed thereafter, conditions for astronomical observations were compromised, and in 1893, the observatory moved to higher ground on Massachusetts Avenue. The site and buildings then were adapted for the Naval Medical Center, and eventually for the Naval Medical Command.

The hillside is dotted with yellow and red brick and limestone buildings dating from 1843 to the 1930s in a landscaped setting of shrubs and oaks. The centerpiece is a two-story Italianate style building constructed of creamy yellow brick with a wooden dome sheathed with copper, known as Building Two. During the years that it served as the Naval Observatory, the dome of the building revolved on six-pound cannonballs set in a grooved cast-iron rail; within, a 9.6-inch German telescope rested on a stone and brick pier designed to lessen vibration. Ornate wrought-iron railings and Doric pilasters decorate the front and rear facades. From the top of the hill, spectacular views are afforded of monumental Washington, the Potomac River, and the Arlington, Virginia, skyline.

FB12 State Department

1941, Gilbert Stanley Underwood and William Dewey Foster. 1958, Graham, Anderson, Probst, and White, with A. R. Clas, associate architect. 23 and C streets NW

The first of two major sections, the block facing 21st Street was built after designs by Underwood and Foster for the War Department on the eve of World War II. Impatient with the piecemeal approach to building, the War Department decided to construct the huge Pentagon across the Potomac River, and the State Department then acquired the building.

The 1941 block, clad in rough limestone and enlivened by polished granite in the spandrels between the metal casement windows, exhibits classical massing and proportions but expresses its function as a modern office building. A large portico of four stark piers rising four stories above a two-story base marks the entrance on 21st Street. Six-story wings flank the entrance pavilion. Simple casement windows on the first and second stories are placed on the same plane as the walls. On the wings, the windows from the third to the sixth stories are recessed, offering interplay of light and shadow. Interest in the recessed windows is further heightened by the extension of each casement's center pane from the window line for a three-dimensional effect, and by the dark pink polished granite in the spandrels between floors. The original design called for sculptural groups to accent the main elevation, but the only portions that were executed are five square medallions in the frieze.

In the mid-1950s, the State Department extension expanded the complex to the west and south, with entrances on C, 23rd, and E streets. This smooth-limestone-sheathed structure is constructed in the modern style of the 1950s and is evenly punctuated with two-pane casement windows.

FB13 Columbia Plaza

1963, Keyes, Lethbridge & Condon. 23rd St. and Virginia Ave. NW

Columbia Plaza is the only executed part of what was planned as two extensive urban renewal development areas for Foggy Bottom. Since the 1940s, planners had deemed the area ripe for a massive reconstruction effort similar to the plan implemented in the District's Southwest Quadrant. The project was scaled back gradually to a single, albeit large, block: a "packaged living" composition, with a hotel, apartments, commercial plaza, and underground parking. The plan called for four groups of high-rise apartments and one hotel arranged around a shopping center and a low-rise serpentine building containing

FB14 Kennedy Center for the Performing Arts

apartments and duplex town houses following the line of the freeway to the rear. The architects likened the shopping area to a "town square," with retail shops at the perimeter. The entrance to the shops from the street was through an arcade, a device intended to differentiate the plaza from the street.

Finally, an office block replaced the hotel, and the supposed town center is usually devoid of pedestrian traffic, for few people chose to live, work, and shop within a single block.

FB14 Kennedy Center for the Performing Arts

1971, Edward Durell Stone. 2700 F St. NW

One of Edward Durell Stone's last major works, the Kennedy Center represents an enlarged version of a form he developed to great acclaim in the U.S. Embassy in New Delhi—a low-slung box with a surrounding single row of thin columns supporting an overhanging roof. In New Delhi, metal filigree grilles softened the building's severe geometry. The Kennedy Center program called for three major auditoriums, greatly magnifying the box, and the building's size then outweighed the relief provided by the narrow, bronze-painted exterior columns.

For many years, the DAR Constitution Hall (see FB05) and Lisner Auditorium at George Washington University (see FB17.10) had been the only sizeable auditoriums available for performing arts groups in the city. After World War II, plans for a national cultural center were made by a congressionally appointed committee. Prospective sites included the Southwest Renewal Area and Foggy Bottom.

By 1960, Stone had proposed plans for a curvilinear structure along the Potomac River north of Memorial Bridge to include three major theaters and a prominent overlook adjacent to the river; it was later altered. Commenting on his approach, Stone once said, "In considering the general building type, I would say that Washington is primarily a city of white buildings in a park-like setting. I would see no reason for departing from that." After the death of President Kennedy in 1963, Congress decided to build the center as a memorial.

Critics condemned the building, though general public reaction to this modern rendition of a classic Washington monument has been enthusiastic. Its larger-than-life hallways, thickly carpeted in red, convey the sensation of a grand and important place. Moreover, the building fulfilled its purpose: to draw performing artists of national and international stature to the city.

FB15 Watergate

1963–1967, Luigi Moretti; Milton Fischer, associate architect. Virginia Ave. between 24th and 27th streets NW

The first privately financed architectural extravaganza built on the Potomac River shore, Watergate was named for the modest band shell and restaurant that once stood there. The departure of the gasworks, which had been central to defining the industrial char-

FB15 Watergate

acter of the Foggy Bottom lowlands, made available the 10-acre site. The Società Generale Immobiliare of Rome, an Italian investment corporation, underwrote the project. Italian architect Luigi Moretti expressed interest in deviating from traditional Washington building types, and he designed five curvilinear buildings that included apartments, a hotel, and office buildings. All are placed in a landscape of gardens and a below-street-level shopping center. Horizontal ribbon windows reinforce the curves, as do balconies with toothlike cladding.

Critics decried the complex as "great curvaceous hulks." The complex, which established a new standard for height and bulk in a formerly low-density, low-rise area, remains one of Washington's most distinctive apartment house designs.

FB16 Saint Mary's Episcopal Church

1886, James Renwick, Jr. 730 23rd St. NW

This little-known architectural treasure was designed by James Renwick, Jr., who undertook the church for an African-American congregation. In order to reduce costs, Renwick modified his original plans, lowering walls, simplifying the roof truss, and omitting much decorative detail. Within the restricted budget and the requirement that the church, offices, and living quarters be placed on the perimeter of the site, Renwick provided an ensemble of red brick Gothic buildings and connecting walls. The low lines of the facade are accented by the picturesque tower with

its well-proportioned entrance. A central courtyard unites the elements of the ensemble. The overall massing of gables and towers, embellished with terracotta panels and stained-glass windows, provides a pleasing picturesque effect.

FB17 George Washington University

1850s–present, George S. Cooper; Victor Mindeleff; Albert L. Harris; Arthur B. Heaton; Alexander B. Trowbridge; Waldron Faulkner; Mills, Petticord and Mills; Keyes Condon Florance; Skidmore, Owings and Merrill. Pennsylvania Ave., 19th St., F St., and 23rd St. NW

Finding itself landlocked on its site in the city's financial district, the university in 1912 secured a hold in the Foggy Bottom area, at 2023 G Street NW. Initially, the university occupied row houses, but as building funds increased, most of these were demolished, and distinctly academic, institutional structures were erected. Some single or small groups of row houses survive, sheltering academic departments. The once-thriving residential community shrank as the university expanded to become the second-largest landholder in Foggy Bottom, after the federal government. University-sponsored real estate development activities included speculative office buildings, which were justified as potential classrooms.

Several campus buildings that date from Foggy Bottom's mid-nineteenth-century heyday as an elite residential neighborhood are the Woodhull House (FB17.1) at 2033 G Street NW and the Alumni House (FB17.2) at 714

21st Street NW, substantial Italianate buildings constructed of red brick and detailed in stone, terracotta, and wood. Notable surviving town houses are the President's Office (FB17.3) at 700 20th Street NW, designed by George S. Cooper, and the adjoining town house (FB17.4) at 2003 G Street NW, designed by Victor Mindeleff, both dating from 1892. Both are typical late nineteenth-century row houses fashioned of brick with sandstone trim. Their mansard roofs denote the Second Empire style, but the form and massing of each resembles more closely the Romanesque Revival.

The first attempt at a comprehensive campus plan is seen in the quadrangle (FB17.5) at 20th, G, 21st, and H streets. Here a yard is bordered to the east and west by Colonial Revival academic buildings of the 1920s, while the south side is lined with 1930s Moderne academic structures. Architect Albert L. Harris, a former apprentice to Henry Ives Cobb of Chicago, provided the classic university quadrangle plan. In 1924, Harris with Arthur B. Heaton designed Stockton Hall (FB17.6) on 20th Street for the law school and Corcoran Hall (FB17.7) on 21st Street for classrooms. In 1970, the modern style law library (FB17.8), designed by Mills, Petticord and Mills, augmented the law school. In the 1980s, Keyes Condon Florance designed the flanking Postmodern classroom extensions.

On the south side of the quadrangle, Bell, Lisner, and Stuart halls (FB17.9), as well as boldly geometric Lisner Auditorium (FB17.10) by Waldron Faulkner, were constructed in 1934–1941 in a spartan Moderne mode. More recently, in an effort to create a harmonious red brick backdrop for the quadrangle, these buildings' protective paint has been removed, revealing depression-era soft brick. In 1987, Skidmore, Owings and Merrill redesigned the entire yard, which uses Neo-Moderne light fixtures to recall the 1930s era.

FB18 Lenthall Houses

c. 1800, John Lenthall. 606–610 21st St. NW

Two of the oldest buildings in the city are these adjoining houses, built about 1800 by John Lenthall, superintendent of construction of the U.S. Capitol. The two-story houses offer a sense of the scale and form of the early middle-class residential neighborhoods in the city. The red-brick, Federal-style edi-

FB16 Saint Mary's Episcopal Church

fices show restrained elegance and well-proportioned elements, such as the windows and double doorway, the end chimneys, and the dormer windows punctuating the roof. Originally located on 19th Street, they were occupied as residences well into the 1970s, when they were moved for a university construction project. Today, the houses are used a residences for university personnel.

FB19 General Services Administration Building

1915–1917, Charles Butler with the Office of the Supervising Architect. F St. between 18th and 19th streets NW

The General Services Administration Building is the federal government's first frankly modern office building where function predominates over style. It was intended to house the scientific and technical staff of the Interior Department, such as the Geological Survey and Reclamation Service, leaving the secretary and his immediate deputies ensconced in the monumental old Patent Office Building (see DE15.2, p. 189). The building's location, far from the Mall and the White House–Capitol corridor, was viewed as another reason for designing a purely practical structure. As the building project evolved and the secretary increased his interest in the project and determined to locate his offices in it, the building took on monumental aspects.

The important feature of the General Services Administration Building is its E-shaped floor plan, with the back along F Street and the arms stretching south forming two open courts. This arrangement provided for abundant natural light to reach the offices located on the interior of the structure. On F Street, then a major streetcar route, three entrances were located, each corresponding to a wing of the building. Workers occupying offices in a particular wing were supposed to use their respective entrance in order to sort themselves out efficiently and to increase the ability of each bureau of the Interior Department to supervise their movements.

When the construction bid came in lower than the appropriation, Secretary of the Interior Franklin E. Lane persuaded the Office of the Supervising Architect to substitute limestone for the intended gray brick on the building's exterior. Thus, the building took on a monumental appearance. Three doors framed by pilasters, each with a modillion cornice above, mark the main entrance. Ernest C. Bairstow carved the eagle over the central cornice and executed the limestone panels in the sixth-story frieze and ornamental work at the F Street entrance.

The Interior Department made its headquarters here until 1936, when the new Interior building to the south was constructed. Thereafter, this structure served as Interior North, the office of the Federal Works Agency in 1939, and the General Services Administration beginning in 1949.

FB20 Interior Department Building

1935–1936, Waddy B. Wood. C St. between 18th and 19th streets NW

President Franklin Delano Roosevelt and Interior Secretary Harold L. Ickes regarded the new Interior Department Building as symbolic of "a new day" for government in the management of natural and historic resources. A block south of the first Interior Department building, it drew on the earlier building's floor plan and utilitarian character. Together, the pair was envisioned as part of a Northwest Rectangle, a proposed group to include a new War Department building.

The plan consists of a north-south connecting wing between C and E streets, from which six wings running east-west project, each separated by a light court. The building, sheathed with Indiana limestone above a pink granite base, rises seven stories, with an eighth-story setback over the connecting wings. The north and south sides are designed with a two-story base, a three-story superstructure, a heavy cornice above, and a two-story attic with a monumental frieze.

Although the building projects pure utility, it is replete with ornamentation and artwork. On the C Street frieze are the seals of the thirteen original states. Ornamental bronze doors and railings and marble urns may be seen at the entrances and embellished panels in the loggia. Murals, sculptures, bas-reliefs, and ornamental bronze and plasterwork adorn the interior of this building.

FB21 Octagon

1800, William Thornton. 1799 New York Ave. NW

William Thornton, architect of the Capitol, designed the splendid Octagon house for a wealthy client, Col. John Tayloe. At the time

FB20 Interior Department Building

FB21 Octagon

with decorative railings and light standards. The unusual building shape allows for a circular entrance hall, an oval stairhall with a winding staircase, and other curved rooms. The entry hall with its gray and white marble floor, enriched trim, and imported cast-iron stoves conveyed wealth and formality. All of the public rooms were placed on the first floor, with the exception of the library, which commanded an imposing position in the circular room above the entry hall. Throughout, great attention was paid to the functional aspects of the public spaces, family and service areas, and the mixing of these functions according to customs of the day.

The once-glorious outbuildings and garden are either gone or much abbreviated by the walkway to the new American Institute of Architects headquarters at the rear. Today the Octagon serves as a historic house museum.

FB22 American Institute of Architects

1972–1974, The Architects Collaborative. 1735 New York Ave. NW

The American Institute of Architects headquarters is one of the earliest of the now-common "background buildings" tied to historic buildings. Located throughout the central city, these ensembles represent an effort to provide new structures behind historic buildings without competing with, or overpowering, them.

In 1963, the organization sponsored a competition, calling for a building of "special architectural significance" and "a symbol of the creative genius of our time," while protecting the Octagon house in front of the site. From several hundred submissions, the AIA in 1964 selected a design prepared by Mitchell-

it was built, when small game could still be hunted on Pennsylvania Avenue, it was one of the grandest and most progressive private houses in the new city. The Octagon served as a temporary presidential house after the British burned the city in 1814, and the Treaty of Ghent was signed there. After the Civil War, the house was given over to institutional use and eventual disrepair. When the American Institute of Architects moved its headquarters from New York City to Washington at the end of the nineteenth century, it leased the building and then purchased it in 1902.

Actually a hexagon with a semicircular tower at the entrance, the three-story red brick house represents the Federal style at its height. It is embellished with wrought-iron grilled railings and marble panels above the second-floor windows. An Ionic portico defines the main entrance and is reached by a staircase

Giurgola that called for a five-story building with a concave semicircular glass wall, a nod to the semicircular brick tower of the Octagon. The design, in revised form, was rejected by the Fine Arts Commission as "unsympathetic" to the Octagon, and Mitchell-Giurgola abandoned the project.

The AIA then hired The Architects Collaborative (the firm founded by Walter Gropius, who had died in 1969). The firm's seven-story, poured-concrete building with bands of tinted glass has a broad V-shaped floor plan. The Fine Arts Commission praised it for not competing with the Octagon, and some critics complimented its sculptural shape and the active environment in the walkway between the new and old buildings. Although others found it cold and monotonous, the building has gained advocates in recent years. They especially like the welcoming first story that attracts visitors to the exhibition spaces in the lobby and mezzanine. It is now widely seen as a warmhearted building, designed to enhance and shelter the Octagon.

Downtown West (DW)

Antoinette J. Lee

DOWNTOWN WEST REPRESENTS THE EXPANSION AFTER World War II of the downtown commercial core west of 16th Street into an area of low-rise buildings. The topography of the area is more varied than its architectural form suggests. The land rises north from Pennsylvania Avenue, reaching a high point at I Street, then falls toward K Street, where it flattens out before rising again north of M Street. West of 23rd Street, the land flattens before reaching Rock Creek Park.

In the early years of the capital city, commercial activity centered on the juncture of the Washington City Canal and Pennsylvania Avenue near 7th Street. From that beginning, the downtown spread north to G Street and west where, by the early twentieth century, it met the financial district along 15th Street. Commercial development continued north to Scott Circle and west to 16th Street. By the late 1930s, it had trickled into Farragut Square. While the downtown was moving westward, residential activity continued its spread at the edges of the District of Columbia.

Following a construction hiatus during the Second World War, pent-up demand for new office accommodations and the readiness of investors to respond released a wave of new construction by the late 1940s. The federal government's increased need to lease office space further fueled the redevelopment of Downtown West. Over the next four decades, the former residential streets were transformed into an almost solidly commercial enclave, redeveloped in a scattershot fashion wherever a site had been assembled along with the necessary planning and zoning approvals. By the 1980s, few nineteenth- and early twentieth-century buildings survived in the area enclosed within Rock Creek Park, Pennsylvania Avenue, and Dupont Circle, in spite of its historic preservation and special zoning regulations. After Downtown West had been virtually filled, development pressed back into the old central business district, Down-

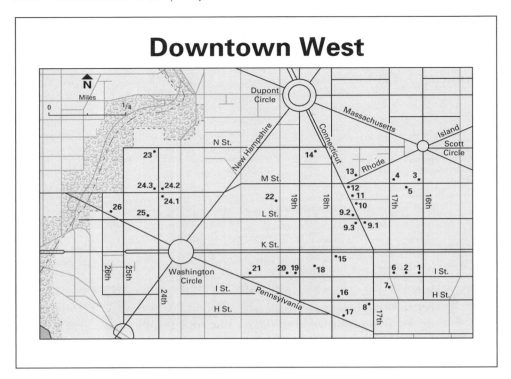

Downtown West

town East, and erupted around new Metro stops throughout the District of Columbia, Virginia, and Maryland.

Early modernism in commercial building design came in the form of modernized classicism with most of its three-dimensional details shorn off. These buildings remained symmetrical, showing the vestigial definition of base, shaft, and entablature. As late as 1941, the Longfellow Building on Connecticut Avenue at M Street appeared revolutionary, with its purely functional ribbon windows and sunshade balconies. Designed by Swiss-born William Lescaze, who also designed the famous Pennsylvania Savings Fund Society Building in Philadelphia, the Longfellow Building has been ruthlessly disfigured by developers, who frosted it with a pink Postmodern glaze.

As simplified classicism fell out of favor in the 1950s, the glass box made its presence felt in the expanding downtown. The seeming resemblance to the majestic glass and steel slabs of famed architect Mies van der Rohe gave these buildings the aura of fashion. As street after street was filled with these superficial versions of serious modern architecture, but rising only to the city's height limit, "K Street Corridor" took on a pejorative meaning, signifying dull streets defined by spare, speculative, glass-enclosed office buildings.

In the 1970s, architects attempted to break out of this predictable building formula and to attract office tenants thirsting for an alternative. Building corners were scooped out or slashed. Retail shopping facilities at the ground floor and in indoor atriums were expanded. In a few instances, only the facades of older buildings survived as frontispieces to new office blocks.

In the 1980s, alternative treatments for new office buildings included towers affixed to building corners, pediments above doors, rusticated stone veneers, new colors, and novel textures. Red brick was used in greater profusion, as were polished stone strips reminiscent of Streamline Moderne buildings of the 1930s and 1940s. Office lobbies blossomed into grand public spaces. For much of Downtown West, these changes came too late to affect the predominant character of this commercial area, which became a ghost town in the evenings. Planning incentives were initiated in an attempt to encourage mixed use in the former light-industrial area called the "West End," which became a haven for hotels and apartment houses interspersed with office blocks. The Golden Triangle formed by Connecticut Avenue, New Hampshire Avenue, and K Street became an entertainment core of restaurants, bars, and nightclubs. In the blocks along Connecticut Avenue and to its immediate west, fashionable shops appeal to the professional people who work in nearby offices.

More older buildings survive on Connecticut Avenue than on many other streets in Downtown West. Plantings of trees set 19th Street apart from its surroundings. In the West End, the mixed uses, hotels, and residential condominiums create forms that differentiate the area from blocks to the east. Occasional sculptural displays are token amenities amid the glass boxes. A few schools and building facades survive to recall the former ethnic character and industrial activities in the area, and except for those located on the fringe of Downtown West, no churches survive.

Downtown West exhibits both the best and the worst of a large area developed during a limited period. The blocks of buildings offer a consistency of scale, treatment, and use, which critics see as a characterless mass of glass boxes, one block of them virtually indistinguishable from any other. Nevertheless, the concentration of similar uses makes for a lively area during office hours and one that offers the efficiency of location.

DW01 **Christian Science Complex**

1970, I. M. Pei. 900–910 16th St. NW

This dark pink reinforced-concrete complex on a landscaped plaza is made of an octagonal Christian Science church facing a rectangular office slab for the news bureau and radio and television stations of the Christian Science church. It was Pei's first major work in the city outside of the Southwest Washington Redevelopment Area.

Both buildings are sandblasted to a smooth finish. In the office block, clear strips of plate glass mark each story. In the nearly windowless church, the articulation of solids and voids is less predictable. A thick and a thin ribbon of plate glass run across the main facade. A bell tower projects laterally from the building near its top, underscoring the horizontal lines of the building. Inside, the auditorium extends from the second to the third floors, placed between the lobby and offices of the plaza level and the storage spaces and educational offices of the fourth and fifth floors.

DW02 **Cafritz Building**

1949–1950, LeRoy L. Werner. 1625 I St. NW

One of the earliest speculative office buildings to be constructed in Downtown West after the close of World War II, the Cafritz Building also provided for one third of the building's area to be turned over to parking spaces

DW01 Christian Science Complex

at the center of the building with offices around the perimeter. When complete, a large compressor in the penthouse fed air throughout the windowless garage core to ventilate the interior space.

The main facade, facing I Street, was designed with elements that recall the Streamline Moderne period of the pre–World War II years. Above that base, the facade is divided into a central section of fourteen bays flanked by sections of ribbon windows that extend around the corners. The corner window treatment provides a sense of weightlessness to the rest of the facade, where a solid limestone wall is punctuated with simple sash windows. The polished granite sheathing of the first floor is the only vestige of the older classical treatment of office facades that were divided into base, shaft, and entablature.

DW03 **Jefferson Hotel**

1922, Jules Henri de Sibour. 1200 16th St. NW

One of the earliest apartment houses along fashionable 16th Street south of Scott Circle, the Jefferson, constructed in 1922, soon was followed by other apartment houses for the affluent and by private clubs. After World War II, as commercial uses increased, apartment living in the area became less desirable. Now operated as a hotel, the Jefferson appeals to visitors who prefer a more intimate

environment than that found in the mass-market hotels.

The Jefferson's U-shaped plan offers natural light and ventilation to the interior of the building. The eight-story facade of carved limestone is divided into a base, shaft, and entablature; it is embellished by stone quoins at the building's edge, heavy window surrounds, and wrought-iron balconies. A welcoming one-story Renaissance entrance and corridor fill in the court of the U and leads to an elaborate lobby enlivened by niches, pilasters, and fine plasterwork.

DW04 **Sumner Square**

1871–1872, Sumner School, 1887, Magruder School, Adolph Cluss, Office of the Building Inspector. 1984–1986, office block, Hartman-Cox. 17th and M streets NW

Sumner Square is a mixed-use project organized around the major landmark, the Charles Sumner School. Completed in 1872 after designs by German-born architect Adolph Cluss, the Sumner School was the first permanent school building in the District of Columbia constructed for black students. On its east side, the William Beans Magruder School of 1887 exemplifies the nineteenth-century method of expanding overcrowded schools in the District—building a detached structure adjacent to the existing school.

The Sumner-Magruder School's decrepit condition led to concerns about its future in the late 1970s, but landmark status and structural fitness allowed it to become the center-

DW04 Sumner Square

piece of a complex of restored, reconstructed, and contextual new architecture. Sumner School was restored by the Ehrenkrantz Group / Building Conservation Technology, expanded to the north, and adapted for use as a cultural center for the D.C. Public Schools. In order to provide underground space, the Magruder School was dismantled and reconstructed over a concrete basement. To the east and rear, a reticent new office structure sheathed in black glass was built with brick towers. Designed by Hartman-Cox, the new building was intended to harmonize with the schools and with the neighboring Jefferson Hotel.

The centerpiece of the complex, the Sumner School, is situated on a commanding site because street regradings placed the building on a raised terrace. Its main facade facing M Street is marked by a central clock tower that terminates in a steep belfry and by Moorish arches above the principal entrance. Flanking the tower are three bays of double windows, each capped by decorative arches. A stone belt course between the first and second stories and a heavy brick cornice above the third story tie together the elements of the composition. Ornamental slate, dormer windows, and iron cresting make the roof one of the building's outstanding features.

The modest Magruder School is typical of the red brick schoolhouses that were produced in large numbers by the Office of the Building Inspector. Its facades are adorned by projecting central bays and decorated with flat- and round-arch brick window lintels, corbeled brick at the cornice, and brick stringcourses.

DW05 National Geographic Society Complex

1902, Hornblower and Marshall. 1932, Arthur B. Heaton. 1964, Edward Durell Stone. 1985, Skidmore, Owings and Merrill. M St. between 16th and 17th streets NW

Beginning at the southwest corner of 16th and M streets, the National Geographic Society now occupies four distinct buildings extending a whole city block to 17th and M streets. The earliest building in the complex, Hubbard Memorial Hall, was constructed in 1902 after designs by Hornblower and Marshall. The adjoining Administration Building, completed in 1932 after designs prepared by Arthur B. Heaton, makes a compatible Re-

DW05 National Geographic Society Complex

naissance Revival style building; both are fashioned of buff brick with limestone trim.

At the corner of 17th and M streets, the ten-story building completed in 1964 represents a dramatic departure for the society. It is a sleek, modern structure designed by Edward Durell Stone. Narrow vertical fins of white Vermont marble separate vertical strips of glass pane, each framed in black Swedish granite spandrels and bronze. These luxurious materials form a curtain around a reinforced-concrete frame. On the interior, marble from the same quarry is used in the lobbies and entrance hall columns. The lobby leads to an "explorers' hall," intended as a museum of science and discovery.

Tying together the older buildings along 16th Street with Stone's slab on 17th is the new office block of 1985 by Skidmore, Owings and Merrill facing M Street. The building resembles a pink concrete terraced mountain set back from the street and sidewalk. It offers a gardenlike respite in the midst of the downtown, as its large street-level plaza is furnished with plantings and large boulders, and its stepped-back stories are lined with shrubs.

DW06 Army Navy Club

1911, Hornblower and Marshall. 1985–1987, addition, Shalom Baranes Associates. 901 17th St. NW

Completed in 1911, the Army Navy Club formed part of a cluster of private clubs in the Farragut Square area that included the Racquet Club (now the University Club) and the Metropolitan Club. In the 1950s, the club building was extended to the side by one bay, and a ballroom was added to the top. By the early 1980s, the club's need for additional revenue led to plans for the expansion of the structure upward by six stories, realized by Shalom Baranes Associates.

The original six-story club building was similar in design to many apartment houses in the city, with its rusticated base, a smooth shaft, and entablature. The shaft is adorned with balconies and large round-arch windows at the first story, indicating the location of the two-story library, and at the fifth story, marking the location of the original ballroom. In the rebuilding of the 1980s, the interior was gutted, leaving the outer facades intact. A four-story foundation was built below ground for garage space and a health club. The club's facilities were compressed into the first four of the original six stories, with the upper stories and the whole of the addition given over to office use. The addition is broken into stepped-back spaces and is punctuated with large windows crowned with triangular pediments. These elongated windows are placed directly above the large round-arch windows of the former ballroom. The architects attempted to reconstruct portions of the old interior by employing original light fixtures, wood paneling, and murals.

DW07 **Office Building**

1987, Shalom Baranes Associates. 816 Connecticut Ave. NW

A pencil-thin office building fit snugly between two conventional-sized modern office blocks, 816 Connecticut Avenue illustrates how a replacement for a single town house in the downtown area might be handled. The Washington architectural firm of Shalom Baranes Associates, which is experienced in enlarging and renovating historic buildings, designed the eleven-story building in a modern style, with each story defined by horizontal stone strips and stone pilasters at the ends. Above the first two stories, the glass panes are pushed out at the center, forming a V-shaped window. Above the eleventh story, a glass-enclosed penthouse offers one of the finest views in the city.

DW08 **Metropolitan Club**

1908, Heins and La Farge. 17th and H streets NW

The Metropolitan Club, situated in the midst of commercialism, is part of a cluster of club-

houses, providing a bulwark of old money and political influence. The prominent firm of Heins and La Farge from New York had probably gained the attention of the club's leaders by its work on Saint Matthew's Cathedral a few blocks to the north.

The main facade of the club building faces H Street, making for a quieter entrance than would one on 17th Street. The symmetrical three-story structure, which is formed of buff brick and trimmed in limestone, resembles a Renaissance Revival residence entered through a portico flanked by bowed bay windows. To the rear is an accordionlike Postmodern office addition designed by Keyes Condon Florance. Its design provides a breathing space between the club and the offices.

DW09 **Washington Square**

1984, Chloethiel Woodard Smith. Connecticut Ave. and L St. NW

In a very real sense, the crossing of Connecticut Avenue and L Street can be claimed by Washington-based architect Chloethiel Woodard Smith. She designed three of the four corner buildings. The northeast corner building, situated over the multilevel shopping and restaurant mall called the Connecticut Connection, was designed by Skidmore, Owings and Merrill. Smith's Blake Building (DW09.1) at the southeast corner resembles a finely curved computer card that turns the corner. At the northwest corner, her 1100

DW10 Mayflower Hotel

Connecticut Avenue (DW09.2) is clad in sleek, polished stone slabs punctuated with dark rectangular windows.

In the massive Washington Square project, Smith best exemplifies the modern design approach to new office blocks of the 1980s. With two glass towers at the north and south corners, the structure breaks out of the glass box formula. Stretching west an entire city block, Washington Square offers upscale shopping at the street level and at a ground-level mall closest to Connecticut Avenue. The entire composition is defined with glass ribbon windows, projecting at equal intervals to create the effect of projecting bays.

DW10 **Mayflower Hotel**

1924, Warren and Wetmore, Robert Beresford. Connecticut Ave. at DeSales St. NW

Warren and Wetmore, architects of Grand Central Terminal in New York, designed the venerable Mayflower Hotel. Robert Beresford of Washington assisted the firm in executing the design. The Mayflower offered first-class hotel accommodations, dining rooms, and ballrooms in the sections of the building closest to Connecticut Avenue. To the rear, with its own private entrance off a quiet street, was the apartment house tower. Today, nearly all of the apartments have been converted to hotel rooms and the public rooms restored to their original elegance.

The Mayflower Hotel rises ten stories and extends east an entire city block from Connecticut Avenue to 17th Street. The buff brick building is set upon a limestone base. Its main facade on Connecticut Avenue is shaped into a pair of curved towers flanking a deep narrow court above the hotel's main entrance. Stone quoins set off the building's corner. Classical urns and carved cornucopias, wreaths, and swags adorn the facade. On the interior, a grand lobby encrusted with plaster ceilings, marble, and gilding extends the length of the building.

DW11 **Raleigh's Building**

1988–1989, David M. Schwarz. Connecticut Ave. and DeSales St. NW

As if mirroring the footprint of the Mayflower Hotel on the south side of DeSales Street, the large new Raleigh's Building exploits its corner location with an appealing three-part curved entrance to the clothing store. A few yards north along Connecticut Avenue, a stone pediment and extended canopy announce the entrance to the office floors. The design of the building is a hybrid between the traditional classical style with base, shaft, and entablature and the common modern glass box that makes up so much of Downtown West. The base is sheathed in stone and accented with pilasters. The shaft is divided into vertical strips of stone sheathing and broad strips of dark glass wall. In the center of each glass strip are simplified two-story pilasters supporting a balustrade. The entablature is made up of a cornice, two stories of office space, and a balustrade cap.

DW12 **Demonet Building**

1846, architect unknown. 1983, Skidmore, Owings and Merrill. Connecticut Ave. and M St. NW

Through the survival of even such modest structures as a former candy factory, the Demonet Building, Connecticut Avenue remains a distinctive thoroughfare. The Demonet Building is a pivot at the meeting of Rhode Island Avenue, M Street, and Connecticut Avenue. Skidmore, Owings and Merrill incorporated the Demonet Building into the corner of a larger development that included a new office block to the rear. The old and the new are joined together with steel beams, which replaced the floor joists of the old building and are attached to the floors of the new.

DW13 **Saint Matthew's Cathedral**

1893–present, Heins and La Farge. 1725 Rhode Island
Ave. NW

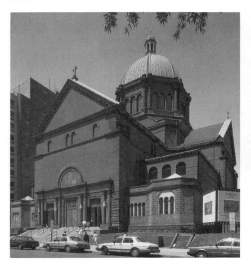

DW14 1818 N St. NW

represents the work of Edwin Blashfield and
Thomas La Farge.

DW14 **Row Houses**

1984, David M. Schwarz. 1818 N St. NW

On N Street, a boundary between new construction and historic buildings, the 1818 N
Street project preserves low-rise town houses
in front of a contextual addition. The row
houses show consistent scale and building materials but a range of historical styles, from
the Romanesque Revival town houses typical
of much of late nineteenth-century residential Washington to an early twentieth-century
Colonial Revival corner house. At the rear,
the new office block, also of red brick, steps
back as it approaches the center of the block
and is marked by gabled bays. The walls are
punctured with window openings and crossed
with red stone strips.

DW15 **Republic Place**

1987, Keyes Condon Florance. 1776 I St. NW

Of all the Postmodern office buildings constructed in Downtown West, Republic Place,
a ten-story office block, ranks among the most
eccentric. Here, the brick of the facade is laid
out in a Flemish bond, with gray and red
headers interspersed with tan stretchers. Beneath the red-mullioned windows are panels
formed of red square bricks. The colorful
surfaces seem to have been designed to attract attention to the distinctive building rather
than to harmonize with nearby buildings. The

The principal church of the Catholic Arch-
diocese of Washington, Saint Matthew's Cathedral is one of the few remaining active
churches in Downtown West. Heins and La
Farge were students of architecture together
at MIT and later trained in H. H. Richardson's office. In 1888, two years after forming
their partnership, these young architects won
the competition for the Cathedral of Saint
John the Divine in New York City and quickly
established a reputation for ecclesiastical design. C. Grant La Farge, son of the painter
John La Farge, provided the design for this
red brick structure. The massing of the building is based on a Latin cross, formed by the
nave, transept, and chancel. At the crossing,
a green copper dome rises to a height of 190
feet from an octagonal drum encircled by
columns and triple round-arch windows and
is crowned by a domed lantern and cross.
Before office buildings surrounded the church,
the dome could be seen from many points in
the Downtown West area. The sparsely ornamented facade facing Rhode Island Avenue is designed to emphasize the color of the
materials: red brick, sandstone, and brownstone with copper and terracotta trim. Designed by John de Rosen, a red mosaic depicting Saint Matthew was added in 1970 at
the tympanum over the central door. The
sumptuous interior includes piers carrying
arcades, mosaics, marble, and statuary and

DW15 Republic Place

DW16 Bachelor Flats

octagonal corner tower is topped by concrete urns, which also adorn the parapet along both facades.

DW16 **Bachelor Flats**

1904, Waddy B. Wood. 1737 H St. NW

The Bachelor Flats, one of several similar service apartment buildings for single men, appealed to affluent tenants who wished to live in a residential area near the private clubs around Farragut Square and close to the

principal departments of the executive branch of government. Servants provided house-keeping and cooking services. When the area was converted to commercial uses after World War II, the Bachelor Flats was adapted for offices. The stone-sheathed bay windows on the facade mark the locations of two of the five apartments on each floor; the apartments consisted of a living room, a bedroom, and a bathroom. Originally, a roof garden shel-tered with a pergola provided private out-door space.

DW17 **National Permanent Building**

1976, Hartman-Cox. 1775 Pennsylvania Ave. NW

In the mid-1970s, the National Permanent Building differentiated itself from nearby glass-covered office buildings by its design of a reinforced-concrete frame around recessed windows. On its prominent trapezoidal site, the poured concrete frame of columns and notched spandrels projects several feet be-yond the glass wall, thus providing a sense of depth to the building while reducing the gray glass windows' exposure to the sun, thereby reducing air-conditioning costs. The circum-ference of the columns becomes smaller as they ascend the building, expressing the lesser load they carry. Flanking the columns, pairs of steel tube utility ducts narrow as they de-scend. At the penthouse, these ducts are en-closed in huge tubes that slant toward the building line, an idea inspired by the Centre Pompidou in Paris.

DW18 International Square

1974–1981, Vlastimil Koubek. 1850 K St. NW

By the early 1970s, real estate developer Oliver Carr, who contributed substantially to the transformation of the West End, had wearied of critics' charges that his buildings were unfriendly, bare-bones glass boxes. In this building, his architect, Koubek, designer of so many of the earlier glass boxes, gave the District one of its earliest privately developed interior food courts and office building atriums. Covering an entire city block, International Square was constructed in three phases between 1974 and 1981. Its exterior is formed of alternating strips of reinforced concrete and dark ribbon windows. At the northwest and southeast corners of the building are open cuts in the otherwise solid block in order to indicate entrances. Overhead walkways connect two corner entrances of the building, providing a pedestrian shortcut. Below the walkways is a large open area, lined with plants and fast-food establishments, an idea derived from projects such as Boston's Faneuil Hall. Pedestrians pass through the food court on the way to and from the Metro stop underneath International Square.

DW19 Presidential Plaza

1986, Keyes Condon Florance. 19th and I streets NW

Located on the site of the former Presidential Hotel, Presidential Plaza recalls the Art Deco and Streamline Moderne apartment houses formerly in Downtown West. The eight-story Presidential Plaza includes a clock tower to anchor the corner, from which strips of pol-

ished light and dark pink granite trace the line of each floor. At the first floor, the rows of granite strips resemble rustication and form an agreeable frame for the retail outlets. Balconies are provided at the corners of the building and on either side of the tower. With the success of its Republic Place and Presidential Plaza, the firm of Keyes Condon Florance joined forces with Hartman-Cox and Skidmore, Owings and Merrill to bring a new style of office building to the District's commercial core.

DW20 Office Building

1981–1983, Swaney Kerns Architects. 1915 I St. NW

Rather than building a modern but compatible eight-story addition behind a small, four-story apartment house, the architects stepped back each new story with a roofline that matches the shape and materials of the original one. The award-winning design was described as a "Tudor facade and its four echoes" as well as a "simple, witty solution" to the need to expand office space while preserving the appearance of the original building.[40] At the lower level, the curved walls define a two-story indoor/outdoor space suitable for a restaurant or cafe.

DW21 Arts Club of Washington

1802–1881, unknown. 2017 I St. NW

One of the earliest surviving structures in Downtown West, the Arts Club of Washington is a fine example of a residence of the capital city's early years. The precise geometry of the house and its flatness of detail convey the design simplicity of the Federal period. Its first owner, Timothy Caldwell, built the rear kitchen wing in 1802 and the front rooms between 1805 and 1808. In 1881, a later owner, Dr. Cleveland Abbee of the weather bureau, raised the former third story to a fourth and crowned it with an attic story similar to the original.

In 1918, the Arts Club of Washington purchased the building for its clubhouse and thus saved it from redevelopment. The club restored the house several times and installed chandeliers and mantles removed from other old buildings. In 1988, the Arts Club and the developers of the new James Monroe Building at the northwest corner of 20th and I

DW20 1915 I St. NW

DW21 Arts Club of Washington

DW22 **Lafayette Center**

1979–1987, Welton Becket. 1120 20th St. NW

A cluster of four red brick buildings located in the center of a city block, Lafayette Center attracts pedestrians to its site by enlarging the arched entrances on its 20th Street facade, just where one enters an interior walkway to 21st Street. Black wrought-iron balconies at each ninth-floor window provide a modest three-dimensional effect to an otherwise flat surface of red brick walls and black glass windows.

The pedestrian then turns a corner and proceeds through a walkway lined with sculpture, dotted with coordinated planters and trash cans, and lit by oversized Baroque sconces. Midway along the walkway is the Galleria, a special events facility available for use by corporations and associations. An effort was made to add amenities and public functions to a speculative office building project.

DW23 **U.S. News and World Report Headquarters**

1984, Skidmore, Owings and Merrill. 2400 N St. NW

The U.S. News and World Report Headquarters is part of a building group designed to create a "sense of place" at the northern section of the West End. Developed by Mortimer Zuckerman of Boston Properties, who is also owner of *U.S. News and World Report,*

streets NW agreed to a transfer of development rights from the former's lot to the latter. In exchange, the developer agreed to preserve the facade of the Arts Club building and its late nineteenth-century annex to the east.

Between the stone foundation and a slate gable roof, walls of Flemish bond brick are articulated into four bays, the westernmost on the first story being the arched entrance. Stone belt courses separate the stories; stone also forms the window lintels and sills. The door is flanked by side lights and crowned by a transom rail and fanlight.

the grouping also includes a twin office building—2300 N Street and its neighbor to the south, the Park Hyatt Hotel. The plan called for future buildings along 24th and N streets.

The buildings' more distinctive features are the large hemicycles at the corners of the two office buildings. They provide an "entrance" to this project and to the rebuilt West End from the north. The materials, precast concrete bands and deep red brick facing, were intended to act as a transition from gray Federal Washington to the red brick town houses of Georgetown. A four-story atrium gives a sense of transparency to the main facade of the magazine's building.

DW24 **Grand Hotel, Park Hyatt, Westin Hotel**

1983–1986, Grand Hotel and Park Hyatt, Skidmore, Owings and Merrill; Westin Hotel, Vlastimil Koubek. 24th and M streets NW

The luxury-class hotels occupying three of the corners at 24th and M streets NW are a product of the 1973 West End Plan's call for a mix of office and residential projects in order to breathe life into the area after office hours and for contemporary retail and entertainment facilities. Hotels qualified as residential uses and were viewed as more profitable than apartments. The three hotels epitomize the recent gentrification of the West End.

Skidmore, Owings and Merrill designed the Grand Hotel (DW24.1) at the southeast corner and the Park Hyatt (DW24.2) at the northeast corner. The Grand Hotel features a circular domed corner tower, a heavily rusticated stone base, and glass and steel marquee. The Park Hyatt's red and brick stone facade is highlighted with green copper roofs over glass canopies and green balconies. Vlastimil Koubek designed the Westin Hotel (DW24.3) at the northwest corner; it is connected with an office block on the west, One Westin Center. The Westin's stone window pediments and a balustrade over the entrance canopy are accents in the tan brick and rusticated stone base. Its unusual U-shaped floor plan creates an appealing interior garden court off a glass-enclosed loggia.

DW25 **Columbia Hospital for Women**

1916, Nathan C. Wyeth. 24th and L streets NW

Although much altered over the years, the Columbia Hospital for Women is still one of the few hospital buildings in the District of Columbia that date from the early twentieth century. The building is a result of a logical organization of uses rather than a concern for style, which is generally Italianate.

Ventilation towers and a roof garden add interest to the tapestry brick, limestone-trimmed exterior. Oriented to the south on the highest point of its site, the hospital is organized around a main block with Y-shaped wings extending at each end to allow exterior windows for each room and corridor. Originally, the east wing was devoted to obstetrical service and the west to gynecological. The assignment of spaces reflects the racial and economic strictures of the times: the nonpaying patients occupied the first two floors, the first for blacks and the second for whites. The third floor housed private patients, presumably only white. Operating and delivery rooms were located on the fourth story, kitchens and dining rooms on the fifth.

DW26 **Westbridge**

1978–1979, Weihe, Black, Jeffries, and Strassman. 25th St. and Pennsylvania Ave. NW

Westbridge, one of the earliest projects to rise in the new West End section of Downtown West, best exemplifies the hoped-for results of the mixed-use zone. A nine-story office building at the north and a ten-story condominium block at the south frame an open, U-shaped courtyard, which is oriented west toward Georgetown. Brick-sheathed balconies define the facade of the condominium tower and those sections of the office blocks that face the condominiums, while simple flat bands of brick and glass define the remainder of the office block. Retail shops line the first floor, and a swimming pool and terrace are located at the second-story level of the courtyard, all offering amenities appropriate for the project's affluent tenants and residents.

Southwest Quadrant (SW)

Antoinette J. Lee

T HE ARCHITECTURAL UNITY OF THE CITY'S SMALLEST QUAD-
rant derives from an ambitious 1950s urban redevelopment plan. Although the developers and architects undertook similar projects in other
American cities, such as Hyde Park in Chicago, none has surpassed the com-
prehensiveness of the Southwest Washington Redevelopment Area. With its
new high-rise and town house residential clusters, shopping centers, office
structures, parks, and cultural facilities, the Southwest became the most complete post–World War II urban renewal community in the nation.

Redevelopment was tumultuous, however, for building owners challenged
the legality of the undertaking. In the famous Supreme Court decision of 1954
on the case of *Berman* v. *Parker* upholding the 1945 D.C. Redevelopment Act,
Justice William O. Douglas found it "within the power of the legislature to
determine that the community should be beautiful as well as healthy, spacious
as well as clean, well-balanced as well as carefully patrolled." The legality of the
Redevelopment Land Agency to condemn land occupied by deteriorated housing was thus confirmed, but the effort suffered in the eyes of the public because extended delays between demolition and new construction left entire blocks
empty for years.

Located at the confluence of the Anacostia and Potomac rivers, the Southwest Quadrant had attracted some settlement even before the federal city was
founded. Recognizing the area's strategic advantages, Pierre Charles L'Enfant
designated its southernmost point as Greenleaf Point or Washington Arsenal,
and it became the site of a fort, arsenal, and penitentiary. Now, as Fort Leslie
J. McNair (see SW14), the spot is best known as the site of the National Defense
University. In the wake of L'Enfant's plan, speculators were quick to construct
houses for residents of the new national capital. One of these ventures, Wheat

Row on 4th Street, dating from 1794–1795, remains among the oldest surviving row houses in the District. Other early development centered on the river: wharves and maritime facilities were constructed, and it also became the center of fishing activity.

In the early nineteenth century, the Southwest evolved more slowly than other neighborhoods contiguous to the Capitol and the President's House, resulting in less desirable housing. The construction of the Washington City Canal along today's Constitution Avenue and then southward on a diagonal path from South Capitol Street to Greenleaf Point isolated much of the area from the rest of the city, and port facilities along this portion of the Potomac River were hampered because of unpredictable water depths. Construction of the railroad tracks in the post-World War II era and the Southwest Expressway further removed "the Island," as it became known, from the fortunes of the District.

By the mid-twentieth century, the area generally was considered a slum. Politicians and planners proposed several solutions, including rehabilitating many of the largely nineteenth-century brick row houses. Urban visionaries, however, preferred that cities conform to modern planning and architectural practices. Planner Harland Bartholomew of Saint Louis and architects Louis Justement and Chloethiel Woodard Smith of Washington provided a scheme reflecting the times: a plan calling for superblocks, created by closing many streets; starkly functional architecture; and planned commercial, cultural, and employment centers. These elements promised to reverse the stampede of middle-class families to the burgeoning suburbs and to rebuild the tax base.

The D.C. Redevelopment Land Agency commissioned William Zeckendorf of Webb and Knapp in New York to prepare a detailed plan. Together with staff architect I. M. Pei and architect Harry Weese of Chicago, Zeckendorf presented a showcase of twentieth-century architecture and planning. The major elements of the Southwest Washington Redevelopment plan consisted of the 10th Street Mall, a north-south corridor linking the federal buildings just south of the Mall with the Maine Avenue waterfront and the residential blocks to the south. Lining the 10th Street Mall were to be federal government buildings, hotels, restaurants, shops, and other tourist facilities. The proposed cultural complex that later became the Kennedy Center for the Performing Arts was sited to the east and could have connected to the 10th Street Mall by a cross-axial promenade.

Clusters of high-rise apartment houses and related town houses, an innovative concept at the time, were sited loosely throughout the quadrant in order to provide light, air, and splendid views to the occupants. The town houses were arranged around residential squares of parking and green spaces, following London's example of private parks. Portions of old Federal style row houses were incorporated into the clusters. Neither urban nor suburban, the high-rise and town house clusters were hybrids. Unlike many speculative suburban developments, the architectural design and landscape standards for the clusters

Southwest

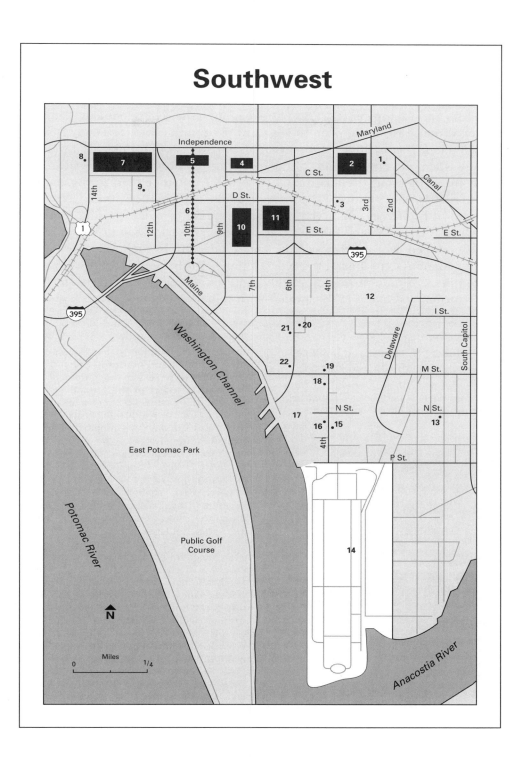

were exceedingly high. The result was a Southwest Quadrant style of development distinctive in the District. The shopping center, churches, schools, public library, and parks filled the interstices.

Much of Zeckendorf's vision was fulfilled, even though the financial collapse of Webb and Knapp cut short his participation in the redevelopment plan. The major variance from the plan, the loss of the cultural center to Foggy Bottom, resulted in an eerie, lifeless 10th Street Mall. Larger social problems developed as well when affluent residents of the new housing found themselves near public housing hugging the quadrant's eastern side. Rather than luring middle-class families, the Southwest drew single adults and childless couples, creating an aura of transiency, while the wholesale clearing of older housing displaced hundreds of low-income families. In the process, strong community ties that had developed over nearly a century and a half were severed.

An ambitious experiment, the redevelopment of the Southwest is still a study in contrasts. Although predominantly modern and sleek, a suggestion of the old informality remains in the waterfront fish market, along with a few graceful old buildings.

SW01 Hubert H. Humphrey Building, Department of Health and Human Services

1976, Marcel Breuer and Herbert Beckhard. Independence Ave. between 2nd and 3rd streets SW

Set back from Independence Avenue and approached by a stark concrete plaza, the Hubert H. Humphrey Building seems to be a modern boxlike sculpture poised on a low glass-and-concrete pedestal. The second of Marcel Breuer's two federal government buildings in the capital (the other is the United States Department of Housing and Urban Development [see SW10]), this precisely articulated office building stands just above the freeway tunnel and houses its exhaust ducts as well as its own mechanical equipment shaft.

The most recent of the federal buildings that line Independence Avenue and form a backdrop for the south side of the Mall, the Humphrey Building was intended as the permanent headquarters of the United States Department of Health and Human Services (formerly Health, Education, and Welfare). Its location just to the west of the Bartholdi Fountain Park at the foot of Capitol Hill serves as a symbolic reminder of Senator Humphrey's long association with the Capitol and with social legislation.

Interest in the building derives from the arrangement of precast concrete panels fitted into the poured concrete frame. The precast panels alternate between double and single window panes, with each window placed in a deep recess with wide horizontal sun screens forming pitched hoods over each panel. A less austere aspect can be found at the concrete corners of the building, where the marks of the wooden forms are visible.

SW02 Health and Human Services Building

1939–1941, Office of the Supervising Architect. Independence Ave. and C St. and 3rd and 4th streets SW

SW02 Health and Human Services Building (Mary E. Switzer Memorial Building)

The Office of the Supervising Architect designed and constructed these two buildings at the same time, using similar designs and adjacent blocks, to house two bureaus serving federal retirement programs. The intent was to draw the center of employment away from the Capitol–White House axis and to stimulate a revival of this part of the Southwest.

The northern building, now the Wilbur J. Cohen Federal Building, is sheathed in limestone on Independence Avenue facing the Mall and yellow brick with limestone trim elsewhere. The building is developed around open light courts, vertical strips of casement window, and unornamented pilasters at the corners. Egyptoid decorative motifs appear above groups of four window strips and above the corner pilasters. At the parapet is a flared limestone strip. Polished pink granite door surrounds mark the entrances. Of special interest are the overdoor panels carved by Emma Lu Davis and Henry Kreis. In low-relief incised lines, the scenes depict the benefits of Social Security.

The companion building to the south, now the Mary E. Switzer Memorial Building, was designed with open light courts on the D Street side and is sheathed in yellow brick and limestone trim. Egyptoid decorative trim ornaments this building, too. Sculptor Robert Kittredge executed the overdoor panels depicting railroad employment and retirement.

SW03 **Design Center**

1983, rebuilding, Keyes Condon Florance. 300 D St. SW

Fashioned from a 1920s refrigeration warehouse associated with the railroad tracks that

SW03 Design Center

once ran across the northern part of the quadrant, the Design Center houses the showrooms of interior designers and decorators and purveyors of building materials for interiors. With the addition of a new glass-sheathed section, the replacement windows, and the rebuilding of the old brick base, Keyes Condon Florance transformed the functional factorylike structure into a showcase. Its massive red-brick facades contrast with the surrounding gray limestone of federal buildings. More recently adorned in a pink and green color scheme, the building reflects a trend of the 1980s.

SW04 **Federal Office Building #10**

1963, Holabird and Root. 800 Independence Ave. SW

This building type developed in the late 1930s to accommodate large numbers of federal office workers. Their office functions required no special facilities and federal office buildings of this type could house workers of

SW04 Federal Office Building #10

SW05 James Forrestal Building

one bureau as well as another. Standard requirements led to standard buildings and materials; movable interior partitions divided the space into offices of varying sizes. Today, the United States Department of Transportation's Federal Aviation Administration and the National Transportation Safety Board occupy the building.

The marble exterior of Federal Office Building #10, one of the most elaborate of these structures, is appropriate to its location on Independence Avenue. At ten stories, it is one of the tallest buildings on the thoroughfare. Set back from the building line and with the top eight floors perched above two stories of glass, nonetheless it exhibits stark, flat detailing that denies it the complexity of neighboring structures. The evenly spaced double windows set in the same plane as the exterior wall are an affirmation of that mode of articulating modular office space that was brought to refinement by Mies van der Rohe at mid-century and later became ubiquitous.

SW05 **James Forrestal Building**

1969, Curtis and Davis. Independence Ave. between 9th and 11th streets SW

The James Forrestal Building, initiated in 1961, contains an imaginative floor plan, a manifestation of President John F. Kennedy's effort to improve the quality of federal government architecture. The major section, a long narrow structure running parallel to Independence Avenue between 9th and 11th streets SW, is raised on 36-foot pilotis, or piers, bridging the 10th Street Mall at its northern entrance. The unusual configura-

tion resulted from the need to improve circulation for the Defense Department, which was to occupy building spaces on both sides of the 10th Street Mall. At street level, the vista from the rear of the Smithsonian Castle south along the 10th Street Mall is nearly unbroken. Pedestrian and automobile traffic pass unimpeded below the building. Clad in concrete panels with double windows, the building and its landscaping stand in stark contrast to the Smithsonian Castle and its lush gardens directly across Independence Avenue.

SW06 **10th Street Mall / L'Enfant Plaza**

1960–1973, I. M. Pei, Dan Kiley, Vlastimil Koubek. 10th St. between Independence Ave. and Banneker Circle

The centerpiece of the Southwest Washington Redevelopment Area was to be the 10th Street Mall / L'Enfant Plaza, a two-block thoroughfare extending from Independence Avenue south. As its name and symbols suggest, the complex's planners aspired to the standards and architectural excellence set by the city's first planner. Bridging the railroad tracks and the Southwest Expressway, this complex was to become a commercial and cultural hub of the city, as well as the entrance to the new Southwest. Office buildings, a hotel, a shopping center, restaurants, and a cultural center were to be located along the 10th Street spine and on the eastern cross axis. The cultural center ultimately was located instead in Foggy Bottom as the John F. Kennedy Center for the Performing Arts. The shopping arcade adjacent to the plaza serves nearby office

SW06 10th Street Mall / L'Enfant Plaza

SW07 United States Department of Agriculture, South Building

workers and bustles on weekdays but is otherwise moribund. The hotel atop the shopping center is isolated from other downtown hostelries.

William Zeckendorf of Webb and Knapp and his staff architect I. M. Pei developed the master plan for the site. While the main axis of 10th Street can be viewed as the link between the new Southwest and the rest of the city, L'Enfant Plaza is the heart of the complex, the vital organ pumping activity into the area. L'Enfant Plaza consists of twin office towers, executed by Araldo A. Cassutta, on either side of the plaza, from which stairs descend to the underground parking arcade. Architect Vlastimil Koubek of Washington undertook the design of the hotel, which encloses the east side of the complex. The plaza itself merges into the 10th Street Mall, a band of pink concrete and red granite. The Mall terminates in the south at Banneker Circle, named in honor of Benjamin Banneker, the black mathematician who assisted with the first survey of the District of Columbia. Land-

scape architect Dan Kiley designed this oval area that serves both as an overlook and the centerpiece of the thoroughfares connecting the mall with the street system to the south.

SW07 United States Department of Agriculture, South Building

1930–1937, Office of the Supervising Architect. Independence Ave. between 12th and 14th streets SW

The seven-story South Building of the Department of Agriculture, with its 4,500 office bays, was envisioned as a functional annex to the main departmental building on the Mall. Two arched bridges at the third-floor level over Independence Avenue link the buildings, which together suggest the importance of agriculture to the country.

The elevations of the South Building on 12th and 14th streets were to be visible from the Mall. The 14th Street side is sheathed in limestone, with a central entrance pavilion composed of sixteen monumental Corinthian columns. The 12th Street side is also of limestone. The two long elevations are clad in variegated tan brick and terracotta trim.

Interior lightwells along the C Street side provide natural illumination to the huge building. The spandrels between windows are ornamented with relief panels depicting animals native to the United States, among them turkeys, eagles, horses, bulls, and rams. The animal motif is carried out in the medallions in the frieze on the 14th Street side. All are the work of sculptor Edwin Morris. Pilasters articulate the large wall masses and separate windows of varying widths. Terracotta fretwork and strips at the water table and parapet further adorn this massive structure.

SW08 United States Holocaust Memorial Museum

1986–1993, James Ingo Freed. between 14th St. and Raoul Wallenberg Pl. SW

In 1980 Congress approved the 1.9-acre site just south of the Mall for the United States' Holocaust museum; $147 million in private monies were to be raised for the museum's construction and endowment. Six years later the German-born architect James Ingo Freed, a partner of I. M. Pei who trained under Mies van der Rohe at the Illinois Institute of Technology, was chosen to design the building. He worked in association with the Washington firm Notter, Feingold and Alexander, whose initial design in 1985 was not approved by the Commission of Fine Arts. The cornerstone was laid on 5 October 1988, after Freed's altered design was given final approval by the commission in March 1988. The building's dual function as museum and memorial is ostensibly divided between its two structures, the five-story limestone and brick rectangle that faces 14th Street and the blind windowed hexagon, the Hall of Remembrance, that overlooks the Tidal Basin. In reality, because of its nature as a place to record, remember, and learn from the German Nazi party's systematic murder of 6 million European Jews between 1933 and 1945, both parts will function interchangeably in expanded definitions of museum and memorial. The formality, regularity, monumentality, and materials of the exterior are a response to the site and design parameters regulated by the Commission of Fine Arts. The main entry on 14th Street is monumental, through a wedge faced by a freestanding curved screen articulated

with abstract classical forms and details. Freed used both limestone and brick on the museum's western side, both as a contextual response to James G. Hill's adjacent Bureau of Engraving (1880) and as a reminder of the materials found in concentration camps that he visited in Germany and Austria. In the interior central space, the rectangular, multistory, skylit Hall of Witness, the exterior's harmony and repose begin to disintegrate. Jarring asymmetries, cracks in walls, an apparent fissure in the floor are all meant to invoke a sense of disquiet and unease as a prelude to the horrors displayed and re-

SW09 Central Heating Plant

SW10 United States Department of Housing and Urban Development Building

counted in adjacent exhibition spaces. Each of the six sides of the Hall of Remembrance is dedicated to a million victims of the Holocaust; its single-volume interior, lit from above, is enclosed within a lower outer shell of unconnected wall segments that form an ambulatory around four of its sides. Consciously symbolic and emotive, the Holocaust Museum promises to be a positive architectural force on an ugly street, drawing strength from the nearby Mall. The adjacent Bureau of Engraving, from which Freed adopted brick towers that face it, will house the museum's administrative offices. (Pamela Scott)

SW09 Central Heating Plant

1934, Paul Philippe Cret. 13th and C streets SW

In few other Washington buildings are sheer function and architectural beauty so well integrated as the Central Heating Plant. It was one of three greatly admired public buildings designed by Cret for the city in the 1930s. Although less familiar than his Folger Shakespeare Library and the Federal Reserve Board buildings (see CH15 and FB08, pp. 146, 210), it was pivotal in translating the classical idiom into modern terms. Modernism did not take the city by storm; it seeped in gradually with buildings such as Cret's, which were beautifully proportioned, carefully detailed, and functional.

The Central Heating Plant supplies all federal government buildings near the Mall. A modern garment fashioned of buff brick and limestone trim clothes this facility. The exterior is designed with vertical ribbons of louvered windows, separated by slightly protruding pilasters. The parapet and the setback are detailed with a geometric pattern. Three massive octagonal smokestacks rise 42 feet along the setback. At the 13th Street entrance, the building's purpose is related in decorative limestone panels illustrating a generator, boiler safety valve, fan, and heat exchanger. The large panel above the central window depicts coal furnaces, boilers, and machinery that traps steam and pipes it to other buildings.

SW10 United States Department of Housing and Urban Development Building

1963–1968, Marcel Breuer and Herbert Beckhard. 451 7th St. SW

More than any other federal government edifice of the 1960s, the United States Department of Housing and Urban Development (HUD) building fulfills the directives President John F. Kennedy issued in an effort to improve the quality of public building design, "Guiding Principles for Federal Architecture."[41] For a city accustomed to boxy containers for federal workers, the HUD Building seemed a radical departure. It was also an important architectural statement for the newly created cabinet-level department that was devoted to upgrading the nation's cities and housing.

One of the world's leading architects, Marcel Breuer epitomized modernity. His body of work fit perfectly President's Kennedy's call for the "choice of designs that embody the finest contemporary American architectural thought." Inspired in part by his buildings for UNESCO and IBM in France, Breuer's design for a ten-story structure resembled a curvilinear X. The four curved walls allowed for open plazas on each side and for optimal window-distance ratio while minimizing distances between offices and reducing the apparent length of corridors. The walls were fitted with precast window panels, each with recessed windows and a sharp diagonal slope behind the mullions. The building frame was made of a cast-in-place concrete "tree" that rested the bulk of the building on a series of stubby pilotis, or piers. It was the first federal office building to be made of precast concrete.

At completion, the HUD building was acclaimed for its imaginative plan and the boldness of the forms. It was, in fact, a major achievement and set a high standard for public buildings. A walk around the building provides an experience in architectural movement and drama that lifts it dynamically above its surroundings—the freeway to the south and the monolithic office buildings on the other three sides.

SW11 United States Department of Transportation Building

1969, Edward Durell Stone. 7th and D streets SW

In contrast to the HUD Building, the United States Department of Transportation (DOT) Building, across 7th Street, represents a commercial building type—a speculative office building that is leased to the federal government. Many such speculative buildings are

SW11 United States Department of Transportation Building

SW12 Capitol Park

constructed to the specifications of a federal agency or bureau but could be leased as readily to the private sector. While providing flexibility to the federal government by providing only as much space as it needs for a fluctuating work force, such buildings also tend to diminish the symbolism so essential to government buildings and blur the lines between the public and private sectors.

The building was designed by Edward Durell Stone, whose Kennedy Center was taking form in Foggy Bottom, and is based on a large rectangular plan, the center of which is cut out to form a courtyard plaza. On each side, an opening at the base allows for easy circulation between street and courtyard. The walls are made up of narrow vertical ribbons of windows separated by equally narrow piers, each sheathed in a white marble veneer from the same Carrara quarry in Italy as that of the Kennedy Center; the broadly overhanging eaves also echo the design of the performing arts center.

SW12 **Capitol Park**

1959–1963, Satterlee and Smith; Chloethiel Smith and Associates. 4th, G, 1st, and I streets SW

The pioneer housing cluster in the Southwest redevelopment area, Capitol Park, secured Chloethiel Woodard Smith's reputation, and she became the designer of choice for subsequent projects in Southwest Washington. Capitol Park embraces two freestanding apartment towers, one set of "twin towers," and several blocks of town houses. The houses were intended for families, while most of the

units in the apartment houses are efficiencies, intended for single career people.

The apartment houses are notable for their planning and for their detailing—balconies protected with decorative tile screens laid out in flat planes, in curved configurations, and in lattice and basketweave patterns. Large glassed-in spaces on the first floors provide light for lobbies. The lowest floor that contains tenants is higher than the top of nearby town houses, thereby addressing concerns about the juxtaposition of high-rise and town house dwellings. Dan Kiley's landscaped open space, pools, and pavilion separate the apartment houses from their low-rise neighbors.

The town houses are organized into groups around small squares of open space, and each group is woven into the whole with walkways, linear green strips, and common rear gardens. Paint colors and variations in the rooflines differentiate each house from its neighbor. During the three decades since the completion of this complex, the trees, shrubs, and vines have grown to maturity, providing a richly verdant setting for this imaginative small-scale town plan. The open feeling here differs notably from the sense of containment in later area development projects.

SW13 **William Syphax School**

1901, Marsh and Peter. Half and N streets SW

The William Syphax School is one of several elegant public school buildings designed by the local firm of Marsh and Peter in the District of Columbia between 1900 and 1910. It is located on the eastern edge of the Southwest Quadrant, an area traditionally inhabited by African Americans. Constructed for black children, the school was named in honor of the first black trustee of the "colored schools," William Syphax, who served from 1868 to 1871.

For the school, Marsh and Peter provided a rendition of the Colonial Revival based on a predictable plan of four classrooms arranged around a large central hallway on each floor. The front presents a symmetrical design with a recessed pavilion flanked by balanced pavilions three bays wide. The architects' skill in addressing this routine structure lies in subtle variations in brickwork, in decorative detail, and in the shapes and sizes of window openings. White terracotta belt courses, white keystones and springline blocks at the second-floor windows, and a wooden cornice painted white enliven the dark red of the walls. The oversized colonial door surround, the projecting wrought-iron balcony at the second floor, and the flat dormer window at the roof emphasize the center of the composition.

SW13 William Syphax School

SW14 Fort Leslie J. McNair

SW14 **Fort Leslie J. McNair**

1903, McKim, Mead and White. 4th and P streets SW

This site at the confluence of the Potomac and Anacostia rivers has been in use since the 1790s, when a battery and official reservation were situated at Greenleaf Point. During the nineteenth century, a federal prison was located on the grounds and the Lincoln conspirators were hanged there. As other military installations developed in the region, the functions of this site were transferred to locations farther from the center of the city, and the Army War College (now National War College) was established. As an outgrowth of his work on the 1901–1902 McMillan Plan, Charles McKim provided the plan and architectural form. Later the National War College became part of the National Defense University.

Closest to the Fort McNair entrance, tightly packed brick buildings house barracks for enlisted persons and support services. The dense geometrically arranged cluster on either side of a north-south thoroughfare opens into the expansive parade ground that runs south to the National War College building. This vista is punctuated, some say spoiled, by two penitentiary buildings adapted to the needs of the installation. East of the parade ground is a row of noncommissioned officers' quarters, all identical brick duplex houses. West of the parade ground, with scenic views of the Washington Channel, Hains Point, the Potomac River, and the Virginia shore, is a row of officers' quarters—large, detached, single-family houses that reflect their occupants' rank. The penultimate building is the domed National War College with its great interior vaults fashioned of Guastavino tile. The design and composition of the final academic building at the center of the U-shaped configuration of residences invoke Thomas Jefferson's University of Virginia and his love of Roman forms. A pleasant tree-lined promenade encircles the site at the water's edge.

SW15 **River Park**

1962, Charles M. Goodman Architects. 4th St. and Delaware Ave. and N and O streets SW

The most unusual housing cluster in the Southwest redevelopment area is River Park, a cooperative completed in 1962 south of Carrollsburg Square. The project's developer, Reynolds Aluminum Service Corporation, had resolved to demonstrate the use of aluminum in urban renewal projects and wielded influence over Charles M. Goodman's design. The project also represents the first use of a central heating and cooling plant for town houses.

The apartment towers form a wall-like configuration along Delaware Avenue, as if to block their residents' view of public housing across that thoroughfare. The town houses are distinctive for their barrel-vaulted roofs, a feature intended to contribute visual excitement to the project. Aluminum is used throughout the high rises and the town houses in window frames, doors, sunscreens, garden fences, outdoor sculpture, and staircases. Of particular note is the grillwork, punched from aluminum sheets.

The town houses are arranged around smaller courtyard spaces and parking is removed to the periphery of the site. While the landscaping is admirable for its uncluttered directness, it appears bleak when compared to the verdure of Capitol Park and the variety at Tiber Island and Carrollsburg Square.

SW16 **Wheat Row**

1794–1795, Joseph Clark. 1315–1321 4th St. SW

This stately residential row resulted from the speculative activities of a syndicate headed by James Greenleaf. The complex was named for John Wheat, an early owner-occupant.

Now restored and integrated into the Harbour Square complex, the three-story brick row is articulated by a central pavilion of four bays, flanked by four-bay sections. An oculus window punctuates the pediment at the roofline above the central pavilion. Brick stringcourses and a heavy cornice reinforce the horizontality of the composition. The windows are crowned with stone lintels with keystones, while the doors are finished with arched lintels over elegant fanlights.

SW17 **Harbour Square**

1963–1966, Chloethiel Woodard Smith; Dan Kiley. 4th, N, and O streets and the waterfront

Following the triumph of Capitol Park, Smith designed another innovative housing cluster, Harbour Square. Apartment towers dominate a U-shaped water garden court and ground-level motor court. The complex faces the Washington Channel; at the rear closest to 4th Street, low-rise apartments and town houses are arranged around the perimeter of the block. Incorporating Wheat Row and several other remnants of the Southwest Quadrant's housing history, this section aimed to re-create around a quadrangle the complexity of an urban form evolved over several centuries.

The outstanding feature of the project, however, is the careful landscaping, beginning with the pedestrian and automobile entrance. Hanging plants suspended from the terrace above the motor court give this otherwise utilitarian feature the character of a botanical garden. Beyond the terrace, a one-acre water garden is ornamented with fountains, sculpture, and platforms; a green lawn and grove of trees beyond the water provide a sense of privacy. In the distance, the Washington Channel and Potomac River form appropriate backdrops.

SW18 **Tiber Island / Carrollsburg Square**

1965, Keyes, Lethbridge & Condon. Waterfront to Delaware Ave. and M to N streets SW

In the design of Tiber Island, the architects aimed to re-create a medieval sense of urban space with a large plaza uniting a pinwheel configuration of apartment houses. Town house clusters were arranged around smaller irregular enclosures. The unbroken system of plaza, town house courts, greenways, and walkways was made possible by the placement of parking below ground, with the plaza serv-

SW15 River Park

SW17 Harbour Square

ing as the roof of the parking facility. In the adjacent Carrollsburg Square section, also designed by Keyes, Lethbridge and Condon, who won design competitions for both projects, the space over the underground parking was divided into smaller courts and gardens for a more informal character.

The architectural treatment of the buildings in the two sections was similar. The high rises were constructed of exposed reinforced-concrete frames, filled in with gray-tan brick panels. The town houses are of brick bearing-wall construction, trimmed with precast concrete. The paving throughout is of similarly colored brick and concrete, with flagstone added for interest. Unlike the Capitol Park project where the apartment-house towers and town house groups present different architectural images, Tiber Island and Carrolls-

burg Square achieve unity of design on a human scale. At their completion, these liveable complexes were widely considered to set a new standard for architectural quality in American urban renewal.

sw19 **Waterside Mall**

1968–1972, Chloethiel Woodard Smith. 400 M St. SW

Conceived as the neighborhood commercial center for the Southwest Washington Redevelopment Area, the mall consists primarily of a U-shaped shopping center. A small indoor mall is located to the north, and beyond that, an open plaza. Flanking office towers, joined by a single-story bridge, house employees of the Environmental Protection Agency. In color and material, this complex

SW19 Waterside Mall

SW21 Waterside Towers

SW20 Town Center Plaza

I. M. Pei used a poured concrete structural system and tinted glass sheets that reach nearly from ceiling to floor. Railed "French doors," placed between paired structural columns, create the illusion of balconies. Stock draperies address the problem of consistency behind the large window surfaces. At the ground floor, the paired columns become single columns that seem rooted into the ground, providing the effect of a colonnade for the lobby. This project was one of several cited by the National Institute of Arts and Letters in awarding the architect the 1961 Brunner Award.

SW21 Waterside Towers

1970, Chloethiel Woodard Smith and Associated Architects. 905–947 6th streets SW

Chloethiel Woodard Smith also designed this complex, but it lacks the humanity of Capitol Park and the magic of Harbour Square. A U-shaped apartment complex, it has a tall glassed-in lobby that permits views toward the inner court, but the stark setting does not lure the pedestrian. Tan brick and concrete trim, unrelieved by the simple metal balconies, present an image of monotony rather than of unity. The row houses to the rear are sited as if to protect residents of the complex from the perils of the city.

echoes the 10th Street Mall / L'Enfant Plaza. Pink concrete panels envelop the complex and towers, while beige brick is used in the shopping center. Reflective glass in the office towers creates a forbidding appearance.

SW20 Town Center Plaza

1961–1962, I. M. Pei. 3rd and 6th streets, M and I streets SW

The four identical apartment towers located just off the four corners of Waterside Mall were designed mainly as efficiencies for middle-income occupants. Underwritten with Federal Housing Authority funds, the project conformed to the agency's construction cost restrictions.

SW22 Arena Stage / Kreeger Theatre

1961–1970, Harry Weese and Associates. 6th and M streets SW

Harry Weese designed the Arena Stage / Kreeger Theatre complex in response to the collective experience of members of the local repertory company who were then housed in a former brewery. Weese, who had never designed a theater, came to the project without preconceived ideas about the building type, an advantage to the company. The first phase, Arena Stage, was designed as a theater-in-the-round with four tiers of seats placed around the stage and housed within an octagonal structure. An adjacent elongated administrative wing, set off from the theater by a glass bay, provides space for the theater and ticket offices. A decade later, the fan-shaped Kreeger Theatre was appended to the rear of the administrative wing. This theater, with its centerpiece a pie-shaped stage, provides an intimate setting for experimental productions.

Both buildings were constructed of poured concrete frames and gray-buff brick crowned with dark gray sheet-metal roofs. Their appeal lies in the forthright expression of the functions housed within. In form and materials, the complex further offers itself as a compatible neighbor to the Southwest Quadrant's housing clusters.

Capitol Hill Neighborhood (CN)

Antoinette J. Lee and Pamela Scott

T HE CAPITOL HILL NEIGHBORHOOD IS LOCATED IN THE shadow of the Capitol. The extent of the shadow is subject to question, but for the purposes of this guidebook, the neighborhood encompasses the area beyond the Capitol and the institutional buildings that make up the Capitol Complex and extends east and south to the Anacostia River. The northern boundary is Florida Avenue, marking the northernmost extent of the L'Enfant City. The later extension of Benning Road to the Anacostia River completes the northern boundary. With the exception of an unrealized cathedral fronted by a great plaza five blocks south of the Capitol, the public spaces planned by L'Enfant exist nearly in the form he intended.

Within this area are block after block of low-rise town houses, row houses, and a few apartment houses. Punctuating this remarkable homogeneity are school buildings, firehouses, churches, and occasional commercial structures. Slicing through the neighborhood are the major commercial thoroughfares of Pennsylvania Avenue SE, Eighth Street SE, and H Street NE. Ringing the area's borders are large public installations. On the south is the sprawling Navy Yard, a major employment center on the Anacostia River. Institutions such as the District Jail complex, D.C. General Hospital, the D.C. National Guard Armory, the Robert F. Kennedy Stadium, and parklands are located along the eastern boundary of the neighborhood.

While the neighborhood derives its name from its proximity to the Capitol, it actually is not located on a hill. The Capitol is situated on the highest point of land between the Anacostia and Potomac rivers, hence its name Capitol Hill. The Capitol Hill neighborhood developed on the high plateau extending east from the crest of the hill.

The deep waters of the Anacostia River south and east of the area appealed

246

to the city's early planners. L'Enfant suggested that the shoreline be devoted to major port facilities, which, in turn, would generate commercial activities. East Capitol Street, running due east from the Capitol to the Anacostia River, was to be 160 feet wide. Along this major axis, "shops will be most conveniently and agreeably situated." Midway along East Capitol Street, on the site of Lincoln Park, was to be a "historic column, from whose station, (a mile from the Federal house) all distances of places through the Continent, are to be calculated."[42] Present-day Lincoln Square on East Capitol Street, midway between the Capitol and the Anacostia River, is in the form and location originally planned. It was the outer boundary of the residential neighborhood in 1876, when Thomas Ball's Emancipation Monument was erected solely from the contributions of freed slaves.

From the area's northern boundary, roads led to Bladensburg, Maryland, then a thriving commercial port along the Anacostia. Public reservations or parks are placed at intersections of major diagonal streets that emanate from the Capitol with other diagonal thoroughfares. Several of these parks gave names to their immediate surroundings, such as Stanton Park, Lincoln Park, and Seward Square.

L'Enfant's expectations for a commercial East Capitol Street did not materialize, but his growth plan for the city and for the area known today as the Capitol Hill neighborhood did. The Capitol and the Navy Yard (see CN45) served as two major nodes of growth, while the public parks and the Eastern Market (see CN33) generated their own modest settlements. By the mid-nineteenth century, the Capitol Hill neighborhood was densely settled in a five-block radius around the Capitol and a radius of nearly equal size around the Navy Yard.

During the early years of the city, boardinghouses near the Capitol housed members of Congress. Laborers who were employed in the construction of the Capitol lived in shanties and barracks. Frame and brick houses were erected for the skilled workers and supervisors. In lands beyond, freestanding houses surrounded by extensive grounds were constructed. After the Civil War, substantial brick town and row houses were constructed to appeal to the increased rolls of middle-class civil servants. They made their homes in these two- and three-story houses, many of which followed a predictable design of a side entrance and a projecting bay window. Terracotta, pressed brick, stone trim, and cast-iron railings and stairs adorned these houses.

Urban development along the Anacostia River caused siltation and created marshy areas. The waterway's role as the site of deep-water ports was precluded. The McMillan Plan of 1901–1902 recommended that the river's edges be reclaimed for much-needed parkland in the eastern section of the city. The Army Corps of Engineers accomplished this work during the 1920s and 1930s, providing for large expanses of parklands on both sides of the river. By then, row house development had reached nearly to the river's edge.

In 1929, the National Capital Park and Planning Commission resurrected L'Enfant's idea of East Capitol Street as a major axis. Instead of a commercial thoroughfare, the planning commission produced a scheme for an East Capitol Street mall of public and semipublic buildings terminating at the Anacostia River in a sports center. In keeping with that plan, the headquarters of several states are located along the street. With this scheme, the planning commission hoped to relieve traffic congestion west of the Capitol. The plan's appeal endured for decades, and as late as the early 1960s East Capitol Street was designated part of a network of "special streets and places."

By the mid-twentieth century, many middle-class families had left Capitol Hill and the area had deteriorated. Studies of blighted and obsolete areas of the District depicted large sections of the Capitol Hill neighborhood as ripe for urban redevelopment. Fortunately for the historic character of Capitol Hill, the Southwest Quadrant was given higher priority. In the meantime, the charm of the older buildings attracted a new group of affluent residents to the area. Starting in the 1950s, the restoration of Capitol Hill gradually gentrified housing closest to the Capitol and then proceeded to outlying blocks of older town and row houses, displacing lower- and lower-middle-class residents. Today, a large swath of Capitol Hill falls within the Capitol Hill Historic District. Much of Capitol Hill, both within and outside the historic district, looks much as it did in the early twentieth century, a testament not only to private preservation efforts but also to lesser development pressures when compared with the forces that overtook areas to the west of the Capitol.

The Capitol Hill Historic District is the largest residential historic district in the city, embracing over 150 city blocks. Its boundary is an irregular rectangle, generally running east from the Capitol Complex to 14th Street, north to F Street, and south to the Southeast Expressway. Its construction history spans that of the Capitol Hill neighborhood, from its founding in the L'Enfant Plan of 1791 to recent infill construction. However, the greatest concentration of buildings dates from the post-Civil War era. Many of the earlier buildings were demolished or greatly altered, and the twentieth-century buildings made modest and compatible contributions to a character that was already well formed.

One of the distinctive aspects of the historic district is the street pattern. L'Enfant specified that the diagonal avenues and principal streets, such as East Capitol Street, be 160 feet wide while the remaining grid streets be 90 feet wide. These dimensions have been achieved not through the width of the thoroughfares alone but also through the use of green space, the open space or front yards of each house. Thus, on East Capitol Street, the building line is set far back from the street curb, creating a privately maintained strip of green carpet that stretches from the Capitol grounds to the D.C. National Guard Armory, punctuated midway by Lincoln Park. The narrower grid streets provide for narrower green front yards for the rows of houses.

Development on Capitol Hill occurred piecemeal, involving many single houses

Capitol Hill Neighborhood 1-47

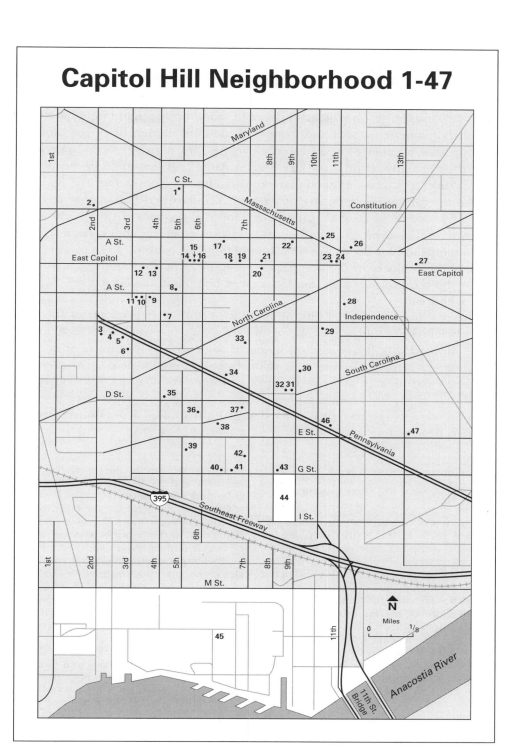

set close to their neighbors and larger groups of houses with common-party walls. Because of the fragmented nature of construction, houses and groups of houses were scattered throughout a large area, with later houses constructed to fill in empty lots. The row and town houses bordering the streets range from one-of-a-kind, large, three-story brick and stone houses standing adjacent to two-story frame structures and groups of identical modest brick row houses. The greatest number of houses were developed during the last three decades of the nineteenth century and are Queen Anne and Romanesque Revival in style. While architects designed many of these houses, contractors and builders played a significant role in producing fairly standardized houses that met the taste and income level of the middle-income civil servants. In the Navy Yard and Marine Barracks area, the houses tended to be more modest because they accommodated blue-collar workers. In addition, the concentration of the black population in blocks in the Southeast Quadrant from the Capitol east to 11th Street also resulted in a more modest scale of housing in the Navy Yard–Marine Barracks area.

The row houses of the 1880s and 1890s were in part products of the District's building regulations that allowed for projecting bay windows. These houses were adorned with heavy window lintels of stone or cast iron, rows of decorative pressed brick and terracotta, stained-glass windows, decorative cast-iron staircases and railings, and heavily rusticated stone foundations. The variety of decorative treatments within a limited range of scale and material resulted in both the variety and the consistency that give the Capitol Hill Historic District its special character.

CN01 George Peabody School

1879–1880, Office of the Building Inspector. 5th and C streets NE

The transition of municipal government in the late 1870s in the District of Columbia from the territorial experiment to the appointed commission system was particularly reflected in municipal architecture and in the George Peabody School. Where the territorial period was criticized for profligate spending on public works, the three District commissioners placed a heavy hand of economy on spending. The opulent public school buildings of Adolph Cluss gave way to spartan red brick designs of the Office of the Building Inspector that provided a fiscally sound solution to the need to provide dozens of such facilities for the city's expanding population. The municipal architecture program produced the Peabody School and its successors for the next two decades, under the direction of the engineer commissioner, who tradition-

ally was a member of the Army Corps of Engineers, and his design staff in the Office of the Building Inspector.

With the Peabody School, the Office of the Building Inspector was still groping for the right model for future schools. It was one of the largest elementary schools the Office of the Building Inspector designed; the later ones were shorter and the hallways and staircases less spacious. The Peabody School gains some of its prominence from its commanding position along the southern boundary of Stanton Park, one of L'Enfant's growth nodes at the intersection of Massachusetts and Maryland avenues NE. The red brick facades are articulated with projecting and recessed pavilions. Heavily corbeled brick designs, round-arch windows, and a third-floor bull's-eye window adorn the central entrance pavilion of the main facade. The unusual fourth-story penthouse is recessed from the building line and is sheathed in wood siding punctuated by circular arch windows. Although nearly double the size of its residential neighbors, its design and materials make it a harmonious element in the Victorian neighborhood.

CN02 **Sewall-Belmont House**

1790–1800, unknown. 144 Constitution Ave. NE

This is the only surviving example in the Capitol Hill Neighborhood of a major house in the Neoclassical style as practiced by Latrobe. Although altered through various rebuildings, it still provides the silhouette of a Federal style house constructed close to the Capitol during the city's nascent years. Robert Sewall had the house built on the corner lot of 2nd Street and Constitution Avenue NE, incorporating an existing brick structure dating from 1750. Secretary of the Treasury Albert Gallatin rented the house as both residence and offices. During the British invasion of the capital city in 1814, the house was partially burned. It was rebuilt soon after, establishing its essential form, which has endured through the years. The property remained in the Sewall family until 1922, when Porter H. Dale, senator from Vermont, purchased it and restored the house and grounds. Seven years later, Alva Belmont acquired the house as headquarters of the National Women's party. From this location, the organization lobbied Congress on women's rights issues. In 1958, when Congress voted to expand its grounds, it decided not to incorporate the house because of its historical associations.

Although many will view the Sewall-Belmont House as a spoiled Federal style house because of the extensive alterations of the late nineteenth and early twentieth centuries, it is a worthy specimen of adaptation and redesign. The house is two and a half stories over a raised basement. The balanced three-bay facade retains its Federal style articulation and its original Flemish bond walls. The mansard roof with three dormer windows was added in the late nineteenth century. The exterior staircase dates from the turn of the twentieth century. The entrance has side lights and a late nineteenth-century peacock fanlight under an early molded arch with keystone. The flat window lintels with sunken bull's-eye corner blocks, a motif employed by late eighteenth-century English Neoclassical architects, were probably introduced into this country by Latrobe. They were quickly adopted by local builders here and in Philadelphia.

CN03 **George Watterston House**

between 1802 and 1819, attributed to Nicholas King. 224 2nd St. SE

Flat window lintels such as those on the Sewall-Belmont house (CN02) appear on the much-restored Watterston house, attributed to Nicholas King, the Washington city surveyor who was also an accomplished architect.

CN04 **Mayers Block**

1887, John Granville Meyers. 221–225 Pennsylvania Ave. SE

The Mayers Block was built by Jonathan Shane for developer Theodore Mayers at a cost of $15,000. The three buildings were designed by J. G. Meyers in the Queen Anne style to have shops at street level with residences above. His composition of triple-arch windows on

the two upper stories of equal height on each building, as well as the expansive pediments—triangular in the center flanked by arched end ones—offered ample opportunities for a rich collection of molded terracotta and corbeled brick patterns.

CN05 S. Fred Hahn Building

1894, John Granville Meyers. 233 Pennsylvania Ave. SE

In response to the change in the 1890s from Victorian forms, materials, and details to those inspired by classicism, Meyers designed the Hahn Building with an exceptionally wide central projecting two-and-a-half-story bay window sheathed in molded copper. Its principal ornament is a great floral swag between the second and third floors. Two of the four original terracotta lion-head window brackets survive on the top story.

CN06 Theodore Mayers Row

1887, John Granville Meyers. 215–221 3rd St. SE

These four houses are fine examples of a typical late Victorian row house type built in wide areas of the city as speculative housing. Their form is characterized by wide, square, pedimented bays with large front and narrow side windows. Inexpensive brick is used in a variety of corbeled patterns with molded terracotta tiles often introduced for additional texture and pattern. In the best examples, details of the facades vary to establish rhythmical patterns within a row. Mayers Row, where the houses are smaller in scale than many similar rows, was erected for $10,000, or $2,500 per house.

CN07 House

before 1887. 120 4th St. SE

The architect and date of this particularly fine three-story Italianate house are unknown, but it does appear in the 1887 *Hopkins Real Estate Atlas* for Washington. Hard-burned brick is laid with butter joints to achieve a flat, taut wall surface to better throw into relief the cast-iron window hoods, door surround, and elaborate triple-arched and bracketed cornice.

CN07 120 4th St. SE

CN08 Mary L. Hill House

CN08 Mary L. Hill House

1892, Nicholas T. Haller. 408 A St. SE

Haller designed a number of Capitol Hill houses in which the predominant influence was that of the Richardsonian Romanesque style. The Hill house, built by John H. Nolan at a cost of $8,500, is a particularly imposing example. Intensely architectonic in its forms and details, its two 6-foot-wide bays were designed as separate fields with different window patterns and cornices. The entrance arch and the balcony bay above the double-story projecting circular bay window provide diagonal points of richly articulated surfaces in an otherwise rather stark composition.

CN09 **Row Houses**

1878, Hugh McCaffrey. 325–327 A St. SE

The builder, McCaffrey, erected these two-story homes, which are wider than most row houses in the area, with wood bracketed cornices. They are particularly well proportioned.

CN10 **House**

c. 1903, perhaps by William T. Davis. 321 A St. SE

The popularity of the Italianate style persisted into the twentieth century, as exemplified by this house, which is a twin to the D. K. Meredith House (1903) at 631 G Street SE, also attributed to Davis.

CN11 **Saint Mark's Episcopal Church**

1888–1889, T. Buckler Ghequier. 1894, addition. 1926, addition, Delos Smith. 1930, addition. 3rd and A streets SE

The asymmetry of Baltimore architect T. Buckler Ghequier's Romanesque Revival Saint Mark's Church was due both to its late Victorian design ethos and the original condition of its site, where row houses abutted it on the east edge as they still do at the southwest corner. The church complex was built in several stages, with the main section of the nave constructed in 1888–1889. It was extended to 120 feet and given a tower, chancel, and parish hall in 1894. In 1926–1927 Smith designed a sympathetic, larger parish hall, and in 1930 the small chapel in the southwest corner was built.

The three-aisled church has three oak doors (with elaborate wrought-iron hinges) arranged asymmetrically, two at the base of the corner tower and the third in the sloping wall that leads directly to the east aisle. Several molded terracotta belt courses of different widths (repeating three patterns) add textural richness to the dark handmade brick; in conjunction with red Seneca sandstone trim, the

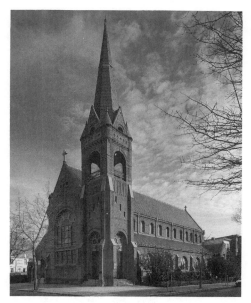

CN11 Saint Mark's Episcopal Church

building's materials achieve richly varied monochromatic surfaces. The lovely 103-foot tower has buttresses on its two lower stages, an arched and balustraded open belfry, and corbeled corner turrets and gables supporting the hexagonal spire.

The direct relationship between the church's external form and its open brick interior (where slender cast-iron columns only nominally separate the nave and side aisles) is a particularly satisfying aspect of its architectural quality. Each of the seven bays has a low, wide tripartite window in the aisles and two arched windows in the clerestory, all in stained glass, which are the glory of the church. Louis C. Tiffany's great baptistery window (1888–1889) is a reproduction of the central section of Gustave Doré's *Christ Leaving the Praetorium* and measures 16 feet by 25 feet. The majority of the other windows were made by Mayer of Munich, which had a studio in New York at the time. The Mayer windows resemble medieval German glasswork and English Gothic Revival work.

CN12 **Two Row Houses**

1870s, Emil S. Friedrich. 321–323 East Capitol SE

This pair of neighboring row houses would seem to be Greek Revival in style, even though they were not erected until the 1870s. Very outmoded for their time with their denticulated cornice and austere appearance, they were designed by an architect who had worked as an architectural draftsman for Robert Mills in the early 1850s.

CN13 Two Houses

c. 1880, August G. Schoenborn. 325, 327 East Capitol St. SE

This pair of three-story, bay-fronted Italianate houses was designed by Schoenborn, a draftsman on the Capitol extensions under Thomas U. Walter during the 1850s and 1860s. He claimed credit as the designer of the Capitol dome's structural system. The attenuated and well-balanced proportions, restrained use of fine quality cast-iron ornament, and attention to subsidiary decorative details distinguish these two houses from less expensive builder-erected examples in the same mode.

CN14 S. W. Tullock House

1887, remodeled, attributed to William Sheets. 506 East Capitol St. NE

The Tullock house facade, a monumental fusion of Richardsonian and Queen Anne elements, is a $4,000 "improvement" to an existing house. The two arches in the 18-inch-thick rusticated stone first story were "relieved by iron beams," installed by builder T. J. Holmes. The composition was an unusual one, with the facade dominated by a swelling second-story corbeled bay that spans

CN14 S. W. Tullock House; CN15 Sarah McC. Spofford House

most of the house's 18-foot width and more than a third of its 26-foot height. An equally wide arch shelters a recessed balcony set atop the bay. Although the windows are expansive, they are of stained and leaded glass and the walls and bay window framing are massive to ensure privacy within.

CN15 Sarah McC. Spofford House

1896, remodeled, William Yost and Brothers. 508 E. Capitol St. NE

The overscaled second-story oriel window faced in pressed tin provides the major interest on Yost's rather erratically composed Spofford house facade. Its 23-foot circumference and 5-foot projection, as well as the deep anthemion frieze that spans the house's width, suggest that it was a stock part intended for a much larger building. Like its neighbor (see CN14), the Spofford house received an entirely new face, including a slate-covered attic story in 1896, but the rectilinearity of the openings, flat brick walls throughout, and classicizing details bespeak the waning of the Victorian era and the waxing of the Arts and Crafts and Classical Revival styles.

CN16 Row Houses

before 1887. 512–516 and 602–608 East Capitol St. NE

The growing sense of East Capitol Street's monumental character during the 1880s, a result of its great width and the deep "parking," or front gardens (actually city rights of way) of its houses, was expressed by increased building heights. Two sets of anonymous undated row houses in the 500 and 600 blocks demonstrate how imposing sheer size and repetition of elements can be. Tautly stretched brick walls are merely overlaid with cast-iron and wood stock parts, perhaps ordered from the catalogs of ironmongers in Baltimore or New York.

CN17 Thomas Healy House

1892, remodeled, William Sheets. 617 A St. NE

This rather imposing example of a full-blown Queen Anne wood row house was the result of renovation of an earlier flat front. The facade was entirely covered by a boldly projecting (4 feet by 8 feet), two-story, double-windowed square bay. The porch has bulbous turned posts, colonial balusters, and fan brackets, a mixture of decorative details typical of the Queen Anne style, as is the delicate linear iron cresting rail above the porch and at the roofline. Sheets was described as the "mechanic" at the time of the modernization.

CN17 Thomas Healy House

CN18 House

c. 1885, Appleton P. Clarke, Jr. 616 East Capitol St. NE

The purest example of the Queen Anne style on Capitol Hill is this early house by Clarke, whose later work was primarily in the Georgian Revival style. After three years of training with Alfred B. Mullett, Clarke opened his own Washington office in 1886. For this house he employed a common 1880s formula for brick houses, a square projecting bay rising from the basement to a gabled roofline to become the major focus of the facade. However, Clarke's adept handling of the surface details, as well as his sure sense of comfortable proportional relationships between the walls and windows, resulted in a thoroughly satisfying textured Queen Anne facade. Horizontal corbeled brick rows and molded terracotta bands of ornament occur at all structurally and visually significant levels, bringing coherence and control to the whole through simple linear patterns. The building's actual sculptural qualities interact with the implied surface layering created by this linear system to create a complex and sophisticated composition.

CN19 638–642 East Capitol St. NE

CN19 Row Houses

1890, Charles Gessford. 638–642 East Capitol St. NE

One of the finest and most prolific architect-builders on Capitol Hill was Charles Gessford, who is best known for his earlier Philadelphia Row (see CN28). This row is one of four distinguished later projects, including the 200 block of 11th Street SE, 200–208 10th Street SE (see CN29), and 824–832 D Street SE (see CN31), adjacent to Philadelphia Row. Much more numerous and distinctive than Gessford's Philadelphia Row were single houses and rows in the Queen Anne style. They are confined to two- or three-story buildings with massive bays, usually square but occasionally alternating with round ones. The maximum effect of a richly textured surface is achieved for the least cost by extensive use of corbeled brick and molded terracotta. High, rusticated stone basements are accompanied by large, solid entry stairs; each floor above is demarcated by several thin bands of corbeled brick or ornamental terracotta moldings, as are intermediate zones established by the segmental arches over doors and windows. Inset corbeled brick panels between stories were common, but the most distinctive use of corbeling was on the beveled corners of the bays and the cornices, which recall Romanesque corbel tables. The best examples have gable roofs, but they extend only the depth of the bays. Stained-glass transom windows with colors so deeply saturated as to be almost opaque were set above tall, narrow double windows often divided by a split turned post. Builders such as Gessford consulted published sources, for example A. J. Bicknell's *Wooden and Brick Buildings with Details* (1875), but they often freely invented their own combinations of forms and details.

CN20 Dr. Richard Kingsman House and Office

CN20 **Dr. Richard Kingsman House and Office**

1895, Appleton P. Clarke, Jr. 711 East Capitol St. SE

The Kingsman house partakes of two traditions, standing between late Victorian eclecticism and the Neoclassicism of the new century. Clarke simplified and abstracted the vocabularies of each, retaining some forms (the two-story semicircular bay) and surface treatments (rusticated limestone basement walls and frieze) of the Victorian era but introducing new compositional devices (pyramidal ordering of windows on the eastern two-thirds and an odd sunken bay window) and depending on architectural rather than sculptural details (smooth limestone for intermediate belt courses, quoins at the entrance, and sawtooth gabled dormer windows). The cost of this double house was $8,000, with the lower story equipped for the doctor's office.

CN21 Antonio Malmati House

CN21 **Antonio Malmati House**

1902, George S. Cooper. 712 East Capitol St. NE

The site, orientation, and architectural vocabulary of the Malmati house are unique in the urban context of East Capitol Street and imply both added expense and bold personalities. Less than half of the triple lot is covered by the large three-bay house with its flat front. A large side garden is overlooked by two octagonal bays. The house, constructed of dark monochromatic brick with brownstone details, was erected by the owner, a building contractor, for $10,000. Cooper's design, a restrained and muscular version of Neoclassicism, is simple and forceful, with windows punched directly into taut brick walls and the skyline broken by stepped end gables.

Vastly overscaled keystone brackets above first-story windows and smaller ones connecting second-floor windows to the simple entablature are unusually sophisticated, even idiosyncratic, design elements.

CN22 **Mrs. S. A. Lawton House**

after 1903, J. A. Rodbird, builder. 28 9th St. NE

The French flavor of the Lawton house is the result not only of its Mansard roof but also of its elegant, self-contained proportions, ashlar masonry construction with corner quoins, and raised window frames. The architect is unknown; the builder erected the house for $4,700.

CN23 **D. T. and Eugenia E. Donohoe House**

1889, Edwin H. Fowler. 1014 East Capitol St. NE

Unadulterated Richardsonian Romanesque buildings on Capitol Hill are rare, although influence of this style pervades most of the late Victorian styles erected here. Two canonical Richardsonian examples are neigh-

boring houses, both substantial, rock-faced, white limestone buildings with deep entry porches set off by foliated columns. The light color of the stone somewhat offsets the ponderousness of the walls, as do intermittent bands of smooth stone that reflect more light than do the textured surfaces.

CN24 **Samuel C. Heald House**

1895, John Granville Meyers. 1016 East Capitol St. NE

Openness resulting from an unusually even balance between walls and windows, variety in window shapes and coherence in their groupings, sensitive handling of rock-faced limestone walls with smooth surfaces emphasizing tectonic seams, and intertwined foliated decoration used in an entirely personal, rather than standardized, manner: all characterize the well-designed and very well-crafted Heald house. The builder, Robert Collins, erected it for $7,000, a considerable sum in 1895.

CN25 **William Hutton House**

1891, Warring Brothers. 1012 Massachusetts Ave. NE

The Warring Brothers, architects and builders, designed the capacious Hutton house in the Colonial Revival style and erected it in

CN25 William Hutton House

brick for $3,500. Its three-story, three-bay format retains some late Victorian forms and details, principally a double-story semicircular bay and small square panes in upper sashes of windows on the first and second stories, an echo of the Queen Anne style. As was common on Washington Colonial Revival houses, decorative and structural elements from both the eighteenth-century American Georgian style and its successor the Federal style have been freely combined on the Hutton house facade. The robustness of some of these details, such as the modillion cornice, and the delicacy of others, the decorated limestone lintels and door arch, are not truly integrated into a unified whole but coexist as harbingers of a new age.

CN26 Fowler Houses

1892, Edwin H. Fowler. 1124, 1126 East Capitol St. NE

The Richardsonian Romanesque and Arts and Crafts styles had natural philosophical affinities, although divergent architectural expressions. However they could be successfully combined, as they were in these two houses designed by their owner and built by William Thompson. Although row houses erected at the same time, each is a distinct composition, consciously individualized by differing forms

and details yet sharing common materials and a fundamental aesthetic approach. In addition to this vertical separation between the two compositions, a horizontal one occurs as the weight of the stylistic influences shifts between the first and second stories. The basements and first levels are covered with rock-faced limestone, with the entries decorated with particularly beautiful Richardsonian ornament. The second stories and wide attic gables, constructed of tan brick but with rough limestone for lintels-cum-belt courses, depend primarily on compositional devices (an abstract Palladian motif on 1124 and the hip-roof dormer at 1126) that speak of Arts and Crafts influence.

CN27 Bartholomew Daly House

1908, Clement A. Didden and Son. 1312 East Capitol St. NE

August Getz and Son were the builders of this unusual Neoclassical house erected for $8,995. The two-story Ionic portico of the Daly house breaks the area's typical row house streetscape, with the facade partially shaded by it and the attic dormers shaded by the tall balustrade. Yellow brick and a red tile roof add to the house's Mediterranean flavor, an early twentieth-century version of a rural or suburban temple house updated for an urban context.

CN28 Philadelphia Row

1865–1867, Charles Gessford. 132–144 11th St. SE

One of the finest and most prolific architect-builders on Capitol Hill was Gessford, who is best known for this, his least typical group of houses. One of the longest unbroken blocks of row houses in the city, the sixteen flat fronts would be mistaken for Federal period buildings except for the very timid bracketed cornice and unusual window pattern. They sit lower to the ground than other rows of the same period, with only five plain granite steps to the front doors and light wrought-iron banisters. Thus the emphasis was on the unusual rhythm of double doors separated by four windows on the three-bay ground story contrasted with two bays stretched across the upper two stories, a subtle asymmetry that would have been unacceptable in the Federal period.

CN29 **George W. Gessford Row**

1891. Charles Gessford. 200–208 10th St. SE

All five of these two-and-half-story brick Queen Anne row houses were erected by architect-builder Charles Gessford for $10,000. They represent the most common type of middle-class speculative row house on Capitol Hill. Projecting square bays with double windows on the fronts and narrow side windows were particularly advantageous on the numbered, north-south running streets. High basements raised the principal rooms above the noise of the streets and afforded privacy from passersby. The houses on this row retain their original steep cast-iron stairs; their simple rails and cut-out patterns allow light to filter through to the basement level as well as to complement the patterned surfaces of the corbeled and molded brick walls.

CN30 **Thomas Simmons House**

1967, 1976–1977, Thomas Simmons. 314–316 9th St. SE

The Thomas Simmons house is one of the few aggressively modern infill additions to the Capitol Hill neighborhood that invite admiration rather than scorn. It was designed in two phases: the first in 1967 and the second in 1976–1977, when an adjacent lot became available. In all, the large site contains the main living quarters, two rental apartments, and one small architectural office. The three living units share a swimming pool at the rear and a garden. At the completion of the second and last phase, the architect described the ensemble as a kind of affluent commune except that its occupants do not experience the loss of privacy felt by those in real communes.

The Simmons house owes its appeal to its oriental-like tranquility. A wooden strip screen and landscaped front yard shield the entry court from the public. The main living spaces are set behind the court, connected to the ends of the front wall with a sloping roof covered with metal sheeting. The viewer can catch a glimpse of the living quarters to the rear, where the motif of wooden strips is repeated, as is the metal roof at the pent. New shapes are also introduced, such as wheel windows on the front of the living quarters. It is doubtful that such a boldly modern design for an infill building in the regulated Capitol Hill Historic District could be approved today. As a product of its era and of preregulation, the Simmons house demonstrates that modern and historic design need not be incompatible.

CN31 **Charles Gessford Row**

1892. Charles Gessford. 824–832 D St. SE

These five Queen Anne row houses are more substantial than many of Gessford's similar Capitol Hill speculative houses. The builder-architect was also the owner-developer of this row, which he erected at a cumulative cost of $26,500. Their height—three tall stories above a high basement—is increased by the conical or gabled roofs that terminate only the rectangular or semicircular bay towers. In addition to size, the alternation of bay shapes and thus skyline treatment, rock-faced stone basement walls, and the proliferation of pressed and corbeled brick patterns account for the more expensive version of Gessford's stand of Capitol Hill row houses.

CN32 **Henry Rabe House**

1891, Frederick G. Atkinson. 820 D St. SE

Of the many substantial, individually designed Capitol Hill houses in which the Richardsonian Romanesque and Queen Anne styles were used together, the Rabe house is one where the two idioms were successfully separated into distinct zones. The house's forms—a massive square front bay intersected by a subsidiary volume whose shallow, gabled bay faces the adjoining alley—are robustly sculptural with the Richardsonian in-

CN32 Henry Rabe House

fluence predominant on the bottom half, evidenced in the wide, arched openings, with Queen Anne playfulness of the small oriel window, evident at the roofline. The dark, rich coloration of the rock-faced Seneca sandstone that covers the basement and first story is matched by the hue of the brick on the upper story and attic walls. The verdigris of the patinated copper, used for roof flashing and pressed ornament as well as for the conical top of the oriel, concentrates intense color on numerous small-scale roof elements. Nearly opaque, densely patterned stained glass, which is used in the semicircular light above the front door and in second-story transom win-

dows, complements the ruddiness of the surrounding walls. The paneled double door is original; spare interlaced Richardsonian ornament beautifully designed and carved. The builder was E. J. Fitzgibbon; the cost, $9,000.

CN33 Eastern Market

1873, Adolph Cluss. 7th St., C St., and North Carolina Ave. SE

The Eastern Market is one of the few remaining market structures in the old L'Enfant City. L'Enfant envisioned farmers' markets located throughout the city as a focus of commercial activity and as a spur to growth of the surrounding community. Many of these market structures fell victim to development pressures close to the center of the city, the replacement of residential functions with commercial activity, and the development of the supermarkets in outlying areas close to emerging residential areas. The survival of Eastern Market is testimony to the retention of the Capitol Hill neighborhood as a residential enclave. Its power as a commercial node spilled over into a few short blocks of shops along Seventh Street, just north of Pennsylvania Avenue. Architect of many municipal structures in the 1860s and 1870s, German-born Adolph Cluss also was a designer of market structures.

This market is the finest in the city to retain its nineteenth-century architectural integrity. Twenty bays long (180 feet) by five bays deep (50 feet), the one-story brick building has a hip monitor roof covered by gray slate shingles. The market's outstanding characteristic

CN33 Eastern Market

CN34 Penn Medical Building

is the adaptation of its brick cladding to its modest *Rundbogenstil,* or Round Arch style. Narrow bays with doors surmounted by large bull's-eye windows alternate with wider sunken window bays. Common bond is used throughout, implying a veneer over a metal frame. The corbeled brick cornice is supplemented on the three projecting entrance bays by massive, double wood brackets carrying a deep overhanging molded wood cornice. The single-volume interior is miraculously unchanged with its iron bar trusses supporting the exposed roof. The addition on the north dates from 1908. The Eastern Market also reinforces the ornamental red brick character of the surrounding Capitol Hill neighborhood.

CN34 **Penn Medical Building**

1983–1986, David M. Schwarz. 650 Pennsylvania Ave. SE

The Penn Medical Building is a Postmodern complex with an office building composed around the marquee and lettering of John Eberson's 1935 Penn Theater and connected by a courtyard to 649 C Street, an apartment house designed by Schwarz as part of the complex. Its refreshingly imaginative glazed terracotta facade is composed in five parts with the three central sections stepping back to create a series of balconies and large windows, welcome amenities for office workers. The fine proportional relationship of the masses, variety of shiny surfaces (polished marble and granite at ground level), and soft but vibrant colors, all echo the flavor of the original building but far surpass it in architectural quality.

CN35 **Ebenezer United Methodist Church**

1897, Crump and Wagner. 400 D St. SE

Tucked away in a residential enclave of Capitol Hill, the Ebenezer United Methodist Church represents the separate religious facilities black residents established for themselves. The southeast section of Capitol Hill, closest to the Navy Yard, spawned modest brick and frame row houses distinctive from their grander neighbors along major diagonal thoroughfares. Prior to 1827, the members of the black population attended the integrated Methodist Episcopal Church, but they were assigned to the galleries. By 1827, the black membership outgrew the space reserved for them, and the Little Ebenezer was established in a frame building at 4th and D streets SE. Over the years, the church served important community functions, including the sponsorship in 1864 of one of the first publicly funded schools for black students.

Constructed in 1896, the current church is the third such structure to occupy the site. The firm of Crump and Wagner designed the modest red brick structure. Its long elevation along 4th Street meets the entrance elevation on D Street in a commanding corner tower. The 4th Street elevation is articulated with a bowed section and stained-glass windows, while the D Street facade is marked by a large rose window above a double entrance door with a stone surround. A short two-story tower anchors the southeast corner of the building. Stone window lintels and white trim enliven an otherwise dark red brick structure.

CN36 **Carbery House**

1813. 423 6th St. SE

Some of the features of the freestanding Maples (see CN37) house are repeated in row houses of the period, such as the Carbery house. This three-bay house, with its side-gable roof, splayed window lintels, and minimal decoration, is typical of the houses built in either brick or wood for the first half of the nineteenth century on Capitol Hill.

CN37 **The Maples**

1795–1796, William Lovering. 619 D St. SE (main facade faces 630 South Carolina Ave.)

The Maples represents the ambitions of speculators who hoped to reap profits from the founding of the federal city. The first owner, William Mayne Duncanson, was one such entrepreneur who, with Thomas Law, invested in city lots. For his own house, Duncanson selected a lot six blocks southeast of the Capitol, along South Carolina Avenue, one of the diagonal thoroughfares. Lovering, designer of houses for other city speculators, provided the designs for Duncanson's house. Speculation in real estate far exceeded the actual demand for housing, and by 1809 Duncanson fell into bankruptcy. Subsequent owners included Francis Scott Key and Constantino Brumidi, who decorated a ballroom addition with his own frescoes. A new owner in 1871 enlarged the house to twenty-one rooms. In 1936, the oldest settlement house in the District, Friendship House, purchased the property. Well-known Washington architect Horace W. Peaslee "colonialized" The Maples and enlarged it to fifty-five rooms in adapting it for Friendship House.

In this work the building was reoriented to its current address on D Street, leaving the original main facade of the house on South Carolina Avenue to the rear of the lot. The new five-bay facade is articulated with a three-bay pavilion supporting a triangular pediment with a bull's-eye window. The door surround and fanlight date from the 1930s, as do the replacement windows throughout. Peaslee's remodeling with large additions to the east and west provide a symmetrical framing for the house. A new theater was constructed on the site of Brumidi's ballroom.

The floor plan of the original block with a central hall flanked by two rooms on either side remains, as do the original cherry railing of the main staircase and the chair rails in the first-floor rooms. Despite all the alterations, The Maples still conveys the spatial relationship of an early Capitol Hill house on a city lot and the scale of residential development of the late eighteenth century. At the same time, it preserves the work of Peaslee, one of the city's most accomplished Colonial Revival architects.

CN38 James H. Grant House

1889, James H. Grant. 1988, additions, Hector Alvarez. 613 South Carolina Ave. SE

Symmetrical one-story additions on either side of the Grant house nearly a century after its placement in the center of a double lot are

CN38 James H. Grant House

complementary modern interpretations of its simple Victorian proportions, forms, and details. The original owner was his own builder, erecting a particularly well-proportioned two-story, three-bay brick house for $4,000. His choices of stock cast-iron door and window hoods and wood bracketed cornice resulted in a pleasant interplay between naturalistic molded curves of the windows, stylized incised ornament over the door, and the layered, lathe-turned, and carved entablature and cornice. The elegance and simplicity of the Italianate style flat front was a perennial favorite in the neighborhood, witnessed by this very late example.

CN39 Annie M. Mulhall House

1879, Owen Donnelly. 520 5th St. SE

Nice proportions with tall slender windows and a particularly fine bracketed cornice distinguish the Mulhall house, one of the architect-builder's many Capitol Hill homes. Donnelly repeated the curve of the slight arch over the windows in the triple arch of the entablature, a small detail that added greatly to the house's sophistication. The $1,600 Italianate Mulhall house seems never to have had cast-iron window hoods.

CN40 Christ Church

1807–1966, Robert Alexander. 620 G St. SE

The earliest structure in the city built to serve an ecclesiastical purpose is the Episcopal

CN40 Christ Church

church on Capitol Hill. For many years, Christ Church, the oldest and probably the first Gothic Revival structure in Washington, was cited as an example of the work of Benjamin Henry Latrobe. In actuality, the original section of Christ Church was designed by Robert Alexander, a member of the vestry, a builder, and Latrobe's chief contractor for the Navy Yard. As successive architects expanded the church structure beyond the simple original block, the Latrobe legend persisted and influenced the most recent rebuilding efforts.

The original 1807 block likely was a simple, hastily erected two-story Flemish bond brick structure that was distinguished for its pointed-arch windows and vaulted cove ceiling. Its service to the population that clustered near the Navy Yard won it the name "new church in the Navy Yard." This original block is now sandwiched between the 1824 expansion to the north and the 1849 narthex and bell tower to the south. Stucco was applied to the narthex and bell tower in 1868, an exterior treatment that was extended to the entire structure by the end of the century.

In 1877–1878, architect William H. Hoffman Victorianized the structure by adding the elegant, slender cast-iron columns in the interior and the stained-glass windows around the exterior. In 1891, the central bell tower was raised and the interior adorned with frescoes. A successful practitioner of the Colonial

Revival style, Washington architect Delos Smith in 1921 removed the frescoes and reformed the interior walls to resemble Venetian marble blocks. Finally, in 1955–1954, Horace W. Peaslee attempted to return the church to what was considered Latrobe's original intentions by simplifying the interior. He provided for simple plaster walls and ceiling and had the cast-iron columns painted white.

The present building bespeaks a Latrobian simplicity in its form. It is located far back from the sidewalk in a wide expanse of lawn. The most prominent feature, the bell tower, is punctuated with a projecting pointed-arch entrance vestibule flanked with small lancet windows. Small corner towers crown the main tower. Buttresses frame the bell tower and the narthex walls. At the fifth level of the tower is a large, circular stained-glass window composed of six circles surrounding a central one. The modest church structure masks the several additions to the rear that house the rectory, offices, parish hall, and support facilities.

CN41 Isaac Kaufman House

1893, remodeling, Charles Meade, Jr. 634 G St. SE

In 1893 Isaac Kaufman hired mechanic Charles Meade, Jr., to reface his house at a cost of $4,000. The result is a successful mixture of Richardsonian and Queen Anne elements, with rock-faced limestone used for the basement and first floor, red brick with limestone details for the second, and a slate mansard roof with pressed metal dormer windows in the attic. Unusually fine Richardsonian ornament serves as a continuous capital-cum-frieze for a series of slender colonnettes that enframe the arched door and bay window at the ground level.

CN42 House

c. 1850–1870. 541 7th St. SE

No large-scale Gothic Revival houses exist on Capitol Hill, but there are numerous wood cottages with Gothic trim of varying degrees of richness. Most of this jigsaw-made trim is attached to two-story, flat-fronted houses without the characteristic high cross first designed by A. J. Davis and published in Andrew Jackson Downing's *Cottage Residences* (1842) and available in similar publications up to the 1870s. This modest example of a

Gothic Revival form is ornamented with Queen Anne windows (a central square of clear glass circumscribed by small squares of colored glass) and a bargeboard.

CN43 **Washington Mechanics Savings Bank** (The City Bank)

1908, Harding and Upman. Corner of 8th and G streets SE

Harding and Upman's design for the City Bank followed a common Beaux-Arts model for small, inexpensive bank buildings. Solid granite for the base and deep entablature plus attic, wide tan brick pilaster-fronted wall segments, and iron-barred ground-story windows were combined to give an image of secure, impenetrable structures. Large upper-story windows that fill the span between pilasters imply a single volume, top-lit interior, a typical bank business room. August Getz and Sons built the bank for $16,000.

CN44 **Marine Barracks**

1805, George Hadfield. 1902–1906, Hornblower and Marshall. 8th St. between G and I streets SE

In 1801, President Thomas Jefferson designated this site for the headquarters of the Marine Corps in Washington. Its location, just north of the entrance to the Navy Yard, likely reinforced the importance of the 8th Street thoroughfare and encouraged its development as a commercial strip as far north as Pennsylvania Avenue.

The barracks consist of a walled enclosure, around which are placed administrative buildings, duplex houses for officers, and barracks for enlisted persons. The 9th Street facade is of particular interest because of the articulation of the long wall into a central tower, hyphens, and end towers. The central tower is crowned with a castellated parapet, while the end towers are topped with hip roofs. A lineup of officer's duplex houses forms much of the 8th Street elevation. The center quadrangle is used as a parade ground. Today, the installation serves as home for the Marine Corps band and special ceremonial details. The number of corpsmen attached to the barracks far exceeds the accommodations available, so modern dormitory blocks were constructed nearby.

The original barracks structures were replaced in 1901–1902, according to a comprehensive scheme prepared by the Washington firm of Hornblower and Marshall. The Commandant's House on the G Street side of the complex at the far northern end was retained. Dating from 1805, it was designed with a four-bay, two-and-a-half-story main block, flanked by one-and-a-half-story wings. While its walls are unchanged, the roofline has taken the form of the Second Empire mansard roof lined with prominent dormer windows. The original form of the Commandant's House is attributed to George Hadfield, although alterations over the years have obscured its original appearance.

CN45 **Washington Navy Yard**

1799–present, Lovering and Dyer, Benjamin Henry Latrobe, and others. Bounded by M St. SE, 1st St. SE, Anacostia River, and 11th St. SE

A city within a city, the Washington Navy Yard possesses its own street system, post office, parks, gasoline station, housing, chapels, and work houses. The Navy Yard also is a unique enclave of 115 acres in the District of Columbia, essentially an industrial center set amid a nonindustrial city.

The Navy Yard was established in 1799 as a shipbuilding facility. By 1803, a few buildings stood on the site, but they did not conform to any particular plan. In that year, Benjamin Henry Latrobe was hired to de-

CN45 Washington Navy Yard, before remodeling

velop a long-range plan for the development of the facility. Latrobe's work on the Navy Yard included a unifying plan that tied together the existing officers' housing with anticipated new buildings, wharves, and industrial structures. His most enduring contribution is the 1804–1805 Navy Yard Main Gate, a long, narrow building along M Street at its axis with 8th Street. The original Main Gate rose one story and presented distinct north and south facades. The opening of the north facade often is described as a miniature triumphal arch, the opening for which is supported by solid Doric columns. The opening on the south facade was a low, semicircular brick arch, a shape identified with Latrobe's architectural style. Guardhouses flanked the gate opening. Major rebuilding of the 1870s replaced Latrobe's gate houses and sandwiched the openings with a three-story brick structure on the sides and a two-story addition on the top.

During the nineteenth and twentieth centuries, the Navy Yard became populated with long, rectangular industrial structures, lined up with geometric precision along the grid street pattern. The buildings served shipbuilding activities until 1876, when the requirements of the vessels exceeded the Navy Yard facilities. After that time, the Navy Yard focused on ordnance design and technical experiments on material. One of the most prominent industrial buildings is the Optical Tower, constructed 1918–1919, which takes calibrated sightings of the Capitol, Washington Monument, and Masonic Temple in Alexandria, Virginia. Several of the other in-

dustrial buildings have been converted to museums and centers for the study of naval history.

A few patches of greenery remain, most notably Leutze Park close to the Main Gate. Here, the site's historic residential structures are located, as well as historic bronze ordnance. Of special interest are the Second Officers House of 1801 and the Tingey house of 1804, both designed by Lovering and Dyer. While significant for their antiquity, both houses have been altered to suit a succession of occupants.

CN46 Row Houses

1894, William Yost. 1000–1010 Pennsylvania Ave. SE

The builder William Yost was resident at 1002 in this intact row of six Richardsonian brick houses. Although their design lacks sophisticated details and refined proportions, it compensates with robust forms, a variety of stoops, bays, and balconies so asymmetrically composed that it is difficult to discern where vertical divisions occur.

CN47 James Buchanan School

1894–1895, Office of the Building Inspector. 13th and E streets SE

The James Buchanan School was one of the last public school buildings the Office of the

Building Inspector designed before municipal building design was opened to architects in private practice. It can be described as one of the last gasps of the Romanesque Revival in District public school buildings and one of the most robust examples of the style. Its construction near 13th Street for white students signifies the sizeable population that had settled east of Lincoln Park. For many years, black housing in the Capitol Hill neighborhood was concentrated closest to the Capitol, while whites settled in the outer rings in newer housing. The original eight-room school proved too small for the growing population, and in the 1920s, additions were appended to the north.

Many of the red brick schoolhouses of the 1880s and 1890s employed common design features. The Buchanan School was an exception to the common pattern. Its bowed central pavilion creates a towerlike effect, accentuated by a conical roof and a flagpole at the top. The heavy stone lintels give the two double windows in the bow a distinct prominence. The flanking pavilions, measuring two bays each, are made up of double round-arch windows on the first floor and double segmental-arch windows at the second floor. The side entrances are notable for the large, circular-arch entrances; each arch springs from elaborately carved imposts.

To the east of the Buchanan School and its later additions is the Buchanan School playground, a highly sculptural array of concrete, wood, and brick forms intended to serve as a new "play plaza." Inspired by First Lady Mrs. Lyndon B. Johnson's interest in "beautification," Mrs. Vincent Astor of New York City hired architect Simon Breines and landscape architect M. Paul Friedberg, both of New York City, to create an innovative recreational area for Capitol Hill children. The park was conceived in 1966 and constructed in early 1968, just before the riots that accompanied the assassination of Martin Luther King, Jr., swept through the city. At the time of the park's completion, this section of Capitol Hill was viewed as possessing dispiriting ghetto conditions. The playground was "aimed directly at the relief of human despair."

CN48 Congressional Cemetery

1807. G–H streets and 17th–19th streets SE

Originally founded as a neighborhood cemetery by Capitol Hill residents, Congressional

CN48 Congressional Cemetery, Cenotaphs

Cemetery is located on L'Enfant's third largest public square after the Capitol and White House. L'Enfant intended a large U-shaped building to be placed on this site; by 1793 it was known as the marine hospital site. In 1816 the cemetery was renamed when part of it was set aside for the interment of congressmen. In that year Benjamin Henry Latrobe designed the congressional cenotaphs that continued to be used until 1877, when Arlington National Cemetery became the national burial ground. Starkly abstract in their geometry, they are some of the few examples in this country of the influence of late eighteenth-century French visionary architecture.

CN49 District of Columbia National Guard Armory

1940–1942, Nathan C. Wyeth. East Capitol Street between 19th and 22nd streets SE

A stake in securing East Capitol Street as a mall of public and semipublic buildings, the District of Columbia National Guard Armory is sited along that major thoroughfare and its easternmost point before meeting the Robert F. Kennedy Stadium and the Anacostia River. Constructed at the outbreak of World War II, its design and location coincided with a renewed interest in shifting the focus of "official Washington" to the east of the Capitol. Nathan C. Wyeth, who served as the District

Capitol Hill Neighborhood 48-53

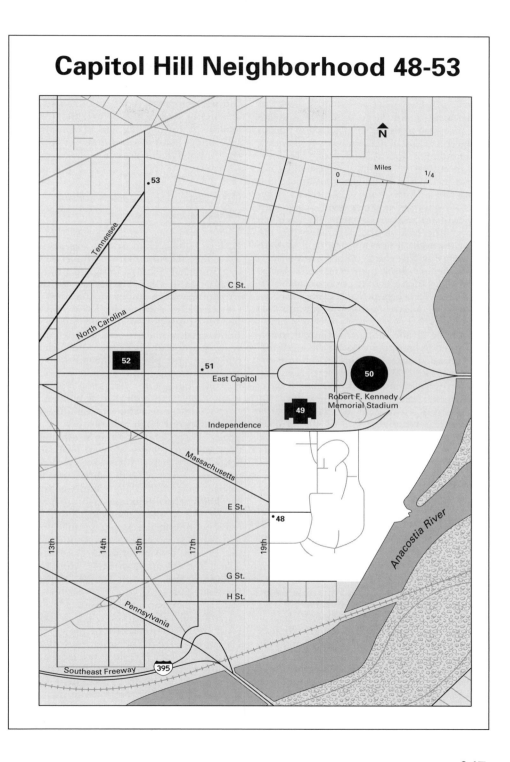

of Columbia's municipal architect from 1934 to 1946, oversaw the design and construction of the project. The armory was intended as the focal point for the National Guard in the District of Columbia and to house its administrative offices.

The armory is a large symmetrical structure of several parts. Its central section houses a large rectangular drill hall, covered with a commanding elliptical shed roof. The shed roof resembles an anchored white sheet billowing in the windy heights of Capitol Hill before the land descends to the river's edge. The roof is formed of a limestone arch around the perimeter and vertical strips of glass block between the base of the perimeter and the top of the walls. Encircling the drill hall are four office wings: the general headquarters, the engineers' offices, quartermasters' offices, and artillery quarters to the rear of the building. The office wings provide space for classrooms, rifle ranges, meeting rooms, and dining rooms.

The main facade, along East Capitol Street, is sheathed in limestone and cut through with five vertical strips of windows over five entrance openings. Metal panels separating the floors are ornamented with a military stars-and-stripes design. Incised lines give an impression of rustication and reinforce the essentially horizontal effect of the armory complex. Incised lines at the center of the frieze create a stylized eagle design, a Moderne version of a classic public building motif.

CN50 Robert F. Kennedy Stadium

1960–1965, George A. Dahl. 22nd and East Capitol streets NE

The Robert F. Kennedy Stadium is located at the easternmost terminus of East Capitol Street, near the banks of the Anacostia River. It forms a commanding focal point for this vista, although from the residential areas, it is somewhat obscured by the heavy tree lines of East Capitol Street. Its large size makes it visible from many parts of the northeast and southeast sections of the city. Constructed in the early 1960s, it was named in honor of Kennedy after his assassination in 1968.

Dallas architect George A. Dahl designed the stadium in a nearly perfectly circular plan. The stadium slopes toward the playing field, much of it protected with a cantilevered roof

over the upper deck. From the exterior, the waving lines of the stadium walls and the slope of the stadium seats give the impression of an elliptical structure in motion—a roller coaster-like form of reinforced concrete bents and steel supports. In an era of roofed sports behemoths and artificial turf, the Kennedy Stadium is a reassuring symbol of sportsmanship under natural conditions set within an appropriately heroic arena.

CN51 Eastern Senior High School

1921–1923, Snowden Ashford. 17th and East Capitol streets NE

Eastern Senior High School was one of the last public school buildings Municipal Architect Snowden Ashford designed prior to his resignation in 1921. He had served the District government for more than two and a half decades, starting in 1895 as assistant building inspector in the old Office of the Building Inspector. He possessed definite ideas as to appropriate styles for municipal public buildings and placed a strong Elizabethan and Gothic stamp on the public school buildings he designed. His design philosophy meshed perfectly with that of William B. Ittner of Saint Louis, who was commissioned to design Central High School (today Cardozo Senior High School). Ittner's adaptation of the Collegiate Gothic style to Central High School likely inspired Ashford's own designs for Dunbar Senior High School (now demolished), completed in 1916, and for the Eastern High School building. Ashford persisted in the use of the Collegiate Gothic in this building, despite the growing public popularity of the Colonial Revival style and the urging of the Eastern Alumni Association to abandon the "Anheuser-Busch Gothic" style.

Eastern Senior High School, constructed for white students, covers a spacious site of four city blocks on the eastern edge of the Capitol Hill neighborhood. Its location is a reflection of the tendency of the white population to locate in the newer outlying areas, leaving the older housing stock closest to the Capitol to the black population. The large building is laid out in a rectangular plan arranged around a central auditorium. Two turreted towers astride a two-story porte-cochère with Gothic arch openings give prominence to the central pavilion. Elliptical driveways encircle a small terraced landscape

CN52 East Capitol Street Car Barn

and staircase. Broad banks of windows define the flanking classroom hyphens, each of which terminates in a projecting end pavilion embellished with limestone sheathed bay windows. Limestone belt courses hold together the sprawling structure. When completed, the building was noted in a national educational journal as possessing generous facilities for academic, business, and technical training. Eastern's architecture was cited as representing the ultimate in eastern school architecture and its facilities as constituting a veritable embarrassment of riches.

CN52 **East Capitol Street Car Barn**

1896, Waddy B. Wood. 1983, Martin and Jones. 1400 East Capitol St.

A tour de force in brick, the East Capitol Street Car Barn demonstrates that an essentially industrial structure can exist in harmony with its residential surroundings. The Car Barn, located at the terminus of the Metropolitan Railroad Company's streetcar lines, was intended as a storage shed for the streetcars, a repair shop, and administrative offices for the streetcar company. The construction of this substantial car barn testifies to the successful electrification, with a conduit system, of Washington's rapid transit system. It was constructed seven years after congressional legislation required Washington trolley companies to operate by mechanical means rather than by animal traction. A narrow

office structure measuring 433 feet long by 46 feet wide occupies the south side of the block, while sheds and shops were located to the north side. Today, only the walls of the shed and shops survive, which enclose and form the framework for modern low-rise apartment houses constructed to resemble town houses. The firm of Martin and Jones designed the conversion of the office structure to the new apartments.

The most compelling element of the Car Barn is the original office structure, running along East Capitol Street NE, between 14th and 15th streets. Designed in the Romanesque Revival style, its massing is classical in inspiration and its brickwork among the most elaborate in the Capitol Hill neighborhood. A central pavilion is linked to two end pavilions at the corners of the block with long hyphens. The main pavilion rises three stories, is crowned with a steep mansard roof, and is flanked by two-story square towers with mansard roofs. Panels of brick diaperwork formed of glazed headers encircle the frieze line of the pavilion and towers. A circular arch marks the entrance to the pavilion. The end pavilions are downsized versions of the central pavilion.

CN53 **William Benning Webb School**

1899–1901, Glenn Brown. 601 15th St. NE

Well-known lobbyist for the American Institute of Architects, Glenn Brown designed the William Benning Webb School, a school for whites located in the Rosedale section of the Capitol Hill neighborhood. The Webb School building is a curious one, given Brown's highly partisan articles favoring a larger role for architects in private practice in the federal government's architectural program. One of his arguments in favor of private practitioners was that the government's architects were content to design federal government buildings in the Romanesque Revival style while private architects had moved on to classical styles, inspired by the World's Columbian Exposition of 1893.

If Brown had a problem with Romanesque Revival public buildings, the Webb School is a contradiction of his public pronouncements. However, in the Webb School, Brown may have offered a glimpse into how the Romanesque style might be integrated into a simple red brick block while displaying Colonial Revival design motifs. Flemish bond with glazed headers forms the wall surface as far as the sill line of the first-floor windows. The brick lintels above the first- and second-floor windows are subtly different from the rest of the wall surface brick, giving the impression of rubbed brick. At the frieze is a diamond-shaped design formed of two rows of glazed headers laid in a zigzag pattern. Brick stringcourses at the second-floor round-arch spring line and at the first-floor window sill line tie together the composition. Today, the old Webb School serves as an adjunct to the modern Myrtilla Miner Elementary School to the south.

Southeast of the Anacostia River (SE)

Pamela Scott

WHILE THE BOUNDARIES OF THE DISTRICT OF COLUMBIA were under consideration, Thomas Jefferson suggested that a substantial area on the eastern shore of what the English settlers called the Eastern Branch of the Potomac River be included in the District of Columbia for reasons of military security. Jefferson was responsible for reviving and including the original Indian name Anacostia for the name of the river, as it appeared on early engraved maps of the city. Anacostia is the Latinized version of the Indian village Nacochtanke (meaning a town of traders), which appeared on John Smith's 1612 map of the region. Today it is used generically to refer to the southeast segment of the city east of the river.

As with all outlying areas of the city, Anacostia developed haltingly, but nonetheless, due to its proximity to the Navy Yard (see CN45, p. 264), it has the distinction of being Washington's first suburb. Pierre Charles L'Enfant had determined that the best harbors were along the northern shore of the river and planned major military installations there. This development became a significant factor in Anacostia's development, as the Navy Yard Bridge at 11th Street SE, erected in wood early in the nineteenth century, connected Anacostia directly to the most important industrial installation in the city. The bridge was burned during the British invasion of Washington in August 1814, not to be replaced until 1846. Three years later the community was large enough to warrant a post office at the foot of the bridge. In 1853 the government purchased a large tract of land in Anacostia for the Government Hospital for the Insane at the urging of social reformer Dorothea Dix (see SE06). Renamed Saint Elizabeths in 1916, it was designed by Thomas U. Walter to be a model hospital set within spacious grounds laid out along picturesque landscape principles, although its elevated site already provided many natural advantages.

271

Southeast of Anacostia
SE 1-6

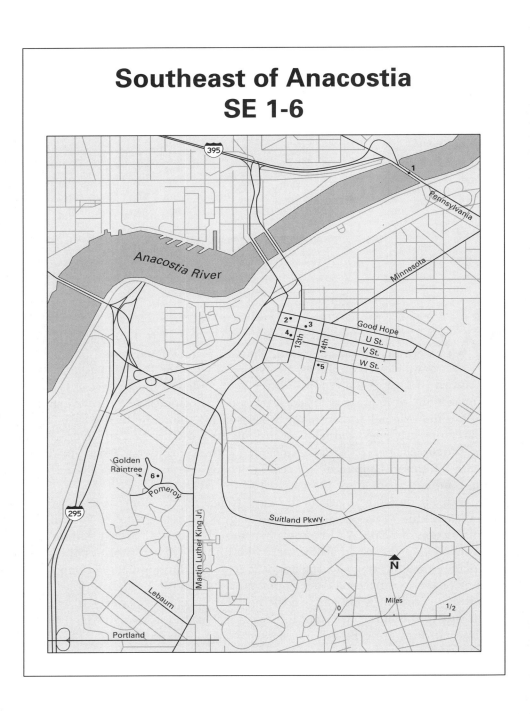

As the sections of the city east of the Anacostia River developed later than other areas, the intact contiguous ground of several Civil War forts now serves as a series of interconnected public parks. Most of the forts in the southeast sector were located on strategic high commanding positions and still retain much of their perimeter walls. Fort Stanton, off Morris Road SE, was built on a ridge 279.7 feet above the Potomac and retains some well-preserved rifle pits in the sides of its parapet walls. This continuous green chain winds through numerous neighborhoods laid out by developers with their own widely varying street patterns in response to the area's diverse landscape conditions. All of the shoreline is occupied by public parks or the extensive grounds of the Naval Research Laboratory at the Bolling Anacostia Tract. The high ground that runs through the area and the large unbuilt areas provide two natural amenities lacking in many parts of the city.

Streetcars did not reach Anacostia across the 11th Street Bridge until 1875, thirteen years later than other areas of the city. The wood bridge carrying Pennsylvania Avenue across the Anacostia River that had burned in 1845 was not replaced by an iron bridge until 1890. It was subsequently replaced in 1939 by the present John Philip Sousa Bridge (SE01) designed by McKim, Mead and White. These lags in services were to be typical of Anacostia's later development. By the 1970s only 16 percent of the houses in the area southeast of the river had been built prior to 1940. Wartime housing needs and private and government-sponsored housing developments during the 1940s, 1950s, and 1960s still account for the majority of structures in the city's Southeast Quadrant.

SE02 F. W. Woolworth Co. Store

1930s, unknown. 1231 Good Hope Rd. SE

This Woolworth's is the best preserved of all of Washington's five-and-ten-cent stores, a rapidly disappearing typology. Miraculously, it retains its shiny red metal frieze with original gold lettering and logo. The rectilinear glass storefront was designed to display merchandise as openly as possible (while keeping it under cover) in order to entice shoppers into the interior. Angled glass walls lead to two deeply set glass doors, intended to allow easy access to the shopping area or the soda fountain. Even the Rococo pressed-tin ceiling and vaguely classical wall paneling and window frames survive. Sleek, slick, and cheap in its Art Deco style, it is a remnant of another

SE02 F. W. Woolworth Co. Store

era now most often found in small-town America.

SE03 House

c. 1875, unknown. 1312 U St. SE

The Union Land Association, formed in 1854, transformed 100 acres of farmland north of the 11th Street Bridge into a fifteen-block suburban grid with graded streets and paved gutters. Uniontown was initially restricted to white residents, but due to the financial failure of the Union Land Company it became the nucleus of an important black neighborhood. The proximity of Uniontown, or Old Anacostia, to Barrys Farm was another stimulus to the entire area's development as a black community. James Barry was an early landowner who in 1802 had been voted president of the newly formed First Chamber of the City Council. Barry Farms, as it was later known, was a post–Civil War settlement for freed slaves sponsored by the United States Government's Freedmen's Bureau. It comprises seventeen blocks bounded by Martin Luther King, Jr., Avenue, Good Hope Road, and 16th and W streets, with the widening of 14th Street between U and V streets to serve as a market area. One-acre plots, which sold for between $125 and $300, came with the lumber to erect houses. Its 500 residents built their own houses, primarily after their regular working hours.

Many of the cottages and row houses of Old Anacostia survive. Although some have lost their decorative wood bargeboards, most have retained front porches with turned posts

and spindles and brackets with stylized plant forms cut out with jigsaws. One of the grandest is the wide, three-bay clapboard house at 1312 U Street, with a distinctive cupola, deep cornice, and square-columned porch. The builder's repeated use of elaborate brackets of differing sizes and details to support the overhangs of the porch, second-floor window hoods, cornice, and cupola roof resulted in a particularly sculptural and architectonic composition. Allied to these qualities are its fine proportions with tall French windows on the ground floor. The flat door and window frames have eared architraves and bases with profiles that replicate those of the porch column bases.

SE04 Saint Teresa of Avila Church

1879, Baldwin and Pennington. 13th and V streets SE

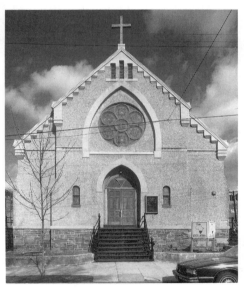

E. Francis Baldwin of the Baltimore firm of Baldwin and Pennington designed Saint Teresa's for a mixed German, Irish, and African American Catholic parish; it was built by Isaac Beer. A brick hall church, Saint Teresa's facade is framed by a corbeled cornice set in a false stepped gable pattern and a high, uncoursed fieldstone basement. Gothic Revival in style, it has buttresses to support the side walls with round-arch windows on the flanks, but its round-arch entry is set within a pointed-arch frame, as is the large rose window above it. Later stucco obscures some of the original

SE06 Saint Elizabeths Hospital (Government Hospital for the Insane)

limestone trim, principally a belt course located at the top of the door, and imitates limestone in areas that are actually brick, including the arches surrounding the door and rose window. The wide central section steps forward slightly to give added prominence to the main axis. Subtle changes in plane—the corbeled cornice, a single course of bricks set diagonally, the projecting central bay, slightly recessed doorway, and projecting upper arch—all cast narrow shadows to enliven what are now planar but rough-textured surfaces. Saint Teresa's retains its unusually wide cast-iron steps and balusters, a characteristic prevalent in Washington's domestic architecture of the period.

SE05 Frederick Douglass House, National Park Service (Cedar Hill)

c. 1855–1859, unknown. 1411 W St. SE

Although modest in its scale and ornamentation, the Frederick Douglass House exhibits characteristics promulgated by Andrew Jackson Downing and his followers for a romantic cottage situated in natural surroundings. The gable intersecting the roof in the center bay of the main facade is an external expression of the cross-axial flow of interior space associated with Downing's picturesque principles for homey domestic architecture. The second-story bay window together with those added later on the ground story brought in more light at the same time that they provided wider views of the surrounding countryside. The porch traversing the entire front (an American invention) helps to break down the division between inside and outside space, while it provides a partially sheltered locale from which to enjoy prospects and fresh air. Floor-to-ceiling windows on the first floor, which are obscured by the porch, admit additional light and could be opened for cross ventilation. The front door with side lights harks back to earlier nineteenth-century styles. The overlay of classical details, the Doric porch

columns and bay window pilasters, on what Downing proposed as a medieval revival form with cross gables, shows how each builder or owner interpreted the new style according to individual tastes and needs.

SE06 Saint Elizabeths Hospital (Government Hospital for the Insane)

1852–1953, Thomas U. Walter. Martin Luther King, Jr., Ave. between Pomeroy Rd. and Lebaum St. SE

Few of the more than one hundred structures within the 336 acres comprising Saint Elizabeths Hospital are architecturally significant. The grounds immediately surrounding the first hospital building were laid out following picturesque landscaping principles within a year or two of Andrew Jackson Downing's picturesque plan for the Mall, but the only remnant of them is the orientation of the original building. The hospital was designed by Thomas U. Walter in consultation with the hospital's first superintendent, Charles H. Nichols, following organizational and therapeutic principles developed at the Pennsylvania Hospital for the Insane by its superintendent, Thomas M. Kirkbride (1809–1883). About thirty mental hospitals based on Kirkbride's twenty-six rules for their design and construction were erected in the United States during the 1850s and 1860s. Saint Elizabeths was unique among state and private institutions for treatment of the mentally ill in that it was national in character and accepted patients from anywhere in the country, as well as residents of the District of Columbia. Part of its congressional mandate was to admit members of the military who became ill while serving the country.

Constructed in brick, Saint Elizabeths was designed in a functional Elizabethan Revival style with angled corner buttresses on the three central towers, battlemented cornices, label molding over windows, and a two-story oriel window above the main entry. The central section was the administration building, which provided offices and housing for the staff. The sexes were segregated in flanking, setback wings, which also diminished in height as they receded from the main block, thus admitting abundant light and air to all parts of the building. The setback or staggered wings were an innovation at Saint Elizabeths urged by Nichols, who argued that they were an improvement on Kirkbride's strictly linear arrangement. Kirkbride urged implementation of Nichols's improvement in the 1880 edition of his book *On the Construction, Organization, and General Arrangement of Hospitals for the Insane.* Private rooms for a maximum of 250 patients, each with a view of the "pleasure grounds," line the central corridor that forms the central spine of Saint Elizabeths. Kirkbride believed that a pastoral setting, comparative privacy afforded by division of each wing into sixteen wards or "families" housing ten to twenty patients, and ample light and ventilation would provide a humane environment and effect a cure for the insane.

Dependence on congressional approval and funding was a constant problem in obtaining high quality architectural facilities at Saint Elizabeths when additional facilities were needed. By the 1870s, overcrowding due to admission of Union veterans mandated additional buildings; an improved variation of the original building intended solely for women patients was proposed by Nichols in 1874 but not funded. In 1878 the first of eighteen cottages, Atkins Hall, a plain but substantial two-story brick building, was built for long-term patients. Statistics compiled in the early 1870s had revealed that only about one-fifth of patients treated in institutions following Kirkbride's model recovered. In 1879 the first of two large dormitory-type structures to house 250 male patients, the Relief Building, was built. Subsequently, small dormitories were the type favored. The most significant additions were a group of fifteen H-shaped, hip-roof buildings designed with Mediterranean details, such as tile roofs, deeply projecting bracketed eaves, and classical forms and details. They were built between 1901 and 1903 following plans produced by the Boston architectural firm of Shepley, Rutan and Coolidge.

SE07 Anacostia Park Pavilion

1975–1977, Keyes Condon Florance. Anacostia River Park

The impressively monumental open pavilion in Anacostia River Park, originally planned as a skating rink, was erected by the National Park Service as a shelter, public toilets, snack bar, and storage facility. From the adjacent freeway the pavilion is experienced as a massive floating rectangular slab, alternately solid and void. Its flat reinforced-concrete truss roof, engineered by James Madison Cutts, constitutes more than a third of the structure's height. The roof is lightly carried by two ranges of thin columnar supports and shelters a series of blank-walled, curvilinear forms with an open axis between them. The pavilion is a particularly powerful joint exercise of both architectural formalism and the honest expression of structural engineering. The roof truss patterns—king posts of the ends, a cross in the center, and diagonals facing inward to join them—form a geometry of triangles at once simple and complex. The pavilion's structure is particularly appropriate given its location, as many of Washington's numerous early bridges that spanned both the Potomac and Anacostia rivers were trusses carried by posts.

SE08 Dr. M. S. Fealty House

1935, John Joseph Earley. 2911 W St. SE

Earley's Art Deco Fealty house is atypical of its neighborhood but notable both for the quality of its modern design and the use of the Washington-based architect's own patented method of precast concrete slab wall construction. Earley's system was designed to have particularly thin walls built by imbedding steel rods in 2-by-4-inch wood studs set sideways. Exterior concrete wall panels and doors were decorated with colorful and often

Southeast of Anacostia
SE 7 - 10

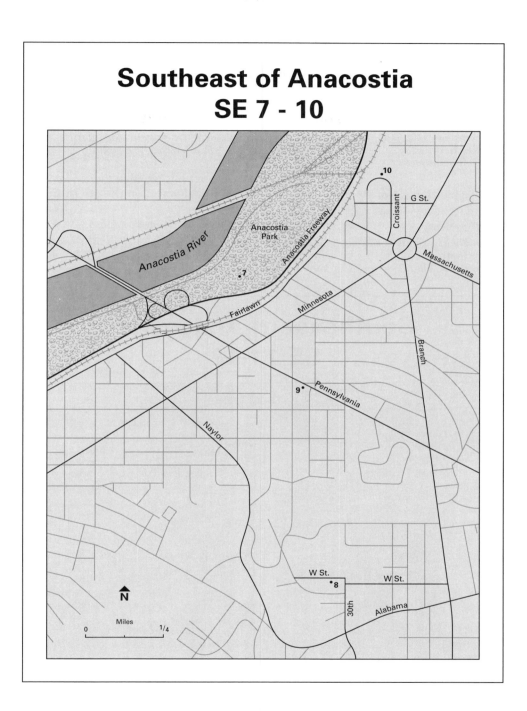

elaborate mosaic patterns. Earley's architectural vocabulary depended on primary geometric forms with large circular and square windows centered in prefabricated panels manufactured by the Earley Process Corporation located in Washington. The simplicity of his designs and prefabricated system, often employed on small, single-story houses, did not compromise either aesthetic or construction quality.

SE09 Engine House No. 19

1910–1911, Averill, Hall and Adams. 2813 Pennsylvania Ave. SE

Although its original brick walls have been covered with stucco and its roof with rubber, the romantic charm of the Arts and Crafts

style Engine House No. 19 flourishes. Its charm depends primarily on the picturesque massing of its form. The octagonal hose tower with rough, primitive quoins; the irregularly formed, stone arched entries; and the steeply sloping roofs with bungalow dormers and overhanging bracketed eaves were meant to complement the domestic architecture of the nearby suburban neighborhood.

SE10 District of Columbia Center for Therapeutic Recreation (Joseph H. Cole Recreation Center)

1977, Cooper-Lecky Partnership. 3030 G St. SE

The Cole Recreation Center is a landmark facility in both social and architectural realms. It is the second public recreation facility in

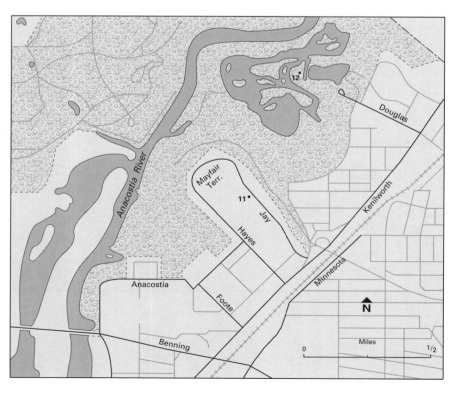

Southeast of Anacostia
SE 11-12

SE09 Engine House No. 19

the country specifically designed to serve re-
tarded and handicapped persons. The
Washington-based firm of Kent Cooper and
William Lecky designed the double-story, irregularly formed, two-part building to provide physical and psychological shelter on the
exterior as well as on the interior. Set on the
edge of Fort Dupont Park, the site includes
outdoor recreation areas, including a baseball
diamond that is reached by a series of paved
pathways specifically scaled for wheelchairs.
The triangular day-care center is connected
to the polygonal main building by a continuous terrace, with entry beneath a deeply
cantilevered roof. The brick materials, small
scale, and noninstitutional style of the buildings were specifically keyed to residential architecture both for user and neighborhood
acceptance. The interiors are lit by clerestory
strip windows that allow the light to make
patterns as it filters through the structural
space frames that support the roof. As in the
surrounding grounds, the interiors were designed to be barrier free, with easy access
from the central courtyard-amphitheater to
the swimming pool, gymnasium, and work
rooms. Doors are not only wide but often set
on angled walls for easy maneuverability and
gradual, unthreatening changes from one
space to another.

SE11 Mayfair Mansions Apartments

1942–1946, Albert I. Cassell. 3819 Jay St. NE

Mayfair Mansions was designed by black architect Albert I. Cassell and codeveloped with
black radio evangelist Elder Lightfoot Solomon Michaux with the encouragement of
Eleanor Roosevelt while she was honorary
chairperson of the Washington Committee
on Housing. The seventeen Colonial Revival
garden apartments are organized around a
long central common overlooking the Anacostia River. Only 18 percent of the 28-acre
site was built on, with the tall, three-story,
rectangular brick buildings facing one another across the mall. Originally their gables
were painted white to increase the historical
allusions made by pedimented doorways, brick
quoined corners, and regular, balanced compositions. As late examples of the Colonial
Revival style, they show some influence of
modernism, most notably tripartite windows
and a planar wall-window relationship. Cassell, a native of Towson, Maryland, who had
received his architectural education at Cornell University, graduating in 1919, had a
long, prolific, and distinguished architectural
career in Washington.

SE12 Kenilworth Aquatic Gardens

1882–1921, W. B. Shaw. Kenilworth Ave. and Douglas St. NE

The Kenilworth Aquatic Gardens were acquired by the National Park Service in 1938.
They had been developed between 1882 and
1921 by Civil War veteran W. B. Shaw, who
dammed 37 acres of his farmland on the
eastern shore of the Anacostia to create a
series of ponds for an extensive private pleasure garden. He was particularly interested
in the cultivation of water lilies, of which
there are now about seventy-five varieties. In
1912 Shaw's garden became a commercial
venture that was open to the public on Sun-
day mornings.

North and Northeast (NE)

Pamela Scott

L ARGE TRACTS OF LAND CONCENTRATED ALONG THE NORTH
Capitol Street corridor were set aside in the nineteenth century as spacious grounds for three distinct types of institutions—cemeteries, educational institutions, and retirement facilities. They were joined in the twentieth
century by the National Arboretum (NE01), at 24th and R streets NE, whose
412 acres contiguous to the Anacostia River offered both wetlands and uplands
for a wide range of specimen plantings. Although established in 1927, its permanent road system was not begun until twenty years later and completed in
1958. The administration-laboratory building, dating from 1964 and located
near the R Street entrance, was designed by Deigert and Yerkes as three interconnected low pavilions composed asymmetrically along a central spine. Landscape architect Hideo Sasaki's master plan dating from 1968 brought coherence to the arboretum's series of disparate gardens. Two features of architectural
interest are the remains of Native American habitation on the site and twenty-
two of the original Aquia sandstone Corinthian columns from the east front of
the Capitol. They were erected atop a hill according to a landscape plan, including a fountain, designed by Russell Page that was completed in 1990.

Two of the three large cemeteries in the area were designed as part of the
rural cemetery movement to function as public parks and thus were consciously
laid out with winding roadways that conform to the natural and sometimes
improved landscape. It was in 1712 that religious services were first held on
the site of Rock Creek Cemetery, located at Rock Creek Church Road and
Webster Street NW, with the first interment in 1719. Its 86 acres have an irregular internal road system that is less contrived than those of Glenwood and
Mount Olivet cemeteries, both founded in the 1850s in response to a city ordinance forbidding new cemeteries within the city limits. Glenwood Cemetery,

NE01 National Arboretum

located at 2219 Lincoln Road NE, was chartered by Congress on 27 July 1854. Mount Olivet Cemetery, at 1300 Bladensburg Road NE, was founded as a Roman Catholic cemetery in 1858; graves from three churches in the city were moved there, including that of James Hoban, architect of the White House.

Four universities in the area were founded in the nineteenth century: Gallaudet in 1856 (see NE04), Howard University in 1867 (see NE12), Catholic University in 1887 (see NE08), and Trinity College in 1897 (see NE07). Their campuses are now nearly filled with buildings, as are the grounds of the Old Soldiers' Home (see NE11), set aside by Congress in 1851 for retired army men, and Walter Reed Hospital, laid out in 1905 as a general hospital for the army. Remnants of seven Civil War forts remain in the area east of Rock Creek Park, but Fort Totten and Fort Slocum are the only ones whose contiguous grounds function as public parks. The city's only significant industrial corridor parallels the railroad tracks that run along the north side of New York Avenue, creating an indelible gash that in conjunction with the Anacostia River divides the northeastern sector of the city into three distinct areas.

NE02 Langston Terrace

1935–1938, Hilyard R. Robinson. Benning Rd., H, 21st, and 24th streets NE

Langston Terrace represents a pioneering architectural effort by and for Washington's black community during the depression. Named for United States representative from Virginia John Mercer Langston (1829–1897), the 274-unit complex was designed by Washington's outstanding African-American architect as the city's first low-rent housing erected for blacks under the Public Works Administration. Langston was briefly the acting president of nearby Howard University,

its only black president before 1926, and later dean of the law school. Construction was begun within a year after passage of the landmark public housing legislation and completed three years later in 1938.

Robinson graduated from Columbia's School of Architecture, afterward traveling extensively in Europe, where he was inspired by experimental new housing developments of the time. He designed Langston Terrace following avant-garde European ideas concerning suburban habitations within a dense urban environment. Architectural critic Lewis Mumford, who saw the model exhibited at the Museum of Modern Art in New York in

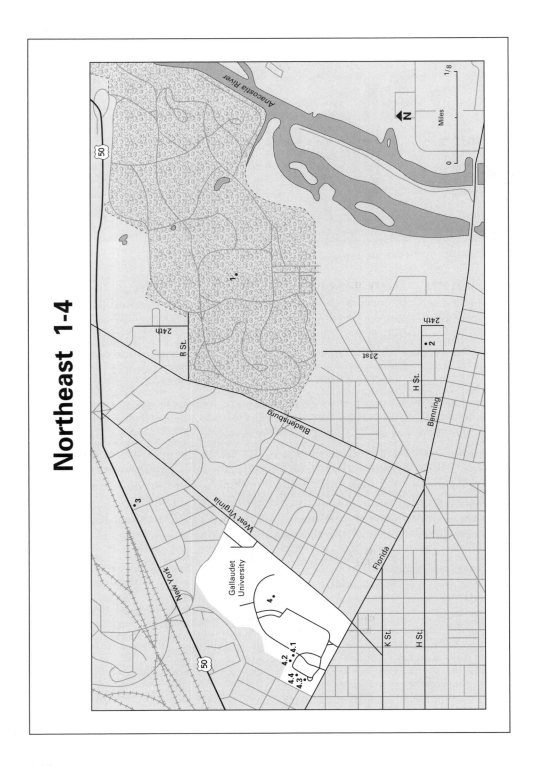

Northeast 1-4

NE02 Langston Terrace

1938, praised the high standard of the complex's exterior design. The fourteen housing blocks, intermingling row houses with apartments, were arranged in a U-shape around a common. The buildings cover only 20 percent of the 13-acre site and vary in height from two to four stories. Although Robinson's training was largely in the International style and the materials at his disposal (concrete with brick fronting) were spare due to a limited budget of $1.85 million, he managed to provide for a decorative and commemorative life-sized bas-relief frieze and statue grouping in unglazed terracotta that still adorns the pedestrian archway leading into the complex. Executed by sculptor Dan Olney, the cycle depicts Langston leading black farm laborers to industrial jobs in cities.

NE03 Hecht Company Warehouse

1936–1937, Abbott, Merkt and Company. 1401 New York Ave. NE

The elegance of line and massing belies the Hecht Company Warehouse's function. In its slab construction with streamlined alternating layers of brick walls and strip windows, the New York architects and engineers Abbott, Merkt and Company created a sophisticated yet functional shell to enclose and light large industrial spaces. Their glazed strata, composed primarily of glass blocks but punctuated with clear industrial metal frame windows, define subtle bays and fill five open floors with diffuse light. The horizontal lay-

ering of solid and translucent materials is subtly complemented by their three-dimensional relationship. The buff brick strips slightly overlap the glass layers, and the seam between them is defined by a course of black bricks. The interplay of the reflective surfaces of glazed bricks and the strip windows must have been striking when new.

The nearly solid, tall black brick ground story originally had three large windows on the ground floor for the display of merchandise; the central one is framed by glass bricks and a fluted aluminum lintel. From the corner facing downtown rises a glass brick tower submerged behind the brick strips that wrap around it, keeping its exuberance in check until it bursts forth at the roofline as a multifaceted abstract beacon light that is almost German expressionist in inspiration.

NE04 Gallaudet University

1862–1865, Emil S. Friedrich. 1865–1885, Frederick Clarke Withers. 800 Florida Ave. NE

The Columbia Institution for the Deaf, Dumb, and Blind was founded in 1856 by former Postmaster General Amos Kendall on the site of his farm. It was the third educational institution in the country (after West Point and Annapolis) to receive financial support from the federal government. The first building for the school was designed in 1859 by the institution's first teacher, Edward Miner Gallaudet. A major addition to it in 1862 by architect Emil S. Friedrich (who had been a draftsman for Robert Mills), the primary department buildings for the younger students, was in the Italianate style, a brick structure with a square central tower, arcade across the entire front, and tall arched windows. On 8 April 1864, President Abraham Lincoln signed the legislation establishing the National Deaf Mute College. The following year Friedrich designed four additional buildings, a gasworks, carriage house, shop building, and a brick and brownstone collegiate department building for older students.

In 1865–1866 Frederick Law Olmsted and Calvert Vaux prepared a master plan for the college campus. The existing institutional buildings, which faced south and west, were to be supplemented by a central multifunctional building to connect the primary and collegiate department buildings. A south-facing arcade overlooking "terrace gardens"

NE04.1 Gallaudet University, Chapel Hall

was planned along the facade of the new building to connect the three structures. It was only partially executed. The school buildings were clustered on the eastern third of the 16-acre site, separated from a row of five faculty villas by an open meadow. Dense plantings along the north, west, and south boundaries isolated the school from the city. Clumps of trees and shrubs at the intersections of winding pathways and roads created a seemingly expansive campus on the scale of a small estate. Within the grounds, functions were clearly controlled by the landscape treatment, a fundamental design tenet that was implemented nearly simultaneously by Olmsted and Vaux on a much larger scale in New York's Central Park.

Frederick Clarke Withers, the English-born and trained architect associated with the Olmsted and Vaux firm, designed the college's buildings for the next twenty years, including those new ones noted on the master plan. Withers's buildings were carried out during two campaigns. The first began in 1867 with Chapel Hall, which made a picturesque transition between the extant Friedrich buildings on the east and the new President's House in the southwest corner, and House No. 1 to its north, the first of the small villas on Faculty Row. Withers brought an entirely new design vocabulary to Gallaudet, creating the most coherent and best-designed enclave of High Victorian Gothic style buildings in Washington.

Chapel Hall's (NE04.1) (1868) massing reflects its original internal functions as chapel and separate refectories for the primary and college students, each attached by corridors or porches to their residence halls. The double-story chapel separated the dining halls, rising above them; it is marked on its southwest corner by a bell tower. In form, function, and style Withers drew his inspiration from Ware and Van Brunt's Memorial Hall of 1865–1878 at Harvard College, albeit on a much smaller scale and with a simpler architectural vocabulary.

The south-facing, triple-arched entry topped by five "church" windows clearly bespeaks a religious function for this section of the building, in spite of the eagle in the pediment over the central arch, a reference to the college's government sponsorship. The arches on both stories have banded voussoirs contrasting the warm hue of the Connecticut brownstone with the same white sandstone as is employed in the belt courses. Stout and squat granite columns at the entry with overscaled foliate capitals are typical of Withers's Venetian-inspired decoration, which also includes colonnettes set into the corners and simple repetitive sculpted ornament in the belt courses. Following the tenets set down by John Ruskin for "truthfulness" in composition and construction, the fenestration and wall treatment is much simpler for the refectories, befitting their more utilitarian function. Unfortunately, the interiors have been gutted.

Withers's second campaign was initiated with the construction of College Hall (NE04.2) in 1874–1875, an administration and dormitory building set at right angles to Chapel Hall and connected to it by an open loggia. Although it is much more aggressive in its broken massing and bold contrast of multiple wide and plain white belt courses set against orange-hued bricks, one nonetheless discerns the architect's transition from his earlier building by the maintenance of the horizontal lines of the belt courses as well as the lower massing of College Hall on its southern end in response to the more modestly scaled Chapel Hall.

A striking change in taste within the High Victorian Gothic style can be easily discerned not just in the differing modulations of composition and change from muted to robust materials but also in the character of the ornament. The handcrafted quality of Chapel Hall's decoration gives way to a hard-edged, even machinelike, quality at College Hall. Here the overall effect is more dependent on strident relationships between forms and materials in contrast to the subtle harmonies of the earlier building.

The President's House (NE04.3) in the southwest corner of the campus and House No. 1 (NE04.4) to its north at the beginning of Faculty Row were erected during the first campaign; the remaining professors' houses were finished during the second. All followed Downingesque precepts of integrating residences into the landscape. This was accomplished by using porches as intermediate spaces between indoors and out, by breaking massing to soften profiles, and by using earth-toned materials to harmonize with nature. However, Withers designed the villas in the High Victorian Gothic style with overall surface polychromy and juxtaposition of parts that departed from Downing's smooth transitions.

NE05 **Ralph J. Bunche House**

1941, Hilyard R. Robinson. 1510 Jackson St.

Robinson focused on public housing and educational complexes (see NE02) during his long career as an educator and practicing architect in Washington. Single-family houses were uncommon in his oeuvre, the most notable having been erected for fellow Howard University professor Dr. Ralph J. Bunche,

NE05 Ralph J. Bunche House

who later achieved national fame as a Nobel Peace Prize recipient and undersecretary of the United Nations. Robinson designed a two-story brick residence with shallow hip roof employing the vocabulary and planning principles of the International style that he had witnessed firsthand in Europe. As such it was one of Washington's first modern buildings, a modest house with entry not on its south-facing facade but on the west, behind a brick wall that spans the lot and divides it into a public front yard and private patios. The front facade's asymmetrical composition utilizes five stock rectangular sash windows and one circular one deriving architectural distinction by their placement and interrelationships. Three are grouped together on the ground story to indicate the public nature of the room they light, a reference to International style strip windows. Those on the second story are placed near the house's corners to emphasize both Robinson's abstract facade composition and the private nature of the bedroom story.

NE06 **Glenwood Cemetery Mortuary Chapel**

1892, Glenn Brown. 2219 Lincoln Rd. NE

In 1854, Glenwood Cemetery was located on a 51-acre tract well outside Washington in compliance with an 1852 ordinance forbidding cemeteries within the city limits; the city did not yet fill the entire District of Columbia. It was laid out by civil engineer George F. de la Roche (1791–1861), who had designed Oak Hill Cemetery in Georgetown in 1851 (see GT27, p. 414), as a rural cemetery landscaped in the picturesque tradition of wind-

Northeast 5-8

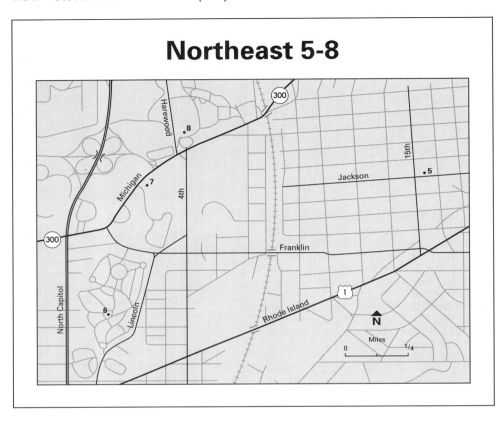

ing roads and paths following the contours of the land.

In 1892, Washington architect Glenn Brown's chapel was sited in a small circle at the confluence of six of the cemetery's carriageways along its central north-south axis. Rectangular in plan, the single-story brick chapel in Flemish bond has battered walls and two sets of substantial dormer windows along its flanks that rise nearly to the peak of its steeply pitched roof. The simple east-facing facade is dominated by a wide, low-arched entrance traversing a third of its width and an equally monumental circular window set above it in the slate gable of the roof. The present stained-glass window, a replacement after 1918 of the original, which had been set in a spoked wheel pattern, is the chapel's only alteration. Brown, who had worked for H. H. Richardson's contractors, Norcross Brothers, on the Cheney Building in Hartford upon graduation from MIT, based Glenwood Chapel on Richardson's Emmanuel Episcopal Church in Pittsburgh, completed five years earlier. Elemental, earthbound geometric forms and simple arched openings outlined by double and triple rows of brick voussoirs link Brown's chapel to Richardson's slightly more elaborate church; both achieve architectural quality by very simple means.

NE07 Notre Dame Chapel, Trinity College

1920–1924, Maginnis and Walsh. 125 Michigan Ave. NE

Notre Dame Chapel's irregular placement in relation to the college's first structure, the Main Building (1899–1909, Edwin F. Durang and Son of Philadelphia), was due to the church's ritualistic alignment, with the entrance facing west and the altar located at the east end. The college's site, including hills and ravines, was not landscaped until the Olmsted Brothers of Brookline, Massachusetts, undertook the work in 1929.

The chapel's Neo-Byzantine style is primarily expressed in its low saucer dome set

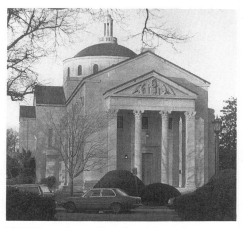

NE07 Notre Dame Chapel, Trinity College

NE08 National Shrine of the Immaculate Conception

atop a 67-foot-high circular drum and by its compact massing and tall proportions. Four arms tightly hug the dome, which rises above stepped gradations of the simple geometric porticoed arm. Plain Kentucky limestone surfaces and red tile roofs all contribute to the impression that Notre Dame's stylistic origins lie in eastern Christian churches.

The chapel's decoration refers throughout to the Virgin Mary, beginning with Mary and Child enthroned attended by angels in the pedimental sculpture on the west portico and

continuing with scenes of her life in the nave's stained glass executed by Connick of Boston. The fine quality mosaics above the altar depicting the Coronation of the Virgin, designed by Bancel La Farge and executed at the Ravenna mosaic factory in Munich, are the glory of the interior.

NE08 National Shrine of the Immaculate Conception

1919–1959, Maginnis and Walsh. 4th and Michigan Ave. NE

In order to ensure that the National Shrine of the Immaculate Conception on the Catholic University campus would be a recognizable and important architectural element on Washington's skyline, the Boston architect Charles D. Maginnis of the firm Maginnis and Walsh included both a lofty dome (237 feet) and tall carillon (329 feet) in his design. The National Shrine is America's largest Roman Catholic church, and although shorter at 459 feet than many other churches, its 77,500 square feet of space place it eleventh largest in the world. Its massiveness, as well as the combination of Byzantine and Romanesque styles of architecture, were conscious attempts to vie with, but distinguish it from, the Neo-Gothic Episcopal National Cathedral (see NW40, p. 381), begun in 1909 on a similar elevated site along Washington's perimeter skyline.

Although French Gothic had been the choice of style when the National Shrine was first contemplated in 1914, an important factor in the selection of the predominantly Neo-Byzantine style was the possibility of erecting the entire exterior shell concurrently from the foundations upward, with the interior decoration finished after the church was in use. The Gothic system of construction demanded that exteriors and interiors be built bay by bay, typically beginning at the altar end.

The National Shrine is entirely masonry construction—Indiana limestone, brick, and tile vaults—with no structural steel used. The lower church was completed by 1927; the superstructure was carried out in five years from 1954 to 1959 under the direction of Eugene F. Kennedy, Jr., of Maginnis and Walsh.

Although the church is large, the coherence of the Latin cross design manifests itself in the clarity and sharpness of the building's silhouette when viewed from every perspective. Treatment of the smooth limestone walls is so sculptural that the church seems to be carved out of rock rather than built up piece by piece. The walls, into which minimal windows are deeply set, are preeminent, with figural and decorative sculpture concentrated on the south-facing entrance front, transept porches, and rose window tracery atop shallow buttresses. The accumulation of porches, radiating chapels, sacristies, aisles, and clerestories to buttress the 100-foot-tall nave, arcaded dome, and multifaceted chancel and sanctuary seem to be a sculptural rather than architectural process.

Only one of five interior domes is expressed on the exterior. It is decorated in colorful blue, gold, and red tiles and rises above the transept crossing. Its symbols are all Marian—as are its colors—with the tile prefiguring the church's interior mosaic decoration. The intertwined A and M stand for Ave Maria; the fleur-de-lis, cedar of Lebanon, tower of ivory, and star of the sea are all traditional emblems of Mary. The carillon is almost Gothic in feeling as its upper stages are physically and visually lightened by open columnar screens, behind which a smaller tower terminated by a blue-tiled and gilded spire emerges.

The triple entrance portal is set within a vast recessed arch 96 feet high and 22 feet deep. Both are framed by hierarchically arranged sculptured figures. Those surrounding the entrance relate to the historical role of women in the Catholic church, particularly to the Virgin Mary, to whom the church is dedicated. The freestanding Mary accompanied by two angels above the central portal was sculpted by Ivan Mestrovic. John Angel was the sculptor of the Annunciation tympanum over the central door. The figures in the eight panels that divide the three doors are women of the Hebrew scriptures on the west and New Testament on the east; Lee Lawrie was the sculptor. Double figures, identified by name beneath each panel on the buttresses that flank the great arch, are twenty-four pairs of patriarchs, prophets, and apostles, with Saint Peter above those on the west and Saint Paul those on the east; all were carved by Joseph Fleri. The sculptural and mosaic program of the east wall and transept porch relates the history of American Catholicism; that of the west, charity. John An-

gel sculpted both cycles. Although various artists were involved, stylistic consistency of the abstract, stocky, and hieratic figural sculpture contributes significantly to the sense of a unified work of art where architects and sculptors shared a common aesthetic. All exterior sculpture was complete by 1959, when the basilica was dedicated.

The relative austerity and sculptural qualities of the church's exterior are carried over to the interior, where the fulsome, curvilinear spaces are defined by smooth, solid walls and tentlike vaulted surfaces of tile. The National Shrine offers a decidedly different architectural experience than the National Cathedral, where space and light are broken into a multitude of parts. Maginnis's crypt (completed 1931) is an exceptionally broad and low triple-apsed room with massive vaults covered in gray Guastavino tiles set in a herringbone pattern, each spatial change marked by bands of iridescent glazed ceramic tiles in muted colors. Short variegated marble columns with square Neo-Byzantine capitals in finely and intricately carved white marble provide more architectonic spatial definitions.

Kennedy's model for the main interior was Saint Mark's in Venice, the major Byzantine-inspired church in Italy. The ring of small arched windows at the base of the central crossing dome, through which seeming pinpricks of intense light are admitted, is particularly associated with Byzantine domes, including Saint Mark's. Large spatial divisions clearly marked by plain piers support central domes and lateral barrel vaults. Open balconies above aisles, with arcades composed of square limestone piers and variegated marble Corinthian columns, reinforce the spatial clarity of the nave, crossing, and chancel. Domed chapels constitute the third horizontal spatial layer.

The interiors are at once immediately comprehensible yet richly complex. Architectural masses rather than sculpture predominate, and stained-glass windows are significant only in the chancel and sanctuary. The even illumination of the interiors is not due to abundant natural light. Rather, large expanses of highly polished limestone wall, glistening marble columns and inlaid floors, and mosaic surfaces reflect natural and artificial light to provide a soft, clear luminosity to every part of the upper church.

Mosaics provide the basilica's main decoration in keeping with its Neo-Byzantine ar-

Northeast 9-11

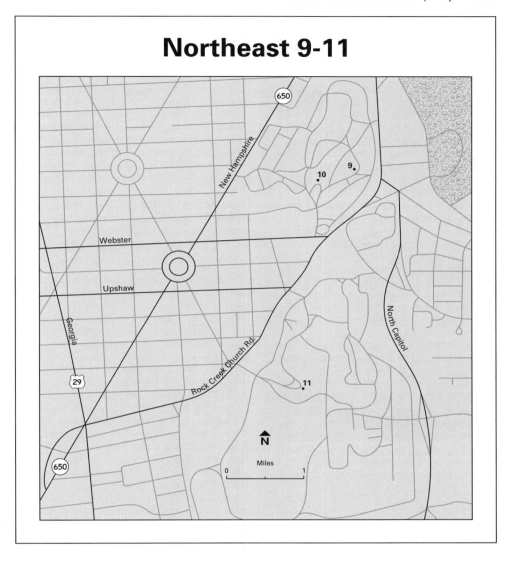

chitectural framework. Gold, blue, and red predominate, all colors associated with Mary, just as the major iconographic scheme of the main church revolves around Mary's story. Three principal companies were responsible for the mosaics in the aisles, fifty-eight chapels, and domes over the chancel and sanctuary: the Vatican Mosaic Studio, Ravenna Mosaic Company, and Venetian Arts. There are long-term plans to decorate the two nave and crossing domes. The Botticino marble main altar and baldachin were designed by George Snowden and completed in 1960.

NE09 Adams Memorial, Rock Creek Cemetery, Section E

1886–1891, Augustus Saint-Gaudens and Stanford White. Webster St. and Rock Creek Church Rd. NW

Augustus Saint-Gaudens's and Stanford White's memorial to Marian Adams (commonly, but mistakenly, called "Grief") is not a portrait of the wife of historian and author Henry Adams, who had died a suicide in 1885, but rather a contemplative, introspective sibyl that expresses the intellectualized pantheism of its patron and designers. White

NE09 Adams Memorial, Rock Creek Cemetery, Section E

NE11 United States Soldiers' and Airmen's Home

designed a simple granite stele and plinth with low, angular wings as an elegant foil for Saint-Gaudens's seated and cloaked bronze figure, setting the whole amidst a sacred holly grove.

NE10 Saint Paul's Episcopal Church

1775, unknown. 1922, Delos Smith. Rock Creek Church Rd. and Webster St. NW

The brick walls of Saint Paul's Church date from 1775. The second church to be erected on the site, it is located within the grounds of Rock Creek Cemetery, the oldest burial ground in the District of Columbia, where interments first took place in 1719. The first church, constructed of wood, was contemporaneous. The present Saint Paul's was remodeled in 1868 but gutted by fire in 1921. Its square

brick tower and octagonal wood belfry as well as all the interior woodwork were designed in a simple Neo-Georgian style by Delos Smith. Some evidence suggests that the church prior to 1868 had a three-bay facade with three round-headed windows on the second floor and two entries topped by rectangular fanlights separated by a central rectangular window. The proportions of Smith's narrow two-story windows immediately suggest the Georgian Revival, as does the elaboration of the belfry on such a simple country church.

NE11 United States Soldiers' and Airmen's Home (United States Military Asylum; Old Soldiers' Home)

1851–1857, Barton S. Alexander. 1869–1872, Edward Clark. Rock Creek Church Rd. at Upshur St. NW

Although naval asylums had existed since the early nineteenth century, the first soldiers' homes were not established until midcentury, when Gen. Winfield Scott earmarked tribute money from the Mexican-American War for them. All twenty-year veterans of the army and disabled soldiers who contributed to the asylums from their pay were eligible for admittance to the homes' residential, recreational, and medical facilities.

One of three such homes established by Congress in 1851, Washington's Old Soldiers' Home is the only one still in operation. Because the 256-acre site was one of the highest and coolest points in the District, it became the unofficial summer White House for Presidents Buchanan, Lincoln, Hayes, and Arthur. The oldest structure on the site is the two-story Gothic Revival cottage, now called Anderson Cottage (architect unknown). Dating from 1843, the brick house with two bargeboarded gables gracing its facade was stuccoed in 1897. Lt. Barton S. Alexander was named architect of the Washington asylum upon its founding and was responsible for its other three extant pre–Civil War structures, the main building, now Sherman South, and the governor's and secretary-treasurer's residences, Quarters No. 1 and 2, respectively. All three stone buildings were constructed between 1854 and 1857. In its round arches and massing, the original Sherman Hall (the lower two stories) was a simplified version of the recently completed Smithsonian Institution building, with a square central clock tower projecting in front of sym-

Northeast 12-18

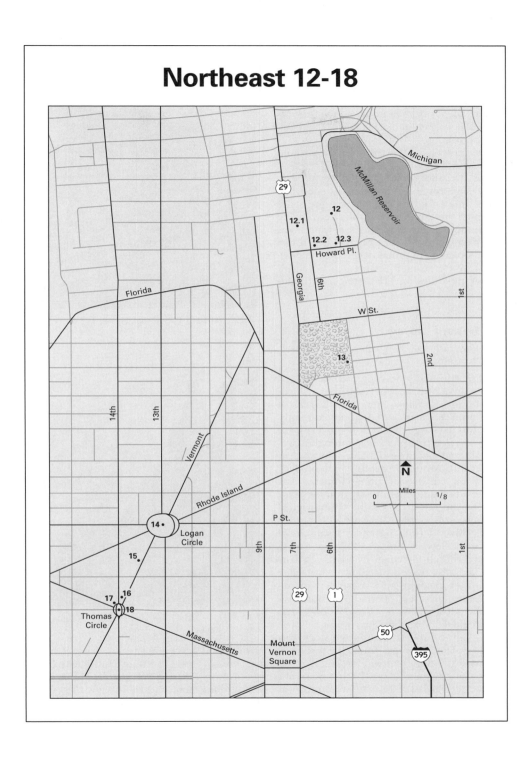

metrical flanking blocks that receded in two stages. Architect of the Capitol Edward Clark designed Sherman Hall's third-story addition between 1868 and 1872, replacing the bell tower with a castellated belfry and introducing such Richardsonian Romanesque features as circular corner pinnacled turrets and foliated decoration.

The cross-axial massing, wraparound porches, and medieval architectural vocabulary of Alexander's two Gothic Revival cottage residences were common to suburban houses influenced by the picturesque styles promoted by Andrew Jackson Downing at midcentury. Their most unusual aspect was their material, New York marble, which dictated simpler, more planar details than wooden or cast-iron bracketed cornices and eyebrow window moldings on brick and wood buildings.

NE12 Howard University

1867–1869, unknown. 1934–1939, Albert I. Cassell. 2400 6th St. NW

Howard University was granted a federal charter on 2 March 1867. Maj. Gen. Oliver Otis Howard, commissioner of the Bureau of Refugees, Freedmen, and Abandoned Lands, which was in charge of allocating government funds for freedmen's schools after the Civil War, assisted Congregationalist minister Dr. Charles B. Boynton in establishing the college named for him. It was initially founded as a Congregationalist seminary for training black men for the ministry. Of the four original buildings, the single survivor is Howard's house, Howard Hall (NE12.1), a substantial three-story Second Empire building with a mansard-roofed tower on its southwest corner. The walls are constructed of hollow white bricks later painted red; a porch with an entablature that replicated those found on both the house's main block and its tower has been removed. Flat but bold granite lintels over tall, graceful first- and second-story windows are plain in comparison to the two types of pressed-metal dormer window frames used on the attic story and tower. Both have scrolls and are set against slate mansard roofs, but the more elaborate arched ones on the tower are accompanied by a pressed metal frieze that sits atop the plain classical entablature. The description of the house that appeared in the *Washington Evening Star* upon its com-

NE12.1 Howard University, Howard Hall

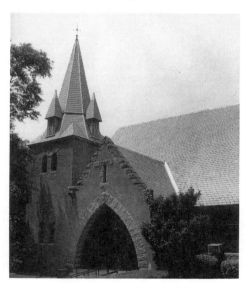

NE12.2 Howard University, Andrew Rankin Memorial Chapel

pletion on 29 November 1867 described it as a "Mexican castle" and noted that its sixteen rooms were dry and well ventilated due to its granite basement and the hollow bricks. All of the original buildings at Howard University were constructed of the new hollow brick as both an economy and a health measure.

The lovely Andrew Rankin Memorial Chapel (NE12.2) was completed in 1895, a

NE12.4 Howard University, Founders Library

Neo-Gothic brick interpretation of Richardsonian Romanesque principles of low, heavy-walled structures that seem to grow out of the earth rather than sit on it. Entry is through a simple rock-faced granite pointed arch with its spring line at ground level. Individual voussoirs of the arch have the letters "Memorial Chapel" and simple floral motifs carved on them. Attached to the entry porch is a squat square tower topped by a shingled broach spire. The only architectural ornament is the rough stone outlining windows and gables; its appeal is achieved by applying materials simply and directly to a finely proportioned Arts and Crafts form.

The most architecturally interesting building, Thirkield Science Hall (NE12.3), was designed by Department of Interior architects in 1910. Booker T. Washington called to the attention of the univesity's board of trustees that no black workers were employed in its erection. The double-story limestone Ionic portico and other limestone elements—entablatures, door frame, belt courses, pilaster caps and bases, and keystones—provide a bold and pleasing contrast to the four brick stories.

During the first decade of the twentieth century, a number of three- to four-story brick buildings focused on a central quadrangle were built at Howard in the Colonial Revival style. This style was common for academic buildings of the period, whether for

city schools or for college campuses. It was continued into the 1930s at Howard when the most significant exemplar, Founders Library (NE12.4), was built. Its design was by Louis E. Fry, Sr., who had joined the Washington firm of Albert I. Cassell, a black architect who, as superintendent of buildings and grounds at Howard, oversaw the design and construction of a number of the university's buildings during the 1920s and 1930s. Fry, a native of Texas, had received his architectural education at Kansas State University and had been the college architect at Prairie View College, Texas, before joining Cassell's office. His design for Founders Library was based on a reinterpretation of the Pennsylvania State House, Independence Hall, in Philadelphia, one of the most potent and long-lasting architectural icons in America. It was used for many academic buildings during the 1930s; Fry's version is particularly fine. The two-story gabled wings abut directly the three-story central block, and limestone trim, which sets off red brick walls, is used extensively for carved frames and swags for circular windows in the pediments of the wings. Fry's fenestration pattern with a tall third story above the cornice is a variation on the proportional relationships associated with Independence Hall, a two-story building. He integrated this top story into the tower by covering its width by a single tripartite win-

NE13 Le Droit Park

dow. Roman Doric columns frame the entrances, while Ionic columns articulate the tower's first stage, and Corinthian its second, an application of the superposition of the classical orders not present on Fry's model. The tower rises from the center in three stages to a height of 165 feet. Its copper-roofed open octagonal cupola sits above an intermediate stage with four clock faces.

NE13 Le Droit Park

1873–1883, James H. McGill. 2nd and 7th streets, Florida Ave. and W St. NW

In 1873 Amzi L. Barber, acting president of Howard University, and his brother-in-law, Andrew Langdon, purchased from the university a 55-acre triangular site on the north side of Florida Avenue (then the District of Columbia boundary) between 2nd and 7th streets NW and began developing Le Droit Park. Within four years forty-one substantial detached and semidetached villas were built in the exclusive suburban community, following designs by local architect James H. McGill. During the next decade he designed an additional twenty-three brick and wood houses. Approximately two-thirds of the McGill-designed houses survive. All were set in a picturesque parklike setting with continuous lawns within a fenced enclave with its own street pattern that deliberately did not coincide with the city's. The predominant styles were Gothic Revival, Italianate, and Second Empire, with a plethora of cross-axial plans,

multiple porches with jigsawn wooden filigree ornament (much of it lost), octagonal single- and double-story bay windows, mansard roofs, multicolored slate roofs, and decorative iron cresting rails atop towers (much of which remains).

McGill's basic source book seems to have been Calvert Vaux's *Villas and Cottages* of 1864, although he freely altered many of the prototypes. *Villas and Cottages* was one of the numerous up-to-date pattern books influenced by the publications of Vaux's partner, Andrew Jackson Downing, during the 1840s, when he provided Americans with a wide range of style, plan, and economic choices for newly created suburban homes. From the mid-1880s onward, however, most of the residences erected were undistinguished two-story row houses; McGill was not their architect. In 1901 the streets in Le Droit Park were formally given to the city, and the community's population changed. It became a pleasant upper-middle-class haven for the city's black social, educational, and cultural leaders, convenient to Howard University, the Howard Theatre, and downtown.

NE14 John A. Logan Statue

1891, Franklin Simmons and Richard Morris Hunt. Logan Circle, Vermont Ave. at 13th and P streets NW

Iowa Circle, renamed Logan Circle in 1930, was not formally landscaped until 1874, although it had been designated on L'Enfant's 1791 plan of Washington. The bronze statue of John A. Logan, a Civil War general, was dedicated on 9 April 1901. It was the second collaboration of the New England sculptor Franklin Simmons with Richard Morris Hunt, although the Parisian-trained American architect had previously designed the bases for several sculptural works including the *Statue of Liberty* in New York Harbor and an elaborate gateway entrance to Central Park. The Logan monument is unique in Washington in being entirely of bronze; Hunt's Italian Renaissance–inspired base has at least as much prominence as the equestrian figure it carries. High-relief panels on the two flanks depict events in Logan's career (criticized as inaccurate in Washington newspapers at the time), while single figures on the ends are allegorical. All are set within a densely architectural framework reminiscent of Renaissance tombs, rectangular boxes decorated with a full complement of architectonic sculpture derived from the column and all its parts, emphasizing in this case multitiered pedestal and base moldings and an entablature with spread-winged eagles at the corners.

NE15 Mount Olivet Lutheran Church
(Vermont Avenue Christian Church)

1881–1883, R. G. Russell. 1302 Vermont Ave. NW

The Vermont Avenue Christian Church was dedicated as a memorial to recently assassinated President James A. Garfield, who had been a member of the congregation. Its architect from Hartford, Connecticut, R. G. Russell, designed the church following a common formula for High Victorian Gothic churches: an asymmetrical corner tower with a broach spire serving as an entry abruptly abuts a tall gabled facade divided horizontally into several zones. Although Russell employed the same architectural vocabulary as Judson York's Luther Place Memorial Church (see NE16) and followed the compositional rules of the style more closely, his building is of inferior architectural quality in that he lacked Clark's sense of proportion and response to the possibilities of materials.

NE16 Luther Place Memorial Church

1870–1883, Judson York. 1226 Vermont Ave. NW

Judson York effectively combined rough quarry-faced, smooth-sawn, and carved red Seneca sandstone for the walls and decorative

trim for his High Victorian Gothic Lutheran church. Its unusual plan and external forms respond to its acute triangular site with a hexagonal broach tower and needle spire facing Thomas Circle and bowed walls terminating in lower broached towers at the rear. Some subtle color variation occurs because of the differing textures of the stone; the original roof and spire would probably have been covered with multicolored slates laid in striated bands, a common feature of High Victorian Gothic buildings where massiveness was often combined with strong color changes. York contained the power of his sculptural forms and faceted surfaces by fragmenting each into a number of parts and carefully proportioning them to one another. The multitude of parts tends to distract one's attention from the fact that York designed a symmetrical church to sit on an irregular lot, with the 13th Street side shorter than the Vermont Avenue.

NE17 National City Christian Church
(Disciples of Christ Church)

1929–1930, John Russell Pope. 1952, Leon Chatelain. 5 Thomas Circle NW

The limestone National City Christian Church was erected at a cost of $1.2 millon as the mother church for the Church of the Disciples of Christ. John Russell Pope designed its Ionic portico surmounted by a 164-foot tower (from the portico's stylobate) as a twentieth-century reinterpretation and refinement of English Baroque churches. He was particularly influenced by James Gibbs's Saint Martin-in-the-Fields (1722–1726) in London, which had provided the model for numerous eighteenth- and early nineteenth-century American churches. Pope commonly choose such familiar architectural prototypes, subtly transforming them by passing them through his exceptional intellectual and visual process of simplification. He probably consulted Gibbs's *A Book of Architecture* (1728), in which Saint Martin's as built was illustrated in addition to an alternate design. Pope's hexastyle portico is Ionic while Gibbs's is Corinthian, but Pope passes his square tower through a secondary pediment set above and behind the entry portico, a motif common in the Baroque architectural tradition but not used by Gibbs at Saint Martin's. One distinctive change was setting the National City Christian Church upon a high podium entered by a broad and long flight of stairs. For the lower two stages of his spire, Pope followed the Gibbs prototype with only minor alterations, adding quoins to the corners of the tower as it emerges from the roof and framing the arched opening above with single engaged Ionic columns rather than Gibbs's double Ionic pilasters. For the third stage, where the transition from square to circular begins, Pope used Gibbs's alternate, unbuilt Saint Martin's tower design, which had a more sculpturally elaborate scrolled frame for its circular clock, replaced by Pope with a blank panel. Gibbs's tower terminated in a tall spire, while Pope designed a circular Corinthian tholos topped by a small rotunda and dome to complete his composition. Gibbs's pointed spire may have suggested medieval architectural form to Pope, who probably found the fusion of medieval and classical vocabularies totally inadmissible. Pope was not averse to medieval architecture; when the church committee was undecided between a Neo-Gothic and a Neoclassical church, he provided sketches in both styles. However, his sense of the correctness and purity of architectural traditions was contrary to the kind of eclecticism that borrowed indiscriminately.

NE18 George H. Thomas Statue

1879, John Quincy Adams Ward and John L. Smithmeyer. Thomas Circle, Massachusetts Ave. and 14th St. NW

The architect of the multitiered base for Ward's bronze statue of Civil War General Thomas was John L. Smithmeyer, whose major architectural work was the Library of Congress (see CH12, p. 142) done in partnership with Paul Pelz. While its ovoid form was well adapted to the shape of an equestrian sculptural group, the building up of a series of pedestals from four plain steps to intermediate walls broken by four coffered column bases to an elaborate superstructure buttressed by large carved console brackets was unusual and expensive when executed in granite.

16th Street
and Meridian Hill (MH)

Pamela Scott

DEVELOPMENT OF MERIDIAN HILL, THE VISIBLE EDGE OF THE city from the White House area, was the result of private initiative. In 1888, former Sen. John B. Henderson and his wife, Mary Foote Henderson, erected a house on a 6-acre site with commanding prospects in this still rural part of the city. Designed by architect E. C. Gardner of Springfield, Massachusetts, the Henderson house was built in a rusticated Seneca brownstone in Romanesque revival style. Subsequent additions and renovations over the next fifteen years by local architects Thomas Franklin Schneider, George Oakley Totten, Jr., and Laussat R. Rogers, who were partners between 1899 and 1907, resulted in an impressive but architecturally incoherent mass of battlemented towers of varying sizes and shapes. The retaining wall between Florida Avenue and Belmont Street on the west side of 16th Street is all that remains of the original complex.

The influence of the Hendersons during their forty-three-year residence at Meridian Hill was far more significant than the house they built. Socially active, they were concerned with developing 16th Street, the major northern thoroughfare leading to the White House, as the Avenue of Presidents. Although today the street extends 7 miles to the District of Columbia line, Meridian Hill was not incorporated within the city limits and mapped until 1903.

Meridian Hill was originally the site of a major farm, Mount Pleasant, owned by the prosperous Georgetown merchant Robert Peter, and derives its name from the official meridian of the United States on the White House north-south axis, established on 20 December 1793. Commodore David Porter's famous house on Meridian Hill was located on the White House axis at the top of the hill. Reputedly designed by George Hadfield in 1816 (burned 1863),

Pope's design for Lincoln Memorial

Henderson Castle

Porter's house and extensive gardens were considered to be one of the most elegant of Washington's early estates.

Beginning in 1890 the Hendersons began buying land in the area, choice lots eventually developed by Mrs. Henderson as an enclave of embassies. Initially, however, the Hendersons sought to interest the government in developing the area as a major focus for new or enlarged public buildings. In 1898, Mrs. Henderson retained Paul Pelz to design a new presidential mansion on the heights of Meridian Hill. Reminiscent of John Nash's Carlton House Terrace (1827–1833) in London, Pelz's grand pile was to sit atop the hill, on the site of the present park, behind a massive retaining wall approached by a vast forecourt and double staircase. Franklin W. Smith, in his illustrated *Designs, Places, and Suggestions for the Aggrandizement of Washington* (1900), reinforced the scheme of Henderson and Pelz by proposing an even larger version to span 16th Street, with the roadway passing through an arch beneath the building. In 1911 John Russell Pope suggested placing the Lincoln Memorial, a Greek temple approached by an extraordinarily long run of steps, in this same central location. Mrs. Henderson vociferously supported this proposal even after the Commission of Fine Arts had selected the western end of the Mall as the site for the Lincoln Memorial.

In 1906 Mrs. Henderson proposed an urban park, Meridian Hill Park (MH01), opposite her home on the east side of 16th Street. Approved by the Commission of Fine Arts in 1914, the 12-acre garden was not completed until 1930. Designed in 1919 by Ferruccio Vitale of the landscape firm of Vitale, Brinckerhoff and Geiffert and completed by Horace W. Peaslee, the sloping site lent itself to a water staircase on the model of those in Italian and English Baroque gardens. Its main feature, the central cascade, was based on the best-preserved seventeenth-century Italian example, that at the Villa Aldobrandini at Frascati. The architectural framework of Meridian Hill Park, including the retaining wall along 16th Street, the water staircase, and the upper and lower terraces, were all constructed of concrete with an aggregate of small stones.

The iconography of the sculptural program is multinational. The monument to President James Buchanan (1930; sculptor, Hans Schuler; architect, William Gordon Beecher), located at the northern terminus of the lower terrace, was part of the plan first approved by the Commission of Fine Arts. The standing figure of Dante (1920; sculptor, Ettore Ximenes; architect, Horace W. Peaslee) was a gift by Carlo Barsotti on behalf of Italian Americans. The equestrian statue of Joan of Arc (1922; sculptor, Paul DuBois; architect, McKim, Mead and White), a copy of the one in front of Reims Cathedral, occupies the central position of the upper terrace above the cascade. It was a gift of friendship by the women of France to American women.

When Mrs. Henderson initiated development of the park, she hired local architect George Oakley Totten to design a series of mansions, which she proposed to lease or sell to embassies. The first was the Venetian-inspired Pink

Palace (see MH20), completed in 1906; the last, the present Embassy of Ecuador at 2437 15th Street, was finished in 1927. In all, Totten designed nine mansions in the neighborhood, as well as his own house. Others designed by various architects supplement Totten's group. They cover a range of historical styles from Italian Renaissance to French Second Empire, apparently as a conscious attempt to provide as much historical and visual variety as possible. Although historical eclecticism was the norm of the period, there may have been an added dimension at Meridian Hill, where the intent to make them embassies of many nations contributed to their stylistic diversity.

By 1915 Totten had purchased a sufficient number of lots on 15th and 16th streets to begin his own residence, having by this time completed designs for numerous speculative mansions for Mrs. Henderson. It was a small house with a separate studio (his wife was a potter) and pavilions set well within the boundaries of a formally landscaped garden that ran between the two north-south streets. The garden and studio are gone, and the five-bay house with its side entrance is now attached to the back of H. H. Richardson's Warder house (see MH22), which Totten purchased during its demolition in 1924 and reerected in his front garden. Totten renovated the Warder house to serve as luxurious apartments, many of which were rented to embassies. It later served several functions, undergoing renovations each time it changed hands.

Three religious congregations moved to Meridian Hill during the 1920s, erecting churches close to one another on the crest of the hill. All have tall spires, adding distinctive vertical notes to the horizontally organized neighborhood of urban mansions. Each has its own architectural merit, but the sum is greater than the parts. The visual interrelationships between the three spires, each distinctly different in form and inspiration, provide Neo-Georgian, Neo-Baroque, and modern stripped classical elements to complement the stylistic diversity of the embassy buildings. In general, and due to its artificially imposed development, Meridian Hill proper was an architecturally sophisticated but isolated enclave rather than a neighborhood with an adequate social and service infrastructure.

Sixteenth Street from Scott Circle to the foot of Meridian Hill is anchored at each end by large, well-designed apartment houses and lined with a few freestanding substantial houses and three major institutional complexes, two of which are exceptional architecturally, the Carnegie Institution (see MH05) and the Scottish Rite Temple (see MH12). Sculptor Henry Kirke Brown's bronze equestrian statue of Mexican War hero General Winfield Scott (MH02) was placed atop its monolithic granite base in Scott Circle in 1874. The architect was George E. Harvey of Newburgh, New York; his drawing for the stark, abstract ovoid pedestal is dated 1871.

Sixteenth Street and Meridian Hill

MH03 **General Scott Apartment Building**

1940–1941, Robert O. Schultz. 1 Scott Circle

The nine-story, yellow brick General Scott was planned to have 175 compact and convenient pieds-à-terre, 151 efficiencies, and 24 one-bedroom apartments. Its modest Art Deco vocabulary consists of strip windows on its curved corner, square projecting bays where black brick panels alternate with picture windows in front of glass-enclosed atriums within, and a polished black marble, aluminum, and glass brick entrance facing Massachusetts Avenue. Although the apartments were renovated in a 1982 conversion to condominiums, the sunken lobby retains its original linoleum floor, its bowed front desk faced with formica to imitate marble, its sinuously carved formica walls, circular recessed ceiling with indirect lighting, and aluminum elevator doors.

MH04 **Susan Shields House**

1888, Samuel Edmonston. 1401 16th St. NW

Although not academically trained as a designer, Samuel Edmonston is listed on the building permit as the architect of the Susan Shields House, with his uncle, Charles Edmonston, as the builder. They had been the contractors for numerous large Washington projects. One was H. H. Richardson's Hay-Adams house (1884–1886), which probably accounts for their use of Richardsonian motifs specifically derived from that great house, also set on a corner. The corner location of the Shields house allowed for a variety of bay designs at its three visible facades. Above a low, red sandstone base the rectangular windows, cut directly into the walls, are single bays grouped in pairs to form a tripartite composition. The subtle decorative patterns on the brick walls are created by various bonds, hexagonal tiles, and the corbeled cornice. The low, sandstone, Syrian-arched porch is divided into two sections; the front part projects in front of the wall, but the inner porch is embedded within the volume of the building, an interesting interpretation of Richardson's deep entrances. Although the Shields house does not approach the design sophistication of its model, it shows how Richardson's influence filtered into mainstream American vernacular architecture.

MH05 Carnegie Institution of Washington

1908, Carrère and Hastings. 1937, addition, Delano and Aldrich. 1530 P St. NW

The purpose of the Carnegie Institution of Washington, founded in 1902, was "to discover the exceptional man and to promote original research." From the beginning, discussions focused on the way in which the inherent dichotomy between these functions might be expressed architecturally. The difficulty was reconciling in a single structure the visual symbol of such an exalted endeavor and yet providing such amenities as scientific laboratories. Carrère and Hastings of New York were selected as the architects. Their design for a three-story pavilion dominated by an unpedimented hexastyle Ionic portico on the exterior and monumental rotunda behind it was based on late eighteenth-century Parisian models. Separation of office functions from the public reception areas (which included a hall on the main axis behind the rotunda) is clearly articulated on the exterior by the interpenetration of two volumes, the subordinate single-bay wings dominated by the overscaled, balustraded portico. The limestone walls are treated with great restraint, with three different shallow quoin patterns demarcating the basement level, enframing the wings, and articulating the wall behind the slender Ionic columns.

On the interior, the 37-foot rotunda continues the exterior's Renaissance-inspired vocabulary in its interpenetration of ancillary spaces at two levels, alternation of in antis framed openings with protruding double-Corinthian-column piers that frame richly ornamented shell niches. The elegance of the walls is complemented by the radiating floor pattern in gray granite, white marble, and red and green variegated marbles. The walls are cast stone to imitate ashlar masonry, and the wooden columns are painted to resemble marble. The addition to the north by Delano and Aldrich (1938) provided an alternate business entrance on P Street, thus making the main portico a ceremonial entrance.

MH06 Saint Luke's Episcopal Church

1876–1879, Calvin T. S. Brent and Alexander Crummell. Southwest corner 15th and Church streets NW

Calvin T. S. Brent (1854–1899), Washington's earliest-known African American architect, was first listed as an architect in *Boyd's Directory of the District of Columbia* in 1875. Church tradition attributes Saint Luke's design to him. The only building we can be certain that he designed is a two-story brick row house at 1704 V Street NW. Brent probably collaborated with Saint Luke's rector, Alexander Crummell, an African American clergyman who had spent six years in England at midcentury and would undoubtedly have been influenced by the Ecclesiological movement. The purpose of Ecclesiology was to reform Gothic Revival church design in keeping with liturgical practices rather than with picturesque compositions. In 1876 in a national appeal for $20,000 to build the church, Crummell stressed the national character of Saint Luke's, noting that Washington's black population of 43,000 came from every state in the union. The simple hall church—60 feet wide by 100 feet deep—is built of randomly laid Potomac blue stone. Four large pointed-arch openings dominate the facade: a double-lancet door divided by a limestone trumeau and topped by a stone tympanum with a carved roundel surmounted by a five-part window of equal width with tracery based on English curvilinear decorated models and large stained-glass windows (by "Mr. Gernhardt") that fill the fields of each of the aisle walls. Two rows of interior iron columns support the roof; the steel tie rods were installed in the 1940s. The original wood wainscoting has been replaced; interior walls are plastered and painted.

MH07 Hightowers

1937–1938, Alvin E. Aubinoe, Sr., and Harry L. Edwards. 1530 16th St. NW

This Art Deco apartment building designed for the Cafritz Company demonstrates how an established formula—skyscraper with projecting bays—could be modernized not just in its outward appearance but also through fundamental changes in concept. Curved strip windows divided vertically by a series of distinct window mullions articulate the two projecting bays of Hightowers. Each bay is subtly separated from the building block by narrow vertical strip windows and in turn is outlined by flat brick frames surmounted by stepped pinnacles, a modest rendition of the ziggurat motif that was popular during the 1930s. The

MH07 Hightowers

MH08 The Cairo

building's edges repeat the plain stepped brick surround of the projecting bays, thus framing the compact, relatively small-scale design. Central and side bays have darker brick recessed spandrels. Aluminum double doors punctured by large semicircular windows are set slightly behind elegant square frames made up of smaller squares of dark glazed tiles. The subtle composition and fine sense of proportion give the modest Hightowers great architectural character.

MH08 The Cairo

1894, Thomas Franklin Schneider. 1615 Q St. NW

Designed as a luxurious apartment house, The Cairo is now a condominium, renovated in 1976 by local architect Arthur Cotton Moore. Numerous additions, including an 1897 conservatory at the rear, were made over the years, and in the mid-1920s The Cairo was converted to a hotel and then reconverted to low-cost apartments. Twelve stories tall (146 feet), with a perilously projecting capped roof, the steel-frame skyscraper prompted zoning laws limiting building heights to 90 feet on residential streets and 110 feet on commercial streets.

Schneider was Washington's preeminent developer-architect. The many row houses he built, primarily in his own interpretation of the Richardsonian Romanesque style, were similar to the buildings adjacent to and across the street from The Cairo on the 1500 block

of Q Street. For the lower floors of The Cairo, Schneider used rock-faced limestone, the same surface treatment that characterized many of his row houses. The Cairo's glory is its exuberant entrance, where a wide, low, and deep arch is set within an intricately carved rectangular band of Moorish ancestry. The whole recalls Louis Sullivan's great entrance to the Transportation Building at the World's Columbian Exposition in 1893. (The Cairo was designed and built between February and December 1894.) Additional and intermittent carved stone ornamentation, particularly the spread-winged gargoyles that support each corner of the projecting balconies, felicitously enriches the plain brown brick walls. The Cairo's height, its form with continuous vertical bays, its entrance, and the interwoven character of its ornament are all more suggestive of Chicago school developments than of the Richardsonian tradition with which its style is usually connected.

MH09 The Green Door (Denman-Werlich House)

1886, Fuller and Wheeler. 1623 16th St. NW

H. P. Denman's house on 16th Street is the finest surviving example of Richardsonian Romanesque in the city, other than Richardson's own Warder house (see MH22). Albert

W. Fuller was the author of five illustrated books of architectural designs in the Queen Anne and Richardsonian styles between 1882 and 1890. Unlike Thomas Franklin Schneider (see MH08), Fuller and Wheeler, who were from Albany, New York, understood and applied Richardson's basic compositional principles, rather than merely copying the superficial motifs—low-springing arches, sculpted foliate decoration—of his style. The Denman house, as published in the June 1886 issue of *The American Architect and Building News,* was initially planned to be brick on all stories with sandstone trim, its battered base emerging from the ground. As erected, the base and first story were built with rock-faced Long Meadow, Massachusetts, sandstone cut in small pieces and set in random courses. The architects thus responded to Richardson's dictate that buildings should seem to grow out of their sites, demonstrably part of the earth, not appear as objects that sit on the land.

Like Richardson, the architects viewed entry as an event, penetrating the massiveness of the wall through a sequence of spaces. However, they did not here adhere to Richardson's practice of placing his inner door off-axis with the outside wall arch. Their placement and variation of the window sizes, shapes, and compositions is particularly successful. In some areas they created subtle asymmetries and in others, elegant, rationally organized groupings of tripartite windows. Queen Anne details—partial, small-paned colored-glass windows, a corbeled chimney springing from the ground story, and small-scale geometric wood details in the gables and window frames—are well integrated to the balanced asymmetries of the total design. Varied materials, such as the buff-colored sandstone, deep red brick, and wood shingles in the gables, were chosen for their contrasts in color and texture; their use is in harmonious balance.

Although the entrance is on 16th Street, the main rooms face south, beginning with the drawing room expressed on the exterior by the corner tower, the library lit by three windows of the octagonal bay, and a small dining room with a single, wide tripartite window. An extended suite of rooms consisting of a sun room, gallery, and large dining room or perhaps ballroom is lit by a sequence of almost continuous tall rectangular windows. A continuous enfilade runs through these rooms from the front to the back of the building (73 feet), although room divisions are marked by wide openings with doors that slide into the walls.

MH09 The Green Door (Denman-Werlich House)

Residence at Washington D.C. for Hon. H. P. Denman; Messrs Fuller & Wheeler, Arch'ts Albany. N.Y.

MH10 **Chasteleton**

1920, Philip M. Jullien. 1701 16th St. NW

As soon as the southern half of the Chasteleton was completed in 1920, the architect was hired to replicate his U-shaped, Neo-Gothic design on the north half of the block. In total, the Chasteleton covers an acre of ground, the largest apartment block in Washington (with 310 units) for three years, erected at a total cost of $1.7 million. It remains the city's largest and most ornate Neo-Gothic apartment house, with brown brick walls embellished with terracotta-clad bays in a lighter buff color. The two lowest of the eight stories are constructed of limestone; the carved Gothic details around the two 16th Street entrances (reflective of its two-phase construction) are particularly ornate. This ornament correctly interprets a wide range of English Gothic motifs, including curvilinear or flowing tracery, pseudo-buttresses, and gargoyles. Jullien, a native Washingtonian, was an architect educated at Catholic University who specialized in apartment buildings.

MH11 **Toutorsky House** (Henry B. Brown House)

1892–1894, William Henry Miller. 1720 16th St. NW

Miller, who conducted a fifty-year architectural practice in Ithaca, New York, was, in 1872, the first student to graduate from Cornell University's School of Architecture. He worked in a variety of late Victorian styles, primarily influenced by contemporaneous developments in England, a common practice among provincial American architects of the period. In his Brown house, Miller employed a vocabulary associated with Flemish architecture, whose revival was popularized in England by Richard Norman Shaw. Three major vertical masses intersect at right angles and relate to the house's corner site and its plan, which has two major entrances and a biaxial arrangement of rooms. Each of the three-and-a-half-story brick masses (one facing 16th Street and the others Riggs Place) has a stepped gable, and each is composed using different fenestration patterns. The scrolled stepped gable on the 16th Street facade surmounts a wall with tall vertical windows that span its five-bay width, while the gables facing Riggs Place are angular and less ornate in outline. Continuous rock-faced brown sandstone belt courses circumscribe the house, merging with window sills and lintels on all stories. These strong horizontals blend with the deep red of the brick and subtly balance the vertical thrust of the numerous, compactly placed, deeply set windows. Although picturesque in outline and arrangement of masses, Miller's composition is totally controlled and coherent when viewed from 16th Street and hierarchically spread out as its masses diminish in size and importance on Riggs Place.

MH12 **Scottish Rite Temple**

1911–1915, John Russell Pope. 1733 16th St. NW

The mausoleum at Halikarnassos (353–c. 340 B.C.E.) was a model for many buildings in this period, including Masonic temples, because as one of the seven wonders of the ancient world it was associated with the beginnings of Western architectural traditions. The origins of freemasonry are linked to the lodges of medieval stonemasons and with a practice of architecture based on fundamental rules of the universe, with its most esoteric aspects expressed through a language of symbols. The definition of freemasonry as "a peculiar system of morality, veiled in allegory, and illustrated by symbols" explains why the buildings housing such organizations are themselves expressive of symbolic meaning.

Thrown down by an earthquake in the thirteenth century and quarried in the sixteenth century by the Knights of Saint John for the building of one of their castles, King Mausolos's tomb, a Hellenistic monument located on the Turkish coast, was the subject of numerous reconstructions by historians, archaeologists, and architects based on two ancient texts that describe its huge dimensions, colonnaded base, and stepped pyramidal top supporting a quadriga.

John Russell Pope's design, based on Newton and Pullman's 1862 restoration of the mausoleum, is centered on a nearly square site (217.5 by 212 feet) and raised above 16th Street on a podium with steps that extend the width of the block and that are organized according to arcane numerology. Three, five, seven, and nine steps converge on the central entry, which is guarded by Sphinxes, sculpted by Adolph A. Weinman, representing wisdom and power, contemplation and action. Thirty-six Ionic columns 33 feet high circumscribe the temple room, where the highest degree of freemasonry (the thirty-third) is conferred. The attic, marked by acroteria and the stepped pyramid, covers a square Guastavino dome; thus, the basic form above the base encloses a single volume. The compact base, with its expanses of smooth walls broken only by windows and doors, the peripteral colonnade set against nearly solid walls, and the faceted surfaces of the roof demonstrate Pope's unerring sense of balanced proportional relationships between masses and details. The light, monochromatic Indiana limestone is particularly well suited to the combination of planar surfaces and finely carved Greek and Egyptian details. Although Pope, with the advice of local architect and mason Elliott Woods, was responsible for incorporating some basic symbolism, the inscriptions and symbolic decorative details were planned by the grand commander of the lodge,

George Fleming Moore, after the architectural design was completed.

The ground story is represented by the monolithic base on the exterior; on the interior an apsed atrium is ringed by offices, meeting rooms, banquet hall, and libraries. The atrium's form and decoration were intended as symbolic imitation of a Roman impluvium. Two sets of four massive Doric columns in a highly polished green Windsor, Vermont, granite establish a pathway leading to the apse on the east, where the main stair rises to the temple room. The oak-beam ceiling is painted in deep shades of red, brown, blue, yellow, and green, as are the walls in recesses behind the column screens. The decorative vocabulary mixes Greek frieze motifs and Egyptian hieroglyphics. The variation of rich and beautifully crafted materials continues in the main space. The temple room, a square with beveled corners that continue up into the dome, is constructed of limestone walls, Botticino marble dado, black and white marble floors, and a Guastavino tile dome. Windows are screened by Ionic columns set in antis made of green Windsor, Vermont, granite. Their gilded bronze capitals and bases echo the lavish use of gold or bronze in the entablature, windows, screens, and doors. The vault nearly doubles the height of the room, a proportional relationship that complements the subdued richness of the architectural surface. American architectural critic Aymar Embury so admired Pope's Scottish Rite Temple that he maintained, "Roman architects of two thousand years ago would prefer [it] to any of their own work."[43]

MH13 Universalist National Memorial Church

1926–1930, Allen and Collens. 1810 16th St. NW

Dr. Frederic Perkins, chairman of the Universalist church's Committee on Church Architecture, was named minister of the Washington congregation to oversee construction of their national memorial. He approved the Neo-Romanesque design by Francis H. Allen and Charles Collens of Boston; both had studied at the Ecole des Beaux-Arts after completing American university educations. Their design replaced an initial classical proposal by Coolidge and Shattuck that was deemed too expensive to build, although its stylistic heritage was more acceptable to the

Commission of Fine Arts. Collens preferred Gothic designs; the round-arch Romanesque style was a compromise.

The Universalist Church has an unusually long (115 feet, 9 inches) frontage on 16th Street. The sanctuary and parish hall are balanced by the truncated Peace Tower, whose mass is embedded in both of them. In the eyes of the nineteenth- and early twentieth-century revivalists, this asymmetrical arrangement of masses, forms, and details had its roots in Romanesque architecture, and it offered a welcome flexibility in planning and designing that they exploited to the utmost. The architects' intention was to give the appearance of a church that had evolved slowly over time; construction in buff brick with limestone trim actually took twelve months. Collens's design is a synthesis of harmoniously integrated structural and decorative details derived from English, French, and Italian traditions. As with his contemporaries working in alternate historicist traditions, Collens viewed this kind of eclecticism as an appropriate American innovation.

Entry to the church is unusual, as is its orientation with the altar at the west end. The main door is at the base of the tower (a secondary one opens at the east end of the S Street facade) rather than at the end of the church. The tympanum of the tower portal, depicting Christ in glory surrounded by the symbols of the evangelists, is beautifully carved, as is all of the interior and exterior ornament. The sculptor is unknown. Superior craftsmanship is evident in all other decorative details, such as the intricate iron strapwork hinges of the oak doors and the altar mosaic by Tiffany and Company. Nonfigural, predominantly blue and red triforium windows and the rose window at the east end were made by the New York firm Calvert, Herrick and Reddinger.

The interior structure of the four-bay church is deceptive, as the arches, piers, colonnettes, and chancel and south aisle vaults appear to be ashlar blocks of variegated sandstone but are in fact terracotta, including the molded capitals. The plaster on the masonry walls was patinated to give the impression of great age. The oak tie-beam truss ceiling, however, follows traditional construction methods. The Universalist National Memorial Church is an excellent demonstration that it is good design—where forms, spaces, textures, and details are harmoniously integrated—that results in pleasing architectural experiences, not dogmatic adherence to a "superior" style of architecture, stylistic purity, or "truthfulness" in construction.

MH14 **Balfour** (Westover)

1900, George S. Cooper. 2000 16th St. NW

The Westover was the earliest fine quality apartment building to be erected at the foot of Meridian Hill, designed as a large Neo-Renaissance palace in what was then a fairly open and isolated location. At a cost of $100,000 for thirty-six apartments, the limestone and buff brick Westover was an expensive building, notable for its well-composed, but uninnovative, facades. Cooper, a local architect, divided its cubic mass into three horizontal zones, a standard Beaux-Arts solution to control visually the height of multiple-story structures. The lower part of the basement story is rock-faced limestone, but its upper walls as well as the entry story demarcated by tall arched windows are smooth limestone. Sculptural details include splayed limestone supports for the main facade's two oriel windows, numerous brackets, keystones, and an elaborate modillion cornice and deep frieze.

MH15 **Roosevelt Hotel**

1919–1920, Appleton P. Clarke, Jr. 2101 16th St. NW

The first architects for the Roosevelt, planned in 1918 to be Washington's finest apartment house, were Carrère and Hastings of New York. Construction was delayed due to the shortage of materials during World War I, and a design by local architect Appleton P. Clarke, Jr., was implemented beginning in 1919. Clarke planned five identical, three-bay wings to face 16th Street and project from a long central spine; they are connected by single-story limestone screens at ground level and serve as the entrances through gardens to each wing. Using a variety of materials for discrete sections and specific purposes of the building was a common solution on other contemporaneous large buildings: variegated brown brick for the walls, limestone to cover the lowest stories, and glazed terracotta for details on the upper stories, as the quoins and sunken two-story balconies ornamented with twisted columns and segmental pediments. The architectural language of the Roosevelt is vaguely Neo-Renaissance with subdued ornament but resolutely rectilinear, self-contained wings. The southernmost wings are nine stories tall, but in order to present an absolutely flat roofline, they decrease in height to eight on the north as Meridian Hill rises. An unrealized, pergolaed roof garden planned by Clarke would have provided a fitting top for the massive and stately structure.

MH16 **Embassy of Ghana** (Embassy of France)

1907–1908, George Oakley Totten, Jr. 2460 16th St. NW

Totten designed what is now the Embassy of Ghana knowing that it would be rented to the French for their embassy, an arrangement Mrs. John B. Henderson had made with Ambassador Jean Jules Jusserand, who lived there until his retirement in 1925. Thus Totten chose a style associated with the great age of French political and artistic life, the Louis XIV style, the Baroque classicism of the late seventeenth and early eighteenth centuries.

Triangular sites were common in Paris due to the street patterns, and prototypical designs, frequently employing corner towers, had been established to deal effectively with them. Totten articulated his prominent corner tower to be separate from the sides of the main mass of the building, which present two, triple-bay facades to those ascending Meridian Hill from the south. The north facade with a double-story bay topped by an open balcony is treated in a minor key, as it faces Kalorama Road. The basement level is very plain, giving way to the richness of the two linked main floors. Giant Corinthian pilasters and unfluted corner piers frame sunken windows separated horizontally by elaborately sculpted panels, those on the facades set within semicircular arches and those on the towers separated by smooth variegated marble slabs set within frames. The fabric of the building is limestone cut in ashlar blocks, but most of the ornament is molded terracotta, including balustrades, capitals, decorative panels between the main stories, and the entablature. Elaborately framed dormer windows on two attic stories—carved limestone for the rectangular ones just above the cornice and copper bull's-eye and square windows in the mansard roof—continue the florid ornamental character of the principal floors. The patina of the copper tower roof provides a striking (almost strident) color contrast to the monochromatic walls. Totten's composition is a particularly coherent one, historically correct to the Louis XIV period in massing, proportions, and details. The plan is elegant with the corner tower acting as a hinge with openings into long rectangular rooms; circulation and services are contained in the building's triangular core.

MH17 **Meridian House International** (Henry White House, White-Meyer House)

1910, John Russell Pope. 1624 Crescent Pl. NW

The Henry White house was the first of two mansions designed by John Russell Pope for friends on Meridian Hill. Set at the back of a sloping trapezoidal site, the house is protected visually by a high brick wall on the street in the French manner and by a tall retaining wall at the foot of the double curved entrance drive. A two-story, five-bay brick house with attached single-bay wings, it is a modern transformation of an English Georgian country house. The Tuscan entrance portico serves as a porte-cochère, and the garden facade loggia—also Tuscan—faces a narrow paved terrace, which was once the vantage point for uninterrupted views of the entire city. French doors and windows throughout the ground floor allow in abundant natural light and open onto small walled gardens that block out the nearby cityscape.

All of the architectural elements reveal Pope's extremely refined sensibility, where attenuated proportions are coupled with abstract, often sinuous details, such as his exterior window brackets or the curved corners of his portico entablatures. The axiality of the entrance sequence and main facade imply a central hall plan, in keeping with the design principles of its Georgian antecedents. Therefore one is surprised by the closing of the main axis in the entrance hall and its diversion to double axes established by the windows flanking the main door. In the entrance hall, engaged Ionic columns carrying a full entablature establish a formality that continues throughout the building. Parallel to the hall, the dining room and library suite traverse the garden side of the main block, with the service wing to the west and the drawing room to the east. As on the exterior, the decorative vocabulary of the interiors is derived from the Anglo-Palladian tradition, but Pope's affinity with sixteenth-century Italian motifs—such as his elongated brackets and entablatures composed of multiple, continuous moldings—subtly changes the robust, sculptural quality of the English tradition into a new and highly refined interpretation of classicism. Open to the public.

MH18 **Meridian House International**
(Irwin B. Laughlin House)

1920–1929, John Russell Pope. 1630 Crescent Pl. NW

Of all the French-inspired mansions in Washington, none is more successful than Meridian House. John Russell Pope's rendition of an early eighteenth-century urban villa is not a reinterpretation of any single prototype or group of prototypes. Rather, its architectural excellence results from his absorption of the

MH18 Meridian House International (Irwin B. Laughlin House)

planning principles, spatial arrangements, surface treatment, and restrained details of the Louis XV style. Set within extensive walled grounds with landscaping specifically planned to complement it, the restrained volumetric cube is broken on the entrance facade by a semioctagonal bay and on the garden front by a semicircular one. Ostensibly two stories high, Meridian House actually has four floors, including a sunken basement level for services and a servants' floor under the mansard roof set behind the deep balustrade that circumscribes the building. Each side measures 78 feet 6 inches and is five bays wide, with the same plain molded entablature dividing the two main stories used at the cornice line. Bracketed keystones over the windows provide minor three-dimensional accents to otherwise planar walls punctuated by shallow panels and unfluted pilasters at the corners. Fine limestone was used for the walls and sculptural details, as in the leaf enframement of the bull's-eye window over the main door and the garlanded mascaron above it.

Due to the difference in ground levels, the entrance is at the basement level with the rise to the main garden level accomplished immediately upon entering by an elegant double staircase contained within a circular room 12 feet in diameter. On the landing the main axis opens visually to the garden through two sets of floor-to-ceiling glass doors. A long rectangular drawing room (43 feet by 24 feet 10 inches) and a dining room (40 feet by 24 feet 10 inches) parallel the central hall, with access to the garden through French doors at their short ends. Tall casement windows on the sides open onto balconies on both main floors, thus flooding all the rooms with natural light. The interconnection of these public rooms, through a series of axially aligned openings, results in a clarity of plan replicated in the treatment of interior walls. The built-in bookcases in the library situated in the northeast corner are original, a typical French *poché* effect rarely encountered in American buildings. Like its neighbor (MH17), the Laughlin house is owned by Meridian House International and open to the public.

MH19 **Apartment Building**

1925, Joseph Younger. 1661 Crescent Pl. NW

Younger's elegant irregular E-shaped apartment building was built as a cooperative, with the cost of its fifty apartments ranging from $6,000 to $29,000. Unusually large and gracious apartments were planned to have three exposures as they span the width and depth of each of the three wings that face Crescent Place. Younger designed in an elegant but restrained version of the Neo-Renaissance style. The lower two of the six stories are faced with limestone in which the thickness of a masonry wall is alluded to in a remarkably shallow layering of rustication, smooth double-story blind arches, and pilasters carrying short segments of entablature. In reality the structure behind the limestone (and brick above) is a steel frame; Younger's careful and ironic imitation of solid masonry construction functions as a mere historical reference. In contrast to the thinness of these limestone walls, the central arch of each three-bay wing is framed by freestanding Roman Doric columns topped by fully developed entablatures and even finials. Beautifully proportioned Doric screens span the two landscaped courtyards.

MH20 **Inter-American Defense Board**

1905–1906, George Oakley Totten, Jr. 2600 16th St. NW

Known locally as the Pink Palace because of its original color, this building was the first speculative mansion undertaken on Meridian

MH20 Inter-American Defense Board

Hill by Mrs. John B. Henderson and her architect, George Oakley Totten. The building has had many residents and undergone numerous changes, including a two-story ballroom addition on the north by Totten in 1912. Under Mrs. Marshall Field's ownership (1920–1937), interior and exterior renovations were undertaken, the most notable being the closing of the two open loggias on the Euclid Street facade. In 1984 eight of nine original balconies were removed, and an office addition was attached to the west wall. The building was painted a cream color at that time but has recently been painted white.

The building's orientation with the entry on the short side facing 16th Street and the greater architectural development on the long Euclid Street facade was probably due to a combination of factors: a southern exposure and its view of the city when it stood in splendid isolation on top of Meridian Hill. In form and details the Pink Palace is a composite of Venetian Renaissance elements, notably the rectangular mass with hip roof and strong horizontal divisions between floors accomplished by projecting moldings, grouped windows, inset loggias, spiral colonnettes (including one inset into the corners), and variegated marble columns. Its most striking features are the Venetian Gothic trefoil arches on second- and third-story windows supplemented by additional medieval decorative details. The smooth, ground-floor walls are polished Beaver Dam marble, while the three upper stories are brick covered with marbleized plas-

MH22 Benjamin H. Warder House

ter, since painted white. The surviving balcony over the main entrance is of terracotta-encased concrete, including the lion's-head consoles supporting it. Most of the ornament is molded terracotta. Unfortunately, the pink variegated marble columns have been painted.

Like its immediate successor, the French Embassy (see MH16), the Pink Palace is a rationally composed and proportionally balanced design in which the correct use of a historical vocabulary has been reinterpreted in modern materials and building methods. It has long been beloved in Washington because it is an architecturally pleasing and believable fantasy.

MH21 **Meridian Hill Studio**

1922, George Oakley Totten, Jr. 2633 15th St. NW

Totten's design of a small apartment complex for Mrs. Henderson in 1922 was horizontal and sprawling in contrast to contemporaneous high-rise apartments, undertaken by professional developers, that were close to it. E-shaped, with two- to three-story gabled wings, its composition and detailing were derived from French vernacular architecture but influenced by the picturesque planning principles of the English Arts and Crafts movement. The reinforced-concrete wall construction was prefabricated on the site, with each wall segment poured into forms and then raised into place, a technique developed by the Army Corps of Engineers.

MH22 **Benjamin H. Warder House**

1885–1888, H. H. Richardson. 2633 16th St. NW

The Benjamin H. Warder house is the sole remaining example among H. H. Richardson's four houses erected in Washington between 1882 and 1888. It has suffered considerably by being dismantled and rebuilt for use as an apartment house, numerous subsequent incarnations, and recent neglect. Until 1923 the Warder house stood at 1515 K Street NW, when it was replaced by an office building. At that time architect George Oakley Totten bought all of the exterior stonework (except for the main doorway) as well as window frames and sashes, roof tiles, and copper trim and cresting. The present door and its surround are replicas, as the originals had already been sold and are now owned by the Smithsonian Institution. Totten also acquired the wood paneling from the vestibule, central hall, and staircase; the mahogany ceiling from the picture gallery; and the white holly woodwork from the front reception room.

The Warder house is an L-shaped building. Its 73-foot street frontage consists of a four-story, gabled entrance wing originally connected by a wall spur to a single-story blank garden wall and entrance drive leading into a sunken forecourt. Five wide elliptical arches carried by piers and polygonal columns have replaced the plain wall, and the courtyard is now level with the main entrance. Elaborate iron gates once closed the drive, which abutted the building on the east and led down to a round-arch service entrance. A conical tower at the intersection of the two rectangular masses served as a courtyard entrance, directly opening into the large central hall and staircase whose L-shape spans the width of both wings. Together the hall and stairs lock into the larger L formed by the wings, isolating rooms at each end and in the back corner. The site arrangement, tower, and balconies on the upper two floors of the south facade create the appearance of a French country manor house rather than Richardson's normal urban use of almost impenetrably thick walls.

Even within Richardson's vocabulary, the composition of solids and voids is a particularly sophisticated one. All windows are rectilinear and cut directly into wall surfaces with a sharpness and clarity peculiarly sympathetic to the shape of the house. On the entrance facade, double windows are grouped into two bays. As large basement windows are set level with the ground, the bottoms of the main-story windows are high on the wall relative to the main door. The door's semicircular blind arch projects into an expanse of unbroken wall above it. This subtle asymmetry of openings set in large fields placed in a triangular relationship to one another is balanced by three small windows grouped together in the gable. The main-story fenestration is consistent throughout: windows are grouped in pairs with their transoms (which once contained stained glass) separated by narrow wall slabs. Openings on the second and third stories vary according to internal function, with those on the south courtyard facade recessed behind elliptical arches or a shallow, balustraded balcony. As the east and west walls were originally attached to neighboring houses, all rooms were lit from the north or south.

The dressed ashlar sandstone is creamy in texture and color, with not even a hint of the rock-faced masonry common in Richardson's work. His battered foundations are exploited compositionally in relation to the wall spur that connects house and courtyard wall. Sculptured foliate decoration was kept to a minimum, appearing in the semicircular arches and columns at the main entrance, on the capitals of squat columns supporting elliptical arches on the third-floor balcony, and on the outer edges of the tall, narrow voussoirs of the flat arches above second- and third-story windows.

MH23 **Embassy of Poland**

1909–1910, George Oakley Totten, Jr. 2640 16th St. NW

Totten's third building on Meridian Hill is Louis XVI in style and immediately followed his design for the Louis XIV French Embassy. In this case, he and his client, Mrs. Henderson, did not know who the international occupant would be. In 1919 the house was sold to the Polish government, apparently having been unoccupied until that time, and was briefly inhabited by the ambassador from Imperial Russia. As originally designed, the three-bay house was a cube, but in 1912 Totten added a two-story ballroom to the rear. Since then it has undergone only minor interior changes and the exterior is intact. The understated elegance and simplicity of the design is reinforced by the smooth monochromatic limestone. Double Corinthian pilasters frame the two upper stories of the central bay, which is marked on the ground-floor level by the original glass and iron marquee and by a Palladian dormer window set in the mansard roof behind the balustrade. The major deviation from a substantially correct reinterpretation of a French Louis XVI mansion is the gradual opening of the central bay, with narrow windows set between the pilasters on the third floor and inset windows beside the central dormer. Decoration is limited to the balcony balustrades and consoles beneath the French windows on the principal story, the Corinthian pilasters, and roof balustrade and dormers. Totten was particularly adept at reinterpreting French historical styles.

MH24 **Embassy of Italy**

1923–1924, Warren and Wetmore. 2700 16th St. NW

Gelasio Caetani, the Italian ambassador in 1924, was a trained architect and engineer and reputedly was involved in the design of the embassy from its site selection to its interior decoration. Caetani and the architects of record, Warren and Wetmore of New York, followed Italian Renaissance models both in the embassy's three-story elevation and in its plan. Proportions and details are more historically correct on this building than on its more eclectic neighbors. As in Italian Renaissance mansions, the ground story is decidedly separated from the piano nobile by a wide belt course. Projection of the bracketed triangular pediments of the main-story windows—based on those of the Palazzo Farnese in Rome—gives sculptural relief to the smooth limestone walls. The two main stories are door set beneath John Joseph Earley's striking concrete and stone mosaic. The architects reinforced the geometry of each individual mass of the temple by using limestone slabs of the appropriate shape for each section: square ones on the cube, rectangular ones set horizontally for the recessive rectangle, and rectangular ones set vertically in the arch. Earley's mosaic of pulsating rays of color is autumnal in hue, focused on a bronze eagle, and framed by a filigreed bronze screen of animals of symbolic importance to masonic rites. Massive mosaic amphorae decorated by Earley flank the entrance arch; his technique of outlining each decorative motif's color change with incised lines can be readily seen.

MH26 Embassy of Spain

integrated by an elaborate entrance motif with the segmentally pedimented second-floor window set within the broken triangular pediment of the doorway. The rectilinear main block is separated from the chancery by a single-story connector on the north, whose windows originally were open onto an arcaded loggia overlooking the square courtyard. The chancery wing on the east was part of the original design but enlarged about 1930.

MH25 Scottish Rite Temple

1938–1939, Porter, Lockie and Chatelain. 2800 16th St. NW

The local Scottish Rite Masonic Temple that serves Supreme Council 33 (distinct from the national function of MH12) is a good example of the application of modernized historical decoration to a modernist formal vocabulary. Raised on a terrace 5 feet above and set back from the sidewalk, the temple is purposefully remote and self-contained as befits a building serving an organization with limited membership and secret ceremonies. Monolithic in massing, it is composed of two intersecting volumes, a 70-foot cube that rises above and projects slightly in front of a rectangle that extends back 129 feet. It is difficult to conceive that this shell contains 81 rooms; it was erected at a cost of $350,000. Front facade surfaces are unbroken by windows or moldings of any kind, with the exception of the magnificent overscaled entry portal set in a massive rectangular arch and consisting of a forbidding handleless bronze

MH26 Embassy of Spain

1921–1923, George Oakley Totten, Jr. 2801 16th St. NW

The Spanish Embassy, built by Mrs. John B. Henderson as part of her speculative development of Meridian Hill, was first offered as a gift to the American government to serve as the vice president's residence. It was vacant for three years before the Spanish government purchased it in 1926. When the federal government declined Mrs. Henderson's gift, she offered it to the Mexican government, presumably on the basis of the building's historical precedents, which perhaps influenced officials of the Spanish government in their choice. The new owners extensively remodeled the existing building and hired Jules Henri de Sibour in 1926 to design the chancery at the back of the property facing 15th Street. Both structures have been renovated numerous times in the intervening years, mainly in the interiors.

The composition of Totten's building is asymmetrical with a central, stepped cube forming the main block, an octagonal bay (originally with an open porch above) projecting to the south, and two separately articulated pieces on the north. The main drawing room is behind the four grouped arched windows; the ballroom is identified by the mansard roof and large thermal window opening. The whole is raised and set behind low balustrades that provide terraces for each section of the building. The structure is of stuccoed brick, and the exterior decoration is classical in derivation with suggestions of Spanish Renaissance architecture in the strapwork details of the pilasters and arch spandrels.

MH27 **Embassy of Mexico** (Franklin MacVeagh House)

1910–1911, Nathan C. Wyeth. 2829 16th St. NW

Built for Secretary of the Treasury Franklin MacVeagh, whose Chicago residence had been designed by H. H. Richardson, 2829 16th Street has served as the Mexican Embassy since 1921, at which time the overscaled Tuscan porte-cochère was added to a somewhat stark urban villa notable on Meridian Hill for its relative plainness. Wyeth's design was unusual among its contemporaneous neighbors in the simplicity of its self-contained form and the predominance of buff-colored brick, which set it apart from the elaborately sculpted and more colorful mansions common to the area. The building is a vertically oriented rectangle of four stories (the top two of which read as attic stories with minimal fenestration). The relatively small amount of window area in comparison to plain, unbroken wall surfaces emphasizes the sense of tautly contained volumes within.

MH28 **Unification Church** (Washington Chapel, Church of Jesus Christ of Latter-day Saints)

1932–1933, Don C. Young, Jr., and Ramm Hansen. 2810 16th St. NW

The architecture of the Mormon Chapel is associated in numerous ways with the history of this American-founded church: one of its architects, Don C. Young, was the grandson of Brigham Young; the mosaic of Christ on the Mount of Olives over the main entrances is by another of his grandsons, Mahonri Sharp Young. The exterior cladding, an unusual bird's-eye marble, was quarried in Utah, and the church's form and many of its details recall the mother church, the Mormon temple in Salt Lake City. From 16th Street the church appears to consist of a large attenuated block that forms the first stage in a four-part spire. It contains the sanctuary that is in front of a larger rectangular meeting hall that spreads out behind it, as in traditional Latin cross churches. The main entrance, however, is located in a north transept arm consisting solely of a foyer; a secondary entrance is opposite in a shallow octagonal bay containing a staircase. The exterior architectural articulation is an interesting fusion of stripped classical elements (pilasters carrying entablatures), medieval features (finials and embryonic buttresses), and modern decorative details abstracted from both traditions.

MH29 **All Souls Church**

1924, Coolidge and Shattuck. 16th and Harvard streets NW

Henry Shepley, grandson of H. H. Richardson, provided the winning design submitted by the Boston firm of Coolidge and Shattuck in the 1920 competition for All Souls Church. The program for the church required that it "typify Unitarian ideas and ideals, harmonize with the architecture of Washington and fit into the surroundings of the chosen site." The third Unitarian church to be erected in Washington (the first was by Charles Bulfinch), it is clearly based on James Gibbs's Saint Martin-in-the-Fields (1720–1727), one of the best known of English Baroque churches. However, a large service wing with courtyard set perpendicular to the church's main axis that extends and expands on the English model was integral to Shepley's design. Apparently Saint Martin's was deemed an appropriate prototype because numerous versions of it had been built in eighteenth-century America. Although not hitherto found in the Meridian Hill area, the Colonial Revival styles of architecture were well represented in other Washington neighborhoods by the early 1920s.

MH30 National Baptist Memorial Church

1922–1926, Egerton Swartwout. 16th St. and Columbia Rd. NW

The present National Baptist Memorial Church replaces an earlier mission church, Immanuel Baptist Church (1908–1909), a Neo-Gothic structure by George W. Stone, Sr., that also featured a tall tower placed to advantage at the acute corner of the site. The cornerstone was laid on 11 April 1922, but

MH30, National Baptist Memorial Church (left); MH28 Unification Church; MH29 All Souls Church

the church was not dedicated until May 1933. The education building at the rear was built in 1941, and the entire complex was renovated and remodeled in 1950. The initial inspiration for New York architect Egerton Swartwout's three-part circular tower was probably John Nash's Church of All Souls, Langham Place (1824), in London. Its two lower stages are colonnaded rotundas with the superposition of the orders reversed (Corinthian above Ionic in Nash's case, Doric above Corinthian in Swartwout's), although Nash's church is topped by a pointed spire. National Baptist's domed upper tier is more Baroque than Neoclassical, with heavy frames of bull's-eye windows making an elaborately sculptural transition from the severity of the second stage to the lighter upper part.

MH32 Church of the Sacred Heart

MH31 **La Renaissance** (Kenesaw)

1903, George W. Stone, Sr. 3060 16th St. NW

The importance of the original Kenesaw is urbanistic rather than outstanding design or innovative interior planning. It was finally located on a narrow triangular site on the crest of Meridian Hill, despite congressional opposition that sought to keep the top of the hill open as a public park. The intent of the original investors, who included Sen. John B. Anderson, was to capitalize on spectacular views in all directions. The seven-story, F-shaped building was the second apartment house in the city to have all of its facades facing streets. Designed by Stone in a bland version of the Neo-Renaissance style, the buff brick and limestone walls are faceted with a series of bay windows, octagonal bay windows and projecting corners.

MH32 **Church of the Sacred Heart**

1923, Murphy and Olmsted; Maginnis and Walsh, associate architects. 16th St and Park Rd. NW

The Neo–Early Christian Roman Catholic Church of the Sacred Heart was the earliest structure in Meridian Hill's small enclave of religious buildings. The additive plasticity of its volumes, basic Latin cross plan, and architectural and sculptural details are faithful renditions of its prototypes, chosen because the Romanesque was an era when all Western Christians were Catholics. The tall and exceptionally wide central nave, transept arms, and colorful low rotunda and dome rise as pure geometric forms above the nearly solid Kentucky limestone walls, broken only by narrow arched windows. Red clay Mediterranean tile roofs and multicolored slate tiles on the dome contribute to its Italian ambiance. The arcaded porch attached to the facade is composed of eight polished pink Milford granite monolithic columns set between slender corner piers; its tall proportions correspond to the aisle heights and reinforce the sense of intersecting horizontal and vertical volumes, a common spatial concern of Beaux-Arts era architects, whether they were designing in medieval or classically inspired styles. Deeply undercut square porch capitals are modeled on those found in Ravenna. The early Byzantine flavor of the interior is due both to its circular vaults and domes as well as to the extensive mosaic cycle that retells the history of the church. Marble, stone, and ceramic in rose, green, blue, and gold are the mosaic aggregates held in place by portland cement, executed by John Joseph Earley. The solidity and spareness of the stone walls interact with the lightness and delicacy of the mosaics to create a particularly satisfying balance of architectural form and decoration.

Dupont Circle (DU)

Pamela Scott

DUPONT CIRCLE IS ONE OF SEVEN CIRCLES THAT APPEAR on Pierre Charles L'Enfant's plan of the city and one of four that are of large circumference. Although it is located on high ground—a considerable advantage in a metropolitan area plagued with drainage problems—and relatively close to the White House, it remained undeveloped until 1867, when army engineers suggested laying it out along with the contiguous streets. By 1871 Connecticut Avenue was paved to the circle, which was enclosed by a wooden fence and graded, and a landscape plan was prepared. A bronze portrait statue of the Civil War naval hero Adm. Francis S. Dupont was authorized by Congress in 1882, when the circle was officially named. When the Dupont statue was dedicated two years later, there were about 850 ornamental trees and shrubs in the 2.25-acre site; by 1886 fifty-six cast-iron settees were in use by a substantial community. In 1877 water and drainage pipes for a fountain in the center were laid, but they were not utilized until 1922, when the present fountain, the work of the architect Henry Bacon and the sculptor Daniel Chester French, was erected.

A syndicate of California investors developed the area's housing, and by 1873 the first large mansion was built. The British Legation, erected on the site of the present Dupont Circle Building (see DU01) between 1873 and 1876, stimulated development of Dupont Circle as a fashionable residential neighborhood. Unlike Meridian Hill, which had had wealth and the international community thrust upon it, Dupont Circle's natural growth process included an infrastructure of houses and businesses for a varied population. The mansions for the wealthy were built primarily on the avenues, while those for the middle and working classes were dispersed throughout the ten radiating wedges formed by the confluence of Connecticut, Massachusetts, and New Hampshire avenues

317

DuPont Circle

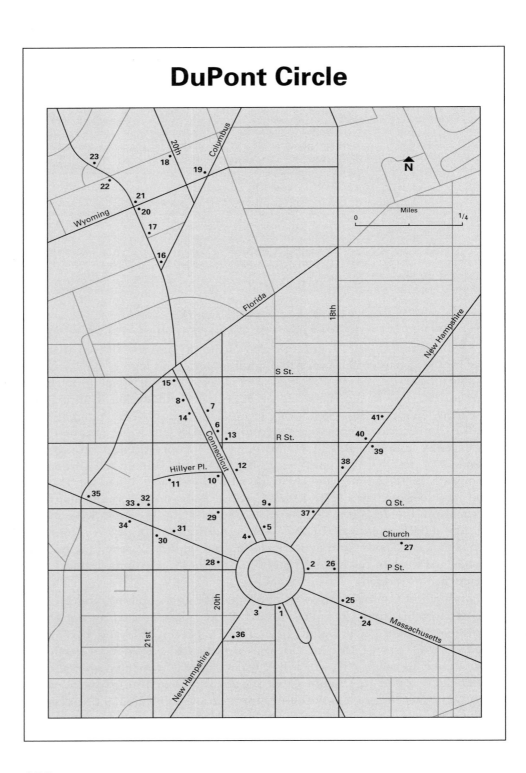

and 19th and P streets. Although only three of the original mansions on the circle survive, the vast majority of those built on Massachusetts Avenue up to and including Sheridan Circle to the west and Scott Circle to the east still exist.

In the 1888 edition of his *Picturesque Washington,* Joseph West Moore estimated that about 50,000 people, or one-sixth of Washington's total population, were winter residents only. The majority of that contingent was made up of congressmen, their families, and their employees, but a significant and highly visible number were wealthy self-made Americans, some of whom were unacceptable in New York and Philadelphia society. Since the residences of this large community served as party houses for a transient population, their internal organization accommodated frequent entertaining, with large dining rooms, ballrooms, and salons. Often as much, or more, private space was allotted to domestic servants as to the owners themselves. Most of these houses today function as embassies or as headquarters for prestigious organizations, where the public life-style of their inhabitants is similar to that of the original occupants.

The major surviving works of the turn-of-the-century Washington firm Hornblower and Marshall are located near Dupont Circle. Unlike the majority of local architects who had studied at the Ecole des Beaux Arts in Paris, Hornblower and Marshall created their own strongly identifiable image, dependent as much on American prototypes as on European ones. Their personal synthesis of pan-European forms, French academic planning, and Richardsonian details was realized in decisively cubic houses built with taut Roman brick skins ornamented with light or red stone trim, carved or plain.

Connecticut Avenue

The major commercial street in the Dupont Circle neighborhood has always been Connecticut Avenue. Large office buildings recently erected predominate below the circle, while late nineteenth- and early twentieth-century shops and offices, designed on a domestic scale and primarily built as residences, line three blocks to the north. Whatever their origins, their architectural integrity has been compromised by poorly designed storefronts, awnings, and signage. Classical Revival styles of many persuasions predominate, but the most ubiquitous are Renaissance and Georgian Revival buildings, with just a few exuberant late Victorian examples providing textural and formal variety.

DU01 **Dupont Circle Building**

1931, Mihran Mesrobian. 1346 Connecticut Ave. NW

A triumph of design over scale, form, and materials characterizes Mesrobian's Dupont Circle Building. An early office building in the area, this structure is a long, tall, thin

wedge that rises twelve stories and extends for half a block, yet its size and shape are modulated by the complex changing grid of the ornamental pattern Mesrobian devised to tame them. Within the confines of a regular window placement, Mesrobian avoided both monotony and anonymity by creating varied spatial fields in five distinct horizontal and ten alternating vertical zones. He used limestone (in conjunction with a soft variegated pink brick) as a structural material for vestigial pilasters and friezes, both plain and decorated, with low-relief sculpture. The limestone has been so widely distributed over the facades and projects so slightly from the brick wall surfaces that both surfaces seem to be only light sheathing materials, which they essentially are. The lowest horizontal layer is two stories of limestone with shop fronts at the ground level. In the next five Mesrobian arranged the pilasters to divide the long facades vertically into groups of four bays, imitating the rhythm and appearance of alternating bay windows, although they do not project from the walls. In the third two-story layer the architect changes the rhythm from units of four to five with intermittent hieratic female figures carved in low relief. In the next two floors, narrow limestone pilasters separate each bay, with wide ones occurring every five bays to maintain the new rhythm established below. The top floor is recessed, and a penthouse tower emerges from the center of the building. All of the ornament is Mesopotamian in origin, perhaps Mesrobian's statement about his own origins and history. Of Armenian origin, he was born in Turkey and educated at the Academy of Fine Arts in Istanbul. He emigrated to America at age thirty-two in 1921, becoming chief architect to Washington developer Harry Wardman.

DU01 Dupont Circle Building

DU02 **The Washington Club** (R. W. Patterson House)

1901, McKim, Mead and White. 15 Dupont Circle

McKim, Mead and White's response to half of one of Dupont Circle's obtuse-ended wedges was to address the circle obliquely (not parallel to the site line) and P Street frontally, with triple-bay, rectangular wings, and to place the entrance between them facing their point of intersection. Thus, when approached from the south, the building's eleven bays appear as a single faceted facade, its two wings tied together by a deep loggia set above the single entrance doorway. The composition derives from a traditional Renaissance palace, with the plain ground story connoting service areas, two highly ornamented principal stories, and a short attic story tucked under the low-slung roof. The highly ornate facade, where the wall surfaces are encrusted with garlands, swags, putti, and escutcheons, specifically recalls several sixteenth-century Roman palaces, such as the Palazzo Spada of 1550. The white, highly polished marble walls are so reflective and the surface ornamentation so profuse that the observer initially suspects glazed terracotta as the sheathing material.

DU03 **Euram Building**

1972, Hartman-Cox. 21 Dupont Circle

Washington's numerous planning review boards have not favored innovative or bold office building design during the last century. Therefore Hartman and Cox's Euram Building, which addressed Dupont Circle as an important urban open space, was a minor triumph under restrictive circumstances. Curtain wall construction on the Connecticut Avenue and 19th Street facades expresses "office," but the dichotomy between open and closed monumental forms on the entrance facade emphasizes the importance and nature of the site. Two brick towers form wedges that open onto a triangular court overlooked by glass-walled offices. Three concrete and glass bridges that contain executive offices are arranged as an inverted stepped pyramid and span the towers. Interior courtyards were common in 1970s office buildings and hotels, and in the Euram they increase the sense of spaciousness, as views across the light-filled court seem to expand laterally the long, open-plan offices that have windows on the court as well as on the street. The Euram Building represents an embryonic return to contextualism in its response to the materials and color contrasts of Mihran Mesrobian's Dupont Circle Building of 1931, which occupies the adjacent wedge to the west.

DU10 1614 20th St. NW

Clarke Waggaman and George N. Ray, who designed the majority of the commercial and many of the residential structures along this strip on Connecticut Avenue during the 1910s and 1920s, left a subdued but distinctive legacy. For tightly knit urban contexts, they favored compositions with tall and open ground stories for business buildings and wide, tripartite second-story windows for residences. Shallow articulation of wall surfaces—usually limestone—might be rusticated, composed of a series of thin, receding panels, or left plain. Examples include the five buildings between 1512 and 1520 Connecticut Avenue NW (DU04) designed as interrelated units, 1509 and 1511 Connecticut Avenue NW (DU05) (1922), the wedge-shaped Wonder Building (DU06) at 1709–1711 Connecticut Avenue NW, and 1721 and 1723 Connecticut Avenue NW (DU07) (1926). The architect for the fine Neo-Renaissance building at 1714 Connecticut Avenue is unknown; Waggaman and Ray are the most likely candidates.

Joseph Younger designed in the same etiolated Neo-Renaissance style as Waggaman and Ray during the same period; his compositions are more varied, as evidenced by 1726 Connecticut Avenue NW (DU08), where the lower two stories are glass walls framed in metal, a common solution for medium-density commercial areas in the 1920s.

The Moorings (DU09) (1927), at 1909 Q Street NW, compact apartments designed by Horace W. Peaslee for bachelor naval officers, has a roof terrace where the building's functional elements are reminiscent of a ship's bridge; rope and shells provide appropriate motifs at the entries, and even porthole windows express its nautical theme. Thomas Franklin Schneider's Romanesque Revival house (DU10) at 1614 20th Street NW (1891) is one of his most exuberant buildings, taking advantage of the corner site to raise a turreted corner tower above a deep, hollow porch in apparent defiance of gravity. Joseph C. Hornblower's own house (DU11) at 2030 Hillyer Place NW (1897) could not be more of a contrast. The extreme simplicity of form covered by Roman brick, gradated in color from brown to tan, was in part provided by an intense desire for privacy and a distaste for ostentation.

The William F. Burch House (DU12) at 1627 Connecticut Avenue NW was designed by Alfred B. Mullett and Company in 1908 in a Georgian Revival style strongly influenced by the Baroque, a style popular in contemporaneous English architecture.

In the George S. Fraser House (Scott-Thropp Mansion) (DU13) at 1701 20th Street, the Washington firm of Hornblower and Marshall in 1890 melded together a wide range of national styles and historical periods to create a highly personal architectural idiom immediately identifiable as their work. Particularly notable was the subtle introduction of the American Richardsonian Romanesque style (with its medieval sculptural details) into a composition that fused principles and elements derived from Italian and French Renaissance traditions. The house's cubic massing is distinctive—three bays by three bays (60 feet by 65 feet), and three stories in

DU13 George S. Fraser House (Scott-Thropp Mansion)

brick above a high pink sandstone basement. This geometric solidity is reinforced by the cube of the square-columned porte-cochère and in the cubic entrance hall.

Although the Fraser house is located on a corner within the grid of narrow streets, the nearby intersection of Connecticut Avenue opens a vista to prominent adjacent facades. Each is a separate two-dimensional composition with differing center lines and articulation. The rusticated base, two belt courses and entablature in sandstone, and the sandstone quoins at the corners and window frames outline tic-tac-toe grids on each facade. Hornblower and Marshall manipulated this grid to avoid monotonous regularity by devising sophisticated deviations on it. For example, the fanlight of the Palladian window directly above the entrance porch rests on the belt course, while on the top floor the bottom third of the tripartite window (itself a variant on the nine-part grid) displaces the belt course below it. The architectural interest of the R Street facade is concentrated at its east end, where a multisectioned, two-story bay window swells out and subtly usurps the central bay to alter irrevocably the balance of the nine squares.

The most significant Postmodern building in the area is a mixed-use commercial structure at 1718–1720 Connecticut Avenue NW (DU14) designed by David M. Schwarz in 1982. Although Neoclassical limestone architecture is more prevalent than Victorian polychromy on Connecticut Avenue, Schwarz chose forms, compositional devices, and strongly contrasting materials associated with

Victorian architecture, particularly the Richardsonian Romanesque style, for his referent in designing his large, complex building.

Marsh and Peter's house at 1742 Connecticut Avenue NW, now the National Science Teachers Association (DU15), was published in the 1901 annual of the Washington Architectural Club. It originally had a single-story octagonal bay window overlooking a minuscule garden on its Connecticut Avenue facade, the only bucolic aspect of its location as it is wedged tightly between Connecticut and Florida avenues. More reminiscent of English than American Georgian architectural traditions, the house's scale and stylistic antecedents imply extensive grounds rather than a confined urban site. Marsh and Peter basically conformed to the design principles of their models: a self-contained rectangular brick

DU14 1718–1720 Connecticut Ave. NW

DU15 National Science Teachers Association

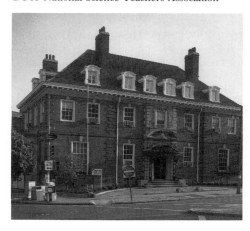

block with a hip roof and symmetrical facade composition focusing on the central entry bay. However, they introduced a subtle irregularity in the fenestration pattern of the wings, placing single large windows on the ground story centered beneath two smaller ones on the second story with a single dormer window above the inner of the two just below. The effect is visually to pull the slightly projecting wings toward the dominant center. Brick quoins (rather than limestone ones) enframing ground-story windows as well as each wing act as a slight counterbalance, but the overall monochromatic effect of the sides prevents them from competing with the entrance bay. Here an exuberant English Baroque–inspired two-story limestone door and window combination provides both contrasting color and sculptural plasticity. The deep, overscaled segmental pediment is filled by a carved cartouche, reminiscent of a family coat of arms but actually displaying the street number. The window above is framed by curved consoles and an elaborate keystone-cum-lintel, the whole squeezed between powerful quoins. The original semicircular fluted metal hood above the door is a distinct intruder, an attached rather than integrated element that seems to have been (and was) ordered from another catalogue of styles.

The architect James Crocroft designed the tall, tapered granite base to support Frederick MacMonnies's bronze equestrian statue of the Civil War general George B. McClellan (DU16) (1907), located at the intersection of Connecticut Avenue and Columbia Road. Its height was intended to allow views of the statue from lower elevations and for the display of bronze military trophies and eagles supporting garlands of oak and laurel leaves, a particularly French treatment of such a base.

The Russian Consulate (DU17), at 2001 Connecticut Avenue NW, was built in 1908–1909 by Hornblower and Marshall as the Lothrop residence. Protectively placed behind its walled terrace, the Lothrop mansion retains superb views of the Washington skyline from its position astride the brow of the hill that was just on the outside edge of L'Enfant's plan. Its cubic form with a hip roof was a common volumetric choice for its architects Hornblower and Marshall, but its stylistic heritage, a mélange of American Georgian and French Beaux-Arts architecture, was not often found in their repertoire. While the elements

DU17 Russian Consulate

from each tradition can be identified and dissected, its architectural quality and character are defined by a successful fusion of these traditions into a distinctive new idiom. The common Renaissance heritage of these styles predicated similar design solutions. While the practice of locating the tall principal story at ground level and equipping it with French windows is most often associated with French mansions of the eighteenth century, Thomas Jefferson had adopted it for Monticello.

Public transportation by trolley car to downtown Washington along Connecticut Avenue, which began in the 1890s, and the area's generally irregular topography (not always suited to row house development) contributed to the development of apartment buildings near this major thoroughfare. Of the dozens of luxurious buildings erected in the neighborhoods, six apartment houses on or near Connecticut Avenue stand out as architecturally superior. Some of those located less prominently are still of interest, including the first to be erected (in 1901), James G. Hill's Mendota (DU18), located at 2220 20th Street NW. A seven-story, U-shaped building with angular and curved bays, it was very much influenced by early Chicago skyscrapers, with its two rusticated ground stories, plain intermediate floors, and strong horizontal entablature. Groupings of windows in sets of twos and threes across the flat facades of Arthur B. Heaton's Altamont (DU19) Wyoming Avenue NW and its two open pavilions set in towers that flank an open loggia off a public dining room indicate

DU20 Apartment house, 2029 Connecticut Ave. NW

dicate the architectural and social changes that quickly took place in apartment house design. Opened in 1916 and designed using an Italian Renaissance vocabulary, the Altamont's additional services included a billiard room, barber shop, beauty parlor, and servants' dining hall in the basement.

The apartment house on the corner of Connecticut and Wyoming avenues, 2029 Connecticut Avenue NW (DU20), was designed in 1915 by Hunter and Bell, who specialized in Washington apartment houses. It exhibits a feature common to many similar buildings of the era, a disparity between the richness of materials and ornamentation at the ground level and rooflines and that of the plain brick walls between them. In this instance the two bottom stories and top story are uniformly clad in cream-colored terracotta, which provides a decided frame and contrast to the four stories of brick walls. The terracotta ornament at the octagonal entrance on Connecticut Avenue and the semicircular one on Wyoming Street as well as the arch enframements into which the two lower stories of windows are set are derived from French Renaissance architecture. It is associated specifically with Francis I, whose personal symbol was the salamander, two of which are found above the main arch of each door (one retains its original mahogany revolving door). Additional decorative motifs associated with the French style include shal-

low arabesque reliefs in the pilaster panels that frame the entrances, fleurs-de-lis, escutcheons, and banded colonnettes. All of this ornament replicates terracotta found on the most elaborate of New York's terracotta apartment buildings, Alwyn Court, on West 58th Street, which demonstrates that they were stock items to be ordered from catalogues rather than uniquely carved, as one is meant to believe.

The terracotta ornament of Joseph Abel and George T. Santmyers's apartment house at 2101 Connecticut Avenue NW (DU21) (1927) can also be traced to an earlier New York building, the Shelton Club Hotel. The ornament there is known to have been manufactured by the Atlantic Terra Cotta Company. In this case the building's form is also reminiscent of New York apartment buildings in its central spine that connects four wings whose setbacks allow sunlight to filter down to lower levels. Large apartments (seven to nine rooms) had three exposures because of this wing arrangement. Open loggias on tower tops and a faceted skyline contrast with the rather severe variegated brick walls and terracotta entrance (which imitates grainy limestone). Originally sixteen 5-foot-tall horned demons holding massive balls or boulders aloft stood above the cornice line; many are still visible. They are associated with the decorative, almost iconographic, program of the entrance, whose five arch spandrels contain cantilevered parrot gargoyles with lion heads above them, an imagery reinforced by the sculpted terracotta lintels above the ground-story windows, which contain birds and squirrels. The decorative vocabulary is

DU22 The Dresden

medieval, eclectic, but mainly dependent on Venetian models.

Two contemporaneous apartment buildings, the Dresden and the Woodward, obliquely face one another as Connecticut Avenue makes a decided shift before crossing Rock Creek Park. Designed in 1909, they represent the antithesis of architectural attitudes of the day. The Dresden (DU22), at 2126 Connecticut Avenue NW, designed by Albert H. Beers to respond to its unusual site conditions, is a staid and stately structure in the Georgian Revival–Beaux-Arts mixture of forms and details so common in Washington during the first decade of the century. The rusticated limestone base is treated as an arcade, punctured by arched windows whose widths respond to the inconsistent pattern of single and double windows above. The building's architectural statement is dependent on the enframement of these windows, which are linked vertically by simple, rectilinear limestone panels and outlined by limestone quoins making a continuous pattern against the red brick walls. The Dresden's understated elegance results not just from its fine materials, workmanship, and design but also from the formality and rigor of the classical system and the associations it evokes.

In contrast, the historical antecedents of Harding and Upman's Woodward Apartments (DU23) (1909–1910), at 2311 Connecticut Avenue—Spanish Renaissance and Spanish Colonial architecture—evoke an entirely different response, one more informal, even playful. These adjectives aptly describe the Woodward's plan, external organization, and decorative details. Harding and Upman responded to the polygonal corner site by balancing asymmetrically two towers of uneven width at the junctures where Connecti-

DU23 Woodward Apartments

cut Avenue shifts and by locating the main entrance between them. The taller, narrow open tower served as a summer pavilion and roof garden. Deep, overhanging eaves supported by a double arrangement of brackets support low-pitched, red-tiled hip roofs that definitely identify the building's stylistic origins as Mediterranean. The walls are composed of light brown Roman brick that successfully blends with light shades of ivory, yellow, green, and brown terracotta ornament arranged pyramidally on three stories over the main door and on the top two levels and towers. Colorful glazed terracotta was a natural choice for decorating in the Spanish Colonial Revival style, and its application as three-dimensional sculpture is particularly successful here. Two tiers of double Ionic columns, richly ornamented entablatures and pedestal-level friezes, giant scrolls, and a cartouche are the most prominent of the terracotta architectural sculptures.

Massachusetts Avenue

DU24 **Embassy of Canada** (Clarence Moore House)

1906, Bruce Price and Jules Henri de Sibour. 1746 Massachusetts Ave. NW

At 59 feet wide and 80 feet tall, the facade of the Moore house is a greatly enlarged version of a typical three-bay row house composition. Within this seemingly restrictive model, the architects created a complex and

highly successful interplay between the three bays and sets of twos. Two main stories marked by tall French windows open onto two sets of balconies, limestone on the second story and wrought iron on the third. Two "attic" stories, each defined by a full (but different) entablature, comprise fully one-third of the building's height. Two side bays, treated in the same elegant manner as those on the front, are visible from the street. Buff brick walls in conjunction with elegant architectural details carved in limestone are rarely an elegant combination, but Price and Sibour balance each material so that the finely carved limestone blends with the brick but predominates as the appropriate vehicle for the sculptural decoration. Total compositional control and integration, evidenced by such correlations as the segmental pediments on the dormer windows vis-à-vis the second-story arched French windows and the differentiation and transition between solids (walls) and voids (windows and doors), make the Moore house one of Washington's finest Beaux-Arts era mansions.

DU25 **National Trust for Historic Preservation** (McCormick Apartments)

1917–1922, Jules Henri de Sibour. 1785 Massachusetts Ave. NW

Washington's ultimate luxury apartment house was modeled on a Parisian formula probably suggested by the similarity of Washington's corner sites to those of Paris. The obtuse angle formed by Massachusetts Avenue crossing the grid at 18th Street suggested to Sibour a corner tower to act as a hinge and to absorb the internal irregularities caused by the disparate geometries established by the two regular main facades. Like its Parisian prototypes, the McCormick Apartments' high rusticated ground floor and tall mansarded top story bracket three intermediate levels in order to minimize the building's large size and to relate it to individual neighboring mansions that were also clearly divided into distinct horizontal layers.

Superb quality carving of sculptural details, such as the brackets that support balconies,

the entablatures and pediments above second- and top-story windows, and the relief panels set between the third and fourth stories, contribute significantly to the refined beauty of the entire building. Restraint in the use of limestone architectural and sculptural ornament was repeated in the fine wrought-iron marquees above the entry and the balcony and balustrade railings, elements that also evoke Parisian streetscapes.

DU26 **Chancery of Iraq** (William J. Boardman House)

1893, Hornblower and Marshall. 1801 P St. NW

The self-contained form, earthy color, and seemingly stark composition of the Boardman house set it apart from the majority of its more flamboyant contemporaneous neighbors. A low hip roof covers three stories of brown-yellow Roman brick walls set upon an ashlar basement, a compact form derived originally from Italian Renaissance palace models. This heritage is emphasized further by the wide brick frieze that divides the blocky structure into a tall ground story and two upper floors. Its Greek key pattern, made by the long thin bricks, is the same height as the Ionic balustrade order of the balcony rail above the single-story bay window on P Street (and the top-story balcony above it), a detail borrowed directly from the Pitti Palace in Florence. As strong as these Renaissance elements are, they were not used in an archaeological manner but rather as one set of fundamental design principles guiding the architects. The second, seemingly contradictory tradition at work, the medieval, has been so well integrated into the classical that the two seem natural allies. The grouping and asymmetries of window placement, low archway with carved Richardsonian Romanesque details, and mottled wall surfaces due to the vagaries of brick firing all suggest the organic, natural, and accidental associated with the long periods of construction during the medieval period. The conflation of the two historical languages transcends them both to result in an architectural idiom both European and American that was personal to Hornblower and Marshall. Elegance was achieved through the sophisticated and very abstract placement of the frameless windows on the tautly stretched wall surfaces and by the excellent craftsmanship and integration of the sandstone base, Roman brick walls, and simple terracotta details.

DU27 Saint Thomas Episcopal Church

1894–1899, Theophilus P. Chandler. 1772 Church St. NW

All that survives of Philadelphia architect Theophilus P. Chandler's rock-faced Neo-Gothic church is its fragmentary east end, essentially two bays with English perpendicular blind tracery that flank a partially preserved carved altar screen set between clustered piers. Originally the Latin-cross church seated 850 people and its lantern tower rose 100 feet above the crossing. The decision by parishioners in 1970 not to rebuild Saint Thomas after it had been nearly destroyed by arsonists, but to stabilize the ruin and make it the centerpiece of an urban park, was due to the small size of the congregation and its commitment to the needs of the socially evolving neighborhood. Romantic ruins as memorials or landscape garden elements are common in Europe, but such a pensive interlude is entirely unexpected in Washington and therefore quite evocative.

DU28 James E. Blaine House

1881–1882, John Fraser. 2000 Massachusetts Ave. NW

The oldest remaining mansion in the Dupont Circle area is the residence of James E. Blaine, the sole surviving example of at least seven imposing Second Empire and Queen Anne residences executed in Washington by the transplanted Philadelphia architect John Fraser. Built in 1881–1882, the monochromatic brick and terracotta Blaine house was designed for a rectangular lot on 16th Street, which accounts for its odd relationship to Dupont Circle, especially its third entrance

DU28 James E. Blaine House

facing the adjoining lot rather than being located on its P Street facade (where there was a commercial addition in 1921). The exterior massing is organized around a cruciform plan superimposed upon a square, which finished in a massive tower rising above the mansard roof. The skyline is further enlivened by seven chimneys (now truncated, having lost their bulbous tops), which emerge on different stories supported by corbeled brick tables, and by the building's prominent corbeled brick entablature. Variegated slate roof tiles cut in differing patterns, pressed tin dormers, and large fields of molded brick provide additional surface decoration whose intricacy is matched by the original wood porte-cochère. Clusters of incised, chamfered, and turned posts support a frieze of filigreed jigsawn panels and a simple bracket cornice. All of these features are stock elements from the Queen Anne repertoire, but Fraser's facility in combining them results in a building of a dense and intricate surface consistency. One of the Blaine mansion's most arresting features is the 20th Street entry, where huge molded terracotta brackets and an iron fence are both ornamented with sunflowers, treated naturalistically in the terracotta, but stylized when rendered in iron.

DU29 Embassy of Colombia (Thomas T. Gaff House)

1904, Bruce Price and Jules Henri de Sibour. 1520 20th St. NW

The unusual entrance to the Gaff house, under a glass canopy and through a detached

DU29 Embassy of Colombia (Thomas T. Gaff House)

DU30 Embassy of Indonesia (Walsh-McLean House)

transoms and securely locked between wide belt courses and a water table, while those on the second story are suspended from the entablature by their keystones. Major interior spaces are expressed by exterior changes in volumetric massing and grouping of windows. The tall gable that dominates the Q Street facade has a great arched window set between the two major stories to mark the main stairhall. Extensive and regular use of terracotta quoins in imitation of limestone to mark the edges of every brick volume (including the chimneys) and to outline all the windows (except the dormers) produces a tessellated surface pattern. (Actual limestone is used in the basement story.) Structure and decoration are so integrated that the smoothness of the terracotta and limestone is imitated on the walls by having mortar joints of the same mellow red as the bricks.

DU30 **Embassy of Indonesia** (Walsh-McLean House)

1902, Henry Andersen. 2020 Massachusetts Ave. NW

Although reputedly commissioned by its original owner, gold miner Thomas F. Walsh, to be Washington's most expensive residence, the $835,000 spent on the fifty-room Walsh-McLean house did not result in a building of outstanding architectural quality. Danish-born and -educated architect Henry Andersen's Neo-Baroque square palace sits uncomfortably on its irregular corner lot. Its two major facades have different entry sequences, with the porte-cochère on 21st Street oriented to vehicular traffic. The Massachusetts Avenue entrance, marked by a wide arch flanked by double Ionic columns in an imported variegated yellow marble and a recessed loggia above, does not adequately express the three-story, galleried central hall. Limestone trim used for all the windows on three stories plus the attic dormers, and for three horizontal bands encircling the building, is not strong enough to subdue the tan Roman brick walls, so that the less expensive material predominates. Andersen provided some imposing curved elements for each facade, but the total effect is bulbous and vulgarly overblown, rather than gracefully curvilinear. Windows too widely spaced and not graduated in size (traditional in palace architecture) contribute to the sense of an incoherent composition. The copper-clad conservatory on the east fa-

vestibule set obliquely in an open courtyard on the south side of the house, is a French planning device particularly appropriate to its stylistic heritage. A modern American rendition of an early seventeenth-century manor house (François Mansart's Balleroy of about 1626 is the most famous example), Price and Sibour's compact and elegant residence displays great clarity of geometric form and sharpness of detail. The sculptural quality of its masses and their interrelationship and the control of proportions through volumetric and linear geometry are the basis for the Gaff house's striking beauty. The relative heights of the three major horizontal layers—the second story compressed between the taller ground story and high hip roof—reversed the normal practice of having the principal story above the street level. Tall ground-story French windows are elongated further by deep cade, with its spectacular stained-glass windows, is one of the house's best features.

DU31 Headquarters of the Church of the Savior Ecumenical Church (Samuel M. Bryan House)

1885, W. Bruce Gray. 2025 Massachusetts Ave. NW

Regrettably few buildings remain of those designed by W. Bruce Gray during his eighteen-year Washington architectural practice (1879–1897) before he became one of San Antonio's leading architects. The Bryan house is a fortunate survivor, an excellent example of the Richardsonian Romanesque–Queen Anne mixture that characterized many lost late nineteenth-century houses in the Dupont Circle area. Its site, wide but shallow, resulted in an exceptionally expansive facade which Gray divided into four distinct vertical zones of nearly equal width. Those that flank the entry—a slightly projecting double bay to the left and a semicircular tower to the right—have large windows on all three stories to amply light the interiors, as does the fourth, which is set slightly back from the tower. Canonical Richardsonian Romanesque features include the recessed doorway set beneath and behind a broad arch supported by foliate columns and battered, rusticated red Seneca sandstone walls on the basement and first floor. The asymmetrical composition, stained glass, dormer window details (particularly the sunflower), and conical tower were all common to the Queen Anne style. While these individual ingredients were typical, Gray's inventive variations were unexpected and felicitous, particularly his play of smooth versus rusticated surfaces in the sandstone walls, belt courses, and entablature.

DU32 Phillips Collection (Duncan Phillips House)

1897, 1907, Hornblower and Marshall. 1989, Arthur Cotton Moore. 1612 21st St. NW

The Phillips Collection has grown from two exhibition rooms in the Duncan Phillips home in 1921, when it opened as the first museum of modern art in America, to two buildings in which the domestic scale and ambiance of the original house have been maintained. Hornblower and Marshall's 1897 reinterpretation of early American architecture drew

DU32 Phillips Collection (Duncan Phillips House)

upon elements from both the eighteenth-century Georgian vocabulary (a modillion cornice and flat arches over the windows) and the Federal style that followed it (ovoid and semicircular bays and Adamesque decorative details).

Contrary to both of these traditions, the main facade composition is asymmetrical, with a tall projecting chimney breast bisecting the two bays to the south of the entrance, balanced by a wide Palladian window occupying the northernmost first-story bay. Shallow relief ornament carved in sandstone was used liberally on the bay entablatures, sandstone attic story, and particularly notably, on the shell motif in the lunette of the Palladian window. Moreover, the architects set the brick building upon a high basement of rock-faced sandstone, an element familiar from the Richardsonian Romanesque style. Both eclectic mixtures of styles and free compositions were design strategies inherited from the Victorian era. When classicism returned as the primary inspiration, such mixtures were frequently more synthetic than during the Victorian era, as the historical styles chosen shared design principles and architectural vocabularies derived from a common source. As in the Phillips house, the resulting forms are subdued, but, paradoxically, surface ornament is often as rich or richer than in the Victorian eclectic styles. Hornblower and Marshall were particularly adept at combining English and American Georgian and Adamesque motifs and manipulating them to create a new Colonial Revival style.

The historical precedent for the library wing added to the north in 1907 by Hornblower and Marshall is the Italian Renaissance. It is expressed on the exterior by bracketed window frames and a large square bay window with heraldic devices carved in stone below and in stained glass among the leaded panes. On the interior, oak-paneled walls, a coffered ceiling, and a monumental, carved oak and limestone fireplace, set behind a Scamozzi style Ionic columnar screen, provide a more vigorous and evocative setting than the subdued and refined Federal-style interiors of the 1897 house. In 1920 McKim, Mead and White added a skylit second story to the library wing to prepare it for use as a public exhibition area. Three years later a mansarded top story was added to the original house by Washington architect Frederick H. Brooke for private family use.

In 1989, when Arthur Cotton Moore renovated Wyeth and King's 1960 addition, the Goh Annex, he responded to the building as a whole, deriving his massing and horizontal lines from the 1897 house and his architectural vocabulary from the later Renaissance-inspired addition. The bird logo over the entrance to the Goh Annex was inspired by a Braque painting. Moore's annex is divided into four levels, with the principal story raised high above a modern rusticated basement, an apsidal entry treated in antis, bracketed rectangular windows on the main story, and square windows in the attic. All of these elements are associated with the Italian Renaissance tradition in architecture, particularly as it was filtered through English Georgian buildings. Both sections of the earlier building are astylar; Moore introduced embryonic pilasters on the facade of the Goh Annex. His major contribution to the interior is the flying oval staircase that spirals up through three stories. Its heritage in terms of location, form, and details is generically Renaissance.

DU33 **Embassy of India** (Thomas Murray House)

1901, Chase and Ames. 2107 Massachusetts Ave.

The setting of the Murray house, part of the continuous urban fabric rather than isolated in its own grounds, contributes to its cosmopolitan European character. Its facade is a particularly coherent, rich, and assured design. Two main floors predominate, each with tall, wide windows overlooking balconies; individual stone balustrades stand before French

DU33 Embassy of India (Thomas Murray House)

DU34 Anderson House, Headquarters of the Society of Cincinnati (Larz Anderson House)

doors below and an elegant wrought-iron screen spans the entire facade above. All are supported by ornately carved brackets; these, as well as the mascarons over the first-floor windows, garland above the entrance, and cartouche over the window above the door, provide sculptural counterpoints to linear layered walls. In Chase and Ames's hands limestone, whether carved or flat, curved or rectilinear, becomes a particularly supple material, capable of being architectonic yet astylar, solid yet light. The asymmetries of their design are subtle but contribute greatly to its quality: vertically the wide entrance bay on the left occupies two bay widths, horizontally the entrance is sunken below the ground-story level. The genesis of this refined architectural treatment is the eighteenth-century French Louis XV style where astylar compositions were decorated with delicate but rich sculpture and ornament was drawn from decorative rather than architectonic vocabularies. Its application on the Murray house is more robust, with elements more densely packed, resulting in its reinterpretation into an American idiom.

DU34 **Anderson House, Headquarters of the Society of Cincinnati** (Larz Anderson House)

1902–1905, Little and Browne. 2118 Massachusetts Ave. NW

Anderson House is considered the masterwork of its Boston-based architects, Arthur Little and Herbert W. C. Browne. Their clients, diplomat Larz Anderson and the writer Isabel Weld Perkins Anderson, probably played an active role in the design of their house. (Larz Anderson's parents had commissioned their house at 1530 K Street, now destroyed, which was designed by H. H. Richardson.) The imposing exterior massing of Anderson House (138 feet wide, 106 feet deep, and 66 feet, 6 inches tall) and architectural forms relate directly to the solidity and proportions associated with English late Baroque architecture. Two massive wings are connected across the front by two arched and pedimented gates and a low courtyard wall and across the back by a seven-bay central block entered through an attenuated semicircular Corinthian portico. The tan limestone walls on the street facade act as protective covering penetrated by few and relatively small windows; this approach is reversed on the south-facing garden front, where large and copious windows flood the major public and private rooms, including an orangerie, with sunlight. Sculpted details are limited to the gates and portico; shallow linear outlining of rectangular and semicircular elements completes the sober and restrained decoration of the planar surfaces.

Although the rooms of Anderson house are decorated in a heterogenous collection of historical styles, their interrelationships are such that there is no sense of disjunction as one passes between them. The symmetry implied by the exterior massing is not replicated in the house's plan, but the separation of private life from the bustle of the street is, as

there are no through vistas upon entering. The three-part hallway (with lovely illusionistic paintings on the ceiling) runs perpendicular to the central axis and directs visitors to the wing and, via a circuitous route, into the two-story ballroom that traverses the south front. Principal public rooms are located on both the ground and second stories with English Baroque and several French eighteenth-century styles, the primary decorative vocabularies used.

DU35 **Cosmos Club** (Richard H. Townsend House)

1901, Carrère and Hastings. 2121 Massachusetts Ave. NW

Carrère and Hastings's remodeling of the Second Empire Curtis J. Hillyer house into the Townsend residence (whose center block incorporated the mass of the original building) is an excellent example of the French academic strategy of using dominant and subordinate parts as compositional and expressive devices. Gradation of massing, window openings, and architectural ornamentation resulted in a particularly coherent and beautiful facade. Each of the building's five parts—central block, wings, and garden walls—is of equal width but unequal height, thus establishing primary, secondary, and tertiary zones. This diminution of mass from the center outward is accompanied by a concurrent movement from an open center to closed edges. Large windows fill each of the three bays in the central block while only the central bay of the wings is punctured; the garden walls are solid, broken only by minor articulation of their surfaces.

Intersection of the two main volumes, one oriented vertically and one horizontally, is further emphasized by their distinctly different surface treatments. In the center the walls are completely subordinated to the architectural framing elements, five giant Corinthian pilasters and elaborate window frames and entablatures. In contrast, the cubic solidity of the wings, literally reinforced by corner quoins and a parapet, is broken by shallow layering of the rectilinear details, imposing balus-

traded balconies and luxuriant masks and swags. All these volumetric and surface tensions are masterfully resolved by the balance of the masses, the same treatment of the rusticated basement, and the elegant and academically correct use of the entire range of the refined Louis XVI decorative vocabulary. The interplay between thin slices of moldings or panels and the exuberantly three-dimensional sculptural decoration, crisp sculptural details that pop out of the smooth limestone walls, attest to the sophistication of the talents of Carrère and Hastings.

New Hampshire Avenue

DU36 **Historical Society of Washington** (Christian Heurich House)

1892–1894, John Granville Meyers. 1307 New Hampshire Ave.

The Heurich house is the finest of Meyers's 115 known Washington buildings, the culmination of a thirty-year career in which he progressed from carpenter to architect. Born into a Pennsylvania German family of builders, Meyers had no academic training as an architect, yet produced complex designs in a variety of mid-Victorian styles. On the Heurich house's exterior, Meyers used the Richardsonian Romanesque vocabulary in an as-

sured manner, gradating it in a hierarchy of primary forms and details to subordinate ones. A distinctive feature was dictated by the different responses to site conditions on New Hampshire Avenue and Sunderland Place. The main facade on the avenue is more elaborate and was executed in dark rock-faced brownstone, while that facing the narrow side street was built in brick and terracotta with brownstone details. Both facades were organized into two sets of projecting bays to respond to the rhythms common among row houses of the period, the immediate urban fabric amidst which the house was designed to stand. The sculptural character of the fabulous porte-cochère and the corner tower are enhanced by the textural richness of all the surfaces.

The architectonic treatment of the exterior gives way to a "decorated" interior, where each room was executed in a different historical period related to contemporaneous ideas about the relationship between style and function. The circular salon located in the tower is decorated in the Louis XV, or Rococo style, while the dining room, with its massive carved oak fitments, is German Renaissance in style.

DU37 **Women's National Democratic Club** (Sarah Adams Whittemore House)

1894, Harvey L. Page. 1967, Nicholas Satterlee. 1526 New Hampshire Ave. NW

Still the finest Arts and Crafts style exterior in the city, the Whittemore house has been

DU37 Women's National Democratic Club (Sarah Adams Whittemore House)

DU38 International Eastern Star Temple (Perry Belmont House)

sadly altered in a large portion of the interior. The monolithic concrete formalist addition to the east, visible only on Q Street, was consciously set apart from the original house so as not to mar Page's beautifully composed building. The octagonal corner tower is echoed by wide octagonal bays on both street facades, the whole covered by a sheltering roof whose form (including hip dormers) resembles an English thatched roof carried out in slate shingles. The faceted volumes are covered in

a very distinctive Roman brick in speckled shades of brown, gold, and cream, the earth from which they were made coming from a unique clay deposit in New Jersey. A punched and tooled copper-covered semicircular bay hangs over the expansive entry, its dull patina a lovely complement to the mottled brick. The clarity of the volumetric composition is repeated in the unframed windows punched directly through the walls. The brickwork is superb; belt courses made up of rows of headers subtly underline each floor, while panels of brick set in lozenge patterns mark the division between the first and second stories in the bays. The upper sashes in the windows are leaded clear glass in a diamond pattern. The Whittemore house's immense charm is due as much to the natural beauty and treatment of its materials as to its sculptural form and the rhythmical variations of its parts.

DU38 **International Eastern Star Temple** (Perry Belmont House)

1909, Sanson and Trumbauer. 1618 New Hampshire Ave. NW

Isolation on its own wedge-shaped block makes the Belmont house appear as monumental as its large scale warrants. Designed by the fashionable Parisian architect Eugène Sanson (with Horace Trumbauer's Philadelphia office overseeing construction), the Belmont house was a true party house, the main floor being dominated by a ballroom whose dimensions measure 78 feet by 33 feet. The building's height to the cornice is divided in half, with the 25-foot principal story sitting high above two "basement" levels; an attic story is contained within the mansard roof. The plainness of the lower stories gives way to increasing richness culminating in the spandrel sculpture above the arched windows and garlanded finials atop the balustrade. The striking fenestration on the main story consists of French doors topped by glass lunettes, an arcade set within a double trabeated framework of Doric and Ionic pilasters. The clarity of the design is enhanced by the precise cutting of the limestone, alternately hard-edged and fully plastic in treatment. The Belmont house's elegance is full blown but not excessive, with gradation from simple to complex, from plain to ornate depending on function and orientation, a primary tenet of its design.

DU39 **A. B. Butler House**

1912, Clarke Waggaman. 1744 R St. NW

Clarke Waggaman's canonical Italian Renaissance urban palace composition with the principal story raised a full level above a rusticated basement and the third-story attic with square windows is distinguished particularly by the elaborate sculptural treatment of the window enframement on the end bays of the main story. Cartouches flanked by putti and garlands that hang down the length of the windows contrast nicely with the shallow handling of the walls, a characteristic of all of Waggaman's work.

DU40 **Thomas Nelson Page House**

1896, McKim, Mead and White. 1759 R St. NW

The Page house is an example of Stanford White's synthesis of Colonial and Federal vo-

cabularies to create a new Colonial Revival idiom for use in a modern urban context. Trapezoidal in plan, two of the house's adjacent sides address New Hampshire Avenue: the symmetrical entrance facade faces it obliquely and the more expressive asymmetrically composed end, directly. The tension between the two dissimilar facades—the six-bay entrance front treated as a traditional grid and the end with a cluster of six elaborately framed French doors that span the two principal stories—is heightened by their juncture at the corner, a frank, almost abstract, transition from freestanding to row house dimensions and articulation.

White chose a minor design element, flat limestone arches above the windows, to demonstrate both function and two-dimensional order on his main facade. Those on the basement and attic levels are plain and heavy, with the central keystone slightly emphasized; those on the two main levels lighter and configured in five parts instead of three, with voussoirs wedged at the corners. Further gradation occurs between the second and third stories. On the more important principal floor the windows are recessed in blind arches whose limestone keystone and impost blocks form an abstract triangular pattern of points and baseline.

DU41 **Anne Thorneburne Johnson House**

1909, Clarke Waggaman. 1716 New Hampshire Ave. NW

The Johnson house exhibits Waggaman's characteristic flat wall treatment in a style of architecture normally associated with a very robust three dimensionality, the Italian Baroque. Even the intricate wrought-iron balconies hug the planar walls more closely than one expects. The house's unusually tall proportions are emphasized by the high placement of the ground-story windows in relation to the simple arched entry and are increased by extension of the walls above the cornice line to encase the dormer windows. Naturalistic and stylized decorative details—brackets to carry the balconies, a floral swag above the door, and ornamented keystones and over-window sculpture on the second story—provide contrasting kinds of three-dimensional relief to enliven the smooth surfaces of the upended rectangular form.

Sheridan Circle and Kalorama (SK)

Pamela Scott

S HERIDAN CIRCLE IS AMONG THE RAREST OF AMERICAN PHE-
nomena, a time capsule. Nothing has been added or taken away since
1920; noisy traffic along Massachusetts Avenue is all that disturbs its
serenity. As Washington's population of part- and full-time wealthy residents
increased, the large domestic structures of Dupont Circle spread westward along
Massachusetts Avenue and soon engulfed the new circle that lay outside of
L'Enfant's plan. The focus of one of Washington's most elite residential neighborhoods since its development at the turn of the century, Sheridan Circle
demonstrates the kind of architectural eclecticism associated with American individuality. In addition to ad hoc private development, its location on the edge
of Rock Creek Park and the irregular way the grid streets intersect the circle
contribute to the lack of continuity and conformity among Sheridan Circle's
dozen structures, originally private residences but now primarily embassies and
chanceries.

The oldest houses on the circle were designed by Washington architect Waddy
B. Wood in a variety of Mediterranean styles, as he apparently felt its quasi-
rural setting suggested an informal ambiance. Within five years, the work of
the equally prolific local architect George Oakley Totten, Jr., began to trans-
form the circle and its environs into Washington's most important enclave of
formal, French-inspired urban mansions. As the neighborhood spread northward and joined Kalorama, a wider range of historical styles by numerous good
and a few excellent architects created an upper-class urban suburb comprising
mansions, large freestanding houses, substantial row houses, and early garden
apartments.

When Sheridan Circle was first laid out, both Stephen Decatur and Gen.
John A. Logan were considered as possible heroes to be honored with statues

336

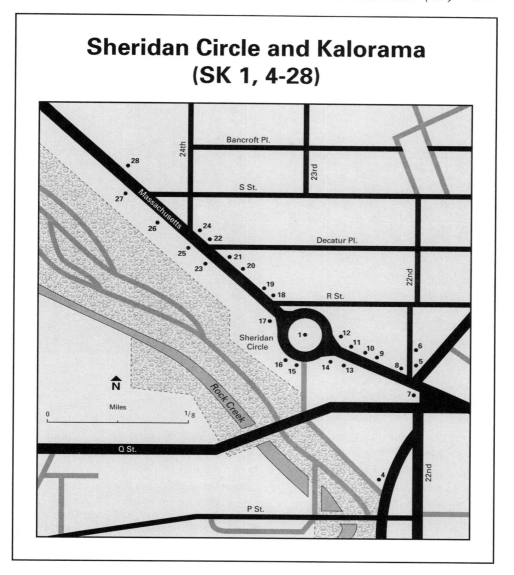

Sheridan Circle and Kalorama
(SK 1, 4-28)

in its central garden. However, Gutzon Borglum's animated bronze figure of the Civil War general Philip H. Sheridan astride his famous horse Rienzi (SK01) was dedicated in 1908. Its base with fountains on the sides and stairs on the north and south, designed by architect Henry Winslow, acts as a pivot for Massachusetts Avenue's abrupt shift in axis. Minimal planting on the interior of the circle creates a low, green oasis that throws into relief the light-colored, three- to four-story buildings around its perimeter. Unlike European urban circles, traditionally composed of buildings with a consistent style, shape, and

Panoramic view of Sheridan Circle

scale, the precarious unity of Sheridan Circle is provided primarily by its color and materials. Its architectural value is the sum of its parts, a rare opportunity in America to view a large group of surviving pre–World War I houses built for the wealthy. These residences, like the majority along the Massachusetts Avenue corridor, escaped replacement by apartment houses because their scale, internal planning, and decoration were keyed to lavish and formal entertaining and could thus be readily adapted to the needs of embassies.

Kalorama, Greek for "beautiful view," takes its name from the poet Joel Barlow's estate, which he named in recognition of the extensive prospects to be had from its elevated position. The 90-acre estate remained intact until subdivided into several developments in 1887. Kalorama and Sheridan circles define the northern and southern boundaries of the district; Massachusetts and Connecticut avenues were extended along and across Rock Creek Park to define its east and west perimeters. The Highway Act of 1893 mandated that streets in subdivisions beyond L'Enfant's northern boundary (now Florida Avenue) conform to street patterns established by the original plan, effectively halting development of the Sheridan-Kalorama area until the law was amended in 1898 to exempt subdivisions created before its enactment.

The present single-span Massachusetts Avenue Bridge (SK02) that crosses Rock Creek Park above Belmont Road was designed by Washington architect Louis Justement in 1940 to replace a viaduct built by the Army Corps of En-

gineers in 1901. As its height was not as great as the bridges farther upstream, its massive, quarry-faced stone surfaces and low, semicircular arch continue the image of a culvert rather than of a soaring feat of engineering. The Taft Bridge (SK03) (1897–1907), which carries Connecticut Avenue across the park, was designed by railroad bridge architect George S. Morison as the largest unreinforced concrete bridge in the world. Its four concrete lions were sculpted by Roland Hinton Perry. The picturesque rectilinear street pattern laid out in 1887 sacrificed little of the character of the hilly Kalorama estate, serving nearly as effectively as winding streets (the norm for earlier and later suburban developments). Retention of natural topographical features and dense planting of trees are the deciding factors.

Kalorama has two areas of architectural interest. Some substantial row houses line a few streets that abut Connecticut Avenue, but the region's glory is its urban mansions located on the high ground between Massachusetts and Connecticut avenues. It contains predominantly Colonial Revival, Mediterranean Revival, and Beaux-Arts-inspired homes set within their own grounds. Kalorama Road NW and Kalorama Circle NW wind around the north ridge of land before it descends into Rock Creek Park. The majority of houses were designed in the 1920s following English models in styles compatible with the natural, picturesque setting in which the predominantly fieldstone houses were placed. The influence of the late English Arts and Crafts movement is evident in many of them where vernacular domestic forms, natural textures of materials, and mildly picturesque compositions were the basic concerns of the architects. Close to downtown, high enough in elevation to benefit from summer breezes, and enjoying panoramic views, Kalorama became a preferred locale for those who could afford to live here.

SK04 Presbyterian Church of the Pilgrims

1928, Flournoy and Flournoy. 2201 P St.

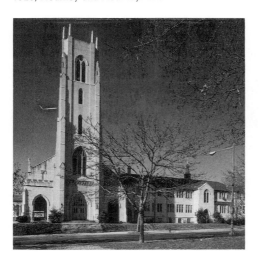

Benjamin Courtland Flournoy's English education is very much in evidence in his Church of the Pilgrims with its attached cloisters. The forms and surfaces are a greatly reduced modern adaptation of the decorated phase of English Gothic ecclesiastical structures. The light-colored, smooth Alabama limestone was perfectly suited to the sleek lines and surfaces and to the soaring 112-foot tower, with lancet windows, corner buttresses, and finials that are the recognizable descendants of their ancestors.

SK05 American News Women's Club
(J. H. Cranford House)

1906, Alfred B. Mullett and Company. 1607 22nd St. NW

Thomas A. and Frederick W. Mullett practiced architecture in Washington until the 1930s, operating under the name of the firm that they had founded with their illustrious father, Alfred B. Mullett, shortly before his

suicide in 1890. Not enough data have been compiled on the work of the Mullett sons to determine whether the Cranford house is typical of their work, although it is a compositional formula and stylistic tradition employed by many Washington architects at the beginning of this century. Three generous stories with an equally tall attic composed of large dormer windows provide four distinct horizontal zones. They are countered by three widely spaced bays with windows treated distinctly on each level. The basic architectural vocabulary of Flemish-bond brick walls, flat arches, and modillion cornice was rooted in the Georgian style, but, when fused with Renaissance elements, resulted in the Edwardian style in England and was accepted in America as a variation on the Georgian Revival.

At the Cranford house the Mullett firm designed an elegantly detailed entrance story in lightly rusticated limestone where the topmost band has three subtle undulations that provide balcony ledges to support the wrought-iron rails of the tall French doors on the second story. Limestone for the keystones and irregular arch abutments on the two brick stories provide striking accent notes, a popular Colonial Revival variation on the monochromatic flat arch of the American Georgian style.

SK06 Permanent Mission of Colombia to the Organization of American States
(Otto Heinl House)

1905, Wood, Donn and Deming. 1609 22nd St. NW

Buff-colored bricks in place of or in conjunction with more costly limestone were used widely for row houses at the turn of the century in reaction to the deeper hues of red brick and sandstone (black when embedded with soot) employed for their Victorian counterparts. Pressed tin (and sometimes copper) entablatures and cornices often replaced those of cast iron and wood, as at the Heinl house.

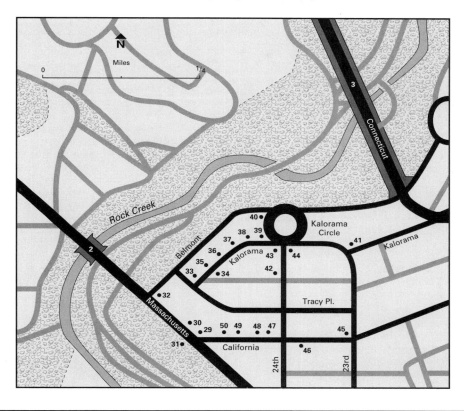

Sheridan Circle and Kalorama (SK 2, 3, 29-50)

SK07 Embassy of Luxembourg (Alexander Stewart House)

1908–1909, Jules Henri de Sibour. 2200 Massachusetts Ave. NW

Jules Henri de Sibour designed Congressman Alexander Stewart's residence. Built at a cost of $92,000, it was one of the costliest mansions in the area. Sibour's approach to angular sites was to absorb their irregularities in the building plans, achieving a simple geometric structure that maintains a rectilinear edge on the streetscape. The triangular site of the Stewart house dictated three important facades; with the exception of the entry porch

on Massachusetts Avenue, they are all articulated by channeled rustication on the ground story with the two astylar upper floors connected by spandrel sculpture and ornamental panels. The exterior utilizes numerous design elements derived from French eighteenth-century architecture. The relatively planar wall treatment with sunken windows framed by double-story, vertical panels, nearly equal proportions of alternating solids and voids, and the subdued use of curvilinear elements and sculpture are associated with the Louis XVI style. Sibour's plan is also French-inspired in its composition of interconnecting rooms that serve similar functions, either

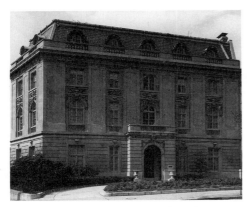

SK07 Embassy of Luxembourg (Alexander Stewart House)

public or private. In contrast, the interiors are decorated in the English Jacobean and Georgian styles, odd historical combinations being common in mansions erected during America's Gilded Age. The Stewart mansion is one of three in the area that Sibour designed early in his career while in partnership with Bruce Price (see Embassy of France, SK41, and Embassy of Colombia, DU29, p. 327). These mansions established his practice of applying correct, although eclectic, histor-

ical vocabularies to beautifully proportioned buildings free of the whimsicalities that his chief rival, George Oakley Totten, often employed.

SK08 Frederick A. Miller House (Argyle Terrace)

1900–1901, Paul Pelz. 2201 Massachusetts Ave. NW

The building permit for the Miller house, issued on 27 March 1900, stipulated a dwelling and "automobile house." This small garage, apparently the first in Washington, still stands on 22nd Street and was untouched by the 1984 fire that gutted the main house. Although the exterior of the main house was rebuilt carefully following the original design, the new buff Roman bricks reveal the extent of the damage. Pelz is best known as one of the architects of the Library of Congress. Like it, the stylistic heritage of the Miller house is French, but Renaissance rather than Baroque in inspiration. Although the house is officially on Massachusetts Avenue, Pelz utilized the depth of the corner lot for the main facade, which has additional prominence due to the open street junction just in front. Two conical towers, ornamented by elaborate dormers, flank the imposing entrance that retains its

SK10 Embassy of United Arab Emirates, Military Department (second from left); SK11 Embassy of Greece, Commercial Section (Irene Rucher Sheridan House) (far left)

ornate but weathered sandstone porch sculpture and extensive walls of its wide double entry staircase. Buff brick walls complement the richly carved sandstone details. Numerous nautical motifs were used in the decorative elements because Miller was a navy captain.

SK09 Headquarters of the National Society, Daughters of the American Colonists (E. H. Alsop House)

1920, Waddy B. Wood. 2205 Massachusetts Ave. NW

Examples of Wood's Colonial Revival row houses abound in the general area, and the Alsop house exhibits many features common to them: limestone lintels above triple windows in a greatly swelling bay whose sunken corner blocks join to form distinctive continuous horizontal belt courses; the door set back beneath an elliptical arch; and pedimented Philadelphia-inspired scroll dormers with switch-back tracery set at the edge of the roof.

SK10 Embassy of United Arab Emirates, Military Department

1907, Wyeth and Cresson. 2209 Massachusetts Ave. NW

Buff brick and limestone in a subdued Beaux-Arts style were Wyeth and Cresson's challenge to red brick neighbors. They responded most directly to an all but equally monumental row house by Wood, Donn and Deming (see SK11) by continuing its horizontal regulating lines and mansard roof but opted for a strongly axial and symmetrical three-bay row house facade. Unusual design features include placing the ornate segmental pedimented door frame on the second floor (rather than at the entry) and a separately composed roof, with two elaborate rectangular dormer windows framing a small oval one rather than adhering to the vertical lines established by three floors of windows below.

SK11 Embassy of Greece, Commercial Section (Irene Rucher Sheridan House)

1903, Wood, Donn and Deming. 2211 Massachusetts Ave. NW

Wood, Donn and Deming's sophisticated hybrid of Colonial Revival and Beaux-Arts motifs was applied to a two-bay facade, an unusual rhythm for row houses where space was not constricted. Elegant and unusual details are found on all four floors. Channeled limestone rustication curves inward to frame the ground-story entry and window; second-story French windows open onto shallow balustraded balconies; carved limestone garlands are set beneath unframed third-story windows; and brick dormer windows are integrated into the upper wall, which continues above the cornice.

SK12 Embassy of Greece

1906, George Oakley Totten, Jr. 2221 Massachusetts Ave. NW

Buff or light gray bricks were an inexpensive alternative to limestone when a light-colored building in the Italian Renaissance Revival style was desired, although rarely used on a structure on the scale of the Greek Embassy. The proportions of the entire building, including the small-scale decorative details executed in limestone in conjunction with the broken surface treatment occasioned by the bricks, resulted in a rather uninspired building, albeit on a prominent site.

SK13 James C. Hooe House

1907, George Oakley Totten, Jr. 2230 Massachusetts Ave. NW

Decoration of the Hooe house facade is Totten's work at his most exotic and flamboyant, yet its triple-bay, four-story composition is strictly controlled with elaborate three-dimensional detailing held within specific zones, primarily concentrated at the roof and cornice lines. Walls of red brick with glazed headers set in a lozenge pattern provide a sharp color contrast with the cream color of the ashlar limestone base and quoins and the exuberantly molded terracotta ornament. Totten derived his design and decorative elements from a French Renaissance vocabulary, where fantastic creatures (salamanders and rampant winged lions) are set among a profusion of shells, arabesques, balusters, and pinnacles. A major second-story room is expressed on the facade by compression of three bays into a single, tripartite window visually supported by a balcony, the gentle curves of which provide a foil for the rectilinearity of the deeply sunken windows.

SK13 James C. Hooe House

SK14 **Chancery of Ireland** (Henrietta M. Halliday House)

1908–1909, William P. Cresson. 2236 Massachusetts Ave. NW

The difficulty of designing two adjacent facades of unequal length yet nearly equal prominence was solved in an atypical manner by William Penn Cresson in the Halliday house. Entrance to the three-bay Sheridan Circle facade (located at the corner rather than in

the center) is demarcated by individualized treatment of the openings on three stories, culminating in an elaborate dormer window set against the mansard roof. The single bay on the 23rd Street facade replicates the width of the entrance bay, but its window details are drawn from the secondary bays on the Massachusetts Avenue facade, with the exception of a projecting balcony supported by garlanded brackets on the second story. As the corner is ignored, juxtaposition of one asymmetrical and one symmetrical facade creates a somewhat truncated overall composition. Cresson combined elements from two French eighteenth-century styles: the quietly dignified limestone exteriors are Louis XVI in origin, but the interiors draw on the lighter and more delicate decoration of the Louis XV period.

SK15 **Embassy of Turkey** (Edward H. Everett House)

1910–1915, George Oakley Totten, Jr. 1606 23rd St. NW

Sheridan Circle's largest mansion is also its most picturesque, a mélange of French-inspired elements spreading 91 feet along its north-south axis with its widest east-west segment (66 feet) balanced precariously on the edge of Rock Creek Park. The main, east-facing, facade is dominated by an imposing central block with a conservatory and roof garden addition to the south. One barely perceives the thin wedge on the north, added to present a suitable facade oriented to the circle. The long west side overlooking the park is multifaceted, as the site is very irregular, and its many projections allow for extensive vistas. In these asymmetries Totten attempted to fuse formality with a picturesque composition, perhaps intending to suggest that the structure had grown by accretions over time. The more open portion at the south end is not sufficiently subordinate to the main block, and its local symmetries are at odds with the building's overall asymmetrical organization.

With its broad semicircular frontispiece enriched by a giant Corinthian colonnade, the Everett house recalls numerous late eighteenth-century chateaux. This same basic arrangement had been used by Benjamin Henry Latrobe in his alterations to James Hoban's south facade of the White House (see WH03, p. 152); comparison of the two buildings indicates how differing window patterns and surface treatment can create such widely divergent designs using the same envelope. Shallow sculpted details of arabesques, pilasters, and friezes are derived from the vocabulary of French Renaissance architecture, and their delicate treatment on a small scale contrasts sharply with the size of the building they ornament. Increasing openness in the fenestration from the basement to the third story of the main block is accompanied by increasingly ornate detailing, resulting in a somewhat top-heavy composition.

SK16 Alice Pike Barney House, Smithsonian Institution

1902, Waddy B. Wood. 2306 Massachusetts Ave. NW

The most outstanding of Waddy Wood's houses on or near Sheridan Circle was designed for the socialite artist Alice Pike Barney and acquired intact with the artist's furnishings by the Smithsonian Institution in 1971. Its curvilinear gable, yellow stuccoed-brick exterior, and strapwork frames ornamenting the main door and two lobed, second-story windows give the house a Spanish flavor. All other openings are unframed, cut directly into the roughly textured planar walls. Wood's composition is an unusual one, as the windows on the two middle stories are not aligned horizontally: those in the center bay run from floor to ceiling, giving the center bay visual prominence that is reinforced by the recessed fourth-story loggia and the open arch set in the gable. The prominence is belied by the ground story, where the principal entrance (set deep within a fenced courtyard) on the left does not correspond to the central main axis. The secondary entrance on the right is given special attention by a mosaic set in the wall above it. Such informality of facade composition is in direct opposition to the prevalent architectural stateliness of the circle's Beaux-Arts buildings, as is its handcrafted appearance.

SK17 Embassy of Korea (Harry Wardman House)

1920, Frank Russell White. 2320 Massachusetts Ave. NW

Frank Russell White made no concessions to Sheridan Circle's shape in his imposing and massive limestone house for developer Harry Wardman. Its rectilinear form and details are derived from Italian Renaissance palace models: channeled rustication on the ground level surmounted by two floors with regularly spaced windows. However, the Wardman house lacks the grace of its antecedents, with large windows more at home on a school or factory and decoration thin and minimal.

SK18 Egyptian Embassy (Joseph Beale House)

1907–1908, Glenn Brown. 2301 Massachusetts Ave. NW

Glenn Brown's very beautiful reinterpretation of an Italian Renaissance facade suffers somewhat from its disjointed relationship to its two immediate neighbors in terms of their

SK18 Egyptian Embassy (Joseph Beale House)

relative siting and scale. The gentle swell of the Beale house's curved facade is an attempt to respond to its awkward location at the corner of R Street and Massachusetts Avenue, as it partially faces, but is not wholly on, Sheridan Circle. Despite these contextual issues, it is the finest architectural work in the immediate area, with well-integrated facade, plan, and decorative program. Division of the four-story, curved facade into three self-contained but interrelated fields demonstrates Brown's sophistication as a designer, although he is generally remembered as an architectural historian. Neo-Renaissance in style, the building has a two-story recessed loggia framed by a Palladian window, the focus of the masterfully proportioned composition. Its depth is a perfect foil for the shallow sunken planes and barely projecting quoins and door and window frames that are carefully placed on the broad expanse of the facade. The Beale house demonstrates that reduction to the primary elements of scale, balance, harmony, and proportion by the solvent of classicism can produce timeless architecture regardless of where or when it was constructed.

SK19 Embassy of Chile (Sarah Wyeth House)

1908, Nathan C. Wyeth. 2305 Massachusetts Ave. NW

Sparsely decorated, smooth limestone walls, a flat, balustraded roofline, and the unusual

profile of its oval bowfront are the basic compositional elements with which Wyeth designed this self-contained Louis XV style mansion. Emphasis is on its volumetric sense, which is enhanced by Wyeth's elegant articulation of the wall surfaces. The importance of the second story as the floor with the principal public rooms is announced on the exterior not by increased decoration, as was traditional, but through its taller proportions. There are only simple bracketed keystones over these windows while those of the third story are ornamented with garlands beneath them but very simple lintels above, also an inversion of traditional practice. The keystones over the ground-story windows are slotted into a wide, ornamented belt course that continues under the bracketed balcony, which traverses the entire width of the bow. The central axis is marked by an overdoor

SK19 Embassy of Chile (Sarah Wyeth House)

SK20 Embassy and Chancery of Haiti (Gibson Fahnestock House)

panel of acanthus sculpture framed by double garlanded brackets, by a light and delicate cast-iron balcony rail, and by a cartouche that connects the second- and third-story windows.

SK20 Embassy and Chancery of Haiti
(Gibson Fahnestock House)

1909–1910, Nathan C. Wyeth. 2311 Massachusetts Ave. NW

The adjoining Fahnestock and Moran houses were under construction simultaneously and succinctly exhibit two basic approaches to high-style Beaux-Arts architecture in America. Both depend upon eighteenth-century French prototypes; Totten's Moran house is a freely composed, eclectic design while Wyeth's Fahnestock house is more academically correct in its composition and architectural vocabulary. Its four-and-a-half-story limestone facade is a finely proportioned composition in which the richness implied by the Corinthian pilasters is achieved by restrained elegance rather than by abundant ornament. Nonetheless the comparatively thin front plane is activated across its entire surface with variously proportioned and detailed windows locked into a subtly defined and perfectly balanced grid. Although less imaginative than its adjoining neighbor, Wyeth's design is visually coherent and viscerally satisfying, its restraint a positive influence on the avenue.

SK21 Embassy of Pakistan (F. B. Moran Residence)

1909, George Oakley Totten, Jr. 2315 Massachusetts Ave. NW

Totten's response to the triangular sites created by the grid of streets crossing Massachusetts Avenue on the north of Sheridan Circle was to create circular elements as pivots around which rectilinear facades (and interior rooms) are disposed. The Moran house's corner tower makes an effective transition between the comparative level of Massachusetts Avenue and the steep incline of Decatur Street. Its physical separation from each of its lateral facades is achieved both by deep undercutting as it adjoins them and by the quoins that define the edges of each of them. Sculpture on the tower, in the form of sunken reliefs (female figures carrying water urns reminis-

SK21 Embassy of Pakistan (F. B. Moran Residence)

cent of Jean Goujon's sculpture on the Renaissance Fountain of the Innocents in Paris), garlanded oval and rectangular frames containing marble slabs, and richly decorated window surrounds, is confined to the two major stories.

The focus of the Massachusetts Avenue facade is a two-story, tripartite window composition framed by double Corinthian pilasters, which in turn are flanked by relief panels of additional urn carriers that float on blank walls beneath wide double windows. The tertiary facade facing Decatur Street is enlivened by a dramatic, countersunk, two-story bay window with a copper dome framed by a bold arch that breaks the entablature line. These three disparate facades are held together by two strong horizontals that anchor the building to its site, a simply treated rusticated basement and an unusually deep and plain entablature. Separate high mansard roofs also help define each facade's composition.

The major source of inspiration for the Moran house was the Château of Chantilly, a palimpsest of numerous building campaigns and thus itself implicitly eclectic. The direct relationship between the exterior disposition of elements and the interior plan was a major intellectual tenet of the Beaux-Arts system of design that Totten fully exploited at the Moran house. Its massing predicates round and rectilinear rooms; its window clusters indicate the relative size and importance of rooms they light. Totten often explored the possibilities of asymmetrical, picturesque compositions and eclectic mixtures of French-inspired details: the Moran house is one of his most successful essays. The lower, copper-faced conservatory, which links the Moran house to its neighbor, the Fahnestock house, was part of Totten's original design.

SK22 **Embassy of Republic of Austria** (William A. Hill Company)

1928, George N. Ray. 2343 Massachusetts Ave. NW

The architectural energy of this compact, beautifully proportioned three-bay Neo-Renaissance house is focused on three second-floor French windows. Here an unusual combination of arched openings crowned by flat lintels is nicely resolved by the keystones that physically connect them and the console brackets that visually frame them.

SK23 **George Cabot Lodge House**

1905, Wood, Donn and Deming. 2346 Massachusetts Ave. NW

Overtones of the Arts and Crafts movement (in the squat, shingled dormers) and the Beaux-Arts in the Lodge house's general scale and proportions were melded to a basically Georgian Revival vocabulary.

SK24 **Embassy and Chancery of Cameroon** (Christian Hauge Residence)

1906–1907, George Oakley Totten, Jr. 2349 Massachusetts Ave. NW

French Renaissance chateaux were less common sources for American Beaux-Arts architecture than were French Baroque and Neo-classical buildings. When architects or clients chose this style—where a medieval vocabulary was applied to the Renaissance system of symmetrical and balanced compositions—the effect was always charming and frequently highly successful. Whether it was the choice of such a prototype or adherence to a stylistically and formally unified composition, the Hauge house is Totten's outstanding design in the Sheridan Circle neighborhood.

The original site was a nearly triangular polygon with two street fronts of unequal length, a condition directly reflected in Totten's design. The house's truncated appearance, where both outside edges come to an abrupt halt, might have been eliminated if buildings of a comparable scale, rather than additions to the Hauge house, had been built on the adjoining lots. (The broad, single-story addition on the northwest corner dates from 1934; the single-bay, two-story addition on the opposite side is part of the original design.)

The smooth, tightly jointed limestone walls provide an excellent surface against which to set the label moldings of double windows, deep balconies ornamented with columnar and tracery balustrades, and the entablature composed of three types of medieval tracery. Totten's concentration of sculptural enrichment within the top third of the building's composition creates an effective balance, with the plain lower walls punctuated by the regular double-window pattern. Variations in the decorative details, whether among the crocketed dormer windows, balustrade tracery, window size and enframement, or differing balcony treatment, give the Hauge house its especially sophisticated character because of the subtlety with which they are handled.

SK25 **Embassy of Korea, Chancery** (Alice W. B. Stanley House)

1930, Smith and Edwards. 2370 Massachusetts Ave. NW

Enclaves of late Arts and Crafts houses inspired by English Neo-Tudor architecture dating from the 1920s and 1930s are rare within the city boundaries. Few examples are as beautifully designed or sited as the Stanley residence. Originally set within a miniature

English garden, it has a picturesque composition of offset and intersecting masses culminating in curved and stepped gables with unusual silhouettes that are uninterrupted by competing structures. An unfortunate rear addition destroys its three-dimensional beauty. The rosy-hued brick sheathing creates a richly toned surface, the texture of which is enhanced by patterned fields of brick, and both Flemish bond (in the front gable) and English bond (the remaining wall surfaces). Although its stylistic heritage is at odds with the predominant architecture of the area, the Stanley house's composition, dependent on local symmetries (seen in the double-bay front gable) and controlled asymmetries (as in the three-bay main facade), is found on many neighbors with designs derived from high-style continental architecture.

SK26 **Embassy of Malawi** (Granville Fortesque House)

1911, Nathan C. Wyeth. 2408 Massachusetts Ave. NW

Wyeth's complete control of proportions is evident in this reserved, even severe, Beaux-Arts facade. Its composition is only atypical in the large window area; notable is Wyeth's suggestion of multiple wall layers in a shallow depth.

SK27 **Embassy of Ivory Coast** (Frederick Atherton House)

1930, Wyeth and Sullivan. 2412 Massachusetts Ave. NW

The horizontality of Wyeth and Sullivan's compact Neo-Renaissance house and its prismatic, barely broken surfaces herald the waning of the tradition.

SK28 **Embassy of Zambia**

1906, Nathan C. Wyeth and William P. Cresson. 2419 Massachusetts Ave. NW

Unsympathetic additions to Wyeth and Cresson's gambrel-roofed Georgian Revival house mar its modest form, but its siting with extensive terraced gardens retrieves some of the damage.

SK29 **C. H. Harlow House**

1916, Waddy B. Wood. 2501 Massachusetts Ave. NW

SK25 Embassy of Korea, Chancery (Alice W. B. Stanley House)

This stuccoed brick and limestone Spanish Renaissance Revival house repeats the composition of Wood's Fitzhugh house (see SK75), built a dozen years earlier, of three stories crossed by three bays topped by a deeply projecting bracketed cornice.

SK30 **House**

1925, unknown. 2507 Massachusetts Ave. NW

One of the finest works of the Wardman Construction Company is this house, where Federal Style elements (the round-headed windows on the principal story set in blind frames and the semicircular portico) have been used on a house of Beaux-Arts form and composition.

SK31 **Embassy of Japan**

1931, Delano and Aldrich. 2516 Massachusetts Ave. NW

Unlike the majority of its neighboring mansions, this group of three buildings was designed as an embassy complex. It is not known what instructions the Japanese government gave the New York architects that resulted in the fine Georgian Revival mansion that is the centerpiece of the U-shaped arrangement. The main residence is set back from Massachusetts Avenue behind a fence and apparent gate houses (actually the end walls of office buildings) so that entry can be controlled. The house's seven-bay facade depends upon the proportional relationships of its solids and

SK31 Embassy of Japan

voids for its architectural merit, as it is almost devoid of decoration. Quoins outline the corners of the house and the edges of the wide projecting portico that encompasses three full bays, a distinct departure from eighteenth-century practice. The main entrance is marked by a great apse on the second story that was intended to be complemented by a single-story, semicircular columnar porch, which was not built.

SK32 **Islamic Center**

1949–1957, Egyptian Ministry of Works and Irwin S. Porter and Sons. 2551 Massachusetts Ave. NW

The Islamic Center's minaret is one of Washington's few identifiable skyline elements that rise out of the dense green of the city. Among the other religious structures that occupy prominent positions on the city's high ground—the National Cathedral and the National Shrine of the Immaculate Conception—its exoticism is unmatched. The architects provided a modernized rendition of the forms and decorative vocabulary of Islamic architecture: the minaret, horseshoe arches, corbeling, and sculpted crenellations. The symmetrical composition of corner blocks frames an arcaded entry and courtyard whose glory is its blue and gold mosaics crafted by the John Joseph Earley Studio in 1953.

SK32 Islamic Center

SK33 **House**

1927, John J. Whelan. 2447 Kalorama Rd. NW

Kalorama Road and Circle (SK33–SK41) form the northern boundary of this district, which

follows a high ridge of land before it descends to Rock Creek Park, a particularly desirable residential area that was developed primarily in the 1920s. Many of the homes were speculative ventures by a series of developers and builder-architects. Whelan's exploded Georgian Revival house, although constructed in coursed rubble stone, suggests southern American Georgian prototypes due to its hip roof and very fine swan's neck pedimented doorway. It was designed as part of a series of brick and fieldstone houses for the developer Malcolm McConihe.

SK34 House

1926, John J. Whelan. 2446 Kalorama Rd. NW

This brick house, built for the developer Malcolm McConihe, recalls the butterfly plan of English Arts and Crafts houses. Its steep slate roof gathers together a conical tower and the two wings set at 140 degrees to one another.

SK35 Embassy of Iceland

1927, George N. Ray. 2443 Kalorama Rd. NW

This large brick house has vertical emphasis that is achieved by two steep, offset gables facing the street and a high hip roof. The main architectural interest consists of the differing textures of various brick patterns set within the black wood frame of the half timbering on the entry gable.

SK36 House

1927, John J. Whelan. 2435 Kalorama Rd. NW

In two contemporary neighboring houses, Whelan commented on the nature of formal and informal in architecture through the historical precedents of his designs and the manner in which he cut and laid fieldstone on each of them. For developer Malcolm McConihe he designed 2435 Kalorama Road in a currently popular English medieval vernacular revival mode. His asymmetrical composition consists of two gabled wings intersecting at right angles. An enclosed entry porch is nestled next to the front-facing gable, its only striking feature a wide bay window supported and framed by corbeled layers of limestone. Small, asymmetrically placed windows frame, and in one instance are framed by, a massive chimney with a double flue that Whelan used as a major compositional and decorative element.

SK37 William A. Scully House

1927, John J. Whelan. 2431 Kalorama Rd. NW

Whelan designed the Scully house following a very traditional and regular undormered Georgian Revival composition but constructed it of uncoursed fieldstone. In contrast to his contemporary house at 2435 Kalorama Road (see SK36), which is irregular in composition, this house is built of small but rectilinear ashlar blocks laid in even courses, a subtle inversion of what one might expect. The Scully house is unadorned except for a columnar porch and Palladian window above that establish a strong central axis.

SK38 Charles D. Drayton House

1926, Thomas J. D. Fuller. 2425 Kalorama Rd. NW

In 1929 Fuller's house was awarded a prize by the Washington Board of Trade as one of the year's outstanding contributions to the beautification of Washington. Massive end chimneys and uncoursed fieldstone construction suggest eighteenth-century Georgian houses of rural Pennsylvania and New Jersey.

SK39 The Lindens (Robert Hooper House)

1754, unknown. 2401 Kalorama Rd. NW

The reason The Lindens has such an authentic air of eighteenth-century architecture is that it is an authentic American Georgian house. Erected in Danvers, Massachusetts, in 1754 by an unknown architect, it was moved to Kalorama in 1935 and rebuilt under the guidance of Walter Macomber. It is an archetypal example of the mid-Georgian period in its impressive size, gambrel-roofed form, all-wood construction, and concentration of architectural interest on its main facade. The latter was constructed of wood planks with their edges set flush then grooved horizontally and vertically to resemble ashlar masonry, as the owners and builders wanted at least the appearance of monumentality and permanence. Sand was added to a stone-colored paint in order to enhance the illusion. The five-bay composition, flat arches over windows, and modillion cornice were typical of colonial houses, but quoins framing the edges and a giant portico marking the central axis were innovations that came in about mid-century. This vocabulary, a slightly old-fashioned colonial expression of English and Dutch eighteenth-century architecture, was not a revival of any style. Rather it was a late survival of Italian Renaissance architecture that had undergone two changes, once when it was transferred to England via architects and illustrated books and then again when the English and Americans utilized the same books on this continent.

SK40 Two Houses

1925, Horace W. Peaslee. 29 and 33 Kalorama Circle

These houses are typical of the influence of the late English Arts and Crafts movement in the Kalorama Hill area. They owe their forms and details to small stone medieval manor houses. They share the same three-dimensional organization, as they are composed of two rectangular, gabled blocks set at right angles to one another. The entries, consisting of closed porches, are located at or near the crossing of the two wings. Decoration is sparse—label moldings over doors and discrete panels of half-timbering. Small, irregularly placed casement windows, minute dormers with diamond quarrel panes, and thick slate roofs reinforce the medieval forms and sculptural details. Both houses were erected for about $45,000 by their developer, Leslie E. F. Prince.

SK41 Embassy of France (William Watson Lawrence House)

1910, Jules Henri de Sibour. 2221 Kalorama Rd.

Square towers, dormer windows, and then low wings that recede in steps from the wide central entrance gable establish a symmetrical composition of an imposing monumentality. Subtle asymmetries of window placement and the medieval details used in the composition and detailing of the limestone window frames suggest an earlier tradition than the Renaissance-inspired axiality and symmetry of the building's overall composition. This combination of styles is associated with early French Renaissance architecture. The flavor is strengthened by the use of multitoned brown brick in imitation of fieldstone for the walls and the carved limestone trim.

SK42 Embassy of Oman (Devore Chase)

1930, Bottomley, Wagner and White. 2000 24th St. NW

The year before he designed Devore Chase, William L. Bottomley said that a good quality revival house should reflect the best cultural traditions of its locality. By 1930 the houses on the top of Kalorama hill demonstrated a variety of historical styles, but Georgian Revival predominated, while the nearby Sheridan Circle mansions were largely influenced by eighteenth-century French architecture. These dual influences account for Devore Chase's fusion of the two historically concurrent traditions on this house at the corner of Wyoming Avenue and 24th Street. It was designed at the height of Bottomley's powers, after he had been a practicing architect for a quarter century. Built in limestone that has a striated texture, the low, two-story house has two major facades treated in a similar fashion: projecting porticoes are outlined by shallow, regular rustication blocks as are the edges of each five-bay composition. Pedimental sculpture consisting of an escutcheon, shell, urn, and fruit provide the only three-dimensional relief to extraordinarily restrained surfaces. Entries are subdued with minimal architectural detail or sculpture to draw attention to them; horizontal regulating lines are undecorated and kept to a minimum; widely spaced windows have barely discernable frames; and the roofs are low without balustrades or parapets. All contribute to a sense of compact volumes, elegant in their simplicity and restraint, powerful in their solidity and clarity.

SK43 Mary E. Stewart House

1938, Paul Philippe Cret. 2030 24th St. NW

Paul Philippe Cret's quiet and elegant Stewart residence is a masterful reinterpretation of an eighteenth-century French country house, which he consciously integrated into its immediate surroundings. Situated between Devore Chase (see SK42) (whose debt to French eighteenth-century architecture is manifest) and The Lindens (see SK39) (an actual eighteenth-century American Colonial mansion), Cret's building mediated between, and expanded the parameters of, their respective traditions. The design is deceptively simple in form and detail, asymmetrical in massing and facade organization in response to its corner site.

Cret chose to reflect the volumetric sense of The Lindens and replicate some of the details (flat window frames) of Devore Chase, but he nonetheless created an independent design notable for its strong architectonic character. Brick walls covered with tan roughcast are accented by gray limestone trim used for corner quoins, a simple cyma recta cornice, and planar window and door frames. The entrance bay is emphasized by a quoined doorway whose long, rectilinear brackets support a lintel-cum-balcony that carries an intricate, wrought-iron railing and by a larger and more elaborately framed dormer window. The mascaron above the door imparts a specifically French flavor to the sophisticated house, a sculptural interlude in a building dependent on proportional relationships, simplicity of line, and harmonious colors and textures for its architectural quality.

SK44 House

1928, Wyeth and Sullivan. 2340 Kalorama Rd. NW

The English-inspired Arts and Crafts house is effectively removed from the street by its siting on a walled embankment. Composed symmetrically of two, two-and-a-half-story gabled wings framing a one-and-a-half-story central block, its multicolored slate roof, mixture of brick and half timbering, and asymmetrical window placement are integrated into a pleasing composition.

SK45 Harry B. Wilson House

1928, David L. Stern. 2301 California St. NW

California Street (SK45–SK50) consists primarily of sophisticated Colonial Revival houses built in the 1910s and 1920s. Stern's house and its neighbor, 2303, erected fifteen years earlier and designed by Boal and Brown for Leroy Goff, demonstrate the evolution from an academic interpretation of American Colonial architecture to a later application of the style that was concerned with evoking its associations in a less rigidly controlled composition.

SK46 Robert B. Roosevelt House

1924, Porter and Lockie. 2336 California St. NW

Porter and Lockie applied sparse classical details to a cubic form in an unusual manner, with slender colonnettes marking the corners, an equally thin twisted rope molding outlining the arched doorway, and shallow anthemion friezes above ground-story windows and enlivening the entablature. The result is a building with Spanish overtones strongly influenced by European modernism.

SK47 John S. Flannery House

1915, Marsh and Peter. 2411 California St. NW

The careful and sometimes playful detailing of Marsh and Peter's gambrel-roofed house is typical of their work, which took license in small ways with the Colonial Revival vocabulary while carefully adhering to its accepted proportional relationships. The belt course composed of upended stretcher bricks, tripartite windows hugging the entablature, and French doors overlooking an iron balcony above the main door are all pleasing variations on the Colonial tradition.

SK48 Brazilian Delegation to the Organization of American States, Ambassador's Residence (Daniel J. Callahan House)

1916, George N. Ray. 2415 California St. NW

Ray designed this gambrel-roofed house in a freely interpreted combination of Georgian and Federal forms and details to capitalize on its corner site. Arched ground-story windows set within wide ornate blind arches flank the entry and carry one double bay around the corners. The Baroque-inspired rusticated doorway with a deeply projecting but suppressed swan's neck pediment is particularly fine.

SK49 Embassy of Venezuela (Mrs. Wilber E. Wilder House)

1929, Wyeth and Sullivan. 2437 California St. NW

The limestone facade of Wyeth and Sullivan's highly unusual and elegant Art Deco house is so flat that shallow relief sculpture of classical details barely breaks the stone's surface.

SK50 Berkeley L. Simmons House

1922, George N. Ray. 2445 California St. NW

Ray designed the Simmons house with orthodox Georgian Revival forms, proportions, and details, with the exception of the monolithic limestone frame around the door, which he interpreted as a Roman gate decorated with niches, swags, and paterae.

SK51 Embassy of Colombia, Chancery

1907, Frederick B. Pyle. 2118 LeRoy Pl. NW

The only unusual feature of Pyle's six-bay Georgian Revival house is the patterned brickwork and tiles in blind arches above the five ground-story windows. The pedimented doorway, modillion cornice, and simple dormers are all common elements drawn from the eighteenth-century vocabulary. It was built for Samuel W. Woodward, the developer of many of the substantial houses on Bancroft Place.

SK52 Lester A. Barr House

1906, Stanley B. Simmons. 2120 LeRoy Pl. NW

Simmons designed this small row house as a canonical Philadelphia Georgian town house with elaborate scrolled and pedimented dormer windows, a fine early Federal doorway, and Aquia sandstone flat arches over ground- and second-story windows.

SK53 John J. Hemphill Row Houses

1909, Lemuel Morris. 2108, 2110 Bancroft Pl. NW

The 2100 block of Bancroft Place (SK53–SK60) demonstrates some sympathetic ideals shared by Victorian and Classical Revival architecture at the turn of the century, as well as the bond that existed between grand Beaux-Arts-inspired buildings and the more modest heritage of the Georgian or Colonial Revival. The six houses on the south side of the street, designed by two architects in units of two and four, were intended to be differentiated from one another yet harmonize with their neighbors. Their unity derives from their common classical heritage, scale, and materials. Lemuel Morris's two bowfronts, built for John J. Hemphill, demonstrate how the Georgian Revival drew upon both American Georgian and Federal architectural styles, casually mixing elements from each. Morris's two doorways have fanlights common to the Federal style, but their plastically conceived porches are more Georgian in inspiration. The flat arches and glazed headers set in Flemish bond on 2108 are associated with the Georgian style, while the flat, cast-stone lintels on 2110 and Chippendale-like balustrade are Federal, as is the bowfronted form.

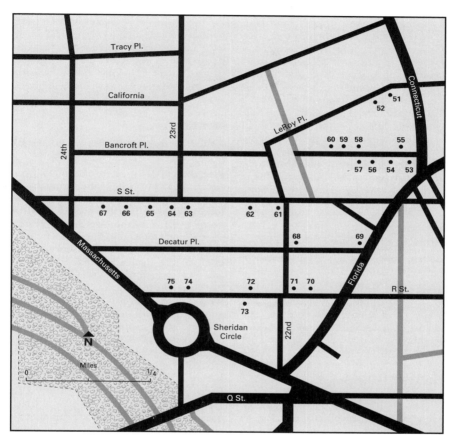

Sheridan Circle and Kalorama (SK 51-75)

SK54 **Row Houses**

1908, Albert H. Beers. 2112–2118 Bancroft Pl. NW

Beers designed these four houses for developer Harry Wardman. All flat fronts, they explore the richness of the Georgian tradition through varied fenestration patterns on their main stories, dormers, and miscellaneous details. Their breadth comes from the use of steel beams, employed in most of the well-constructed houses carried out under Wardman's aegis. The eclecticism demonstrated here, although not as flamboyant as that of the Victorian era, owes its existence to the earlier period. Young turn-of-the-century architects were conscious that diverse contemporaneous styles should harmonize with one another, and they generally believed that the abstract elements of design—scale, proportion, balance—regardless of style, would achieve this goal.

SK55 **Row Houses**

1895, Thomas Franklin Schneider. 2111–2121 Bancroft Pl. NW

When Schneider built the six corresponding houses on the opposite side of the street in Richardsonian Romanesque style, they were out of date, as advanced taste was already returning to styles determined by the classical language of architecture. Schneider designed his row of rusticated limestone units to appear as a single mansion when viewed from Connecticut Avenue. He achieved this effect partially by foreshortening the perspective as he decreased the width of each house ascending the incline of Bancroft Place and partially by varying the forms and details of each house to diminish the regularity commonly associated with row houses. Their color, materials, and stylistic vocabulary provide the continuity that bespeaks a single structure. But for the fact that 2121 was refaced by Waddy Wood in 1917, Schneider's Bancroft Place row would be one of his most coherent compositions among his vast number of mature Richardsonian row house complexes in the city.

SK56 James Kerrick House

1907, Beecher, Friss and Gregg. 2120 Bancroft Pl. NW

This Arts and Crafts house, with its low, sloping roof and second-story, cantilevered porch, breaks the predominantly three-story, flat-fronted lines of its Colonial Revival and Beaux-Arts neighbors.

SK57 Frederick Eichelberger House

1907, Arthur B. Heaton. 2122 Bancroft Pl. NW

A course of orange terracotta tile panels gives Heaton's Georgian Revival house a slight flavor of the Arts and Crafts movement, where obviously handmade objects were greatly valued.

SK58 Three Houses

1909, Albert H. Beers. 2123–2127 Bancroft Pl. NW

The upper half of Bancroft Place (SK58, SK59) has a commanding presence due to the reciprocity between both sides of the street, where exceptionally wide, three- and four-story town houses face one another across a fairly narrow street, an atypical urban experience in Washington. The majority are substantially Beaux-Arts in style but have overtones of

Georgian influence in their use of bricks as a primary building material and extensive use of decorative elements common to the Georgian vocabulary. Contrary to the Georgian tradition, however, doors set into rusticated ground stories of smooth, buff limestone are subdued rather than celebrated.

These three large Beaux-Arts houses were designed for developer Harry Wardman, yet each facade, as in his 1908 row on the opposite side of the street (see SK54), was organized as an individual unit meant to harmonize with, but not copy, its neighbors.

SK59 Houses

1903, 1907, Frederick B. Pyle. 2126, 2128, 2129, 2131, 2132, 2137 Bancroft Pl. NW

Pyle designed six important houses on the street, 2137, in 1903, and numbers 2126, 2128, 2129, 2131, and 2132 four years later following the same strategy. His bowfronted house at 2137 in the Georgian Revival style uses white stone keystones above the windows. Pyle exaggerated the Georgian Revival motif in the Beaux-Arts flat fronts at 2129 and 2131, which are more elaborate and formal than at 2137, across the street. Not only the keystones but also the end stones of the arches were executed in limestone to create a strong color contrast and distinct checkerboard pattern. Pyle's houses on the south side of the street have more plastically developed facades, employing a vocabulary derived from Baroque rather than Renaissance sources. Deep cornices supported by richly sculpted brackets or substantial modillions partially mask (at 2126 and 2132) round and oval bull's-eye dormer windows. Their stone details—whether cornices, quoins, or Gibbs surrounds on the door and window frames (on the ground story of 2132)—are exuberant but carefully balanced elements within his overall compositions.

SK60 House

1918, Waggaman and Ray. 2135 Bancroft Pl. NW

This five-bay house for developer William A. Hill is an interesting admixture of Georgian Revival and Beaux-Arts styles. Its most unusual feature is a magnificently carved window frame on the main story, signifying entry, set above a perfectly plain doorway below.

SK61 W. R. Castle, Jr., House

1929, Carrère and Hastings. 2200 S St. NW

S Street has a remarkable series of Colonial Revival mansions (SK61–SK67) that exhibit differing expressions of the style. Two neighboring houses by Carrère and Hastings, at 2200 and 2222 S Street NW (see SK62), are the latest in the group and are linked by elegant compositions and subtle details. Closer to English Regency architecture than any American manifestation of Georgian architecture, they employ all header bricks for their ground stories, bold and elaborate door frames, and widely spaced fenestration in unusual patterns. The Castle house's Greek Doric limestone porch topped by bold and varied sculpted anthemion antefixes is an exciting contrast to planar brick walls.

SK62 Embassy of Lao People's Democratic Republic (David A. Reed House)

1929, Carrère and Hastings. 2222 S St. NW

The Reed house's wide five-bay facade provided Carrère and Hastings with an expansive brick wall that they subdivided in a symmetrical but irregular manner. Small unframed windows are cut directly into the ground-story brick walls, concentrating attention on the limestone frames of five second-story French windows. Blind brick arches above them repeat the regular end-brick pattern used on the ground-floor walls, carrying this subtle textural variation to the house's upper tier. Windows on the top story are confined to the middle three bays, leaving broad blank corners and focusing the eye on the door's broken pediment complete with escutcheon.

SK63 Embassy of Ireland (Frederic and Mathilda Delano House)

1924, Waddy B. Wood. 2244 S St. NW

Wood, Washington's premier Colonial Revival architect, designed the Delano residence in a remarkably restrained manner. The attic story is recessed behind a parapet wall of alternating segments of brick wall and classical balusters. Two floors of brick walls with plain but finely proportioned window frames in limestone act as a foil for an elegant semi-circular limestone porch composed of six unfluted Corinthian columns with sculptural details that are so reduced as to be almost suppressed.

SK64 Embassy of Myanmar (Thomas M. Gales House)

1902, Appleton P. Clarke, Jr. 2300 S St. NW

The Gales house is the earliest of the series of Georgian Revival mansions on S Street and as such is more archaeological in its reinterpretation of American eighteenth-century architecture than many later examples. End chimneys, a gambrel roof, corner quoins, pedimented dormer windows with switch-back tracery, and prominent flat arches over rectangular windows are all common to the tradition. Clarke's wide projecting central bay, however, is forceful in its parts and eclectic in its elements. A broad, elliptically curved Ionic porch shelters a Federal style doorway with side lights and an elliptical fanlight. Its classical balustrade is repeated only in front of the wide central dormer, itself unusual in its broken pediment and abstract Palladian motif.

SK65 The Textile Museum (George Hewitt Myers House)

1912, John Russell Pope. 2310 S St. NW

It is appropriate that the central axis of the Myers house is now visible from the sidewalk to the terraced garden through a glass door (replacing the original), as John Russell Pope focused the facade's and house's architectural energy there. Limestone walls extend beyond the Doric porch whose two columns abut their corresponding pilasters, the whole severe in detailing and refined in proportions. Above, an Ionic Palladian window with a delicately carved limestone tympanum occupies the central field of both upper stories.

SK66 The Textile Museum (Martha S. Tucker House)

1908, Waddy B. Wood, with Edward W. Donn and William L. Deming. 2320 S St. NW

Wood's three houses on S Street span two extremes of Georgian Revival—from the archaeological interpretation to a sophisticated

SK65 and SK66 The Textile Museum

reordering of its elements. This house, done in partnership with Donn and Deming, now provides exhibition rooms for the Textile Museum. Wood applied the basic Colonial Revival bay system to an elongated composition but adopted elements frequently used in contemporaneous Beaux-Arts architecture, a raised and rusticated limestone basement containing the entrance with a swan's neck enframement for a two-story window above it.

SK67 **Woodrow Wilson House, National Trust for Historic Preservation**

1915, Waddy B. Wood. 2340 S St. NW

The best of Wood's three buildings on the street (also see SK63 and SK66) is the home Woodrow Wilson lived in subsequent to his

presidency. Its facade composition was directly inspired by Robert Adam's Society of Arts in London (1772–1776). Three Palladian windows outlined by shallow fluted stone arches define the prominent main story of the cubic building. The countercurves of the delicately wrought portico and the oval panels that mark the centers of the bays on the third story are an inversion of the forms and compositional elements that one expects. The sophistication of Wood's facade is not replicated in the house's spatial development, but it nonetheless merits a visit.

SK68 **Martha Codman House**

1906–1907, Ogden Codman. 2145 Decatur Pl.

The Codman house, one of Washington's most beautiful residences, was designed for his cousin by the wealthy dilettante architect Ogden Codman, most of whose work was as an interior decorator. He married a typical eighteenth-century French urban mansion plan to an English Georgian stylistic vocabulary. The entire U-shaped building is separated from the street by a tall balustraded brick wall in the French manner, with a courtyard entered through wrought-iron gates. By cutting into the sharp slope of a slight incline to situate his house, Codman was able to take advantage of the site to create a broad terrace along the southwest corner. French doors in the living room open onto it, as does an orangerie. Thus the service floor at ground level is subordinated to the upper three stories, which sit back and tower above the street.

SK69 Friends Meeting House

SK69 **Friends Meeting House**

1930, Walter F. Price. 2111 Florida Ave. NW

The picturesque setting for the Friends Meeting House was designed by the landscape architect Rose Greely to complement the picturesque composition of the two fieldstone buildings that consciously recall buildings in Pennsylvania where the Society of Friends, or Quakers, was established in America. Domestic in scale and form, the story-and-a-half buildings were patterned on a timeless vernacular type in order to evoke the simple, unpretentious life-style and beliefs of the church's members. Only the paneled shutters indicate a vague eighteenth-century heritage.

SK70 **Edward Lind Morse Studio**

1902, Hornblower and Marshall. 2133 R St. NW

Hornblower and Marshall's Arts and Crafts style studio house for the artist Edward Lind Morse represents a fundamentally modern attitude about the relationship between facades and streets. It is intensely private and introverted, with only three relatively small windows and a solid oak door fortified by handcrafted metal hinges facing the street. Brown brick walls upon which the abstract composition of windows and door seem to float is terminated in a stepped gable, the whole an uncommonly sophisticated architectural statement made with a minimum of elements.

SK70 Edward Lind Morse Studio (right); SK71 Captain Theodore F. Jewell House

SK71 **Captain Theodore F. Jewell House**

1900, Waddy B. Wood. 2135 R St. NW

Perfect control of the proportions between the three major masses and within each block is fundamental to the architectural superiority of Codman's design. Two-bay wings project two bays of equal width from the building's spine and flank a three-bay recessed central section. The windows occupy a spacious field, with no sense of being cramped by the brick walls in which they are set. White marble quoins, balustrades, keystones, cornices, and simple sculpted panels inset between the second and third stories provide crisp outlines and a sharp color contrast to the deep red brick walls. The overwhelming impression given by the Codman house is one of repose and serenity, a result of both its superb design and unique setting.

Two contiguous row houses in the 2100 block of R Street share brick as a common material, English architectural traditions as a common heritage, and the opening years of this century as a common era. Yet each is a distinct architectural statement realized through differing compositions, proportions, and details. Comparison of the Jewell house with its neighbor at 2137 R Street also in the Georgian Revival style (and designed by Waddy Wood) indicates the difference in effect that scale and sculptural elaboration can make. Both were designed with the same stock design elements common to the style—red brick walls and white window frames, flat arches in limestone, columnar door frames, modillion cornices, and dormer windows—yet the Jewell house is infinitely more pleasing. Its compactness brings its more vigorously sculptural door, cornice, and gables into a closer relationship with one another to better contrast with its flat walls.

SK72 **Embassy of Cyprus** (E. G. Davis House)

1891, R. G. Crump. 1922, remodeling and addition, Waddy B. Wood. 2211 R St. NW

The 2200 block of R Street (SK72–SK74) is more diverse than the 2100 block, the location of several detached houses in a wide range of styles. In 1922 Wood designed a new facade and east addition for Mabel Langhorne in the currently popular French Renaissance mode of rough coursed fieldstone with irregular limestone quoins marking all the building's perimeters, including an asymmetrical gabled section that incorporated a garage door.

SK73 **John D. Patten House**

1901, Hornblower and Marshall. 2212 R St. NW

The Georgian Revival was not a common stylistic choice of architects Hornblower and Marshall, but the deviations here from an archaeological rendition of that style give it a personalized architectural character. Treatment of the entire central bay—the overscaled Ionic portico attached to the wall by brackets with no pilaster to give it visual support—contradicted the Renaissance heritage of the Georgian style. Three small square windows grouped together above the portico are elements common to the Georgian vocabulary, but their positioning by Hornblower

and Marshall is a free interpretation of their original function as attic windows.

SK74 **Embassy of Kenya** (F. A. Keep House, 1906, and C. Russell Peyton House, 1908)

1906, 1908, Nathan C. Wyeth and William P. Cresson. 1937, renovation, Frederick H. Brooke. 2249 and 2251 R St. NW

Wyeth was involved in the design of both of these houses. In partnership with Cresson, he erected 2251 in 1906; two years later he designed 2249 on his own. The buildings are linked by the same cubic massing, common cornice lines, limestone facades, and by a double arch leading to garages, probably done in Brooke's 1937 renovation to accommodate the Swedish Embassy. Their similarities are striking and their differences subtle: the Peyton house has five bays in comparison to the Keep house's three.

SK75 **Embassy of the Philippines** (Emma S. Fitzhugh House)

1904, Wood, Donn and Deming. 2253 R St. NW

More subdued than its later neighbors, this stucco building has low, overhanging bracketed eaves and a red tile roof that give its simple, three-bay classical facade a vaguely Spanish Renaissance appearance or a Mediterranean flavor. The uneven grid created by the widely spaced but vertically linked bays of the upper two stories sits uncomfortably on the ashlar basement story, partially due to the low roofline but also perhaps because the architects were attempting to create a hybrid, an urban country house.

Rock Creek Park and Northwest Washington (NW)

Pamela Scott

NORTHWEST WASHINGTON HAS RETAINED EXTENSIVE NATural areas, either as public parks and parkways or as large institutional grounds. In combination with its pervasive suburban neighborhoods, these open, often wooded, spaces have extended L'Enfant's original vision of the city as a picturesque environment from its central core into its outlying districts.

Rock Creek and Connecticut Avenue

Preservation of the Rock Creek valley as an extensive and varied public park, where the natural landscape was to be used for recreation, sports, and the simple enjoyment of nature, had its genesis in plans of the 1860s to find a healthier location for the president's house. Proposals in 1867 by army engineer Nathaniel Michler for sites on the high ground in present-day northwest Washington were based upon Frederick Law Olmsted's principles of retaining a site's natural features and enhancing them with public amenities, ideas instituted in New York's Central Park just a decade earlier. In the late 1880s, Washington banker Charles C. Glover, whose grandfather had known L'Enfant, led local business leaders in promoting Rock Creek Park in Congress, as general public health issues, particularly the creek's increasingly polluted waters, were of great concern. The 1890 congressional legislation that established the park for the "benefit and enjoyment of the people of the United States" promoted its national rather than local importance in order to ensure public funding. Washington as a national resource was also envisioned as a model of American

361

civic beauty, a city of gardens, where the country's much-vaunted natural resources would be preserved for all citizens.

Army engineers who were members of the Rock Creek Park Commission, led by Gen. Thomas Lincoln Casey, established the park's boundaries by 1891, while its civilian members, led by Samuel P. Langley, secretary of the Smithsonian Institution, oversaw purchase of the privately held land, a process that lasted until the end of the decade. The park's boundaries were predicated on its topography, a narrow creek bed in its lower third, and broad, rolling meadows and woods where the valley widened above the rugged terrain of the National Zoological Park, about 175 acres, set aside by Congress in 1889, in the ravine that divided northwest suburbs developed in the 1860s and 1870s just outside the city's original boundaries. Frederick Law Olmsted, Jr., the landscape architect for the 1902 McMillan Commission, whose main objective was the revitalization of monumental Washington, was a vociferous supporter into the 1910s of preserving Rock Creek's scenic beauty in its natural state.

The parkway road system, where pleasure driving was included as one of the recreational benefits of the park, was designed in the 1920s and 1930s by the National Capital Planning Commission. Automobile access at limited east-west intersections and a winding and varied roadway that ran from the park's mouth at the Potomac through the Maryland extension of Rock Creek Park, Sligo Creek Park, made the park available to a much larger population than just inhabitants of its contiguous suburban neighborhoods.

In 1892 Frederick Law Olmsted was consulted about the layout of the National Zoological Park (NW01). As it had been founded to shelter all species of North American animals at the very time when the frontier was closing, the emphasis was on providing natural habitats for the animals insomuch as possible. Thus, in addition to conventional animal houses, extensive pastures for grazing were planned along with natural rock quarries to contain bears, a scheme that was unsuccessful. Two of the original buildings survive, the Principal Animal House (NW01.1), now the lion house, designed by William R. Emerson of Boston in 1892, and the New Mammal House (NW01.2), at present the monkey house, completed in 1906 from a design by Washington architects Hornblower and Marshall.

Linnean Hill (NW02), or the Pierce-Klingle House, located in the park at 3545 Williamsburg Lane NW, was built by nurseryman and mill owner Isaac Pierce (see NW03) in 1823 and named in honor of the Swedish botanist Carolus Linnaeus. Pierce's house is constructed of gray granite fieldstone and follows the common American Georgian vernacular form for an end-chimney type of five bays and two stories. A single-bay, two-story gabled wing replacing the front door was added at an unknown date before 1859. The single-story west wing is an 1843 addition. The house's glory is its south facade, with an elaborate two-story cast-iron veranda (c. 1855) and the remnants of Pierce's gardens framed by two cubic outbuildings set into the slope of a lower terrace.

Northwest 1-32

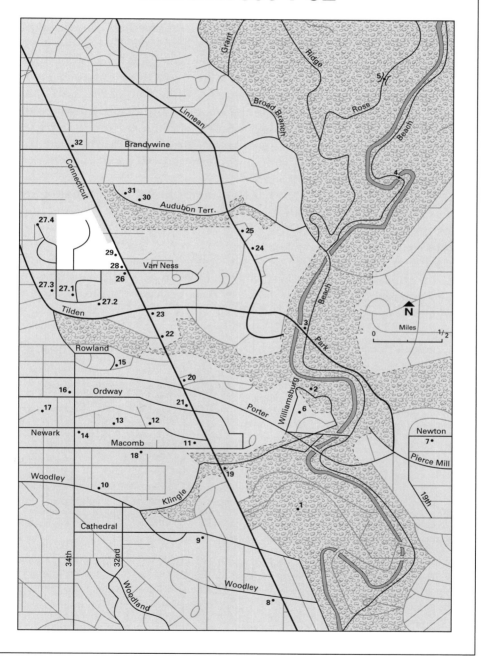

Between 1856 and 1859 Pierce designed and constructed an extensive picturesque garden on his 82-acre estate. Linnean Hill, currently undergoing restoration, was first restored by the National Park Service in 1935–1936.

Rock Creek waters had turned numerous mill wheels even before the city's
founding. Pierce Mill (NW03), restored by the National Park Service in 1934–
1936 and again in 1984–1985, is a rectangular, two-and-a-half-story, gable-
roofed structure built of uncoursed blue-gray granite and brownstone quarried
locally. The "BIP 1829" inscribed in the south stone gable may refer to "Betsy
and Isaac Pierce" or "Built by Isaac Pierce" and the date of the mill's completion. It was probably begun in 1820; the wooden north gable attests to an earlier construction date. Adjacent buildings—the springhouse on Tilden Street, a
private house that originally had been a distillery, and a nearby stone barn—
were also once part of the plantation, whose extent was comparable to the size
of the park today, about 2,000 acres.

Two surviving twentieth-century bridges across Rock Creek typify the dichot-
omous romantic and pragmatic concerns surrounding the park's genesis. Boulder
Bridge (NW04), which carries Beach Drive over the creek, was designed in
1902 by W. J. Douglas as a single-span arch whose steel-reinforced concrete
structure was faced with large stones to achieve a rustic and natural appearance. In contrast, the Ross Drive Bridge (NW05) of 1907, with its unornamented exposed open-spandrel concrete arch, expressed a functionalist engineering aesthetic much admired for its directness and simplicity.

NW06 **Gearing House**

1914, Nicholas R. Grimm. 2329 Porter St. NW

The Gearing house is one of Washington's
most substantial and best-preserved bunga-
lows, retaining its particularly fine and complex system of overhanging eaves on the house
itself as well as on its porches.

NW07 **Stoddard Baptist Home** (Ingleside)

1851, Thomas U. Walter. 1818 Newton St. NW

In 1860 Walter included Ingleside on a list
of his fifty most important works. Apart from
its architectural quality (marred by later alterations and additions), Ingleside is significant in Walter's oeuvre because it marks a
change in his architecture. Famous as one of
the country's leading practitioners of the Greek
Revival style, Walter shifted to the modern
Italianate style at Ingleside. This change coincided with his Renaissance Revival wing additions to the United States Capitol.

The house's wide and sweeping profile was
unusual among American Italianate villas,

NW07 Stoddard Baptist Home (Ingleside)

which tended to be more compact, with the
conjunction of two intersecting cubes marked
by a square tower. Walter's low rectangular
massing was probably a response to the site
and to its source. Until its extensive grounds
were subdivided in the early 1890s for suburban development, Ingleside sat on the crest
of a hill overlooking a varied and rolling
landscape that was reputed in the nineteenth

century to have been designed by Andrew Jackson Downing. Ingleside's massing and articulation closely resemble those of design 33, "Southern Villa—Romanesque Style," published in Downing's *The Architecture of Country Houses*. This relationship can no longer be appreciated fully because the orientation of the house was reversed in the 1896 remodeling by local architect William J. Marsh. The present entrance on the street was originally the garden facade; the terraces and arcaded porticoes date from 1911, changes made by Washington architect Nicholas T. Haller. In their additions, both architects respected Walter's building by conforming to the simple lines of the arched windows and bracketed overhanging eaves of the stuccoed-brick country villa.

NW08 Wardman Tower

NW08 **Wardman Tower**

1928–1929, Mihran Mesrobian. 2600 Woodley Rd. NW

The Greek-cross-shaped Wardman Tower was designed as a luxury apartment complex of fifty-five three-bedroom units but later converted to a hotel and connected to developer Harry Wardman's 1918 Wardman Park Hotel, now the Sheraton Washington Hotel. Its location on a promontory above Connecticut Avenue gives units in each of its four arms expansive views, good cross ventilation, and direct sunlight for 90 percent of its rooms. The impression of a streamlined version of Colonial Revival architecture comes from the balconies, thin quarter and half circles with white edges that create the building's unusual facade patterns, as do the white framed windows set against red brick walls. Each wing and bay is framed by brick quoins with columns, pilasters, pediments, Palladian windows, and console brackets distributed from the ground level to the mansard roofs nine stories above. An arcade mimicking the Hall of Mirrors at the Palace of Versailles later joined the two original structures.

NW09 **Embassy and Chancery of Switzerland**

1957–1958, William Lescaze. 2900 Cathedral Ave. NW

NW09 Embassy and Chancery of Switzerland

By the late 1950s the Swiss-born and -trained architect William Lescaze (1896–1969), one of the earliest practitioners of European modernism in America, was beginning to be influenced by the movement's later phases, notably the regular linear facade patterns created by exposed skeletal structures promoted by Mies van der Rohe. Miesian elements at the low and sprawling Swiss Embassy complex are still embryonic. Its cubic massing, planar wall treatment, and organization into a series of blank or unfenestrated walls set against glass ones are all so beautifully proportioned and detailed that the modern buildings fit comfortably into a residential neighborhood dominated by 1930s and 1940s historicist architecture.

Cleveland Park

In 1904 a promotional booklet, real estate agents Moore and Hill boasted, "Cleveland Park is unquestionably the handsomest and most desirable suburb of the national Capital." The area just north of the Washington National Cathedral was a favored locale for summer homes in the nineteenth century. The most famous, Red Tops, President Grover Cleveland's Queen Anne retreat, was demolished in 1927. One major house from this era, Twin Oaks (NW10), survives at 3225 Woodley Road. It was designed by the Boston architect Francis Richmond Allen in 1888 in a mixture of Queen Anne and Colonial Revival styles for Gardiner Green Hubbard; of the original 50 acres of densely wooded hills, 17 acres remain undeveloped as a reminder of the appearance of many of Washington's outlying districts before they underwent suburbanization.

In 1892, the Rock Creek Railway Company began running electric streetcars up Connecticut Avenue. Shortly thereafter the Cleveland Park Company initiated the first phase of the area's development. Beginning in July 1894 the Brookline, Massachusetts, landscape architect Frederick Law Olmsted was consulted by government officials concerning extension of Washington's streets and avenues beyond the city's original boundaries. Those in the eastern sector of Cleveland Park between 34th Street and Connecticut Avenue adhere to the Olmsteds' principles of conforming to a site's original terrain to minimize costs, prevent erosion, and provide a natural setting for habitations, evidence of that firm's influence on the city engineers.

Between 1895 and 1909 the Cleveland Park Company hired many Washington architects to design numerous sprawling residences in a mixture of Colonial Revival, late Queen Anne, and Arts and Crafts styles. The president of the company, John Sherman, and his wife, Ella Bennett Sherman, a trained artist, also designed many of the houses beginning in 1902. In addition, the company provided a lodge on Connecticut Avenue to serve as a streetcar stop and entrance to the community, a stable for common use, and a chemical fire station, all lost to later commercial development.

Newark, the first street to be developed, retains its original character. Among the more interesting houses are Ella Bennett Sherman's 1905 design for a Shingle style residence at 2930 Newark Street NW (NW11), where the wide gables of the roof and porch are offset, a simple asymmetrical composition that reinforces the expansive openness implied by the arch sunk deep into the roof gable and the Japanese-inspired construction of the porch brackets. Robert T. Head's 1898 house at 3035 Newark Street NW (NW12) is a bold mixture of Queen Anne diamond-quarrel windows and half timbering and large, but delicately detailed, Colonial Revival swags that traverse both its wide gable and octagonal tower. Head's best composition is the Queen Anne house at 3149 Newark Street NW (NW13); the complex geometry of its masses—steep double gables filled with half timbering set into pebble-dashed surfaces—is balanced asymmetrically by a generous wraparound porch, where curved screens of balusters hung between columnar posts echo both the linearity and curved lines of the exposed framing of the gable walls. Frederick B. Pyle's much simpler composition for the house at 3314 Newark Street NW (NW14) of 1908 recalls the severity and solidity of some Chicago school houses of the 1890s in the rectilinearity of its single mass punctured by symmetrical tripartite windows and its Greek-columned porch treated as a pergola.

Cleveland Park is not without contemporary houses. William Lescaze's 1939–1940 Harold Spivacke House at 3201 Rowland Place NW (NW15) is in a modified International style, with horizontal strip windows turning corners on both its brick ground story and wood second level and a broad deck on the second story above the main living area. In 1962 I. M. Pei and Associates designed a split-level house for William M. Slayton at 3411 Ordway Street NW (NW16). A walled courtyard on the street ensures privacy, as both the entrance and garden facades are composed of triple glass-filled arches that replicate the reinforced-concrete barrel-vaulted interiors.

NW13 3149 Newark Street NW

NW17 **Rosedale**

c. 1793–1795, unknown. 3501 Newark St. NW

The high and varied landscape, where the main residential section of Cleveland Park is located, was valued for its healthful atmosphere and panoramic views as early as 1793–1795, when Georgetown merchant and federal city proprietor Uriah Forrest began this country house on a large tract of land called Pretty Prospects. Now owned by Youth for Understanding International Exchange, Rosedale consists of an L-shaped series of connected structures, the oldest a single-story stone double house called the Cottage. The Cottage may be the oldest building in the city; tradition dates it to 1740, but no scientific studies have been undertaken. Forrest's original house resembles Mount Vernon before George Washington made additions to it, a frame five-bay house sheathed in clapboards, with brick end chimneys and a simple single-story porch, supported by spindly columns, that traverses its entire south facade.

A similar two-story gabled addition of three bays was added to it at right angles and a lower single-bay saltbox connected the wood sections of the house to the stone ones. Rosedale is an eighteenth-century vernacular type still commonly found in the Virginia and

Maryland tidewater region but a unique survivor in Washington, though many Colonial Revival houses in the city's extensive early twentieth-century suburbs were based on just such a structure.

NW18 **Tregaron** (The Causeway)

1911, Charles Adams Platt. 3100 Macomb St. NW

NW19 Kennedy-Warren Apartments

low service wing on the east to maintain the impression of a symmetrical and formal facade.

NW19 **Kennedy-Warren Apartments**

1930–1931, Joseph Younger. 1935, Alexander H. Sonnemann. 3133 Connecticut Ave. NW

In 1911, 20 acres of Twin Oaks (see NW10) were sold to Ohio financier James Parmelee, who commissioned Charles Adams Platt to design an estate that included a gardener's cottage, carriage house, and extensive formal and informal gardens, large areas of which survive in neglected condition. When Ambassador Joseph Davies and his wife Marjorie Merriweather Post bought the estate in 1940, they renamed it Tregaron and added a wood dacha as part of their famous Russian art collection. The Washington International School is the present owner.

Tregaron's Neo-Georgian design owes more to English than to American eighteenth-century traditions. Its shallow portico of four monolithic limestone attenuated Corinthian columns encompasses three out of nine bays of its long facade. Platt's plain, even severe, basement walls, pilasters, entablature, and main door and bull's-eye window enframements are a subdued gray in contrast to the brick walls. The only sculpted elements are limestone panels that mark the division between the two stories behind the portico and the pediment's festooned circular window, both of which exemplify the refined elegance associated with the architect's decorative sensibilities. Platt's landscaping successfully masks an octagonal conservatory on the west and

Only about two-thirds of Joseph Younger's original design for the spectacular Art Deco Kennedy-Warren apartment complex was built. Two additional wings were planned; they were to have been joined by a spine set parallel to Connecticut Avenue that would have created an asymmetrical arrangement of increasingly wider end blocks as one ascended the avenue. The composition of the setback entrance tower is a slightly narrower version of the existing end facade closest to Connecticut Avenue: layers of horizontally grouped windows alternating with buff brick walls are recessed slightly behind corner piers decorated with pilasters and ornamental aluminum spandrels set beneath double windows. The entrance tower is capped by a pyramidal copper tile roof and two limestone griffins. Younger's repetition of horizontally grouped windows versus single bays, in conjunction with stepped corner towers, creates alternating vertical rhythms of compression and expansion that effectively and rationally counteract the structure's massiveness. Art Deco decorative details, whether carved in limestone or pressed into the extensive dull and burnished aluminum panels, are totally integrated into Younger's tectonic system, resulting in one of the city's finest buildings from this era. It is claimed that the Kennedy-Warren has the earliest natural air cooling system in the country. A left rear wing was added by the B. F. Saul Company in 1935 with architect Alexander H. Sonnemann replicating Younger's original design.

NW20 Park and Shop

1903, Arthur B. Heaton. 3507–3523 Connecticut Ave. NW

Basic services were not available to Cleveland Park residents until the 1920s, when commercial activity expanded rapidly along three blocks of Connecticut Avenue. Although the business area is generally characterized by three-story limestone structures, the most notable building is this Park and Shop, the earliest suburban shopping center with its own off-street parking in the city. It was designed as a low, L-shaped complex, where several shops are unified by a continuous overhanging roof to shelter pedestrians moving from shop to shop. This convenience and its simple vernacular Colonial Revival style barnlike structure are elements long associated with markets in America. In 1934 the Park and Shop was featured in an article in the *Architectural Record* by noted planner Clarence Stein, where it was cited as an excellent example of this new type of retail complex.

NW21 Uptown Theatre

1936, John J. Zink. 3426 Connecticut Ave. NW

The Baltimore firm of Zink, Atkins and Craycroft built more than 200 movie theaters in large eastern cities during the heyday of movie theater design. For the 1,500-seat Uptown Theatre, Zink designed a sizeable facade as a frontispiece composed of a series of vertical limestone planes stepping up to and set against a large rectangular yellow brick wall. Triple sets of wide fluted bands rise vertically from above the storefronts that flank the theater's central cantilevered marquee and pass onto the stepped brick wall behind, where they simply disappear at its edges, having either continued upward or been turned horizontally. This simple surface embellishment on otherwise unrelieved planes gives a sense of scale and balances the vertical thrust of the windows and the large overall rectangular street facade.

Etched-glass windows, neon lights, and a long marquee of silver aluminum bands compete with other Art Deco contrivances such as long, uninterrupted brick courses, decorative stone panels with zigzag motifs, and setbacks and recessed bays, all to produce the prevailing sense of streamlining most associated with the Art Deco style. Greeting the patron at pedestrian level is an entrance of polished pink granite, which continues on into the lobby.

NW22 The Broadmoor

1928–1929, Joseph Abel. 3601 Connecticut Ave. NW

Joseph Abel sought to provide maximum light and cross ventilation for each of the south-facing Broadmoor's 194 units (originally 179 apartments and the remaining hotel rooms). Two L-shaped wings meet at a central pavilion with the entrance through an elaborate

NW22 The Broadmoor

porte-cochère. Shallow projecting bays provide numerous windows and sun porches for each apartment. The Broadmoor occupies only 15 percent of its 5-acre site, with expansive landscaped lawns covering one of the first underground parking garages in the city. Abel used rough-textured tapestry brick for the walls, with some projecting in a random pattern to create artificially rustic surfaces, apparently to blend the massive structure into its consciously preserved natural setting. However, the disparity of scale between landscape and architectural elements tends to dilute this goal. Sparse historically eclectic carved limestone decorative details are confined primarily to edges with the intention of increasing the building's picturesque appearance by visually breaking up its nine-story masses into a series of smaller units.

NW23 Tilden Gardens

1927–1930, Parks and Baxter; Harry L. Edwards. 3000 Tilden St. NW

The developers, brothers Monroe and R. Bates Warren, planned Tilden Gardens to be the largest luxury apartment complex in Washington designed as a cooperative. Parks and Baxter, working in association with Harry L. Edwards, organized the six buildings containing a total of 200 units on the rugged 5-acre triangular site to take advantage of its existing sloping landscape. The three cruciform and three double cruciform five-story structures are built of textured brown tapestry bricks with minimal limestone trim. Decorative detailing is sparse, with rectangular windows punched directly into the walls. Stepped battlements and square and triangular gables define the irregular skyline of the complex with cross-shaped arrangements based on New York and Philadelphia models. Three formal gardens with terracing, fountains, and pergolas are interconnected to one another and to the apartment buildings through a variety of picturesque and formal walkways. Parking is concealed in basement garages built into the slope of the hill.

Large apartment complexes continue intermittently to line Connecticut Avenue as far as the Maryland border at Chevy Chase Circle. Broken and rolling land on both sides of the avenue is now covered by single-family house lots, with more affluent homes located contiguous to Rock Creek Park. Few large estates escaped subdivision into suburban housing developments during the 1930s, 1940s, and 1950s.

NW24 Hillwood Museum (Hillwood; Abremont)

1926, Jack Diebert (?). 1955–1957, Alexander McIlvaine. 4155 Linnean Ave. NW

Hillwood is associated with the heiress Marjorie Merriweather Post, who purchased the 24.4-acre estate in 1955 and had its interiors entirely renovated by Alexander McIlvaine of New York to provide an appropriate setting for her extensive collection of French and Russian art. The "refurbishing" of the interiors, which comprise thirty-six rooms, at a cost of $680,000 was probably a complete rebuilding. McIlvaine designed them in an eclectic range of neo-Beaux-Arts styles, but primarily in the popular eighteenth-century French Rococo and Neoclassical styles considered at the time as the epitome of good taste.

The house was originally erected for Mrs.

Henry Parsons Erwin by her mother, Mrs. Thomas Walsh (see Embassy of Indonesia, DU30, p. 328), who had a twin mansion built on the other side of Rock Creek Park for another daughter, Mrs. David St. Pierre Gaillard. The architect of both houses seems to have been Jack Diebert, about whom no biographical information has been located.

Hillwood today is very grand in scale. There have obviously been additions, but it is unclear where, when, or by whom. Diebert designed Abremont in a free rendition of the American Neo-Georgian style, two very tall stories in red brick. A very attenuated tetrastyle portico on the south or garden facade has columns based on the Grecian Tower of the Winds order, a simplified Corinthian capital with two levels of leaves and no volutes. A single-story north entrance porch spans the wide central projecting portico.

The mansion sits near the center of the

property surrounded by a series of designed landscapes, including a Japanese garden, French parterre, and circular rose garden. Two subsidiary structures are part of the museum, a Russian dacha or cubic log house and a museum of American Indian artifacts in the style of a rustic Adirondack camp. They were completed in 1984 from a design by O'Neil and Manion for which they won an *Architectural Record* Honor Award.

NW25 Thomas Patten House

1985, Joseph E. Wnuk. 4205 Linnean Ave. NW

Historically the Van Ness area has been a center for contemporary domestic architecture. Numerous modern and Postmodern houses clustered around Lenore Lane and adjoining blocks on Linnean Avenue take advantage of natural settings or wide vistas afforded by wooded lots or hilly terrain on the edge of Rock Creek Park. The Patten house exemplifies how Postmodernism retained modernist structural systems and the aesthetic of transparency that together had changed the house's fundamental relationship with the ground and nature yet reintroduced historical forms, materials, and details. Much contextually conscious Postmodern architecture in Washington is ironically not integrated into traditional neighborhoods but isolated or grouped with like structures, as is the Patten house. Its two-story facade is formal, symmetrical, and private, composed of three gabled pieces in addition to a porticoed porch, It serves as the front for the house's main core, a gabled rectangle set perpendicular to it, out of which cubic and semicircular glass pavilions are extruded on the back to take advantage of its orientation and elevated site. The facade's flat two-dimensional squares,

rectangles, triangles, and circles are played off against their volumetric equivalents, a composition that intellectually regularized, reduced, and abstracted elements from the basic vocabulary of the "colonial" house, the most potent and meaningful of American house types and styles. Clapboard walls and shingled roofs maintain the allusion. In 1986 the Patten house won a design excellence award from the Washington Chapter of the American Institute of Architects.

NW26 INTELSAT Headquarters Building

1980–1985, John Andrews International Ltd. 3400 International Dr. NW

The only outstanding work of contemporary architecture among many examples in the Van Ness area is John Andrews's INTELSAT Building, appropriately a Space Age crystal palace to house the 110-nation cooperative that owns and operates communications satellites. Nominally its formal entrance faces the International Center, on whose grounds INTELSAT's 12-acre site is located. The most important view and approach to the building, however, is from Connecticut Avenue, and the wedged-shaped entry that faces it obliquely replicates the main entrance; both prepare users for the scale, geometries, and luminous effects to be experienced both outside and within.

A series of octagonal office pods and atriums interlock as in a honeycomb in an L-shaped configuration set diagonally across the slightly inclined site. Their arrangement, shapes, and surfaces were designed to take maximum advantage of the sun. The five glass-domed atriums set along the central spines contrib-

NW27.1 Federal Office Building, Department of State

ute to the energy efficiency of the building through passive solar gain and air venting. In addition, these light-filled gardens help fulfill the client's requirement that all offices have both windows and a view. Sodded roof gardens atop the office pods are part of the energy conservation system, and the strip windows of the office pods are equipped with three levels of reflective, solar-gray sun screens to shade interiors while still providing views.

The atriums also function as the main streets of the large, self-contained environment. Intersections occur between each set of symmetrical office pods, with vertical circulation towers rising in the centers of the atriums and extruded on the exteriors, where their smooth, mirrored-glass walls spiral upward as they follow the staircase paths within circular towers. Structure is omnipresent, providing decoration as well as support. The way faceted exterior forms are put together and held together becomes the dominant interior experience, with the space frames of the atrium domes and sun-screen trusses breaking up and scattering light while they provide ever-changing linear patterns of great complexity.

NW27 **International Center**

1968–present, Edward Durell Stone, James Van Sweden, and others. International Drive, International Place, and International Court, NW

In 1968 Congress charged the secretary of state with responsibility for developing a neighborhood for foreign chanceries (office buildings for embassy staff) that had difficulty finding convenient locations after passage in 1964 of the city's strict zoning plan. The master plan for the International Center, located on the west side of Connecticut Avenue at Van Ness Street on a large tract of land formerly held by the Bureau of Standards, was designed by Edward Durell Stone, Jr., and approved by the National Capital Planning Commission in 1970. The 6-acre lot between Tilden and Van Ness streets that faces Connecticut Avenue was reserved for an international organization (see INTELSAT, NW26), and twenty-three lots of about an acre each were divided into two groups, the street patterns of which are based on the model of suburban housing developments. The sites south of Van Ness Street winding around a central park began to be developed in 1979, while nine lots to the north organized around a double cul-de-sac were reserved for future expansion. The plan mandated that buildings be on a domestic scale—not more than four stories—in recognition of the large residential neighborhood along the site's western perimeter. The natural topography was to be preserved; between 1980 and 1985 James Van Sweden was the landscape architect for the park, a plateau overlooking all the contiguous buildings. From the outset the stylistic language of the chanceries represented a new international eclecticism, with national architectural traditions of each country reinterpreted within the framework of contemporary design. Many contain central atriums, de rigueur in late modern office buildings but here sometimes conceived as symbolic ceremonial spaces or actual gathering places for cultural and social events.

NW27.1 **Federal Office Building, Department of State**

1986–1990, Leo A. Daly Associates. 3507 International Pl. NW

The State Department's administrative center for the adjacent chanceries as well as for those located elsewhere in the city was conceived by its architect as a town hall with architectural antecedents that were generically early twentieth-century American. The composition of its facade is highly formal—two symmetrical wings arranged around a recessed entry. The whole building is a three-story cubic block; all facades are treated alike, with low, wide central pediments and the red barrel clay tile roof giving it a decidedly Mediterranean look. The architectural language is an abstract version of classicism, with the Renaissance tradition contributing its major features. The building material is cast stone treated to resemble stuccoed walls with most horizontal joins masked to give the appearance of continuous surfaces. Scoring of the walls in discrete areas into rectilinear panels is unrelated to structure but an effective proportioning device that visually breaks down the building's large mass. The middle story is articulated with triple windows reminiscent of the Palladian motif, and top-floor windows form a continuous band of green solar-glass window wall, faceted to form recessed octagonal bays that hark back to window shapes of Victorian row houses. Green aluminum for the narrow window frames makes an elegant transition between sand-colored walls and green glass.

NW27.2 **Embassy of Kuwait, Chancery**

1979–1980, Paul Vieyra of Skidmore, Owings and Merrill. 3500 International Dr. NW

Initially it does not seem that Middle Eastern building traditions influenced Paul Vieyra's design for the Kuwait Chancery in any way. Its form and materials—an off-white stainless

steel and tinted-glass cube—are integral to the whole design concept of the high-tech phase of modernism. The cube set on a paved terrace is only partly visible from the street, with the entry cut into its northeast corner. This focus on the diagonal informs the architect's remaining design decisions. Four large second-floor windows on adjacent sides are pulled to the entry corner, their diagonal braces pointing downward to it. The lobby is dominated by a square reception desk rotated 90 degrees to the entry and partially enclosed by light metal screens with a small repetitive pattern derived from Islamic geometric decoration. Corner entry and rotated squares were integral to the vocabulary of this intensely geometric phase of late modernism. On an abstract intellectual level (which this building exemplifies), the entire building is an intricate and flat geometric pattern exploded in scale and made three dimensional and architectonic. Both the flat roof and the floors are cantilevered from massive square pylons; additional floors beneath the entry level are terraced at the rear.

NW27.3 **Embassy of Ghana, Chancery**

1974–1989, Brown and Wright. 3512 International Dr. NW

The architects of all the buildings in the International Center complex have been conscious of energy conservation in their designs. Brown and Wright's solution was to hang an external cage of interconnected rectangular marble panels in front of bronze glass walls, treating each side of the T-shaped structure in the same regular manner. The result is a complex interplay between both of the two-dimensional surfaces and the three-dimensional spaces above, beneath, and between them. Entry is not specifically marked architecturally; the building's focus is inward to a central multilevel courtyard and garden organized on principles derived from traditional palaces of the Paramount Chief of Ghana.

NW27.4 **Embassy of Austria, Chancery**

1989–1992, Boeckl/Gates. 3524 International Ct. NW

Leopold Boeckl's strikingly beautiful Postmodern Austrian chancery is the most "foreign" of those yet built at the International Center in that its historical references—early

NW27.4 Embassy of Austria, Chancery

twentieth-century Secessionist architecture of Vienna—had no contemporaneous American version. Its freshness and clarity belong to the most recent wave of European architectural traditions to be imported, one where cultural and national diversity are celebrated. The elegance of its forms, materials, and details is matched by its lyrical proportions. Each corner of the self-contained block is marked by diagonal towers clearly delineating the formal bowed front facade from the sides where dark-tinted windows are organized in a regular pattern of tall rectangles below and squares above. Granite squares set into the limestone walls just below the cornice recall the work of the Viennese architect Josef Hoffmann and reinforce the sense that Boeckl's design is informed by a model endlessly applied to every detail as well as the building's overall form. Its volumetric exteriors give little indication of interior spaces, which include a large interior atrium for cultural activities, a large library, and several apartments in addition to offices.

NW28 **University of the District of Columbia** (Washington Technical Institute)

1972–present, Bryant and Bryant and Ellerbe Becket, Inc. 4200 Connecticut Ave. NW

In 1972 two local firms, the brothers Charles and Robert Bryant and Ellerbe Becket, Inc., collaborated on the master plan for the 21.8-acre Washington Technical Institute campus; construction began in 1976. Twelve asymmetrically arranged buildings were planned

NW28 University of the District of Columbia (Washington Technical Institute)

in a tight configuration with only the U-shaped administration building directly facing Connecticut Avenue. The remaining buildings climb the rising ground behind Van Ness Station (see NW29) and are grouped in clusters between Van Ness and Yuma streets. The stylistic language established by the master plan, the International style, has been maintained in all three construction phases. The result is an unusually unified architectural ambiance for a group of buildings erected over a twenty-year period. The cantilevered reinforced-concrete volumetric masses are balanced above recessed glass and concrete entries, with several of the buildings connected by elevated walkways and by continuous paved plazas terraced to conform to the changing grades. The 1960s Brutalist aesthetic in which the concrete's surface imperfections reveal its process of manufacture and construction was descended from the nine-

NW29 Van Ness Station

teenth-century preoccupation with truthfulness to materials in architecture.

NW29 **Van Ness Station**

1982–1984, Hartman-Cox. 4250 Connecticut Ave. NW

Van Ness Station is one of Washington's earliest mixed-use office and retail complexes to break away from both the modernist box and monochromatic surfaces. It is composed of two masses, the lower stepped one joining a seven-story office block at a slight angle to form a wedge-shaped plaza-cum-sidewalk. This juxtaposition is a response to the open space in front of the adjacent University of the District of Columbia buildings and provides an entry for a Metro stop. Hartman-Cox won a Metro-sponsored competition for the complex because their building's faceted massing organized around an interior court met the client's space needs and was inexpensive as well as elegant. The cladding is brick, predominantly buff colored, interwoven with thin red stripes spaced and located vis-à-vis deep openings and planar strip windows in order to recall colorful early twentieth-century buildings by the Viennese architect Otto Wagner. Concurrently the architects referred to the colors (and even faceting) of earlier large-scale Connecticut Avenue buildings (see The Broadmoor, NW22) built of brick with buff limestone trim. Hartman-Cox reversed the tonal values reinforcing the red brick detailing with window frames painted to match. More significantly, they explored the relationship between decoration and struc-

ture—the way in which linear patterns dematerialize volumes perhaps even more effectively than glass.

NW30 **James Newmyer House**

1967, Hugh Newell Jacobsen. 3003 Audubon Terrace

Even in his early Newmyer house, Jacobsen's interest in the history of architecture, particularly mid-Victorian composition and planning, informs all parts of the building, as public and private wings are articulated separately by their own massing and mansard roofs and distinguished by their relative scale. Black anodized-aluminum bay windows, a contemporary version of a common nineteenth-century window type, let in generous but controlled light and allow wide vistas onto the surrounding wooded landscape. Yet the formality of classicism dominates, with local symmetries, balance between horizontals and verticals, self-contained cubic forms, and even monumentality in the unbroken, pier-like light brown brick walls.

Single-story and L-shaped, the Newmyer house sits high on a raised brick podium that serves as entry porch, pathway, basement wall, planter, berm, and garden terrace. Particular hallmarks of Jacobsen's work include the arrangement of rooms or suites of rooms into separate pavilions, the uncompromising way walls meet the ground or the podium, standing-seam metal mansard roofs, and subtle changes in brick patterns to define edges.

NW31 **Ann and Donald Brown House**

1968, Richard Neutra. 3005 Audubon Terrace NW

In the 1960s there were few sites remaining in Washington that could accommodate a house such as that designed by Neutra, for it demands both a beautiful natural setting and enough space to allow for privacy. Situated atop and into the end of a small ridge, the Brown house resonates with echoes of early twentieth-century modernism. Resolute horizontals defined by thin, cantilevered slab floors and roofs, all-enveloping glass walls, a tall, white, and planar garden wall, each bespeaks the training and orientation of the architect. Viennese-born and -educated, Neutra's interest in American architecture dates from before 1911, when he became aware of Frank Lloyd Wright. Neutra emigrated to America

NW31 Ann and Donald Brown House

in 1923, working both in Chicago and with Wright at Taliesin, his architecture school in Spring Green, Wisconsin. Neutra's move to California in 1925 was decisive, for there he was instrumental in defining the image of California modernism during the 1930s, 1940s, and 1950s, along with his countryman, Rudolf Schindler. A feature of that tradition in the Brown house is the carport created by cantilevering the main story out of the end of the ridge.

The Brown house's picturesque composition—asymmetrical in its plan and its stepped horizontals—owes much to Wright's influence. However, the ambiguous nature of its setting and materials—rooted in nature at one end as it emerges from the ridge, yet subduing it in the wall sculpture garden at the other—and the use of rough natural materials alongside smooth industrially produced ones indicate a fundamental conflict between American and European perceptions of modernism.

NW32 Saratoga

1989, David M. Schwarz. 4601 Connecticut Ave. NW

Schwarz gives us an updated version of the brick and limestone apartment building by responding to the contrasting colors and materials of this common early twentieth-century Washington type as well as to their unusual site planning. In his bold decorative bands, relegated to the lowest and highest stories, Schwarz used limestone look-alike panels made of cast concrete and brick-colored mortar to intensify the red of the bricks. The rectan-

gular ends of the Saratoga's two wings, oriented parallel to the regular grid of Brandywine Street, meet Connecticut Avenue at an angle to form triangular lawns and an entry court. The recessed court not only brings more light and air to some individual apartments but also provides for all occupants the amenity of a quiet, green zone between street and lobby. The rhythmical repetition of octagonal bays along the Brandywine Street facade is another desirable feature adapted from the standard apartment house vocabulary to which Schwarz gives a contemporary form without historicist clichés.

NW33 Chevy Chase Arcade

1925, Louis R. Moss. 5520 Connecticut Ave. NW

Moss's perfectly preserved early arcade exemplifies many of the amenities of the small neighborhood shopping, business, and office arcades that led to their burgeoning into contemporary shopping centers. The concentration of goods and services in an enclosed, weatherproof environment equipped with large plate-glass windows both on the street and facing the central mall simplified the shopping process. Moss's limestone facade responded to the new typology by filling a gridded Neoclassical armature two stories in height and five generous bays in width with glass on both levels. Entry to the mall is through an archway that has no door (inviting, but also a convenience when hands are full), given special importance by its scale and architectural embellishment equivalent to small public buildings.

Northwest   33-41

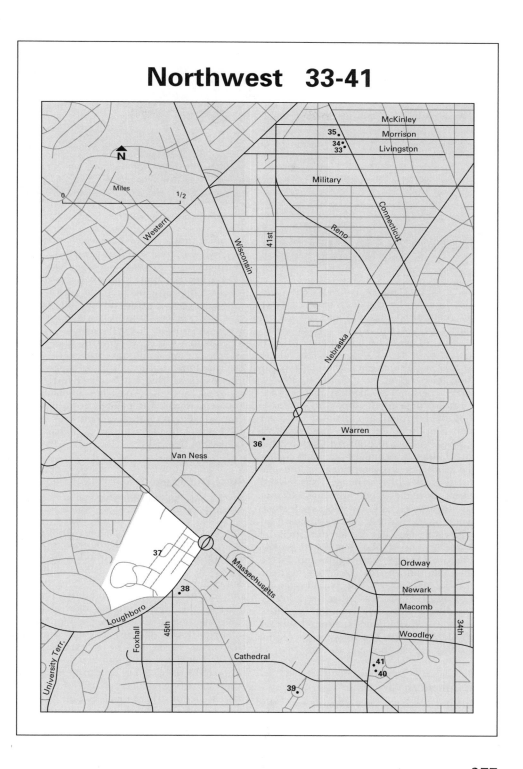

NW34 **Riggs National Bank, Chevy Chase Branch** (Chevy Chase Savings Bank)

1926–1927, Arthur B. Heaton. 5530 Connecticut Ave. NW

Heaton's slightly angled two adjacent main facades hint at the disparity between their highly regularized organization and the irregularity of the site for this lovely Neo-Renaissance bank. The tall arch of the entrance (now shorn of its original elaborate white marble door frame) is replicated for the side fenestration, now almost double its original length. The bank's architectural qualities are dependent upon the combination of finely tuned proportions, exquisite workmanship and detailing, and excellent materials. The base of polished black marble is nearly hidden by plantings; pink- and cream-veined sandstone walls sawn to a smooth surface are particularly striking. Exaggerated voussoirs above the arched openings lock into the uniformly rectangular blocks of stone contributing to Heaton's tightly composed facades, a refinement not carried out when the bank was extended. Relief sculpted profile portraits of George Washington and Pierre Charles L'Enfant in rondels set high on the front facade indicate the nature and intensity of the nostalgic historicism that swept Washington during the early twentieth century. The image of Washington is genuine, but that of L'Enfant is ersatz, as no portrait of the city's designer was known at the time.

NW35 **American City Diner**

1987, Kullman Industries. 5532 Connecticut Ave. NW

This shiny blue and silver aluminum, stainless steel, and glass-block diner incorporates features from 1940s diners originally made by

NW35 American City Diner

Kullman Industries of Newark, New Jersey. In 1948 there were thirteen manufacturers of diners; in 1987 there were four. In hopes of reviving the diner, Kullman Industries put together the most striking and typical diner elements, relying principally on photographs of a 1945 classic design (for which the plans are lost) to make this prototype at a cost of $1 million. Curved corners of glass blocks and the curved aluminum cornice give a snug exterior appearance to a surprisingly large interior, measuring 1,800 square feet. To increase its "authentic" nostalgic ambiance, the billboard mural was painted from a photograph taken by Margaret Bourke-White in 1937 for *Life* magazine of a billboard in Louisville, Kentucky.

NW36 **Dumblane**

1912, Gustav Stickley. 4120 Warren St. NW. Not visible from the road

One of the country's largest and most elaborate Craftsman homes, Dumblane was built in 1912 by Samuel Hazen Bond, who wholeheartedly embraced the ideals of independence, individuality, and simplicity of the Arts and Crafts movement. Bond himself made much of the house's original oak furniture; the remaining furnishings were handcrafted (many to Bond's designs) at Gustav Stickley's Craftsman Workshops near Syracuse, New York. Dumblane was published in the February 1913 issue of *The Craftsman* magazine, where its setting amidst orchards and gardens was extolled nearly as much as Bond's up-to-date house. Its design was a variant of a symmetrical, two-and-a-half-story gabled rectangle that had appeared in the October 1904 issue of *The Craftsman;* it is not certain whether

Stickley's office or Bond was responsible for the slight changes made to the prototype.

Three distinct horizontal levels of the house are emphasized by a wide pergola that wraps around three-quarters of the ground level, deep eaves that shelter three groups of strip windows set high beneath it on the second floor, and three broad, deep dormers that spring near the ridgepole and slope down to meet and continue the plane of the wall below. The garage and Bond's workshop was designed as an adjacent Arts and Crafts cottage. Bond incorporated many modern constructional techniques (concrete foundations; reinforced steel beams), and conveniences (built-in vacuuming system; electric clothes washer and dryer), but the impression of a handmade house predominated because of the way natural materials were used. Oiled or stained cypress for exterior woodwork brought out its grain; the patina of copper gutters complemented the unglazed deep blue-green roof tiles. The most unusual material is the rough-textured tapestry brick from which the walls were constructed. Each brick measures 12 inches by 2 inches by 4 inches and weighs 12 pounds. Their colors range from salmon pink to brown to dark blue, and they were laid in common bond with mortar joints three quarters of an inch wide. Unfortunately the exterior walls are now painted, so the interplay between texture and color that originally enlivened the house's exterior surfaces has been lost.

NW37 American University

1891–1902, Frederick Law Olmsted, Van Brunt and Howe, Henry Ives Cobb. 4400 Massachusetts Ave. NW

American University's first landscape plans by Frederick Law Olmsted, developed between 1891 and 1896, were picturesque in organization in response to the irregular and rocky site. His collaborators, Kansas City-based architects Henry Van Brunt and Frank Howe, initially envisaged all of the university buildings in the Romanesque Revival style to create a unity between them and Olmsted's landscape treatment. However, the university's founder, Methodist Bishop John Fletcher Hurst, intended that American University be a protestant institution modeled on his conception of George Washington's vision for a national university, one devoted to postgraduate studies. Hurst insisted on a formal plan and classically inspired buildings as one step toward extending L'Enfant's city plan to the university's outlying district. Olmsted and Van Brunt had worked together on the Chicago World's Columbian Exposition of 1893, a triumphant application of Beaux-Arts planning principles on a large public scale. Van Brunt's Hall of History (1898), now called Hurst Hall (NW37.1), follows a standard Neoclassical form of a long rectangle with a low hip roof bisected by a giant portico. It is unusual only in the treatment of the portico, two Ionic columns set in antis framed by a

NW37 American University, plan by Henry Ives Cobb

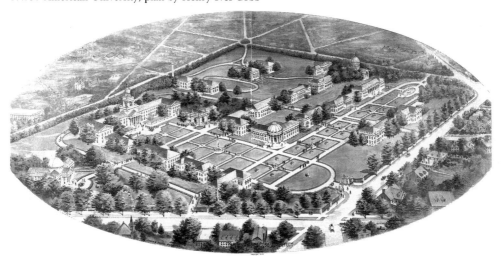

single bay and set between simple Doric pilasters.

In 1898 Van Brunt's successor at American University, Henry Ives Cobb (who had laid out the University of Chicago), moved from Chicago to Washington and formalized Olmsted and Van Brunt's final scheme of two intersecting open-ended quadrangles, adding an enclosed quadrangle behind the open quadrangle parallel to Nebraska Avenue. These long rectangular lawns, called the Court of Ceremony, were the foci for a plan of twenty-three marble and granite buildings spread out over the 93-acre campus. The buildings were to be uniformly two stories in height and sober and functional in their design. Stimulated by the state buildings at the World's Columbian Exposition, Hurst promoted state support of individual buildings to cultivate American University's national character. Only one of these buildings was erected, the key structure located at the intersection of the open quadrangles. It was originally the Ohio Building but was renamed in honor of the assassinated president, William McKinley, who had been one of the university's trustees. Cobb designed McKinley Ohio Hall of Government (NW37.2) (1902) to act as a hinge around which the two main landscaped spaces pivoted, as it was set on the inside corner of the intersecting quads. Its two arcaded flanks come together at a colonnaded and copper-domed rotunda. The building was never completed. Its Doric capitals were left in the rough, the finish carving to be done in situ. It is almost more appealing in this unfinished state, as the boldness of the capital's two flat rings is in keeping with the layered plasticity of the adjoining walls.

NW38 Metropolitan Memorial United Methodist Church

1930–1932, Harold Wagoner. Nebraska Ave. and 45th St. NW

Architect Harold Wagoner of Philadelphia worked within an ethos espoused and popularized by the American medievalist architect and author Ralph Adams Cram (1863–1942), who viewed European medieval architecture as the foundation of a living tradition. Cram believed that medieval-style buildings erected in America must be Gothic rather than Romanesque, which had already run its course evolving into the structurally more

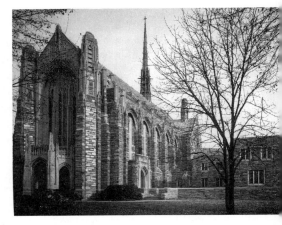

NW38 Metropolitan Memorial United Methodist Church

sophisticated Gothic style. American Neo-Gothic structures were logically to continue developing the forms, structural systems, and decorative language of their European ancestors. Therefore twentieth-century "Cram" Gothic churches were not composed of pastiches of famous European examples where quotations, however transformed, can be identified but were individual solutions to site-specific problems of liturgy, congregation, and sect. The open site on which the Metropolitan Memorial United Methodist Church stands offered Wagoner the opportunity to exploit the verticality of the Gothic tradition. His tall nave with shallow aisle thrusts upward, supported both physically and visually by all the church's forms. Tall, unpierced buttresses predominate, even replacing towers at the entrance; all windows are tall, narrow lancets, even on the west front, where one might expect to find a round rose window. Wagoner treated materials in the canonical Neo-Gothic fashion: walls and buttresses are built up of rough quarried variegated sandstone and limestone; dressed and carved limestone was used to cap them and was employed for tracery and window frames and the lovely octagonal entrance porch. One quotation, the metal flèche modeled on that of Notre Dame in Paris, marks where 1959 additions begin at the eighth bay.

NW39 The Westchester

1929–1931, Harvey Warwick, Sr. 4000 Cathedral Ave. NW

In 1929 Washington developer Gustave Ring envisioned The Westchester as the largest apartment complex south of New York City. His ambitious plan—eight apartment buildings with more than 1,000 units spread over 28 acres at the southwest corner of Cathedral Avenue and 39th Street—was halted by the Great Depression. The scope of the intentions of developer and architect is obvious, even in The Westchester's incomplete state. Four buildings containing 556 units cover less that 10 percent of the beautifully landscaped site. Two freestanding irregular I-shaped units flank the entrance drive, a divided road that curves around the main landscape feature, a sunken formally designed elliptical garden. Two large connected buildings irregularly arranged around staggered spines were to have been replicated across the main drive. Although only eight stories tall, the blockiness of each brick-covered unit, unrelieved by either bay windows or balconies, gives them a looming appearance. The placement and scale of The Westchester's limestone ornamental details do little to relieve the powerful effect of its massive blocks. Its stylistic heritage—Neo-Georgian, Neo-Tudor, and Neo-Moorish—is composed of the same ingredients as contemporaneous Hollywood movies, opulence with tasteless style.

NW40 Cathedral of Saint Peter and Saint Paul (Washington National Cathedral)

1906–1990, George F. Bodley and Henry Vaughan; Frohman, Robb and Little; Smith, Segreti and Tepper. Massachusetts and Wisconsin avenues NW

Conceived as a national cathedral free and open to all denominations, the Cathedral of Saint Peter and Saint Paul was inspired by Pierre Charles L'Enfant's plan for such a structure to have been located in the heart of the city on the block bounded by F and G and 7th and 9th streets NW. He envisaged a church "for national purposes, such as public prayer, thanksgivings, funeral Orations, &c. and assigned to the special use of no particular Sect or denomination, but equally open to all."[44] Although Congress granted the Protestant Episcopal Cathedral Foundation a charter on 6 January 1893 for a national cathedral for the "promotion of religion and education," Washington National Cathedral is in no way affiliated with the federal government nor does it have a congregation. Rather, its twofold mission is to provide ecumenical worship services and education via its four schools—Beauvoir Grammar School, the College of Preachers, the National Cathedral School for Girls, and Saint Albans School for Boys.

In 1895 the New York architect Ernest Flagg was commissioned to submit designs in Gothic and Renaissance styles. Flagg convinced the cathedral committee that a classical building was superior in terms of modern construction technology. His white marble cruciform church with a 208-foot-high central dome and a capacity of 3,500 people was selected in 1896. The controversial design was conceived by Flagg as the most monumental Neo-Renaissance structure in America, as New York's contemporaneous Saint John the Divine was the largest Neo-Gothic building in the country. Although Flagg's design was abandoned, a vestige of its classical heritage is seen in Hearst Hall, located within the cathedral grounds at the corner of Wisconsin Avenue and Woodley Road.

By 1907 sufficient funds had been collected to commence the cathedral. Henry Y. Satterlee had been consecrated as the first bishop in 1896 and spent his entire twelve-year term promoting and raising money for the complex. Between 1898 and 1903 he purchased the site he preferred, 57 acres on Mount Alban above Georgetown with commanding views of the city. In 1906 the cathedral established an advisory commission consisting of architects Daniel Burnham, Charles F. McKim, Charles H. Moore (professor of architecture at Harvard), Bernard Green (superintending architect of the Library of Congress), and Casper P. Clarke (director of the Metropolitan Museum of Art). They recommended the highest site within the compound for the cathedral and that an architect be appointed in preference to holding a competition. The commission was divided over whether the design should be classical or medieval in inspiration. Bishop Satterlee led the movement for "a *genuine* Gothic Cathedral on this side of the Atlantic," because, he said, "American Churchmen are so weary of designs which glorify the originality of the architect, that they are longing more and more for a pure Gothic Church which is built simply for the Glory of God."[45] After consulting church authorities in England to seek the best Neo-Gothic architect, Satterlee invited George Frederick Bodley to visit Washington. He was concerned that an American architect work on the project, so he selected Henry Vaughan as associate architect, an Englishman who had been Bodley's chief draftsman before his immigration to America in 1881.

Bodley and Vaughan's design, finished in the spring of 1907, was for a Latin-cross church with an octagonal baptistery attached to the south nave and a vestry located between the north transept and polygonal choir. The central tower was to rise 220 feet; two lower towers presented an almost solid mass of masonry at the west end. The design was based on typical fourteenth-century English models in its plan and elevation, in that it was not seen as a skeletal framework for stained glass, as in French Gothic cathedrals, but as a more solid structure, where the linear patterns of stone colonnettes, moldings of pointed arches, and vaulting ribs predominate. Bodley and Vaughan proposed a soft rosy-red stone; the material eventually selected was a buff Indiana limestone.

Bodley died within a month of the cornerstone ceremony on 29 September 1907, leaving Vaughan in charge until his death a decade later. During those ten years Vaughan was responsible for carrying out the Bethlehem Chapel of the Nativity (1908–1910) (underneath the sanctuary and choir), the bishop's residence (1913–1914), the Chapel of the Annunciation (1913–1914), and the sanctuary and choir (1915–1918). Vaughan's successor was the Boston-based firm Frohman, Robb and Little, appointed in 1921. Philip Hubert Frohman, chief architect of the cathedral for fifty years, was descended from four generations of French engineers and architects. He began altering Bodley and Vaughan's design as early as 1919, raising the crossing tower to 330 feet, extending the buttresses, altering the nave, and revising the west front. Donald Robb and Henry Little had both apprenticed with Cram and Ferguson, the best Neo-Gothic architectural firm in the country. When Frohman retired in 1971, both transept arms, the crossing tower, and eight of the nine nave bays were complete; the west front was under construction. Washington architects Anthony J. Segreti and Robert C. Smith were retained as superintending architects to finish Frohman's design. Construction was completed in 1990, but ornamental work, principally carved-stone details and additional stained-glass windows, is ongoing.

In plan the Washington Cathedral most closely resembles England's Wells Cathedral, with its polygonal east end, wide transepts, and choir about half the length of the nave and narthex. However, it truly represents a mingling of interrelated national styles, a traditional American solution when reviving European architectural styles. Its overall exterior form (514.5 feet in length), with its pinnacled Gloria in Excelsis crossing tower, is reminiscent of the tower at Canterbury Cathedral; the 219-foot nave, supported by buttress walls and flying buttresses, fuses principles borrowed from both French and English Gothic cathedrals; and the twin-towered west front, with three separate entries and five distinct horizontal levels, derives from Notre Dame in Paris.

Frohman's genius was to synthesize these diverse Gothic influences and integrate them in such a way that the prevailing historical authority at National Cathedral appears to be the Curvilinear phase of the Decorated style, the second phase of the middle period of English Gothic architecture. Its characteristics are manifested here by richly carved decoration, particularly in pinnacles and bosses, elaborate window tracery that fills the pointed arches, and multiple ribs that outline the structure of vaults.

The change of reins from Vaughan to Frohman can be discerned easily on the exterior by comparing the buttressing system of the choir with that of the nave. Two levels of flying buttresses span the distance between freestanding buttress piers to support the upper walls of the octagonal east end, even though solid walls beneath tripartite traceried windows render them superfluous. Bodley and Vaughan's planned ambulatory would have connected these buttresses to low walls, but it was eliminated in order to insert windows into the Bethlehem Chapel in the crypt. Their single-aisle, six-bay choir has buttresses that rise interrupted only by unoccupied, canopied niches to the triforium level before the springing of the flying buttresses. Additional surface decoration in the form of quatrefoil and arcaded balustrades, sculpted figures, gargoyles, and a textual frieze enrich its surfaces. Although greater in number, the individual sculpted pieces outside the choir are simpler in form and detail than those in the nave.

As Frohman's nave has double aisles (a French feature), its much wider buttresses are partially subsumed into the outer aisles at ground level and then rise in steps to support the inner aisle walls before their flying buttresses are thrown against the clerestory walls. In both choir and nave a second, lower level of flying buttresses, hidden beneath the inner aisle roofs, supports the walls at the triforium level. The massive nave buttresses are more three-dimensionally, or architecturally, sculptural than those of the choir, with three setbacks before their paneled and crocketed pinnacles rise above the springing line.

These variations between the pyramidal composition of the nave and the more vertical choir are separated by two exceptionally wide transept arms. The entry level of each differs in response to site and orientation, but their upper walls are similar, composed of a level of three triple-lancet windows intervening between the portals and the large rose windows that are in turn surmounted by an exuberantly decorated range of double-lancet windows from which plain gables emerge.

Frohman's north transept was constructed first (1922–1930); its complex two-level, biaxial Women's Porch absorbs the slope of the hill and abuts a cloister of the cathedral close. The crossing and south transept were under construction into the 1960s. The wide south transept door is the most sculpturally ornate part of the cathedral exterior. Eight-foot-tall figures of the archangels Gabriel and Michael occupy elaborate canopied open side niches atop the buttresses that flank the rose window. The iconography of the deeply recessed south portal tympanum focuses on the Last Supper above a frieze entitled *On the Road to Emmaus.* The trumeau figure is Saint Alban of England and the eight jamb figures represent Those Who Came to Christ. Forty-four canopied angels decorate the voussoirs of the four receding arches that enframe the tympanum.

These reliefs and figures, executed between 1959 and 1971, demonstrate the inherent conflict, as does much of the cathedral's sculpture, of creating meaningful and expressive modern works within the context of another historical period. For Frohman, the architectural response to this conundrum was to synthesize the best Gothic solutions—whether English or French—to create a "perfect" Neo-Gothic cathedral untainted by stylistic principles of modern architecture, although some concessions were made to modern structural principles. Steel trusses span the transept and nave roofs, and reinforced-concrete beams support the transept balconies and were used in floors above the nave and in the west towers. The walls, however, are traditional masonry construction, with some vertical steel reinforcing rods imbedded in them. The number of sculptors who have contributed to the cathedral's fabric, however, has resulted in a wide variety of attitudes ranging from representational to abstract. All the architects have been actively involved in the design of the sculpture, whether architectural, symbolic, or figural.

The 301-foot crossing tower, dedicated in 1964, has two levels of triple-lancet windows separated by a nearly solid section of horizontal wall, because it houses two sets of bells. Music from ten hand-rung peal bells is emitted from the upper louvered windows, while the fifty-three-bell carillon is located behind the lower windows. The elaborate tracery patterns of the gables above the top windows, pierced balustrades, and crocketed pinnacles in three sizes establish the distinctive broken outline of the cathedral's highest and most visible element.

Frohman revised the National Cathedral's west facade four times, finally organizing it in a manner similar to the facade of Notre Dame in Paris but rendered in an English Gothic vocabulary. The entrance story is separated from the rose window at the clerestory level by an arcaded gallery; a second arcade serves as the Pilgrim Observation Gallery just above roof level. The two towers rise 235 feet with double-lancet windows on each face and a decorative vocabulary similar to, but not exactly copying, that of the crossing tower.

The architectural details of the three entrance portals is Early English in inspiration, with plain receding archivolts supported by simple colonnettes, with the exception of the central door, where canopied niches await jamb figures. The cathedral's sculptural masterpieces are the tympanums of the central portals designed by Frederick E. Hart and dedicated in 1983 and 1984. The iconographical theme of the west facade, Creation of the Universe, centers on these exciting works and Rowan LeCompte's west rose window. Hart's trumeau figure of Adam that bisects the central door is depicted in the process of becoming, appropriate for the first human being. In the tympanum above, a great swirl of human forms emerges from earth, water, and (presumably) air. Their exposed anatomical parts are wholly formed, but they all remain submerged to some degree in the earthly elements. The north Saint Peter tower is presided over by Hart's trumeau figure; the fiery orb in the tympanum above represents the Creation of Day. The south tower is dedicated to Saint Paul; the sphere in its tympanum illustrates the Creation of Night. The pierced bronze gates, which read equally from the inside or from without, were designed by Ulrich Henn. The shift to a more abstract sculptural vocabulary in recent years has produced finer quality sculpture.

Development of a coherent program of iconography has always been in the hands of the cathedral's clergy. Dean George C. F. Bratenahl, working with Vaughan, planned a symbolic scheme organized around the central theme of the Christian creed. Bosses at the intersection of the ribs in the nave, crossing, choir, and aisle vaults relate to the Nicene and Apostles' creeds. Those over the west balcony depict the Ten Commandments, a break in this iconography necessitated by Frohman's early 1960s design of rib vaults for this narrow bay. In 1961 Dean Francis B. Sayre, Jr., expanded the iconographical program to encompass a wide range of historical figures of many callings who contributed to Christianity. National and Christian symbols are now intermingled in the recent sculpture and stained-glass windows.

Upon entry at the west end, the initial experience of the nave is of a lofty space where the three horizontal divisions of arcade, triforium, and clerestory are subjugated to a vertical linear cage unbroken until the ribs meet at the bosses that define the ridgeline. As early as 1921 Frohman was planning to incorporate refinements in his design that would correct for numerous visual illusions that occur within such a large structure, including the perception of the nave's horizontal lines meeting at infinity. Most are so subtle as to be invisible, as they were intended to be. However, his offsetting of the central west door by more than 6 feet to the north of the center line of the apse, which is a tenth of a mile away, in order to give a wider vista of the nave and a view into the sanctuary, is perceptible from the narthex.

As the height builds from the outer aisles to the nave, so does the complexity of the vaulting. Two bays of ribbed groin vaults above the outer aisles correspond to single bays with complex tierceron vaults above the inner aisles and nave. The nave can be perceived as a totality from any point along its central axis, either as an entirely integrated structural system that exists in order to open walls on three levels to admit colored light filtered through stained-glass windows or as a transcendent space dominated by architectural form and structure.

Typical of the Decorated style, the nave and aisle capitals are composed of a series of plain molded rings that perfectly complement the simplicity of the uncarved column shafts. Sculpted bosses (some yet to be carved) not only serve structurally as the keystones of the pointed arches but also resolve aesthetically the vertical linear system of colonnettes and ribs, flowerlike terminations atop long, slender stems. National Cathedral's collection of 650 vaulting bosses is the most comprehensive in the world.

The only aisle bay to break the rhythm of simple molded capitals and columnar piers is the Woodrow Wilson Bay, the sixth bay on the south side. Its carved screen of trefoil and cinquefoil tracery and its foliated capitals introduce a sculptural elaborateness generally reserved for the cathedral's altars.

Artificial light, introduced via lanterns hung from the triforium level and spotlights in the vaults, supplements natural light to the degree that all internal spaces are clearly visible while maintaining the necessary contrast of light and shadow for architectural forms to retain their distinct articulation. National Cathedral's stained-glass windows are an integral part of the building, and, like its sculpture, range from traditional to abstract patterns. The pale palette and subtle painted surfaces of the first windows installed in the crypt in 1912 led to the decision that all windows in the upper church would be large and in vivid primary colors in the French Gothic tradition.

The scale, form, and elaborateness of the architectural framework for all 214 windows are graded by their location at ground level in the outer aisles, above the inner aisles, or in the clerestory. The nave outer aisle windows are generally composed of three separate lancets, some with simple pointed arches and some with foiled tops. Triple-lancet windows, with complex stone tracery following typical English Decorated patterns terminated by sexfoils at the apex of the arches, light the inner aisles. There is no comprehensive symbolic scheme governing the two lower ranges of windows; rather, they are the work of many artists depicting a variety of Christian and national themes.

When the cycle is complete, all the nave clerestory windows will have been designed by Rowan LeCompte, who received his first commission for a National Cathedral window in 1941. The nave clerestory windows depict Old Testament themes up to the easternmost pair, which relate the calling of Saint Peter and the conversion of Saint Paul. The rose and clerestory windows in the transepts and choir are based on the New Testament, culminating in Christ in Majesty above the high altar. The twelve-petaled south rose window celebrates the church triumphant, and that in the north, the Last Judgment.

Many of the south-facing clerestory and aisle windows cast sparkling colored light disks on interior walls, intense and concentrated on nearby vaults and ribs but diffuse and soft hued on lower walls. This enlivening of the cathedral's interior surfaces is an effect that has been lost in older buildings due to dirt, deterioration of glassy surfaces, or paint filming applied to the glass. Windows installed in National Cathedral prior to 1962 had painted interior surfaces and were spattered with black paint on the exterior in imitation of old glass.

LeCompte's masterpiece is the twelve-petaled west rose window (1973–1976), abstract in its design and unusual in its use of chunks of faceted glass to create a kaleidoscopic effect. The perception of the predominant colors of the more than 11,000 pieces of glass changes depending upon the angle and intensity of light shining through them.

The Canterbury Pulpit located in the crossing, designed in 1906 by William Douglas Caroe, architect of Canterbury Cathedral, was carved from blocks of the French limestone originally destined for use at the English cathedral. The miniature Children's Chapel at the southeast intersection of the south transept and choir was designed by Frohman, Robb and Little in 1932 in the English Perpendicular style with fan vaults covering the cubical space. Saint John's Chapel adjacent to it has a reredos carved in situ that was designed by Robb.

A drawing of the high altar reredos designed by Bodley and Vaughan was published in 1907, before the cornerstone was laid, but its design was modified by Donald Robb, and carving in Caen stone did not begin until 1937. Completed in 1973, this *Ter sanctus* ("Holy, Holy, Holy, Lord God of Sabbath") reredos is the center of all the apse iconography that is based on the fourth-century hymn *Te Deum*. Saint Mary's Chapel to the north of the sanctuary has a polychromed and gilded-wood reredos that was designed by Frohman, Robb and Little and carved in 1933.

The Bethlehem Chapel beneath the sanctuary was designed by Bodley and constructed under Vaughan's direction between 1908 and 1910. In the Early Decorated Gothic style, its quadripartite vaults spring from plain columns and span a five-bay nave flanked by three aisles and terminated by a polygonal apse that contains the tomb of Bishop Satterlee behind the altar. An unusual feature for such a crypt chapel is direct natural light admitted through painted stained-glass windows executed in 1912 by John Lisle of Thomas Kempe and Company of London. Their theme is the Incarnation of Christ. The simple columns and capitals of the Bethlehem Chapel established the order that Frohman employed throughout the nave and on the west front.

The Resurrection Chapel beneath Saint John's Chapel was designed by Frohman in the Norman style of architecture, with low groin vaults and simple geometric decoration. As many Gothic cathedrals were begun during the Romanesque period, or were built on the foundations of earlier churches, Frohman was deliberately archaizing in this chapel as well as the chapel beneath the crossing. The Resurrection Chapel contains the cathedral's only mosaics, designed and executed by Rowan LeCompte.

The Chapel of Saint Joseph of Arimathea beneath the crossing was designed in the Transitional style in order to provide National Cathedral with the full range of English medieval styles. Four massive circular columns, only a quarter of which are visible, support the crossing tower and define a Greek-cross-shaped space, one arm of which contains Jan Henryke de Rosen's mural of Christ's burial painted in 1938.

As in medieval Gothic cathedrals, there is a distinct sense that National Cathedral was constructed over time under the aegis of many architects and artists. However, the architectural time line and the decorative time line represented by the sculpture and stained-glass windows do not always mesh. Under Frohman's direction the architectural vocabulary became both more archaeologically correct and more synthetically eclectic, in that precise proportions and details were of paramount importance, resulting in a nave of great beauty and architectural integrity. The recent freedom of expression granted to sculptors and stained-glass artists never extended to the architecture, the outcome being a building that appears to have had modern additions inserted into its medieval fabric.

NW41 Hearst Hall, National Cathedral School for Girls

1890–1900, Robert W. Gibson. Washington National Cathedral grounds

The I-shaped composition of the four-and-a-half-story limestone school is common within the historical vocabulary of its models, French Renaissance mansions. The main entry on the short end facing Woodley Road is, however, unusual, particularly as the Wisconsin Avenue facade organization implies that it is the main facade. Four recessed central bays set off by arches with Louis Amateis's low reliefs in their spandrels illustrate five roles deemed appropriate at the time for women—purity, faith, art, motherhood, and nursing. Ionic pilasters span the two main stories and their restraint is characteristic of the wall treatment, although the school's three-dimensional massing, with high, slate-covered hip roofs, is bolder, set off with two levels of copper-trimmed dormer windows.

NW42 Babcock-Macomb House

1912, Arthur B. Heaton. 3415 Massachusetts Ave. NW

Heaton's large number of Washington buildings, ranging from residences to firehouses, were most often a mixture of Colonial Revival and Arts and Crafts styles. His design for the brick Colonial Revival house for Kate W. Babcock was estimated to cost $24,500 by its builder James L. Parsons. Unusual was the organization of the facade's windows, five bays wide with the center three clustered together to form a triple entry, a motif very probably inspired by John R. Pope's nearby McCormick house (see NW48).

NW43 Embassy and Chancery of Norway

1930–1931, John J. Whelan. 3401 Massachusetts Ave. NW

The composition and details of Whelan's fifteen-room ambassador's residence and original small chancery (six main rooms) recall the late phase of European Renaissance

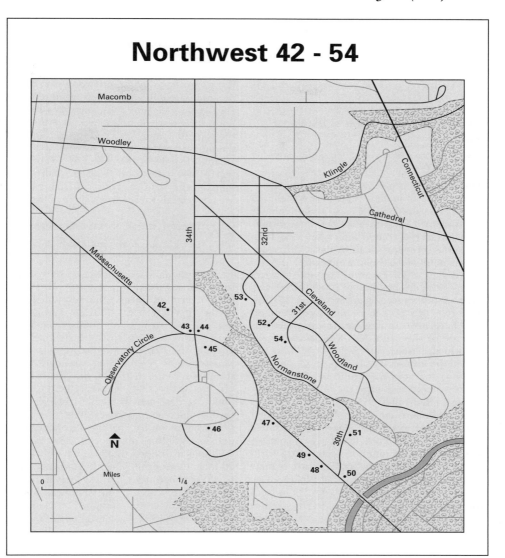

Northwest 42 - 54

architecture that had the most significance for America, the English Georgian that flourished and was exported to the colonies throughout the eighteenth century. The English Georgian model spawned an even greater number and variety of American versions in the early twentieth century; the decision of several foreign governments to build their Washington embassies in an American style of architecture rather than one associated with their own national traditions bespeaks its wide-ranging success. The embassy's second story is the principal floor of the three-story, five-bay mansion, its prominence signified by tall windows topped by markedly sculptural triangular pediments supported by side consoles. So much emphasis is given to the middle layer that the broken segmental pediment above the entrance, set into a low rusticated basement, is pushed up into the field above, the only feature that deviates from a strict adherence to eighteenth-century rules. Whelan's unpretentious design, pleasing proportions, and well-executed details indicate why the style had such force for so long: following the rules produced very high quality architecture. In 1941, while the Norwegian government and royal family were in exile, a new wing was added on 34th Street. Its central hall was hung with murals transferred from the Norwegian Pavilion at the New York World's Fair.

NW44 Apostolic Legation of the Papal State

1938–1939, Frederick V. Murphy. 3339 Massachusetts Ave. NW

The lavish Apostolic Legation (serving ecclesiastical, not diplomatic functions) was guided through its design and construction phases by Amleto Giovanni Cicognani, Apostolic Delegate to the United States between 1933 and 1958. Murphy, head of the architecture department at Catholic University, did his first design in 1932 and his second six years later, both unconventional modernized versions of Italian Renaissance palaces. His updating of this potent architectural tradition may have been in reaction to the overt historicism of the many Neo-Renaissance mansions in the immediate area, it may have reflected the influence of European modernism on him, or it may have reflected Cicognani's desire to express at once the modern mission of the Catholic church while referring to its strongly Roman heritage. Murphy designed the U-shaped complex to have a separately articulated main block facing Massachusetts Avenue, its self-contained rectangular form and division into three stories with regular vertical bays a traditional format followed by Renaissance urban palaces. His deviations from this formula are subtle. He gave the ground level and second floor equal prominence (rather than focusing most of the architectural attention on the second floor) in direct response to internal function. Wall articulation is linear rather than sculptural, with the alternation of narrow and wide stone courses on the tall "rusticated" basement very refined and centered on the plain door surround decorated simply with the papal tiara in a coat of arms. Framing on three sides of each second-story window is unusual, a treatment usually reserved for entries. Three ground-floor reception rooms—the Popes' Room, American Cardinals' Room, and Apostolic Delegates' Room—are decorated with portraits of the appropriate group. The second floor contains two large salons and a large

dining room. There are three chapels among the building's fifty rooms. The expense ($475,000) and opulence of the complex are not overtly expressed by the facades, faced with Indiana limestone treated with three different finishes. The slightly rough surface of the rusticated basement was achieved with abrasion wheels and rubs, smoother second-floor walls were sand rubbed, and those on the top story chat sawn. The three sides of the interior courtyard are surrounded by an arcaded loggia; in the center is a reproduction of the pine cone from the Cortile del Pigna at the Vatican. Formal Italian gardens are terraced down the steep slope at the rear.

NW45 United States Naval Observatory

1887–1893, Richard Morris Hunt. Observatory Circle. Massachusetts Ave. and 34th St. NW

In 1881 the navy selected the present 73-acre site for a new naval observatory, a large, high tract of ground outside the developed parts of the city. A circle 1,000 feet in diameter was laid out so that vibrations from future road traffic would not disturb delicate timekeeping and astronomical instruments. When Massachusetts Avenue was extended during the 1890s, it curved around the circle's northern perimeter. All of the large group of buildings designed by Richard Morris Hunt for the observatory survive. Some were purely utilitarian in nature, including a boiler house, dynamo building, and stables. The scientific buildings include a circular observatory for a 26-inch telescope and a multifunctional, four-part structure (the James Melville Gilliss Building) that appears to have been built in stages but was in fact designed as a unit and completed in 1892. Its central portion, a long two-story rectangle intersected by three projecting wings, contains administrative offices. A circular library with a low conical roof is attached at the east end; on the west a three-story tower rising above the main block is topped by a revolving dome housing a 12-inch Clark refractor telescope. To the west of the tower is a single-story gabled utilitarian looking building that was designed to house a transit telescope (which observes only stars that pass overhead along the meridian).

The simple geometries, severe architectural treatment, and disjointed nature of the Gilliss Building's design led Washington architect and critic Glenn Brown, writing in the *American Architect and Building News* in No-

NW45 United States Naval Observatory

vember 1892, to express disappointment with Hunt's building. Certainly its plainness and irregular planning do not initially suggest the style of America's leading exponent of French Beaux-Arts architecture, renowned for his lavish mansions. Yet Hunt's planning was highly rational, an enlargement of the operational dictates of the observatory. The two sections containing telescopes had to have separate foundations to ensure structural stability as well as to accommodate separate heating systems that would maintain the temperature of the outside air on the roof in order to minimize local atmospheric interference when the telescopes were in use. Hunt balanced the necessary western shed and tower with the library rotunda on the east, articulating each form to emphasize its distinct function in a sophisticated, albeit sober, architectural idiom. With each form Hunt expressed a different aspect of structure, varying its geometry, treatment of material, and architectural decoration.

The metal transit telescope shed is most distinct, visually linked to the rest of the complex only by rusticated stone foundations. The tower walls are battered, with solid corners erected of rock-faced marble, but belt courses, central tripartite window frames, entablature, and balustrade are smooth, sawn marble. Classical details alternate between very reduced to totally abstract. Doric pilasters used to divide and frame the windows are plain but recognizable. The entablature above the second-story windows distinguishes this level as most important; its frieze is composed of three narrow bands (used with Ionic and Corinthian orders) upon which Hunt superimposed a plain raised circular disk above each pilaster, a Doric feature. The cornice and balustrade are more boldly abstract, solid marble slabs with triangular, arched, and oblong shapes set side by side with pronounced seams to stress a different aspect of tectonic structure from the rough and smooth walls below.

The central administration building has the least surface decoration but is the most sculpturally composed, with interpenetrating volumes clearly demarcated. With the exception of the Ionic in antis porch above the south entrance, Doric pilasters are used to divide double windows. Those on the first floor carry their entablature moldings around three sides while those on the second story have moldings only on their front face. Their resulting abstract, linear profiles are yet another comment on the nature of architectural structure. Two distinctive abstract features of the tower and office block are combined on the library's walls. The Ionic-Doric frieze encircles the top of the rotunda, while wide superimposed profile pilasters cut through five horizontal bands. Despite their broken massing and textural variations, all three of the building's marble sections are horizontally bounded by two wide plain belt courses and a common cornice line. Hunt employed many strategies of avant-garde French rationalist thinking in his design for the Naval Observatory, the architectural expressions of which are rare in America.

NW46 Vice President's House

NW46 **Vice President's House**

(Superintendent's House; Admiral's House; Quarters A, United States Naval Observatory)

1891–1893, Leon E. Dessez. Observatory Circle

Failure of an attempt in 1966 to build a permanent official home for the vice president on 10 acres adjoining the Naval Observatory led to renovation in 1974 of the original superintendent's house on the observatory grounds. Dessez's sprawling two-story house is an appealing late Victorian mixture of Queen Anne and Colonial Revival stylistic features designed in the tradition of summer resort architecture, probably in response to its high (and then rural) location, where there were always breezes. The formal vocabulary—a semicircular, conical-capped tower protruding from its southeast corner; broad, squat dormers (originally with copper roofs) set low in the high hip roof—was primarily drawn from the Queen Anne tradition. However, the house's basically rectangular form and wraparound Colonial Revival porch with double Ionic columns that terminates at a porte-cochère set on the central cross axis (and main door) indicate the new stylistic tendency, as do a plethora of closely spaced windows on both stories and broad, plain entablatures throughout. In 1961, the red brick walls were painted white and the shutters were painted black, further colonializing its appearance. Dessez's very reductivist architectural vocabulary was probably a result of the same no-frills attitude that pervaded the Naval Observatory's scientific and administrative buildings.

NW47 **British Embassy**

1927–1931, Sir Edwin Lutyens. 3100 Massachusetts Ave. NW

The British Embassy is one of many overseas projects by the great English architect Sir Edwin Lutyens. The imposing U-shaped chancery faces Massachusetts Avenue and is attached to and set at right angles to the residence, the whole complex similar to a sprawling English country house in the eighteenth century set amidst extensive gardens. It was a style appropriate to express the official British presence in America, as it shared its genesis with the predominant eighteenth-century American style of architecture.

Lutyens's interpretation of traditional English forms, however, was one he had pioneered at the turn of the twentieth century, a period when classically derived, post-Renaissance architectural traditions were combined to formulate a new idiom. Lutyens fused the exuberant and sculptural qualities of the English Baroque with the basic forms, graceful proportions, and brick with stone trim of the English eighteenth century. Because his handling of these two formal traditions was informal and quirky in plan, massing, and detailing, multiple tensions were created, and then masterfully resolved in amusing and subtle, but always intellectually and visually satisfying, ways. An example visible from the street is the use of interlocking second-story window surrounds with the wide pilaster strips that separate them, juxtaposed to the archaeologically correct eighteenth-century doorway of the consulate entry. Lutyens's siting and organization of the British Embassy affords protection and privacy to its occupants but offers observers limited views of its architectural complexity and beauty. Its imposing scale is evident, but its richness is masked by the formality of the entrance sequence.

NW48 **Embassy of Brazil** (Robert and Katharine McCormick House)

c. 1908–1910, John Russell Pope. 3000 Massachusetts Ave. NW

Pope placed the McCormick house near the center of its triangular lot obliquely facing Whitehaven Street so that all the principal rooms would benefit from southeastern exposure. Hence its short end faces Massachusetts Avenue, with the entrance facade masked by trees and plantings that ensure privacy and relative quiet. The architect modeled the rectangular house (87 feet 8 inches by 49 feet 9 inches) on early Italian Renaissance models, with three of its five bays grouped in the center above a recessed loggia entrance and the single end bays occupying the middle of their respective fields. Stone balconies beneath second-story French windows at each end indicate the locations of the main public rooms—the dining room facing Massachusetts Avenue and the salon at the opposite end. Quoins outline all four corners of the building from the ground to the eaves. Pope's horizontal composition is similarly subtle, each floor diminishing in height with the fourth-floor attic windows compressed between up-

per stringcourse and the entablature and overhanging modillion cornice. Pope handled the walls with his characteristic restraint; quoins, window frames, stringcourses, and the wide frieze that separates the ground and first floor barely break the smooth limestone surfaces. (The limestone is a veneer over brick walls reinforced with steel beams.) The single entrance door and flanking windows are set within the wide loggia demarcated by two sets of Tuscan columns, the simplest of the classical orders to generate the most measured and tranquil architectural vocabulary.

NW49 **Chancery of Brazil**

1973, Olavo Redig de Campos. 3006 Massachusetts Ave. NW

The three-story floating gray glass box daringly cantilevered above a transparent lobby is actually suspended from roof trusses supported by a single row of interior columns. The elements of the structural system—the purity of its unbroken geometric form, dark monochromatic color, and regular but asymmetrical facade articulation by thin vertically and horizontally organized I-beams—are all canonical late modern architectural principles espoused and disseminated principally through the teachings and buildings of the German-born architect Ludwig Mies van der Rohe. His vision of an airy architecture where tectonic structure becomes decoration transformed American architecture from the 1940s

NW47 British Embassy

through the 1970s. The international nature of modernism—expressive of new industrial materials, structural systems, and life-styles in opposition to regional or national traditions—espoused by Mies and others during its formative years in the early twentieth century is realized by the nationality of the chancery's architect, a native of Brazil and head of the Department of Building for the Brazilian Foreign Ministry, who worked in association with Hans-Ullrich Scharnberg, a German-trained architect who had a Washington architectural practice during the 1970s.

NW50 Count Laszlo and Countess Gladys Vanderbilt Széchényi House (Maie H. Williams House)

1917, Clarke Waggaman. 1927, George N. Ray. 2929 Massachusetts Ave. NW

Waggaman's sophisticated reinterpretation of Neoclassical traditions in the cubic block of the Williams house is evident in the composition and details of its simplified forms. The relationship of the windows—voids punched directly into brick walls—to two limestone belt courses that divide the house into the three stories changes on each floor, as window sizes and shapes vary according to internal function. The interplay on the limestone frontispiece of a very abstract rendition of a Palladian window above the entrance with the simple but academically correct porch below is one of sunken versus projecting elements and a nearly solid masonry wall segment above visually supported by a skeletal wall and columned porch below. The single-story ballroom addition to the north, designed in 1927 by Waggaman's partner George Ray, is visu-

ally connected to the tightly composed main block by replication on a smaller scale of the house's cube and retention of its lower belt course to encircle it.

NW51 Scott B. Appleby, Jr., House

1925, Laurence P. Johnston. 2501 30th St. NW

This stately late Beaux-Arts mansion was erected in limestone by the Metropolitan Construction Company for $40,000, a significant sum in 1925. Its stylistic references to late Italian Renaissance palace forms, a two-story, flat-roofed rectangular block, are reinforced by the structural vocabulary of a rusticated ground story, quoins outlining second-story edges (projecting wings on the front and sides that are two bays wide), and a balustrade around the building's entire perimeter. Other strongly Neo-Renaissance aspects are the regularly spaced rectangular windows framed by segmental pediments on the ground story and flat lintels on the second story and the Palladian window above the entrance. The architect's statement of the house's individual character is most evident on the side elevations, where narrow two-story projections set close to the corners read as bay windows (lit from the sides by very narrow openings) when viewed from the ends but as extensions of the house's main volumes when viewed from the front.

NW52 Charles E. and Anita Eckles House

1928, Porter and Lockie. 4 Thompson Circle NW

Tudor Revival mansions, the twentieth-century equivalent of the English-inspired Gothic Revival of a century earlier, were composed following similar picturesque principles but were often larger, more formally and spatially complex, and combined many materials in their construction. Porter and Lockie's composition of a long, steep-gabled rectangle, which is oriented parallel to the road and intersected by cross gables of varying dimensions, originated in late nineteenth-century British transformations of traditional native house forms. However his British precedents, such as the work of C. F. A. Voysey, concentrated almost exclusively on interpenetrating abstract geometric masses rather than on surface details. For Porter and Lockie such formal vocabulary demanded appropriate surface articulation and materials in order to re-create the look and feel of an "olde Englishe" manor house. Irregularity and asymmetry were fundamental: wood half timbering was set in a stone gable at one end and in a different pattern on a stucco wall at the other. Uncoursed blocks of stone in shades of gray and brown, varicolored bricks not just for the chimney but set haphazardly into the stone walls, and gray slate covering all slanted surfaces rather than just the roofs resulted in an impressive range of textures and colors already consciously aged at the time they were assembled.

NW53 **Arthur S. Henning House**

1932, James W. Adams. 2728 32nd St. NW

A large group of early twentieth-century mansions is nestled among the steep slopes and winding roadways of Massachusetts Heights, a narrow corridor between 34th Street and Massachusetts Avenue to the east of the Naval Observatory that was first developed in 1911. Like their more modest contemporaneous counterparts in many other areas of the city, these mansions ranged widely in style and materials. Although most of its neighbors were inspired by English architectural prototypes, none is as intensely English as the Arthur S. Henning House, where the complementary relationship between the gardens and sprawling residence is reminiscent of small Edwardian estates. With an end wall facing the street and the main entrance masked by a pergola, glimpses of discrete parts of the picturesquely composed, L-shaped house were planned to create the impression of an old and venerable estate slowly built over time. The wing farthest from the street has a conical tower set in front of the main rectangle, both constructed in Elizabethan black and white exposed half timbering. Set at a right angle to it is a gabled, two-story wing with a simple scalloped bargeboard in brick and a large end chimney; the rough texture of the walls comes more from the intentionally sloppy mortar joints than from the surfaces of the bricks. Irregular, slightly curved terracotta tiles that cover all the roofs contribute to the sense of the house's great age, as their varied color modulations harmonize well with the multitoned bricks. Diamond-quarreled casement windows finish the effect: a romantic and sophisticated, rustic and vernacular stage set for gracious living.

NW54 **Dr. W. Calhoun Sterling House**

1927, Horace Peaslee. 2618 31st St. NW

An arch designed by H. H. Richardson that once surrounded Henry Adams's kitchen window has been much narrowed and now outlines the main door at 2618 31st Street; the entrance arch of the Adams house (slightly narrowed) now frames the garage door. These elements were salvaged when the adjoining Hay and Adams houses, built 1884–1885 on Lafayette Square, were demolished in 1927 to make way for the hotel that bears their names. Together these arches were determining factors in the design of Horace Peaslee's picturesque one-and-a-half-story suburban residence, where housing the automobile is at least symbolically more important than providing for humans. His compact, asymmetrical composition is dominated by steep, slate-covered gabled and hip roofs that shelter the light brown stuccoed walls and blend nicely with the intricately carved sandstone of the Richardsonian fragments.

NW55 **German Chancery**

1964, Egon Eiermann. 4645 Reservoir Rd. NW

The seemingly simple design and construction of the International Style glass box led to so many bad imitations in America that it is difficult for many to appreciate the lyrical beauty that could be achieved with this type. Much of the excitement of the best of early German modernism, which depended on the precise detailing, exquisite proportioning, and resilience of exposed steel frames holding large expanses of window glass, can be experienced at the German Chancery. The prominent German architect Egon Eiermann drew upon his native Bauhaus and Werkbund design and craft traditions to mix the

NW55 German Chancery

NW56 Mount Vernon College, Florence Hollis Hand Chapel

Responding further to the residential neighborhood, Eiermann provided hidden parking for one hundred cars. He minimized the chancery's scale by dematerializing its mass through an exterior steel and wood armature enclosing a series of rectangular boxes (50 feet by 300 feet), terraced perpendicular to the site's declivity, that are one-and-a-half stories near the street but six stories at the building's central core.

NW56 Mount Vernon College, Florence Hollis Hand Chapel

1971, Hartman-Cox. 2100 Foxhall Rd. NW

In 1968 the Washington firm Hartman-Cox devised a master plan for the small, densely wooded campus of Mount Vernon College, where all the previous buildings from the 1940s were in a bland Neo-Georgian style. Three of their proposed buildings were erected, the gate house at the W Street entrance, two sections of a dormitory complex, and a nondenominational, 300-seat chapel that also serves for public musical and dramatic productions. In all three buildings the architects responded sensitively to existing natural and man-made conditions, scaling their brick buildings to the earlier structures and nestling them into the rolling or gullied landscape.

Siting the chapel across the axis of a small ravine is particularly successful, as views from the single-volume interior scan the meandering streambed. Entry into the multifaceted, shed-roofed form is asymmetrical, with the door set on the upper corner high on the chapel's facade. Experience of the central space is delayed by the long staircase that winds down to ground level. The architects took the most salient site conditions—steepness and sinuousness—and slowly introduced architectural order. It is completed in the symmetrical auditorium, which is dominated by the space frame of the shed roof. The architects used a rectangular module to great effect, playing vertical doorways off against horizontal balconies, glass walls, and the individual units of the roof. There is little direct sunlight; rather it is reflected off the smooth white walls of the space frame from downward-angled windows. Muted and diffused interior lighting conditions thus respond to the light outside that filters down through surrounding trees.

mechanistic and industrial with the natural and romantic to create an architecturally and metaphorically complex building perfectly suited to its difficult sloping site and not unsympathetic to its residential neighborhood.

In the early 1960s Eiermann stood at the vanguard of architects who wished to invigorate modern architecture by combining structural and decorative elements. In the German Chancery, designed and constructed near the end of his career, he explored the interplay between enclosure and openness in which the decorative and colorful external framing has affinities with Victorian houses.

Northwest 55-60

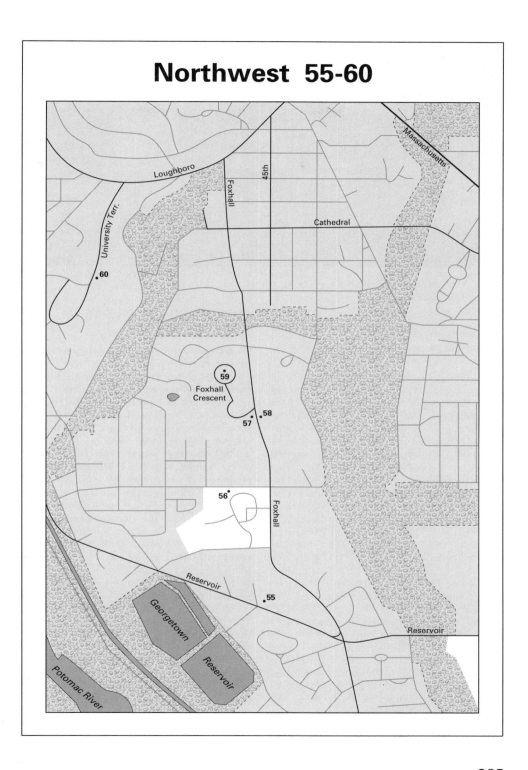

NW58 David Lloyd Kreeger House

NW57 **Embassy of Belgium** (Anna Thomson Dodge House)

1930–1931, Horace Trumbauer. 2300 Foxhall Rd. NW

Philadelphia architect Horace Trumbauer designed four Washington mansions, the last toward the end of his career for Anna Thomson Dodge in 1930. Most of Trumbauer's numerous opulent American palaces were inspired by classic examples of late seventeenth- and early eighteenth-century French models, including Versailles. He occasionally worked in partnership with French architects and frequently quoted directly from famous French prototypes. Pierre Lassurance's Hôtel de Rothelin of 1700 at 101 Rue de Grenelle in Paris provided Trumbauer with the frontispiece for the Dodge house. The three compressed center bays of the exceptionally wide nine-bay facade replicate the two-story Ionic portico of Lassurance's composition. Trumbauer repeats the double engaged columns and pilasters that frame the portico, the arched French doors on the ground story, and arched entablature above the second-story central arched window. Unlike many Washington mansions inspired by similar prototypes, Trumbauer's house has elaborate pedimental sculpture in imitation of its original model. Fine quality limestone and finely tuned proportional relationships among the portico elements themselves, and the portico's correlation with the overall facade, result in a building with elegance and grace that approaches that of its famous model.

NW58 **David Lloyd Kreeger House**

1966–1969, Philip Johnson. 2401 Foxhall Rd. NW

Washington's premier modern mansion was designed to incorporate museum-scaled spaces for the display of the client's outstanding collection of nineteenth- and twentieth-century paintings and sculpture. Johnson created a lyrical modernization of a Roman villa, complete with sculpture terraces, pools, and extensive gardens, indoor and out. Set behind a 435-foot, rough-textured travertine wall that faces Foxhall Road, the Kreeger house is composed of asymmetrically arranged, groin-vaulted cubes with travertine walls facing the street and glass ones that open views onto the wooded 5.5-acre site. Articulation of structure—whether the travertine-covered reinforced concrete frame, the shallow vaults that cover each 22-foot module, or the baluster-like posts of the steel trusses that separate each vault—is paramount and complements the clarity of the plan.

Art galleries on all three levels do not invade the private areas but are adjacent to them, free-flowing spaces as opposed to the contained cubes of family rooms. Walls of the main gallery, a two-story great hall that rises to 25 feet, are covered with cream-colored carpet to blend with the travertine yet facilitate changing the paintings. Johnson's melding of historicism and modernism results in a romantic yet functional house in the grand manner, where the same module, same clerestory lighting, and same tentlike vaults shelter intimate and public spaces alike.

NW59 **Foxhall Crescents**

1982–1986, Arthur Cotton Moore. Foxhall Crescent Dr.

The 26 homes that constitute Foxhall Crescents are clustered on 25 acres that formerly were the Nelson Rockefeller estate. The developer's initial plan was for a subdivision of 150 houses to cover the entire site. Moore's scheme to leave a 30-foot broad band of trees around the perimeter of his single curved street that terminates in a circle won neighborhood approval. Consequently the large houses (each about 4,000 square feet) nearly fill each lot, and Moore's overall design for seven different models responded particularly to their propinquity. All have curved facades, some convex and some concave, for unlike most expensive suburban houses they sit very close to the sidewalk. Perhaps it was their quasi-urban, quasi-suburban setting that prompted Moore to think of them in terms of fragmented English crescents. Their Postmodern stylistic vocabulary is English Regency in origin, with variegated light brown brick walls (ubiquitous in London) on the second floors sandwiched between rusticated limestone ground stories and plain limestone entablatures. Moore's Mannerist reinterpretation of historical sources simultaneously extols and mimics them.

NW60 **Jane Couser Barton House** (John C. Dreier House)

1977, Hugh Newell Jacobsen. 2927 University Terrace NW

The Dreier house is composed of four staggered, single-story Cape Cod cottages (recalling the smallest houses in the game of Mo-

NW60 Jane Couser Barton House (John C. Dreier House)

nopoly), pristine in the clarity of their separate geometries as well as the starkness of their black and white materials. Although anchored on the ridge of a steep incline, from the street the house seems to hover slightly above grade, as the walls meet the barely elevated decks or the ground at sharp right angles. Jacobsen's definition of a house as a series of interconnected rooms, each clearly expressed formally on the exterior, is fostered in this case by his choice of a vernacular prototype. This compartmentalization and fusion of exterior form and interior space is a heritage of his education in the 1950s at Yale University under Louis Kahn.

Organization of the units along a diagonal was dictated by the triangular site but turned to advantage in the lighting of each room, where a single window, or sliding glass door, suffices for each facade. Jacobsen's own structural vocabulary, the line formed by hidden gutters or triangular transom windows set flush with wall surfaces, is critical to his absolute mastery of proportion.

NW59 Foxhall Crescents

Georgetown (GT)

Antoinette J. Lee

THE BUILDINGS OF GEORGETOWN CAN BE FOLLOWED IN A time line from the oldest along the shores of the Potomac River to later development on the steep heights as far north as Dumbarton Oaks, Montrose Park, and Oak Hill Cemetery. Founded in 1751, forty years before Washington, Georgetown was linked to the new capital by a bridge over the crevice of Rock Creek at Pennsylvania Avenue that connected to Georgetown's M Street, a major east-west commercial thoroughfare. From the waterfront, Wisconsin Avenue carried commercial development northward. The prosperous merchants of the late eighteenth and early nineteenth centuries built large freestanding Federal style houses on high ground along Prospect and N streets. Farther north, substantial estates were established. As Georgetown became urbanized, detached and attached houses filled the empty lots and surrounded the large estates. Constructed from the middle to the end of the nineteenth century, these houses were in picturesque Italian Villa and Romanesque Revival styles.

Many of the row houses of the Romanesque Revival period resembled those on Capitol Hill and in Dupont Circle. The basic house form consisted of a side entrance and bay window ornamented with corbeled brick and terracotta and cast-iron stairs and railings. At the beginning of the twentieth century, simple red brick row houses with porches, a form found throughout much of the city, made their way into Georgetown.

Georgetown had flourished as a port city from the Revolutionary War to the end of the eighteenth century. Its location at the head of the tidewater secured its strength as an international trade center. Its prosperity, along with that of its sister city, Alexandria, on the Virginia side of the river, contributed to George Washington's selection of this part of the Potomac River for the capital.

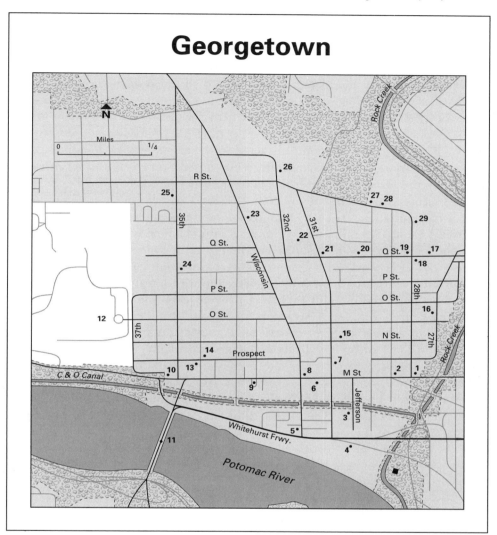

Georgetown

The L'Enfant Plan, however, left "George Town" just outside the boundary of the new city, and it thus developed and retained its own street system. During the capital city's early years, Georgetown provided fully developed commercial and social services for its residents, and it continued to operate as a separate entity until it merged with Washington in 1871.

As a port, Georgetown declined by the 1820s, as the tobacco trade in that area became exhausted and as Baltimore became the center of the flour trade. Construction of a bridge over the Potomac River at 14th Street added to siltation, also diminishing its suitability as a port. Although completion of the Chesapeake and Ohio Canal in 1850 spurred the local economy, it did not compensate for the eclipse of the port facilities. In the 1880s, a far superior harbor was created in Southwest Washington, and by the early twentieth century, the Georgetown waterfront was devoted to industrial uses, such as a power plant, meat-processing plant, and the warehousing of construction materials. Working-class white and black residents occupied much of the housing, particularly on low ground close to the river.

In the 1920s, at the urging of resident activists, a zoning amendment limited the size of new construction in Georgetown. In the following decade, with an influx of affluent new residents attracted to the area's historic buildings, many houses were remodeled dramatically, while others were restored to an earlier period by the removal of latter-day accretions. Inspired by efforts to preserve the old sections of Charleston and New Orleans, Georgetown civic leaders sought protective legislation. In 1950, Congress designated the area a historic district.

Today, Georgetown is a major center of employment as well as a fashionable residential neighborhood. Its shops and dining establishments attract large crowds during the after-work hours. The major commercial routes of M Street and Wisconsin Avenue are lined with restored and recent but compatible construction. The most recent infill buildings provide examples of Postmodern and contextual architecture. Away from these well-trodden streets, residential Georgetown reveals itself in its variety of housing. Around the periphery are large institutions and public facilities. Georgetown University is to the west. To the north are the old reservoir site now occupied by the Georgetown Public Library, Dumbarton Oaks, Montrose Park, and Oak Hill Cemetery. Completing the eastern boundary of an area that has retained a distinctive cultural identity for more than two centuries, Rock Creek Park serves as a natural green link to the rest of the city.

GT01 Corcoran at Georgetown

1889, Office of the Building Inspector. 1986, Arthur Cotton Moore/Associates. 28th and M streets NW

Composed of an 1889 red brick public school, a fine and typical example of the work of the Office of the Building Inspector, together with a mews of town houses to the east and a mixed-use structure along M Street by Arthur Cotton Moore/Associates, this complex is a fine example of adaptive use of a surplus school combined with compatible new construction on the remains of the schoolyard.

In the transformation of the site, the exterior of the old Corcoran School was restored and embellished with new entrance approaches, while the interior was rebuilt as offices for the Hotel Employees and Restaurant Employees International Union. The town house mews to the rear of the school, complete with circular towers, appears to be an enlarged version of the post–Civil War row houses found in Georgetown and elsewhere in the District. The mixed-use structure fronting on M Street is devoted to shops and offices. A portion of the rear serves as residential units. In design, this structure echoes the towers and basket-weave brickwork of the Corcoran School. The courtyard between the town house mews and the M Street building is a virtual stage set of design motifs drawn from the Capitol and the Mall, including L'Enfant's cascade, the McMillan Plan's reflecting pool, and a diminutive colonnade. This group of objects, which can only be described as disconnected architectural models embedded in concrete, defies conventional explanations as to purpose or meaning and in this respect is typical of the recent work of Arthur Cotton Moore/Associates.

GT01 Corcoran at Georgetown

GT02 **Building**

1980, Martin and Jones. 2833 M St. NW

One of the earliest Postmodern buildings in the District of Columbia, this mixed-use structure attempts to address its surroundings and blaze a path between colonial and Federal styles. By means of an irregular roofline and recessed elevations, the building differentiates the commercial and residential functions. The commercial space is announced by a single asymmetrically placed classical column and entablature, a nod to the Biograph Theatre to the east. This motif is repeated at the corner and on the 29th Street side at the entrance to the apartments above. Oversized fanlight windows are punched into the gables, and a bowl-shaped bite has been taken out of the parapet at the third floor on M Street. While providing an unusual treatment, the firm of Martin and Jones created a modern structure compatible with a complicated array of architectural neighbors.

GT03 **The Foundry**

1973–1976, ELS Design Group; Arthur Cotton Moore/Associates. 1055 Thomas Jefferson St. NW

Imbued with a desire to help rebuild cities and with a belief that good design yields a healthier bottom line, the Inland Steel Development Corporation purchased the Foundry site in 1970. The ELS Design Group of Berkeley, California, and Arthur Cotton Moore/Associates conducted feasibility studies and developed the design, along with Sasaki Associates, the landscape architecture firm, and Washington architect Vlastimil Koubek, who oversaw construction.

The original setting directly south of the C & O Canal was not inspiring. A sand and gravel plant stood on the site and to the east was the mid-nineteenth-century Duvall Foundry Building, which had withstood various uses including that of a veterinary hospital for canal mules. The Duvall Foundry Building was moved a hundred feet to allow construction of a new foundation. The new building was set back from the C & O Canal with a large outdoor public space. A mall occupies the first two levels of the new building, and shops line an internal "street" that cuts through the space at angles. Five floors of offices occupy the upper levels. The separation of functions is expressed in the jutting and angling back of the exterior walls. Outdoor rooms and terraces mark the junctures. The idealism and hard-nosed business sense that carried the Foundry project to completion produced an organic, orderly, model project for the Georgetown waterfront. Few subsequent developments in the area have been as successful in reconciling these potentially contradictory attitudes.

GT04 **Washington Harbour**

1987, Arthur Cotton Moore/Associates. 3000 K St. NW

Washington Harbour ranks among the city's most loved and hated new buildings. On the waterfront between 30th and 31st streets, it connects in its monumentality with the Potomac River, the Kennedy Center, and Watergate, rather than with Georgetown. For this project, Moore abandoned his usual red brick contextual palette and opted for a tan brick

and limestone Postmodern mix of surfaces, shapes, and decorative elements, producing a seemingly forced juxtaposition of elements.

The most admirable aspect of Washington Harbour is its plan. The project includes four structures, two on either side of Thomas Jefferson Street, which defines the center line and concludes in a monumental elliptical plaza and fountain. Virginia Avenue extended bisects the project on a roughly east-west thoroughfare lined with shops. A wooden boardwalk runs along the river's edge. With this site plan, a strong sense of place is created in what was formerly a postindustrial wasteland. The design, which repeats motifs from previous projects by Moore such as a limestone arch that had appeared in the rehabilitation of the Old Post Office in the Federal Triangle (see FT01, p. 169), can be viewed as the architect's effort at autobiography.

GT05 **Dodge Center**

1974–1975, Hartman-Cox. 1000–1006 Wisconsin Ave. NW

Another new development in the waterfront area, this aggressively geometric project conformed to a tightly circumscribed set of design conditions. Hartman-Cox designed the Dodge (now Waterfront) Center to wrap around three late eighteenth- and early nineteenth-century warehouses, which took on the appearance of a retaining wall for the new development. The three buildings, in-

GT04 Washington Harbour

cluding the Dodge warehouse, were erected on the foundations of an old stone building thought to have been a tobacco rolling house, and typify the utilitarian design of much of Georgetown's waterfront architecture. The new building, constructed of reinforced concrete and brick, is composed of two major blocks—the smaller facing Wisconsin Avenue and the larger facing the Whitehurst Freeway. The upper floors of each section are stepped back to form balconies. On Wisconsin Avenue, this setback minimizes the height differential between new and historic buildings. Along K Street, the building appears to be pulling back from the ill effects of the Whitehurst Freeway, which forms the project's southern boundary. The silhouette of Dodge Center marked significant change in Georgetown building projects from highly contextual designs to those that assert their individual presence.

GT06 **Canal Square**

1970, Arthur Cotton Moore. 31st and M streets NW

A pioneering example of the adaptive use of an old, spacious warehouse structure, Canal Square served as a model for similar structures in the nation's worn out industrial centers. New construction also wove the old into the new in a compatible fabric. At completion, it was the largest building effort in Georgetown since early in the century.

Canal Square is barely visible from M or 31st streets, although access is announced with marked passageways. The project is best seen from the interior of the block. Here a plaza serves as the centerpiece for the warehouse at one side and for the new building that

encircles the rest of the site. Shops and restaurants are housed on the lower floors, with offices above. Walkways provide easy pedestrian access to the shops; elevator towers serve the offices. The new section of the complex displays glass ribbons of windows and red brick walls.

Moore's treatment of the warehouse, the first of his contextual projects in Georgetown, established an approach to adaptive use that, while efficient, popular, and profitable, robbed the historic structure of its characteristic detail. In a number of cases, including this one, historic buildings were shorn of untidy and hard-to-maintain details, cleaned up, and presented as viable alternatives to modern buildings.

GT07 **Georgetown Custom House and Post Office**

1857–1858, Ammi B. Young. 1221 31st St. NW

On upward sloping land just north of M Street sits the Georgetown Custom House and Post Office, one of several dozen federal buildings designed by Supervising Architect Ammi B. Young in the 1850s for emerging cities nationwide. Young earlier had designed Boston's Greek Revival Custom House and customhouses for Norfolk and Cincinnati. For the rest of the 1850s, when building construction accelerated with the growth of cities, economical and standardized designs became increasingly attractive. In his development of this approach, Young turned to the London clubhouses of Sir Charles Barry for inspiration. Based on the Italian palazzo of the high Renaissance, especially the Palazzo Farnese in

Rome, these elegant buildings provided the simple rectangular massing and refined Renaissance detail that Young then adapted with such discretion to his own thoroughly American ends. Along with this stylistic freshness, however, the building is also distinguished for another and equally important innovation. The interior construction utilizes the then recently introduced fireproof method of iron posts and beams, with segmental brick vaults between the latter. This revolutionary technique was, in fact, used in all Young's customhouses and post offices. From then on it became standard for all federal buildings, and it remained as such until the introduction of the steel frame late in the nineteenth century.

By the time Georgetown received a federal customhouse, the port city had existed for a century; its scale of operation compared to that of emerging cities such as Chicago and Cleveland, which also received a federal building in that decade. The Barryesque palace design of the Georgetown customhouse was replicated elsewhere, as in Galena, Illinois.

The appeal of the Georgetown Custom House and Post Office rests in the subtle differentiation between the carved granite trim and the flat granite walls. The five-bay, two-story design is ornamented with granite window lintels, sills, and trim as well as projecting granite stringcourses and a rough cut stone water table. An elegant granite cornice with simple moldings and a delicate dentil band crowns the building. The structure rises from a granite terrace, which distinguishes the building from its immediate neighbors. While not as imposing as federal buildings closer to the city center, the Georgetown Custom House and Post Office nevertheless serves as a dignified reminder of Young's contribution during the early years of the Office of the Supervising Architect and of Georgetown's once active port.

GT08 **Farmers and Mechanics Branch, Riggs Bank**

1921–1922, Marsh and Peter. 1201 Wisconsin Ave. NW

Situated at Wisconsin Avenue and M Street, the Riggs Bank responds to the topography and the tempo of the place and is one of the most effective corner buildings in the District of Columbia. Here, Wisconsin Avenue con-

GT08 Farmers and Mechanics Branch, Riggs Bank

tinues its steep rise to the north, and on M Street, commercial activity, no longer following a strictly linear path, fans in four directions. The building addresses the corner with its dramatic gold-leafed dome crowned by a lantern. Under the dome, at the building cornice, a clock, with a design of garlands and swags beneath, surveys the scene. One enters at the corner between Corinthian columns. On the flanks of the building colossal pilasters articulate the vertical piers; between the piers the first- and second-story windows are separated by decorative spandrels to form recessed curtain walls.

The local firm that designed the building was also responsible for the admirable Evening Star Building (see DE24, p. 197) on Pennsylvania Avenue and a small number of Beaux-Arts commercial structures, but it was best known for its residential and public school commissions.

GT09 **Georgetown Market**

1865, unknown. 3276 M St. NW

This modest red brick market house extends more than 500 feet south from its narrow three-bay front on M Street. The market was constructed in 1865 on an earlier stone foundation; in the 1930s, after farmers had stopped using it as a traditional produce market, the building became a grocery and later an auto parts store. In the late 1970s, it was resurrected as an upscale market to serve Georgetown residents. At that time, the "stage set" interior contained a mezzanine restaurant overlooking a choreographed group of sellers offering produce and meats as well as "con-

GT09 Georgetown Market

diments" and "ready-made hors d'oeuvres to full meals." This experiment with a transformed market collapsed because of competition from surrounding commercial establishments; it drew throngs of visitors but few residents.

The red brick market structure is instructive nonetheless for its scale and location, recalling the homey presupermarket neighborhood whose residents sought daily provisions at establishments along M Street and Wisconsin Avenue. The one-story common bond red brick structure is notable for its brick pilasters that separate round-arch window openings along the side elevations. A similar treatment can also be seen at Eastern Market on Capitol Hill, where the brickwork is more ornate.

GT10 Capitol Traction Company Union Station

1895–1897, Waddy B. Wood. 3600 M St. NW

At the western end of M Street, where the city's streetcar lines joined those that ran through the rolling hills of Northern Virginia, this commanding structure was built to store streetcars. Whereas the car barn on Capitol Hill is horizontal (see CN52, p. 269), this one is vertical. Architect Waddy B. Wood designed both car barns, which reveal not only his understanding of the transportation technology of the times but also his ability to use appropriate architectural forms expressive of function.

The most prominent feature is the 140-foot-high brick clock tower, once containing passenger elevators, that rises from a four-story brick and stone base. The main part of the building housed four systems of tracks,

streetcar offices, and passenger waiting rooms. It reaches north to Prospect Street, where a small entrance pavilion four floors above M Street is announced with red brick end turrets projecting through and above the red tile roof. A major addition in 1910–1911, prompted by the need to accommodate larger streetcars, extended the original building along M Street.

Sheathed in stone blocks that suggest strength, the first floor is punctuated with large round-arch openings that admitted the streetcars. Stone medallions carved with "1895" and "CT Co." adorn the building. The vigorous Richardsonian imagery is particularly expressive of the building's dynamic function.

GT11 Francis Scott Key Bridge

1917–1923, Nathan C. Wyeth. Potomac River between Georgetown and Rosslyn

Connecting the District of Columbia with Virginia across the Potomac River, the Francis Scott Key Bridge is one of the vital segments of the economic dreams of the city's early promoters. Key Bridge replaced the 1833–1834 Aqueduct Bridge, which was part of the man-made water-based system linking Alexandria to the Chesapeake and Ohio Canal. The Aqueduct Bridge enabled products in canal boats to cross the Potomac River without being unloaded into other vessels. After the Civil War, a roadway replaced the boat channel.

As streetcar and later automobile traffic proliferated by the early twentieth century, Aqueduct Bridge was deemed inadequate.

GT10 Capitol Traction Company Union Station

GT11 Francis Scott Key Bridge

Architect Nathan C. Wyeth designed the new bridge, named in honor of Francis Scott Key, whose house stood near the District terminus of the bridge. (Key's house was demolished during construction of the Whitehurst Freeway.) The reinforced concrete bridge reaches across the Potomac River in five large segmental arches in a manner reminiscent of the great viaducts of ancient Rome. Each spandrel is open ribbed, allowing for the repetition of the arched design in the structure itself and creating a light, lacy pattern. The project was an architectural and engineering feat of the day, as well as an important example of Wyeth's work.

GT12 **Georgetown University**

1792–present, Smithmeyer and Pelz; John Carl Warnecke; Hugh Newell Jacobsen; Mariani and Associates; Daniel F. Tully Associates; Metcalf and Associates. Bounded by Reservoir Road, 37th St., M St., and Glover Archbold Parkway

Founded in 1789, Georgetown is the oldest Catholic university in the United States. Since 1805, the Society of Jesus has assumed responsibility for the school. The university occupies a commanding site on the Potomac Palisades. The oldest buildings are on the highest points, while later structures occupy the slopes and lowlands. The plan for the campus revolved around the "old quadrangle" with Healy Hall forming the eastern boundary. The medical school–hospital complex forms the northern rim of the campus along Reservoir Road. Unusual features of the university include an astronomical observatory and a cemetery.

Healy Hall (GT12.1), the most compelling architectural work, was designed by Smithmeyer and Pelz. Construction began in 1877, but interior details were not completed until 1909. Its 200-foot-high central clock spire juts into the sky, echoed by a secondary spire rising from the building's southwest corner. Of dark gray Potomac gneiss ashlar, the building forms a somber, stately presence on the campus. Sandstone trim, green copper gargoyles, and a polychromatic roof provide light accents to the exterior. Interior spaces of interest include Gaston Hall, an auditorium adorned with wall paintings and elaborate plasterwork. The recently restored Riggs Library is distinctive for its four tiers of cast-iron stacks.

The rear of Healy Hall is built of red brick to harmonize with the oldest campus buildings. Old North Building (GT12.2), forming one boundary of the old quadrangle, was begun in 1792. Its red brick is marked by a central five-bay projecting pavilion, a one-story wooden porch, and belt courses between the stories. The small Chapel of the Sacred Heart (GT12.3), on the west, a row of red brick academic buildings, and the old Infirmary, on the south, complete the old quadrangle.

In contrast to this tightly enclosed space, the quadrangle facing 37th Street is open and spacious. The front of Healy Hall forms part of the quadrangle's western boundary. The remainder and the northern boundary are formed by Copley and White-Gravenor halls

GT12.1 Georgetown University, Healy Hall

GT12.9 Georgetown University, Village C Student Housing

(GT12.4), both stone-faced Collegiate Gothic structures that complement Healy Hall. To the south is John Carl Warnecke's Lauinger Library (GT12.5), completed in 1970. Constructed of gray granite aggregate poured in place, the modern library is given vertical emphasis with extended stair towers and supporting columns.

Modernity and energy conservation characterized the university building program of the late 1970s and the early 1980s. Daniel F. Tully Associates of Melrose, Massachusetts, designed an underground gymnasium (GT12.6) over which the football field and track were constructed. This innovative structure, built in 1977–1979, offered savings in real estate and energy consumption. The dramatically modern Intercultural Center (GT12.7) was another exercise in expanded educational facilities with energy-saving potential, supported by funds from the Department of Energy. Metcalf and Associates designed this classroom building in the early 1980s with a large, sloping solar-paneled roof facing south.

Postmodernism is represented at the university by newer student housing projects. Hugh Newell Jacobsen designed Village B Student Housing (GT12.8) on 37th Street, a residential area particularly sensitive to the impact of university facilities. The U-shaped project resembles typical Georgetown low-rise Italianate row houses "with Federal undertones." At the western edge of the campus, Mariani and Associates designed the sprawling Village C Student Housing project (GT12.9), a three-building complex that hugs the base of the hill on which the original

quadrangle is located. The red brick structure is arranged with stepped elevations and dormered rooflines, contextually sympathetic stone trim, bay windows, and round-arch doorways. The most recent addition to the campus is the multipurpose Postmodern Leavey Center (GT12.10), intended to accommodate traditional student center activities as well as those associated with a profit-oriented conference center. Designed by Mariani and Associates, the Leavey Center has at its base a three-story garage below a student activities level. A landscaped flat roof lies above, and two towers contain offices and hotel rooms. From a distance, the towers make the Leavey Center immediately recognizable.

GT13 Prospect House

1788–1793, unknown. 3508 Prospect St. NW

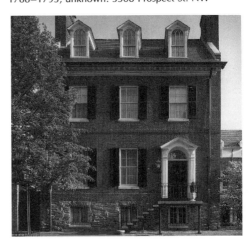

Prospect House is typical of the houses that prosperous Georgetown merchants built for themselves in the late eighteenth century. It represents as well the building traditions of the era when lot sizes and the technical capabilities of building elements significantly affected design. Thus, residences such as Prospect House exhibit a planar quality with decorative details seemingly pasted on rather than integrated.

Despite design limitations, Prospect House exhibits an urban sophistication appropriate to a thriving port city. It is of Flemish bond brick on a raised rubble basement. The entrance is trimmed with reeded pilasters, a wooden pediment, and a semicircular leaded-glass fanlight. The verticality of the door, window openings, dormer windows, and end chimneys is balanced by the horizontal water table, brick belt course between the first and second stories, and the carved wooden cornice. The bay window and veranda on the east as well as the service wing are later additions. Stately Prospect House served as an official federal government guest quarters from 1949 to 1951.

GT14 **John Thomson Mason House**

1797–1798, unknown. 3425 Prospect St. NW

The Mason house, also known as "Quality Hill," is one of the largest of the late eighteenth-century houses that grace Prospect Street, home to Georgetown's upper class. Its first occupant, John Thomson Mason, came from a prominent family with substantial landholdings in Maryland and Virginia, and this house provided him with an appropriate setting for socializing with the leaders of the young nation.

Like many of its contemporaries in Georgetown, the design of the Mason house was in part determined by the nature of the building materials. The house is fashioned of brick (now painted) laid out in Flemish bond. Decorative detailing includes keystone window lintels, a molded water table, a modillion cornice, and dormer windows. A carved wooden door surround barely adds a third dimension to the planar wall surfaces. During a major restoration of 1942–1944, the arch in the center hall, salvaged from the Francis Scott Key House, was added, as was flooring in the vestibule, reportedly from a historic house on Capitol Hill.

GT15 **Wheatley Town Houses**

1854–1859, unknown. 3041–3045 N St. NW

This row of three dwellings was constructed over a period of four years. The first section, 3045 N Street, apparently was for the owner, Francis Wheatley, who built the adjacent houses on the east, 3041 and 3043 N Street, by 1859. Unlike the nearly flat facades of earlier row houses, these are ornamented with polychromatic or sculptural detail. Tall, narrow windows bestow a strong sense of verticality. The first house bears details notable in Georgetown. Each window presents a flat geometric design made of sandstone and red brick to resemble a hood mold. The same design tops the door, except that the frame projects slightly. At the sill line of the second and third stories, bands of diamond-shaped bricks invite the play of light and shadow. The adjacent row houses are more pronounced in their sculptural detail. Elaborate segmental cast-iron hood molds with a central medallion and deep brackets crown each window, although the quantity of detail diminishes from the first story to the third. At the roofline is a richly bracketed cornice. As a group, these houses represent a trend toward the sculptural qualities of stone and cast iron.

GT16 **Trentman House**

1969, Hugh Newell Jacobsen. 1350 27th St. NW

Modern yet respectful of its historic environment, Hugh Newell Jacobsen's design repre-

GT16 Trentman House

GT17 Dumbarton House

sents an alternative to the Colonial and Federal Revival in-fill houses constructed in Georgetown well into the 1960s. In an era of Postmodernism and contextualism, the Trentman house demonstrates that a structure in the modern style can enhance a historic area as well as a building decked in architectural fragments copied from its neighbors.

Jacobsen employed burgundy brick and dark gray slate; the ground-floor openings for the entrance door and garage are recessed segmental archways. The three large windows of the first story project from the wall plane with convex brick embrasures. The nine windows at the second story are in long narrow recesses. At the rear of the building's sloping roof, four narrow windows admit natural light to the third-floor rooms. The interior is starkly modern, with a floor plan arranged around two circular stair towers rising the height of the house.

GT17 **Dumbarton House**

1799–1805, unknown. 1928, Fiske Kimball; Horace W. Peaslee. 2715 Q St. NW

Appearing aloof from the city surrounding it, Dumbarton House sits like a country dwelling on high ground north of Q Street. By all accounts, United States Treasury First Registrar Joseph Nourse built the original rectangular block with its hyphens and wings. The

house passed through several owners and renovations until 1915, when its location on Q Street became an impediment to a new route across Rock Creek Park and the District government moved the house to its current site.

In 1928, the National Society of Colonial Dames of America purchased the house and hired Kimball of Philadelphia and Peaslee of Washington to restore it as their headquarters. Kimball, who was also a well-respected historian, offered the major ideas; Peaslee was the on-site architect of record. The two-story house originally was designed on a central hall floor plan with two rooms on each side. At the rear, two large bow-shaped wings attractively frame the garden. On the exterior, a carved wooden basket-weave frieze, stone window lintels, a stone belt course, wrought-iron balconies, and a Doric portico leading to the entrance door are the principal decorative features. Restoration work of the 1930s included installation of mantles salvaged from houses in Georgetown and Philadelphia, the Colonial Revival rear garden wall and landscaping, and the rebuilt, enlarged wings of the house.

GT18 **Robert P. Dodge House**

1850–1853, Andrew Jackson Downing and Calvert Vaux. 1534 28th St. NW

This is one of two Italian Villa houses designed by Downing and Vaux in the heights of Georgetown. The second house, designed for Dodge's brother, is nearby on 30th Street. Robert P. Dodge began his career as an engineer for the C & O Canal, later developing business interests with the Georgetown Gas

GT18 Robert P. Dodge House

Light Company and the Columbia Flour Mill.

Dodge commissioned the residence on the mid-nineteenth-century outskirts of Georgetown, an appropriately bucolic setting for a country house. An illustration of it appeared in Calvert Vaux's *Villas and Cottages* (1857). (It was designed for Robert P. Dodge, not Francis Dodge, as is described in Vaux's book.) The original plan featured a porch tower that rose above the roofline, with the rest of the house arranged asymmetrically around the tower. A veranda along the northeast side of the house abutted the porch tower; the library-bedroom block adjoined the other side of the tower.

Urbanization and changing tastes have altered the Dodge house. Its grounds have been hemmed in by more recent dwellings, and Neoclassical elements have overwhelmed the Italian villa design. The porch tower was shortened and enclosed and the northeast veranda replaced by a two-story porch of large square pillars. Italianate decorative details such as window hood molds and brackets have been removed. The major surviving feature is the ground-floor plan, although the interior decorative features have been modified as well to reflect the exterior alterations. Despite all this, the original design intentions can still be perceived.

GT19 **Residence**

1964, Hugh Newell Jacobsen. 2813 Q St. NW

The sight of this residence may produce a double take. Its western wing concludes a string of pleasant row houses dating from the 1880s. As an extension to the end house are

an entrance hyphen, and, at first glance, a replica of the original house as the eastern wing. Here the basic form, openings, materials, and decorative flourishes have been carried over from one side of the site to the other. The new wing is not, in fact, a replica of the western block because the windows differ and the interior spaces were opened to provide dramatic deep spaces and fine views of the garden. In this project, the architect and review board sought relief from the pressure to provide creative modern designs for buildings in historic Georgetown by seeking solutions through the selective use of historical precedents. This residence thus became a precursor to the Postmodern buildings of the 1980s.

GT20 **Cooke's Row**

1868–1869, Starkweather and Plowman. 3000 block of Q St. NW

Cooke's Row represents the last phase in the efflorescence of the Italian Villa style in the heights of Georgetown. At the same time, it also is one of the few examples of the Second Empire style in the neighborhood. As a group, the row presents an irregular, picturesque silhouette in an area otherwise defined by geometric forms and many common cornice lines. Georgetown banker Henry David Cooke commissioned the group of four duplex row houses set back from the north side of Q Street. It was designed by the architectural and engineering firm of Starkweather and Plowman, which made its mark in the area with the Theological Seminary in Alexandria and several private schools and churches in Georgetown. The row included Second Empire duplexes on the ends, sandwiching two Italian Villa duplexes in the center, yielding eight units. Although in different styles, these duplexes share common spatial relationships. Changes in floor-to-ceiling heights, the extended towers and cupolas, the high chimneys, and bay windows, as well as differences in window shapes and heights, provide picturesque irregularity and variety.

GT21 **W. Taylor Birch House**

c. 1888, Thomas Franklin Schneider. 3099 Q St. NW

In red brick Victorian Georgetown, the W. Taylor Birch House is an anomaly, one of the few residences that can be described as Richardsonian for its flamboyant use of stone and brick. A round tower underscores the house's prominent location. The heavy stone at the first floor and the opposition of stone and brick at the window surrounds convey a kind of raw power. Abundant foliage around the house contributes to its forces-of-nature character.

Architect and entrepreneur Schneider, who designed the sky-piercing Cairo (see MH08, p. 303), was responsible for the Birch house, and it seems fitting that he should have defied the genteel traditions of Georgetown with such an earthy building.

GT22 **Tudor Place**

1794–1816, William Thornton. 1644 31st St. NW

In Tudor Place, Thornton realized a design as austerely geometric as could be found in

GT21 W. Taylor Birch House

the work of Benjamin Henry Latrobe, Robert Mills, or John Soane. Unlike much of Georgetown's Federal architecture, Tudor Place derives its appeal from three-dimensional composition and the play of light and shadows. Its drama is enhanced by the setting at the crest of a hill with an excellent view of the Potomac River.

When Thornton undertook the design for Thomas and Martha Custis Peter, he found two wings on the property, which were the only completed portions of what the previous owner envisioned as a large country house. Thornton provided the central structures and hyphens and joined the elements with buff

GT22 Tudor Place

stucco over brick. The central block is marked by a semicircular, half-domed porch, which is supported on four Doric columns that reach to the cornice line. The circular form continues in the house itself, where a recessed portion of equal volume is extracted, so that the circle begun by the outside porch is completed. The circular form is echoed in the recessed arches above the first-floor windows, enhancing the sculptural effect. The hip roofs over the central block and wings reinforce the house's overall geometric character.

GT23 Wisconsin Avenue Vocational School

1911–1912, Snowden Ashford and Thomas J. D. Fuller. 1640 Wisconsin Ave. NW

In harmony with its surroundings, this small building was wedged into a triangular site formed by the intersection of Wisconsin Avenue and 33rd Street. The previous building on the site was a general purpose elementary school that served white students. The replacement school, constructed in 1911–1912, offered industrial education, including training in mechanical drawing and shopwork, also for white students. In 1950, the building was converted to offices for the public school system, and thereafter to a private office building.

At the time the building was designed, the Office of the Municipal Architect had only recently been formed. As its first head, Snowden Ashford tried to assert governmental control over architectural design. That the Wisconsin Avenue School was designed in the Colonial Revival style, rather than in the Collegiate Gothic or Elizabethan Style favored by

Ashford, may be due to its appropriateness for Georgetown or to the taste of Washington architect Thomas J. D. Fuller, whose name appears with Ashford's on the drawings.

The Wisconsin Avenue School is considered Colonial Revival because of the robust decorative framing of the painted brick exterior. The corners of its central pavilion and of the building itself are edged in brick quoins. At the main entrance, Ionic pilasters support a segmental-arch pediment; other highlights of the central pavilion include swags under the second-floor windows and carved stone ornaments around the second-floor central window.

GT24 Volta Bureau

1894–1896, Peabody and Stearns. 1537 35th St. NW

Alexander Graham Bell's achievements in science and his interest in advancing the education of deaf children are both evoked by the Volta Bureau. With the $10,000 Volta Prize he won in 1880, Bell established a laboratory at the rear of his parents' house at 35th and Volta Place. His patents for a telephone and a phonograph record yielded additional funds that helped to endow the Volta Bureau for the Increase and Diffusion of Knowledge Relating to the Deaf.

Bell commissioned the prestigious Boston firm of Peabody and Stearns to design the building, which incorporated his laboratory, on a lot just north of his parents' house. Its design probably was derived from the Volta Temple at Lake Como, Italy, named in honor of physicist Alessandro Volta. The long, nar-

GT25 Ellington School of the Arts

row building that houses the Volta Bureau has a Composite distyle in antis porch fronting on 35th Street. The massive columns support an entablature surmounted by a high parapet punctuated with balusters. Terracotta bands crisscross the yellow brick building. A major renovation of 1948–1949 closed the soaring interior spaces with a floor of offices. Because of zoning restrictions, a facility such as the Volta Bureau could not now be built in residential Georgetown. Like the quiet nineteenth-century public school edifices, however, the Volta Bureau demonstrates how well institutional and residential buildings have coexisted throughout much of the city's history.

GT25 **Ellington School of the Arts**

1896–1898, Harry B. Davis. 35th and R streets NW

In the mid-1890s, an estate called the "Cedars" for its trees was selected as the site for an expanded Western High School. The first District school with a significant landscape setting, Western High was designed during the period when the District Commissioners had opened the design of municipal buildings to private architects, thereby ending the exclusive hold of this design work by the Office of the Building Inspector. Unlike the functional red brick edifices of Central, Eastern, and M Street high schools of the 1890s, this new school was a Classical Revival structure with a templelike central motif and flanking wings. The present building is the version rebuilt following a devastating fire in 1914. The two-story portico over a rusticated and arcaded base was widened and extended to balance the addition of twelve rooms to the wings. The expansion provided for a larger assembly hall and stage. When the roof was rebuilt, a pressed metal cornice replaced the balustrades. During the 1920s and 1930s, enrollment increased and additional wings were constructed. The Ellington School of the Arts, a District-wide arts school, now occupies the structure. A nineteenth-century wrought-iron fence encloses the landscaped setting along 35th Street.

GT26 **Dumbarton Oaks**

1801–present, unknown; Beatrix Farrand; Philip Johnson. 1703 32rd St. NW

A privately maintained academic research center, Dumbarton Oaks offers an unmatched experience in the built and natural environments. Its research facility, museum spaces, and exquisite gardens cover 16 acres, a fraction of the District's open space and parkland. Yet, per square foot, Dumbarton Oaks provides greater pleasure than any other open space in the District, the Mall and the Capitol grounds excepted.

Constructed in 1801 as part of a large estate, the house has been altered by several owners. Its full blossoming commenced in 1920 when Mr. and Mrs. Robert Woods Bliss

GT26 Dumbarton Oaks

each of the perimeter sections is a low dome. The plan provides for interconnected circular rooms, each containing small exhibits of Pre-Columbian artifacts. The luxurious materials used throughout the house include white Illinois marble sheathing on the columns in the circumference of each circular room and teak floors edged with green Vermont marble.

A visit to Dumbarton Oaks is a memorable experience. Here, a commitment to quality has achieved an enchanting rightness of form—of shapes, color, texture, light, and shadow—a rightness that evokes a delicious serenity in which time itself seems to pause and rest. It is a welcome enclave in an ever-changing and power-burdened city.

GT27 Oak Hill Cemetery Gatehouse

1850–1853, George F. de la Roche. 3001 R St. NW

purchased it. During the next two decades, the house was enlarged, and under the careful hand of landscape architect Beatrix Farrand, the grounds were molded into their present form. In 1940, the Blisses bequeathed the house and landscaped grounds to Harvard University for use as a research center for Byzantine and medieval studies; 27 acres of grounds were given to the city as parkland. In the 1960s, a Neo-Georgian wing was built at the west to accommodate Mrs. Bliss's landscape and garden library. On the north, Philip Johnson designed a modern pavilion to display Mr. Bliss's collection of Pre-Columbian art.

The original Federal style house sits on the highest point of land, and its later appendages flow from this center. The property's most extraordinary feature is its gardens, lovingly arranged according to Farrand's classical Mediterranean garden plan. Set on a series of terraces are cascading pools and "outdoor rooms," which can be viewed from the upper terraces. On the north, the landscape moves from formality to informality as it merges into the wooded parklands.

The construction of the Pre-Columbian museum during 1962–1965 may have appeared an anomaly in design-regulated Georgetown; however, its location in a downhill slope hidden from public streets made it an acceptable addition. A modern interpretation of a Byzantine church plan, the museum wing is laid out with eight circles arranged in a square configuration around a central circle left open for a fountain. Atop

The Oak Hill Cemetery Gatehouse marks the entrance to a large wooded expanse of land on the northern boundary of Georgetown. Banker William Wilson Corcoran, who donated the land for a cemetery, hired de la Roche, an engineer who had worked on the grounds of the old Naval Observatory in Foggy Bottom, to survey and lay out the cemetery grounds. It has been assumed that de la Roche also designed the gatehouse, intended to house offices and two stories of living quarters for the gatekeeper and his family.

Resembling a miniature Italian villa with an irregular, picturesque silhouette, the brick building is organized around a tower at the southeast corner. Red sandstone accentuates

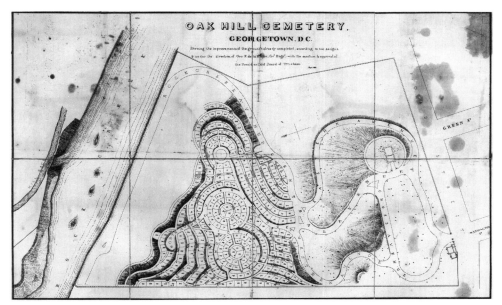

GT27 Oak Hill Cemetery plan

the building's shape and detail at the water table, window hood molds, window sills, buttress caps, steps, and stringcourse around the tower. Heavy wooden brackets at the eaves support the roof. Attached columns and floral capitals decorate the sandstone pillars at the entrance to the cemetery. Separated by several blocks from other Italian villas, the cemetery gatehouse documents the short appearance of this style in mid-nineteenth-century Georgetown.

GT28 Oak Hill Cemetery Chapel

1850, James Renwick, Jr. 3001 R St. NW

Just inside the gates of Oak Hill Cemetery, on a ridge to the north, is a small elegant chapel by Renwick. Renwick's versatility with churches in the Gothic style is nowhere more evident than in a comparison between this modest commission and the imposing Grace Church of 1846–1847 or Saint Patrick's Cathedral of 1858–1879 in New York City. It was Renwick's work on the Smithsonian Institution (see ML05, p. 94) that led him to this commission and to his later work on the first Corcoran Gallery of Art (see WH15, p. 164) and Saint Mary's Episcopal Church (see FB16, p. 214) in Foggy Bottom.

The diminutive chapel measures approxi-

GT28 Oak Hill Cemetery Chapel

mately 23 feet by 41 feet. Its one-story walls are formed of random courses of Potomac gneiss, a charcoal gray rock with high mica content. As trim, red sandstone is used at the water table, belt courses, window enframements, frieze, and finial. On the sides, four Gothic windows are separated by buttresses, each of which is capped with sandstone. Sandstone also appears at the front door frame, where moldings are anchored with sandstone floral drops. In its composition, Renwick's chapel exemplifies the aesthetic possibilities of building materials indigenous to the region.

GT29 Evermay

1801, Nicholas King. 1628 28th St. NW

High on Georgetown's northern rim and close to Rock Creek Park, Evermay occupies one of the largest surviving plots of open land in the vicinity. The site provides a superlative view of Georgetown, descending south to the Potomac River. Although diminished from its earlier size, the Evermay property is an especially impressive estate. The house, a five-bay, two-story brick structure, is trimmed with stone and wood. The northern and main facades are nearly identical, although the latter is slightly more ornamented, particularly in the round-headed window above the door in the central bay. Three dormer windows on the roof and double chimneys rising above the sides enhance the vertical forces of the building; the hyphens and wings of the main block reinforce the horizontal. The house

GT29 Evermay

had been Victorianized in the mid-nineteenth century with verandas, balconies, and brackets but was restored in the 1920s by Ambassador F. Lammot Belin. Admired for its elegant detailing, it represents the form and scale of the best of the builders' tradition in Georgetown.

Notes

1. Edward C. Carter II, John C. Van Horne, and Lee W. Formwalt, *The Journals of Benjamin Henry Latrobe, 1799–1820: From Philadelphia to New Orleans*, 3 vols. (New Haven: Yale University Press, 1980), 3:70.
2. Charles Dickens, *American Notes* (reprint, New York: St. Martin's Press, 1985), p. 106.
3. Carter, Van Horne, and Formwalt, *The Journals of Benjamin Henry Latrobe*, 3:71–72.
4. *Philadelphia General Advertiser*, 23 August 1793.
5. Library of Congress, Thomas Jefferson Papers.
6. Quoted in Susan L. Klaus, " 'Some of the Smartest Folks Here.' The Van Nesses and Community Building in Early Washington," *Washington History* 3, no. 2 (1991–1992):38.
7. Records of the U.S. Senate, Petitions, National Archives, RG 46, SEN 25A–G5.
8. Records of the U. S. Senate, Petitions, National Archives, RG 46, SEN 34A–H5–H6.
9. Quoted in Louise Mann Madden and Sheila Dressner Ruffine, *Cleveland Park: Washington, D. C., Neighborhood* (n.p., n.d.), p. 50, typescript on deposit in the Prints and Photographs Division, Library of Congress.
10. Quoted in Hugh Morrison, *Louis Sullivan: Prophet of Modern Architecture* (New York: Norton Library, 1962), p. 184.
11. Quoted in Sue A. Kohler, *The Commission of Fine Arts: A Brief History, 1910–1990* (Washington, D.C.: Commission of Fine Arts, 1991), p. 203.
12. Aymar Embury, "Are We On Our Way?" *Arts and Decoration* 21 (January 1921): 285.
13. *Washington Post*, 25 September 1940.
14. Pierre Charles L'Enfant to George Washington, 22 June 1791, Library of Congress, Manuscript Division.
15. Ibid.
16. Pierre Charles L'Enfant to Commissioner of Public Buildings, 30 August 1800, Library of Congress, Manuscript Division.
17. Smithson's will outlining the bequest went into effect on his death on 27 June 1829. His nephew was the primary heir, but when he died, in 1835, Smithson's fortune passed to the U.S. government.
18. Robert Dale Owen, *Hints on Public Architecture* (New York: Putnam, 1849), p. 6.
19. Andrew Jackson Downing, "A Talk About Parks and Gardens," *The Horticulturalist* (October 1848); reprinted in *Rural Essays* (New York: G. P. Putnam, 1853), p. 192.
20. Downing's description, dated 3 March 1851, which accompanied his plan, is in the National Archives, RG42, Records of the Commissioners of Public Buildings and Grounds.
21. The statement was actually a paraphrase of Burnham's thinking made by San Fransisco architect Willis J. Polk.
22. Richard Rathbon, *A Descriptive Account of the Building Recently Erected for the Departments of Natural History of the United States Nation Museum* (Washington, D.C.: Government Printing Office, 1913), p. 16.
23. Quoted by William B. Rhoads, "Franklin D. Roosevelt and Washington Architecture," *Records of the Columbia Historical Society* 52 (1989): 148.
24. Lin's statement was an integral part of her design, preserved in the Prints and Photographs Division, Library of Congress.
25. Quoted in Keith N. Morgan, *Charles A. Platt: The Artist as Architect* (Cambridge: MIT Architectural History Foundation, 1985), p. 69.
26. George Wetterston, Officer's Journal, 1833–1849, National Archives, Record Group 42, Records of the Washington National Monument Society.
27. Frederick L. Harvey, *History of the Washington National Monument and Washington National Monument Society* (Washington, D.C.: Government Printing Office, 1902–1903), p. 116.
28. *Washington National Monument*, broadside, 1848, Library of Congress, Rare Books Division.
29. Library of Congress, Manuscript Division.
30. Quoted in Sual K. Padover, ed., *Thomas Jefferson and the National Capitol* (Washington, D.C.: Government Printing Office, 1946), p. 59.
31. John L. Smithmeyer, "The National Library Building—The Proposed Plan," *Library Journal* 6 (1881): 77–81.
32. Latrobe to Thomas Jefferson, 5 November 1816, *The Correspondence and Miscellaneous Papers of Benjamin Henry Latrobe*, Vol. 3, *1811–1820* (New Haven, Conn.: Yale University Press, 1988), pp. 622–23.
33. Papers of Pierre Charles L'Enfant, Library of Congress, Manuscript Division.
34. "Justice on a Pedestal," *Architectural Forum* 127 (September 1967): 77.
35. Michael J. Crosbie, "On the Avenue," *Architecture*, April 1991, p. 61.
36. "Simplicity of Design in New Library, Work of the Late Mies van der Rohe," *AIA Journal* 58 (October 1972): 6.
37. "Preservation with Personality," *Washington Post*, 19 December 1987, D1.
38. "Memorial Continental Hall," *Architects and Builders Journal* 5 (May 1904): 19.
39. Charles Butler, "Competition—Federal Reserve Board Building," *Octagon: A Journal of the AIA* 7 (January 1935): 11.

40. "Awards Update," *Progressive Architecture* 64 (March 1983): 36.

41. "Headquarters for HUD by Breuer and Beckhard: A Major Landmark for a Political Era Which Aspired to a Public Architecture of Quality," *Architectural Record* 144 (December 1968): 99–106.

42. L'Enfant's description of his plan hand printed on the manuscript placed before Congress on December 1791 and first published in the Philadelphia newspaper, *Dunlop's American Daily Advertiser,* December 26.

43. Aymar Embury, "Are We on Our Way?" *Arts and Decoration* 21 (1921): 285.

44. Written on L'Enfant's manuscript map and first published in the Philadelphia newspaper, *Dunlop's American Daily Advertiser,* December 26, 1791.

45. Richard Feller, *For Thy Great Glory* (Culpeper, Va.: Community Press, 1965).

Suggested Reading

Adam Davidson Galleries. *I. M. Pei & Partners: Drawings for the East Building, National Gallery of Art.* Washington, D.C.: Adam Davidson Galleries, 1978.

Applewhite, E. J. *Washington Itself.* New York: Alfred A. Knopf, 1983.

Art in the United States Capitol. Washington, D.C.: Government Printing Office, 1978.

Beauchamp, Tanya. "Adolph Cluss and the Building of the U.S. National Museum. An Architecture of Perfect Adaptability." M.A. thesis, University of Virginia, 1972.

Berk, Sally Lichtenstein. "The Richest Crop: The Rowhouses of Harry Wardman (1872–1938), Washington, D.C. Developer." M.A. thesis, George Washington University, 1989.

Bowling, Kenneth R. *Creating the Federal City, 1774–1800: Potomac Fever.* Washington, D.C.: American Institute of Architects Press, 1988.

Brown, Glenn. *History of the United States Capitol.* Reprint. New York: Da Capo Press, 1970.

Bryan, Gray MacWhorter, III. "Waddy Wood's Residential Structures in Washington, D.C." M.A. thesis, University of Virginia, 1980.

Bryan, John M., ed. *Robert Mills, Architect.* Washington, D.C.: American Institute of Architects Press, 1989.

Bushong, William, Judith Helm Robinson, and Julie Mueller. *A Centennial History of the Washington Chapter, The American Institute of Architects, 1887–1987.* Washington, D.C.: Washington Architectural Foundation Press, 1987.

Bustard, Bruce I. *Washington Behind the Monuments.* Washington, D.C.: National Archives, 1990.

Butler, Jeanne F. "Competition 1792: Designing a Nation's Capitol." *Capitol Studies* 4 (1976): 10–96.

Caemmerer, H. P. *Washington: The National Capital.* Washington, D.C.: Government Printing Office, 1932.

Cantor, Jay. "The Public Architecture of James Renwick, Jr." M.A. thesis, University of Delaware, 1967.

Carr, Lynch Associates. *Anacostia Conserved.* Washington, D.C.: D.C. Department of Housing and Community Associates, 1979.

———. *Le Droit Park Conserved.* Washington, D.C. : D.C. Department of Housing and Community Associates, 1979.

Collins, Kathleen. *Washingtoniana Photographs.* Washington, D.C.: Library of Congress, 1989.

Commission of Fine Arts. *Massachusetts Avenue Architecture.* 2 vols. Washington, D.C.: Government Printing Office, 1973–1975.

Davis, Deering, Stephen P. Dorsey, and Ralph Cole Hall. *Georgetown Houses of the Federal Period.* New York: Architectural Book Publishing Company, 1944.

District of Columbia Sesquicentennial. Washington, D.C.: Library of Congress, 1950.

Dupont Circle Revisited. Washington, D.C.: L'Enfant Trust, 1981.

Durkin, Joseph T. *Georgetown University.* Garden City: Doubleday, 1964.

Fairman, Charles E. *Art and Artists of the Capitol of the United States of America.* Washington, D.C.: Government Printing Office, 1927.

Feller, Richard T. *Completing Washington Cathedral for Thy Great Glory,* Washington, D.C.: Washington Cathedral, 1989.

Finley, David Edward. *A Standard of Excellence.* Washington, D.C.: Smithsonian Institution Press, 1973.

Georgetown Commercial Architecture. 3 vols. Washington, D.C.: Commission of Fine Arts and National Park Service, 1967.

Georgetown Residential Architecture. 4 vols. Washington, D.C.: Commission of Fine Arts and National Park Service,

Georgetown Historic Waterfront. Washington, D.C.: Commission of Fine Arts and National Park Service, 1968.

Goode, James M. *Best Addresses.* Washington, D.C.: Smithsonian Institution Press, 1989.

———. *Capital Losses.* Washington, D.C.: Smithsonian Institution Press, 1979.

———. *The Outdoor Sculpture of Washington, D.C.* Washington, D.C.: Smithsonian Institution Press, 1974.

Grossman, Elizabeth Greenwell. "Paul Philippe Cret: Rationalism and Imagery in American Architecture." Ph.D. dissertation, Brown University, 1980.

Gutheim, Frederick. *Worthy of the Nation: The History of Planning for the National Capital.* Washington, D.C.: National Capital Planning Commission and Smithsonian Institution Press, 1977.

Gutheim, Frederick, and Wilcomb E. Washburn. *The Federal City: Plans & Realities.* Washington, D.C.: National Capital Planning Commission and Smithsonian Institution Press, 1976.

Hafertepe, Kenneth. *America's Castle: The Evolution of the Smithsonian Building and Its Institution, 1840–1878.* Washington, D.C.: Smithsonian Institution Press, 1984.

Helm, Judith Beck. *Tenleytown, D.C.: Country Village into City Neighborhood.* Washington, D.C.: Tennally Press, 1981.

Herman, Jan K. *A Hilltop in Foggy Bottom.* Washington, D.C.: Department of the Navy, 1984.

Historic American Buildings Survey. "Meridian Hill Park." HABS No. DC–532.

Hoagland, Alison K. "Nineteenth-Century Building Regulations in Washington, D.C." *Records of the Columbia Historical Society of Washington, D.C.* 52 (1989): 57–77.

419

Hutchinson, Louise Daniel. *The Anacostia Story: 1608–1930*. Washington, D.C.: Smithsonian Institution Press, 1977.

Junior League of Washington. *An Illustrated History: The City of Washington*. New York: Alfred A. Knopf, 1977.

Kohler, Sue A. *The Commission of Fine Arts: A Brief History, 1910–1990*. Washington, D.C.: Commission of Fine Arts, 1991.

Kohler, Sue A., and Jeffrey R. Carson. *Sixteenth Street Architecture*. 2 vols. Washington, D.C.: Commission of Fine Arts, 1978–88.

Longstreth, Richard, ed. *The Mall in Washington, 1791–1991*. Washington, D.C.: National Gallery of Art, 1991.

Look, David W., and Carole L. Perrault. *The Interior Building: Its Architecture and Its Art*. Washington, D.C.: National Park Service, 1986.

Lowry, Bates. *The Architecture of Washington, D.C.* 2 vols. Washington, D.C.: Dunlap Society, 1976–1979.

———. *Building a National Image: Architectural Drawings for the American Democracy, 1789–1912*. Washington, D.C.: National Building Museum, 1985.

Lyons, Linda Brody. *A Handbook to the Pension Building*. Washington, D.C.: National Building Museum, 1989.

McCue, George. *The Octagon*. Washington, D.C.: American Institute of Architects Foundation, 1976.

McLoud, Melissa. "Craftsmen and Entrepreneurs: Builders in Late Nineteenth-Century Washington, D.C." Ph.D. dissertation, George Washington University, 1988.

Maddex, Diane. *Historic Buildings of Washington, D.C.* Pittsburgh: Ober Park Associates, Inc., 1973.

Morgan, William. *The Almighty Wall: The Architecture of Henry Vaughn*. Cambridge, Mass.: MIT Press and the Architectural History Foundation, 1983.

Myer, Donald Beekman. *Bridges and the City of Washington*. Washington, D.C.: Commission of Fine Arts, 1974.

Noreen, Sarah Pressey. *Public Street Illumination in Washington, D.C.* GW Washington Studies, No. 2. Washington, D.C.: George Washington University, 1975.

Norton, Paul F., et al. *Decatur House*. Washington, D.C.: National Trust for Historic Preservation, 1967.

The Old Executive Office Building: A Victorian Masterpiece. Washington, D.C.: Government Printing Office, 1984.

Olszewski, George J. *Dupont Circle, Washington, D.C.* Washington, D.C.: National Park Service, 1967.

Owen, Robert Dale. *Hints on Public Architecture*. New York: Putnam, 1849. Reprint, with introduction by Cynthia R. Field. New York, Da Capo Press, 1978.

Padover, Saul K., ed. *Thomas Jefferson and the National Capital*. Washington, D.C.: Government Printing Office, 1946.

Park, Edwards, and Jean Paul Carlhian. *A New View from the Castle*. Washington, D.C.: Smithsonian Institution Press, 1984.

The Pennsylvania Avenue Plan 1974. Washington, D.C.: Pennsylvania Avenue Development Corporation, 1974.

Peterson, Anne E. *Hornblower & Marshall, Architects*. Washington, D.C.: National Trust for Historic Preservation, 1978.

Rathbun, Richard. *United States National Museum*. Washington, D.C.: Government Printing Office, 1913.

Records of the Columbia Historical Society. 1897–1989.

Reiff, Daniel D. *Washington Architecture, 1791–1861*. Washington, D.C.: Commission of Fine Arts, 1971.

Reps, John W. *Monumental Washington*. Princeton: Princeton University Press, 1967.

———. *Washington on View: The Nation's Capital in 1790*. Chapel Hill: University of North Carolina Press, 1991.

Ridout, Orlando, V. *Building the Octagon*. Washington, D.C.: American Institute of Architects Press, 1989.

Santoyo, Elsa M., ed. *Creating an American Masterpiece: Architectural Drawings of the Old Executive Office Building, 1871–1888*. Washington, D.C.: The American Architectural Foundation, 1988.

Schwartz, Nancy B. *Historic American Buildings Survey: District of Columbia Catalog 1974*. Charlottesville: Columbia Historical Society and University Press of Virginia, 1976.

Seale, William. *The President's House*. 2 vols. Washington, D.C.: White House Historical Association, 1986.

Small, Herbert. *The Library of Congress: Its Architecture and Decoration*. The Classical America Series in Art and Architecture. New York: W. W. Norton, 1982.

Smith, D. Mullett. *A. B. Mullett: His Relevance in American Architecture and Historic Preservation*. Washington, D.C.: Mullett-Smith Press, 1990.

Smith, Kathryn Schneider, ed. *Washington at Home*. Washington, D.C.: Columbia Historical Society, 1988.

Vignelli Massimo. *Hugh Newell Jacobsen, Architect*. Washington, D.C.: American Institute of Architects Press, 1988.

Washington History. 1989–1991.

Washington Present and Future. Washington, D.C.: National Capital Park and Planning Commission, 1950.

Wirz, Hans, and Richard Striner. *Washington Deco*. Washington, D.C.: Smithsonian Institution Press, 1984.

The WPA Guide to Washington, D.C. New York: Pantheon Books, 1983. Reprint of *Washington, D.C.: City and Capital*. Federal Writers' Project of the WPA. New York: Hastings House, 1942.

Ziolkowski, John E. *Classical Influence on the Public Architecture of Washington and Paris*. New York: Peter Lang, 1988.

Glossary

AIA See AMERICAN INSTITUTE OF ARCHITECTS.

abacus The top member of a column capital. In the Doric order, it is a flat block, square in plan, between the echinus of the capital and the architrave of the entablature above.

Academic Gothic See COLLEGIATE GOTHIC.

acroterium, acroterion (plural: acroteria). **1** A pedestal for a statue or similar decorative feature at the apex or at the lower corners of a pediment. **2** Any ornamental feature at these locations.

Adamesque A mode of architectural design, with emphasis on interiors, reminiscent of the work of the Scottish architects Robert Adam (1728–1792) and his brother James (1732–1794). It is characterized by attenuated proportions, bright color, and elegant linear detailing. Adamesque interiors, as one aspect of the broader Neoclassical movement, became popular in the late eighteenth century in Britain, Russia, and elsewhere in northern Europe. Simplified versions of these interiors began to be seen in the United States around the year 1800 in the work of Charles Bulfinch (1763–1844) and Samuel McIntire (1757–1811). Adamesque interiors, often emulating original Adam designs, were again popular in the 1920s. See also the related term FEDERAL.

aedicule, aedicular An exterior niche, door, or window, framed by columns or pilasters and topped by an entablature and pediment. Meaning has been extended to a smaller-scale representation of a temple front on an interior wall. Distinguished from a tabernacle (definition **1**), which usually occurs on an interior wall. See also the related term NICHE.

Aesthetic movement A late nineteenth-century movement in interior design and the decorative arts, emphasizing the application of artistic principles in the production of objects and the creation of interior ensembles. Aesthetic movement works are characterized by a broad eclecticism of materials and styles (especially the exotic) and by a preference for "conventionalized" (i.e., stylized) ornament, rather than naturalistic. The movement flourished in Britain from the 1850s through the 1870s and in the United States from the 1870s through the 1880s. Designers associated with the movement include William Morris (1834–1896) in England and Herter Brothers (1865–1905) in America. The Aesthetic movement evolved into and overlapped with the Art Nouveau and the Arts and Crafts movement. See also the related term QUEEN ANNE (definition **4**).

ambulatory A passageway around the apse of a church, allowing for circulation behind the sanctuary.

American Adam style See FEDERAL.

American bond See COMMON BOND.

American Foursquare See FOURSQUARE HOUSE.

American Institute of Architects The national professional organization of architects, established in New York in 1857. The first national convention was held in New York in 1867, and at that meeting, provision was made for the creation of local chapters. In 1889, the American Institute of Architects absorbed the independent Chicago-based Western Association of Architects (established 1884). The headquarters of the national organization moved from New York to Washington in 1898. Abbreviated as AIA.

American Renaissance Ambiguous term. See instead BEAUX-ARTS CLASSICISM, COLONIAL REVIVAL, FEDERAL REVIVAL.

Anglo-Palladianism, Anglo-Palladian An architectural movement in England motivated by a reaction against the English Baroque and by a rediscovery of the work of the English Renaissance architect Inigo Jones (1573–1652) and the Italian Renaissance architect Andrea Palladio (1508–1580). Anglo-Palladianism flourished in England (c. 1710s–1760s) and in the British North American colonies (c. 1740s–1790s). Key figures in the Anglo-Palladian movement were Colen Campbell (1676–1729) and Richard Boyle, Lord Burlington (1694–1753). Sometimes called Burlingtonian, Palladian Revival. See also the more general term PALLADIANISM and the related term GEORGIAN PERIOD.

antefix In classical architecture, a small upright decoration at the eaves of a roof, originally devised to hide the ends of the roof tiles. A similar ornament along the ridge of the roof.

anthemion (plural: anthemions). A Greek ornamental motif based upon the honeysuckle or palmette. It may appear as a single element on an antefix or as a running ornament on a frieze or other banded feature.

antiquity The broad epoch of Western history preceding the Middle Ages and including such ancient civilizations as Egyptian, Greek, and Roman.

apse, apsidal A semicircular or polygonal feature projecting as a major element from an important interior space, especially at the chancel end of a church. Distinguished from an exedra, which is a semicircular or polygonal space, usually containing a bench, in the wall of a garden or nonreligious building. A substantial apse in a church, containing an ambulatory and radiating chapels, is called a chevet. The terms apse and chevet are used to describe the *form* of the end of the church containing the altar, while the terms chancel, choir, and sanctuary are used to describe the liturgical *function* of this end of the church and the spaces within it. Less substantial projections in nonreligious buildings are called bays if polygonal or bowfronts if curved.

arbor 1 An openwork structure covered with climbing plants. Distinguished from a trellis, which is generally a simpler, more two-dimensional structure, often attached to a wall. Distinguished from a pergola, which is an openwork structure supported by a colonnade, creating a shaded walk. **2** A grouping of closely planted trees or shrubs, trained together and self-supporting.

arcade 1 A series of arches, carried on columns or piers or other supports. **2** A covered walkway, one side of which is part of a building, while the other is open, as a series of arches, to the exterior. **3** In the nineteenth and early twentieth centuries, an interior street or other extensive space lined with shops and stores.

arch A curved construction that spans an opening. (Some arches may be flat or triangular, and many have a complex or compound curvature.) A masonry arch consists of a series of wedge-shaped parts (voussoirs) that press together toward the center while being restrained from spreading outward by the surrounding wall or the adjacent arch.

architrave 1 The lowest member of a classical entablature. **2** The moldings on the face of a wall around a doorway or other opening. Sometimes called the casing. Distinguished from the jambs, which are the vertical linings perpendicular to the wall planes at the sides of an opening. Distinguished from surround, a term usually applied to the entire door or window frame considered as a unit.

archivolt The group of moldings following the shape of an arched opening.

arcuation, arcuated Construction using arches.

Art Deco A decorative style stimulated by the 1925 Exposition Internationale des Arts Décoratifs et Industriels Modernes, held in Paris. As the first phase of the Moderne, Art Deco is characterized by sharp angular and curvilinear forms, by a richness of materials (including polished metal, stone, and exotic woods), and by an overall sleekness of design. The style was often used in the commercial and residential architecture of the 1930s (e.g., skyscrapers, hotels, apartment buildings). Sometimes called Art Deco Moderne, Deco, Jazz Moderne, Zigzag Moderne, Zigzag Modernistic. See also the more general term MODERNE and the related terms MAYAN REVIVAL, PWA MODERNE, STREAMLINE MODERNE.

Art Moderne See MODERNE.

Art Nouveau A style in architecture, interior design, and the decorative arts that flourished principally in France and Belgium in the 1890s. The Art Nouveau is characterized by undulating and whiplash lines and by sensuous organic forms. The Art Nouveau in Britain and the United States evolved from and overlapped with the Aesthetic movement.

Arts and Crafts A late nineteenth- and early twentieth-century movement in interior design and the decorative arts, emphasizing the importance of handcrafting for everyday objects. Arts and Crafts works are characterized by rectilinear geometries and high contrasts between figure and ground, and the furniture often features expressed construction. The term originated with the Arts and Crafts Exhibition Society, founded in England in 1888. Designers associated with the movement include C. F. A. Voysey (1857–1941) in England and the brothers Charles S. Greene (1868–1957) and Henry M. Greene (1870–1954) in America. The Arts and Crafts movement evolved from and overlapped with the Aesthetic movement. For a more specific term, used in the United States after 1900, see also CRAFTSMAN.

ashlar Squared blocks of stone that fit tightly against one another.

astylar Term that describes a classical building without columns in the usual locations (e.g., peristyles, porticoes, rotundas).

atelier 1 A studio where the fine arts, including architecture, are taught. Applied particularly to the offices of prominent architects in Paris who provided design training to students enrolled in or informally attached to the Ecole des Beaux-Arts. By extension, any working office where some organized teaching is done. **2** A place where artworks or handicrafts are produced by skilled workers. **3** An artist's studio or workshop.

attic 1 The area beneath the roof and above the main stories (or story) of a building. Sometimes called a garret. **2** A low story above the entablature, often a blocklike mass that caps the building.

axis An imaginary center line to which are referred the parts of a building or the relations of a number of buildings to one another.

axonometric drawing A pictorial drawing using axonometric projection, in which horizontal lines that are perpendicular (usually at two 45-degree angles from the vertical, or at complementary angles of 30 and 60 degrees). Consequently, all angular and dimensional relationships in plan remain the same in the drawing as in the thing depicted. Sometimes called an axon or an axonometric. See also the related terms ISOMETRIC DRAWING, PERSPECTIVE DRAWING.

baluster One of a series of short vertical members, often vase-shaped in profile, used to support a handrail for a stair or a railing. Balusters that are thinner and simpler in profile are sometimes called banisters.

balustrade A series of balusters or posts supporting a rail or coping across the top (and sometimes resting on a lower rail). Balustrades are often found on stairs, balconies, parapets, and terraces.

band course Ambiguous term. See instead BAND MOLDING or STRINGCOURSE.

band molding In masonry or frame construction, any horizontal flat member or molding or group of moldings projecting slightly from a wall and marking a division in the wall. Not properly a synonym for band course. Simpler horizontal bands in masonry are generally called stringcourses.

bandstand A small pavilion, usually polygonal or circular in plan, designed to shelter bands during public concerts in a garden, park, green, or square. See also the related terms GAZEBO, KIOSK.

banister 1 Corrupted spelling of baluster, in use since about the seventeenth century. Now occasionally used for balusters that are thinner and simpler in profile than classical vase-shaped balusters. **2** Improperly used to mean the handrail of a stair.

bargeboard An ornate fascia board that is attached to the sloping edges (verges) of a roof, covering the ends of the horizontal roof timbers (purlins). Bargeboards are usually ornamented with carved, turned, or jigsawn forms. Sometimes called gableboards, vergeboards. Less ornate boards along the verges of a roof are simply called fascia boards.

Baroque A style of art and architecture that flourished in Europe and colonial North America during the seventeenth and eighteenth centuries. Although based on the architecture of the Renaissance, Baroque architecture was more dynamic, with circles frequently giving way to ovals, flat walls to curved or undulating ones, and separate elements to interlocking forms. It was a monumental and richly three-dimensional style with elaborate systems of ornamental and figural sculpture. See also the related terms RENAISSANCE, ROCOCO.

Baroque Revival See NEO-BAROQUE.

barrel vault A vaulted roof or ceiling of semicircular or semielliptical cross section, forming a tunnellike enclosure over an apartment, corridor, or similar space.

Barryesque Term applied to Italianate buildings showing the influence of the English architect Sir Charles Barry (1795–1860), who introduced a derivative form of the Italian High Renaissance palazzo in his Travelers Club in London, 1829–1832. The style was brought to the United States by the Scottish-trained architect John Notman (1810–1865) and was popular from the late 1840s through the 1860s, especially for institutional and government buildings. Distinguished from the Italian Villa style, which has the northern Italian rural vernacular villa as its prototype. See also the more general term ITALIANATE.

basement 1 The lowest story of a building, either partly or entirely below grade. **2** The lower part of the walls of any building, usually articulated distinctly from the upper part of the walls.

batten 1 A narrow strip of wood applied to cover a joint along the edges of two parallel boards in the same plane. **2** A strip of wood fastened across two or more parallel boards to hold them together. Sometimes called a cross batten. See also the related term BOARD-AND-BATTEN SIDING.

battered (adjective). Inclined from the vertical. A wall is said to be battered or to have a batter when it recedes as it rises.

battlement, battlemented See CRENELLATION.

Bauhaus 1 Work in any of the visual arts by the faculty and students of the Bauhaus, the innovative design school founded by Walter Gropius (1883–1969) and an active force in German modernism from 1919 until 1933. **2** Work in any of the visual arts by the former faculty and students of the Bauhaus, or by individuals influenced by them. See also the related terms INTERNATIONAL STYLE, MIESIAN.

bay 1 The interval between two recurring members. A facade is frequently measured by window bays, a skeletal frame by structural bays. **2** A polygonal or curved unit of one or more stories, projecting from the wall and usually containing grouped windows (bay windows) on each story. See also the more specific term BOWFRONT.

bay window The horizontally grouped windows in a projecting bay (definition **2**), or the projecting bay itself, if it is not more than one story. Distinguished from an oriel, which does not rise from the foundation and has a suspended rather than rooted appearance. A semicircular or semielliptical bay window is called a bow window. A bay window with a central section of plate glass in a late nineteenth-century commercial building is called a Chicago window.

beam A structural spanning member of stone, wood, iron, steel, or reinforced concrete. See also the more specific terms GIRDER, I-BEAM, JOIST.

bearing wall A wall that is fully structural, carrying the load of the floors and roof all the way to the foundation. Sometimes called a supporting wall. Distinguished from curtain wall. See also the related term LOAD-BEARING.

Beaux-Arts Historicist design on a monumental scale, as taught at the Ecole des Beaux-Arts in Paris throughout the nineteenth century and early twentieth century. The term Beaux-Arts is generally applied to an eclectic Roman-Renaissance-Baroque architecture of the 1850s through the 1920s, disseminated internationally by students and followers of the Ecole des Beaux-Arts. As a general style term Beaux-Arts connotes an academically grounded discipline for historical eclecticism, rather than one single style, as well as the disciplined development of a *parti* into a fully visualized design. More specific style terms include Neo-Grec (1840s–1870s) and Beaux-Arts Classicism (1870s–1930s). See also the related terms NEOCLASSICISM, for describing Ecole-related work from the 1790s to the 1840s, and SECOND EMPIRE, for describing the work from the 1850s to the 1880s.

Beaux-Arts Classicism, Beaux-Arts Classical Term applied to eclectic Roman-Renaissance-Baroque architecture and urbanism after the Neo-Grec and Second Empire phases, i.e., from the 1870s through the 1930s. Sometimes called Classic Revival, Classical Revival, McKim Classicism, Neoclassical Revival. See also the more general term

BEAUX-ARTS and the related terms CITY BEAUTIFUL MOVEMENT, PWA MODERNE.

belfry A cupola, turret, or room in a tower where a bell is housed.

bell cote A small gabled structure astride the ridge of a roof, which shelters a bell. It is usually close to the front wall plane of the building.

belt course See STRINGCOURSE.

belvedere 1 Any building, especially a pavilion or shelter, that is located to take advantage of a view. See also the related term GAZEBO. 2 See CUPOLA (definition 2).

blind (adjective). Term applied to the surface use of elements that would otherwise articulate an opening but where no opening exists. Used in such combinations as blind arcade, blind arch, blind door, blind window.

board-and-batten siding A type of siding for wood frame buildings, consisting of wide vertical boards with narrow strips of wood (battens) covering the joints. (In rare instances, the battens may be fastened behind the joints. If the gaps between boards are wide and the back battens approach the width of the outer boards, the siding is called board-on-board.) See also the related term BATTEN.

board-on-board siding A type of siding for wood frame buildings, consisting of two layers of vertical boards, with the outer layer of boards covering the wide gaps between the boards of the inner layer.

bowfront A semicircular or semielliptical bay (definition 2).

bow window A semicircular or semielliptical bay window.

brace A single wooden or metal member placed diagonally within a framework or truss or beneath an overhang. Distinguished from a bracket, which is a more substantial triangular feature, and from a strut, which is essentially a post set in a diagonal position.

braced frame construction A combination of heavy and light timber frame construction, in which the principal vertical and horizontal framing members (posts and girts) are fastened by mortise and tenon joints, while the one-story-high studs are nailed to the heavy timber frame. The overall frame is made more rigid by diagonal braces. Sometimes called braced framing.

bracket Any solid, pierced, or built-up triangular feature projecting from the face of a wall to support a projecting element, like the top member of a cornice or the verges or eaves of a roof. Brackets are frequently used for ornamental as well as structural purposes. Distinguished from a brace, which is a simple barlike structural member. Distinguished from the more specific term console, which has a height greater than its projection from the wall. See also the related term CORBEL.

Bracketed style A nineteenth-century term for Italianate.

brick bonds, brickwork See the more specific terms COMMON BOND, ENGLISH BOND, FLEMISH BOND, RUNNING BOND.

British colonial A term applied to buildings, towns, landscapes, and other artifacts from the period of actual British colonial occupation of large parts of eastern North America (c. 1607–1781 for the United States; c. 1750s–1867 for much of Canada). The British colonial period saw the introduction into the New World of various regional strains of English and Scotch-Irish folk culture, as well as high-style Anglo-European Renaissance, Baroque, and Neoclassical design. Sometimes called English colonial. Loosely called colonial or Early American. See also the related term GEORGIAN PERIOD.

Brutalism An architectural style of the 1950s through 1970s, characterized by complex massing and by a frank expression of structural members, elements of building systems, and materials (especially concrete). Some of the work of Paul Rudolph (born 1918) is associated with this style. Sometimes called New Brutalism.

bungalow A low one- or one-and-a-half-story house of modest pretensions with a low-pitched gable or hipped roof, a conspicuous porch, and projecting eaves. This house type was a popular builders' type from around 1900 to 1930. The term bungalow was also loosely applied to any vernacular building of a semirustic nature, including vacation cottages and lodges.

Burlingtonian See ANGLO-PALLADIANISM.

buttress An exterior mass of masonry bonded into a wall that it strengthens or supports. Buttresses often absorb lateral thrusts from roofs or vaults.

Byzantine Term applied to the art and architecture of the Eastern Roman Empire centered at Byzantium (i.e., Constantinople, Istanbul) from the early 500s to the mid-1400s. Byzantine architecture is characterized by massive domes, round arches, richly carved capitals, and the extensive use of mosaic.

Byzantine Revival See NEO-BYZANTINE.

campanile In Italian, a bell tower. While usually freestanding in medieval and Renaissance architecture, it was often incorporated as a prominent unit in the massing of picturesque nineteenth-century buildings.

cantilever A beam, girder, slab, truss, or other structural member that projects beyond its supporting wall or column.

cap A canopy, ledge, molding, or pediment over a window. Sometimes called a window cap. Distinguished from a hood, which is a similar feature over a door. See also the related term HEAD MOLDING.

capital The moldings and carved enrichment at the top of a column, pilaster, pier, or pedestal.

carriage porch See PORTE-COCHÈRE.

casement window A window that opens from the side on hinges, like a door, out from the plane of the wall. Distinguished from a double-hung window.

casing See ARCHITRAVE (definition 2).

cast iron Iron shaped by a molding process, generally strong in compression but brittle in tension.

Distinguished from wrought iron, which has been forged to increase its tensile properties.

cast-iron front An architectural facade made of prefabricated molded iron parts, often markedly skeletal in appearance with extensive glass infilling. Prevalent from the late 1840s to the early 1870s.

castellated Having the elements of a medieval castle, such as crenellation and turrets.

cavetto cornice See COVED CORNICE.

cella 1 The largest interior space in a classical temple or a building derived from a clasical temple. In Greek, called the naos. **2** The walled inner prt of a classical temple or a building derived from a classical temple, i.e., the part within the peristyle colonnade or behind the portico.

cement A mixture of burnt lime and clay with water, which hardens permanently when dry. When a fine aggregate of sand is added, the cement may be used as a mortar for masonry construction or as a plaster or stucco coating. When a coarser aggregate of gravel or crushed stone is added, along with sand, the mixture is called concrete.

chamfer The oblique surface formed by cutting off a square edge at an equal angle to each face.

chancel 1 The end of a Roman Catholic or High Episcopal church containing the altar and set apart for the clergy and choir by a screen, rail, or steps. Usually the entire east end of a church beyond the crossing. In churches that have a long chancel space, the part of the chancel between the crossing and the apse, where the singers participate in the service, is called the choir. The innermost part of the chancel, containing the principal altar, is called the sanctuary. **2** In less extensive Catholic and Episcopal churches, the terms chancel and choir are often used interchangeably to mean the entire eastern arm of the church.

Châteauesque A term applied to masonry buildings from the 1870s through the 1920s in which stylistic references are derived from early French Renaissance chateaux, from the reign of Francis I (1515–1547) or even earlier. Sometimes called Château style, Châteauesque Revival, Francis I style, François Premier.

chevet In large churches, particularly those based upon French Gothic precedents, a substantial apse surrounded by an ambulatory and often containing radiating chapels.

Chicago school A diverse group of architects associated with the development of the tall (i.e., six- to twenty-story), usually metal frame commercial building in Chicago during the 1880s and 1890s. William Le Baron Jenney, Burnham and Root, and Adler and Sullivan are identified with this group. Sometimes called Chicago Commercial style, Commercial style. See also the related term PRAI-RIE SCHOOL.

Chicago window A tripartite oblong window in which a large fixed center pane is placed between two narrow sash windows. Popularized in Chicago commercial buildings of the 1880s–1890s. See also BAY WINDOW.

chimney girt In timber frame construction, a major wooden beam that passes across the breast of the central chimney. It is supported at its ends by the longitudinal girts of the building and sometimes carries one end of the summer beam.

choir 1 The part of a Roman Catholic or High Episcopal church where the singers participate in the service. Usually the space within the chancel arm of the church, situated between the crossing to the west and the sanctuary to the east. **2** In less extensive Catholic and Episcopal churches, the terms choir and chancel are often used interchangeably to mean the entire eastern arm of the church.

Churrigueresque Term applied to Spanish and Spanish colonial Baroque architecture resembling the work of the Spanish architect José Benito de Churriguera (1665–1725) and his brothers. The style is characterized by a freely interpreted assemblage of such elements as twisted columns, broken pediments, and scroll brackets. See also the related term SPANISH COLONIAL.

cinquefoil A type of Gothic tracery having five parts (lobes or foils) separated by pointed elements (cusps).

City Beautiful movement A movement in architecture, landscape architecture, and planning in the United States from the 1890s through the 1920s, advocating the beautification of cities in the image of some of the most urbane places of the time: the world's fairs. City Beautiful schemes emphasized civic centers, boulevards, and waterfront improvements, and sometimes included comprehensive metropolitan plans for parks, parkways, and transportation facilities. See also the related term BEAUX-ARTS CLASSICISM.

clapboard A tapered board that is thinner along the top edge and thicker along the bottom edge, applied horizontally with edges overlapping to provide weathertight siding on a building of wood construction. Early clapboards were split (rived, riven) and were used for barrel staves and for wainscoting. The term now applies to any beveled siding board, whether split or sawn, rabbeted or not, regardless of length or width. (The term is sometimes applied only to a form of bevel siding used in New England, about 4 feet long and quarter-sawn.) Sometimes called weatherboards.

classical orders See ORDER.

classical rectangle See GOLDEN SECTION.

Classical Revival Ambiguous term, suggesting **1** Neoclassical design of the late eighteenth and early nineteenth centuries, including the Greek Revival; or **2** Beaux-Arts Classical design of the late nineteenth and early twentieth centuries. Sometimes called Classic Revival. See instead BEAUX-ARTS CLASSICISM, GREEK REVIVAL, NEOCLASSICISM.

classicism, classical, classicizing Terms describing the application of principles or elements derived from the visual arts of the Greco-Roman era (seventh century B.C.E. through fourth century C.E.) at any subsequent period of Western civilization, but particularly since the Renaissance. More a descriptive term for an approach to design and for a general cultural sensibility than for any particular style. See also the related term NEOCLASSICISM.

clerestory A part of a building that rises above the roof of another part and has windows in its walls.

clipped gable roof See JERKINHEAD ROOF.

coffer A recessed panel, usually square or octagonal, in a ceiling. Such panels are also found on the inner surfaces of domes and vaults.

collar beam A horizontal tension member in a pitched roof connecting opposite rafters, generally halfway up or higher. Its function is to tie the angular members together and prevent them from spreading.

Collegiate Gothic 1 Originally, a secular version of English Gothic architecture, characteristic of the older colleges of Oxford and Cambridge. 2 A secular version of Late Gothic Revival architecture, which became a popular style for North American colleges and universities from the 1890s through the 1920s. Sometimes called Academic Gothic.

colonial 1 Not strictly a style term, but a term for the entire period during which a particular European country held political dominion over a part of the Western Hemisphere, Africa, Asia, Australia, or Oceania. See also the more specific terms BRITISH COLONIAL, DUTCH COLONIAL, FRENCH COLONIAL, SPANISH COLONIAL. 2 Loosely used to mean the British colonial period in North America (c. 1607–1781 for the United States; c. 1750s–1867 for much of Canada).

Colonial Revival Generally understood to mean the revival of forms from British colonial design. The Colonial Revival began in New England in the 1860s and continues nationwide into the present. Sometimes called Neo-Colonial. See also the more specific term GEORGIAN REVIVAL and the related terms FEDERAL REVIVAL, SHINGLE STYLE.

colonnade A series of freestanding or engaged columns supporting an entablature or simple beam.

colonnette A diminutive, often attenuated, column.

colossal order See GIANT ORDER.

column 1 A vertical supporting element, usually cylindrical and slightly tapering, consisting of a base (except in the Greek Doric order), shaft, and capital. See also the related terms ENTABLATURE, ENTASIS, ORDER. 2 Any vertical supporting element in a skeletal frame.

Commercial style See CHICAGO SCHOOL.

common bond A pattern of brickwork in which every fifth or sixth course consists of all headers, the other courses being all stretchers. Sometimes called American bond. Distinguished from running bond, in which no headers appear.

Composite order An ensemble of classical column and entablature elements, particularly characterized by large Ionic volutes and Corinthian acanthus leaves in the capital of the column. See also the more general term ORDER.

concrete An artificial stone made by mixing cement, water, sand, and a coarse aggregate (such as gravel or crushed stone) in specified proportions. The mix is shaped in molds called forms. Distinguished from cement, which is the binder without the aggregate.

console A type of bracket with a scroll-shaped or S-curve profile and a height greater than its projection from the wall. Distinguished from the more general term bracket, which is usually applied to supports whose projection and height are nearly equal. Distinguished from a modillion, which usually is smaller, has a projection greater than its height (or thickness), and appears in a series, as in a classical cornice.

coping The cap or top course of a wall, parapet, balustrade, or chimney, usually designed to shed water.

corbel A projecting stone that supports a superincumbent weight. In medieval architecture and its derivatives, a support for such major features as vaulting shafts, vaulting ribs, or oriels. See also the related term BRACKET.

corbeled construction Masonry that is built outward beyond the vertical by letting successive courses project beyond those below. Sometimes called corbeling.

corbeled cornice A cornice made up of courses of projecting masonry, each of which extends farther outward than the one below.

Corinthian order A ensemble of classical column and entablature elements, particularly characterized by acanthus leaves and small volutes in the capital of the column. See also the more general term ORDER.

cornice The crowning member of a wall or entablature.

Corporate International style A term, not widely used, for curtain wall commercial, institutional, and governmental buildings since the Second World War, which represent a widespread adoption of selected International style ideas from the 1920s. See also the more general term INTERNATIONAL STYLE.

Corporate style An architectural style developed in the early industrial communities of New England during the first half of the nineteenth century. This austere but graceful mode of construction was derived from the red-brick Federal architecture of the early nineteenth century and is characterized by the same elegant proportions, cleanly cut openings, and simple refined detailing. The term was coined by William Pierson in the 1970s.

cottage 1 A relatively modest rural or suburban dwelling. Distinguished from a villa, which is a more substantial and often more elaborate dwelling. 2 A seasonal dwelling, regardless of size, especially one located in a resort community.

cottage orné A rustic building in the romantic, picturesque tradition, noted for such features as bay windows, oriels, ornamented gables, and clustered chimneys.

course A layer of building blocks, such as bricks or stones, extending the full length and thickness of a wall.

coved ceiling A ceiling in which the transition between wall and ceiling is formed by a large concave panel or molding. Sometimes called a cove ceiling.

coved cornice A cornice with a concave profile. Sometimes called a cavetto cornice.

Craftsman A style of furniture and interior design belonging to the Arts and Crafts movement in the United States, and specifically related to *The Craftsman* magazine (1901–1916), published by Gustav Stickley (1858–1942). Some entire houses known to be derived from this publication can be called Craftsman houses. See also the more general term Arts and Crafts.

crenellation, crenellated A form of embellishment on a parapet consisting of indentations (crenels or embrasures) alternating with solid blocks of wall (merlons). Virtually synonymous with battlement, battlemented; embattlement, embattled.

cresting An ornamental strip or fencelike feature, usually of metal or tile, along the ridgeline or summit of a roof.

crocket In Gothic architecture, a small ornament resembling bunched foliage, placed at intervals on the sloping edges of gables, pinnacles, or spires.

crossing In a church with a cruciform plan, the area where the arms of the cross intersect; specifically, the space where the transept crosses the nave and chancel.

cross rib See LIERNE.

cross section See SECTION.

crown The central, or highest, part of an arch or vault.

crown molding The highest in a series of moldings.

crowstep Any one of the progressions in a gable that ascends in steps rather than in a continuous slope.

cruciform In the shape of a cross. Usually used to describe the ground plans of buildings. See also the more specific terms GREEK CROSS, LATIN CROSS.

cupola 1 A small domed structure on top of a belfry, steeple, or tower. **2** A lantern, square or polygonal in plan, with windows or vents, which is located at the summit of a roof. Sometimes called a belvedere. Distinguished from a skylight, which is a lesser feature located on the slope of a roof. **3** In historic English usage, synonymous with dome. A dome is now understood to be a more substantial feature.

curtain wall In skeleton frame or reinforced concrete construction, a thin nonstructural cladding of stone, brick, terracotta, glass, or metal veneer. Distinguished from bearing wall. See also the related term LOAD-BEARING.

cusp The pointed, roughly triangular intersection of the arcs of lobes or foils in the tracery of windows, screens, or panels.

cyma recta A molding of double curvature, with the concave section above the convex section.

cyma reversa A molding of double curvature, with the convex section above the concave section. When viewed from the side, it has the profile of the letter S.

dado A broad decorative band around the lower portion of an interior wall, between the baseboard and dado rail or cap molding. (The term is often applied to this entire zone, including baseboard and dado rail.) The dado may be painted, papered, or covered with some other material, so as to have a different treatment from the upper zone of the wall. Dado connotes any continuous lower zone in a room, equivalent to a pedestal. A wood-paneled dado is called a wainscot.

Deco See ART DECO.

dentil, denticulated A small ornamental block forming one of a series set in a row. A dentil molding is composed of such a series.

dependency A building, wing, or room, subordinate to, or serving as an adjunct to, a main building. A dependency may be attached to or detached from a main building. Distinguished from an outbuilding, which is always detached.

diaper An overall repetitive pattern on a flat surface, especially a pattern of geometric or representational forms arranged in a diamond-shaped or checkerboard grid. Sometimes called diaper work.

discharging arch See RELIEVING ARCH.

dome A major hemispherical or curved roof feature rising from a circular, polygonal, or square base. Distinguished from a cupola, which is a smaller, usually subordinate, domical element.

Doric order An ensemble of classical column and entablature elements, particularly characterized by the use of triglyphs and metopes in the frieze of the entablature. See also the more general term ORDER.

dormer A roof-sheltered window (or vent), usually with vertical sides and front, set into a sloping roof. Sometimes called a dormer window.

dosseret See IMPOST BLOCK.

double-hung window A window consisting of a pair of frames, or sashes, one above the other, arranged to slide up and down. Their movement is sometimes stabilized by a system of cords and counterbalancing weights contained in narrow boxing at each side of the window frame. Sometimes called guillotine sash.

double-pen In vernacular architecture, particularly houses, a term applied to a plan consisting of two rooms side by side or separated by a hallway.

double-pile In vernacular architecture, particularly houses, a term applied to a plan that is two rooms deep and any number of rooms wide.

drip molding See HEAD MOLDING.

drum 1 A cylindrical or polygonal wall zone upon which a dome rests. **2** One of the cylinders of stone that form the shaft of a column.

Dutch colonial A term applied to buildings, towns,

landscapes, and other artifacts from the period of actual Dutch colonial occupation of the Hudson River valley and adjacent areas (c. 1614–1664). Meaning has been extended to apply to the artifacts of Dutch ethnic groups and their descendants, even into the early nineteenth century.

Dutch Colonial Revival The revival of forms from design in the Dutch tradition.

ear A slight projection just below the upper corners of a door or window architrave or casing. Sometimes called a shouldered architrave.

Early American See BRITISH COLONIAL.

Early Christian A style of art and architecture in the Mediterranean world that was developed by the early Christians before the fall of the Western Roman Empire, derived from late Roman art and architecture and leading to the Romanesque (early fourth to early sixth century).

Early Georgian period Not strictly a style term, but a term for a period in British and British colonial history approximately coinciding with the reigns of George I (1714–1727) and George II (1727–1760). See also the related term LATE GEORGIAN PERIOD.

Early Gothic Revival A term for the Gothic Revival work of the late eighteenth to the mid-nineteenth century. See also the related term LATE GOTHIC REVIVAL.

Eastlake A decorative arts and interior design term of the 1860s and 1880s sometimes applied to architecture. Named after Charles Locke Eastlake (1836–1906), an English advocate of the application of Gothic principles of construction and design, rather than mere Gothic elements. Characterized by simplicity and solidity of forms, which are sometimes embellished with chamfered, turned, or incised details. Sometimes called Eastlake Gothic, Modern Gothic. See also the related term QUEEN ANNE.

eaves The horizontal lower edges of a roof plane, usually projecting beyond the wall below. Distinguished from verges, which are the sloping edges of a roof plane.

echinus A heavy molding with a curved profile placed immediately below the abacus, or top member, of a classical capital. Particularly prominent in the Doric and Tuscan orders.

eclecticism, eclectic A sensibility in design, prevalent since the eighteenth century, involving the selection of elements from a variety of sources, including historical periods of high-style design (Western and non-Western), vernacular design (Western and non-Western), and (in the twentieth century) contemporary industrial design. Distinguished from historicism and revivalism by drawing upon a wider range of sources than the historical periods of high-style design.

Ecole, Ecole des Beaux-Arts See BEAUX-ARTS.

Egyptian Revival Term applied to eclectic works or elements of those works that emulate forms in the visual arts of ancient Egyptian civilization.

elevation A drawing (in orthographic projection) of an upright, planar aspect of an object or building. The vertical complement of a plan. Sometimes loosely used in the sense of a facade view or any frontal representation of a wall, whether photograph or drawing, whether measured to scale or not.

Elizabethan Manor Style See NEO-TUDOR.

Elizabethan period A term for a period in English history coinciding with the reign of Elizabeth I (1558–1603). See also the more general term TUDOR PERIOD and the related term JACOBEAN PERIOD for the succeeding period.

embattlement, embattled See CRENELLATION.

encaustic tile A tile decorated by a polychrome glazed or ceramic inlay pattern.

enfilade The alignment of a series of doors through a sequence of adjoining rooms, resulting in a vista through these rooms.

engaged column A half-round column attached to a wall. Distinguished from a free standing column by seeming to be built into the wall. Distinguished from a pilaster, which is a flattened column. Distinguished from a recessed column, which is a fully round column set into a nichelike space.

English bond A pattern of brickwork in which the bricks are set in alternating courses of stretchers and headers.

English colonial See BRITISH COLONIAL.

English half-timber style. See NEO-TUDOR.

entablature In a classical order, a richly detailed horizontal member resting on columns or pilasters. It is divided horizontally into three main parts. The lowest is the architrave (definition **1**), the structural part, and is generally an unornamented continuous beam or series of beams. The middle part is the frieze (definition **1**), which is generally the most freely ornamented part. The uppermost is the cornice. Composed of a sequence of moldings, the cornice overhangs the frieze and architrave and serves as a crown to the whole. Each part has the moldings and decorative treatment that are characteristic of the particular order, but modern adaptations often alter canonical details. See also the related terms COLUMN, ORDER.

entablature block A block bearing the canonical elements of a classical entablature on three or all four sides, placed between a column capital and a feature above, such as a balcony or ceiling. Distinguished from an impost block, which has the form of an inverted truncated pyramid and detailing typical of medieval architecture.

entasis The slight convex curving of the vertical profile of a tapered column.

exedra A semicircular or polygonal space usually containing a bench, in the wall of a garden or a building other than a church. Distinuished from a niche, which is usually a smaller feature higher in a wall, and from an apse, which is usually identified with churches.

exotic revivals A term occasionally used to suggest a distinction between revivals of European styles (e.g., Greek, Gothic Revivals) and non-European styles (e.g., Egyptian, Moorish Revivals). See also the more specific terms EGYPTIAN REVIVAL, MAYAN REVIVAL, MOORISH REVIVAL.

extrados The outer curve or outside surface of an arch. See also the related term INTRADOS.

eyebrow dormer A low dormer with a small segmental window or vent but no sides. The roofing warps or bows over the window or vent in a wavy line.

facade An exterior face of a building, especially the principal or entrance front. Distinguished from an elevation, which is an orthographic drawing of a building face.

false half-timbering A surface treatment that simulates half-timber construction, consisting of a lattice of broad boards and stucco applied as an exterior veneer on a building of masonry or wood frame construction. Most commonly seen in domestic architecture from the late nineteenth century onward.

fanlight A semicircular or semielliptical window over a door, with radiating mullions in the form of an open fan. Sometimes called a sunburst light. See also the more general term TRANSOM (definition 1) and the related term SIDELIGHT.

fasces A symbol of Roman authority consisting of a bound bundle of rods with an axe projecting from them.

fascia 1 A plain, molded, or ornamented board that covers the horizontal edges (eaves) or sloping edges (verges) of a roof. Distinguished from the more specific term bargeboards, which are ornate fascia boards attached to the sloping edges of a roof. Distinguished from a frieze (definition 2), which is located at the top of a wall. **2** One of the broad continuous bands that make up the architrave of the IONIC, CORINTHIAN, or COMPOSITE ORDER.

Federal A version of Neoclassical architecture in the United States popular from New England to Virginia, and in other regions influenced by the Northeast. It flourished from the 1790s through the 1820s and is found in some regions as late as the 1840s. Sometimes called American Adam style. Not to be confused with FEDERALIST. See also the related term ROMAN REVIVAL.

Federal Revival Term applied to eclectic works (c. 1890s–1930s) or elements of those works that emulate forms in the visual arts of the Federal period. Sometimes called Neo-Federal. See also the related terms COLONIAL REVIVAL, GEORGIAN REVIVAL.

Federalist Name of an American political party and the era it dominated (c. 1787–1820). Not to be confused with FEDERAL.

fenestration Window treatment: arrangement and proportioning.

festoon A motif representing entwined leaves, flowers, or fruits, hung in a catenary curve from two points. Distinguished from a swag, which is a motif representing a fold of drapery hung in a similar curve. See also the more general term GARLAND.

fillet 1 A relatively narrow flat molding. **2** Any thin band.

finial A vertical ornament placed upon the apex of an architectural feature, such as a gable, turret, or canopy. Distinguished from a pinnacle, which is a larger feature, usually associated with Gothic architecture.

fireproofing In metal skeletal framing, the wrapping of structural members in terracotta tile or other fire-resistant material.

flashing A strip of metal, plastic, or various flexible compositional materials used at roof valleys and ridges and at chimney corners to keep water out. Any similar material used to protect door and window heads and sills.

Flemish bond A pattern of brickwork in which the stretchers and headers alternate in the same row and are staggered from one row to the next. Because this creates a more animated texture than English bond, Flemish bond was favored for front facades and more elegant buildings.

Flemish gable A gable whose upper slopes ascend in steps rather than in a straight line. These steps may be rectilinear or curved, or a combination of both.

fluting, fluted A series of parallel grooves or channels (flutes), usually semicircular or semielliptical in plan, that accentuate the verticality of the shaft of a column or pilaster.

flying buttress In Gothic architecture, a spanning member, usually in the form of an arch, that reaches across the open space from an exterior buttress pier to that point on the wall of the building where the thrusts of the interior vaults are concentrated. Because of its arched construction, a flying buttress exerts a counterthrust against the pressure of the vaults contained by the vertical strength of the buttress pier.

foliated (adjective). In the form of leaves or leaflike shapes.

folk Not a style term in itself, but a descriptive term, applicable to all the visual arts and all styles and periods. Applied to **1** a regional, often ethnic, tradition in which continuities through the years in the overall appearance of artifacts (including buildings) are more important than changes in stylistic embellishment; **2** the work of individual artists and artisans unexposed to or uninterested in prevailing or avant-garde ideals of form and technique. Approximate synonyms include anonymous, naive, primitive, traditional. For architecture, see also the more general term VERNACULAR and the related term POPULAR.

four-part vault See QUADRIPARTITE VAULT.

foursquare house A hipped-roof, two-story house with four principal rooms on each floor and a symmetrical facade. It usually has a front porch across the full width of the house and one or more large dormers on the roof. A common suburban house type from the 1890s to the 1920s. Sometimes called American Foursquare, Prairie Box.

frame construction, frame Ambiguous terms. See

instead BRACED FRAME CONSTRUCTION, LIGHT FRAME CONSTRUCTION (PLATFORM FRAME CONSTRUCTION), SKELETON CONSTRUCTION, TIMBER FRAME CONSTRUCTION. Not properly synonymous with wood construction, wood-clad, or wooden.

Francis I style See CHÂTEAUESQUE.

François Premier See CHÂTEAUESQUE.

French colonial A term applied to buildings, towns, landscapes, and other artifacts from the period of actual French colonial occupation of large parts of eastern North America (c. 1605–1763). The term is extended to apply to the artifacts of French ethnic groups and their descendants, well into the nineteenth century.

French Norman A style associated since the 1920s with residential architecture based on rural houses of the French provinces of Normandy and Brittany. While not a major revival style, it is characterized by asymmetrical plans, round stair towers with conical roofs, stucco walls, and steep hip roofs. Sometimes called Norman French.

fret An ornament, usually in series, as a band or field, consisting of a latticelike interlocking of right-angled linear elements.

frieze 1 The broad horizontal band that forms the central part of a classical entablature. 2 Any long horizontal band or zone, especially one that has a chiefly decorative purpose, located at the top of a wall. Distinguished from a fascia, which is attached to the horizontal edge of a roof.

front gabled Term applied to a building whose principal gable end faces the front of the lot or some feature like a street or open space. Sometimes called gable front. Distinguished from side gabled.

gable The wall area immediately below the end of a gable, gambrel, or jerkinhead roof.

gableboard See BARGEBOARD.

gable front See FRONT GABLED.

gable roof A roof in which the two planes slope equally toward each other to a common ridge. Sometimes called a pitched roof.

galerie In French colonial domestic architecture, a porch or veranda, usually sheltered by an extension of the hip roof of the house.

gambrel roof A roof that has a single ridgepole but a double pitch. The lower plane, which rises from the eaves, is rather steep. The upper plane, which extends from the lower plane to the ridgeline, has a flatter pitch.

garland A motif representing a rope of entwined leaves, flowers, ribbons, or drapery, regardless of its shape or position. It may be formed into a wreath, festoon, or swag, or follow the outline of a rectilinear architectural element.

garret See ATTIC (definition 1).

gauged brick A brick that has been cut or rubbed to a uniform size and shape.

gazebo A small pavilion, usually polygonal or circular in plan and serving as a garden or park shelter. Distinguished from a kiosk, which generally has some commercial or public function. See also the related terms BANDSTAND, BELVEDERE (definition 1).

General Grant style See SECOND EMPIRE.

Georgian period A term for a period in British and British colonial history, and not, in architecture or the other visual arts, a sufficiently specific style term. The Georgian period begins with the coronation of George I in 1714 and extends until about 1781 in the area that became the United States (and in Britain, until the death of George IV in 1830). See also the related terms ANGLO-PALLADIANISM, BRITISH COLONIAL.

Georgian plan See DOUBLE-PILE, DOUBLE-PEN.

Georgian Revival A revival of Georgian period forms—in England, from the 1860s to the present, and in the United States, from the 1880s to the present. Sometimes called Neo-Georgian. See also the more general term COLONIAL REVIVAL and the related term FEDERAL REVIVAL.

giant order A composition involving any one of the five principal classical orders, in which the columns or pilasters are nearly as tall as the height of the entire building. Sometimes called a colossal order. See also the more general term ORDER.

girder A major horizontal spanning member, comparable in function to a beam, but larger and often built up of a number of parts. It usually runs at right angles to the beams and serves as their principal means of support.

girt In timber-frame construction, a horizontal beam at intermediate (e.g., second-floor) level, spanning between posts.

glazing bar See MUNTIN.

golden section Any line divided into two parts so that the ratio of the longer part to the shorter part equals the ratio of the length of the whole line to the longer part: $a/b = (a + b)/a$. The ratio is approximately 1.618:1. A golden rectangle, or classical rectangle, is a rectangle whose long side is related to the short side in the same ratio as the golden section. It is proportioned so that neither the long nor the short side seems to dominate. In a Fibonacci series (i.e., 1, 2, 3, 5, 8, 13, . . .), the sum of the two preceding terms gives the next. The higher one goes in such a series, the closer the ratio of two sequential terms approaches the golden section.

Gothic An architectural style prevalent in Europe from the twelfth century into the fifteenth in Italy (and into the sixteenth century in the rest of Europe). It is characterized by pointed arches and ribbed vaults and by the dominance of openings over masonry mass in the wall. The Gothic was preceded by the Romanesque and followed by the Renaissance.

Gothic Revival A movement in Europe and North America devoted to reviving the forms and the spirit of Gothic architecture and the allied arts. It originated in the mid-eighteenth century. Sometimes called the Pointed style in the nineteenth century, and sometimes called Neo-Gothic. See also the more specific terms Early Gothic Revival, High Victorian Gothic, Late Gothic Revival.

Grecian A nineteenth-century term for GREEK REVIVAL.

Greek cross A cross with four equal arms. Usually used to describe the ground plan of a building. See also the more general term CRUCIFORM.

Greek Revival A movement in Europe and North America devoted to reviving the forms and the spirit of Classical Greek architecture, sculpture, and decorative arts. It originated in the mideighteenth century, culminated in the 1830s, and continued into the 1850s. Sometimes called Grecian in the nineteenth century. See also the more general term NEOCLASSICAL.

grisaille A technique of painting in different shades (values) of gray, often simulating relief sculpture.

groin The curved edge formed by the intersection of two vaults.

guilloche An ornamental pattern formed by interwoven or braided curing bands or ribbons.

guillotine sash See DOUBLE-HUNG WINDOW.

guttae (L., sing. **gutta**) In classical Doric entablatures, the set of small conical or cylindrical elements seeming to hang into the architrave zone of the entablature beneath each triglyph in the frieze zone. Also, the conical or cylindrical "pegs" in the underside of the horizontal mutule blocks in the cornice zone of the entablature that overhang the triglyphs and intervening metopes in the frieze zone.

HABS See HISTORIC AMERICAN BUILDINGS SURVEY.

HAER See HISTORIC AMERICAN ENGINEERING RECORD.

half-timber construction A variety of timber-frame construction in which the framing members are exposed on the exterior of the wall, with the spaces between timbers being filled with wattle-and-daub (i.e., woven lath and plaster) or masonry materials, such as brick or stone. These masonry materials may also be covered with stucco. Sometimes called half-timbered construction.

hall-and-parlor house, hall-and-parlor plan A double-pen house (i.e., a house that is one room deep and two rooms wide). Usually applied to houses without a central through-passage, to distinguish from hall-passage-parlor houses.

hall-passage-parlor house, hall-passage-parlor plan A two-room house with a central through-passage or hallway.

hammer beam A short horizontal beam projecting inward from the foot of the principal rafter and supported below by a diagonal brace tied into a vertical wall post. The hammer beams carry much of the load of the roof trussing above. Hammer beam trusses, which could be assembled using a series of smaller timbers, were often used in late medieval England instead of conventional trusses, which required long horizontal tie beams extending across an entire interior space.

haunch The part of the arch between the crown or keystone and the springing.

header A brick laid across the thickness of a wall, so that the short end of the brick shows on the exterior.

head molding A molding or set of moldings designed to shelter and embellish the top of a door or window. Sometimes called a drip molding. See also the related terms CAP (for windows) and HOOD (for doors).

heavy timber construction See TIMBER-FRAME CONSTRUCTION.

high style or high-style (adjective). Not a style term in itself, but a descriptive term, applicable to all the visual arts and all styles and periods. Applied to the works of the masters and their schools and disciples, usually reflecting a cosmopolitan awareness of traditions beyond a particular place or time. Usually contrasted with vernacular (including the folk and popular traditions).

high tech Term applied to architecture in which building materials and elements of building systems are used to celebrate contemporary technology. Elemental geometric forms, primary colors, and metallic finishes are used to heighten the technological imagery.

High Victorian Gothic A version of the Gothic Revival that originated in England in the 1850s and spread to North America in the 1860s. Characterized by polychromatic exteriors inspired by the medieval Gothic architecture of northern Italy. Sometimes called Ruskin Gothic, Ruskinian Gothic, Venetian Gothic, Victorian Gothic. See also the more general term GOTHIC REVIVAL.

hip gable roof See JERKINHEAD ROOF.

hip roof A roof that pitches inward from all four sides. The edge where any two planes meet is called the hip.

Historic American Buildings Survey A branch of the National Park Service of the United States Department of the Interior, established in 1933 to produce detailed documentation of American architecture. Such documentation typically includes historical and architectural data, photographs, and measured drawings, and is deposited in the Prints and Photographs Division of the Library of Congress. Abbreviated as HABS. See also the related term HISTORIC AMERICAN ENGINEERING RECORD.

Historic American Engineering Record A branch of the National Park Service of the United States Department of the Interior, established in 1969 to produce detailed documentation of sites and structures associated with industry, transportation, and other areas of technology. Abbreviated as HAER. See also the related term HISTORIC AMERICAN BUILDINGS SURVEY.

historicism, historicist, historicizing A type of eclecticism prevalent since the eighteenth century, involving the use of forms from historical periods of high-style design (usually in the Western tradition) and, occasionally, from favored traditions of vernacular design (such as the various colonial traditions in the United States). Historicist influences are designated by the use of the prefix Neo- with a previous historical style (e.g., Neo-Baroque). Distinguished from the more general term eclecticism, which draws upon a wider range of sources in addition to the historical. See also the more specific term REVIVALISM.

hollow building tile A hollow terracotta building block used for constructing exterior bearing walls of buildings up to about three stories, as well as interior walls and partitions.

hood A canopy, ledge, molding, or pediment over a door. Distinguished from a cap, which is a similar feature over a window. Sometimes called a hood molding. See also the related term HEAD MOLDING.

horizontal plank frame construction A system of wood construction in which horizontal planks are set or nailed into the corner posts of a timber frame building. There are, however, no studs or intermediate posts connecting the sill and the plate. See also the related term VERTICAL PLANK FRAME CONSTRUCTION.

hung ceiling See SUSPENDED CEILING.

hyphen A subsidiary building unit, often one story, connecting the central block and the wings or dependencies.

I-beam The most common profile in steel structural shapes (although it also appears in cast iron and in reinforced concrete). Used especially for spanning elements, it is shaped like the capital letter "I" to make the most efficient use of the material consistent with a shape that permits easy assemblage. The vertical face of the "I" is the web. The horizontal faces are the flanges. Other standard shapes for steel framing elements are Hs, Ts, Zs, Ls (known as angles), and square-cornered Us (channels).

I-house A two-story house, one room deep and two rooms wide, usually with a central hallway. The I-house is a nineteenth-century descendant of the hall-and-parlor houses of the colonial period. The term is commonly applied to the end-chimney houses of the southern and mid-Atlantic traditions. The term most likely derives from the resemblance between the tall, narrow end walls of these houses and the capital letter "I."

impluvium The tank in the center of a Roman atrium designed to receive water draining from the roofs.

impost The top part of a pier or wall upon which rests the springer or lowest voussoir of an arch.

impost block A block, often in the form of an inverted truncated pyramid, placed between a column capital and the lowest voussoirs of an arch above. Distinguished from an entablature block, which has the details found in a classical entablature. Sometimes called a dosseret or supercapital.

in antis Columns in antis are placed between two projecting sections of wall, in an imaginary plane connecting the ends of the two wall elements.

intermediate rib See TIERCERON.

International style A style that originated in the 1920s and flourished into the 1970s, characterized by the expression of volume and surface and by the suppression of historicist ornament and axial symmetry. The term was originally applied by Henry-Russell Hitchcock and Philip Johnson to the new, nontraditional, mostly European, architecture of the 1920s in their 1932 exhibition at the Museum of Modern Art and in their accompanying book, *The International Style*. Also called International, International Modern. See also the related terms BAUHAUS, MIESIAN, SECOND CHICAGO SCHOOL.

intrados The inner curve or underside (soffit) of an arch. See also the related term EXTRADOS.

Ionic order An ensemble of classical column and entablature elements, particularly characterized by the use of large volutes in the capital of the column. See also the more general term ORDER.

isometric drawing A pictorial drawing using isometric projection, in which all horizontal lines that are perpendicular in an object, building, or space are drawn at 60-degree angles from the vertical. Consequently, a single scale can be used for all three dimensions. Sometimes called an isometric. See also the related terms AXONOMETRIC DRAWING, PERSPECTIVE DRAWING.

Italianate 1 A general term for an eclectic Neo-Renaissance and Neo-Romanesque style, originating in England and Germany in the early nineteenth century and prevalent in the United States between the 1840s and 1880s, not only in houses but also in Main Street commercial buildings. The Italianate is characterized by prominent window heads and bracketed cornices. Called the Bracketed style in the nineteenth century. See also the more specific term ITALIAN VILLA STYLE and the related terms RENAISSANCE REVIVAL, ROUND ARCH MODE, SECOND EMPIRE. **2** A specific term for Italianate buildings that are predominantly symmetrical in plan and elevation. Distinguished from Barryesque, which is applied to more formal institutional and governmental buildings.

Italian Villa style A subtype of the Italianate style (definition **1**), originating in England and Germany in the early nineteenth century and prevalent in the United States between the 1840s and 1870s, mostly in houses, but also churches and other public buildings. The style is characterized by asymmetrical plans and elevations, irregular blocklike massing, round-arch arcades and openings, and northern Italian Romanesque detailing. Larger Italian Villa buildings often had a campanile-like tower. Distinguished from the more symmetrical Italianate style (definition **2**) by having the northern Italian rural vernacular villa as prototype.

Jacobean period A term for a period in British history coinciding with the rule of James I (1603–1625). See also the related term ELIZABETHAN PERIOD for the immediately preceding period, which itself is part of the TUDOR PERIOD.

Jacobethan Revival See NEO-TUDOR.

jamb The vertical side face of a door or window opening, amounting to the full thickness of the wall, and usually enriched with paneling, moldings, or jamb shafts (which are engaged columns set into a splayed, or angled, jamb). In an opening containing a door or window, the jamb is distinguished from the reveal, which is the portion of wall thickness between the door or window frame and the outer surface of the wall. (In an opening without a door or window, the terms jamb and reveal are used interchangeably.) Also distinguished from an architrave (definition **2**), which consists of the moldings on the face of a wall around the opening.

Jazz Moderne See ART DECO.

Jeffersonian A personal style of Neoclassicism identified with the architecture of Thomas Jefferson (1743–1826), derived in part from Palladian ideas and in part from Imperial Roman prototypes. The style had a limited influence in the piedmont of Virginia and across the Appalachians into the Ohio River valley. Sometimes called Jeffersonian Classicism. See also the related terms ANGLO-PALLADIANISM, FEDERAL, ROMAN REVIVAL.

jerkinhead roof A gable roof in which the upper portion of the gable end is hipped, or inclined inward along the ridgeline, forming a small triangle of roof surface. Sometimes called a clipped gable roof or hipped gable roof.

joist One of a series of small horizontal beams that support a floor or ceiling.

keystone The central wedge-shaped stone at the crown of an arch.

king post In a truss, the vertical suspension member that connects the tie beam with the apex of opposing principal rafters.

kiosk Originally, a Turkish summer palace. Since the nineteenth century, the term has been applied to any small pavilion or stand, usually found in public gardens, parks, streets, and malls, where it serves some commercial or public function. Distinguished from a gazebo, which may be found in public or private gardens or parks, but which usually serves as a sheltered resting place. See also the related term BANDSTAND.

label 1 A drip molding, over a square-headed door or window, which extends for a short distance down each side of the opening. **2** A similar vertical downward extension of a drip molding over an arch of any form. Sometimes called a label molding.

label stop 1 An L-shaped termination at the lower ends of a label. **2** Any decorative boss or other termination of a label.

lancet arch An arch, generally tall and sharply pointed, whose centers are farther apart than the width or span of the arch.

lantern 1 The uppermost stage of a dome, containing windows or arcaded openings. **2** Any feature, square or polygonal in plan and usually containing windows, rising above the roof of a building. The square structures that serve as skylights on the roofs of nineteenth-century buildings—particularly houses—were also called lantern lights, and, in Italianate and Second Empire buildings, came to be called cupolas.

Late Georgian period Not strictly a style term, but a term for a period in British and British colonial history approximately coinciding with the reigns of George III (1760–1820) and George IV (1820–1830). In the United States, the Late Georgian period is now understood to end some time during the Revolutionary War (1775–1781) and to be followed by the Federal period (c. 1787–1820). In Britain, the Late Georgian period includes the Regency period (1811–1820s). See also the related term EARLY GEORGIAN PERIOD.

Late Gothic Revival A term for the Gothic Revival work of the late nineteenth and early twentieth centuries. See also the more specific term COLLEGIATE GOTHIC (definition **2**) and the related term EARLY GOTHIC REVIVAL.

lath A latticelike, continuous surface of small wooden strips or metal mesh nailed to walls or partitions to hold plaster.

Latin cross A cross with one long and three short arms. Usually used to describe the ground plans of Roman Catholic and Protestant churches. See also the more general term CRUCIFORM.

leaded glass Panes of glass held in place by lead strips, or cames. The panes, clear or stained, may be of any shape.

lean-to roof See SHED ROOF.

lierne In a Gothic vault, a short ornamental rib connecting the major transverse ribs and the secondary tiercerons. Sometimes called a cross rib or tertiary rib.

light frame construction A type of wood frame construction in which relatively light structural members (usually sawn lumber, ranging from two-by-fours to two-by-tens) are fastened with nails. Distinguished from timber-frame construction, in which relatively heavy structural members (hewn or sawn timbers, measuring six-by-six and larger) are fastened with mortise-and-tenon joints.

lintel A horizontal structural member that supports the wall over an opening or spans between two adjacent piers or columns.

living hall In Queen Anne, Shingle style, and Colonial Revival houses, an extensive room, often containing the entry, the main staircase, a fireplace, and an inglenook.

load-bearing Term applied to a wall, column, pier, or any vertical supporting member, constructed so that all loads are carried to the ground through the wall, column, or pier. See also the related terms BEARING WALL, CURTAIN WALL.

loggia 1 A porch or open-air room, particularly one set within the body of a building. **2** An arcaded or colonnaded structure, open on one or more sides, sometimes with an upper story. **3** An eighteenth- and nineteenth-century term for a porch or veranda.

Lombard A style term applied in the United States in the mid-nineteenth century to buildings derived from the Romanesque architecture of northern Italy (especially Lombardy) and the earlier nineteenth-century architecture of southern Germany. Characterized by the use of brick, for both structural and ornamental purposes. Also called Lombardic. See also the related term ROUND ARCH MODE.

lunette 1 A semicircular area, especially one that contains some decorative treatment or a mural painting. **2** A semicircular window in such an area.

Mannerism, Mannerist 1 A phase of Renaissance art and architecture in the mid-sixteenth century, characterized by distortions, contortions, inversions, odd juxtapositions, and other departures from High Renaissance canons of design. **2** (not capitalized) A sensibility in design, regardless of style or period, characterized by a knowledgeable violation of rules and intended as a comment on the very nature of convention.

mansard roof A hip roof with double pitch. The upper slope may approach flatness, while the lower slope has a very steep pitch, sometimes flaring in a concave curve (or swelling in a convex curve) as it comes to the eaves. This lower slope usually has windows, and the area under the roof often amounts to a full story. The name is a corruption of that of François Mansart (1598–1666), who designed roofs of this type, which was revived in Paris during the Second Empire period.

Mansard style, Mansardic See SECOND EMPIRE.

mascaron The representation of a face, sometimes grotesque, used as an architectural ornament. Also called a mask.

masonry Construction using stone, brick, block, or some other hard and durable material laid up in units and usually bonded by mortar.

massing The grouping or arrangement of the primary volumetric components of a building.

Mayan Revival Term applied to eclectic works or elements of those works that emulate forms in the visual arts of the Maya civilization of Central America. See also the relted term ART DECO.

McKim Classicism, McKim Classical Architecture of, or in the manner of, the firm of McKim, Mead and White, 1890s–1920s. See BEAUX-ARTS CLASSICISM.

medieval Term applied to the Middle Ages in European civilization between the age of antiquity and the age of the Renaissance (i.e., mid-400s to mid-1400s in Italy; mid-400s to late 1500s in England). In architecture and the other visual arts, the medieval period included the end of the Early Christian period, then the Byzantine, the Romanesque, and the Gothic styles or periods.

Mediterranean Revival A style generally associated since the early twentieth century with residential architecture based on Italian villas of the sixteenth century. While not a major revival style, it is characterized by symmetrical arrangements, stucco walls, and low-pitch tile roofs. Sometimes called Mediterranean Villa, Neo-Mediterranean. See also the related term SPANISH COLONIAL REVIVAL.

metope In a Doric entablature, that part of the frieze which falls between two triglyphs. In the Greek Doric order the metopes often contain small sculptural reliefs.

Middle Ages See MEDIEVAL.

Miesian Term applied to work showing the influence of the German-American architect Ludwig Mies van der Rohe (1886–1969). See also the related terms BAUHAUS, INTERNATIONAL STYLE, SECOND CHICAGO SCHOOL.

Mission Revival A style originating in the 1890s, and making use of forms and materials from the Spanish and Mexican mission architecture of the eighteenth and early nineteenth centuries. Not to be confused with Mission furniture of the Arts and Crafts movement. See also the more general term SPANISH COLONIAL REVIVAL.

modern Ambiguous term, applied in various ways during the past century to the history of the visual arts and world history generally: **1** from the 1910s to the present (see also the more specific terms BAUHAUS, INTERNATIONAL STYLE); **2** from the 1860s, 1870s, 1880s, or 1890s to the present; **3** from the Enlightenment or the advent of Neoclassicism or the industrial revolution, c. 1750, to the present; **4** from the Renaissance in Italy, c. 1450, to the present.

Modern Gothic See EASTLAKE.

Moderne A term applied to a wide range of design work from the 1920s through the 1940s, in which aspects of traditionalism and modernism coexist and in which eclecticism (from a historical, exotic, or machine aesthetic) is inseparable from the urge for stylization. Sometimes called Art Moderne, Modernistic. See also the more specific terms ART DECO, PWA MODERNE, STREAMLINE MODERNE.

modillion One of a series of small, thin scroll brackets under the projecting crown molding of a classical cornice. It is found in the Corinthian and Composite orders. Distinguished from a console, which usually is larger and has a height greater than its projection from the wall.

molding A running surface composed of parallel and continuous sections of simple or compound curves and flat areas.

monitor An extensive shed-roofed feature on a roof, containing a band of windows or vents. It may be located along one of the roof slopes (a trapdoor monitor) or along the ridgeline (a clerestory monitor), and it usually runs the entire length of the roof. Distinguished from a skylight, which is a low-profile or flush-mounted feature in the plane of the roof.

Moorish Revival Term applied to eclectic works or elements of those works that emulate forms in the visual arts of those parts of North Africa and Spain under Muslim domination from the seventh through the fifteenth centuries.

mortar A mixture of cement or lime with water and a fine aggregate of sand used to secure bricks or stones in masonry construction.

mortise-and-tenon joint A timber framing joint that is made by one member having its end shaped into a projecting piece (tenon) that fits exactly into a hole (mortise) in the other member. Once joined, the pieces are held together by a peg that passes through the tenon.

mullion 1 A post or similiar vertical member dividing a window into two or more units, or lights, each of which may be further subdivided (by muntins) into panes. 2 A post or similar vertical member dividing a wall opening into two or more contiguous windows.

muntin One of the small vertical or horizontal members that hold panes of glass within a window or glazed door. Distinguished from a mullion, which is a heavier vertical member separating paired or grouped windows. Sometimes called a glazing bar, sash bar, or window bar.

mushroom column A reinforced concrete column that flares at the top in order to counteract shear stresses in the vicinity of the column.

National Register of Historic Places A branch of the National Park Service of the United States Department of the Interior, established by the National Historic Preservation Act of 1966, to maintain files of documentation on districts, sites, buildings, structures, and objects of national, state, or local significance. Properties listed on the National Register are afforded administrative—and, ultimately, judicial—review in instances where projects funded or assisted by federal agencies might have an impact on the historic property. Properties listed on the register may also be eligible for certain tax benefits.

nave 1 The entire body of a church between the entrance and the crossing. 2 The central space of a church, between the side aisles, extending from the entrance end to the crossing.

Neo-Baroque Term applied to eclectic works or elements of those works that emulate forms in the visual arts of the Baroque style or period. Sometimes called Baroque Revival.

Neo-Byzantine Term applied to eclectic works or elements of those works that emulate forms in the visual arts of the Byzantine style or period. Sometimes called Byzantine Revival.

Neoclassical Revival See Beaux-Arts Classicism.

Neoclassicism, Neoclassical A broad movement in the visual arts which drew its inspiration from ancient Greece and Rome. It began in the mid-eighteenth century with the advent of the science of archaeology and extended into the mid-nineteenth century (in some Beaux-Arts work, into the 1930s; in some Postmodern work, even into the present). See also the related terms Beaux-Arts, Beaux-Arts Classicism, classicism, and the more specific terms Greek Revival, Roman Revival.

Neo-Colonial See Colonial Revival.

Neo-Federal See Federal Revival.

Neo-Georgian See Georgian Revival.

Neo-Gothic Term applied to eclectic works or elements of those works that emulate forms in the visual arts of the Gothic style or period. The cultural movement that produced so many such works in the eighteenth, nineteenth, and twentieth centuries is called the Gothic Revival, though that term covers a wide range of work.

Neo-Grec An architectural style developed in connection with the Ecole des Beaux-Arts in Paris during the 1840s and characterized by the use of stylized Greek elements, often in conjunction with cast-iron or brick construction. See also the more general term Beaux-Arts.

Neo-Hispanic See Spanish Colonial Revival.

Neo-Mediterranean See Mediterranean Revival.

Neo-Norman Term applied to eclectic works or elements of those works that emulate forms in the visual arts of the eleventh- and twelfth-century Romanesque of Norman France and Britain.

Neo-Palladian See Palladianism.

Neo-Renaissance Term applied to eclectic works or elements of those works that emulate forms in the visual arts of the Renaissance style or period. The mid- to late nineteenth-century cultural movement that produced so many such works is called the Renaissance Revival, though that term covers a wide range of work.

Neo-Romanesque Term applied to eclectic works or elements of those works that emulate forms in the visual arts of the Romanesque style or period. The mid-nineteenth-century cultural movement that produced so many such works is called the Romanesque Revival, though that term covers a wide range of work.

Neo-Tudor Term applied to eclectic works or elements of those works that emulate forms in the visual arts of the Tudor period. Sometimes called Elizabethan Manor style, English half-timber style, Jacobethan Revival, Tudor Revival.

New Brutalism See Brutalism.

New Formalism A style prevalent since the 1960s, characterized by symmetrical arrangements, rich materials (marble cladding, metal grillework), and stylized classical (even Gothic) detailing. Architects associated with this style include Philip Johnson (b. 1906), Edward Durell Stone (1902–1978), and Minoru Yamasaki (1912–1985).

newel post A post at the head or foot of a flight of stairs, to which the handrail is fastened. Newel posts occur in a variety of shapes, in profile and cross section, and are generally more substantial elements than the individual balusters that support the handrail.

niche A recess in a wall, usually designed to contain sculpture or an urn. A niche is often semicircular in plan and surmounted by a half dome or shell form. See also the related terms aedicule, tabernacle (definition 1).

nogging Brickwork that fills the spaces between members of a timber frame wall or partition.

Norman French See French Norman.

octagon house A rare house type of the 1850s, based on the ideas of Orson Squire Fowler (1809–1887), who argued for the efficiencies of an octagonal floorplan. Sometimes called octagon mode.

oculus A circular opening in a ceiling or wall or at the top of a dome.

ogee arch A pointed arch formed by a pair of opposing S-shaped curves.

order The most important constituents of classical architecture are the orders, first developed as a structural-aesthetic system by the ancient Greeks. An order has two major components. A column with its capital is the main vertical supporting member. The principal horizontal member is the entablature. The Greeks developed three different types of order, the Doric, Ionic, and Corinthian, each distinguishable by its own decorative system and proportions. All three were taken over and modified by the Romans, who added two orders of their own, the Tuscan, which is a simplified form of the Doric, and the Composite, which is made up of elements of both the Ionic and the Corinthian. The Romans often used the orders as a structural system in the same manner as the Greeks. Unlike the Greeks, however, they also applied them as decoration to the surfaces of walls that were supported by other means. Sometimes called classical orders. See also the related terms COLUMN, ENTABLATURE, GIANT ORDER, SUPERPOSITION (definition 1).

oriel A projecting polygonal or curved window unit of one or more stories, supported on brackets or corbels. Sometimes called an oriel window. Distinguished from a bay window, which rises from the foundation and has a rooted rather than a suspended appearance. However, a multistory projection in a tall building, whether cantilevered out or built from the foundation, is called a projecting bay or a unit of bay windows.

Oriental Revival Ambiguous term, suggesting eclectic influences from any period in any culture in the "Orient," or Asia, including Turkish, Persian, Indian, Chinese, and Japanese, as well as Arabic (even the Moorish of North Africa and Spain). Sometimes called oriental style. See also the related term MOORISH REVIVAL.

orthographic projection A system of visual representation in which all details on or near some principal plane, object, building, or space are projected, to scale, onto the parallel plane of the drawing. Orthographic projection thus flattens all forms into a single two-dimensional picture plane and allows for an exact scaling of every feature in that plane. Distinguished from pictorial projection, which creates the illusion of three-dimensional depth. See also the more specific terms ELEVATION, PLAN, SECTION.

outbuilding A building subsidiary to and completely detached from another building. Distinguished from a dependency, which may be attached or detached.

overhang The projection of part of a structure beyond the portion below.

PWA Moderne A synthesis of the Moderne (i.e., Art Deco or Streamline Moderne) with an austere late type of Beaux-Arts Classicism, often associated with federal government buildings of the 1930s and 1940s during the Public Works Administration. See also the more general term MODERNE and the related terms ART DECO, BEAUX-ARTS CLASSICISM, STREAMLINE MODERNE.

Palladianism, Palladian Work influenced by the Italian Renaissance architect Andrea Palladio (1508–1580), particularly by means of his treatise, *I Quattro Libri dell'Architettura* (*The Four Books of Architecture*, originally published in 1570 and disseminated throughout Europe in numerous translations and editions until the mid-eighteenth century). The most significant flourishing of Palladianism was in England, from the 1710s to the 1760s, and in the British North American colonies, from the 1740s to the 1790s. Sometimes called Neo-Palladian, Palladian classical. See also the more specific term ANGLO-PALLADIANISM.

Palladian motif A three-part composition for a door or window, in which a round-headed opening is flanked by lower flat-headed openings and separated from them by columns, pilasters, or mullions. The flanking sections, and sometimes the entire unit, may be blind (i.e., not open).

Palladian Revival See ANGLO-PALLADIANISM.

Palladian window A window subdivided as in the Palladian motif.

parapet A low wall at the edge of a roof, balcony, or terrace, sometimes formed by the upward extension of the wall below.

pargeting Elaborate stucco or plasterwork, especially an ornamental finish for exterior plaster walls, sometimes decorated with figures in low relief or indented. Found in late medieval, Queen Anne, and period revival buildings. Sometimes called parging, pargework. See also the more general term STUCCO.

parquet Inlaid wood flooring, usually set in simple geometric patterns.

parti The essential solution to an architectural program or problem; the basic concept for the arrangement of spaces, before the development and elaboration of the design.

patera (plural: paterae). A circular or oval panel or plaque decorated with stylized flower petals or radiating linear motifs. Distinguished from a roundel, which is always circular.

pavilion 1 A central or corner unit that projects from a larger architectural mass and is usually accented by a special treatment of the wall or roof. **2** A detached or semidetached structure used for specialized activities, as at a hospital. **3** In a garden or fairground, a temporary structure or tent, usually ornamented.

pediment 1 In classical architecture, the low triangular gable end of the roof, framed by raking cornices along the inclined edges of the roof and by a horizontal cornice below. **2** In Renaissance and Baroque and later clasically derived architecture, the triangular or curvilinear culmination of a prominent part of a facade. **3** A similar but smaller-scale feature over a door or window. It may be triangular or curvilinear.

pendentive A concave surface in the form of a

spherical triangle that forms the structural transition from the square plan of a crossing to the circular plan of a dome.

pergola A structure with an open wood framed roof, often latticed, and supported by a colonnade. It is usually covered by climbing plants, such as vines or roses, and provides shade for a garden walk or a passageway to a building. Distinguished from arbors or trellises, which are less extensive accessory structures lacking the colonnade.

period house Term applied to suburban and country houses in which period revival styles are dominant.

period revival Term applied to eclectic works—particularly suburban and country houses—of the first three decades of the twentieth century, in which a particular historical or regional style is dominant. See also the more specific terms CoLONIAL REVIVAL, DUTCH COLONIAL REVIVAL, GEORGIAN REVIVAL, NEO-TUDOR, SPANISH COLONIAL REVIVAL.

peripteral (adjective). Surrounded by a single row of columns.

peristyle A range of columns surrounding a building or an open court.

perspective drawing A pictorial drawing representing an object, building, or space, as if seen from a single vantage point. The illusion of three dimensions is created by using a system based on the optical laws of converging lines and vanishing points. See also the related terms AXONOMETRIC DRAWING, ISOMETRIC DRAWING.

piano nobile (plural: *piani nobili*). In Renaissance and later architecture, a floor with formal reception, living, and dining rooms. The principal and often tallest story in a building, usually one level above the ground level.

piazza 1 A plaza or square. 2 An eighteenth- and nineteenth-century term for a porch or veranda.

pictorial projection A system of visual representation in which an object, building, or space is projected onto the picture plane in such a way that the illusion of three-dimensional depth is created. Distinguished from orthographic projection, in which the dimension of depth is excluded.

picturesque An aesthetic category in architecture and landscape architecture in the late eighteenth and early nineteenth centuries. It is characterized by relationships among buildings and landscape features that evoke the qualities of landscape paintings, in which the eye is led past a variety of forms and spaces into the distance and the mind is led to contemplate a sense of age (by means of ruins, fallen trees, weathered rocks, and mossy surfaces on all or these). In actual settings, asymmetrical and eclectic buildings, indirect approaches, and contrasting clusters of plantings heighten the experience of the picturesque.

pier 1 A freestanding mass, supporting a concentrated load from an arch, a beam, a truss, or a girder. While generally rectilinear in plan, piers in buildings based upon medieval precedents are often curvilinear in plan. 2 An upright portion of a wall that performs a columnar function. The pier may be continuous with the plane of the wall, or it may be distinguished from the plane of the wall to give it a columnlike independence.

pier and spandrel A type of skeletal wall organization in which the vertical metal columns (and their square-cornered cladding) project in front of the plane of windows and their spandrel panels. The spandrel panels may be exposed structural spanning members. More often they provide decorative covering for the structure.

pilaster 1 A flattened column, with or without fluting, that is attached to a wall. It is usually finished with the same capital and base as a freestanding column. 2 Any narrow, vertical strip attached to a wall. Distinguished from an engaged column, which has a convex curvature.

pilastrade A series of pilasters supporting an entablature (or a fascia board, in vernacular architecture).

pillar Ambiguous term, often used interchangeably with COLUMN, PIER, or POST; see instead one of those terms. (Although the term pillar is sometimes applied to columns that are square in plan, the term pier is preferable.)

pinnacle In Gothic architecture, a small spirelike element providing an ornamental finish to the highest part of a buttress or roof. It has a slender pyramidal or conical form and is often articulated with crockets or ribs and is topped by a finial. Distinguished from a finial, which is a smaller feature appearing by itself.

pitched roof See GABLE ROOF.

plan A drawing (in orthographic projection) representing all or part of an object, building, or space, as if viewed from directly above. A floor plan is a drawing of a horizontal cut through a building, usually at the level of the windows, showing the configuration of walls and openings. Other types of plans may illustrate ceilings, roofs, structural elements, and mechanical systems.

plank construction General term. See instead the more specific terms HORIZONTAL PLANK FRAME CONSTRUCTION, VERTICAL PLANK CONSTRUCTION.

plate 1 In timber-frame construction, the topmost horizontal structural member of a wall, to which the roof rafters are fastened. 2 In platform and balloon frame construction, the horizontal members to which the tops and bottoms of studs are nailed. The bottom plate is sometimes called the sill plate or sole plate.

Plateresque Term applied to Spanish and Spanish colonial Renaissance architecture from the early sixteenth century onward, in which the delicate, finely sculptured detail resembles the work of a silversmith *(platero)*. See also the related term SPANISH COLONIAL.

platform frame construction A system of light frame construction in which each story is built as an independent unit and the studs are only one story high. The floor joists of each story rest on the top plates of the story below, and the bearing walls or partitions rest on the subfloor of each floor unit or platform. Platform framing is easier to construct and more rigid than balloon framing and has become the common framing method in the twentieth century. Structural members are usually sawn lumber, ranging from two-by-fours to two-by-tens, and are fastened with nails. Sometimes called platform framing, western frame, western framing.

plinth The base block of a column, pilaster, pedestal, dado, or door architrave.

Pointed style A nineteenth-century term for Gothic Revival.

polychromy, polychromatic, polychrome A many-colored treatment, especially the combination of materials in various colors or the application of surface color, to articulate wall and roof planes and to highlight structure.

popular A term applied to vernacular architecture influenced by such publications as books of the orders, builders' guides, style books, pattern books, mail-order catalogs, architectural periodicals, and household magazines. Architecture in the popular tradition may be built according to commercially available plans or from widely distributed components; or it may be built by local practitioners (architects, builders, contractors) emulating buildings that are represented in publications. The distinction between popular architecture and high-style architecture by lesser-known architects depends on one's point of view with regard to the division between vernacular and high-style. See also the more general term VERNACULAR and the related term FOLK.

porch A structure attached to a building to shelter an entrance or to serve as a semienclosed sitting, working, or sleeping space. Distinguished from a portico, which is either a pedimented feature at least one story in height supported by classical columns or a more extensive colonnaded feature.

porte-cochère A porch projecting over a driveway and providing shelter to people leaving a vehicle and entering a building or vice versa. Also called a carriage porch.

portico 1 A porch at least one story in height consisting of a low-pitched roof supported on classical columns and finished in front with an entablature and pediment. **2** An extensive porch supported by a colonnade.

post A vertical supporting element, either square or circular in plan. Posts are the integral vertical members of a frame or truss, whether of wood or metal. Posts may also carry fences or gates, or may serve as freestanding markers (e.g., mileposts).

post-and-beam construction A structural system in which the main support is provided by vertical members (posts) carrying horizontal members (beams or lintels). Sometimes called post-and-girt construction, post and lintel construction, trabeation, trabeated construction.

Postmodernism, Postmodern A term applied to work that involves a reaction against the ideas and works of various twentieth-century modern movements, particularly the Bauhaus and the International style. Postmodern work makes use of historicism, yet the traditional elements are often merely applied to buildings that, in every other respect, are products of modern movement design. The term is also applied to works that are attempting to demonstrate an extension of the principles of various modern movements.

Prairie Box See FOURSQUARE HOUSE.

Prairie school, Prairie style A diverse group of architects working in Chicago and throughout the Midwest from the 1890s to the 1920s, strongly influenced by Frank Lloyd Wright and to a lesser degree by Louis Sullivan. The term is applied mainly to domestic architecture. An architect is said to belong to the Prairie school; a work of architecture is said to be in the Prairie style. Sometimes called Prairie, for short. See also the related terms CHICAGO SCHOOL, WRIGHTIAN.

pre-Columbian Term applied to the major cultures of Latin America (e.g., Aztec, Maya, Inca) that flourished prior to the discovery of the New World by Columbus in 1492 and the Spanish conquests of the sixteenth century. Distinguished from North American Indian, which is generally applied to indigenous cultures within the area that would become the United States and Canada.

pressed metal Thin sheets of metal (usually galvanized or tin-plated iron) stamped into patterned panels for covering ceilings and exterior and interior walls or into molding profiles and other details for assembly into exterior and interior cornices. Loosely called pressed tin or stamped metal. Prevalent from the 1870s through the 1920s.

program The list of functional, spatial, and other requirements that guides an architect in developing a design.

proscenium In a recessed stage, the area between the orchestra and the curtain.

proscenium arch In a recessed stage, the enframement of the opening.

prostyle Having a columnar portico in front, but not on the sides and rear.

provincialism, provincial Term applied to work in an isolated area (such as a province of a cosmopolitan center or a colony of a mother country), where traditional practices persist, with some awareness of what is being done in the cosmopolitan center or the homeland.

purlin In roof construction, a structural member laid across the principal rafters and parallel to the wall plate and the ridge beam. The light common rafters to which the roofing surface is attached are fastened across the purlins. See also the related term RAFTER.

pylon 1 Originally, the gateway facade of an Egyptian temple complex, consisting of a truncated broad pyramidal form with battered (inclined) wall surfaces on all four sides, or two truncated pyramidal towers flanking an entrance portal. **2** Any towerlike structure from which bridge cables or utility lines are suspended.

pyramidion A small pyramid, especially one on top of an obelisk or a larger pyramid.

quadriga A sculptural group on top of a building or monument which consists of a chariot drawn by four horses.

quadripartite vault A vault divided into four triangular sections by a pair of diagonal ribs. Sometimes called a four-part vault.

quarry-faced See ROCK-FACED.

quatrefoil A type of Gothic tracery having four parts (lobes or foils) separated by pointed elements (cusps).

Queen Anne Ambiguous but widely used term. **1** In architecture, the Queen Anne style is an eclectic style of the 1860s through 1910s in England and the United States, characterized by the incorporation of forms from postmedieval vernacular architecture and the architecture of the Georgian period. Sometimes called Queen Anne Revival. See also the more specific term SHINGLE STYLE and the related terms EASTLAKE, STICK STYLE. **2** In architecture, the original Queen Anne period extends from the late seventeenth into the early eighteenth century. **3** In the decorative arts, the Queen Anne style and period properly refer to work of the early eighteenth century during the reign of Queen Anne (1702–1714, i.e., after William and Mary and before Georgian). **4** In the decorative arts, eclectic work of the 1860s to 1880s is properly referred to as Queen Anne Revival.

quoin One of the bricks or stones laid in alternating directions, which bond and form the exterior corner of a building. Sometimes simulated in wood or stucco.

rafter One of the inclined structural members of a roof. Principal rafters are primary supporting elements spanning between the walls and the apex of the roof and carrying the longitudinal purlins. Common rafters are secondary supporting elements fastened onto purlins to carry the roof surfacing. See also the related term PURLIN.

raking cornice A cornice that finishes the sloping edges of a gable roof, such as the inclined sides of a triangular pediment.

random ashlar A type of masonry in which squared and dressed blocks are laid in a random pattern rather than in straight horizontal courses.

recessed column A fully round column set into a nichelike space only slightly larger than the column. Distinguished from an engaged column, which appears to be built into the wall.

reentrant angle An acute angle created by the juncture of two planes, such as walls.

refectory A dining hall, especially in medieval architecture.

regionalism 1 The sum of cultural characteristics (including material culture, language) that define a geographic region, usually extending beyond a single state or province, and coinciding with one or more large physiographic areas. **2** The conscious use, within a region, of forms and materials identified with that region, creating an architecture that is in keeping with the historical architecture of the region, and even a distinctive new regional style.

register A horizontal zone of a wall, altarpiece, or other vertical feature. Usually synonymous with story, but more inclusive, allowing for the description of zones with no corresponding interior spaces.

relieving arch An arch, usually of masonry, built over the lintel of an opening to carry the load of the wall above and relieve the lintel of carrying such load. Sometimes called a discharging arch or safety arch.

Renaissance The period in European civilization identified with a rediscovery or rebirth *(rinascimento)* of classical Roman (and to a lesser extent, Greek) learning, art, and architecture. Renaissance architecture began in Italy in the mid-1400s (Early Renaissance) and reached a peak in the early to mid-1500s (High Renaissance). In England, Renaissance architecture did not begin until the late 1500s or early 1600s. The Renaissance in art and architecture was preceded by the Gothic and followed by the Baroque.

Renaissance Revival 1 In architecture, an ambiguous term, applied to (a) Italianate work of the 1840s through 1880s and (b) Beaux-Arts Classical work of the 1880s through 1920s. **2** In the decorative arts, an eclectic furniture style incorporating a variety of Renaissance, Baroque, and Neo-Grec architectural motifs and utilizing wood marquetry, incised lines (often gilded), and ormolu and porcelain ornaments. Sometimes called Neo-Renaissance.

rendering Any drawing, whether orthographic (plan, elevation, section) or pictorial (perspective), in which shades and shadows are represented.

reredos A screen or wall at the back of an altar, usually with architectural and figural decoration.

return The continuation of a molding, cornice, or other projecting member, in a different direction, as in the horizontal cornice returns at the base of the raking cornices of a triangular pediment.

reveal 1 The portion of wall thickness between a door or window frame and the outer face of the wall. **2** Same as jamb, but only in an opening without a door or window.

revival, revivalism A type of historicism prevalent since the eighteenth century, involving the adaptation of historical forms to contemporary functions. Distinguished from a more pervasive historicism by an ideological conviction that sought to rationalize the choice of a historical style according to the values of the historical period that produced it. (The Gothic Revival, for instance, was associated with the Christianity of the Middle Ages.) Revival works, therefore, tend to invoke a single historical style. More hybrid works are manifestations of a less dogmatic historicism or eclecticism. See also the more general terms HISTORICISM, ECLECTICISM.

rib The projecting linear element that separates the curved planar cells (or webs) of vaulting. Originally these were the supporting members for the vaulting, but they may also be purely decorative.

Richardsonian Term applied to any work showing the influence of the American architect Henry Hobson Richardson (1838–1886). See the note under the more limiting term RICHARDSONIAN ROMANESQUE.

Richardsonian Romanesque Term applied to Neo-Romanesque work showing the influence of the American architect Henry Hobson Richardson (1838–1886). While many of Richardson's works make eclectic use of round arches and Romanesque details, many of his works show a creative eclecticism that transcends any particular historical style. The term Richardsonian, therefore, is a more inclusive term for the work of his followers than Richardsonian Romanesque—a term that continues to be widely used. Sometimes called Richardson Romanesque, Richardsonian Romanesque Revival.

ridgepole The horizontal beam or board at the apex of a roof, to which the upper ends of the rafters are fastened. Sometimes called a ridge beam, ridgeboard, ridge piece.

rinceau An ornamental device consisting of a sinuous and branching scroll elaborated with leaves and other natural forms.

rock-faced Term applied to the rough, unfinished face of a stone used in building. Sometimes called quarry-faced.

Rococo A late phase of the Baroque, marked by elegant reverse-curve ornament, light scale, and delicate color. See also the related term BAROQUE.

Romanesque A medieval architectural style which reached its height in the eleventh and twelfth centuries. It is characterized by round arched construction and massive masonry walls. The Romanesque was preceded by the Early Christian and Byzantine periods in the eastern Mediterranean world and by a variety of localized styles and periods in northern and western Europe; it was followed throughout Europe by the Gothic.

Romanesque Revival Ambiguous term, applied to 1 *Rundbogenstil* and Round Arch work in America as early as the 1840s and 2 Richardsonian Romanesque work into the 1890s. Sometimes called Neo-Romanesque.

Roman Revival A term, not widely accepted, for a version of Neoclassicism involving the use of forms from the visual arts of the Imperial Roman period. Applied to various works in Italy, England, and the United States, where it is most clearly visible in the architecture of Thomas Jefferson. See also the related terms FEDERAL, NEOCLASSICISM.

rood screen An ornamental screen that serves as a partition between the crossing and the chancel or choir of a church.

rosette A circular floral ornament similar to an open rose.

rotunda 1 A circular hall in a large building, especially an area beneath a dome or cupola. 2 A building round both inside and outside, usually domed.

Round Arch mode The American counterpart of the German *Rundbogenstil,* characterized by the predominance of round arches, whether these are accentuated by Romanesque or Renaissance detailing or left as simple unadorned openings. See also the related terms ITALIANATE, LOMBARD, RUNDBOGENSTIL.

roundel A circular panel or plaque. Distinguished from a patera, which is oval shaped.

rubble masonry A type of masonry utilizing uncut or roughly shaped stone, such as fieldstone or boulders.

Rundbogenstil Literally, "round arch style," a historicist style originating in Germany in the 1820s and spreading to Britain and the United States from the 1840s through the 1860s. It is characterized by an eclectic combination of Romanesque and Renaissance elements. See also the related term ROUND ARCH MODE.

running bond A pattern of brickwork in which only stretchers appear, with the vertical joints of one course falling halfway between the vertical joints of adjacent courses. Sometimes called stretcher bond. Distinguished from common bond, in which every fifth or sixth course consists of all headers.

Ruskin Gothic, Ruskinian Gothic See HIGH VICTORIAN GOTHIC.

rustication, rusticated Masonry in which the joints are emphasized by narrow recessed channels or grooves outlining each block. Sometimes simulated in wood or stucco.

sacristy A room in a church where liturgical vessels and vestments are kept.

safety arch See RELIEVING ARCH.

sanctuary 1 The part of a church that contains the principal altar. Usually the innermost space within the chancel arm of the church, situated to the east of the choir. 2 Loosely used to mean a place of worship, a sacred place.

sash Any framework of a window. It may be movable or fixed. It may slide in a vertical plane (as in a double-hung window) or may be pivoted (as in a casement window).

sash bar See MUNTIN.

scagliola Interior plasterwork imitating stone, consisting of mixtures of plaster, marble dust, sizing, and various pigments. The surface, which may contain various inlaid and incised elements, is rubbed and polished.

Secession movement The refined classicist Austrian (Viennese) version of the Art Nouveau style, so named because the artists and architects involved seceded from the official Academy in 1897. Josef Hoffman (1870–1956) is the architect most frequently mentioned in association with this movement.

Second Chicago school A term sometimes applied to the International style in Chicago from the 1940s to the 1970s, particularly the work of Mies van der Rohe. See also the related terms INTERNATIONAL STYLE, MIESIAN.

Second Empire Not strictly a style term but a term

for a period in French history coinciding with the rule of Napoleon III (1852–1870). Generally applied in the United States, however, to a phase of Beaux-Arts governmental and institutional architecture (1850s–1880s) as well as to countless hybrids of Beaux-Arts and Italianate forms in residential, commercial, and industrial architecture (1850s–1880s). Sometimes called General Grant style, Mansard style, Mansardic. See also the related terms BEAUX-ARTS, ITALIANATE (definition **1**).

section A drawing (in orthographic projection) representing a vertical cut through an object, building, or space. An architectural section shows interior relationships of space and structure, and may also include mechanical systems. Sometimes called a cross section.

segmental arch An arch formed on a segmental curve. Its center lies below the springing line.

segmental curve A curve that is a segment (i.e., less than half the circumference) of a circle or an ellipse. The base line of the curve is a chord measuring less than the diameter of the larger circle from which the segment is taken.

segmental pediment A pediment whose top is a segmental curve.

segmental vault A vault whose cross section is a segmental curve. A dome built on segmental curves is called a saucer dome.

setback 1 In architecture, particularly in the design of tall buildings, a series of upper stories that are stepped back to allow more sunlight to reach the streets. **2** In planning, the amount of space between the lot line and the perimeter of a building.

shaft The tall part of a column between the base and the capital.

shed roof A roof having only one sloping plane. Sometimes called a lean-to roof.

Shingle style A term applied primarily to American domestic architecture of the 1870s through the 1890s, in which broad expanses of wood shingles dominate the exterior roof and wall planes. Rooms open widely into one another and to the outdoors, and the ample living hall or stair hall is often the dominant feature of the interior. The term was coined in the 1940s by Vincent Scully for a series of seaside and suburban houses of the northeastern United States. The Shingle style is a version of the Anglo-American Queen Anne style. See also the related terms COLONIAL REVIVAL, STICK STYLE.

shouldered architrave See EAR.

side gabled Term applied to a building whose gable ends face the sides of a lot. Distinguished from front gabled.

side light A framed area of fixed glass alongside a door or window. See also the related term FANLIGHT.

sill course In masonry, a stringcourse set at windowsill level, usually differentiated from the wall by its greater projection, its finish, or its thickness. Not applicable to frame construction.

sill plate See PLATE (definition **2**).

skeleton construction, skeleton frame A system of construction in which all loads are carried to the ground through a rigid framework of iron, steel, or reinforced concrete. The exterior walls are curtain walls (i.e., not load-bearing).

skylight A window in a roof, specifically one that is flush with the roof plane or only slightly protruding. Distinguished from a cupola (definition **2**), which is a major centralized feature at the summit of a roof. Distinguished from a monitor, which is an extensive roof feature containing a band of windows or vents.

soffit The exposed underside of any overhead component, such as an arch, beam, cornice, or lintel. See also the related term INTRADOS.

sole plate See PLATE (definition **2**).

space frame A series of trusses placed side by side and joined to one another by triangulated rods, tubes, or beams, so that the individual planar trusses are united into a three-dimensional structural framework. Often used in roof structures requiring long spans.

spandrel 1 The quasi-triangular space between two adjoining arches and a line connecting their crowns, or between an arch and the columns and entablature that frame it. **2** In skeletal construction, the wall area between the top of a window and the sill of the window in the story above. Sometimes called a spandrel panel.

Spanish colonial A term applied to buildings, towns, landscapes, and other artifacts from the various periods of actual Spanish colonial occupation in North America (c. 1565–1821 in Florida; c. 1763–1800 in Louisiana and the Lower Mississippi Valley; c. 1590s–1821 in Texas and the southwestern United States; c. 1769–1821 in California). The term is extended to apply to the artifacts of Hispanic ethnic groups (e.g., Mexicans, Puerto Ricans, Cubans) and their descendants, even into the early twentieth century. See also the related term CHURRIGUERESQUE.

Spanish Colonial Revival The revival of forms from Spanish colonial and provincial Mexican design. The Spanish Colonial Revival began in Florida and California in the 1880s and continues nationwide into the present. Sometimes called Neo-Hispanic, Spanish Eclectic, Spanish Revival. See also the more specific term MISSION REVIVAL and the related term MEDITERRANEAN REVIVAL.

spindle A turned wooden element, thicker toward the middle and thinner at either end, found in arch screens, porch trim, and other ornamental assemblages. Banisters (i.e., thin, simple balusters) may be spindle-shaped, but the term spindle, when used alone, usually connotes shorter elements.

spire A slender pointed element surmounting a building. A tall, attenuated pyramidal form with any number of thin triangular faces that are unbroken or articulated only with crockets, pinnacles, or small dormers. Distinguished from a steeple, which is divided into stages and which may be topped with a spire.

splay The slanting surface formed by cutting off a right-angle corner at an oblique angle to one face. A reveal at an oblique angle to the exterior face of the wall.

springing, springing line, springing point The line or point where an arch or vault rises from its supports and begins to curve. Usually the juncture between the impost of the support below and the springer, or first voussoir, of the arch above.

squinch An arch, lintel, or corbeling, built across the interior corner of two walls to form one side of an octagonal base for a dome. This octagonal base serves as the structural transition from a square interior crossing space to an octagonal or round dome.

stair A series of steps, or flights of steps connected by landings, which connects two or more levels or floors.

staircase The ensemble of a stair and its enclosing walls. Sometimes called a stairway.

stair tower A projecting tower or other building block that contains a stair.

stamped metal See PRESSED METAL.

steeple 1 A tall structure rising from a tower, consisting of a series of superimposed stages diminishing in plan, and usually topped by a spire or small cupola. Distinguished from a spire, which is not divided into stages. 2 Less commonly used to mean the whole of the tower, from the ground to the top of the spire or cupola.

stepped gable A gable in which the wall rises in a series of steps above the planes of the roof.

stereotomy The science of cutting three-dimensional shapes from stone, such as the units that make up a carefully fitted masonry vault.

Stick style A term applied primarily to American domestic architecture of the 1850s through the 1870s, in which exterior wall planes are subdivided into bays and stories outlined by narrow boards called "stickwork." The term was coined by Vincent Scully in the 1940s for a series of houses with clearly articulated wall panels and sticklike porch supports and eaves brackets. Sources include the English and German picturesque traditions, as well as the French rationalist tradition. See also the related terms QUEEN ANNE, SHINGLE STYLE.

story (plural: stories). The space in a building between floor levels. British spelling is storey, storeys. Sometimes called a register, a more inclusive term applied to horizontal or to vertical plane zones that do not correspond to actual floor levels.

Streamline Moderne A later phase of the Moderne, popular in the 1930s and 1940s and characterized by stucco surfaces with rounded corners, by horizontal banding, overhangs, and window groupings, and by other details suggestive of modern Machine Age aerodynamic forms. Sometimes called Streamline Modern, Streamline Modernistic. See also the more general term MODERNE and the related terms ART DECO and PWA MODERNE.

stretcher A brick laid the length of a wall, so that the long side of the brick shows on the exterior.

stretcher bond See RUNNING BOND.

string In a stair, an inclined board that supports the ends of the steps. Sometimes called a stringer.

stringcourse In masonry, a horizontal band, generally narrower than other courses, extending across the facade of a building and in some instances encircling such features as pillars or columns. It may be flush or projecting; of identical or contrasting material; flat, molded, or richly carved. Not applicable to frame construction. Sometimes called a band course or belt course. More elaborate horizontal bands in masonry or frame construction are generally called band moldings.

strut A column, post, or pole that is set in a diagonal position and thus serves as a stiffener by triangulation. Distinguished from a brace, which is usually a shorter bracketlike member.

stucco 1 An exterior plaster finish, usually textured, composed of portland cement, lime, and sand, which are mixed with water. 2 A fine plaster used for decorative work or moldings.

stud One of the vertical supporting elements in a wall, especially in balloon and platform frame construction. Studs are relatively lightweight members (usually two-by-fours).

Sullivanesque Term applied to work showing the influence of the American architect Louis Henry Sullivan (1856–1924).

sunburst light See FANLIGHT.

supercapital See IMPOST BLOCK.

supercolumniation See SUPERPOSITION (definition 1).

superimposition, superimposed See SUPERPOSITION.

superposition, superposed 1 The use of an ensemble of the classical orders, one above the other, as the major elements articulating a facade. When this is done, the Doric, considered the simplest order, is used on or near the ground story. The Ionic, considered more complex, comes next; and the Corinthian, considered the most complex, is used at the top. Sometimes the Tuscan order or rusticated masonry may be used for the ground story beneath the Doric order, and the Composite order may be used above the Corinthian order. Sometimes called supercolumniation, superimposition. See also the related term ORDER. 2 Less commonly, any vertical relationship of architectural elements (e.g., windows, piers, colonnettes) in any style or period.

superstructure A structure raised upon another structure, as a building upon a foundation, basement, or substructure.

Supervising Architect The Supervising Architect of the United States Treasury Department, whose office was responsible for the design and construction of all major federal government buildings (such as courthouses, customhouses, and post offices) from the 1850s through the 1930s. The Office of the Supervising Architect was formally established by Congress in 1864 and lasted until 1939, when its functions were absorbed into the

Public Buildings Administration (and in 1949, into the General Services Administration).

supporting wall See BEARING WALL.

surround An encircling border or decorative frame around a door or window. Distinguished from architrave (definition **2**), a term usually applied to the frame around an opening when considered as a series of relatively flat face moldings.

suspended ceiling A ceiling suspended from rod-like hangers below the level of the floor above. The interval between the floor slab above and the suspended ceiling often serves as a space for ducts, utilities, and air circulation. Sometimes called a hung ceiling.

swag A motif representing a suspended fold of drapery hanging in a catenary curve from two points. Distinguished from a festoon, which is a motif representing entwined leaves, flowers, or fruits, hung in a similar curve. See also the more general term GARLAND.

tabernacle **1** A niche or recess, usually on an interior wall, framed by columns or pilasters and topped by an entablature and pediment. Distinguished from an aedicule, which more often occurs on an exterior wall. See also the related term NICHE. **2** In the Jewish religion, a portable sanctuary. **3** In Protestant denominations, a large auditorium church.

tempietto Literally, a small temple, usually circular. These structures served as religious monuments and garden ornaments from the Renaissance to the nineteenth century. A well-known example is Bramante's Tempietto in the courtyard of San Pietro in Montorio in Rome (1502). Distinguished from a tholos, a round classical monument with Greek connotations, associated with the Greek Revival of the early nineteenth century.

terracotta A hard ceramic material used for **1** fireproofing, especially as a fitted cladding around metal skeletal construction; or **2** an exterior or interior wall cladding, which is often glazed and multicolored.

tertiary rib See LIERNE.

thermal window A large lunette window similar to those found in ancient Roman baths (*thermae*). The window is subdivided into three to five parts by vertical mullions. Sometimes called a *thermae* window.

tholos In Greek and Greek Revival architecture, any small round building, or such a form incorporated in a larger building. Distinguished from a tempietto, a similar round architectural form with Renaissance or Renaissance Revival connotations.

three-hinged arch An arch in two major segments anchored with cylindrical "hinge" pins at either end and at the crown. Movement within the arch, caused by temperature changes, the torsion of wind movements, or other forces, can be absorbed by the movement of the arch around the pins, thereby avoiding stresses that would occur in the structural frame if the arches were fixed.

tie beam A horizontal tension member that ties together the opposing angular members of a truss and prevents them from spreading.

tier A group of stories or any zone of architectural elements arranged horizontally.

tierceron In a Gothic vault, a secondary rib that rises from the springing to an intermediate position on either side of the diagonal ribs. Sometimes called an intermediate rib.

tie rod A metal rod that spans the distance between two structural members and, by its tensile strength, restrains them against tendencies to collapse outward.

timber-frame construction, timber framing A type of wood frame construction in which heavy timber posts and beams (six-by-sixes and larger) are fastened using mortise and tenon joints. Sometimes called heavy timber construction. Distinguished from light frame construction, in which relatively light structural members (two-by-fours to two-by-tens) are fastened with nails.

trabeation, trabeated construction See POST-AND-BEAM CONSTRUCTION.

tracery Decoration within an arch or other opening, made up of narrow curvilinear bands or more elaborately molded strips. In Gothic architecture, the curved interlocking stone bars that contain the leaded stained glass.

transept The lateral arm of a cross-shaped church, usually between the nave (the area for the congregation) and the chancel (the area for the altar, clergy, and choir).

transom **1** A narrow horizontal window unit, either fixed or movable, over a door. Sometimes called a transom light. See also the more specific term FANLIGHT. **2** A horizontal bar, as distinguished from a vertical mullion, especially one crossing a door or window opening near the top.

transverse rib In a Gothic vault, a rib at right angles to the ridge rib.

trefoil A type of Gothic tracery having three parts (lobes or foils) separated by pointed elements (cusps).

trellis Any open latticework made of strips of wood or metal crossing one another, usually supporting climbing plants. Distinguished from an arbor, which is generally a more substantial yet compact three-dimensional structure, and from a pergola, which is a more extensive colonnaded structure.

triforium In a Gothic church, an arcade in the wall above the arches of the nave, choir, or transept and below the clerestory window.

triglyph One of the slightly raised blocks in a Doric frieze. It consists of three narrow vertical bands separated by two V-shaped grooves.

triumphal arch **1** A freestanding arch erected for a victory procession. It usually consists of a broad central arched opening, flanked by two smaller bays (usually with open or blind arches). The bays are usually articulated by classical columns, supporting an entablature and a high attic. **2** A similar configuration applied to a facade to denote a monumental entryway.

truss A rigid triangular framework made up of beams, posts, braces, struts, and ties and used for the spanning of large spaces. The major horizontal or inclined members are called chords. The connecting vertical and diagonal elements are called the web members.

Tudor arch A low-profile arch characterized by two pairs of arcs, one pair of tight arcs at the springing, another pair of broad (nearly flat) arcs at the apex or crown.

Tudor period A term for a period in English history coinciding with the rule of monarchs of the house of Tudor (1485–1603). Tudor period architecture is Late Gothic, with only hints of the Renaissance. See also the more specific term ELIZABETHAN PERIOD for the end of this period, and the related term JACOBEAN PERIOD for the succeeding period.

Tudor Revival See NEO-TUDOR.

turret A small towerlike structure, often circular in plan, built against the side or at an exterior or interior corner of a building.

Tuscan order An ensemble of classical column and entablature elements, similar to the Roman Doric order, but without triglyphs in the frieze and without mutules (domino-like blocks) in the cornice of the entablature. See also the more general term ORDER.

tympanum (plural: tympana). **1** The triangular or segmental area enclosed by the cornice moldings of a pediment, frequently ornamented with sculpture. **2** Any space similarly delineated or bounded, as between the lintel of a door or window and the arch above.

umbrage A term used by Alexander Jackson Davis (1803–1892) as a synonym for veranda, the implication being a shadowed area.

vault An arched roof or ceiling, usually constructed in brick or stone, but also in tile, metal or concrete. A nonstructural plaster ceiling that simulates a masonry vault.

Venetian Gothic See HIGH VICTORIAN GOTHIC.

veranda A nineteenth-century term for porch. Sometimes spelled verandah.

vergeboard See BARGEBOARD.

verges The sloping edges of a gable, gambrel, or lean-to roof, usually projecting beyond the wall below. Distinguished from eaves, which are the horizontal lower edges of a roof plane.

vernacular Not a style in itself, but a descriptive term, applicable primarily to architecture, covering the vast range of ordinary buildings that are produced outside the high-style tradition of well-known architects. The vernacular tradition includes the folk tradition of regional and ethnic buildings whose forms (plan and massing) remain relatively constant through the years, in spite of stylistic embellishments. The term vernacular architecture is often used as if it meant only folk architecture. However, the vernacular tradition in

architecture also includes the popular tradition of buildings whose design was influenced by such publications as books of the orders, builders' guides, style books, pattern books, mail-order catalogs, architectural periodicals, and household magazines. Usually contrasted with high style. See also the more specific terms FOLK, POPULAR.

vertical plank construction A system of wood construction in which vertical planks are set or nailed into heavy timber horizontal sills and plates. A building so constructed has no corner posts and no studs. Two-story vertical plank buildings have planks extending the full height of the building, with no girt between the two stories. Second-floor joists are merely mortised into the planks. Distinguished from the more specific term vertical plank frame construction, in which there are corner posts.

vertical plank frame construction A type of vertical plank construction, in which heavy timber corner posts are introduced to provide support for the plate, to which the tops of the planks are fastened. See also the related term HORIZONTAL PLANK FRAME CONSTRUCTION.

vestibule A small entry hall between the outer door and the main hallway of a building.

Victorian Gothic See HIGH VICTORIAN GOTHIC.

Victorian period A term for a period in British, British colonial, and Anglo-American history, and not, in architecture or the other visual arts, a sufficiently specific style term. The Victorian period extended across eight decades, from the coronation of Queen Victoria in 1837 to her death in 1901. See instead EASTLAKE, GOTHIC REVIVAL, GREEK REVIVAL, QUEEN ANNE, SHINGLE STYLE, STICK STYLE, and other specific style terms.

Victorian Romanesque Ambiguous term. See instead RICHARDSONIAN ROMANESQUE, ROMANESQUE REVIVAL, ROUND ARCH MODE.

villa 1 In the Roman and Renaissance periods, a suburban or rural residential complex, often quite elaborate, consisting of a house, dependencies, and gardens. **2** Since the eighteenth century, any detached suburban or rural house of picturesque character and some pretension. Distinguished from the more modest house form known as a cottage.

volute 1 A spiral scroll, especially the one that is a distinctive feature of the Ionic capital. **2** A large scroll-shaped buttress on a facade or dome.

voussoir A wedge-shaped stone or brick used in the construction of an arch. Its tapering sides coincide with radii of the arch.

wainscot A decorative or protective facing, usually of wood paneling, applied to the lower portion of an interior partition or wall. Distinguished from a dado, which is the zone at the base of a wall, regardless of the material used to cover it. Wainscot properly connotes woodwork. Sometimes called wainscoting.

water table 1 In masonry, a course of molded bricks or stones set forward several inches near the base of a wall and serving as the cap of the basement courses. **2** In frame construction, a ledge or projecting molding just above the foundation to protect it from rainwater. **3** In masonry or frame construction, any horizontal exterior ledge on a wall, pier, or buttress. Often sloped and provided with a drip molding to prevent water from running down the face of the wall below.

weatherboard See CLAPBOARD.

weathering The inclination given to the upper surface of any element so that it will shed water.

web 1 The relatively thin shell of masonry between the ribs of a ribbed vault. **2** The portion of a truss between the chords, or the portion of a girder or I-beam between the flanges.

western frame, western framing See FRAME CONSTRUCTION.

winder A step, more or less wedge-shaped, with its tread wider at one end than the other.

window bar See MUNTIN.

window cap See CAP.

window head A head molding or pedimented feature over a window.

Wrightian Term applied to work showing the influence of the American architect Frank Lloyd Wright (1867–1959). See also the related term PRAIRIE SCHOOL.

wrought iron Iron shaped by a hammering process, to improve the tensile properties of the metal. Distinguished from cast iron, a brittle material, which is formed in molds.

Zigzag Moderne, Zigzag Modernistic See ART DECO.

Photography Credits

Franz Jantzen has taken a great number of the photographs for this book. Unless otherwise noted, photographs have been taken by him.

INTRODUCTION

Page 6, *The City of Washington,* by George C. Cooke; **p. 7,** Handy Map of Washington, J. C. Entwistle, 1876; **p. 18,** first printed map of Washington, D.C., by Thackara and Vallence, printed 1792; **p. 22,** drawing of Blodgett's Hotel; **p. 25,** George Hadfield's Branch Bank of the United States; **p. 26,** Van Ness house by Benjamin Henry Latrobe; **p. 29,** Charles Bulfinch's design for the Unitarian church; **p. 30,** W. W. Corcoran House; **p. 31,** Trinity Episcopal Church; **p. 34,** 1860 facade of the Third Baptist Church; **p. 36,** Alfred B. Mullett's District of Columbia Jail; **p. 39,** Montgomery Meigs House; **p. 41,** Shepherd's Row; all from the Library of Congress, Washington, D.C. **Page 10,** park system of Washington City, 1902, published in *The Century Magazine* (March 1902). **Page 45,** H. H. Richardson's design for the Washington Casino, by permission of the Houghton Library, Harvard University. **Page 50,** Glenn Brown plan for modernizing Washington; **p. 52,** Cass Gilbert's plan, from *Papers Relating the Improvement of the City of Washington* (Washington, D.C.: Government Printing Office, 1901). **Page 53,** Cass Gilbert's plan for Lafayette Square; **p. 55,** John Russell Pope's plan for Theodore Roosevelt Memorial; Commission of Fine Arts, Washington, D.C. **Page 57,** Hugh Newell Jacobsen's 1976 design for the Pennsylvania Avenue Development Corporation. **Page 60,** Frank Lloyd Wright's rendering of the Crystal Heights Hotel, The Frank Lloyd Wright Archives.

THE MALL

Page 69, Benjamin Henry Latrobe's plan for the Capitol grounds and the Mall, 1815; **p. 66,** plan for a national university on the Mall, 1816, by Benjamin Henry Latrobe; **p. 67,** Robert Mills's 1841 plan for the Mall; **p. 70,** Washington National Monument Society Membership Certificate; **p. 72,** plan of the Mall by Benjamin Franklin Smith, Jr., 1852; **p. 73,** view, to the west, of the Department of Agriculture Grounds; **p. 75,** Baltimore and Potomac Railroad Station; all from the Library of Congress, Washington, D.C. **Page 71,** Andrew Jackson Downing's plan for the Mall, 1851; **p. 82,** Lincoln Memorial, The National Archives.

ML02 National Air and Space Museum, Hellmuth, Obata and Kassabaum, Inc., photographer George Silk; **ML03** Hirshhorn Museum and Sculpture Garden, Smithsonian Institution; **ML04** Arts and Industries Building; **ML09** Washington National Monument; **ML12** Arlington Memorial Bridge; all from the Library of Congress, Washington, D.C. **ML06** Arthur M. Sackler Gallery, National Museum of African Art, photographer Pamela Scott. **ML14** National Museum of American History (National Museum of History and Technology), photograph courtesy of the National Museum of American History, Smithsonian Institution; **ML17** National Gallery of Art, East Building, I. M. Pei and Partners, photographer Esto Photographics Ind.

MONUMENTAL CAPITOL HILL

Page 116, William Thornton's plan for the east elevation of the Capitol; **p. 116,** William Thornton's plan for the principal story of the Capitol; **p. 118,** Section of the Capitol rotunda, by Charles Bulfinch, c. 1822; **CH01** United States Capitol, exterior; **CH01** United States Capitol, c. 1846, daguerreotype by John Plumbe, Jr.; **CH02** Cannon House Office Building; **CH08** Supreme Court; **CH09** United States Post Office; **CH12** Library of Congress, Jefferson Building; **CH13** Library of Congress, John Adams Building; all from the Library of Congress, Washington, D.C. **CH03** Russell Senate Office Building; **CH04** Longworth House Office Building; **CH06** Dirksen Senate Office Building; **CH07** Hart Senate Office Building; photographer Pamela Scott. **CH15** Folger Shakespeare Library, The Folger Shakespeare Library, photographer Julie Ainsworth.

WHITE HOUSE

WH03a White House, north portico; **WH03b** White House, south portico; **WH04** Treasury Building; **WH08** Decatur House, National Trust for Historic Preservation; **WH10** Saint John's Church; all from the Library of Congress, Washington, D.C. **WH09** Chamber of Commerce Building, *Nation's Business.* **WH15** Renwick Gallery, Smithsonian Institution (Corcoran Gallery of Art), Smithsonian Institution.

DOWNTOWN EAST

DE06 Judiciary Square; **DE13** National Bank of Washington; **DE15.3** United States General Post Office; **DE15.4** Le Droit Building; **DE15.5** Washington Loan and Trust Company; **DE17** Greyhound Terminal; **DE19** Franklin School; all from the Library of Congress, Washington, D.C. **DE07** Pension Building; **DE29** National Place; photographer Harlan Hambright. **DE10** Metro Operations Control Center, photographer Robert C. Lautman. **DE18** Masonic Temple, photographer Dan Cunnington; Keyes Condon Florance Architects. **DE15.2** Patent Office Building, National Collection of Fine Arts, Washington, D.C. **DE25** Columbia Square, Cervin Robinson. **DE30** National League of Cities Building, photographer Lawrence S. Williams, Inc.; Frank Schlesinger Architects/Planners. **DE31** Western Plaza, Venturi, Rauch and Scott Brown, photographer Tom Bernard.

FOGGY BOTTOM

FB04 American Red Cross National Headquarters; **FB06** Organization of American States Building; **FB09** National Academy of Sciences; **FB11** Old Naval Observatory; **FB21** Octagon; all from the Library of Congress, Washington, D.C. **FB15** Watergate, Goode-Phillips Collections, courtesy of the Photographic Archives of the National Gallery of Art, Washington, D.C. **FB22** American Institute of Architects, courtesy of The American Institute of Architects, photographer Gordon H. Schenck, Jr.

DOWNTOWN WEST

DW10 Mayflower Hotel; **DW21** Arts Club of Washington; Library of Congress, Washington, D.C. **DW14** 1818 St. NW, David M. Schwarz Architectural Services, photographer Hedrick Blessing. **DW15** Republic Place; **DW19** Presidential Plaza; photographer Dan Cunningham, Keyes Condon Florance Architects. **DW16** Bachelor Flats, Goode-Phillips Collections, courtesy of the Photographic Archives of the National Gallery of Art, Washington, D.C.

SOUTHWEST QUADRANT

SW03 Design Center, photographer James Oesch, Keyes Condon Florance Architects. **SW14** Fort Leslie J. McNair; **SW16** Wheat Row; all from the Library of Congress, Washington, D.C. **SW17** Harbour Square; **SW20** Town Center Plaza; Goode-Phillips Collections, courtesy of the Photographic Archives of the National Gallery of Art, Washington, D.C.

CAPITOL HILL NEIGHBORHOOD

CN04 Mayers Block; **CN05** S. Fred Hahn Building; **CN07** 120 4th St. SE; **CN08** Mary L. Hill House; **CN17** Thomas Healy House; **CN19** 638–642 East Capitol St. NE; **CN20** Dr. Richard Kingsman House and Office; **CN21** Antonio Malmati House; **CN22** Mrs. S. A. Lawton House; **CN24** Samuel C. Heald House; **CN25** William Hutton House; **CN29** George W. Gessford Row; **CN41** Isaac Kaufman House; **CN42** 541 7th St. SE; **CN43** Washington Mechanics Savings Bank (The City Bank); **CN46** 1000–1010 Pennsylvania Ave. SE; photographer Pamela Scott. **CN33** Eastern Market; **CN40** Christ Church; **CN44** Marine Barracks, Marine Commandant's House; **CN45** Washington Navy Yard; all from the Library of Congress, Washington, D.C. **CN34** Penn Medical Building, Goode-Phillips Collections, courtesy of the Photographic Archives of the National Gallery of Art, Washington, D.C.

SOUTHEAST OF THE ANACOSTIA RIVER

SE06 Saint Elizabeths Hospital (Government Hospital for the Insane), The National Archives, Washington, D.C.

NORTH AND NORTHEAST

NE02 Langston Terrace; **NE04.1** Gallaudet University, Chapel Hall; **NE11** United States Soldier's and Airmen's Home; all from the Library of Congress, Washington, D.C. **NE07** Trinity College, Notre Dame Chapel, Office of Public Relations, Trinity College.

16TH STREET AND MERIDIAN HILL

Page 298, Pope's design for Lincoln Memorial, The National Archives, Washington, D.C. **p. 298,** Henderson Castle; **MH07** Hightowers; **MH09** The Green Door (Denman-Werlich House); **MH11** Toutorsky House (Henry B. Brown House); **MH16** Embassy of Ghana (Embassy of France); **MH22** Benjamin H. Warder House; all from the Library of Congress, Washington, D.C. **MH08** The Cairo, Goode-Phillips Collections, courtesy of the Photographic Archives of the National Gallery of Art, Washington, D.C. **MH17** Meridian House (Henry White House, White-Meyer House), photographer Arnold Kramer.

DUPONT CIRCLE

DU01 Dupont Circle Building; **DU10** 1614 20th St. NW; **DU41** Anne Thorneburne Johnson House; photographer Pamela Scott. **DU02** The Washington Club (R. W. Patterson House); **DU24** Embassy of Canada (Clarence Moore House); **DU25** National Trust for Historic Preservation (McCormick Apartments); **DU30** Embassy of Indonesia (Walsh-McLean House); **DU34** Anderson House, Headquarters of the Society of Cincinnati (Larz Anderson House); **DU35** Cosmos Club (Richard H. Townsend House); all from the Library of Congress, Washington, D.C. **DU03** Euram Building, photographer Robert C. Lautman. **DU14** 1718–1720 Connecticut Ave. NW, David M. Schwarz Architectural Services. **DU20** Apartment house, 2029 Connecticut Ave., Goode-Phillips Collections, courtesy of the Photographic Archives of the National Gallery of Art, Washington, D.C. **DU28** James E. Blaine House, Collection of the Historical Society of Washington, D.C. **DU32** Phillips Collection (Duncan Phillips House), The Phillips Collections, photographer Robert C. Lautman. **DU40** Thomas Nelson Page House, photographer Arnold Kramer.

SHERIDAN CIRCLE AND KALORAMA

Pages 338–339, panoramic views of Sheridan Circle; **SK07** Embassy of Luxembourg (Alexander Stewart House); **SK13** James C. Hooe House; **SK14** Chancery of Ireland (Henrietta M. Halliday House); **SK18** Egyptian Embassy (Joseph Beale House); **SK21** Embassy of Pakistan (F. B. Moran Residence); all from the Library of Congress, Washington, D.C. **SK65** and **SK66** The Textile Museum, The Textile Museum.

NORTHWEST

NW08 Wardman Tower; **NW19** Kennedy-Warren Apartments; **NW22** The Broadmoor; **NW23** Tilden Gardens; **NW39** The Westchester; Goode-Phillips Collections, courtesy of the Photographic Archives of the National Gallery of Art, Washington, D.C. **NW28** University of the District of Columbia (Washington Technical Institute), photograph Leon M. Gurley. **NW37a** American University, plan by Henry Ives Cobb; **NW38** Metropolitan Memorial United Methodist Church; National Archives, Washington, D.C. **NW37b** American University, McKinley Building, The American University, photographer F. Harlan Hambright and Associates. **NW56** Florence Hollis Hand Chapel, Mount Vernon College, Robert C. Lautman. **NW59** Foxhall Crescents, Arthur Cotton Moore/Associates.

GEORGETOWN

GT01 Corcoran at Georgetown; **GT03** The Foundry; **GT04** Washington Harbour; **GT06** Canal Square; Arthur Cotton Moore Associates. **GT07** Georgetown Custom House and Post Office; **GT12.1** Georgetown University, Healy Hall; **GT14** John Thomson Mason House; **GT18** Robert P. Dodge House; **GT22** Tudor Place; **GT23** Wisconsin Avenue Vocational School; **GT24** Volta Bureau; **GT27a** Oak Hill Cemetery Gatehouse; **GT28** Oak Hill Cemetery Chapel; **GT29** Evermay; all from the Library of Congress, Washington, D.C. **GT27b** Oak Hill Cemetery plan, The National Archives.

Index

Pages with illustrations are indicated in bold.

Abbott, Merkt and Company: Hecht Company Warehouse, 283

Abel, Joseph, 324; The Broadmoor, 369–370

Abremont, 370–371

Acacia Mutual Life Insurance Company, **181**–182

Ackerman and Ross: Carnegie Library, 196–197

Adams, James W.: Arthur S. Henning House, 393

Adams, John, 20

Adams, Warner and Herbert Adams (sculptors), 144

Adams Memorial, Rock Creek Cemetery, 289–**290**

Adas Israel Synagogue, **186**

Agriculture Department building, 79–80, **99**–100

Aitken, Robert (sculptor), 138

Albert Kahn Associated Architects and Engineers, Inc.: Washington Post Building, **203**

Alexander, Barton S.: United States Soldiers' and Airmen's Home, **290**–292

Alexander, Robert: Christ Church, 262–**263**

Alexandria, Virginia, 16

Alfred B. Mullet and Company: American News Women's Club (J. H. Cranford House), **340**; William F. Burch House, 321. *See also* Mullet, Alfred B.

Allen, Francis Richmond: Twin Oaks, 366

Allen and Collens: Universalist National Memorial Church, 306–307

Allied Architects of Washington: Longworth House Office Building, **136**

All Souls Church, 314–**315**

Alsop, E. H., House, 343

Alvarez, Hector: James H. Grant House, additions, **262**

Amateis, Louis (designer), 135

American City Diner, **378**

American Institute of Architects (AIA), 33–34, 37, 41, 46, 51, 58, 76, 77, **217**–218

American News Women's Club, 340

American Pharmaceutical Association Building, 54, **211**–212

American Red Cross National Headquarters, 207–**208**

American Security and Trust Company, **202**

American University, **379**–380

Anacostia Park Pavilion, 276

Andersen, Henry: Embassy of Indonesia (Walsh-McLean House), **328**–329

Anderson House, Headquarters of the Society of Cincinnati, **330**, 331

Andrei, Giovanni (designer), 131

Andrews, John. *See* John Andrews International Ltd.

Angel, John (sculptor), 288

Apex Building, 187

Apostolic Legation of the Papal State, 388

Appleby, Scott B., Jr., House, 392

Architect of the Capitol, 47

Architects Collaborative, The: American Institute of Architects, **217**–218

Arena Stage/Kreeger Theatre, 244–245

Argyle Terrace, 342–343

Arlington House, 24

Arlington Memorial Bridge, 104–**105**

Arlington National Cemetery, 39, 266

Army Corps of Engineers. *See* United States Army Corps of Engineers.

Army Medical Museum and Library, 75

Army Navy Club, 223–224

Arrasmith, William S.: Greyhound Terminal, **195**

Arthur Cotton Moore/Associates: Corcoran at Georgetown, 400–**401**; The Foundry, 401–**402**; Old Post Office, 169–**170**; Washington Harbour, **402**

Arthur Erickson Associates: Canadian Chancery, **187**

Arts and Industries Building, 41, 74, 92, **93**, 94

Arts Club of Washington, 228–**229**

Ashford, Snowden: Eastern Senior High School, 268–269; Wisconsin Avenue Vocational School, **412**

Atherton, Frederick, House, 349

Atkinson, Frederick G.: Henry Rabe House, 259–**260**

Aubinoe, Alvin E., Sr.: Hightowers, 302–**303**

Averill, Hall and Adams: Engine House No. 19, 278, **279**

Ayres, Louis: Commerce Department Building, **171**–172

B

Babcock-Macomb House, 386

Bachelor Flats, **227**

Bacon, Henry, 82–83, 317; Lincoln Memorial, **103**–104

Bairstow, Ernest C. (sculptor), 216

Baldwin and Pennington: Saint Teresa of Avila Church, **274**–275

Balfour (Westover), 307

Ball, Thomas (sculptor), 247

Baltimore and Potomac Railroad Station, 74, **75**, 76, 82, 121

Banneker, Benjamin, 19, 237

Baranes, Shalom. *See* Shalom Baranes Associates.

Barlow, Joel, estate, 338

Barnes, Edward Larrabee. *See* Edward Larrabee Barnes Associates.

Barney, Alice Pike, House, Smithsonian Institution, **345**

Barr, Lester A., House, 354

Bartholdi, Frederic A. (sculptor), 66

Bartholomew, Harland, 232

Bartlett, Paul Wayland (sculptor), 119, 128, 144

Barton, Jane Couser, House (John C. Dreier House), **397**

Baur, Theodore (sculptor), 144

Beale, Joseph, House, 53, 345–**346**

Becket, Welton: Lafayette Center, 229. *See also* Welton Becket Associates.

Beckhard, Herbert: Hubert H. Humphrey Building, Department of Health and Human Services, 234; United

449

Beckhard, Herbert (*cont.*)
States Department of Housing and Urban Development, 239
Beecher, Friss and Gregg: James Kerrick House, 356
Beecher, William Gordon, 299. *See also* Beecher, Friss and Gregg.
Beers, Albert H.: The Dresden, 325; 2112–2118 Bancroft Pl. NW, 355; 2123–2127 Bancroft Pl. NW, 356
Bell, Maj. William H.: Washington Armory, 72
Belluschi, Pietro, 87
Benjamin Thompson Associates, 122; Union Station, 140, **141**, 142
Bennett, Edward H., 167–168
Bennett, Parsons and Frost: Federal Trade Commission Building, **176**–177; United States Botanic Garden, 66, **90**
Beresford, Robert: Mayflower Hotel, **225**.
Bingham, Theodore A., 153
Birch, W. Taylor, House, **411**
Blaine, James E., House, **327**
Blair House, 164
Blashfield, Edwin (painter), 145, 226
Bleifeld, Stanley (sculptor), 189
Blodgett's Hotel, **22**, 28
Boal and Brown, 353
Board of Public Works, 39–40
Bodley, George F.: Cathedral of Saint Peter and Saint Paul, **381**–386
Boeckl, Leopold: Embassy of Austria, Chancery, 373–**374**
Bomford, George, 162
Bond, Samuel Hazen, 378–379
Bond Building, **199**
Borglum, Gutzon (sculptor), 209
Borie, Charles L., Jr., 174–175.
Bottomley, Wagner and White: Embassy of Oman (Devore Chase), **352**–353
Bottomley, William L., 352
Boulder Bridge, 364
Boyd, William (sculptor), 143
Branch Bank of the United States, 24, **25**
Brazilian Delegation to the Organization of American States, Ambassador's Residence (Daniel J. Callahan House), 354
Breckinridge, Charles (horticulturist), 72
Breines, Simon: Buchanan School playground, 266
Brent, Calvin T. S.: Saint Luke's Episcopal Church, 302

Brent, Daniel C., 27
Breuer, Marcel, and Herbert Beckhard: Hubert H. Humphrey Building, Department of Health and Human Services, **234**; United States Department of Housing and Urban Development, **238**, 239
Broadmoor, The, **369**–370
Brooke, Frederick H.: Embassy of Kenya (F. A. Keep House and C. Russell Peyton House), renovation, 360; Phillips Collection (Duncan Phillips House), addition, 330
Brookland, 9
Brown, Ann and Donald, House, 375–**376**
Brown, Arthur, Jr.: United States Customs Service, Departmental Auditorium, and the Interstate Commerce Commission, 172–**173**
Brown, Glenn, 51–53, 76; Egyptian Embassy (Joseph Beale House), 345–**346**; Glenwood Cemetery Mortuary Chapel, 285–286; William Benning Webb School, 270
Brown, Henry B., House, **305**
Brown, Henry Kirke (sculptor), 300
Brown and Wright: Embassy of Ghana, Chancery, 373
Bruce, Ailsa Mellon, 88
Bruff, J. Goldsborough (designer), 156
Brumidi, Constantino (artist), 119, 132–134, 262
Bryan, Samuel M., House, 329
Bryant and Bryant: University of the District of Columbia, **374**–375
Buberl, Caspar (sculptor), 93, 185, 191
Buchanan, James, School, 265–266
Bulfinch, Charles, 27–29, 59, 65, 117–120, 151, 162, 315; Unitarian Church, **28**; United States Capitol 125–135
Bunche, Ralph J., House, 56, **285**
Bunshaft, Gordon, 86, 87; Hirshhorn Museum and Sculpture Garden, 91–92
Burch, William F., House, 321
Burleith, 9
Burnham, Daniel H., 48–49, 77, 79, 80, 82, 121–122, 159, 166, 202; Union Station, 140, **141**, 142

Butler, A. B., House, **334**
Butler, Charles: General Services Administration Building, 216
Butti, Guido (sculptor), 193

C

Cabin John Bridge, 38
Cafritz Building, 221–222
Cain, Walker O. *See* Steinman, Cain and White
Cairo, The, **303**
Calder, Alexander (sculptor), 111, 138
Callahan, Daniel J., House, 354
Calvert, Herrick and Reddinger (windows), 307
Campos, Olavo Redig de: Chancery of Brazil, 391–392
Canadian Chancery, **187**
Canal Square, **403**
Cannon House Office Building, 51, 122–123, **135**–136
Capellano, Antonio (sculptor), 132
Capital Hilton Hotel, 203
Capitol Hill Historic District, 248
Capitol Park, **240**
Capitol Traction Company Union Station, **405**
Carbery House, 261
Carlhian, Jean Paul: Enid A. Haupt Garden, 71–72, 96; National Museum of African Art, 96; S. Dillon Ripley Center, 96–97; Arthur M. Sackler Gallery, 96
Carnegie Institution of Washington, 51, 302
Carnegie Library, 196–197
Caroe, William Douglas: Canterbury Pulpit, Cathedral of Saint Peter and Saint Paul, 385
Carrère and Hastings, 47, 51, 122–123, 132, 174, 307; Cannon House Office Building, **135**–136; Carnegie Institution of Washington, 302; Cosmos Club (Richard H. Townsend House), **331**–332; Embassy of Lao People's Democratic Republic (David A. Reed House), 357; Hotel Washington, **201**; Russell Senate Office Building, 135–136; W. R. Castle, Jr., House, 357
Carroll, Daniel, 16
Carrollsburg Square. *See* Tiber Island/Carrollsburg Square.
Casey, Edward Pearce, 42, 66, 121; Daughters of the American Revolution Continental Memorial Hall, **208**–209
Casey, Thomas Lincoln, 38, 42,

121, 362; Old Executive Office Building (State, War, and Navy Building), **156**, 157–158; Washington National Monument, **100**–102
Cassell, Albert I.: Howard University, 292–294; Mayfair Mansions Apartments, 279
Cassutta, Araldo A.: L'Enfant Plaza office towers, 237
Castle, W. R., Jr., House, 357
Cathedral of Saint Peter and Saint Paul, **381**–386
Catholic University, 12. 281. **287**
Causeway, The, **368**
Causici, Enrico (artist), 132
Central Heating Plant, **238**, 239
Chamber of Commerce Building, 53, 161–162, **163**
Chanceries: of Brazil, 391–392; German, **393**–394; of Iraq (William J. Boardman House), 326–327; of Ireland (Henrietta M. Halliday House), **344**. *See also* Embassies.
Chandler, Theophilus P.: Saint Thomas Episcopal Church, 327
Charles M. Goodman Architects: River Park, 241–242,**243**
Chase and Ames: Embassy of India (Thomas Murray House), **330**–331
Chasteleton, 305
Chatelain, Leon: National City Christian Church, 295–296
Cheville, T. S., 162
Chevy Chase, 9, 43
Chevy Chase Arcade, 376
Chloethiel Smith and Associates (also Chloethiel Woodard Smith and Associated Architects): Capitol Park, **240**; Waterside Towers, **244**. *See also* Smith, Chloethiel Woodard.
Christ Church, 262–**263**
Christian Science Complex, 221, **222**
Church of the Sacred Heart, **316**
Church of the Savior Ecumenical Church, Headquarters (Samuel M. Bryan House), 329
Clark, Edward, 32; United States Patent Office, 189–**191**; United States Soldiers' and Airmen's Home, **290**, 292
Clark, Joseph, 20; Wheat Row, **242**
Clarke, Appleton P., Jr.,: Embassy of Myanmar (Thomas A. Gales House), 357; Dr. Richard Kingsman House and Office,

256; Roosevelt Hotel, 307–308; 616 East Capitol St. NE, 255
Clarke, Matthew Saint Clair, 163
Clas, A. R.: Capital Hilton Hotel, 203; State Department, 212
Clement A. Didden and Son: Bartholomew Daly House,258
Cleveland Park, 9, 366–370
Cluss, Adolf, 40–42, 191, 250; Eastern Market, 41, **260**–261; Franklin School, 195–**196**; Shepherd's Row, 40, **41**; Sumner School, 41, 222–223
Cluss, Adolph, and Joseph W. von Kammerhueber: Agriculture Department Building, 73
Cluss, Adolph, and Paul Schulze: Army Medical Museum and Library, 75; Arts and Industries Building, 74, 92, **93**, 94; United States Patent Office, 191
Cobb, Henry Ives: American University, **379**–380; McMillan Commission Plan, 76
Cobb, Henry N.: Columbia Square, **198**
Codman, Martha, House, **358**–359
Codman, Ogden: Martha Codman House, **358**–359
Cohen, Wilbur J., Federal Building, 234–235
Cole and Denny: Freer Gallery of Art, 97–99
Colombia, Permanent Mission of, to the Organization of American States (Otto Heinl House), 341
Columbia Heights, 9
Columbia Hospital for Women, 230
Columbian Institute, 22, 23–24, 26
Columbia Plaza, 206, 212–213
Columbia Square, **198**
Commandant's House, Marine Barracks, 24, 264
Commerce Department Building, **171**–172
Commission of Fine Arts, 5, 49, 54, 56, 58, 59, 210, 218
Commission of 100 for the Federal City, 5
Congressional Cemetery, 24, **266**
Connick (stained glass manufacturer), 287
Constitution Gardens, 88
Constitution Hall. *See* Daughters of the American Revolution Constitution Memorial Hall.
Cooke's Row, **410**–411
Coolidge and Shattuck, 306; All Souls Church, 314–315
Cooper, George S.: Balfour

(Westover), 307; Bond Building, **199**; Antonio Malmati House, **256**–257; President's Office, George Washington University, 215
Cooper-Lecky Partnership, 89; District of Columbia Center for Therapeutic Recreation, 278–279; Vietnam Veterans Memorial, **105**–106
Cope and Stewardson: District Building, 170–**171**
Corcoran, William W., 30, 164
Corcoran at Georgetown, 400, **401**
Corcoran Gallery of Art, 30, **207**
Cornelius and Baker, 134
Cosmos Club (Richard H. Townsend House), 60, **331**–332
Costaggini, Filippo (artist), 132
Court of Claims Building, 159–160
Cox, Allyn (muralist), 132, 135
Crandell, Germond: Germond Crandell Building, **189**
Cranford, J. H., House, 340
Crawford, Thomas (sculptor), 119, 123, 127, 128, 135
Cresson, William P., 47–48; Chancery of Ireland (Henrietta M. Halliday House), **344**. *See also* Wyeth, Nathan C., and William P. Cresson.
Cret, Paul Philippe, 55–56, 84, 105, 124, 145; Central Heating Plant, **238**, 239; Federal Reserve Board Building, 210; Folger Shakespeare Library, **146**–147; Mary E. Stewart House, **353**. *See also* Kelsey, Albert, and Paul Philippe Cret.
Crocroft, James, 323
Crump, R. G.: Embassy of Cyprus (E. G. Davis House), 360
Crump and Wagner: Ebenezer United Methodist Church, 261
Crystal Heights, 60, 61
Curtis and Davis: James Forrestal Building, **236**
Cutts, James Madison (engineer): Anacostia Park Pavilion, 276

D

D.C. Redevelopment Act of 1945, 231
Dahl, George A.: Robert F. Kennedy Stadium, 268
Dale, Chester, 83
Daly, Bartholomew, House, 258
Daly, Leo E. *See* Leo E. Daly Associates.
Daniel F. Tully Associates: Georgetown University,406–407

Daon Building, 196
Daughters of the American
   Colonists, National Society,
   Headquarters, 343
Daughters of the American
   Revolution Constitution
   Memorial Hall, 54, 176, 209
Daughters of the American
   Revolution Continental
   Memorial Hall, **208**–209
Davis, A. J., 263
Davis, E. G., House, 360
Davis, Emma Lu (sculptor), 235
Davis, Harry B.: Ellington School
   of the Arts, **413**
Davis, William T., 253
Decatur House, National Trust for
   Historic Preservation, 25, **160**–
   161
Deigert and Yerkes: National
   Arboretum, administration-
   laboratory building, 280
Delano, Frederic A., 58, 84
Delano, Frederic and Mathilda,
   House, 357
Delano and Aldrich: Carnegie
   Institution of Washington,
   addition, 302; Embassy of
   Japan, 349–**350**; Post Office
   Building, **173**–174
Deming, William L., 48. *See also*
   Wood, Donn and Deming.
Demonet Building, 225
Departmental Auditorium, 172–
   173
Department of Agriculture. *See*
   United States Department of
   Agriculture.
Design Center, **235**
Dessez, Leon E.: Vice President's
   House (United States Naval
   Observatory), **390**
Devore Chase, **352**–353
DeWitt, Poor and Shelton: Library
   of Congress, James Madison
   Building, 146
Didden, Clement A. *See* Clement
   A. Didden and Son.
Diebert, Jack: Hillwood Museum
   (Hillwood; Abremont), 370–371
Dirksen Senate Office Building,
   137
Disciples of Christ Church, 295
District Building, 24, 170–**171**
District of Columbia Center for
   Therapeutic Recreation, 278–
   279
District of Columbia Jail, 35–**36**
District of Columbia National
   Guard Armory, 266, 268
District of Columbia Office of
   Planning, 59

District of Columbia
   Redevelopment Act of 1945,
   231
Dodge, Robert P., House, 409–
   410
Dodge Center, 402–403
Donn, Edward W., Jr., 48. *See also*
   Wood, Donn and Deming.
Donnelly, John, Jr., (designer),
   138–139
Donnelly, Owen: Saint Peter's
   Church (builder), 148; Annie M.
   Mulhall House, 262
Donoghue, John (sculptor), 144
Donohoe, D. T. and Eugenia E.,
   House, 257
Douglas, W. J.: Boulder Bridge,
   364
Downing, Andrew Jackson, 30–31,
   70–72, 158, 263, 275, 292, 364–
   365; Robert P. Dodge House,
   409–**410**
Downtown Historic District, 189
Drayton, Charles D., House, 351
Dresden, The, **325**
DuBois, Paul (sculptor), 299
Dumbarton House, **409**
Dumbarton Oaks, 413–**414**
Dumblane, 378–379
Dupont, Adm. Francis S., 317
Dupont Circle Building, 319–**320**
Durang, Edwin F. *See* Edwin F.
   Durang and Son.

E

Earley, John Joseph, 175, 313,
   316, 350; Dr. M. S. Fealty
   House, **276**–277
Earley Process Corporation, 278
East Capitol Street Car Barn,
   269–270
Eastern Market, 41, **260**–261
Eastern Senior High School, 268–
   269
Ebenezer United Methodist
   Church, 261
Eckles, Charles E. and Anita,
   House, 392–393
Ecole des Beaux-Arts, 43–44, 46–
   49, 55
Edbrooke, Willoughby J.: Old Post
   Office, 169–**170**
Edmonston, Charles (builder-
   contractor), 301
Edmonston, Samuel: Susan
   Shields House, 301
Edward Larrabee Barnes
   Associates: Federal Judiciary
   Building, 122, 142
Edwards, Harry L.: Hightowers,
   302–**303**; Tilden Gardens, 370
Edwin F. Durang and Son, 286

Eggers, Otto R., 83
Eggers and Higgins, 87; Dirksen
   Senate Office Building, **137**;
   Jefferson Memorial, 102–**103**
Eggleston, N. H. (designer), 162
Egyptian Ministry of Works:
   Islamic Center, **350**
Ehrenkrantz Group/Building
   Conservation Technology:
   Sumner School restoration,
   223
Eichelberger, Frederick, House,
   356
Eiermann, Egon: German
   Chancery, 393–**394**
Eliscu, Frank (sculptor), 146
Ellerbe Becket, Inc.: University of
   the District of Columbia, **374**–
   375
Ellicott, Andrew, 18–19
Ellicott, Henry Jackson (sculptor),
   143
Ellington School of the Arts, **413**
Elliot, William P., Jr., 154, 190
Elliott Woods, 122–123
ELS Design Group: The Foundry,
   401–402
Emancipation Monument, 247
Embassies: British, 390–**391**:
   Egyptian (Joseph Beale House),
   345–**346**; of Austria, Chancery,
   373–**374**; of Belgium (Anna
   Thomson Dodge House), 396;
   of Brazil (Robert and Katharine
   McCormick House), 391; of
   Canada (Clarence Moore
   House), 325–326; of Chile, **346**;
   of Colombia (Thomas T. Gaff
   House), 327–**328**; of Colombia,
   Chancery, 354; of Cyprus (E. G.
   Davis House), 360; of Ecuador,
   299–300; of France (William
   Watson Lawrence House), **352**;
   of Ghana (Embassy of France),
   308; of Ghana, Chancery, 373;
   of Greece, 343; of Greece,
   Commercial Section (Irene
   Rucher Sheridan House), **342**,
   343; of Iceland, 351; of India
   (Thomas Murray House), **330**–
   331; of Indonesia (Walsh-
   McLean House), **328**–329; of
   Ireland (Frederic and Mathilda
   Delano House), 357; of Italy,
   312–313; of Ivory Coast
   (Frederick Atherton House),
   349; of Japan, 349–**350**; of
   Kenya (F. A. Keep House and
   C. Russell Peyton House), 360;
   of Korea (Harry Wardman
   House), 345; of Korea,
   Chancery (Alice W. B. Stanley

House), 348–**349**; of Kuwait, Chancery, **373**; of Lao People's Democratic Republic (David A. Reed House), 357; of Luxembourg (Alexander Stewart House), **340**, 341–342; of Malawi (Granville Fortesque House), 349; of Mexico (Franklin MacVeagh House), **314**; of Myanmar (Thomas M. Gales House), 357; of Oman (Devore Chase), **352**–353; of Pakistan (F. B. Moran Residence), **347**–348; of the Philippines (Emma S. Fitzhugh House), 360; of Poland, **312**; of Republic of Austria (William A. Hill Company), 348; of Spain, **313**–314; of Turkey (Edward H. Everett House), **344**–345; of United Arab Emirates, Military Department, **342**, 343; of Venezuela (Mrs. Wilber E. Wilder House), 354; of Zambia, 349

Embassies and chanceries: of Cameroon (Christian Hague Residence), **348**; of Haiti (Gibson Fahnestock House), **346**, 347; of Norway, **386**–388; of Switzerland, **365**–366

Emerson, William R.: Principal Animal House, National Zoo, 362

Engine House No. 19, 278

Erickson, Arthur. *See* Arthur Erickson Associates.

Euram Building, 57, 320–321

Evans, Rudolph (sculptor), 103

Evening Star Building, 197–**198**

Everett, Edward H., House, **344**–345

Evermay, **416**

Executive Office Building. *See* New Executive Office Building; Old Executive Office Building.

Ezdorf, Richard von: Old Executive Office Building (State, War, and Navy Building), **156**, 157–158

F

Fahnestock, Gibson, House, 47, **346**, 347

Falguière, J. N. J. (sculptor), 159

Farrand, Beatrix: Dumbarton Oaks, 413–**414**

Faulkner, Waldron: George Washington University, 214–215

FBI Building, **197**

Fealty, Dr. M. S., House, **276**, 278

Federal Home Loan Bank Board, **206**

Federal Judiciary Building, 122, 142

Federal Office Building, Department of State, **372**–373

Federal Office Building #10, 235–**236**

Federal Penitentiary, 27–28

Federal Reserve Board Building, 56, 124, 210

Federal Trade Commission Building, **176**–177

15th Street Historic District, 201–202

First Division Memorial, 105–106, 151–152

Fischer, Milton: Watergate, 213–**214**

Fitzhugh, Emma S., House, 360

Flagg, Ernest, 381–382; Corcoran Gallery of Art, **207**

Flanagan, John (sculptor), 144

Flannery, John S., House, 354

Fleri, Joseph (sculptor), 288

Flour City Ornamental Iron Company, 146

Flournoy and Flournoy: Presbyterian Church of the Pilgrims, **340**

Foggy Bottom Historic District, 206

Folger, Henry Clay, 124

Folger Shakespeare Library, 56, 124, **146**–147

Forrestal, James, Building, **236**

Fort De Russey, 38

Fort Dupont Park, 279

Fortesque, Granville, House, 349

Fort Leslie J. McNair, 27, **241**

Fort Reno, 38

Fort Slocum, 281

Fort Totten, 281

Foster, William Dewey. *See* Underwood, Gilbert Stanley and William Dewey Foster.

Founders Library, Howard University, 3, **293**–294

Foundry, The, **401**–402

Fowler, Edwin H.: D. T. and Eugenia E. Donohoe House, 257; Fowler houses, 258

Foxhall Crescents, **397**

Foxhall Village, 9

Franklin School, 40, 195–**196**

Franzoni, Giuseppe (carver), 130

Fraser, George S., House (Scott-Thropp Mansion), **321**

Fraser, James Earle (sculptor), 105, 138, 152

Fraser, John: James E. Blaine House, 327

Frederick Douglass House, National Park Service (Cedar Hill), 275

Freed, James Ingo: United States Holocaust Memorial Museum, 238–239

Freer, Charles L., 81, 98

Freer Gallery of Art, 81, **97**–99

French, Daniel Chester (sculptor), 103, 144, 151

Friedberg, M. Paul (landscape architect), 200, 266

Friedlander, Leo (sculptor), 105

Friedrich, Emil S., 253–254; Gallaudet University, 283, 284

Friends Meeting House, **359**

Frohman, Robb and Little: Cathedral of Saint Peter and Saint Paul, 381–386

Fuller, Thomas J. D.: Charles D. Drayton House, 351; Wisconsin Avenue Vocational School, **412**

Fuller and Wheeler: The Green Door (Denman-Werlich House), 303–**304**

G

Gaff, Thomas T., House, 46–47, 327–**328**

Gales, Thomas M., House, 357

Gallaudet University, 283, **284**, 285

Gallery Row, **189**

Gardner, E. C., 297

Garfinckel's Department Store, 199

Gearing House, 364

General Accounting Office, 186

General Post Office, 19–20, 28–29, 32

General Scott Apartment Building, 301

General Services Administration Building, 216

Georgetown Custom House and Post Office, 35, **403**–404

Georgetown Market, 404–**405**

Georgetown University, 56–57, **406**–407

Georgetown University Law Center, **181**

George Washington University, 33, 206, 214–215

Germond Crandell Building (Gallery Row), **189**

Gessford, Charles: Charles Gessford Row, 259; George W. Gessford Row, **259**; Philadelphia Row, 258; 638–642 East Capitol St. NE, 255–256

Gessford, George W., Row, **259**

Gevelot, Nicholas (artist), 132

Ghequier, T. Buckler: Saint Mark's Episcopal Church, **253**

Gibson, J. & G. H. *See* J. & G. H. Gibson Company.

Gibson, Robert W.: Hearst Hall, National Cathedral School for Girls, 386

Gilbert, Cass, 52, 53, 77, 124, 151–152, 159; Chamber of Commerce Building, 161–162, **163**; Supreme Court, **138**–140; Treasury Annex, 164

Glenwood Cemetery, 280–281

Glenwood Cemetery Mortuary Chapel, 285–286

Goodhue, Bertram Grosvenor: National Academy of Sciences, 210–**211**

Goodman, Charles M. *See* Charles M. Goodman Architects.

Graham, Anderson, Probst, and White: State Department, 212

Graham, Burnham and Company: United States Post Office, **140**

Grand Hotel, 230

Grant, James H.: James H. Grant House, **262**

Grant Memorial, 66

Gray, W. Bruce, 80: Samuel M. Bryan House, 329

Greely, Rose (landscape architect), 359

Green Door, The (Denman-Werlich House), 303–**304**

Greenleaf, James (developer), 20

Greenough, Horatio (sculptor), 30, 31

Gregory, John (sculptor), 147

Greyhound Terminal, **195**

Grimm, Nicholas R.: Gearing House, 364

Gropius, Walter, 84

Gross, Chaim (sculptor), 177

Guastavino (tile), 108, 241, 288, 306

Guerin, Jules (muralist), 104

Gugler, Eric, 153

H

Hadfield, George, 24, 33, 59, 115–116, 151, 190; Judiciary Square, **183**; Marine Barracks, 264; United States Capitol, 125

Hahn, S. Fred, Building, 252

Haller, Nicholas T., 365; Mary L. Hill House, **252**–253

Hallet, Stephen Sulpice, 20, 22–23, 115

Halliday, Henrietta M., House, 344

Hamer, J. J. Fernand (sculptor), 159

Hand, Florence Hollis, Chapel, **394**

Hansen, Ramm: Unification Church, **314**

Harbeson, Hough, Livingston, and Larson: Organization of American States Building, 209–210; Rayburn House Office Building, 136–137

Harbour Square, 242, **243**

Hardenbergh, Henry Janeway: Willard Hotel, **200**–201

Harding and Upman: Washington Mechanics Savings Bank (The City Bank), **264**; Woodward Apartments, **325**; Woodward Building, 202

Hardy Holzman Pfeiffer, 200

Harlow, C. H., House, 349

Harris, Albert L.: George Washington University, 214–215

Harrison, Wallace K.: National Academy of Sciences, 210–211

Harry Weese and Associates: Arena Stage/Kreeger Theatre, 244–245

Hart, Frederick E. (sculptor), 89, 384

Hart Senate Office Building, 137–138

Hartman-Cox, 57–58, 189; Dodge Center, 402–403; Euram Building, 320–321; Folger Shakespeare Library, 146–147; Mount Vernon College, Florence Hollis Hand Chapel, **394**; National Permanent Building, **227**; 1001 Pennsylvania Ave. NW, 197; Sumner Square, 222–223; Van Ness Station, **375**

Hartman-Cox and Morris Architects: Market Square, 188–189

Harvey, George E. (designer), 300

Hastings, Thomas. *See* Carrère and Hastings.

Hauge, Christian, Residence, **348**

Haupt, Enid A., Garden, 71–72, 96

Hay-Adams House, **44**–45

Head, Robert T.: 3035 Newark St. NW, 367; 3149 Newark St. NW, 367

Heald, Samuel C., House, **257**

Health and Human Services Building, 234–**235**

Healy, Thomas, House, **255**

Hearst Hall, National Cathedral School for Girls, 386

Heaton, Arthur B.: Altamont, The, 323–324; Babcock-Macomb House, 386; Frederick Eichelberger House, 356; George Washington University, 214–215; National Geographic Society Complex, 223; Park and Shop, 369; Riggs National Bank, Chevy Chase Branch, **378**

Hecht Company Warehouse, 283

Heinl, Otto, House, 341

Heins and La Farge: Metropolitan Club, 224; Saint Matthew's Cathedral, **226**

Hellmuth, Obata and Kassabaum: National Air and Space Museum, **91**

Hemphill, John J., Row Houses, 354

Henderson, Mary Foote, 297, 299–300

Henderson, Sen. John B., 297, 299

Henderson, Sen. John B. and Mrs. Mary Foote, residence, 297, **298**

Henn, Ulrich (sculptor), 384

Henning, Arthur S., House, 393

Heurich, Christian, House, 42, **332**

Higgins, Daniel, 83

Hightowers, 302–**303**

Hill, James G., 36–37; Mendota, The, 323; National Bank of Washington, **187**–188; Washington Loan and Trust Company, **194**

Hill, Mary L., House, **252**–253

Hill, William A. (developer), 348, 356

Hillwood (Museum), 370–371

Hirshhorn Museum and Sculpture Garden, 86, 91–**92**

Historical Society of Washington (Christian Heurich House), **332**

Hoban, James, 21–22, 28, 29, 59, 116, 148, 151, 281; United States Capitol, 125; White House, **152**, **153**, 154

Hoffman, William H.: Christ Church, 263

Holabird, John A., 84

Holabird and Root: Capital Hilton Hotel, 203; Federal Office Building #10, 235–**236**; Lafayette Building, 202

Holocaust Memorial Museum, United States, 51, 238–239

Hooe, James C., House, **343**–344

Hooper, Robert, House, 351–352

Hornblower, Joseph C., 45–46, 60, 321
Hornblower and Marshall, 45–46, 80–81, 319; Army Navy Club, 223–224; Arts and Industries Building, 94; Chancery of Iraq (William J. Boardman House), **326**–327; George S. Fraser House (Scott-Thropp Mansion), 321–**322**; Marine Barracks, 264; Edward Lind Morse Studio, **359**; National Geographic Society Complex, 223; Natural History Museum, **108**; New Mammal House, National Zoological Park, 362; John D. Patten House, 360; Phillips Collection (Duncan Phillips House), **329**–330; Russian Consulate, **323**
Hotel Washington, **201**
House Office Building. *See* Cannon House Office Building; Longworth House Office Building; Rayburn House Office Building.
Howard University, 3, 11–12, 56, 281, **292**, **293**, 294
Howe, George, 84
Hudnut, Joseph, 84
Hughes, Charles Evans, 139
Humphrey, Hubert H., Building, Department of Health and Human Services, **234**
Hunt, Richard Morris, 43; John A. Logan Statue, 294–295; United States Naval Observatory, 388–**389**
Hunter and Bell: 2029 Connecticut Ave. NW, **324**
Hutton, William, House, 257–**258**
Hyatt Regency Hotel, 181

I

I. M. Pei and Partners (also I. M. Pei and Associates): Columbia Square, **198**; National Gallery of Art, East Building, 87–88, **110**–112; William M. Slayton House, 367. *See also* Pei, I. M.
Ingersoll, Robert G., House, 164
Ingleside, 33, **364**–365
INTELSAT Headquarters Building, **371**–372
Inter-American Defense Board, **310**–311
Interior Department Building, 48, 216, **217**
Interior South, 210
Internal Revenue Service Building, 174, **175**
International Center, 372

International Eastern Star Temple (Perry Belmont House), **333**
International Square, 228
Interstate Commerce Commission, 172–**173**
Irwin S. Porter and Sons: Islamic Center, **350**
Islamic Center, **350**
Ittner, William B., 268

J

J. & G. H. Gibson Company (glass), 134
Jackson Place, 160
Jacobsen, Hugh Newell, 56–57; Arts and Industries Building, 94; Jane Couser Barton House (John C. Dreier House), **397**; Georgetown University, 407; James Newmyer House, 375; Renwick Gallery, Smithsonian Institution, 165; Trentman House, 408–**409**; United States Capitol, 126
Jaeger, Albert (sculptor), 159
Janes, Fowler, Kirtland and Company (foundry for Capitol dome), 127
Jardella, Francisco (painter), 132
Jefferson, Thomas, 16–17, 19, 22–23, 25, 26, 29, 37, 115, 116–117, 120, 149–150, 271
Jefferson Hotel, 222
Jefferson Memorial, 54, 84–85, 102–**103**
Jennewein, C. Paul (sculptor), 105, 175
Jewell, Captain Theodore F., House, 359–360
John Andrews International Ltd.: INTELSAT Headquarters Building, **371**–372
John Carl Warnecke and Associates: Hart Senate OfficeBuilding, 137–138
Johnson, Anne Thorneburne, House, **334**–335
Johnson, Philip: David Lloyd Kreeger House, **396**; Dumbarton Oaks, 413–414
Johnson, Thomas (commissioner), 16
Johnson, Thomas J., 159
Johnston, Laurence P.: Scott B. Appleby, Jr., House, 392
Judiciary Square, **183**
Jullien, Philip M.: Chasteleton, 305
Justement, Louis, 136, 232; Massachusetts Avenue Bridge, 338

Justice Department Building, 174–**175**

K

Kahn, Albert. *See* Albert Kahn Associated Architects and Engineers, Inc.
Kahn, Louis I., 56
Kammerhueber, Joseph W. von, 40. *See also* Cluss, Adolph and Joseph W. von Kammerhueber.
Kaufman, Isaac, House, 263
Keep, F. A., House, 360
Kelsey, Albert, and Paul Philippe Cret: Organization of American States Building (Pan American Union, International Union of the American Republics), **209**–210. *See also* Cret, Paul Philippe.
Kenilworth Aquatic Gardens, 279
Kennedy, Eugene F., Jr.: National Shrine of the Immaculate Conception, 287, 288
Kennedy, Robert F., Stadium, 268
Kennedy Center for the Performing Arts, **213**
Kennedy-Warren Apartments, **368**–369
Kerrick, James, House, 356
Key, Francis Scott, Bridge, 405–**406**
Keyes, Lethbridge & Condon: Columbia Plaza, 212–213; Metro Operations Control Center, 186; Tiber Island/Carrollsburg Square, 242–243
Keyes Condon Florance: Anacostia Park Pavilion, 276; Design Center, **235**; National Gallery of Art, West Wing, 110; George Washington University, 215; Metropolitan Club, 224; Presidential Plaza, **228**; Republic Place, 226–**227**
Kiley, Dan (landscape architect): Capitol Park, 240; Harbour Square, 242, **243**; 10th Street Mall/L'Enfant Plaza, 236–**237**
Kimball, Fiske, 84–85; Dumbarton House, **409**
King, Martin Luther, Jr., Memorial Library, **194**
King, Nicholas: Evermay, **416**; George Watterson House, 251
Kingsman, Dr. Richard, House and Office, **256**
Kirkbride, Thomas M., 275–276
Kiselewski, Joseph (sculptor), 186
Kittredge, Robert (sculptor), 235
Konti, Isidor (sculptor), 209–210
Koubek, Vlastimil: Foundry, The, 401; International Square, 228;

Koubek, Vlastimil (*cont.*)
10th Street Mall/L'Enfant Plaza,
236–**237**; Westin Hotel, 230;
Willard Hotel, 200–201
Kreeger, David Lloyd, House, **396**
Kreeger Theatre. *See* Arena Stage/
Kreeger Theatre.
Kreis, Henry (sculptor), 235
Kress, Samuel, 83
Kullman Industries: American
City Diner, **378**

L

La Farge, Bancel (mosaicist), 287
La Farge, C. Grant. *See* Heins and
La Farge.
La Farge, Thomas (designer), 226
Lafayette Building, 202
Lafayette Center, 229
Lafayette Square, 158–159
Langston Terrace, 56, 281, **283**
Lantz, Michael (sculptor), 177
La Renaissance (Kenesaw), 316
Latrobe, Benjamin Henry, 20, 21,
23, 24, 25–26, 29, 59, 65, 116–
117, 119–120, 123, 251, 263,
266; Decatur House, National
Trust for Historic Preservation,
160–161; Saint John's Church,
162–163; United States Capitol,
125–135; Washington Navy
Yard, 264–265; White House,
152, **153**
Laughlin, Irwin B., House, 54,
309–310
Launitz, Robert E. (sculptor), 71
Laurent, Robert (sculptor), 177
Law, Thomas (developer), 20
Lawrence, William Watson,
House, **352**
Lawrie, Lee (sculptor), 145, 146,
211, 288
Lawton, Mrs. S. A., House, **257**
Leckie, Robert (engineer and
stonemason), 67
LeCompte, Rowan (stained glass
artisan), 384, 385
Le Droit Building, **193**–194
Le Droit Park, 9, **294**
L'Enfant, Pierre Charles, 5–6, 12,
16–19, 20–21, 22, 61, 62, 64–
65, 67, 68, 69, 90, 113, 115,
149, 158, 166, 178, 231, 248,
260, 266, 271, 317, 338, 381
L'Enfant Plaza. *See* 10th Street
Mall/L'Enfant Plaza.
Lenthall, John: Lenthall Houses,
215–216
Leo A. Daly Associates: Federal
Office Building, Department of
State, **372**–373
Lescaze, William: Embassy and

Chancery of Switzerland, **365**–
366; Longfellow Building, 220;
Harold Spivacke House, 367
Leutze Park, 265
Library of Congress, 38, 42, 119–
120; John Adams Building,
145–146; Thomas Jefferson
Building, 142, **143**–145; James
Madison Building, 146
Lin, Maya: Vietnam Veterans
Memorial, 14, 89, **105**–106
Lincoln Memorial, 51, 54, 79, **82**–
83, **103**–104
Lindens, The, 351–352
Linnean Hill, 362, 364
Lisle, John (artisan), 385–386
Little and Browne: Anderson
House, Headquarters of the
Society of Cincinnati, **330**, 331
Lodge, George Cabot, House, 348
Logan, John A., Statue, 294–295
Longworth House Office Building,
136
Lord, Austin W., 80
Lord and Burnham: palm house,
United States Botanic Garden,
90
Lord and Hewlett, 80
Lorin, Veuve (stained glass
manufacturer), 162
Lovering, William, 20; The
Maples, 261–262
Lovering and Dyer: Washington
Navy Yard, 264–265
Lundy, Victor: United States Tax
Court, **182**
Lutheran Church of the
Reformation, **147**–148
Luther Place Memorial Church,
295
Lutyens, Sir Edwin: British
Embassy, 390–**391**
Lynn, David, 119, 125, 133

M

MacMonnies, Frederick (sculptor),
144, 323
MacNeil, Hermon A. (sculptor),
139
Macomber, Walter, 351
MacVeagh, Franklin, House, 47,
314
Madison Place, 163–164
Maginnis and Walsh: Church of
the Sacred Heart, **316**; National
Shrine of the Immaculate
Conception, **287**–289
Magruder School, 222–223
Malmati, Antonio, House, **256**–
257
Maples, The, 261–262
Mariani and Associates:

Georgetown University, 406–
407
Marine Barracks, 264
Market Square, 57, 188–189
Marsh, William J., 46, 365. *See also*
Marsh and Peter.
Marshall, J. Rush, 45–46, 60. *See
also* Hornblower and Marshall.
Marsh and Peter: Daughters of
the American Revolution
Continental Memorial Hall,
208–209; Evening Star
Building, 197–**198**; Farmers
and Mechanics Branch, Riggs
Bank, **404**; John S. Flannery
House, 354; National Science
Teachers Association, **322**–333;
William Syphax School, 240–
241. *See also* Peter, Walter G.
Martin and Jones: East Capitol
Street Car Barn, 269; 2833 M
St. NW, **401**
Martin Luther King, Jr., Memorial
Library, **194**
Martiny, Philip (sculptor), 144,
196
Mason, John Thomson, House,
408
Mason, Otis T. (ethnologist), 143
Masonic Temple, **195**
Massachusetts Avenue Bridge, 338
Max O. Urbahn Associates:
Federal Home Loan Bank
Board, **206**
Mayer of Munich (stained glass
manufacturer), 253
Mayers, Theodore, Row, 252
Mayers Block, **251**–252
Mayfair Mansions Apartments,
279
Mayflower Hotel, **225**
McCaffrey, Hugh: row houses,
253
McClellan, George B., statue, 323
McConihe, Malcolm (developer),
351
McGill, James H.: Le Droit
Building, **193**–194; Le Droit
Park, **294**
McIlvaine, Alexander: Hillwood
Museum (Hillwood; Abremont),
370
McKim, Charles F., 48, 77, 79, 80,
81, 83, 108, 159
McKim, Mead and White, 108,
172; Arlington Memorial
Bridge, 104–**105**; *Joan of Arc*,
299; Fort Leslie J. McNair, **241**;
National Museum of American
History, 106, **107**, 108; Thomas
Nelson Page House, **334**;
Phillips Collection, 330; Saint

John's Church, 163; John Philip Sousa Bridge, 273; Washington Club, The (R. W. Patterson House), **320**; White House, 153

McLean Gardens, 11

McMillan, James, 76, 77, 81

McMillan Commission Plan, 8, 76, 151, 164, 167, 170, 202, 241, 247, 362. *See also* Senate Park Commission Plan.

Meade, Charles, Jr.: Isaac Kaufman House, 263

Meière, Hildreth (mosaicist), 211

Meigs, Montgomery C., 32, 33, 38, 74, 162; Meigs House, **39**; Pension Building, 183, **184–186**; United States Capitol, 118–119, 125, 128

Mellon, Andrew W., 81, 83, 84, 109

Mercié, Antonin (sculptor), 159

Meridian Hill Park, 299

Meridian Hill Studio, 311

Meridian House International (Henry White House, White-Meyer House), 54, **308–309**

Meridian House International (Irwin B. Laughlin House), 54, **309–310**

Meridian Stone, 69, 70

Mesrobian, Mihran: Dupont Circle Building, 319–**320**, 321; Wardman Tower, **365**

Mestrovic, Ivan (sculptor), 288

Metcalf and Associates: Georgetown University, 406–407

Metro Operations Control Center, 186

Metropolitan Club, 224

Metropolitan Mechanics' Institute, 34–35

Metropolitan Memorial United Methodist Church, **380**

Metropolitan Square, 201

Meyers, John Granville, 42; S. Fred Hahn Building, 252; Samuel C. Heald House, **257**; Historical Society of Washington (Christian Heurich House), **332**; Mayers Block, **251–252**; Theodore Mayers Row, 252

Michaux, Elder Lightfoot Solomon, 279

Michler, Nathaniel, 153

Mies van der Rohe, Ludwig: Martin Luther King, Jr., Memorial Library, **194**

Miller, Frederick A., House, 342–343

Miller, W. C. and A. N. *See* W. C. and A. N. Miller Company.

Miller, William Henry: Toutorsky House (Henry B. Brown House), **305**

Mills, Clark (sculptor), 158

Mills, Petticord and Mills: George Washington University, 215; Natural History Museum, **108**

Mills, Robert, 26, 28–29, 32, 59–60, 66, 67, 68, 95, 118, 151, 158, 162, 254; Treasury Building, **154–157**; United States Patent Office, 189–**191**; United States Tariff Commission Building, 191, **192**, 193; Washington National Monument, 69, **100**–102

Mindeleff, Victor: town house, George Washington University, 215

Minton Tile Company, 134, 191

Moller, Georg (artist), 95

Moore, Arthur Cotton: The Cairo, 303; Canal Square, **403**; Foxhall Crescents, **397**; Phillips Collection, 330; landscape plan, Treasury Building, 156–157. *See also* Arthur Cotton Moore/ Associates.

Moore, Clarence, House, 46–47, 325–326

Moorings, The, 321

Moran, F. B., Residence, 347–348

Moretti, Luigi: Watergate, 213–**214**

Morison, George S.: Taft Bridge, 339

Morris, Edwin (sculptor), 238

Morris, Lemuel: John J. Hemphill Row Houses, 354

Morris, Robert (developer), 20

Morse, Edward Lind, Studio, **359**

Moss, Louis R.: Chevy Chase Arcade, 376

Mount Olivet Cemetery, 280–281

Mount Olivet Lutheran Church, 295

Mount Pleasant, 9

Mount Vernon College, 12, **394**

Mount Vernon Square, 9, 196

Mulhall, Annie M., House, 262

Mullett, Alfred B., 35–36, 255; Apex Building, 187; District of Columbia Jail, **36**; Old Executive Office Building (State, War, and Navy Building), 151, **156**, 157–158; Sun Building, **198**; Treasury Building, **154**, 156. *See also* Alfred B. Mullet and Company.

Mullett, Frederick W. *See* Alfred B. Mullett and Company.

Mullett, Thomas A. *See* Alfred B. Mullett and Company.

Municipal Center, 182–183

Murphy, C. F.: FBI Building, **197**

Murphy, Frederick V.: Apostolic Legation of the Papal State, 388

Murphy and Olmsted: Church of the Sacred Heart, **316**

Myers, George Hewitt, House, 357

N

National Academy of Sciences, 210–**211**

National Air and Space Museum, 86–87, **91**

National Arboretum, 280, **281**

National Archives, 54, 175–**176**

National Bank of Washington, 36–37, **187**–188

National Baptist Memorial Church, **315**–316

National Capital Park and Planning Commission, 58, 84, 85, 248, 362

National Capital Planning Commission, 5, 8, 59, 89

National Cathedral. *See* Cathedral of Saint Peter and Saint Paul.

National City Christian Church, 295–296

National Gallery of Art, 54, 81, 83, 84; East Building, 87–88, **110**–112; West Building, **108**–110, 111

National Geographic Society Complex, **223**

National Institution for the Promotion of Science, 66–67

National League of Cities Building, **199**–200

National Museum of African Art, 88, 96

National Museum of American Art, 86, 189–191

National Museum of American History, 86, 106, **107**, 108

National Museum of History and Technology, 86, 106, **107**, 108

National Park Service, 59

National Permanent Building, 57, **227**

National Place, 199

National Portrait Gallery, 86, 189–**191**

National Savings and Trust Company, **201**

National Science Teachers Association, **322**–323

National Shrine of the Immaculate Conception, **287**–289

National Trust for Historic Preservation, **358**

National Trust for Historic
Preservation (McCormick
Apartments), **326**
National Visitors' Center, 122
National Zoological Park, 362
Natural History Museum, 46, 71,
80, 81, **108**
Navy Yard, 9
Naylor Gardens, 11
Neutra, Richard: Ann and Donald
Brown House, 375–**376**
New Executive Office Building,
159–160
Newmyer, James, House, 375
Nicholson, John (developer), 20
Notre Dame Chapel, Trinity
College, 286–**287**
Notter, Feingold and Alexander,
238

O

Oak Hill Cemetery, 285, 414–**415**
Oak Hill Cemetery Chapel, **415**–
416
Oak Hill Cemetery Gatehouse,
414–415
Obata, Gyo: National Air and
Space Museum, 87, **91**
O'Connor, James L.: Saint Peter's
Church, **148**
Octagon, 23, 216–**217**
Office of the Building Inspector:
James Buchanan School, 265–
266; Corcoran at Georgetown,
400–**401**; George Peabody
School, 250–251
Office of the Supervising
Architect, 32, 35–37, 40, 42, 46,
47; Health and Human Services
Building, 234–**235**; United
States Department of
Agriculture, South Building,
237–238
Old Executive Office Building
(State, War, and Navy Building),
35, 38, 151, **156**, 157–158
Old Naval Observatory, 206, 212
Old Post Office, 169–**170**
Old Soldiers' Home, 82, 83, 281.
See also United States Soldiers'
and Airmen's Home.
Olmsted, Frederick Law, 119, 121,
361, 366; American University,
379–380; Gallaudet University,
283; National Zoological Park,
362
Olmsted, Frederick Law, Jr., 48,
58, 76–77, 362
Olmsted Brothers: Trinity
College, 286
Organization of American States
Building, 25, 56, **209**–210

Owen, David Dale, 69, 95
Owen, Frederick D.: White House
addition proposal, 153
Owen, Robert Dale, 67, 69, 75, 95

P

Page, Harvey L.: Women's
National Democratic Club
(Sarah Adams Whittemore
House), 332–**333**
Page, Russell (landscape architect),
280
Page, Thomas Nelson, House, **334**
Park and Shop, 369
Park Hyatt, 230
Parks and Baxter: Tilden
Gardens, 370
Patten, John D., House, 360
Patten, Thomas, House, **371**
Peabody, George, School, 250–251
Peabody and Stearns: Volta
Bureau, **412**–413
Peaslee, Horace W.: Christ
Church, 263; Dumbarton
House, 409; The Maples, 262;
Meridian Hill Park, 299; The
Moorings, 321; Dr. W. Calhoun
Sterling House, **393**; 33
Kalorama Circle, 352; 29
Kalorama Circle, 352
Pei, I. M.: Christian Science
Complex, 221, **222**; 10th Street
Mall/L'Enfant Plaza, 232, 236–
237; Town Center Plaza, **244**.
See also I. M. Pei and Partners.
Pelz, Paul J., 42, 299; Frederick A.
Miller House (Argyle Terrace),
342–343. *See also* Smithmeyer
and Pelz.
Penn Medical Building, **261**
Pension Building, 38, 183–186
(**184**)
Permanent Mission of Colombia to
the Organization of American
States (Otto Heinl House), 341
Perry, Roland Hinton (sculptor),
144, 339
Persico, Luigi, 128, 132
Peter, Walter G., 46. *See also*
Marsh and Peter.
Pettrich, Ferdinand (sculptor), 155
Peyton, C. Russell, House, 360
Philadelphia Row, 258
Phillips Collection (Duncan
Phillips House), **329**–330
Pierce-Klingle House, 362, 364
Pierce Mill, 364
Pierson and Wilson: Library of
Congress, John Adams
Building, 125, 145–146
Platt, Charles Adams, 105;
Corcoran Gallery of Art, west

wing, **207**; Freer Gallery of Art,
81, **97**–99; Tregaron (The
Causeway), **368**
Pope, John Russell, 54, 82, 83, 85,
299; American Pharmaceutical
Association Building, **211**–212;
Daughters of the American
Revolution Contstitution
Memorial Hall, 209; Embassy of
Brazil (Robert and Katharine
McCormick House), 391;
Jefferson Memorial, 102–**103**;
John R. McLean House, 159;
Meridian House International
(Henry White House), **308**–309;
Meridian House International
(Irwin B. Laughlin House),
309–310; National Archives,
175–**176**; National City
Christian Church (Disciples of
Christ Church), 295–296;
National Gallery of Art, West
Building, **108**–110; Scottish Rite
Temple, **305**–306; Second
Division Memorial, 152; The
Textile Museum (George Hewitt
Myers House), 357–**358**
Popiel, Antoni (sculptor), 159
Porter, Lockie and Chatelain:
Scottish Rite Temple, 313
Porter and Lockie: Charles E. and
Anita Eckles House, 392–393;
Lutheran Church of the
Reformation, 147–148; Robert
B. Roosevelt House, 353. *See
also* Irwin S. Porter and Sons.
Post Office Building, **173**–174
Potter, William Appleton, 36, 120
Powers, Hiram (sculptor), 165
Pratt, Bella Lyon (sculptor), 144
Presbyterian Church of the
Pilgrims, **340**
Presidential Plaza, **228**
President's House. *See* White
House.
Price, Bruce: Embassy of Canada
(Clarence Moore House), 325–
326; Embassy of Colombia
(Thomas T. Gaff House), 327–
328
Price, Walter F.: Friends Meeting
House, **359**
Prince, Leslie E. F. (developer),
352
Proctor, Alexander (sculptor), 105
Prospect House, **407**–408
Public Buildings Act, 167
Public Buildings Commission, 123
Pujol, Paul: base, *Lafayette*, 159
Putnam, Brenda (sculptor), 147
Pyle, Frederick B.: Embassy of
Colombia, Chancery, 354;

houses at 2126, 2128, 2129, 2131, 2132, and 2137 Bancroft Pl. NW, 356; 3314 Newark St. NW, 367

R

Rabe, Henry, House, 259–**260**
Raleigh's Building, 225
Rankin, Kellogg and Crane: Agriculture Department Building, 80, 99–100
Ravenna Mosaic Company, 289
Ray, George N., 321; Brazilian Delegation to the Organization of American States, Ambassador's Residence (Daniel J. Callahan House), 354; Embassy of Iceland, 351; Embassy of Republic of Austria (William A. Hill Company), 348; Berkeley L. Simmons House, 354; Count Laszlo and Countess Gladys Vanderbilt Széchényi House (Maie H. Williams House), **392**
Rayburn House Office Building, 136–137
Redevelopment Land Agency, 231
Reed, David A., House, 357
Reed, Walter, Hospital, 12, 281
Renwick, James, Jr., 29–31; William W. Corcoran Residence, **30**–31, 159; Oak Hill Cemetery Chapel, **415**–416; Renwick Gallery, Smithsonian Institution (Corcoran Gallery of Art), 30, 164–**165**; Saint John's Church, 162; Saint Mary's Episcopal Church, 214, **215**; Smithsonian Institution, 30, 68, 69, **94**–96; Trinity Episcopal Church, **31**; Washington National Monument, 101
Renwick Gallery, Smithsonian Institution, (CorcoranGallery of Art), 164–**165**
Republic Place, 226–**227**
Ricci, Ulysses (sculptor), 211
Richardson, H. H., 44–**45**, 120, 303–304, 314, 331; Hay-Adams House, **44**–45, 159; Benjamin H. Warder House, 300, **311**–312
Riggs National Bank, 36–37, 201–202; Chevy Chase Branch, **378**; Farmers and Mechanics Branch, **404**
Ripley, S. Dillon, 88
Ripley, S. Dillon, Center, 96–97
River Park, 241–242, **243**
Robinson, Hilyard R., 56; Ralph J. Bunche House, **285**; Langston

Terrace, 281, **283**
Roche, George F. de la, Glenwood Cemetary, 285; Oak Hill Cemetery, 414–415
Rock Creek Cemetery, 280, 289, 290
Rock Creek Park, 16, 38, 219, 361–364, 370
Rodbird, J. A. (builder): Mrs. S. A. Lawton House, **257**
Rodier, Gilbert LaCoste, 136
Rogers, Isaiah, 35; Treasury Building, **154**–157
Rogers, Laussat R., 47, 297
Rogers, Randolph (designer), 135
Roosevelt, Robert B., House, 353–354
Roosevelt, Theodore, Memorial, plan, 54, **55**
Roosevelt Hotel, 307–308
Rosedale, 367–368
Rosen, Jan Henryke de (muralist), 386
Rosen, John de (mosaicist), 226
Rosenwald, Lessing J., 83
Ross Drive Bridge, 364
Russell, R. G.: Mount Olivet Lutheran Church, 295
Russell Senate Office Building, 51, 122–123, 135–136
Russian Consulate, **323**

S

Saarinen, Eero, 84
Saarinen, Eliel, 84
Saarinen and Saarinen, 107
Sackler, Arthur M., Gallery, 88, 96
Saint Elizabeths Hospital (Government Hospital for the Insane), **275**–276
Saint-Gaudens, Augustus, 77; Adams Memorial, Rock Creek Cemetery, 289–**290**
Saint-Gaudens, Louis, 140
Saint John's Church, 25, **162**–163
Saint John's Church Parish House, 33, **163**
Saint Luke's Episcopal Church, 302
Saint Mark's Episcopal Church, **253**
Saint Mary's Episcopal Church, 214, **215**
Saint Matthew's Cathedral, **226**
Saint Paul's Episcopal Church, 290
Saint Peter's Church, **148**
Saint Teresa of Avila Church, **274**–275
Saint Thomas Episcopal Church, 327
Sanson, Eugène: International Eastern Star Temple (Perry

Belmont House), **333**
Santmyers, George T., 324
Saratoga, 376
Sasaki, Hideo (landscape architect): National Arboretum, 280
Sasaki Associates (landscape architects), 401
Satterlee, Nicholas: Women's National Democratic Club (Sarah Adams Whittemore House), 332–**333**
Satterlee and Smith: Capitol Park, **240**
Saunders, William (landscape architect), 73
Scaravaglione, Concetta (sculptor), 177
Schlesinger, Frank: National League of Cities Building, **199**–200; National Place, 199
Schmitz, Carl (sculptor), 177
Schneider, Thomas Franklin, 41–42, 297, 304; W. Taylor Birch House, **411**; The Cairo, **303**; 1614 20th Street NW, **321**; 2111–2121 Bancroft Pl. NW, 355–356
Schoen, Paul, 41
Schoenborn, August G., 127; houses at 325, 327 East Capitol St. SE, **254**
Schuler, Hans (sculptor), 299
Schultz, Robert O.: General Scott Apartment Building, 301
Schulze, Paul, 41. *See also* Cluss, Adolph, and Paul Schulze.
Schwarz, David M.: 1818 N St. NW, **226**; Penn Medical Building, **261**; Raleigh's Building, 225; Saratoga, 376; 1718–1720 Connecticut Ave. NW, **322**
Scottish Rite Temple (John Russell Pope, architect), 54, **305**–306; (Porter, Lockie and Chatelain, architects), 313
Scully, William A., House, 351
Second Division Memorial, 105–106, 152
Senate Office Building. *See* Dirksen Sentate Office Building; Hart Senate Office Building; Russell Senate Office Building.
Senate Park Commission Plan, 43, 48–49, 52, 53, 76–**78**, 79–**80**, 81–**82**, 83, 84, 85, 86, 104, 121, 123. *See also* McMillan Commission Plan.
Serra, Richard (sculptor), 200
Sewall-Belmont House, **251**
Shalom Baranes Associates, 199;

Shalom Baranes Assoc. (*cont.*)
816 Connecticut Ave. NW, 224;
Army Navy Club, 223–224
Shaw, W. B.: Kenilworth Aquatic
Gardens, 279
Sheets, William: S. W. Tullock
House, **254**; Thomas Healy
House, **255**
Shepherd, Alexander R., 7, 39–40
Shepherd's Row, 40, **41**
Shepley, Bulfinch, Richardson,
and Abbott: Arthur M. Sackler
Gallery, National Museum of
African Art, S. Dillon Ripley
Center, and Enid A. Haupt
Garden, Smithsonian Insitution,
84, 88, **96**–97
Shepley, Henry R., 84; All Souls
Church, 314–315
Shepley, Rutan and Coolidge, 276
Sheridan, Irene Rucher, House,
342, 343
Sheridan, Philip H., Statue, 336–
337
Sherman, Ella Bennett: 2930
Newark St. NW, 366–367
Shields, Susan, House, 301
Shrady, Henry M. (sculptor), 66
Shreve, Lamb and Harmon:
Acacia Mutual Life Insurance
Company, **181**–182
Sibour, Jules Henri de, 46–47;
Embassy of Canada (Clarence
Moore House), 325; Embassy of
Colombia (Thomas T. Gaff
House), 327–**328**; Embassy of
France (William Watson
Lawrence House), **352**; Embassy
of Luxembourg (Alexander
Stewart House), **340**, 341–342;
Embassy of Spain, 313; Interior
South, 210; Jefferson Hotel,
222; National Trust for Historic
Preservation (McCormick
Apartments), **326**
Simmons, Berkeley L., House, 354
Simmons, Franklin: John A.
Logan Statue, 294–295
Simmons, Stanley B.: Lester A.
Barr House, 354
Simmons, Thomas: Thomas
Simmons House, 259
Simon, Louis A.: Internal
Revenue Service Building, 174,
175
Skidmore, Owings and Merrill:
Connecticut Connection, 224;
Constitution Gardens, 88; Daon
Building, 196; Demonet
Building, 225; Embassy of
Kuwait, Chancery, **373**; George
Washington University, 214–
215; Grand Hotel, 230;

Hirshhorn Museum and
Sculpture Garden, 91–**92**;
Metropolitan Square, 201;
National Geographic Society
Complex, 223; Park Hyatt, 230;
U.S. News and World Report
Headquarters, **229**–230
Slayton, William M., House, 367
Smith, Chloethiel Woodard, 232:
Harbour Square, 242;
Washington Square, **224**–225;
Waterside Mall, 243–**244**. *See
also* Chloethiel Smith and
Associates.
Smith, Delos: Christ Church, 263;
Saint Mark's Episcopal Church,
253: Saint Paul's Episcopal
Church, 290
Smith, James Kellum: National
Museum of American History,
107
Smith, Oliver (church window
designer), 148
Smith, Segreti and Tepper:
Cathedral of Saint Peter and
Saint Paul, **381**–386
Smith and Edwards: Chancery of
Korea (Alice W. B. Stanley
House), 348–**349**
Smithmeyer, John L., 42–43, 121;
George H. Thomas Statue, 296
Smithmeyer and Pelz: Georgetown
University, 406; Library of
Congress, Thomas Jefferson
Building, 38, 120–121, 142–
143, 144–145. *See also* Pelz, Paul
J.
Smithson, James, 59–60, 68, 81
Smithsonian Gallery of Art
Commission, 83–84
Smithsonian Institution, 20, 29–
30, 59–60, 66, **68**, 70–72, 81,
94–96; Alice Pike Barney
House, **345**; Arthur M. Sackler
Gallery, National Museum of
African Art, S. Dillon Ripley
Center, Enid A. Haupt Garden,
96–97; National Museum of
American Art, National Portrait
Gallery, 189–**191**
Snowden, George (church altar),
289
Soane, John, 411
Sonnemann, Alexander H.:
Kennedy-Warren Apartments,
368–369
Southern Building, **202**
Southwest Washington
Redevelopment Area, 231–234,
243
Spivacke, Harold, House, 367
Spofford, Ainsworth, 120, 144
Spofford, Sarah McC., House, **254**

Spring Valley, 12
Stanley, Alice W. B., House, 348–
349
Stanton Park, 250
Starkweather and Plowman:
Cooke's Row, **410**–411
Starrett and Van Vleck:
Garfinckel's Department Store,
199
State, War, and Navy Building. *See*
Old Executive Office Building.
State Department, 212
Stein, Clarence (planner), 369
Steinman, Cain and White:
National Museum of American
History, 106, **107**, 108
Sterling, Dr. W. Calhoun, House,
393
Stern, David L.: Harry B. Wilson
House, 353
Stewart, Alexander, House, 341–
342
Stewart, Mary E., House, **353**
Stickley, Gustav: Dumblane, 378–
379
Stoddard Baptist Home, 364
Stone, Edward Durell, 84;
Georgetown University Law
Center, **181**; International
Center, 372; Kennedy Center
for the Performing Arts, **213**;
National Geographic Society
Complex, **223**; United States
Department of Transportation
Building, 239–**240**
Stone, George W., Sr.,: Immanuel
Baptist Church, 315; La
Renaissance (Kenesaw), 316
Strickland, William, 26, 33, 151
Stubbins, Hugh, 84
Sullivan, Louis, 49, 303
Sumner School, 41, 57, 222–223
Sumner Square, **222**–223
Sun Building, **198**
Supreme Court, 53, 123–124,
138–140
Swaney Kerns Architects: 1915 I
St. NW, 228
Swanson, Robert F., 84
Swartwout, Egerton: National
Baptist Memorial Church, **315**–
316
Switzer, Mary E., Memorial
Building, **235**
Syphax, William, School, 240–**241**
Széchényi, Count Laszlo and
Countess Gladys Vanderbilt,
House, **392**

T

Taft, Lorado (sculptor), 122, 141
Taft Bridge, 339
Tayloe, John, 216

Taylor, Frank: National Museum of American History, **107**
10th Street Mall/L'Enfant Plaza, 236–**237**
Textile Museum, The, 357–**358**
Thomas, Ernest (plasterer), 134
Thomas, George H., Statue, 296
Thompson, Benjamin. *See* Benjamin Thompson Associates.
Thornton, William, 23–24, 59, 151; Octagon, 216–**217**; Tudor Place, **411**–412; United States Capitol, 115, **116**, 117, 125–135
Tiber Island/Carrollsburg Square, 242–243
Tiffany and Company, 208, 253, 307
Tilden Gardens, 370
Tonetti-Dozzi, François M. L. (sculptor), 144
Totten, George Oakley, Jr., 47, 297, 299–300, 336; Embassy and Chancery of Cameroon (Christian Hauge Residence), **348**; Embassy of Ghana (Embassy of France), **308**; Embassy of Greece, 343; Embassy of Pakistan (F. B. Moran Residence), **347**–348; Embassy of Poland, **312**; Embassy of Spain, **313**–314; Embassy of Turkey (Edward H. Everett House), **344**–345; James C. Hooe House, **343**–344; Inter-American Defense Board, **310**–311; Meridian Hill Studio, 311; University Club, **202**–203
Toutorsky House (Henry B. Brown House), **305**
Town and Elliot: United States Patent Office, 189–**191**
Town Center Plaza, **244**
Townsend, Richard H., House, 51, **331**–332
Traquair, Adam (sculptor), 131
Treasury Annex, 53, 164
Treasury Building, 19–20, 28–29, 150–151, **154**–157
Tregaron, **368**
Trentman House, 408–**409**
Trinity College, 281, 286–**287**
Trowbridge, Alexander B., 124, 125; Library of Congress, John Adams Building, 145–146
Trowbridge and Livingston: American Red Cross National Headquarters, 207–**208**
Trumbauer, Horace: Embassy of Belgium (Anna Thomson Dodge House), 396; International Eastern Star Temple (Perry Belmont House), **333**

Trumbull, John (painter), 132
Tucker, Martha S., House, 357–**358**
Tudor Place, 23, **411**–412
Tullock, S. W., House, **254**
Tully, Daniel F. *See* Daniel F. Tully Associates.
Twin Oaks, 366

U

U.S. News and World Report Headquarters, **229**–230
Underwood, Gilbert Stanley: General Accounting Office, 186
Underwood, Gilbert Stanley and William Dewey Foster: State Department, 212
Unification Church (Washington Chapel, Church of Jesus Christ of Latter-day Saints), **314**
Union Land Association, 274
Union Station, 49, 81, 122, 140, **141**, 142
United States Army Corps of Engineers, 7, 37, 58, 74, 247
United States Botanic Garden, 65–66, 71, **90**
United States Capitol, 19, 22–23, 24, 26, 27, 29, 31–32, 33, 38, 39, 40, 64, 65, 66, 67, 69, 70, 71, 77, 78, 79, 81, 82, 95, 101, 103–104, 113–120, 121, 122, 123, 124, 125–**126**, 127–**129**, 130–**133**, 136, 140, 146, 151
United States Customs Service, 172–**173**
United States Department of Agriculture, 71–74
United States Department of Agriculture, South Building, **237**–238
United States Department of Housing and Urban Development Building, **238**, 239
United States Department of Transportation Building, 239–**240**
United States General Post Office, 19–20, 28–29, 191, **192**, 193
United States Holocaust Memorial Museum, 51, 238–239
United States Naval Observatory, 388, **389**, **390**
United States Patent Office (United States Civil Service Commission Building), 19–20, 24, 28–29, 189–**191**
United States Post Office, **140**
United States Soldiers' and Airmen's Home, 12, **290**–292. *See also* Old Soldiers' Home.
United States Supreme Court Commission, 123–124

United States Tariff Commission Building, 19–20, 28–29, 191, **192**, 193
United States Tax Court, **182**
Universalist National Memorial Church, 306–307
University Club, **202**–203
University of the District of Columbia, **374**
Upman, Frank, 136
Uptown Theatre, 369
Urbahn, Max O. *See* Max O. Urbahn Associates.

V

Van Brunt and Howe: American University, 379–380
Van Ness, John P., 25, 27
Van Ness House, **26**
Van Ness Station, 57, **375**
Van Sweden, James: International Center, 372
Vatican Mosaic Studio, 289
Vaughan, Henry: Cathedral of Saint Peter and Saint Paul, **381**–386
Vaux, Calvert, 71; Robert P. Dodge House, 409–**410**; Gallaudet University, 283
Vedder, Elihu (mosaicist), 144
Venetian Arts Company, 289
Venturi, Rauch and Scott Brown: Western Plaza, **200**
Vermont Avenue Christian Church, 295
Vice President's House, **390**
Vietnam Veterans Memorial, 14, 88–90, **105**–106
Vieyra, Paul: Embassy of Kuwait, Chancery, **373**
Vitale, Ferruccio (landscape architect): Meridian Hill Park, 299
Volta Bureau, **412**–413

W

W. C. and A. N. Miller Company, 10
Waggaman, Clarke, 321; A. B. Butler House, **334**; Anne Thorneburne Johnson House, **334**–335; Count Laszlo and Countess Gladys Vanderbilt Széchényi House (Maie H. Williams House), **392**
Waggaman and Ray: 2135 Bancroft Pl. NW, 356
Wagoner, Harold: Metropolitan Memorial United Methodist Church, **380**
Walter, Thomas U., 31–34, 65, 151, 158, 254; Saint Elizabeths Hospital (Government Hospital

Walter, Thomas U. (*cont.*)
for the Insane), 271, **275**–**276**;
Saint John's Church Parish
House, **163**; Stoddard Baptist
Home (Ingleside), **364**–365;
Third Baptist Church, **34**;
Treasury Building, **154**–157;
United States Capitol, 118, 119,
120, 125–135; United States
General Post Office, 192, 193;
United States Patent Office,
189–**191**
Ward, John Quincy Adams
(sculptor), 144; George H.
Thomas Statue, 296
Warder, Benjamin H., House,
311–312
Wardman, Harry (developer), 320,
349, 356
Wardman, Harry, House, 345
Wardman Tower, **365**
Warnecke, John Carl: Georgetown
University, 406–407; Madison
Place, 163; New Executive
Office Building and Court of
Claims Building, 159–160; 718–
726 and 740–744 Jackson Pl.
NW, 160. *See also* John Carl
Warnecke and Associates.
Warner, Olin (sculptor), 144
Warren and Wetmore: Embassy of
Italy, 312–313; Mayflower
Hotel, **225**
Warring Brothers: William Hutton
House, 257–**258**
Warwick, Harvey, Sr.: The
Westchester, 380–**381**
Washington, George, 16, 17, 18–
19, 21, 23, 62, 64, 149
Washington Aqueduct, 38
Washington Armory, 72
Washington Building Company,
27
Washington Casino Association, 45
Washington City Canal, 29, 65, 67,
70, 72, 178, 189, 204, 219, 232
Washington Club, The (R. W.
Patterson House), **320**
Washington Harbour, **402**
Washington Loan and Trust
Company, **194**
Washington Mechanics Savings
Bank (The City Bank), **264**
Washington National Cathedral.
See Cathedral of Saint Peter and
Saint Paul.
Washington National Monument,
20, 24–25, 28–29, 38, 39, 70–
71, 78, 79, 82, **100**–102
Washington National Monument
Society, 69, 70, 100
Washington Post Building, **203**

Washington Square, **224**–225
Washington Technical Institute,
374–375
Watergate, 206, 213–**214**
Waterside Mall, 243–**244**
Waterside Towers, **244**
Watterston, George, House, 251
Webb, William Benning, School,
270
Webb and Knapp, 232, 237
Weese, Harry, 232. *See also* Harry
Weese and Associates.
Weihe, Black, Jeffries, and
Strassman: Westbridge, 230
Weinman, Adolph A. (sculptor),
103, 139, 306
Welton Becket Associates: Hyatt
Regency Hotel, 181. *See also*
Becket, Welton.
Werner, LeRoy L.: Cafritz
Building, 221–222
Wesley Heights, 12
Westbridge, 230
Westchester, The, 380–**381**
Western Plaza, **200**
Westin Hotel, 230
Wetmore, James A., 174
Wheatley Town Houses, 408
Wheat Row, 231–232, **242**
Whelan, John J.: Embassy and
Chancery of Norway, **386**–388;
William A. Scully House, 351;
2447 Kalorama Rd. NW, 350–
351; 2446 Kalorama Rd. NW,
351; 2435 Kalorama Rd. NW,
351
Whistler, James A. M. (artist), 99
White, Frank Russell: Embassy of
Korea (Harry Wardman House),
345
White, Henry, House, 54, **308**–
309
White, Stanford: Adams
Memorial, Rock Creek
Cemetery, 289–**290**
White House, 17, 19, 20, 21, 22,
29, 31, **152**, **153**, 154
White-Meyer House, 54, **308**–309
Widener, Joseph E., 83
Wilder, Mrs. Wilber E., House,
354
Willard Hotel, **200**–201
Williams, Elisha O. (builder), 22
Williams, Maie H., House, **392**
Williamson, Colin (builder), 22
William Yost and Brothers: Sarah
McC. Spofford House, **254**
Wilson, Harry B., House, 353
Wilson, Joseph M.: Baltimore and
Potomac Railroad Station, 74
Wilson, Woodrow, 49, 54
Wilson, Woodrow, House, **358**

Winder Building, 206–**207**
Windham, William, House, 163–
164
Windrim, James: National Savings
and Trust Company, **201**
Winslow, Henry: Philip H.
Sheridan statue, 337
Winslow, Lorenzo S.: White
House, 153
Winter, Ezra (muralist), 146
Wisconsin Avenue Vocational
School, **412**
Wisedell, Thomas: Capitol
grounds, 119
Withers, Frederick Clarke:
Gallaudet University, 283–285
Wnuk, Joseph E.: Thomas Patten
House, **371**
Women's National Democratic
Club (Sarah Adams Whittemore
House), 332–**333**
Wonder Building, 321
Wood, Donn and Deming, 48;
Embassy of Greece, Commercial
Section (Irene Rucher Sheridan
House), 343; Embassy of the
Philippines (Emma S. Fitzhugh
House), 360; George Cabot
Lodge House, 348; Masonic
Temple, **195**; Permanent
Mission of Colombia to the
Organization of American States
(Otto Heinl House), 341;
Textile Museum (Martha S.
Tucker House), 357–**358**;
Union Trust Building, 202
Wood, Waddy B., 48, 336;
Bachelor Flats, **227**; Alice Pike
Barney House, Smithsonian
Institution, **345**; Capitol
Traction Company Union
Station, **405**; Corcoran Gallery
of Art, **207**; Headquarters of
the National Society, Daughters
of the American Colonists (E.
H. Alsop House), 343; East
Capitol Street Car Barn, **269**–
270; Embassy of Cyprus (E. G.
Davis House), 360; Embassy of
Ireland (Frederic and Mathilda
Delano House), 357; C. H.
Harlow House, 349; Interior
Department Building, 216, **217**;
Captain Theodore F. Jewell
House, 359–360. *See also* Wood,
Donn and Deming.
Woods, Elliot: Scottish Rite
Temple, 306; Judiciary Square,
183
Woodward, Samuel W.
(developer), 354
Woodward Apartments, **325**

Woolworth, F. W., Co., Store, **273**–274
Wright, Frank Lloyd, 61, 85, 99; Crystal Heights Hotel, **60**
Wyeth, Nathan C., 47, 136; Embassy and Chancery of Haiti (Gibson Fahnestock House), **346**, 347; Columbia Hospital for Women, 230; District of Columbia National Guard Armory, 266, 268; Embassy of Chile (Sarah Wyeth House), **346**–347; Embassy of Malawi (Granville Fortesque House), 349; Embassy of Mexico (Franklin MacVeagh House), **314**; Judiciary Square, **183**; Francis Scott Key Bridge, 405–**406**; Municipal Center, 182–183; White House, 153
Wyeth, Nathan C., and William P. Cresson: Embassy of Kenya (F. A. Keep House and C. Russell Peyton House), 360;

Embassy of United Arab Emirates, Military Department, **342**, 343; Embassy of Zambia, 349
Wyeth, Sarah, House, **346**
Wyeth and King, 330
Wyeth and Sullivan: Embassy of Ivory Coast (Frederick Atherton House), 349; Embassy of Venezuela (Mrs. Wilber E. Wilder House), 354; 2340 Kalorama Rd. NW, 353

X

Ximenes, Ettore (sculptor), 299

Y

Yellin, Samuel (designer), 210
York, Judson: Luther Place Memorial Church, 295
York and Sawyer, 202; Commerce Department Building, **171**–172
Yoshimura, Junzo, 88

Yost, William: row houses, **265**. *See also* William Yost and Brothers.
Young, Ammi B., 35; Georgetown Custom House and Post Office, **403**–404; Treasury Building, **154**–157
Young, Don C., Jr.: Unification Church, **314**
Young, Mahonri Sharp (mosaicist), 314
Younger, Joseph: Kennedy-Warren Apartments, **368**; 1726 Connecticut Ave. NW, 321; 1661 Crescent Pl. NW, 310

Z

Zantzinger, Borie and Medary: Justice Department Building, 174–**175**
Zeckendorf, William, 232, 237
Zink, John J.: Uptown Theatre, 369